SUPERSONIC SAINTS 2

MORE THRILLING EXPERIENCES OF LDS PILOTS

COMPILED BY

JOHN BYTHEWAY

ILLUSTRATIONS BY CHAD S. BAILEY

DESERET BOOK

SALT LAKE CITY, UTAH

Pencil drawings © 2008 Chad S. Bailey (airartcsbailey.com): 4, 13, 23, 34, 41, 48, 57, 64, 73, 78, 87, 98, 105, 114, 125, 134, 141, 148, 157, 168, 179, 188, 199, 208, 215, 222, 229, 236
Technical drawings courtesy Richard Ferriere (richard.ferriere.free.fr): x, 10, 18, 38, 44, 52, 62, 70, 76, 84, 94, 102, 110, 122, 130, 152, 162, 174, 186, 194, 204, 212, 232
All other technical drawings adapted from various sources
All photos courtesy of the respective authors

Library of Congress Cataloging-in-Publication Data

Supersonic Saints 2 / John Bytheway.
  p. cm.
Includes index.
ISBN 978-1-59038-911-9 (hardback : alk. paper)
1. Church of Jesus Christ of Latter-day Saints—Biography.   2. Mormon Church—Biography.   3. Air pilots—Anecdotes.   4. Air pilots—Religious life.   I. Bytheway, John, 1962–
BX8678.A476 2008
289.3092'273—dc22
[B]   2008024937

Printed in the United States of America
R. R. Donnelley and Sons, Crawfordsville, IN

10   9   8   7   6   5   4   3   2   1

To the memory of
Lieutenant Nathan "OJ" White, United States Navy
December 12, 1972–April 2, 2003

Lieutenant White's story appears in chapter 20.

CONTENTS

CONTENTS

CONTENTS

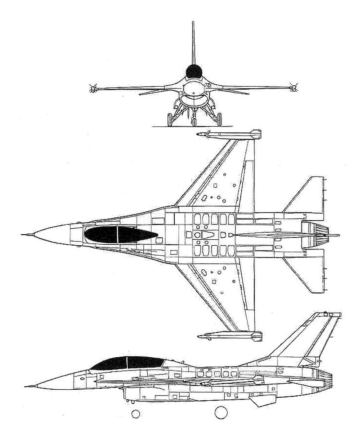

INTRODUCTION

JOHN BYTHEWAY

"Is this what you feel like every day?" I asked Major Derek "Maestro" O'Malley as we approached the F-16 waiting for us on the flight line. I had seen F-16s before, usually behind chain-link fences, or from the bleacher seats at air shows. But this time, the plane that I consider to be the most beautiful aircraft ever designed was not roped off. There was no airman standing guard, making sure people didn't touch. This time, I was going to climb in, buckle up, close the canopy, and take off.

With a bit of awe, and some boyhood giddiness I couldn't seem to contain, I climbed the ladder, settled into the cockpit, connected my oxygen and intercom on the right side and my g-suit on the left side, attached myself to the ejection seat with no fewer than five buckles, and waited for Maestro and the crew chief to prepare the jet for launch.

The hour that followed is one that I will relive for the rest of my life. A full-afterburner takeoff; low-level, high-speed flight over the desert north of Nellis Air Force base; a couple of 360 degree aileron rolls in less than a second; and effortlessly breaking the sound barrier. Was it a blast? Yes. Did I make use of the airsick bag? I most certainly did. Would I go again? Faster than you can say, "Roger."

John Bytheway (left) and Major Derek O'Malley prepare to board the F-16.
Photo by Kimberly Bytheway.

I had a lot of fun that day, but I was sobered by the thought that when these military pilots answer the call, it's not just for the fun of flying. They put themselves in harm's way to defend our borders and promote the cause of freedom around the world. And for that they have my respect, admiration, and gratitude.

When I first laid eyes on an F-16 over twenty-five years ago, my dream was to fly one someday. But my dreams came to a halt when I lost my 20–20 vision at age seventeen and therefore could not fly for the military. Later, as a college student, I settled for a solo in a Cessna 152—not the big dream I had hoped for, but still one of the great thrills of my life.

My affection for all things to do with aviation never waned, however, and last year I got to live my dreams vicariously by putting the stories of other pilots in a book, *Supersonic Saints: Thrilling Stories from LDS Pilots.* Copies "flew" off the shelves (so to speak), and in the months that followed, many more LDS pilots sent us their experiences to share. The first *Supersonic Saints* compilation consisted of sixteen chapters involving pilots and their aircraft ranging from the Cessna 0–2 Bird-Dog to the space shuttle Columbia.

In *Supersonic Saints 2,* we've increased the number of chapters to twenty-eight and broadened the time frame. This edition includes a couple of World War II stories involving the P-38 Lightning and the C-46 Commando. Fast forward to 1995, and we relive Major Chris Stewart's story of the supersonic B-1 Bomber's attempt to set a world record for an around-the-globe flight. In addition, we're excited to have a former Young Women and Relief Society instructor, Captain Janine K. Garner of the U.S. Marine Corps, share two of her flying stories. We also have helicopter experiences in Grenada and the Philippines. Some of the stories involve mechanical problems and weather; others detail actual combat. Of course, none of these pilots love war, but we honor them for answering the call of their country and defending the cause of freedom. Many airplane enthusiasts have experience only in private aviation, so we've included a couple of nonmilitary flying chapters as well.

I'd like to express my gratitude to all the pilots who have so generously shared their experiences. I also owe a particular debt of gratitude to Major Derek "Maestro" O'Malley, the 57th Wing, the United States Air Force Weapons School, and the 16th Weapons Squadron / F-16 Weapons School, who made it possible for me to fulfill my childhood dream of flying in an F-16.

But that's enough taxiing—let's get clearance and take off.

INTRODUCTION

The stories that follow are about two of my favorite things: faith and flying. Since you have this book in your hands, I suspect you like them too. So sit back, buckle up, and get ready for the second sortie of *Supersonic Saints*.

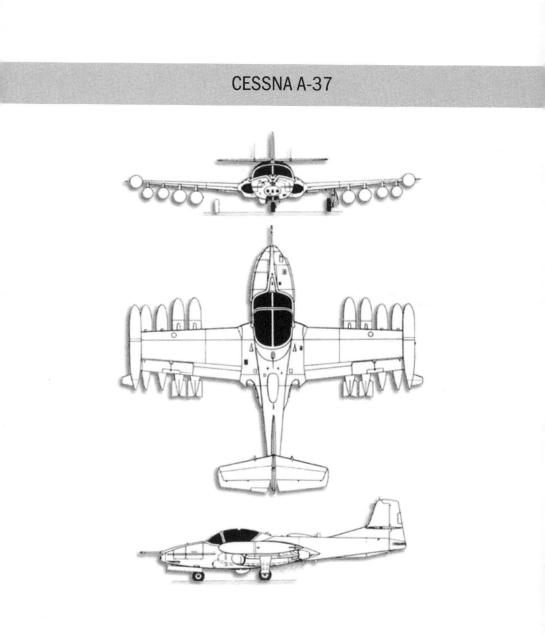

CHAPTER ONE

"SIR! I'M ON FIRE!"

GORDON H. WEED

While flying an A-37B Fighter Bomber in one of my many low-level combat missions in Vietnam, "Sir, I'm on fire" was the emergency call I received from my wingman. We were supporting Troops In Contact (TIC) with enemy forces, and this is one of the most dreaded radio transmissions a flight leader can receive from his wingman—that he is on fire over hostile enemy territory.

During the year I was in Vietnam, I flew 436 combat missions in the A-37B Fighter Bomber. I was a lieutenant colonel at the time of this particular mission, which took place during the siege of An Loc, a city in South Vietnam a short distance north of Saigon with a population of about 15,000 people. I was the commander of the 8th Special Operations Squadron stationed at Bien Hoa Air Base in South Vietnam.

It was June 22, 1972, and the war had intensified around An Loc. I was flying lead in a two-ship formation flying out of Bien Hoa Air Base. The base is about ten minutes flying time south of the city. Bill Harrell, a young first lieutenant who had recently graduated from the Air Force Academy, was my wingman. He was an exceptional pilot for someone of his age and experience.

1

He was well trained and much disciplined. He followed instructions implicitly and displayed the demeanor one would expect from a graduate of the Air Force Academy. Of course, he had to be good in order to be assigned to the 8th SOS, an elite and distinguished squadron with a long history of significant achievements.

One of our missions that day was to destroy a heavily fortified enemy bunker that was causing numerous casualties at the perimeter of An Loc. (A "bunker" in a combat area is a well-constructed log-and-sand dugout with antiaircraft gun emplacements and a sizable concentration of enemy troops in and around it.) The army ground commander wanted this bunker silenced as soon as possible. He had briefed the Airborne Forward Air Controller (FAC) on its location and requested an immediate air strike.

According to the ground commander, this bunker had wall-to-wall 51-caliber machine guns and a lot of enemy troops in close proximity with AK-47 rifles. There were also heat-seeking ground-to-air missiles in the area. The FAC flew over the bunker, shooting a white phosphorous smoke to mark its exact location. The bad guys knew they were in serious trouble and opened up with massive ground fire directed at the FAC and the circling A-37s. At the FAC's direction I was cleared to drop two 500-pound bombs on the bunker. I rolled in at a low angle and released the bombs as directed. As I came off the target, the ground commander yelled over the radio that I was taking heavy ground fire—which was no surprise, with so many enemy guns in the area. I kept jinking and dodging until I reached a safe altitude. (Jinking is a radical maneuver pilots use to avoid the ground fire and make it difficult for the gunners to hit the aircraft.)

A bombing run of this kind is normally followed close behind the lead aircraft by the wingman dropping two 500-pound canisters of napalm on the same bunker. Napalm is especially effective in knocking out tanks and bunkers. Close air support delivers the kind of ordnance the ground commander requires for a specific target. The A-37 can carry and deliver, precisely on target, whatever he requests. The ground commander in this case was delighted, but wanted more napalm put down in the same area to eliminate the remaining forces and some guns that were still active. I asked the FAC to mark the target again with smoke to make sure we wouldn't hit the friendly forces that were also in the area. He marked the target with white smoke and cleared us in "hot," meaning that we were to hit the target with napalm as requested. Bill was carrying the napalm, so as flight leader I made a low-level pass at the target area, firing my Gatling gun to minimize ground fire and lead the way for Bill to drop the napalm. He followed close behind and released two 500-pound canisters of napalm that split the smoke down the middle.

In spite of previous ground fire suppression, we were still taking heavy 51-caliber and AK-47 ground fire. As I pulled off the target with a tight turn to the left, I observed Bill jinking and doing his best to avoid the ground fire. I leveled off and kept Bill in sight. Everything appeared to be normal until I heard Bill calmly say: "Sir! I'm on fire!" My response was: "You're on fire?" It was more of a question because he was still below me and I couldn't see any smoke coming from his aircraft. He came back again with a very patient and calm statement: "I think I'm going to have to get out, sir." By this time, I could see flames coming from the nose section up over the canopy and streaming back over the fuselage and tail section.

My first impression, which was in accordance with standard operating emergency procedures, was to confirm the fire, assure Bill that I had him in sight, and encourage him to actuate the rocket seat and eject immediately. But instead, I heard the Spirit whisper to me as plainly as I have ever heard anything, *"Don't let him bail out."* Why? To my surprise and his consternation, I said: "Hang in there a minute; you're not smoking." Bill, with great composure and exceptional discipline, replied: "Roger that, sir, but it's getting hot as hell in here." There was another A-37 flight in the area, and one of the pilots was taping this dialogue between Bill and myself. He came up on the radio frequency and said, "Turn off your bleed air," which is an emergency procedure for an engine fire.

Apparently he thought I didn't know what I was doing because he couldn't imagine that a flight leader would instruct his wingman to stay in an aircraft that was burning as profusely as this aircraft was burning.

This was obviously a fuel fire coming from the nose section—but where was the fuel coming from? The fuel was in the wings and the fuselage and the wing pylon tanks. The nose section had electrical equipment and the Gatling gun with 1100 rounds of 7.62 ammunition. Could it be that those shells were cooking off (getting so hot they would explode), causing the fire? No! That couldn't be! This was a fuel fire. Why couldn't I tell him to bail out? This aircraft was bound to explode—and even if it didn't explode in the next few seconds, the fire was sure to burn through the windshield, with disastrous consequences.

For some reason unknown to me, I had to keep Bill busy in the cockpit, lest he decide to leave it. I said, "Turn off your electrical; see if it's electrical." He obediently complied and started turning off some electrical switches. This was not logical, but he did it anyway. In spite of the serious nature of the fire, I still couldn't bring myself to give the bail-out order. Of course, every pilot has the prerogative of leaving a disabled aircraft at his discretion. Bill was getting impatient with this dialogue, but he was doing everything I was asking him to do. Except for the fire, the aircraft was performing beautifully, gaining altitude and getting farther away from the bad guys every minute. I told Bill once again that he wasn't trailing smoke, but we both knew that it was time to eject. About the time he was reaching for the ejection handles, he calmly announced: "Okay! The fire is pretty

5

much out, sir, and I am heading south." As I flew in closer to Bill, I could see that the fire was out.

I asked him if he had good stability and if his engines were okay. He said everything looked good in the cockpit but that he couldn't see anything outside of the canopy—it was all frosted over from the fire. On closer observation, I could see the source of the fire. He had taken a bad hit from a 51-caliber slug in the in-flight refueling line just forward of the canopy and in the same spot where the in-flight refueling light is mounted. The electrical wiring for the light had probably ignited the fuel as it came spewing out of the refueling line, causing the flames to stream up over the canopy. When all of the trapped fuel in the in-flight refueling plumbing had siphoned out, the fire went out.

If Bill had tried to bail out during the critical phase of the fire by blowing off the canopy, the flames would have engulfed the cockpit. He would have been critically burned and incapable of pulling the jettison handles to eject. He never would have made it.

Now, with the canopy badly burned and frosted over, the question became how to get Bill back to the base when he couldn't see outside of his cockpit. Rather than fly an instrument approach and landing, we decided that he should fly off my wing in tight formation and I would lead him back to the base. By lowering his seat and bending down in the cockpit, he could see enough of my aircraft to stay in formation.

I instructed Bill to jettison his remaining ordnance and perform a "before-landing" check. It appeared that all systems were functioning properly: speed brake, flaps, and landing gear. We set up a straight-in approach to the runway. Crash and emergency equipment were standing by in the event of a mal-function. Bill flew off my wing on final approach all the way down to the runway. When we touched down, I saw that he could use the side of the runway for visual reference and that he was rolling down the runway. To give him the full benefit of the entire runway, I applied power to my engines and flew around for another approach.

After Bill had cleared the runway, I landed my aircraft, shut down the engines, and jumped out of the cockpit. The fire trucks and ambulance were there, and the ground crew got Bill out of the cockpit in short order. They said his flight suit was soaking wet and the cockpit was still pretty warm. I ran over to Bill to see how he was and he came up to me and said, "Thanks."

I said, "Don't thank me," and I looked up into a beautiful blue sky.

He paused a moment and then said, "Yes, I know."

A note in the crew chief's maintenance log for Bill's aircraft reads as follows: "June 22, 1972 Aircraft #6358 returned to base having been on fire, bullet thru I.F.R. (in-flight refueling probe), windshield and canopy burned, fire damage to top forward nose section. Pilot Lt. Harrell was OK. What a feat bringing this one back! Aircraft repaired and returned to service.—Master Sergeant Bill Stevens."

There is no question in my mind that divine intervention prevented the death of a fighter pilot that day. Bill's exceptional composure and his outstanding training, discipline, and obedi-ence saved his life. This episode was audiotaped by the A-37 pilot I mentioned, and I have a copy of the tape. The dialogue between Bill and myself is verbatim. There are a number of stories, similar to this one, that characterize the caliber of the pilots and crew members in the 8th Special Operations Squadron. One of the highlights of my career was to fly combat in one of the most distinguished squadrons in the United States Air Force.

PILOT'S BIOGRAPHY

Colonel Gordon H. Weed,
United States Air Force, retired

Hometown: Salt Lake City, Utah; currently living in Centerville, Utah

Family: married to Patricia Lunt; four children, twenty-one grandchildren, and four great-grandchildren

Church experience: served a mission to Stockholm, Sweden, 1946–1949; has served as a branch president, Gospel Doctrine teacher, and Gospel Essentials teacher; served a couples mission to Seoul, Korea, from 1987–1989; later served as a high councilor and Public Affairs host; traveled back to Vietnam in 1989 with the group Veterans Assisting Saints Abroad; currently teaching Temple Preparation class

Awards and recognitions: Distinguished Flying Cross, Air Medal, Vietnamese Cross of Gallantry, and the Legion of Merit

Colonel Gordon Weed inspects Lieutenant Bill Harrell's A-37.
Note the smoke damage on the canopy.

LOCKHEED F-104 STARFIGHTER

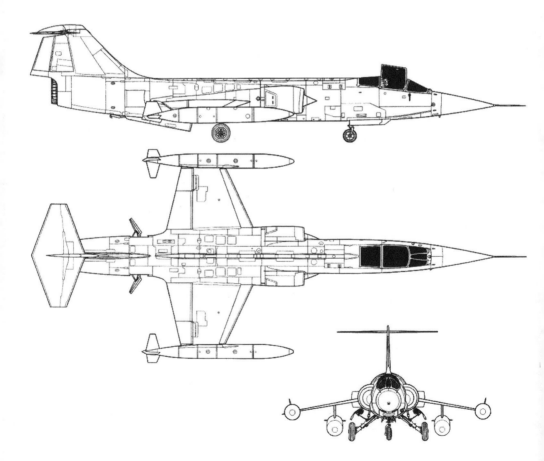

CHAPTER TWO

BLESSINGS AND MISSILES

HAROLD R. ALSTON

At the age of eighteen, I received my patriarchal blessing. In it I was promised that I would be "preserved from the ravages of the elements whether on land, the sea or in the air." I had no perception as to the impact that promise might have on my life; at that time I had never been on a boat or in an airplane. However, eighteen months later, I began training as an aviation cadet, which led to a twenty-five-year career as a United States Air Force jet fighter pilot.

In January of 1965, I requested and received orders to George Air Force Base near Victorville, California. In late February, my very pregnant wife and I loaded our three sons, aged eight, seven, and three, into our station wagon and drove from Hampton, Virginia, to California. On March 19 our fourth son was born. I had already begun training in the F-104 Starfighter. The Starfighter is nicknamed "the missile with a man in it" because of its long fuselage, short wingspan, and capability of flying at mach 2, or twice the speed of sound. By May, I was at DaNang Air Base, South Vietnam, flying combat in my new airplane with the 436th Tactical Fighter Squadron, 479th Fighter Wing.

After only a few months at home, I volunteered to transfer to the 435th TFS and deploy to Udorn Royal Thai Air Base, Thailand, for a second combat tour. This was after much prayer and discussion with Patsy, who would be left with our young family. We felt the sooner I returned to inevitable combat, the sooner I would come back home and we could settle into a new, stable assignment. I was assigned to leave two months early with a small advance party of eight airplanes and fifteen pilots. When the squadron arrived, nine of those pilots returned home, and the remaining six of us stayed until we completed a full combat tour of 100 missions each over North Vietnam. It was a daunting goal: Odds were that a pilot would be shot down once in 52 missions over the North. The advance party's tasks were to establish liaison with other squadrons already in the theatre, work out combat tactics, fly combat missions to become familiar with the area, procedures, and threats; then lead the rest of the squadron, after they arrived, by teaching them the lessons we learned.

Because of the design and performance of the airplane, our mission, among others, was to provide combat air patrol (CAP) and escort of the strike force. In other words, we were to keep enemy fighters from hindering our bombing forces who were interdicting North Vietnam. Things were much different from what I had experienced at DaNang, South Vietnam, the year before. The enemy order of battle had increased, with many more surface-to-air missiles, radar-controlled 37, 57, 85, and 100 millimeter antiaircraft weapons. There were still enemy Mig-17, 19, and 21 fighters to worry about. Most of our missions were in the Hanoi area of North Vietnam, which was extremely well defended and considered the most dangerous area in which to fly.

Our most dangerous mission was to fly Mig CAP with the F-105 Wild Weasels. The Weasels had special radar detection equipment. Their purpose was to detect and destroy antiaircraft artillery (AAA) and surface-to-air missile (SAM) sites before they could shoot at the flights of tactical bombers interdicting targets in North Vietnam. Our job was to keep the Mig aircraft from shooting down the Weasels. It was like trolling for fish. We had to fly a combat formation on the F-105s and clear the skies behind us. We were "bait" because enemy aircraft had to get through us to get at the more prized target. Typically we flew below 10,000 feet altitude, at high subsonic speeds. This envelope placed us in range of every gun and missile in the North Vietnamese arsenal. It was not a happy thought, as on top of

our work with the Migs we had to watch extra diligently for ground fire as well.

My twenty-fifth mission was an additional fulfillment of the promise made in my patriarchal blessing. We were scheduled with a flight of four to fly Mig CAP on two F-105 Wild Weasels. Flight lead was assistant operations officer Major Charley Ward. Number two was Captain Jack Kwortnik, a new pilot in the squadron. This position provided the most protection for a less-experienced pilot. Jack had spent hours with me after he arrived and picked my brain about every aspect of combat flying he could think of and any additional information that I could add. He was particularly concerned about SAMs and how to defeat them. Leading the second element in the number-three position was my roommate Captain Howie Sargeant. I was scheduled in the number-four aircraft.

We flew north from Thailand and rendezvoused with the air refueling tankers over Laos. After topping off our fuel tanks we proceeded into North Vietnam with the F-105s. As we crossed the Black River we assumed combat formation, ours being one mile behind the F-105s. We descended to about 4,000 feet above the ground. At 600 knots this did not give much maneu-vering space below us but did allow a little terrain masking if needed. Our target area was close to Hanoi.

Near the famous "Thud Ridge," just northwest of Hanoi, the Wild Weasels detected radar activity from a SAM site. Almost immediately missiles were launched at us. We were in a slight right turn at the time and I was on the left of the formation look-ing across all the airplanes. A missile was coming from our 4 o'clock position. Missiles previously fired at me had been at much higher altitude, where I could roll inverted and pull the aircraft down with 5 or 6 g's. SAMs could not turn that tightly and would crash into the ground. But, being so low, I didn't have the option of that evasive maneuver. To defeat this SAM we all pushed over with negative g's and descended close to the ground. The idea was to get the missile trajectory downward so it would not be able to track us in ground clutter and would be unable to maneuver without crashing. I saw Jack roll inverted in a "split s" to keep positive g's. Unfortunately, the time it took to roll rather than pushing did not change his aircraft position in space and allowed the SAM to intercept him. The missile hit Jack's aircraft in the fuselage behind the cockpit and a fireball developed. I saw the seat with Jack eject so quickly that I thought he had been blown out of the airplane. His F-104 crashed into the ground in about a 30-degree dive. The other members of my flight turned north toward China and accelerated to exit the high-threat area. I was still concerned about Jack and was probably the only one who knew he had been out of the airplane when it crashed.

It is never prudent to be alone and without support from a wingman in combat, but I had to check on Jack. It is amazing how fast the human mind works to scan the departing flight, watch for other SAMs, watch an aircraft crash, maintain visual sight of a pilot in peril, and pray at the same time. It may have been the quickest prayer I ever uttered when I asked Heavenly Father to let me look closely at Jack and protect me while doing so.

As the rest of my flight disappeared, I accelerated and made a hard turn around the descending parachute that held my friend. I could see no movement; the parachute was partially scorched, and the survival kit we carried and dropped before

15

landing on the ground had not been released. I was now between Jack and the SAM launch site in a hard right turn. As I looked at Jack and anticipated where he would land, my thoughts were immediately jarred back to combat when I visually acquired another SAM fired at me. It passed close but harmlessly by my aircraft. At the time I wondered how it had missed me, or why it had not detonated from the proximity fuse. Perhaps some would say my supersonic speed, closeness to the ground, and 6+ g forces saved me, but I know differently. Throughout this whole encounter I was perfectly calm, without apprehension or concern that I would be shot down. As He had done so many times before, the Lord saved me that day. Unfortunately, Jack landed in tall elephant grass and I could not see him on the ground. I did not think it prudent to make another orbit around him, but mentally memorized where he had landed so I could debrief Intelligence. Then I departed to find my flight and return to land at Udorn. Captain Jack Kwortnik was listed as missing in action and has never been accounted for.

I have always been grateful for an unseen, but not unfelt, "copilot" even though I always flew a single-seat jet fighter.

PILOT'S BIOGRAPHY

Lieutenant Colonel Harold R. Alston,
United States Air Force, retired

Call sign: Sheik

Hometown: Salt Lake City, Utah

Family: married to Patsy Casper, four sons, Doug, Brad, Russ, and Rod (all pilots), sixteen grandchildren

Church experience: Eagle Scout, bishop, bishop's counselor, ward clerk, elders quorum president, Young Men president, missionary with Patsy in Canada Winnipeg Mission, presently serving as Gospel Doctrine teacher

Hobbies: flying own airplane, being at cabin on the Smith & Morehouse River, and being with sons and grandchildren

Awards and recognitions: Distinguished Flying Cross with V device (valor), Air Medal (11), Meritorious Service Medal; first USAF pilot to fly 100 combat missions over North Vietnam in the F-104

Captain Harold Alston in the F-104.

NORTH AMERICAN F-100 SUPER SABRE

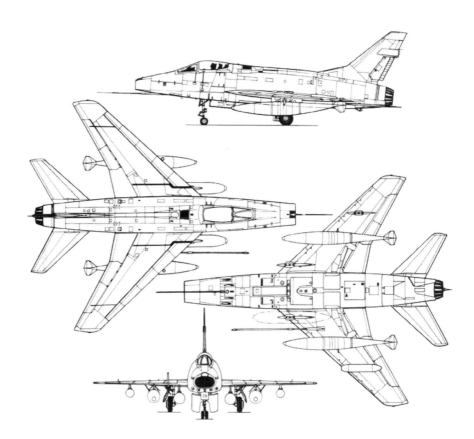

CHAPTER THREE

LIGHTNING STRIKES TWO!

THALES A. "TAD" DERRICK

The year was 1963. The "West," western nations led by the United States, and the "East," Communist Bloc nations led by Russia, were nuclear powers with huge arsenals of thermonuclear (hydrogen) bombs and missile warheads. Tensions were very high during this Cold War period, since both West and East had the capability to destroy the other as viable societies.

The United States Air Force (USAF) 48th Tactical Fighter Wing, to which I was assigned, was based at Lakenheath, England. Lakenheath, which belonged to the Royal Air Force (RAF), was loaned to the USAF as a key component of the western nations' nuclear deterrent. The "Heath," as it was affectionately called by fighter pilots, was home to three fighter squadrons. These squadrons had the main mission of maintaining a certain number of single-seat, F-100D Super Sabre fighter aircraft on nuclear alert around the clock, 365 days per year.

Geographically, Lakenheath was located on the East Anglia low-lying wetland plain in Suffolk County, about ninety miles north-northeast of London and approximately eighty miles inland from the North Sea. The English weather was typically cloudy and the temperature cold. The pilots joked that England had about one week per year of what Americans would call summer.

Fighter pilots and ground personnel were assigned with their families to three-year tours of duty. Most personnel lived off the base in small towns and villages nearby since housing on the base was very limited. My wife, our two young sons, and I lived in the town of Brandon just east of the base. We attended the Bury St. Edmund's Branch of The Church of Jesus Christ of Latter-day Saints, where I served as branch president and my wife as Relief Society president.

We had passed the two-year point of our assignment in England. I had spent my first two years as a fighter pilot in the 492nd Tactical Fighter Squadron, pulling my share of nuclear alert as well as acting as a squadron instructor pilot. I also taught aircraft weapons ground school classes.

After two years as a squadron pilot and instructor, I was selected to become part of the Wing Tactical Evaluation unit. Pilots in this unit administered various types of written and flight evaluations to squadron pilots. Pilots were required to have annual instrument flight checks and annual tactical/proficiency flight checks. For instrument flight checks, a "Tac Eval" pilot conducted the evaluation from the front seat of the two-seat F-100F aircraft, and the squadron pilot flew under a fold-down "hood" in the rear seat. Instrument checks required pilots to demonstrate that they could fly an F-100 after takeoff, put it through a variety of maneuvers, and return and land safely referring only to the flight instruments. Tactical/proficiency flight checks were conducted in two single-seat F-100D aircraft, with the "Tac Eval" pilot flying as the wingman/chase pilot to the squadron pilot being evaluated. Tactical/proficiency checks were to ensure the pilot could accomplish the assigned fighter missions.

One day, I was scheduled to give a pilot his annual tactical evaluation flight check. The sky was overcast and the ever-present damp, cold chill was in the air. I left my office in the Tac Eval unit and drove to the squadron building about two and one-half hours prior to the scheduled takeoff time. I met the pilot to be evaluated, and together we listened, on an intercom, to the base meteorologist give us the weather forecast for take-off time and for our return about two hours later. The local weather was 1,000 feet overcast with tops at 20,000 feet and two miles visibility. The forecast was to remain the same for the next six hours. There were no abnormal or severe weather advisories. According to the forecaster, it was just a regular English day. The weather over France was good with just a few scattered clouds at 5,000 feet. Visibility was greater than five miles. It seemed like an acceptable day for a tactical evaluation check.

I selected an equivalent target route in France. Equivalent target routes were low-altitude, visual navigation routes that closely simulated the type of route a pilot would fly if scrambled to attack a Communist Bloc target with a nuclear weapon. These were the days long before GPS navigation, and pilots had to learn to fly at altitudes below 500 feet to avoid enemy radar and to navigate to their assigned target using precise headings and precise times while confirming their position by visually acquired ground references such as power lines, roads, bridges, railroads, rivers, and other topographical features. Airspeed would be between 420 and 575 miles per hour, with the higher speed used as aircraft approached the equivalent target.

21

The pilot being evaluated conducted the flight briefing. He gave a fine briefing that covered the entire flight from engine start to engine shutdown after landing. After engine start, we would assemble on the taxiway and proceed to the takeoff runway. I would note the takeoff time, as there was a requirement to be over the equivalent target at an exact time. We would make a formation takeoff with me on his right wing. We would have our exterior white, red, and green lights in the "bright steady" position since we would be entering the clouds almost immediately after takeoff. I would maintain close formation until we were on top of the clouds—expected to be at 20,000 feet. The pilot being evaluated would then signal me to take a "chase position" about 1,000 feet behind his aircraft, 1,000 feet to the side, and 200 feet above his altitude. This would give me a good vantage point to evaluate his navigation and also help look out for other aircraft.

The pilot would begin a visual descent at a predetermined point over France, level off at 500 feet above the ground, and navigate to the equivalent target. I would note his Time-On-Target (TOT). Making the TOT was very critical since timing in a nuclear conflict is unimaginably vital. We would then climb back to altitude, return to the radio beacon in England that marked our location for beginning the planned instrument approach, make a formation descent, be acquired by Ground Controlled Approach (GCA) radar, and make a formation landing. Piece of cake! We had both flown similar profiles dozens of times, and this one seemed no different.

Everything went as outlined initially in the briefing. We entered the clouds at about 1,000 feet above the ground, and I moved in closer because the clouds were a bit more dense than usual. I held his green right wingtip light about four feet from my canopy and aligned with the white light behind his canopy. Then, at about 7,000 feet above the ground, it happened! There was a brilliant flash of lightning and a number of events occurred simultaneously: My engine compressor stalled violently (a compressor stall in a jet engine occurs when the airflow entering the engine intake is suddenly disrupted, the compressor airfoils "stall," and dynamic pressure in the engine that normally proceeds from front to rear attempts to reverse); the compressor stall was accompanied by a very loud bang and a resulting sharp thump on the cockpit floor; the cockpit air-conditioning system sent a flow of ozone into the cockpit; the aircraft began to vibrate severely; several caution and warning lights illuminated; my engine oil pressure registered zero; all communication and navigation radios ceased to function; and

a realization dawned on me that my aircraft been hit by a bolt of lightning!

The pilot in the lead aircraft peered at me through the mist of the clouds and soon realized that my radio was inoperative. We communicated via hand signals. He too had been hit by the same bolt of lightning! Since I was technically in command of the flight as the check pilot, he asked via hand signals if I wanted to take the lead. I shook my head in the standard reply of "no." I was "blind" as to our location and could not contact any agency by radio. I signaled him to begin a 180-degree turn. He did an excellent job of maintaining aircraft control. He was now my lifeline to be able to return to base, if the aircraft held together that long. He did have a functional radio and was able to contact GCA and request an emergency return to base. His aircraft damage seemed less severe than mine.

We began a descent, and the vibration of my aircraft seemed to increase. My theory was that the lightning had damaged the engine compressor and perhaps a compressor blade or two had broken off and damaged other engine components, causing a complete loss of oil pressure, and this was the cause of the vibration. We had been taught that the engine would run for only a very few minutes if oil pressure was lost. I realized that I would need to eject from the aircraft if the engine failed. Flight controls would also be lost with engine failure since they were hydraulic and used engine-driven pumps for pressure. A ram air turbine might provide some temporary flight control if hydraulic fluid was still available.

The thought of the ejection itself didn't worry me as much as where a pilotless airplane might go. I knew we were now somewhere north of the base, and there were several villages in that area. There were also marshes and woodlands. I began to pray, "Heavenly Father, if it be possible I would like to get this aircraft on the ground safely. However, if that is not to be, please help me maintain control until I get below the clouds and can point the airplane toward an unpopulated area and then eject." I had felt calm throughout the emergency, but the trained calmness was now replaced with a divine, secure feeling of peace. The Spirit assured me all would be well.

No sooner had I begun to feel comforted than I realized that if the engine kept running, our flight of two fighters would soon be turning to the final approach heading. Our final approach path would take us near RAF Mildenhall, a neighboring airbase, and the Mildenhall Elementary School. Another prayer: "Heavenly Father, whatever happens, please keep my aircraft away from Mildenhall and especially the elementary school." The Spirit was almost reproving, "All will be well."

The lead pilot signaled that we were on final approach and to lower the speed brake, landing gear, and wing flaps. All three systems worked fine on both aircraft. At last, about two miles from touchdown, our aircraft descended out of the clouds, and although my head was turned toward the lead aircraft and I was concentrating on flying good, close formation, I could see the runway at Lakenheath straight ahead out of the corner of my right eye. I kept telling myself, "Be smooth on the throttle. No abrupt changes. Don't cut the throttle until you know you have the runway made." We passed over the 1,000 foot overrun, and the lead pilot reduced power smoothly. I followed his action, and soon my wheels were rolling down the runway, as were those on the lead aircraft. We both deployed our drag-chutes, and I shut my engine down to prevent what I feared might be a post-landing fire. Fire suppression trucks followed me as I coasted off the runway and onto a taxiway. Other fire trucks followed the lead aircraft.

"Whew! I thank Thee, Heavenly Father, for getting me back safely. That was one spooky ride."

I noticed the firefighters pointing and looking at my aircraft's vertical fin and shaking their heads. I wondered what those actions meant. Maintenance personnel supplied me with a ladder, and after the cockpit and ejection seat were secured, I climbed out of the cockpit and looked at the vertical fin. It was shredded!

Both aircraft were towed back to the maintenance area, and the other pilot and I looked at both airplanes and reconstructed what had happened. The lightning bolt had hit his aircraft in the left wing, traveled through the wing center box, exited his right wing, and entered my left wing. It had then traveled through my aircraft electrical and avionics system, followed the large electrical cable down the top of the fuselage behind the canopy, and exited through the vertical fin—shredding it on the way out. Both engines had compressor stalled when the lightning burned up the air nearby, but neither engine was damaged. The ozone we both smelled in our cockpits was caused by the lightning. The zero oil pressure was due to burned wiring. The severe vibration I felt was not due to engine damage, but to the vertical fin sheet metal flapping in the airstream. (The top of the vertical fin looked much like an umbrella that had been turned inside out by a strong wind that had ripped the fabric off, leaving only the metal "fingers" of the frame.) The lead pilot had no reason to suspect the vertical fin problem and probably could not have seen it anyway in the dense clouds.

The Director of Operations, my boss, met us at the squadron. The Chief of Maintenance had briefed him on the aircraft damage. He gave us both a handshake and an "atta-boy." After we debriefed the flight, I asked the other pilot when he would be ready for his Tac Eval check flight, since we had not completed it. He said, "How about tomorrow?" I smiled and said, "Fine, but let's get a different guy to give us the weather briefing." We laughed and went to the weather intercom and told the briefer who had given us the forecast that we had a "Pirep" (a *Pirep* is a pilot report of weather conditions). We said, "We report an imbedded thunderstorm with forked lightning at 7,000 feet about 40 miles east of Lakenheath." He said he had heard all about it and was as surprised as we were at the imbedded thunderstorm. We said, "We doubt you were quite as surprised as we were."

Kneeling at my bedside that night in personal prayer, I reviewed the events of the flight in my mind, and again and more formally thanked our Heavenly Father for His watchful care and for allowing my role as son, husband, father, branch president, and fighter pilot to continue, that I might be of service to His children in all of my roles.

PILOT'S BIOGRAPHY

Lieutenant Colonel Thales A. "Tad" Derrick,
Unites States Air Force, retired

Call sign: Meteor

Hometown: Salt Lake City, Utah; St. George, Utah

Family: married to Willa Nita Brooks; children are David, Daniel, Dennis, Dana, and Douglas; twenty-three grandchildren

Church experience: bishop, high councilor, stake president, mission president, now a counselor in stake presidency

Hobbies: Church and community service (active in CERT); caring for small orchard; computers; flying own aircraft, a C-172 SkyHawk

Awards and recognitions: Distinguished Flying Cross, Distinguished Service Medal (3 awards), Air Medal (five awards), among others

Captain Thales A. "Tad" Derrick in the cockpit of an F-100D Super Sabre. The shoulder patch designates the 48th Tactical Fighter Wing, known as the "Statue of Liberty Wing."

CH-53D HELICOPTER

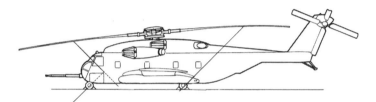

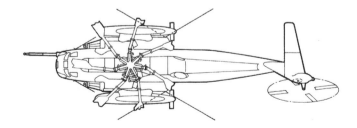

CHAPTER FOUR

THE NIGHT THE LIGHTS WENT OUT

DAVID WASSINK

In 1991, most Marine units were involved in Operation Desert Storm. It was my lot in life to be assigned at the time as one of the active duty instructors at a Reserve helicopter squadron, HMH-772, stationed in Willow Grove, Pennsylvania. I was a well-seasoned captain who had recently graduated from the Marine Corps Weapons and Tactics Instructor's course, the helicopter equivalent of "Top Gun."

Like many, we watched the progress of the war with Iraq from home on the television. It was like being in the stands while your teammates are on the field playing the game. Finally, in March of 1991 we were told the unit would be mobilized. We initially moved the squadron down to New River, North Carolina, and became members of the 2nd Marine Air Wing. About a month later, still with no real indication of what we were going to do, since the war was pretty much over by then, we were ordered to Tustin, California, where we joined the 3rd Marine Air Wing. After arriving there we were informed that we would deploy to Okinawa, Japan, to relieve the squadron there that had been forced to extend their deployment when Desert Storm kicked off. A couple of weeks after arriving in California, we were boarding a plane to Okinawa, where we then became a part of the 1st Marine Air Wing, giving us the dubious distinction of having been part of a squadron assigned to that many different Marine Air Wings in less than ninety days.

Once in Okinawa, life quickly settled into a routine interrupted only by the occasional typhoon. That is, until Mount Pinatubo erupted in the Philippines, covering Clark Air Force Base and the Subic Bay Naval facility in a foot or more of volcanic ash. The ash caused roofs to collapse, shorted out electrical systems, and fouled air-conditioning units and drinking water without discrimination. The American servicemen and women with their families at those two installations were in some pretty rough circumstances, so the decision was made to evacuate them.

We flew four of our CH-53Ds aboard the USS *Midway*, loaded up with supplies, and set sail for the Philippines in short order. The *Midway* was an old aircraft carrier that was preparing to be decommissioned. It was ironic that the last actual mission she would fill would be with helicopters aboard, not jets. Along the way we did what research we could on the effects of volcanic ash on aircraft, particularly turbine engines. We wanted to be ready for anything once we started operating near a live volcano.

Our arrival at Subic Bay was rather eerie. It looked as if the whole area was covered with a gray, thick layer of snow— except it was June in the Philippines. All the utilities on the shore were out. Later, as we flew over the area, we noted our maps weren't worth much since the terrain had changed so dramatically. Valleys that had been lined by hills reaching 700 feet above the valley floor no longer existed, with ash filling in the valley completely.

The families and nonessential servicemen were loaded aboard the *Midway* with row upon row of cots set up on the hangar deck. It was a noisy place but all were happy to be someplace with working lights and fresh water. As soon as the last evacuee was aboard, we pulled anchor and headed south to Cebu, the Philippines. There we would fly all our guests off to the airport to await further transportation back to the States.

Since we had almost 4,000 guests aboard the *Midway* and only four CH-53Ds to move them with, we knew we were in for a long day shuttling passengers with their few bags ashore. The operation extended well into the night and I was designated as one of the night flyers. The aircraft commander had been flying for several hours when I hot-seated in to get current again before carrying passengers off the ship at night.

It was a dark, moonless night. The use of night-vision devices was still somewhat novel and not completely accepted as it is today. Our night flying off the ship would be unaided, partly because of policy and partly because there just wasn't enough light to make the night vision goggles (NVGs) useful.

After strapping in, the aircraft commander gave me the controls and we were given permission to take off. I climbed straight ahead and climbed to establish single-engine parameters in case we lost an engine. Once we had sufficiently climbed and accelerated, I started a crosswind turn. It was then that the number one generator dropped off the line.

As a crew, we had briefed electrical problems, including both single and dual generator failures. Single generator failures were not uncommon and not a big event because we always had the second generator to carry the load. We were briefed that if the second generator failed, an extremely unlikely event, the pilot not at the controls would use his flashlight to illuminate the nonelectric gauges for the flying pilot. We would then signal the tower using flares that we needed to land. The aircraft commander went through the procedures to try to reset the generator but it wouldn't come back on line. It didn't reset, so I started to call the tower to let them know we needed to land. I had just started the call when the second and only remaining generator dropped off.

Flying in the dark without reference to any gauges is not something I would recommend to anyone. The only references I had to maintain level flight were the stars above and the lights from the shore, which looked suspiciously like the stars above. Of course we had smooth seas too, so there were reflections off

the water that were starlike in their quality as well. The aircraft commander tried to reset the generators, but no luck. Meanwhile I was anxiously trying to keep the wings level and avoid a descent. Swimming that night was *not* on my agenda. Unfortunately I had nothing I could trust to tell me if I was succeeding in keeping things flying. Also, without electrical power there is no augmentation on the flight controls, requiring the pilot to use significantly more effort to move the controls. It is kind of like losing the power steering in your car. The steering wheel becomes rather difficult to turn.

We are taught not to trust the "seat of our pants" when we have no reference to the horizon. Instead, we are to follow our instruments. The problem was that the instruments requiring electricity to run were useless and I couldn't see the static gauges. The aircraft commander was yelling things to the crew chief and they seemed to be discussing things, but I couldn't tell what they were saying. Meanwhile, I was only guessing at flying the aircraft. This seemed to go on for an eternity. I kept waiting for the aircraft commander to use his flashlight to help me see the gauges.

Finally, the crew chief fired up the auxiliary power plant (APP) and tried to reset the number two generator. This is not a normal or briefed practice. It is not mentioned anywhere in our emergency procedures. To this day I do not know what inspired him to light the APP and try again to reset the generator. I do know that it worked, however, and we were able to regain the essential lights and gauges to fly. The total time for the outage was only about three or four minutes—but at 500 feet, that is more than enough time to descend into the water. Miraculously, I had only gained fifty feet of altitude, our wings were level, and we were on the desired heading. With the radios back on line, I wasted no time in declaring an emergency and turning in toward the ship, hoping the generator would stay on. It did, and we landed safely without further incident.

In reflecting on this episode, it has become clear to me that several factors were at work. First, because of my training and experiences, I was able to feel what the aircraft was telling me, much like we can gain a feel for listening to the Spirit through practice and living the commandments. Second, after all we can do, Heavenly Father will bless us with what we need. In this case, it was trying a way to regain electrical power that was not the standard. Finally, even though we may plan in order to react and minimize difficult situations, sometimes life may bring us the unexpected, and we need to cope with things as best we can, always being guided by the Spirit.

PILOT'S BIOGRAPHY

Colonel David Wassink,
United States Marine Corps, drilling reservist

Call sign: Waz

Hometown: Tonawanda, New York

Family: married to Ruth Van Buskirk Wassink, five children

Church experience: former bishop, counselor in bishopric, Scoutmaster, elders quorum president; currently the servicemen's group leader, Al Asad Air Base, Iraq

Current occupation: technical director, General Dynamics Information Technology, when not mobilized

Awards and recognitions: more than 2000 hours in the CH-53A/D/E, Air Medal with Combat V, two Meritorious Service Medals, two Sikorsky Rescue awards, and numerous other military awards

Colonel David Wassink with the CH-53D.

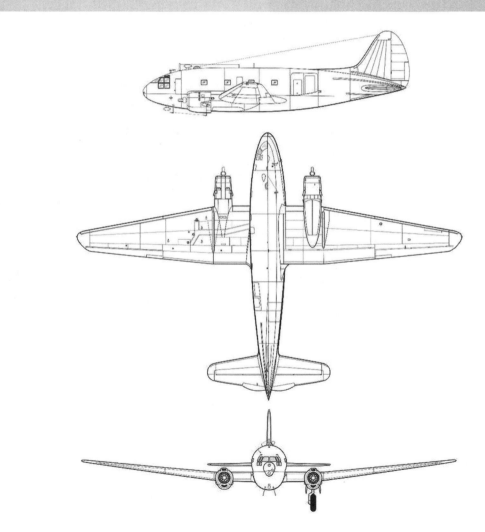

CHAPTER FIVE

EMERGENCY—IS MY ENGINE ON FIRE?

CECIL RAY HANSEN

From the time the Japanese forces gained control of Burma during World War II and were threatening to invade India until the combined American-English-Burmese-Chinese-Indian forces pushed them south and secured the Myitkyina area with the Myitkyina airfield, airplanes flying the "Hump" between India and western China had no emergency place to land. The route between India and China required pilots to fly over the massive Himalayan mountains in Burma. It is from those mountains that the region gained the nickname of the "Hump." Because the Japanese controlled Burma, and landing in the mountains was impossible, flying the "Hump" always meant traveling clear from from India to the destination in China, then a return trip all the way back to India or bail out—not much of a choice. Hence, even if the weather was reasonably good and no enemy aircraft were encountered, every flight could be an emotional as well as a physical challenge.

So it was for me on one return trip from a base in the Kunming (Ynnan) area. The daylight flight to China had been uneventful and I expected the return trip back to India to be the same. We took off and climbed to an altitude of 15,000 feet on our assigned course, leveled off, and settled back in our seats. There were only a few scattered clouds over the mountaintops and there was very little, if any, turbulence. The aircraft seemed to be functioning normally; however, I repeatedly scanned the instrument panel as I had been taught to do on every training base since the beginning of my pilot training. We had flown about one-third of the way back when I saw the oil pressure on the left engine begin to drop. Minutes later, the left engine temperature started to rise.

From my seat I could see the front of the left engine, which appeared to be all right, so I asked the radio operator to go back into the cargo area and make a visual check from one of the windows. He returned quickly and reported some smoke coming from the back of the engine under the wing. By that time, the oil pressure had dropped considerably and the engine temperature was continuing to rise. I told the copilot what I suspected and instructed him to keep the airplane on a straight course while I shut down the left engine, feathered the propeller (to reduce the drag on the airplane), and released the engine fire extinguisher in case we had any fire in the engine area. The radioman made another visual check from the cargo area and reported no more smoke. So far, so good.

Now we had to see if the plane would hold our current altitude on one engine, or at least let us descend slowly enough to keep above the remaining mountain ridges we had to cross. I did not have any feeling of panic although I felt some concern since I had never had the experience of flying a C-46 on one engine. Also, my crew (copilot and radioman) did not seem to be worried and expressed confidence in my flying ability.

It was soon obvious that our plane would not stay at 15,000

feet and that our airspeed had decreased with only one engine. However, our descent was gradual enough that I felt we would clear all the remaining mountain ridges and get back to our base in India. Time passed and we were finally crossing the last ridge with altitude to spare. The radioman called the Sookerating Base control tower and informed them that we would be making a single-engine landing. We were cleared to do so and I began to feel the pressure of having to make such a landing, but all went well and we were soon on the ground and led by the "Follow Me" jeep along with two other jeeps into our assigned parking place.

By the time I had filled out the airplane's log book, the base engineer and the plane's crew chief had the engine's cowling (covering) up and were shaking their heads at what they found. The engine was covered with oil and, as they observed, should have caught fire even with the engine fire extinguisher's use.

There was no logical explanation (to them) why we didn't burn up. We truly had been blessed and saved from a fiery crash or, at least, from having to bail out on the side of the plane where there would have been flames coming from a burning engine. We would have been parachuting into the very steep and rugged Himalayan mountainous terrain, from which some crews who bailed were never found. I was so thankful to return to Sookerating again safely. This is just one of a number of my experiences in the CBI (China-Burma-India) theater where my life and the lives of the members of my crew were spared.

In my patriarchal blessing given some five years later, the Lord reminded me of my blessings during those experiences with these words: "You have been through many trials having been called into the service of your country and . . . you have seen many, many times the workings of the Lord and the things that He has done in your behalf and in your protection."

PILOT'S BIOGRAPHY

First Lieutenant Cecil Ray Hansen, United States Army Air Force

Hometown: American Fork, Utah

Family: married to Nina Elizabeth Sykes; three daughters, one son, and one adopted son; they also have twenty grandchildren and thirty-two great-grandchildren (with two more on the way)

Church experience: served a full-time mission with his wife from 1986 1987 in the Louisiana Baton Rouge/Florida Tallahassee Missions; served in many teaching and leadership positions such as bishop, high councilor, stake clerk, counselor to stake president, counselor to mission president, temple worker, and stake patriarch (1976–2006); currently serving as ward chorister

Education and occupation: served as a pilot in Engineer Battalion Headquarters Company for about three years after World War II; received bachelor's and master's degrees from University of Utah, doctorate of education from Brigham Young University; worked as a teacher, principal, and district administrator; currently retired and serves as a caregiver for his wife

Awards: received two Air Medals; twice received the Distinguished Flying Cross; and received three Unit Battle Stars

Lieutenant Cecil Hansen outside the operations office, Sookerating, India.

BEECHCRAFT T-34C MENTOR

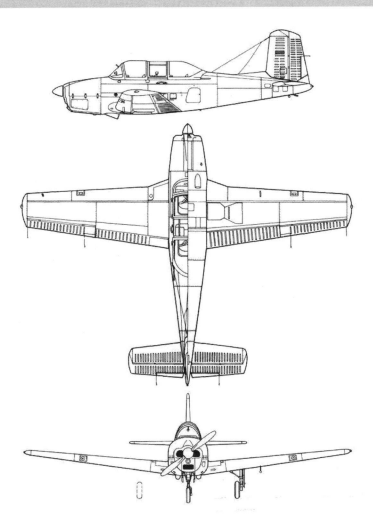

CHAPTER SIX

SOLO

JANINE K. GARNER

Back in the winter of 2001, I was in Naval Primary Flight Training at Whiting Field in Pensacola, Florida. I had completed Aviation Preflight Indoctrination (API), ground school, the half-dozen mandatory Basic Instrument simulator trainers and flights, and the thirteen familiarization (FAM) flights required before you are allowed to sign for a plane and go fly by yourself—to fly "solo." I had a meager forty hours under my belt at that time, and had never flown anything in my life up until I began flight school, but I was ready for anything up in the air while flying the Beechcraft T-34C Mentor.

The T-34C is a delightful little aircraft that thousands of marines, sailors, and even the occasional airman have learned to fly in naval flight school. It is reminiscent of a World War II plane, with a single, prop-driven engine; two seats, one in front for the student, and one in the rear for the instructor; and a bubble glass canopy that was all that kept you from the sky.

Flying was both thrilling and humbling at the same time. Thrilling to put the plane through its paces and recover from a spin or a stall perfectly, or land so smoothly your instructor couldn't even tell if you had touched down. Humbling when you

45

botched up an emergency procedure in practice, or didn't know the answer to the question on the fuel system that you were asked. Constant vigilance and study of the flight manuals and your emergency procedures were necessary in order to pass the syllabus and to survive in the event you did face a real emergency on your solo flight, not just a simulated one that the instructor placed before you.

So, on February 8, 2002, after I had passed my thirteenth FAM flight, my "Check Flight" (the flight where they throw every simulated emergency possible at you to ensure you truly are ready to fly solo), in the early afternoon my instructor signed me off and told the Flight Duty Officer (FDO) that I was ready for my solo flight. So, before I could even call my husband to let him know that I'd passed my Check Flight, I had signed for and walked out to my plane . . . completely and utterly alone. I was thrilled! I knew I would do great, and I knew I was ready for anything.

I completed my walk-around inspection of the plane, climbed inside, ran through my checklists, and started up the engine. Pausing to say a quick prayer on the runway before I took off, I asked Heavenly Father to help me remember all of my training and to bring me and the plane back safely since now I had no instructor in the backseat to bail me out of a tight spot. Then I was in the air all by myself, with no instructor to harp on me, ask me questions about the electrical system, correct my flying, tell me where to go, and so on. Nope, I was on my own. I was free. It was a glorious feeling to fly around Pensacola in that quiet cockpit with nothing but the static of the radio and the hum of the propeller to fill the void. Utilizing the Visual Flight Rules (VFR) that I had been taught, I made my way over to Saufley Airfield to execute my required three solo touch-and-go landings before I returned back to base. I hadn't been taught Instrument Flight Rules (IFR) yet, other than my Basic Instrument (BI) flights, where I had gained a basic understanding of what to do when I couldn't see the ground outside to get a visual reference of where I was. But I wasn't worried—the sun was bright and the sky was clear. Besides, they wouldn't have let a solo take off if the weather was going to be bad; we were allowed to fly only in VFR conditions.

Executing three perfect touch-and-go landings at Saufley (of course they were perfect, since I was the only judge), I turned back to base and started following the course rules to Whiting Field. Everything was going fine until I passed the Chicken Ranch (one of the visual checkpoints we used), when I realized that the ground was getting harder to see. Looking ahead I could see lots of smoke; it turned out that north of Whiting Field there was a controlled burn being done, and the smoke from it was starting to obscure the course rules. In short, I was having a hard time seeing where I was going. To someone trained to fly in IFR conditions, this is no big deal; you've learned to trust your instruments and the data they are giving you, and not to trust your eyes, or what you feel in the "seat of your pants." In IFR conditions, your mind and eyes can play tricks on you, and because of certain G-forces, it can sometimes "feel" like you are climbing, descending, or turning, when in fact you are in straight and level flight. This can be very dangerous for the obvious reason that if you trust what you are "feeling" and the visual illusions before you, and not what your instruments are telling you, you could very easily fly yourself straight into the ground or into a mountainside.

I had been prepared for every eventuality but this one. I had been prepared to lose my engine and have to glide to the ground. I'd been prepared for my landing gear not to work, or for my plane to catch on fire, or to hit a bird. I'd been prepared to have to bail out of my plane and deploy my parachute, but I was *not* prepared to lose sight of my visual guides—my "road" home to safety. In short, I was not prepared to be lost and unable to see where I was going. As I radioed the tower to let them know that I could no longer see the field, they told me to execute "lost sight" procedures and to execute a "TACAN arrival." I had no idea what a TACAN was—only that it was something used to help pilots navigate safely in IFR conditions. Even if I had known, I didn't have an "Approach Plate" (the "map" that tells you how to do a TACAN arrival) on the plane, and I certainly didn't know how to read one. All I knew how to do was to stare at my instruments and maintain my altitude,

heading, and airspeed. I quickly informed the tower that I was on my very first solo flight and certainly did not know how to execute a TACAN arrival. The radio was silent, and the longest moment in my life up until then passed while I waited for a response.

I was completely alone, and with no instructor in the back-seat to help me, the thrill of freedom I had previously felt turned into fear and confusion. I knew safety was nearby, but I had lost sight of the road to it and didn't know how to get there. I focused all my efforts on ignoring the visual illusions that the setting sun was giving me through the layer of smoke outside and concentrated on keeping my wings level according to my gyro, maintaining my airspeed, and flying my last assigned heading. Afraid to close my eyes for even a moment, I said a prayer to Heavenly Father to guide me safely home and to help me fight the urge to follow my "feelings" and what my mind was telling me was "straight and level flight," but to trust my instruments instead. Before I could even finish my prayer, I was quickly filled with a sense of peace and the knowledge that even though my instructor was not in the plane with me, I was not alone.

Just then the tower radioed back to me a new heading and altitude to fly. They had all other aircraft holding while myself and two other solos who were in the same situation as I was were given vectors to the airfield, with hopes that we would break out of the smoke overhead of the airfield and be able to execute a Precautionary Emergency Landing (PEL) onto one of the runways. I was the first one vectored in, and, going against what my senses were telling me to do, I trusted in my instruments and the tower controller and plowed my way through that smoke. After what seemed like an eternity, my eyes beheld the most beautiful sight they'd seen that day: the runway at Whiting Field. I quickly lowered my landing gear and flaps, executed my before-landing checklist, and, intercepting the landing pattern from where I was, brought it in for a safe landing.

As I taxied off the runway, relief flooded into me, and I paused for another moment when safely clear to thank Heavenly Father for guiding me safely home.

I have often recalled in the years since, how easy it is to take for granted the straight and narrow path that leads to our Father in Heaven. So long as we are diligent we will never get lost, and we can always make it safely home to Him, but if we take our eyes off the goal for even a moment through neglect or unrighteousness, we may find the way obscured such that we can no longer see our way clear to safety. During these times we may feel completely alone, scared, and lost, but we must never forget that we are never truly on our own. The Holy Ghost is always in the "backseat of the plane" waiting for us to ask Him to help guide us back onto the path home to Heavenly Father. We may not like the way He wants us to go, and it may be hard, but we need to trust the instruments the Lord has given to guide us (the scriptures, prayer, Church leaders) and not fall prey to the visual illusions that Satan places before us.

PILOT'S BIOGRAPHY

Captain Janine K. Garner,
United States Marine Corps

Call sign: ATIS

Hometown: St. George, Utah

Family: married to Captain Ronald T. Garner, USMC, since 2001

Church experience: former Primary teacher, Young Women's teacher, Young Women's basketball coach; currently a Relief Society teacher

Current occupation: still flying for the USMC

Awards and recognitions: more than 1,000 flight hours in the Marine Corps, over five Air Medals, numerous other military awards, medals, and honors

Captain Janine K. Garner with the T-34C.

MCDONNELL DOUGLAS F-4 PHANTOM

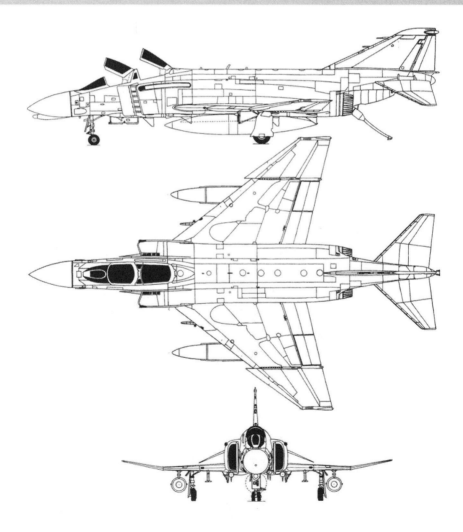

CHAPTER SEVEN

MAYDAY! MAYDAY! MAYDAY!

FRED WILSON

I spent nearly twenty years flying for the Idaho Air National Guard as a Weapons Systems Officer (WSO) on an F-4 Phantom. Flying this airplane was literally a childhood dream come true. I accumulated approximately 2,200 flying hours. This included fifteen years flying the RF-4C, photo reconnaissance version of the F-4 Phantom, and four and a half years flying the F-4G "Wild Weasel" ground attack version of the F-4. It also included two combat tours (1993 and 1994) flying out of Dhahran, Saudi Arabia, into southern Iraq. I retired from the Idaho Air National Guard in December 1994.

This is an account of an incident that happened to me with Captain Greg Engelbreit on April 8, 1982. I was a first lieutenant and had been flying for about four and a half years.

The flight was a normal, night-radar, low-level training mission. I had planned a route at 1,000 feet above the ground flying at 480 knots (550 mph). We took off about 7:00 P.M. from Gowen Field in Boise, Idaho. It was a beautiful evening; the sun was just setting in a clear sky. We entered the low-level about fifteen minutes after takeoff flying west in the general direction of Burns, Oregon.

A radar low-level ride means that the pilot is flying a terrain-following mode on the radar. He gets commands that say *climb* and *descend* to keep us at a relatively constant altitude above the ground. He doesn't have any navigation capability to know where we are. In the backseat, my radar screen showed the ground returns ahead of us, so I could navigate using points that I had predetermined I would look for. But I could not see the terrain clearance on my scope. The pilot and I were each mutually dependent as he flew terrain clearance and I flew navigation.

After about fifteen minutes of low-level, which would have been about 120 miles of flying, we pulled up slightly to make a left turn. Suddenly I felt an impact. Training kicked in, and I grabbed the stick and pulled, causing the airplane to pitch up away from the ground. I tried to talk to Greg but got no response. Looking around, I found the cockpit framed in feathers and knew that we had hit a bird. The bird, later determined to be a twenty-two-pound whistling swan, had broken through the left front-quarter panel of the windscreen, striking Greg in the shoulder and face.

My first thought was, "Wow! We hit a bird!" followed quickly by, "I don't need to be going this fast." I pulled the power back, leveled off, and turned toward Boise. I then made the radio call that I thought I would never make, and had never heard on the radio. I had been taught since I was getting my private pilot's license to make this call in an emergency. It is designed to get everyone's attention. It is a call that fearless jet flyers would never make. I hit the microphone and said, in what I thought was my best soprano voice, "Mayday! Mayday! Mayday!" When I got no immediate reply, I switched to the common emergency frequency, named Guard, and repeated the call. My next thought was, "Heavenly Father, I really need your help to get us out of this."

With the broken windscreen and, I found out later, a hole in Greg's oxygen mask, the noise was quite loud on the intercom, making it very hard to hear any radio calls. When I made the second Mayday call, the other three F-4s from our squadron that were flying low-levels that night, as well as an F-111 returning to Mountain Home, tried to respond to me. I couldn't hear any of them. As I slowed down, the noise decreased and I was more able to hear. About this time, Greg lowered the landing gear and wing flaps—things that I couldn't do from the backseat, but that we had discussed that he would do in an emergency.

One of the other F-4s contacted the air traffic control center and was directed to my position. I didn't know that Major Bill Miller and his WSO, Mike McGrath, had joined with me and were flying formation on my left side. I could not see them because of the bird remains on the inside of my canopy. When center told me they were there, I had Bill move to the other side where I could fly formation with him—something I had really never done before, especially at night!

As we flew toward Mountain Home AFB, a place with longer runways and more rescue facilities, suddenly a warning light came on. It was only about an inch square, but that Master Caution Light looked to fill the whole panel—then it went off. I told Bill about the light, not knowing what was wrong. He told me that Greg had just lowered the tail hook and then reset the Master Caution Light. This was a relief to me as I had no way of putting the hook down, and I needed it for the emergency landing.

I later learned that Greg had done several things for me that

I didn't know about and couldn't do. He had turned his oxygen to 100 percent; he had turned the radar transponder to emergency, which told all of the ground radar people that we had a problem; he had also cleaned off a small area on the side of his canopy so he could see the other airplane. Not bad for a guy who, the doctors said, *was totally unconscious from his injuries.*

We flew formation for what seemed a long time, but probably was only a half hour—we had slowed down to 180 knots (200 mph). When you fly formation on the wing, the only thing you watch is the other airplane. Everything you do involves moving relative to the lead airplane—you don't look around. My first real knowledge of where we were was when I saw the lights of Mountain Home behind Bill. The next time I knew *for sure* where we were was when I saw lights as we were about to touch down. Bill led me to a formation landing and then he did a touch-and-go, leaving me the clear runway. With my hook down, I was able to catch the arresting cable (kind of like on an aircraft carrier) and get stopped. I have been told it was a very smooth formation and landing.

I sat on the runway, holding the brakes, unable to shut the engines off from the backseat. The fire/rescue people came and two men climbed up onto the airplane, looked at my ejection seat, and gave me a thumbs-up indicating it was okay. When I opened my canopy, they asked if I could shut the engines off. I told them it had to be done from the front seat. One of the men on the airplane was the wing commander from Mountain Home AFB, Colonel Coleman. He held onto Tech Sergeant Gardner's belt as he leaned over the intake to open Greg's canopy and shut off the engines.

I got out and used my seat's safety pins to secure Greg's

ejection seat. Greg meantime was securing his lower ejection handle—raising a guard into place to safety it. They got Greg out on a stretcher, and he said, "Fred, what happened?"

I replied, "We hit a bird, we're on the ground in Mountain Home, and you are going to be okay."

He said, "Okay." And then he was really unconscious. Greg was med-evaced to St. Al's Hospital in Boise, and I was examined at the base hospital and flown back, by helicopter, to Boise.

Greg underwent several major surgeries and bone grafts, and was medically retired from the military. He didn't remember the flight at all.

About a week later, I was released to fly again. I attempted to fly close formation again and lower the gear. I was all over the sky! It seems I was not able to do it without adrenaline and heavenly help.

In the aftermath of the event, Greg and I received several awards. In September of 1982, we went to Washington, D.C., and received the Earl T. Ricks Award from the Air Force Association. In July of 1983 we again went to Washington, D.C., to receive the Cheney Award presented at the Pentagon by the Chief of Staff of the Air Force.

I also received the Air Force Well Done Award from the Air Force Safety Office; the Tactical Air Command Air Crew of Distinction Award; and the Distinguished Flying Cross for heroism in aerial flight.

In August of 1983 we made a third trip to Washington, D.C., where I received the Koren Kolligian Jr. Trophy. This was presented in the Pentagon by the Chief of Staff of the Air Force, General Charles Gabriel, with numerous other generals and colonels in attendance. We then had a luncheon with General Gabriel and the Kolligian family. This award is presented for the most outstanding act of airmanship in the United States Air Force for the year.

A lesson that I learned looking back at this experience was the importance of preparation. Before every flight, we would sit down as a crew and discuss the mission we were going to do. We would talk about expected events, and we would talk about possible emergencies and how we would react. One of the emergencies that we talked about before every flight was the possibility of a bird strike. We flew in the altitudes that were used by birds—relatively low. It got to be almost common, like listening to the safety briefing on an airliner; most people listen once, then skim through it. We would say, "I will do this, you will do that"—without having to think about what we were planning to do; it was always the same.

When we hit the bird, we didn't have to think about what to do. We both reacted according to the decisions that we had previously made. The preparations we had done and the decisions we made in advance guided us when there was no time to think, or wonder, or ponder. Many decisions in life can be made in advance in this same way, so that when the choice arrives, the decision has already been made.

An interesting added note: On April 7, 1983, another Thursday night exactly a year later, I was flying another radar low-level mission. We hit another bird that came through the canopy and hit Major Dave Hudlet in the right shoulder. This time it was only a duck and did much less damage. I flew to Mountain Home AFB, where Major Hudlet landed the airplane. The base was having a retirement party that night for Colonel Coleman, who had been seriously injured in an airplane accident several months before. It seemed we were all having a bit of déjà vu. The next year I stayed off the flying schedule that night.

PILOT'S BIOGRAPHY

Lieutenant Colonel Fred Wilson, United States Air Force Reserves (Idaho Air National Guard), retired

Call sign: Famous

Hometown: Boise, Idaho

Family: married to Louise Blacker Wilson; five children; five grandchildren

Church experience: full-time mission, Eastern States; stake high council; military servicemen's group leader at Gowen Field; bishop; bishop's counselor; high priests group leader; Gospel Doctrine teacher; Scout leader (many times)

Current occupation: engineering support technician

Hobbies: ham radio, radio-controlled airplanes, Boise State University football

Awards: the 1982 Koren Kolligian Jr. Trophy, Distinguished Flying Cross, Combat Readiness Medal, Earl T. Ricks Award (Air Force Association), TAC Aircrew of Distinction, Air Force Well Done Award, Air Medal with an oak leaf cluster, forty-four combat missions in Iraq

Lieutenant Colonel Fred Wilson, looking through the hole caused by the bird strike.

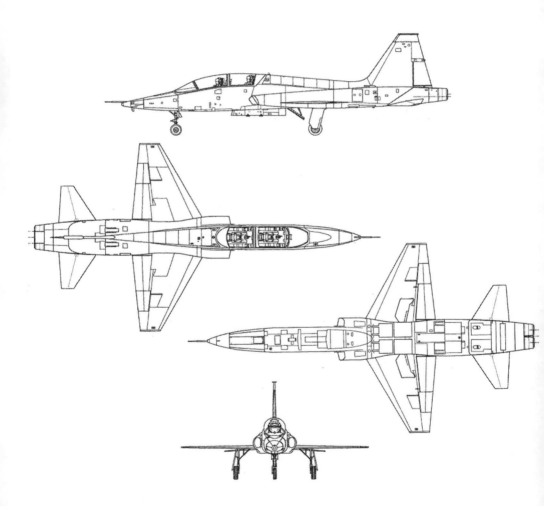

CHAPTER EIGHT

PREPARE EVERY NEEDFUL THING

MILTON R. SANDERS

Doctrine and Covenants 88:119 reads: "Organize yourselves; prepare every needful thing . . ." Nowhere is this commandment from the Lord more critical and millisecond-time dependent than in high-speed flight. To that end, each aircraft has a section in the flight manual for emergency procedures, detailing steps to take when something malfunctions in the highly complex aircraft.

The emergency procedures require intimate familiarity, but for many of them the pilot has a checklist to thumb through as a reminder of the proper steps and the proper order in which to accomplish them. These are the less-critical procedures, where a pilot has time to adequately think through the problem and even perhaps radio for advice to another aircraft or get help from the ground.

Other procedures are called BOLD FACE emergency procedures. Each pilot is required to memorize those and be able to execute them without having to think through every step.

One such bold face procedure is:

ABORT

1. THROTTLES IDLE

2. WHEEL BRAKES APPLY

The pilot needs to be familiar with notes and conditions associated with the procedure, and he is tested in a simulator and in ground evaluations. Some emergency procedures are also practiced and tested when teaching students or during evaluation check flights with flight examiners. Engine-out landings (for multiengine aircraft), no-flap landings, and straight-in approaches are examples of emergency procedures that are practiced and evaluated in flight.

Following my return from Vietnam, flying the F-100 Super Sabre in combat, I was assigned as a T-38 instructor pilot at Vance AFB, Enid, Oklahoma, in the 76th Flying Training Squadron. I was the "G" Flight safety officer and was assigned four students to take through T-38 flight training. As safety officer, I received all the flight incidents and accidents, and selected specific ones to brief to the instructors and students at our daily

flight briefings. I also posted a selection on our Flight Safety Bulletin Board—all to help prepare each of us for recognizing, analyzing, and taking the proper action in case we experienced a similar malfunction.

One of our mottos when experiencing an emergency was "Wind the clock." The T-38 has a spring-operated clock on the instrument panel that the crew chief takes a few seconds each morning to wind up. This phrase reminded us to take a few seconds to analyze the situation before simply reacting and possibly performing the wrong action. The formal initial action as defined in the flight manual was stated as: "Maintain Aircraft Control, Analyze the Situation, and Take Proper Corrective Action." Since that was a mouthful, we preferred the simpler injunction, "Wind the clock."

In the spring of 1970, I reviewed an accident that had killed two instructor pilots who were on a proficiency flight to practice their instructional techniques. They experienced an engine malfunction while making a touch-and-go landing—a landing with a brief touchdown, then taking off without stopping. One of their two engines failed as they advanced the throttles to take off. Since they were already near flying speed, had one good engine, and had very little time to analyze the problem, they decided to continue their takeoff. The T-38 will fly nicely on one engine once you have sufficient flying speed. They got off the ground and started to climb, but made one tragic mistake. By habit, they raised the landing gear to streamline the airplane so it could accelerate faster and climb better. They forgot one thing: The main landing gear doors are closed, whether the gear is up or down. That means that the gear doors must open first, increasing drag, before the landing gear will retract. This extra drag caused them to lose speed and impact the ground, killing them almost instantly. If they had waited another thirty seconds, they would have had speed and altitude to prevent this.

The accident investigation board discovered that the engine failure was caused by a bleed valve malfunction. The bleed valve opens during engine acceleration, venting excess pressure to prevent the compressor section from overpressurizing and inhibiting thrust buildup. When the bleed valve fails, the symptoms include a loud buzzing sound, very little thrust, and the nose yaws (slips sideways) toward the bad engine. This accident, the bleed valve failure, and its symptoms were well publicized throughout the training command, which had eight training bases at the time.

A few weeks after I briefed our pilots about bleed valve failures, the excitement had died down, and everyone was engrossed in other tasks. I was out with one of my students, flying from the backseat, demonstrating a single-engine landing from an overhead pattern. We pitched out over the runway, calculated single-engine pattern and landing speeds (higher than for a normal landing to give us a safety margin), put down the gear and 60 percent flaps (normal landings are with full flaps), and started the turn to final approach. Everything proceeded normally; we touched down in the first 1500 feet of the runway; I lowered the nose slightly while checking the airspeed (145 knots—about right for our touch and go); and advanced both throttles to take off again.

Immediately I heard a buzzing noise and the aircraft yawed ten degrees to the left. The normal tendency at that speed, and with nearly 3,000 feet of the 9,202 foot runway gone, would be to continue the takeoff and sort out the problem later, after having gained some altitude and breathing room. However, having thoroughly analyzed the fatal accident, including all the symptoms of the bleed valve failure, and having thought through all the decision processes, I executed the ABORT procedure listed above. While bringing the throttles to idle and applying the brakes, I made a radio call to mobile control and announced my abort—since there are usually multiple airplanes in the traffic pattern, and mobile control was expecting me to continue my takeoff and clear the runway. I didn't want another T-38 breathing up my tailpipe without anyone else knowing what was happening. Needless to say, there was absolutely no time to "wind the clock."

We got stopped by the end of the runway, turned off, and parked on the apron just off the runway to wait for the emergency crew to come chalk the aircraft, pick us up, and tow the aircraft. It is never a good idea to taxi a malfunctioning aircraft back to the parking area in the middle of fifty other aircraft. Shut it down; give it to maintenance; get a ride back to operations in their truck.

While sitting in the aircraft waiting for maintenance, I mentally reviewed what had just happened. I was very thankful that I had prepared for this possibility by previously thinking through the symptoms, weighing my options, and making my decisions prior to reaching the critical situation. I offered a silent prayer of thanks for the Spirit that, not for the first time, aided my thinking and actions in a critical situation.

A phrase that has stuck in my mind is, "Flying is hours of boredom interspersed with moments of stark terror." By preparing every needful thing and staying as close to the Spirit as you can, these moments are not as stark, nor are they filled with as much terror, and you have gratitude for a loving Heavenly Father who demonstrates that He knows who you are, what you are thinking, and what you need.

By organizing ourselves, preparing every needful thing, and staying focused on the task at hand, we accomplish what the Father has for us to do. The Lord has given us His advice to accomplish His purposes while prolonging our mortal lives and strengthening our spiritual lives in the process. I am thankful for the Spirit and its influence in my life in my normal endeavors as well as those where split-second actions are critical.

PILOT'S BIOGRAPHY

Major Milton R. Sanders,
United States Air Force, retired

Call sign: Sandman

Hometown: Orem, Utah

Family: married to Kay G. Sanders (deceased); five children; eleven grandchildren

Church callings: bishop, served in five other bishoprics; high councilor (three times); high priests group leadership four times (twice as group leader); executive secretary four times; currently in high priests group leadership

Current occupation: computer systems engineer, SirsiDynix— a library automation company

Education: command pilot, commercial license (multiengine, instrument); bachelor's in engineering science, United States Air Force Academy; master's in aeronautical engineering, U.S. Air Force Institute of Technology

Hobbies: ham radio, guitar, computers, radio-controlled model airplanes, photography, home video production, singing Elvis karaoke, building a cabin

Awards and recognitions: Distinguished Flying Cross, Meritorious Service Medal (2), Air Medal (16), Air Force Commendation Medal (3), Army Commendation Medal, Outstanding Unit Award (4), Vietnam Service Medal (4 stars), others

Major Milt "Sandman" Sanders with a T-38 Talon, Vance AFB, Oklahoma.

BOEING 737-200

CHAPTER NINE

I'LL FLY WITH YOU ANYWHERE

KEN SWAIN

This is about a microburst incident that happened to me one day.

A microburst is a very sudden and intense downdraft, usually close to the ground. The first real research into microbursts was after Eastern Airlines Flight 66 crashed at JFK International Airport in June 1975. After the investigation of that accident, weather experts and the FAA (Federal Aviation Administration) went back and researched a large number of accidents that had been labeled "pilot error." Where adequate weather records were available, they discovered that some of those accidents had indeed been weather related, attributable to the presence of microbursts. Some others, in which weather data was insufficient to form a valid conclusion, were possibly also caused by microbursts. One of the most dramatic microburst crashes occurred at the Dallas—Fort Worth Airport, when Delta Airlines Flight 191 crashed on August 2, 1985, killing eight of eleven crew members and 126 of the 152 passengers on board and one person on the ground: a total of 135 deaths.

As for my own experience, I was flying a B-737 into Buffalo one afternoon. This was in 1970, before we really knew much about wake turbulence, wind shears, sudden downdrafts, or microbursts, as noted above.

The runway we were using at Buffalo that day was Runway 23, or, in other words, the runway that pointed 230 degrees on the compass scale. All runways are labeled with their compass headings. One of the unusual things about this runway is that the I-90 tollway is just off the approach end, and there is not a lot of overrun or threshold prior to the runway. The I-90 tollway is about a third of a mile from the end of the runway, which sits up above the tollway about twenty or thirty feet. That makes it imperative that you do not land short in any way.

This particular afternoon as we were approaching the outer marker (the last navigational fix before the runway), there was some wind, but not an excessive amount. I had a bad feeling and told my first officer that I was going to add an additional 30 knots to the 20 that was already added for wind and that I was going to fly the glide slope about 100 to 150 feet higher than I should. The normal approach speed on this flight without any wind would be about 160 miles an hour. With the normal wind addition, it would be about 185 miles an hour. On this day my speed was about 220 miles an hour. The runway at Buffalo is about 700 feet above sea level, and the normal altitude over the end of the runway would be about 150 feet above ground to land about 1000 feet down the runway. I planned to be at about 250 to 300 feet over the end of the runway. The normal procedure for an approach is to add one-half of the steady wind and the full gust value to your approach air speed up to a maximum of 20 knots or about 24 miles an hour. My first officer looked at me, kind of puzzled, and said, "You'll never get it on the ground." I replied that I knew I was going to be high and fast, but that I had a bad feeling and I didn't like it. We would give this a try, and if we were too high and too fast, we would just go around and try it again.

Just as we were passing over the tollway and approaching the runway, we caught a microburst. It slammed us down and we hit on about the first three hundred feet of the runway. We landed hard, but safely, and then rolled to a stop about halfway down the runway.

Had we not been high and fast, the microburst would have put us onto the ground just short of the runway and we would have hit into that rise or onto the tollway. After we got the airplane stopped, my first officer just looked over at me with a look of amazement on his face and said, "I'll fly with you anywhere."

This was just one of the times in flying that the Spirit whispered to do something different than procedure called for and the results were life saving. They can now forecast an area of

microbursts electronically with Doppler radar at larger airports so the pilots can be aware and take proper precautions.

I spent forty years as a pilot—first as a fighter pilot in the USAF and ANG (Air National Guard), and then as a commercial pilot for United Airlines. I flew as captain on most of the airplanes that Boeing produced: the B-727, B-737, B-757, B-767, B-747, and the B-747–400. Several times during my forty-year career in the Air Force and with United Airlines I have had the Spirit direct me to do something that was different from standard procedure, but probably the most dramatic was that flight into Buffalo, New York.

PILOT'S BIOGRAPHY

Captain Ken Swain,
United States Air Force

Call sign: Eagle

Hometown: Salt Lake City, Utah

Family: married to Sylvia Dean; six children; nineteen and a
   half grandchildren; two great-grandchildren

Church experience: served in many callings including as
   bishop, stake executive secretary, stake Young Men's
   presidency, high priests group leader, and Scoutmaster;
   has served three couple missions since retirement,
   including executive secretary to the Area Presidency in
   the Philippines; currently serving as a home teacher

*Ken Swain just prior to his final flight before retirement
(San Francisco to Sydney, Australia, June 1996).*

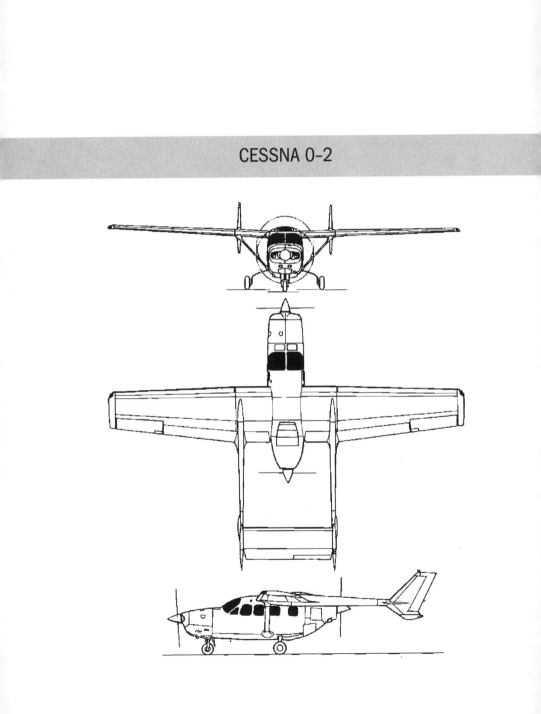

CHAPTER TEN

COMPASS, ALTIMETER, AND AIRSPEED

FRANK LEUCK

In mid-April 1971, I was a young major in the USAF flying in Southeast Asia as a Forward Air Controller and commander of a small detachment of pilots flying missions in support of MACV-SOG. SOG (Studies and Observations Group) was a highly classified covert operation designed to collect intelligence on the enemy throughout Southeast Asia.

I had returned from my third mission of the day with some damage to my O-2 aircraft from small arms fire. After I had gone through the normal maintenance and intelligence debriefings, my Army counterpart informed me they had received information of the likelihood that our Forward Operating Base would be hit by a sapper unit (saboteurs) during the night. Under these circumstances we normally flew the aircraft to a nearby and more secure airfield to ensure their safety.

The pilots, radio operators, and aircraft maintenance personnel were all briefed about the impending attack and were busy preparing for departure. My aircraft was the only one with battle damage, and the crew chief was busy making sure it was flight worthy. Night was approaching and all the aircraft had departed; my crew chief and I were the only ones remaining.

The crew chief told me we were safe for the short flight to a base where more work could be done on the aircraft, so we took off.

We had been in the air for less than five minutes when I got busy on the radio to ascertain the condition of the recovery base. I was informed that the base where I intended landing was experiencing severe thunderstorms and the field was closed for at least several hours. The alternate landing base was nearly an hour away with severe weather en route.

I informed the crew chief that it could be a bumpy ride, meaning we would most likely encounter some violent turbulence. He assured me the aircraft was air worthy, but he was concerned about the low level of fuel on board and whether it would take us to our alternate. I checked my fuel gauge and determined we were okay if we didn't have to divert too far

around thunderstorms. Almost simultaneously we both suggested we say a prayer that this night would end successfully.

It was a very dark night and we could see the lightning in the clouds ahead. I adjusted my instrument lights to low and turned on some red-lighting for the cockpit so we could preserve our night vision.

Without warning, a bolt of lightning struck our aircraft. The flash was blinding and the noise was deafening. It scared us both! The aircraft rocked hard to the right before I noticed that all my lighting was out. Normally the aircraft has safety wiring into the electrical system to avoid damage due to lightning, but sometimes a severe jolt of current will zap right through the protection. There we were—without lighting, radios, navigation systems, and most instruments.

As we surveyed the damage, the only things we could use were the magnetic compass, airspeed indicator, and altimeter. Without cockpit lighting, the crew chief had to shine his flashlight on the few functional instruments. We generally knew where we were and the direction to our alternate, but without a navigational system and a view of the ground, we knew we were in trouble.

We decided what altitude we would have to fly to clear the mountain range between us and the alternate, set our airspeed for optimum fuel conservation, and adjusted our heading using the magnetic compass as our guide to safety.

We cleared the mountains, and as we neared the time we estimated we would be near our alternate, the clouds cleared, and we could see the lights of the runway to our left. We landed without incident, talked to the maintenance people, consoled each other, and felt our prayers had been answered. We found a place to sleep but, although I thought I was deserving of a good night's rest, it didn't happen.

My mind was racing through the events of that night. I prayed with a thankful heart for our safe recovery and the lessons learned that would last a lifetime. My mind began drawing some analogies from the experience. I began likening the few remaining flight instruments to other factors in my life.

That night, my only sense of direction came from a simple magnetic compass. I thought about just how powerful a blessing it is that Christ is our compass. Without a compass that night, our flight would have been doomed to failure and disaster. How many times have I relied on the never-ending direction and the guidance of Deity? I am so grateful for the Father, because of His plan of happiness; the Savior, for His gift of the Atonement; and the Holy Ghost, for that ability to call on Him and, with faith, gain imperceptible impulses for good. As my compass, the Godhead offers me peace, hope, and direction.

I thought of my altimeter and airspeed indicator. Where was the analogy of those two instruments in my life? Without the altimeter, how would I have gained the comfort that I could clear the mountain range on our path? I thought about the ability of setting my altimeter in life. What altitude should I be flying at? Is my altitude set high enough to overfly the "fiery darts of the adversary"? How do I know when it's time to fly low versus flying high? Am I setting my goals (my altitude) high enough to accomplish the deeds in my life necessary to meet the final destination (life eternal)?

My mind flashed back to a college class I took called "vector analysis." The professor put two dots on the chalkboard and said that dot number one is where we are and the dot two is where we want to be. Between these two dots he drew a line with an arrowhead at dot number two, which he called our destination. He completed his scenario by saying, "This is a vector. Life is made up of a series of vectors. In order to get where we need to be, we need both direction (coming from a compass) and velocity (set with an airspeed indicator)."

That dark night in mid-April, I needed direction, altitude, and airspeed to get safely home. This was my analogy, my explanation, for many things I had faced and would confront in my mortal journey home to my Father. I am so grateful for that night when the compass, altimeter, and airspeed indicator gave deeper meaning and direction to my life.

PILOT'S BIOGRAPHY

Colonel Frank Leuck,
United States Air Force

Family: married to Judith Sherwood, a concert violinist, have
been married for forty-seven years; eight children; nineteen grandchildren

Education: attended several professional military schools,
including the U.S. Army War College

Aircraft flown: flew as a navigator on B-52s until selected for
pilot training in 1966; logged several thousand hours in
the T-37, T-38, A-37, O-2, and T-39; served as the commander of units on two different occasions and held key
staff positions in four major commands

Major Frank Leuck in Quon Loi, 1972.

Awards and recognitions:
Legion of Merit, two Distinguished Flying Crosses,
three Meritorious Service
Medals, seven Air Medals,
the Joint Service Commendation Medal with "V" device,
the Presidential Unit Citation, the Combat Readiness
Medal, National Defense
Service Medal, Vietnamese
Cross of Gallantry, and Vietnamese Medal of Honor

LOCKHEED P-38 LIGHTNING

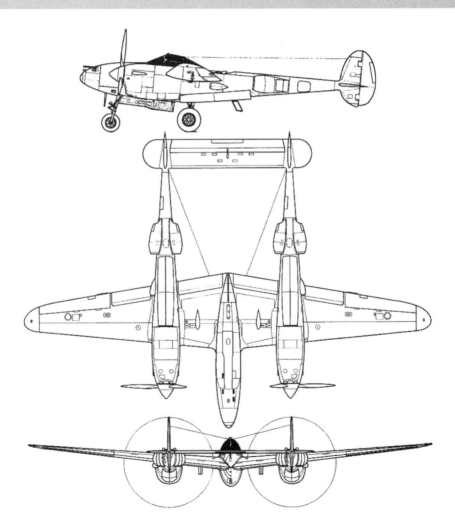

CHAPTER ELEVEN

THAT'S ANOTHER ONE I OWE YOU

JOSEPH VANSETERS

While I was serving in the Northern States Mission, working in Detroit, Pearl Harbor was bombed. Before coming home I took my cadet exams and was told to report when I got off my mission.

Our class went through multiengine schools to become bomber pilots; however, eighteen of us got to fly twin-engine photo reconnaissance. The airplanes we flew were P-38s (or Army F-5s), stripped down, twin engines, no guns, only cameras. Our sole protections were an alert eye and a fast airplane.

Now, this airplane was so fast that they called it the "Lightning." Some guys from back in the hills said this plane could go faster than a scalded dog. All you had to do was push the nose down and push both throttles to the fire wall and break the wire (for water injection) and not even the wind could catch you. However, if you used water for more than two minutes, they would have to overhaul the engine. If you used the water for more than five minutes, you had to junk the engine.

Early one morning in Coffeyville, Kansas, on March 21, 1945, I was scheduled to fly a high-altitude photo-reconnaissance training mission. We would fly these at 32,000 feet. When

I went to check out my parachute and oxygen equipment, they said my parachute was being repacked, so they gave me an oversized loaner chute. They wanted to refit the chute, but I said I never use them and I wanted a loose-fitting chute for a long, six-hour mission (my first mistake).

When I got up to my mission altitude of 32,000 feet, I had to pass up my first two targets because of darkness and/or cloud cover. I would pick them up on my way back home.

The next target was the Ponca City, Oklahoma, railroad yards. I unbuckled the chest strap on my parachute, unzipped my jacket and got my pencil out of my shirt pocket, and wrote down the time of day, the altitude, the intervalometer reading (number of frames you are shooting), the camera I was using, and the airspeed. Then I lined up the railroad yard and rolled into the turn. Everything looked good, so I switched on the cameras, checked the compass, and wrote down the heading, or the direction I was flying.

After the run on the railroad yard, I rolled into a turn to the northwest and lined up with the railroad line to Blackwell. I checked the heading and wrote it down with the time, altitude, direction, and intervalometer number. Then I checked the instruments; everything looked fine except the tachometer was turning fast and fluctuating. There also seemed to be a bit more vibration in the plane than I could account for. About halfway through the run to Blackwell, the right engine revved up to almost 3,000 RPMs. I guess the brake on the right propeller wasn't holding. I reduced the RPMs and cut back the right throttle. I had never had a prop that wouldn't hold steady RPMs.

Shortly after that, the right engine cut out because the right drop tank had run dry (this was standard procedure). As I reached down and switched from the drop tank to the main tank, the plane twisted violently to the right. This startled me. I jammed the left rudder in and grabbed the wheel with both hands, trying to keep the plane on course. The plane seemed to go crazy.

When the right engine lost power, the pitch on the right prop flattened out. The propeller became a brake on the right side holding that side of the plane back. The left engine held full power, which spun the plane to the right. I grabbed the pitch control to adjust the RPMs, but nothing happened. The plane shuddered violently and lurched to the right. All of a sudden, within seconds, the world was spinning very fast. My airplane was in a flat spin.

As the gasoline from the main tank reached the right engine, it came back to cruising power: 1425 horsepower. With no pitch on the right propeller to pull the plane forward, the

prop went wild and ran away. It screamed as it wound up to full bore, tore itself off the engine, and whizzed over the top of the canopy where I was sitting. There was a terrible vibrating and shaking. With nothing to absorb the energy of 1425 horsepower, the right engine accelerated so fast it blew up and tore things up as it wrenched itself from its mountings and fell off the airplane.

As this was happening I grabbed the throttles and retarded them, but the 1425 horsepower of the left engine had spun the plane to the right. I continued to jam the left rudder all the way in and twist the wheel to the left, trying to correct the spin, but none of the controls would respond. Then I tried to push the wheel all the way forward in an attempt to get the plane to dive. But nothing happened, and the world kept on spinning. So I switched off the main switch and shut the left engine down to prevent a fire. I thought, "I don't want to burn up too." I had done everything I could think of to gain control of the airplane, but none of the controls would respond. The airplane was spinning violently, forcing me back into my seat. It was in a tight, flat spin—the type of spin that an airplane will not recover from.

I was worried about what the Old Man (my commanding officer or C.O.) would say if I lost one of his airplanes—until I realized that the right engine was gone. Then I thought, "Nuts to that, I've got to get out of here."

I jettisoned the canopy and undid my safety belt, but I couldn't move. I tried and tried everything I could think of but I couldn't move out of my seat. The centrifugal force was too great. It was holding me back tight against the back of my seat. I rolled down the left window. I twisted and squirmed as I tried to find something to grab on to help me crawl out of the airplane. The centrifugal force was just too great; I still couldn't move. The ground was rushing up. In a few minutes, I would smash into the ground and be killed. I didn't want to die. My life flashed through my mind. I thought of Mom and Dad. I thought of my wife and our little baby, Karen. But, then, all of my life I had never really thought I would live to maturity. My two brothers had both died when I was two years old. Why should I be able to live?

The world was spinning around and around, trying to make me dizzy and soothe me for what was surely going to happen.

The floor of the cockpit was stainless steel, very smooth and slick. My shoes would slip when I tried to push myself up with my feet and legs. I was really getting worried. I looked up and shouted, "Heavenly Father, please help me, I don't want to die, Heavenly Father, I need your help, please help me!" Tears ran down my cheeks. "Please help me now!"

Then I heard a voice say to me, *"Hook your heel in the seat."* The bucket seat in a P-38 is cut down in front. There's a groove in the center to make room for the control stick. I got my heel hooked in the seat to give my leg leverage and I got both hands on the top of the windshield and gave a jerk.

I went headfirst out of the left window. My head hit the turbo supercharger, which was red hot. It knocked my helmet and oxygen mask off and cut my forehead. The live prop nicked my jacket. My legs were cut when they hit the pipes where the other engine had blown off. I was hit a couple more times by the tail and the wing, but then I was free.

Then the instincts of my training took over. I reached my right hand for the D-ring so the rip cord would pull the parachute open. Then a loud voice shouted at me, *"Both hands."* I didn't hesitate. I grabbed the D-ring with both hands and pulled as hard as I could. This forced my arms straight out in front of me. I was coming facedown, and this forced the parachute risers into my armpits and chest. The parachute popped open, and it flipped me right side up. It also pulled the bail-out bottle out of its leg pocket, but with my oxygen mask gone, it didn't matter much.

The wind at about 28,000 feet altitude was over 100 knots that morning and was very rough. Something kept hitting me in the top of the head. I looked up and saw that it was the snap buckle on the chest strap of my parachute. My chest strap was unbuckled. I then realized I had undone it to get out my pencil to write down the intervalometer notes for this run. However, if the chest strap had been buckled, it would have broken my neck because of the way I was falling and because of my big parachute.

As the wind swung my parachute back and forth I could watch my airplane spinning like a falling leaf till it was out of sight. My head hurt like crazy so I put my hand up to my head to soothe the pain. When I brought my hand down, my glove was covered with blood. I wondered how bad it was. I had a stretch-band watch with a shiny back that I had gotten for Christmas. I used the back of the watch for a mirror and looked at my head. A cut was bleeding between my eyebrows up into my hair. My watch said it was about eight forty-five.

The wind whistling through the parachute made a mournful sound and I felt so all alone. I was getting light-headed because I had lost my oxygen mask and my bail-out bottle. I fought hard to stay awake so I wouldn't fall out of my parachute. Then everything seemed to get really dark and I passed out from the lack of oxygen.

I don't know how long I was unconscious. When I started to regain consciousness, the sun looked like a little red apple. The ground was rushing up at me. I looked down and there were a river and trees right below me. I tried to slip my parachute away from the river but I didn't have the strength.

I reached up and grabbed the risers on the parachute and prepared to hit the ground. Within seconds I plunked down in a little clearing just a few feet from the river. My leg hurt like crazy. It had gotten twisted as I was wrenched out of the cockpit and a wing or something had hit me in the small of the back. It was hard to put my weight on that leg for a while.

As I stood up, I looked around, shook my head, and said out loud, "All those open fields and I have to land next to a river and a bunch of trees." I spread out my parachute so someone could find me. Then I realized that I was well and all in one piece and thought of all the reasons I should be dead.

I got down on my knees, looked up to the sky, and said, "Thank you, thank you, thank you, Heavenly Father, you have taken such good care of me. I should be dead ten times over. I really owe you one." Then I looked around at the surroundings and the parachute. I put my hand up to my head because it was still hurting like crazy and it was still bleeding. My flight jacket and flying suit had blood dripped all over them. Then I shook my head and thought, "Never thought I'd live through it. Thank you again, Heavenly Father. Sure hope this isn't habit-forming."

Everything happened so fast that I never had the chance to call "Mayday" (the distress call for an airplane pilot), but another airplane saw the trail of black oil and reported a crash. Some schoolchildren saw my plane go down and saw the parachute, so their teacher called the county sheriff. It only took about half an hour for the sheriff to find me because the schoolchildren told him where my parachute came down.

I asked the sheriff to take me to my downed airplane. The sheriff seemed to know right where it was. It hadn't burned. I went through the wreckage and took out the form one and all other papers. I asked the deputy if he would stand guard on the plane till the Army got there. Then the sheriff and I headed toward town.

As we drove past the school on the way to town, we stopped because the children wanted to see me and the parachute. The kids "oooed" and "ahhhed" because of the big cut on my forehead. I had blood all over my face and on my flying suit and jacket. Everyone had a hundred questions. Then the teacher asked if she could feel the silk parachute.

"Sure can," I remarked as I turned around and gathered up the parachute and handed it to her. She took the silk parachute in her hands and squeezed a handful of silk. She rubbed the silk around on her hands and arms and face. Then she gathered it up and held it close to her. She didn't say anything. Tears came to her eyes. The students and everyone, including myself, noticed the tears. There was silence for a long minute.

With tears still welled up in her eyes, she handed the parachute back to me and squeezed my shoulder and said, "Glad you're okay. Now I don't feel so bad about not having any silk stockings and pretty silk things."

A few days later, after the hospital and the inquiry and the accident review board, the Old Man (the C.O.) called me in and we talked. I told him I was sorry I lost one of his airplanes. He said he was glad we didn't lose the pilot; we had lost two others out of that class. Then he said he was sorry I was still having nightmares. I told him that all night long I was still trying to get out of the airplane. He then asked if I said my prayers. "Sure do," I replied, "many times a day and many more when I'm flying." He asked if I still wanted to go into combat, adding that it would be all right if I didn't want to go. I told him I really wanted to go. Then he shook my hand and said, "That's good. You'll go and you'll be fine." He was right. That's another one I owe You.

PILOT'S BIOGRAPHY

First Lieutenant Joseph VanSeters, United States Army Air Corps

Hometown: born in Blackfoot, Idaho; raised in Salt Lake City; currently lives in St. George, Utah

Family: married to Joan Butler; raised nine children

Church experience: served in Northern States Mission; currently serves in the temple

Hobbies: master herbalist, author of newspaper column and book entitled *Herbs and Oldtime Remedies*

Joseph VanSeters with the P-38.

CH-53D HELICOPTER

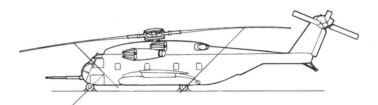

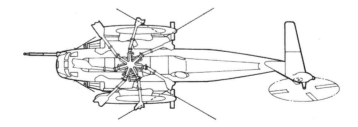

CHAPTER TWELVE

MY CARIBBEAN DETOUR

DAVID WASSINK

In late 1983, much of the world's attention turned to Beirut, Lebanon, where a multinational peacekeeping force was at work trying to settle things down. As a young marine first lieutenant, I was picked to be among the CH-53D helicopter pilots to join HMM-261, the Raging Bulls, and deploy to the eastern Mediterranean Sea to sit off the coast of Lebanon in support of the ground forces ashore. All our training focused on the tasks we anticipated flying in and around Beirut. We studied the anticipated threats while closely watching the political climate to get a sense of how things might go.

We were scheduled to depart North Carolina aboard the USS *Guam* around the 18th of October when we received notice that we needed to leave early. So we packed our bags, boarded our aircraft, and flew aboard the *Guam* while it sat pierside in Norfolk, Virginia, and were under way on the 17th. That was an indicator that things were not going to be normal. Once aboard the *Guam* and under way, we were told that we were not going directly to the Mediterranean but instead would turn south and head for the Caribbean and an island called Grenada. The operation we were entering into was dubbed Operation Urgent Fury.

It was an invasion of the nation of Grenada by the United States, Jamaica, Barbados, and members of the Organization of Eastern Caribbean States in response to the illegal deposition and execution of Grenadan Prime Minister Maurice Bishop.

Before we arrived in the vicinity of Grenada, on October 23rd a terrorist drove a truck bomb into the marine barracks at the Beirut airport, killing 244 marines and sailors. Our hearts went out to our fellow soldiers of the sea but soon enough we would have our own problems to address.

On October 25th, Operation Urgent Fury began in earnest, with the marines landing in the northern part of the island, around the Pearls airport and Grenville, while the army began arriving in the south. Things in the north went pretty smoothly, with little resistance, but in the south things were heating up. Soon the marine AH-1T Cobra helicopter gunships were diverted from supporting the marines to helping the fight around Point Salines.

Major Pat Giguere and his copilot, First Lieutenant Jeff Scharver, along with their wingman, piloted by Captain Tim Howard and his copilot, Captain Jeb Seagle, were dispatched to join the fight. The two aircraft made several runs on various targets until a hidden antiaircraft machine gun opened up, crippling the aircraft flown by Howard and Seagle. Tim Howard was wounded, losing his right hand, and his left leg was severely hit as well. Seagle was knocked unconscious as the rounds slammed into the aircraft. With his aircraft no longer flyable, Howard guided the helicopter into an autorotative landing on a soccer field. He had to fly using his left hand on both the cyclic and collective controls. The landing was hard but the aircraft stayed upright. Fire spread quickly and started cooking off the remaining ammunition. The impact apparently jarred Jeb Seagle awake and he managed to climb out, then pull Tim Howard out of the burning aircraft and drag him away to safety.

Giguere and Scharver remained overhead and called for assistance to pull Howard and Seagle out of the soccer field. The antiaircraft gun continued to fire, and Giguere and Scharver made several runs on it, trying to silence the gun. Soon a CH-46 helicopter piloted by Major Mel Demars and First Lieutenant Larry King would arrive to try to retrieve Howard and Seagle. They knew time was critical because an armed group of enemy troops were nearing the positions occupied by Howard and Seagle. Hearing the troops as they neared, Seagle left Howard to try to distract the enemy troops away while seeking help from friendly forces. Demars and King landed soon afterward and loaded Howard on the aircraft. It was evident that because of his wounds, Howard would need immediate medical attention. Nevertheless, Demars and King waited for Seagle to show himself, but to no avail.

Out of ammunition, Giguere and Scharver had continued to make runs on the antiaircraft gun. All too soon the gun crew figured that out and started firing on the aircraft. As the rescue aircraft was departing, the antiaircraft gun found its mark and Giguere and Scharver were killed instantly as their Cobra plunged into the water below. Jeb Seagle's body was found later. He had been captured by the enemy troops and beaten before he was killed.

The next day, the marines joined the fight to the south. The Army Rangers had located a number of American students who had been studying medicine at the university. Their safety required an immediate extract, and the marine helicopters were best suited for the mission. We landed at Point Salines and briefed the mission with the Rangers. Along with Pat Merrigan, I was flying the third of three CH-53Ds participating in the rescue of the students. The plan was that the CH-46s would land at Grand Anse beach and discharge the Rangers, who would then collect the students and prepare them to be picked up by the CH-53s.

Once the plan was briefed and understood by all participants, we manned up and went to work. I remember feeling detached from the moment and not overly worried about my own safety. We were briefed that our landing area would be along the beach and extended from a wall down to a clothesline with three sheets on it. The CH-46s dropped the Rangers off and the CH-53s waited for the signal to come in and pick up the students. Orbiting a good distance away, we could see explosions from the rockets and TOW missiles being fired by the two

Cobras we had as escorts. There was thick smoke and, judging from the sounds on the radio, it was evident there was a bit of confusion on the ground.

Soon enough the students were ready for extraction and we turned inbound to our designated landing area. Unfortunately, the designated landing zone was too small for all three giant CH-53Ds, so Pat Merrigan and I were forced to land a bit farther back away from the sheets and clothesline. There was a large palm tree to our right, and caution led us to land a little farther into the surf. With the right main landing gear in the sand, the left main was floating a bit, and when the crew chief lowered the ramp, the cabin filled with water. We brought the ramp back up before too much water flowed in, and Pat Merrigan decided we needed to move more to our right to get the left main landing gear further up and into a drier location to load the students. As Pat moved toward the right, the palm tree became a problem that was soon alleviated when we inadvertently cut it down using the rotors. We landed, lowered the ramp, and loaded up with students. I could see looking at the rotor tip path that what was normally a line was a little ragged.

Now, with a damaged aircraft, we evaluated the situation and decided that the best thing to do was to fly to the Point Salines airport, the closest safe place we could land. Our lead aircraft lifted and we followed them out. As we departed I looked over my left shoulder and watched one of the Cobras in a duel with an unseen gun emplacement. The Cobra pitched hard up and to the left as I watched rounds impact the water immediately beneath the low-flying aircraft.

Pat and I followed our flight lead over to Point Salines, where we discharged the students. We taxied clear and shut down our damaged aircraft. On inspection, all six of the rotor tips were damaged and three rotor blades had cracked spars, making them unsafe for flight. We were done and out of the fight. The other two CH-53Ds then returned to Grand Anse and picked up a second load of students. As we looked over our damaged aircraft, I was surprised and humbled as the students lined up nearby began applauding and cheering, offering their thanks for saving them from an uncertain fate. It never occurred to me until then that maybe we were doing something special.

We concluded operations around Grenada about November 1 and headed east at best speed to relieve our friends in Beirut. Eventually we logged 144 consecutive days at sea, flying daily in support of our infantry brethren.

To this day whenever I hear John 15:13, which reads, "Greater love hath no man than this, that a man lay down his life for his friends," my mind turns to the sacrifices offered by Jeb Seagle, Jeff Scharver, and Pat Giguere. I am honored and humbled to have had the opportunity to serve alongside such great men who showed love for their friends by making the ultimate sacrifice. The heroism demonstrated both in Grenada and later in Beirut has been a source of inspiration for me throughout my career.

PILOT'S BIOGRAPHY

Colonel David Wassink,
United States Marine Corps, drilling reservist

Call sign: Waz

Hometown: Tonawanda, New York

Family: married to Ruth Van Buskirk Wassink; five children

Church experience: former bishop, counselor in bishopric, Scoutmaster, elders quorum president; currently the servicemen's group leader, Al Asad Air Base, Iraq

Current occupation: technical director, General Dynamics Information Technology, when not mobilized

Awards and recognitions: more than 2,000 hours in the CH-53A/D/E, Air Medal with Combat V, two Meritorious Service Medals, two Sikorsky Rescue awards, and numerous other military awards

Colonel David Wassink with the CH-53D.

CURTISS C-46 COMMANDO

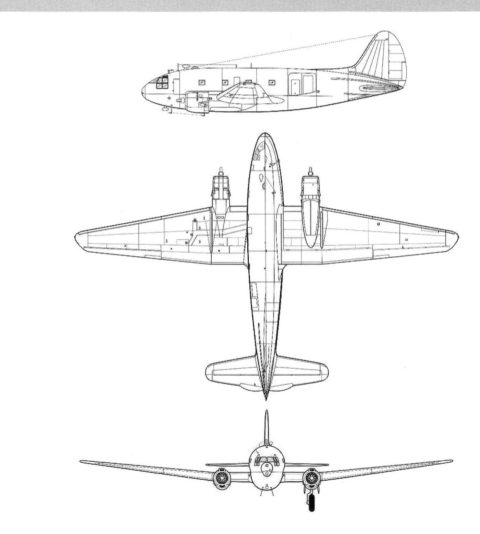

CHAPTER THIRTEEN

THE "STORM FROM HELL"

CECIL RAY HANSEN

This flight to China had begun like so many others from Sookerating, a U.S. Army ATC (Air Transport Command) base in the Assam Valley in northeast India. The flight briefing at three hundred hours (3:00 A.M.) at the base operations center was almost routine, as "there had been no enemy aircraft interference reported during the flights that night and the weather was comparatively good at that time." However, the weather officer noted that west-southwest winds at flight level on our air routes were stronger than usual, which was causing some turbulence over the mountains.

The crew consisted of me as pilot, a copilot who was new to the "Hump," and an experienced radio operator who had flown with me on other flights. The crew chief who met us at the C-46 airplane said he wasn't going along because he needed to do some engine repair on another plane, but that we need not worry about this airplane because it was comparatively new and was in good condition. For this fact we were grateful. He had checked the cargo of high-octane gasoline in fifty-gallon drums and stated that it was secure and there appeared to be no leaks.

The flight from India across northern Burma to either Chanyi or Chengkung Air Base (after all these years I'm not certain which one it was) in the Yunnan Province of China was routine, but enjoyable in those quiet early morning hours, especially as a first trip for the new copilot. To him, the scenic beauty was breathtaking—the jungle, broken only by the Ledo Road and the slow rivers that flowed through it to the south, then, as we turned more eastward, the Burma Road winding up and down the rugged mountains and across swift-running streams, sunup across the Himalayan Mountains, and finally, the Paoshan and Kunming airbases, which we passed before arriving at our destination.

By the time our plane was unloaded and we were ready for our return flight to India, incoming pilots were commenting on what appeared to be a severe storm coming from the west and the speed with which it seemed to be moving. We found their reports to be true, for as we climbed to our 17,000-foot flight level, we were soon engulfed in that storm. Under these circumstances, we were flying blind, totally dependent on instruments and especially our radio compass and the radio checkpoints for our flight path and to know our speed across the ground. By the time we reached our first checkpoint, we realized that we were flying into very strong head winds, which increased dramatically along with the lightning, the rain, and the turbulence as we flew toward the next checkpoint. It was not long, however, before our radio compass began to move erratically due to the electrical disturbances of the storm. Hence it was no longer of any help to us in knowing where we were or what our ground-speed was.

I had experienced severe storms with some electrical

disturbances on previous flights, but not the severity of what we now faced. I knew our situation was serious, and my radioman expressed his concern when he said, "Lieutenant, I'm getting nothing but static, what do we do now?" I tried to give him some positive encouragement by asking him to keep trying for a signal from the next checkpoint or, better, from one of the bases in the Assam Valley, which I hoped would now be to the north or northwest of us and with which he might make contact if we were getting nearer to them.

Standard procedure for this kind of emergency was to now fly directly west until some contact could be made with a ground station to determine our position and the direction to our base. Barring that, we would continue flying west until the plane ran out of gas, at which time we would bail out. So we continued on our westerly course with the hope that we would make some kind of radio contact to determine where we were.

All the time, our fuel gauges were showing less and less gasoline.

Before every flight I always prayed that the flight would be a safe and successful one. And I had done so before I had left my bunk area the previous night. Also, from the letter I had received from home, I knew that my family was praying for me every day even though they did not know where in the world I was stationed. But now, as I felt a need for more help, I silently offered a prayer for some kind of divine intervention. Our radio operator continued to try for contact from checkpoints or from the Assam Valley that would serve to correct our radio compass, and I looked out the side cockpit window into the thick grey clouds. Momentarily, I felt impressed to look down. As I did so, I saw a small break in the clouds directly below us and, through that break, the ground. There, in that small opening and for that moment, there appeared a landmark with which I was very familiar—a bridge on the Ledo-Burma Road over the Salweem River. From 17,000 feet it was like a pinpoint in the sea of green jungle. I explained to the crew what I was going to do, then reduced power on the engines and put the plane into a sharp, descending turn, trying to stay near, if not in, the small opening. Finally we broke out of the clouds at about 2,000 feet above the jungle-covered ground and I felt we had a chance or maybe even a choice of what we could now do.

I presented the options to my crew of either going south to the Myitkyina Air Field, which had recently been taken from the Japanese, and there wait out the storm, or going north toward Sookerating, which was on the other side of the "First Ridge." This latter choice meant going over that ridge of mountains. The minimum instrument altitude over the ridge was 13,000 feet, and the whole ridge appeared to be covered with clouds. There was a way over the ridge through a pass at a much lower altitude if I could locate it and see our way through it in the heavy rainstorm.

The copilot asked if it would be possible to get over the ridge with the uneven base of the clouds, which was just above us and well down on the mountains in the heavy rain. Then he added that he would trust my judgment, and for me to do what I felt was best. The radio operator's response was, "Lieutenant, take us home. You know the pass through that ridge; you have flown it before." So we turned north, located the pass where the Ledo Road crossed the mountains, and began the flight not far above the ground and just under the clouds that seemed to hang just above us regardless of our altitude. Finally, the mountains began to slope down into the Assam Valley toward Ledo and Sookerating and we knew one problem was behind us. There was still, however, the problem of having enough gasoline to reach our base.

By the time we passed Ledo, the fuel gauges reached the empty mark, which meant that we had at best about fifteen minutes of flying time left, exactly the time required to reach Sookerating under normal conditions. The engines were running smoothly and I reduced power to conserve what fuel we had left. When the base came in sight, our radio operator called the control tower and told them of our situation, and we were given clearance for a straight-approach landing since there were no other aircraft in the area. As I banked to the left to make a long final approach to the runway, the right engine sputtered, but it came fully to life as I brought the plane back to a straight and level position on the approach. I continued my silent prayer until I felt the wheels touch down on the runway. At midfield, we had slowed enough to turn onto the taxi strip, but as we began the left turn, the right engine quit completely. Using the now sputtering left engine, I taxied to the revetment parking area, grateful to be "home."

Later, I learned that a number of aircraft and some crews from the bases in the valley were lost before that storm (which was later dubbed the "Storm from Hell") had ended. The number of aircraft lost was placed between thirty-five and forty. My silent prayer, which began at 17,000 feet and continued throughout the remainder of the flight, had been answered by divine intervention. And if no one else knew who had brought us safely home, I knew.

PILOT'S BIOGRAPHY

First Lieutenant Cecil Ray Hansen, United States Army Air Force

Hometown: American Fork, Utah

Family: married to Nina Elizabeth Sykes; three daughters, one son, and one adopted son; they also have twenty grandchildren and thirty-two great-grandchildren (with two more on the way)

Church experience: served a full-time mission with his wife from 1986–1987 in the Louisiana Baton Rouge/Florida Tallahassee Missions; served in many teaching and leadership positions such as bishop, high councilor, stake clerk, counselor to stake president, counselor to mission president, temple worker, and stake patriarch (1976–2006); currently serving as ward chorister

Education and occupation: received bachelor's and master's degrees from University of Utah, doctorate of education from Brigham Young University; worked as a teacher, principal, and district administrator; currently retired and serves as a caregiver for his wife

Awards: received two Air Medals; twice received the Distinguished Flying Cross; and received three Unit Battle Stars

Lieutenant Cecil Ray Hansen.

NORTH AMERICAN F-100 SUPER SABRE

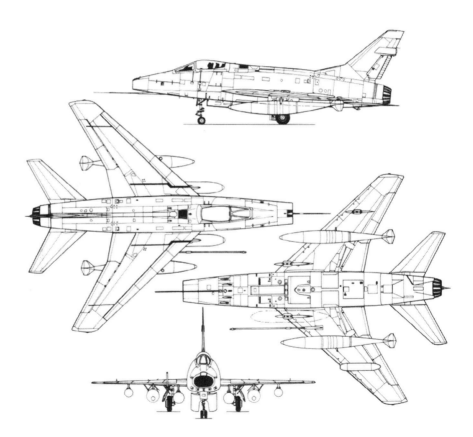

CHAPTER FOURTEEN

ELEGANT FAREWELL PARTY OR NIGHT ALERT?

THALES A. "TAD" DERRICK

There were just four days until the annual Thanksgiving holiday, November 25, 1965. The pilots and ground crews of the 481st Tactical Fighter Squadron, stationed at Tan Son Nhut Air Base, Vietnam, were all in a good mood. The happy mood resulted not so much from the forthcoming holiday as from the realization that on Thanksgiving Day they would be going home!

The 481st, which had received a Presidential Unit Citation in early 1965 for being a top squadron in Tactical Air Command, had been deployed to Vietnam in mid-June. The pilots joked sarcastically that the deployment was their "citation reward." The pilots flew their F-100Ds, and a few F-100Fs, Super Sabres from their home base at Cannon AFB, New Mexico, to Hawaii; then to Guam; then to the Philippines; then to DaNang AB, Vietnam; and later to Tan Son Nhut AB, Vietnam. The F-100s were accompanied by KC-135 aerial tankers for each leg of the trans-Pacific Ocean flight. (The F-100 was affectionately called "The Hun" by those who flew them.) The deployment was forecast to be for three months, to provide interdiction and close air support for the growing number of U.S. Army and U.S. Marine ground forces. The concept was that after three months, a permanent unit would be assigned, and the 481st would return to New Mexico.

The reality that unfolded at the three-month point was that the permanent replacement unit was not ready to deploy to Vietnam. It was announced that the 481st would remain until all pilots had flown 100 combat missions. The pilots were accepting of the 100 fighter combat mission "rule," which had been somewhat of a tradition in other conflicts. It wasn't long, however, until all the pilots had each logged 100 combat missions, and the replacement unit was still not ready. No new artificial number of missions was established. The news was that the 481st would continue to fly combat "until properly relieved." This was not good news, but the pilots were professionals, and they knew that their role in the Air Force was to "fly and fight."

And fly and fight they did! The pilots of the 481st flew 4,500 combat hours and 3,200 combat missions in just five months. Each pilot's aircraft had received battle damage—holes in the aircraft from ground fire. Six pilots were shot down; four were recovered by rescue helicopters; two died in their aircraft. The pilots averaged about 125 combat missions each.

The deployment was now drawing to a close. The 481st would leave their "Huns" for the incoming unit and would get the incoming unit's aircraft upon return to New Mexico. The 481st would return home on an Air Force C-141 Starlifter transport. Large aluminum "mobility boxes" were being packed as the incoming unit's boxes were unpacked. The incoming pilots were beginning to fly combat missions led by 481st pilots, so there could be a seamless transition.

The South Vietnamese vice president, Nguyen Kao Ky, who

was also a general and former fighter pilot in the South Vietnamese Air Force (VNAF), had taken a special interest in the
pilots of the 481st. He appreciated their attitude toward his
country and their total dedication toward the goal of preventing
Communist expansion. He decided to show his gratitude by personally hosting a huge farewell dinner party for the squadron in
a large hotel meeting room. The dinner party was scheduled for
November 21. This date coincided with the last night that the
481st squadron would be responsible for manning the two
fighters on night alert.

My assignment in the squadron was assistant operations
officer and scheduling officer. It was my role to assign pilots to
combat missions as well as to complete various administrative
tasks. I also flew an equal number of combat missions with the
other squadron pilots. The replacement unit scheduling officer
and I agreed that he would take over scheduling the missions
for November 22nd and thereafter. My last scheduling assignment was to schedule two 481st pilots for night alert. This
assignment would traditionally fall upon the two lowest-
ranking pilots because, after all, "rank has its privileges (RHIP)."

I thought it would be interesting to attend the farewell party
and hear the vice president speak, but then felt an impression
that the party would have alcohol as a main ingredient, and that
feature held no interest for me. Further, it had been my policy
not to ask any pilot to fly a mission I would not fly myself, so I
listed my name as the flight leader for the two aircraft on night
alert. I planned to ask for a volunteer to take the wingman role.
Major Pat Berry, the operations officer, walked by the scheduling board and asked why I was pulling night alert. I told him

there were those who would enjoy the party more than I would and that I wanted to finish up some paperwork anyway.

Pat, who usually loved a good party, was quiet for a minute and then said, "I think I'll be your number two. Put my name on the board." I was really surprised and asked him if he wanted to be the flight leader since he was a major and I was a captain. He said, "No, you can lead, if we get scrambled." I was delighted to have Pat on alert with me. We were good friends and had the most F-100 flight experience of any of the squadron pilots. Pat had around 2,600 hours, and I had about 2,400 hours in the F-100. The younger pilots were astonished to see the night alert schedule and left the operations building in a rush before either Pat or I changed our minds.

After an early dinner, Pat and I relieved the afternoon alert pilots, and each one of us did a preflight inspection of his aircraft; each put his parachute in the cockpit and his helmet on

top of the windscreen. We then went back to the squadron building, where we busied ourselves with the last of the paperwork so all would be in order for the next day and the "new guys."

I conducted the standard night-alert briefing and we retired to the alert trailer about 9:30 P.M. and went to sleep on our bunks still wearing our flight suits. The alert protocol required that we be off the ground in fifteen minutes or less, so there was no time for dressing.

The scramble telephone rang at just after 10:30 P.M. A U.S. Army convoy had been ambushed on a road between a series of hills! We were told to get airborne ASAP and the Tactical Air Control Center (TACC) radar would give us a vector to the target. Pat and I sprinted to our aircraft. Our crew chiefs were already there, and as we fired the explosive starter cartridge to get the engine running, our crew chiefs helped us into our parachutes and shoulder harnesses. We were rolling out of the revetments in less than five minutes from the time of the phone call. The control tower cleared us for immediate takeoff, and in just over ten minutes we were roaring down the runway in formation with afterburners blazing! (It should be noted that going in ten minutes from being sound asleep to piloting a jet fighter into the blackness of a moonless night over the dark jungle is a real transition, and the adrenalin really flows!)

Pat and I were directed by the radar site toward the area of the ambush. We were notified by the TACC that there would not be a "flare ship" to illuminate the target. Flare ships were C-130 transport aircraft that had been modified to drop flares and were on airborne alert at various locations over South Vietnam. They would join the fighters over a target and from a higher altitude than the fighters would drop magnesium flares attached to small parachutes. (Pat and I had both completed "Night Owl" training before coming to Vietnam, in which we were trained to use the F-100D as a night fighter, which was never intended in the design. These were the days before night vision goggles or night scopes. We had to depend upon our own eyeballs and were expected to drop munitions that were designed for daylight use. The few flares didn't come close to making it "as bright as day.")

The news of not having a flare ship was a concern. We carried a few flares on each F-100D but would have to ration them carefully. Flare ships usually dropped between five and seven flares at a time and would drop more upon request from the fighter pilots. We would have to limit our flares to two or three at a time—not a comforting prospect in the hilly terrain.

The TACC requested that we contact our Forward Air Controller (FAC), call sign Dingo, when we were a few miles from the target area. A FAC is an Air Force pilot in another aircraft, in this case an O-1 (also known as an L-19) Bird Dog, who is in communication with the troops on the ground and who briefs the pilots on the current status of the battle. He also identifies the locations of friendly and enemy forces. I directed Pat to change radio channels and gave the FAC a call: "Dingo, this is Crusader lead, a flight of two Huns, with a standard night alert load, approaching your location."

"Crusader lead, this is Dingo. Since we don't have a flare ship, I'm holding a bit south of the ambush area. I suggest you 'pickle off' (drop) a couple of flares so I can give you better information."

"Roger, Dingo, here is one flare." The flare illuminated, very dimly, a ravine between some uneven, low-lying hills. A winding dirt road was in the bottom of the ravine. There were U.S. Army trucks stopped on the road. "Crusader, good drop. The flare is almost centered above the area of the firefight. It appears that our convoy was ambushed by a Vietcong patrol, which has now taken up positions on both sides of the road a little north of the trucks. Our guys are returning small-arms fire from the area near the trucks. We need you to drop on both sides of the road starting about even with the trucks, and then stop your drop to the north about one-fourth of a mile."

I began making a tight circle around the target area. "Roger, Dingo. Crusader two, confirm you have the target area in sight."

"Crusader lead, Crusader two has the target area in sight."

The dim-light challenge was compounded by the fact that our munitions were anti-material/anti-personnel weapons designed to be dropped at 450 miles per hour in level flight from an altitude of about one hundred feet above the ground. It was a good weapon in the daytime on flat terrain, but not so good in hilly terrain at night and in really close proximity to friendly forces.

I took a deep breath and pushed my radio mike button. "Crusader two, I'll come in Sierra to November (south to north) on the east side. Suggest you come in November to Sierra (north to south) on the west side, beginning your drop about a quarter-mile north of the trucks."

Pat radioed back, "Roger, Crusader lead."

"Crusader two, take separation, navigation lights off." Navigation lights are a red light on the left wingtip, a green light on the right wingtip, a white light behind the canopy, and a small white and a small orange light on the vertical fin. Lights were turned off to prevent ground gunners from being able to see the aircraft on approach to the target area.

"Crusader two, taking separation, lights off."

"Dingo, Crusader lead's dropping three flares, turning in hot."

"Crusader lead, Dingo, roger cleared hot."

"Dingo, suggest you tell our guys to get their heads way down and as close as practical to the trucks."

"Roger, Crusader, they started that process as soon as they heard you in the area."

Flash! Flash! Flash! My three flares ignited, and now I could refine my attack tactic. I would come in parallel to the road at 450 miles per hour and get as low as I dared. I would try to match my wings' left bank with the angle of the hill and keep the nose straight with the right rudder. Tricky! The trucks are coming up fast now, a little finesse to my right, ready, ready, NOW! Munitions away! Pull-up! There is a higher hill straight ahead! Watch out for my "dead flare," the first one I dropped to acquire the target area, which had burned out but was still "airborne" in its parachute just off to my left. (We called burned-out flares "ghosts" since the white parachutes, which sometimes seem to appear out of nowhere, could be real hazards. The flare's metal canister could damage or bring down a fighter hitting it at high speed.) "Crusader two, lead's off right. Watch for the 'ghost' about over the road and seems to be drifting east."

"Roger, Crusader two. Two flares away and Two is in hot."

"Crusader lead, Dingo, beauty drop. The Army guys are under their trucks, but they are cheering."

"Roger, Dingo, we'll keep the pressure on." Crusader two

made his attack in the opposite direction and on the west side of the road. His munitions were "on the money."

"Crusader two, Dingo. Sweet! Same spot next time just a little higher up the hill as the bad guys are pulling back."

Pat and I alternated our flare drops and munitions runs, continuing to dodge "ghosts" and hills. We then commenced firing on "our sides of the hills" with our four twenty-millimeter cannons. We noticed that our trucks were now turning around and heading down the ravine in the direction from which they had come. Their plan was to wait down the road a couple of miles for some Army tanks that would escort the convoy through the hills.

The flares were expended, as was all of our firepower. I called the FAC, "Dingo, these two Crusaders have done their thing, and we are bugging out."

"Roger, Crusaders, Dingo, the Army guys told me to tell you that Army–Air Force relations were never better."

I replied laughingly, "Roger, Dingo. Tell them we're always happy to be of service. Talk to you later, Dingo."

I turned my navigation lights back on, as did Pat, and he rejoined in formation with me. We flew back to Tan Son Nhut in silence except for a brief check-in and "mission completed" report to the TACC. I noticed for the first time that I had worked up a real sweat during the attack, probably from anxiety about not hitting our own troops, the high humidity, and the series of challenges faced. I now felt cold and clammy, so I turned the cockpit heat up a notch.

After Pat and I landed, had the aircraft dearmed, and taxied back to the parking revetments, we were met by a host of our aircraft maintenance personnel. They wanted to hear the whole story. Those guys were the best! They kept our aircraft in top condition, and I never feared taking a 481st F-100D on any mission!

Pat and I walked into the empty operations building, grabbed a soft drink, and sat down at a briefing table. We just sat there in silence for a few moments. When we did speak, we agreed that this had been the most challenging of any of our night combat missions. There were some other "hairy ones," like flying multiple missions the same night to break up an attack on an army outpost, but those were not as difficult as this one. We wondered if the outcome would have been the same on this night if we had scheduled two of our younger, less-experienced pilots to pull night alert. We feared that the dreaded "last mission curse," where a pilot is lost flying his last combat mission, might have come true.

We agreed we had received divine guidance in choosing night alert over the elegant farewell party. Each of us in our own way acknowledged the guiding hand of a loving God in our lives and especially on this—our last night alert before going home. It would indeed be a happy Thanksgiving!

PILOT'S BIOGRAPHY

Lieutenant Colonel Thales A. "Tad" Derrlck, Unites States Air Force, retired

Call sign: Meteor

Hometown: Salt Lake City, Utah; St. George, Utah

Family: married to Willa Nita Brooks; children are David, Daniel, Dennis, Dana, and Douglas; twenty-three grandchildren

Church experience: bishop, high councilor, stake president, mission president, now a counselor in stake presidency

Hobbies: Church and community service (active in CERT); caring for small orchard; computers; flying own aircraft, a C-172 SkyHawk

Awards and recognitions: Distinguished Flying Cross, Distinguished Service Medal (3 awards), Air Medal (five awards), among others

Major Pat Berry, left, and Captain Tad Derrick, right, discuss their night tactics.

PIPER ARCHER

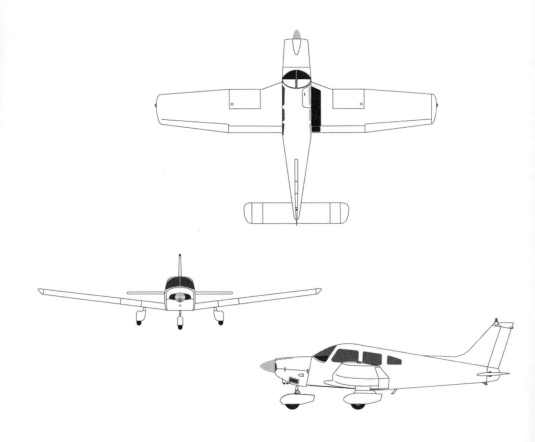

CHAPTER FIFTEEN

CLOUDS AND PRAYER

ANDREW LOWRY

It was a beautiful Saturday morning at Falcon Field in Mesa, Arizona, just the perfect day for a leisurely flight. I had invited my sister Krista to come along on a cross-country flight I had planned the day before. Prior to this flight I had flown only about 70 flight hours total, and had only had my pilot's license for about a year. I was currently building flight time to start a flight program in which I could finish my ratings and become a flight instructor.

My sister and I met at the airport early—about 6:00 A.M.—because the flight we were going on would be about three hours long. We joked around and had fun doing the usual pre-flight check of the airplane. When it came time to check the inside of the plane to make sure all the instruments and switches in the cockpit were in good working order, there were big placards on a couple of the instruments that said, "INOP." The "INOP" sticker basically meant that the instruments were inoperative and did not work. Legally I could still go on the flight, but it was up to me to make the call on whether I felt like I could complete the flight safely without those instruments: the heading indicator and the attitude indicator. I have to admit, when I first saw the placards, the Spirit told me it was not a good idea to go and that I didn't have enough experience to complete the flight without those particular instruments.

Before I go any further, I'll tell you just what those instruments do. The attitude indicator is an instrument with an artificial horizon, or a card that always stays level with the horizon, whether you're turning, climbing, or descending. It also has a miniature airplane or representation of the airplane that shows you what your airplane is doing in relation to the horizon. For example, if you bank or turn to the right, the little miniature airplane on the attitude indicator shows a turn to the right. Pilots can use this instrument to fly in the clouds and know if they are turning, climbing, and so on, without looking outside the airplane. The heading indicator is basically a compass card you can use to see which direction you are flying. As you turn, the compass card turns also, making it easy to fly certain headings or directions. Without these instruments, flying is still pretty easy, as long as you are not trying to follow a specific course to another airport that is far away.

I was flying to specific airports, airports I had never been to. But being the "experienced" pilot I thought I was, I ignored the whisperings of the Holy Spirit and decided to go anyway. After all, I had driven down to the airport already, so I had to go, right? We took off and started to follow the regular compass (which isn't as easy to follow as a heading indicator because it swings around with turbulence and bumps), and also used an aeronautical chart to get to our first destination of Show Low, Arizona. Along the way we watched valleys, roads, lakes, and other landmarks to track our progress. We found the airport and I called the traffic to tell them we were in the area and were going to do a touch-and-go, then depart the area to the north. We entered a downwind, did final checks, executed a nice touch-and-go, and departed to the northwest toward Holbrook, Arizona.

My confidence was building as we flew to Holbrook. I looked down and admired the great beauty of the mountains of eastern Arizona, taking in the full peacefulness of being able to fly and see the greatness of Heavenly Father's creation. It took a little searching around to find Holbrook but we finally did. The wind was starting to pick up and as I tried to do a touch-and-go there, the wind was too strong and I had to go around and not land there. No big deal, we could just keep flying to our next destination, Winslow. That part of the flight was easy because we could just follow Interstate 40 west and that would take us straight there.

As we were flying toward Winslow the wind started to

increase and the weather got pretty turbulent. Let me tell you, there is nothing worse than being in an airplane when you are getting bounced all around and there is nothing you can do about it. Both of us were starting to feel sick, and we welcomed the sight of Winslow. As we drew close to Winslow, I thought, "I didn't need those instruments anyway; I have found all the airports just fine." Boy, was I in for a surprise! When we got to Winslow, the landing was less than stellar because of the wind, and we stopped and got out so we didn't lose our breakfast all over the cockpit! We rested and got ourselves ready for the last leg of the trip.

We were to fly down to Payson, Arizona, do a touch-and-go there, and then return safely to our home airport of Falcon Field. We were both feeling pretty good as we took off and we joked around as we made our way to Payson. I flew the heading I had figured out that would take us to Payson, and we continued to track our progress on our chart. As we continued to fly the weather started to worsen and the clouds started to lower. Pretty soon we were only about 1500 feet off the ground and it was pretty hard to see very far ahead because we had to stay low to keep out of the clouds. So I resorted to using the compass more heavily, and tried to continue tracking our progress with the chart. I looked at the flight plan I had done; the time was drawing near to when we should be able to see Payson. I looked at the chart and tried to figure out where we were. I tried to look at valleys, rivers, lakes, anything! But everything looked the same; it was all mountains! About that time I had a horrible realization, one that no pilot ever wants to admit or ever have happen to them: I WAS LOST!

The time drew closer for our proposed arrival in Payson and

still nothing! So I reverted to my training of what to do when you get lost. I couldn't climb higher to get a better view of everything, I was too low to use any of the navigation instruments in the airplane, but I could probably call air traffic control and see if they could help me. Right before I was going to call ATC, Krista and I agreed that we should say a prayer. If anyone knew where we were, Heavenly Father did. So Krista said the prayer of course, because I still had to fly the plane. She offered up the most simple of prayers, thanking Heavenly Father for the great opportunity we had to go on this adventure of flying, and also asking Him to help us find our way home. Not one second after we said "amen," I looked up and through the low clouds saw the Four Peaks! Yes! The Four Peaks are the most prominent mountain peaks just northeast of Falcon Field! So I turned the airplane toward the peaks and flew the rest of the way home just fine.

After I had tied the airplane down and was sitting in the car before we left, my full appreciation came for how the Lord helped us. Had we not found the Four Peaks, we would have had to land who knows where because we were starting to get low on fuel. As we drove home I offered a prayer of thanks; my emotions were full and thankful for how much the Lord really does watch over us and protect us.

I learned some great things about life on that flight. We always need to listen to the Spirit when we feel those promptings, whether it's about flying, talking to someone about the gospel, whatever the case may be. If we trust in the Lord and do listen to the Spirit, we will be rewarded. I also realized that even when we don't listen to the Spirit the first time, the Lord does not give up on us. When I could not guide my airplane back to the airport, the Lord was there for me, and He led me back safely even though I hadn't listened the first time.

Lastly, when I flew from Winslow toward Payson, I now realize that I was only a few degrees off of what my heading was supposed to be, but by the time I got down to where Payson should have been, I was miles away from where I wanted to be. In life we may think we are only a few degrees off of the straight and narrow path, but if we continue that way, down the road we will be "miles" away from where we need to be spiritually. Thankfully the Lord will always take us in His arms and safely lead us home, no matter how far we may get off course.

PILOT'S BIOGRAPHY

Andrew Lowry

Hometown: born in Salt Lake City; currently living in Queen Creek, Arizona

Family: married to Keri Lowry; two children, Griffin and Ellie

Church experience: served in the Pennsylvania Pittsburgh mission, 1997- 1999; has served as a Primary teacher, in the Sunday School presidency; currently serves as Varsity Scout coach

Hobbies: spending time with family, Church service, playing the violin, martial arts, and, of course, flying! Other airplanes flown include the Cessna 150, Citation 501, Piper Seneca, and currently a Beechcraft King Air 350

Andrew Lowry.

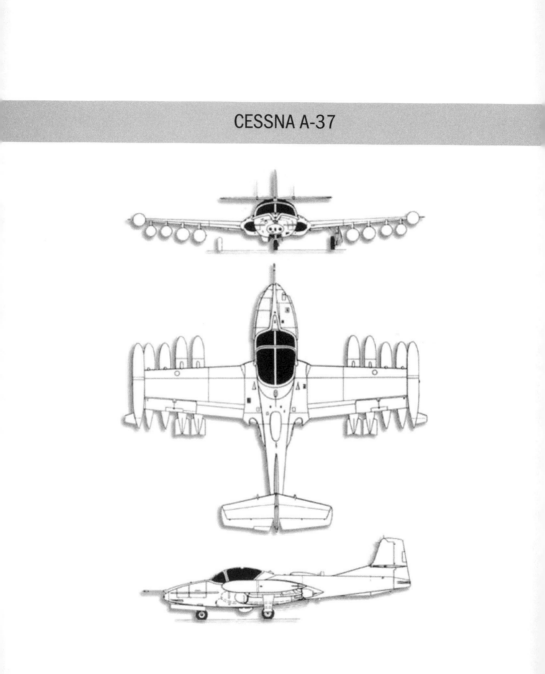

CHAPTER SIXTEEN

SPECIAL OPERATIONS SQUADRON

GORDON H. WEED

The A-37 fighter bomber (the "A" designating "attack" for air-to-ground missions) was specifically designed for low-level close air support of friendly troops in contact with enemy forces in a jungle environment. It had two side-by-side ejection seats but was normally flown by one pilot from the left side. The right seat was used by an instructor pilot for checking out new pilots in close air support combat missions. It was a tailor-made aircraft for such a mission and the pilots and ground troops loved it. It had a low profile, was very maneuverable, and was difficult to bring down with antiaircraft fire. It carried diversified bombs and rockets and a six-barrel, electric-powered Gatling gun with 1100 rounds of ammunition. And it was extremely accurate placing the weapons on target.

In 1970, when other flying squadrons were being transferred to Thailand, the 8th Special Operations Squadron was the only American flying squadron left in Vietnam and was stationed at Bien Hoa Air Base located north of Saigon. Being a special operations squadron, it was self-contained with 25 A-37 fighter bombers, 40 pilots, and 360 support personnel. Our mission was twenty-four-hour-a-day, low-level close air support for the remaining American troops and friendly Vietnamese ground forces.

In 1972, I was fortunate to be the squadron commander of the 8th Special Operations Squadron. These special operations were being directed by higher authority and controlled by airborne Forward Air Controllers (FAC). The FACs, as they are called, are the unsung heroes of close air support missions.

On one particular mission, intelligence ground forces came across a major enemy buildup in a sanctuary located deep inside enemy territory. One of my flight commanders and I were scheduled to fly together that day and were directed to destroy the enemy forces before they had time to disperse. Fighters always fly in flights of at least two aircraft for mutual protection and to keep track of each other during an air strike. When we arrived over the target, the FAC was on scene and in contact with the friendly ground forces. He immediately marked the area where the opposing forces were with white smoke rockets and gave us a briefing on where the enemy gun emplacements were.

The briefing was not encouraging. The enemy was well dug in and had numerous antiaircraft guns in the area, including heat-seeking Strela (Russian-made) missiles. Our A-37s were configured with napalm and cluster bombs, which were more than adequate to destroy the trucks, tanks, and enemy ground forces. The enemies were firing at the FAC with everything they had, and he was very fortunate to have been shot at and missed. "Rampage Charlie" was the code name for the ground commander of the friendly forces, and he was ecstatic when the A-37s arrived over the target. He reported that some high-ranking enemy officers were on scene and that this was at least a force of regimental size and apparently had radar-controlled antiaircraft guns.

As we descended over the target area, we could see that there was a great deal of commotion on the ground. Troops in contact with the enemy, tanks and weapons carriers, trucks and other equipment were in disarray. It appeared that they were trying to pack up and leave. It wasn't difficult for the FAC to identify the target, so he called for a napalm drop and marked the exact target with white smoke. He then gave the A-37s clearance to hit the target with napalm. The enemy gunners either didn't have tracer bullets or were reluctant to use them because tracers reveal the exact location of the enemy guns. We flew in low and saw the muzzle flashes of the 12.7 mm guns that were shooting at us. Past experience indicated that if you can see the gun barrel flashes, they are aiming right at you and the bullets are going behind you. Pilots know this and are not too concerned when they see the gun flashes. It's when the ground commander tells you that you are taking ground fire and you don't see the flashes that it gets hairy. The gunners have you zeroed in and you are very likely to take a hit.

In our first pass at the target, we hit the smoke mark, blasted the enemy, and came off with good results. We could see some vehicles burning and enemy troops running for cover. The FAC was pleased with the strike, but he was concerned about one particular gun that the ground commander wanted silenced. We talked it over and decided that another low-level napalm pass was the best option. With the help of the ground commander, the FAC pinpointed the gun's location, marked it, and cleared us in hot. Once again the opposing forces were shooting behind us so we weren't too impressed with their ability. We came off the target low and fast in order to avoid the other guns and the heat-seeking missiles in the area. The ground commander confirmed that the gun was history and we felt a little more secure.

About the time we figured that the gun and missile threats had been overrated, the enemy started shooting at us with everything they had. It looked like a Fourth of July fireworks display. They opened up with everything that was still operational. The last napalm run made them really mad and they knew we were for real. We were getting low on fuel so the FAC requested that we put our cluster bombs down along the tree line where most of the bad guys were dug in and then return to our air base. It sounded like a good idea, because so far, we had been pretty lucky. We came in low and fast, stabilized, and started pumping out the cluster bombs. The radio crackled, "You're taking fire, you're taking fire," and this time we couldn't see gun flashes.

About halfway through the run, we heard a loud thump. We had taken a bad hit by a 12.7 mm antiaircraft gun. The aircraft shuddered and yawed sharply to the right, and the airspeed dropped to 110 knots, which was just about stalling speed. I was still pumping out cluster bombs in hopes of at least getting the gun that had hit us. Our wingman yelled that we were trailing smoke from the right engine. It was obvious from the instrument panel that the right engine had been hit, so I pulled the firewall shut-off handle, which would shut off all fuel to the engine and hopefully put out the fire.

My main concern at that point was controlling the aircraft. It felt like the speed brakes were out and we were going down. At that low airspeed, I didn't dare pull the left throttle back and I needed full left rudder and considerable aileron to keep the wings level. We were barely above the trees and getting farther away from the target area. The airspeed stabilized at 130 knots and to our surprise we were still airborne. Our wingman had last observed us just above the trees trailing smoke and apparently thought we had crashed. He was circling the area until I called him and told him to join up on us and give us a battle damage check. I jettisoned the cluster bomb pods and was thinking about getting rid of the fuel pylon tanks but we decided to keep them—they were in short supply and didn't seem to be a problem in keeping the aircraft flying.

We were trying without much success to gain some airspeed and altitude. The right wing was vibrating and acting like it wanted to stall. I eased off on the aileron and we regained some stability. I called the FAC and told him that we were still airborne and heading for home. Our wingman couldn't locate us so we gave him our heading and altitude and finally spotted him about 2,000 feet above us doing about 200 knots. We told him to throttle back and descend to our altitude and join up on our wing. We were about 6,000 feet by this time and still climbing very slowly. Aside from excessive drag from an apparent frozen engine, the aircraft was performing pretty well. Our main concern now was fuel consumption, as we had to keep a pretty high throttle setting on the number-one engine.

Our wingman joined up and gave us a battle damage check, which was quite encouraging. He said everything looked good on the outside and asked if we could increase our airspeed a little. He was getting low on fuel like we were, so I told him to gain some altitude, keep us in sight, and alert operations back at the base of our emergency. After what seemed like an eternity we sighted the base and made a straight-in approach. The landing gear came down and locked, the flaps worked okay, and the touchdown was about like most single-engine landings. We pulled off the runway and shut the remaining engine down.

We had taken a 12.7 mm hit in the right engine. The slug had shredded the engine turbine, caused a brief engine fire, and torn into the main wing spar and engine mount. Chunks of the engine mount and wing spar were in the engine shroud. I brought them home for souvenirs. From all indications, it was a good thing we couldn't get a higher airspeed. The chief of maintenance said if the airspeed had been much higher, in all probability the wing would have come off in flight. I don't know who my "guardian angel" was on that flight, but he really let me sweat it out before he intervened and helped me get that aircraft back to the base. I am convinced he is assigned to combat missions of this type and comes through when I ask for his help. Whether through the chain of command or directly from the Lord, it is the same.

PILOT'S BIOGRAPHY

Colonel Gordon H. Weed,
United States Air Force, retired

Hometown: Salt Lake City, Utah

Family: married to Patricia Lunt; four children, twenty-one grandchildren, and four great-grandchildren

Church experience: served a mission to Stockholm, Sweden, 1946–1949; has served as a branch president, Gospel Doctrine teacher, and Gospel Essentials teacher; served a couples mission to Seoul, Korea, from 1987–1989; later served as a high councilor and Public Affairs host; traveled back to Vietnam in 1989 with the group Veterans Assisting Saints Abroad; currently teaching Temple Preparation class

Awards and recognitions: Distinguished Flying Cross, Air Medal, Vietnamese Cross of Gallantry, and the Legion of Merit

Colonel Gordon H. Weed with the A-37 Drangonfly.

LOCKHEED KC-130J

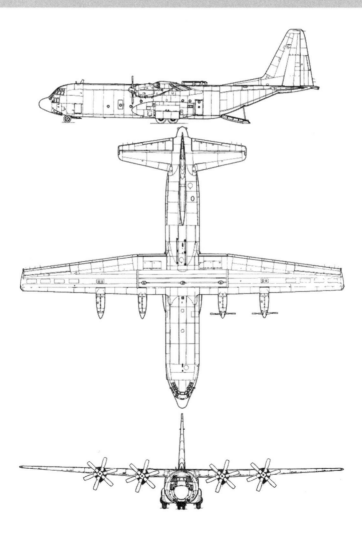

CHAPTER SEVENTEEN

THE FULL ARMOR OF GOD

JANINE K. GARNER

In 2006 I was on my first deployment to Iraq, as a KC-130J pilot for the Marine Corps. It was the middle of the summer, and *hot.* Even at night it seemed we were lucky if it cooled down to 90 degrees. So, after over five months of flying around in Iraq, and never once getting shot at while I was flying, I was getting sick and tired of sitting in my plane for hours on end sweating like crazy in my full flight gear, body armor, helmet, and NVGs (night vision goggles).

I knew why we had the gear; it was there to protect us in the event that an insurgent took a shot at us from the ground, but that still didn't stop me from complaining about wearing it. Aside from being very hot to wear, the required extra gear was also cumbersome and made moving around in the plane extremely awkward. It never hampered my flying ability; it was just an annoyance. It would have been so easy just to remove the required body armor and fly in comfort. I mean, I hadn't been shot at yet, and what were the chances, really?

My entire attitude changed one evening in July as I was flying into Baghdad with the back of my plane full of passengers. It was a routine flight, the first of many my crew and I were to

139

make that night into Baghdad, transporting gear and passengers. Just like every other flight I'd been on in the previous five months, this one was going just as planned. Everything was routine, and we were all having to struggle against getting complacent. Things had been so benign that it was hard to remember that we were technically in a war zone!

So, tired from being up so late, my head hurting from wearing my helmet and NVGs so many nights in a row, my back and shoulders tired from constantly wearing the body armor, and, of course, sweating despite the air conditioner, we began our approach, and I did my duties with all the motivation of a zombie. Suddenly, as we were nearing the approach end of the runway with our landing gear and flaps down, I heard one of the crew yell, "Break right!"

Someone had just launched an RPG (rocket-propelled grenade) or missile or some sort of projectile at us! Our training kicked in, and the entire crew quickly executed the procedures we'd been taught and trained for in this situation. Looking down I could also see small-arms fire coming up at us from the ground, but I didn't really have time to process the information or to be scared. I, like my crew, only had time to react.

Later that evening, once we were safely on the deck in Baghdad, I had time to think about what had happened. Someone had tried to kill me and my crew. I had always known that was possible, from a conceptual level, but I'd never actually been on the receiving end of a weapon before. It shook me to my very core, and I realized the importance of the protective gear worn by me and my crew. How very glad I was then that, despite the heat and the inconvenience of it all, my crew and I had not removed any of the protective equipment we were wearing. But mostly, how thankful I was that the crew had been alert in the back of the plane on the lookout for any potential danger. He could very easily have been sleeping or not paying attention—after five months of no one shooting at us, why would they start now? The answer to that is simple: because they were waiting for a time when we let our guard down; they were waiting for that chink in our armor. They were looking for a "target of opportunity."

Satan is the same way. He is always waiting in the wings for us to let our guard down. He is waiting for us to neglect to put on the full armor of God. It is so easy to slip, to not read our scriptures, say our prayers, go to church, fulfill our callings, pay our tithing, and so on. Sometimes it feels like overkill, almost like a burden, and it would be so much easier not to have to worry and be inconvenienced by all those things the Lord gave us to protect us. Honestly, what will not doing it one time hurt?

But the thing is, had my crew and I not been paying attention or wearing our full armor, it could have hurt us fatally. Just as the men on the ground were trying to destroy my aircraft and all of us on board, so is Satan trying to destroy our spirits. Don't let him—don't become his next "target of opportunity." Remain vigilant and always wear the full armor of God.

PILOT'S BIOGRAPHY

Captain Janine K. Garner,
United States Marine Corps

Call sign: ATIS

Hometown: St. George, Utah

Family: married to Captain Ronald T. Garner, USMC, since 2001

Church experience: former Primary teacher, Young Women's teacher, Young Women's basketball coach; currently a Relief Society teacher

Current occupation: still flying for the USMC

Awards and recognitions: 1000 flight hours in the Marine Corps, over five Air Medals, numerous other military awards, medals, and honors

Captain Janine K. Garner pictured with the KC-130J.

CHAPTER EIGHTEEN

THE JACKSON HOLE ADVENTURE

ALBERT B. KENDELL

In the mid-sixties, I was a captain flying a Convair 580 for Frontier Airlines on a trip from Jackson, Wyoming, to Salt Lake City, Utah. Flying in and out of Jackson Hole is beautiful, interesting, and potentially challenging because of where it sits. The airport is at 6,444 feet above sea level, nestled in a valley surrounded by mountains, with the 14,000-foot Tetons just to the west.

In training, pilots are taught all about flying in and out of high-altitude airports where you must deal with "density altitude" issues, meaning that an airplane performs more poorly at high altitude than it would at sea level because the air is thinner.

But the major area of training is always emergency procedures: what to do when you have an engine fire, an electric failure, or some other "abnormal" occurrence. The one dreaded emergency most pilots never want to experience is not just having an engine fire, but to have an engine fire or lose an engine at the most critical time of all: on takeoff.

Takeoff is when you have your hands full even when things are normal, but to experience this emergency is, well, the reason that more than 70 percent of all aircraft-related fatalities occur when one has engine failure on takeoff. On takeoff your plane is usually full of people, baggage, and fuel. It is heavy. It is trying to get enough airspeed to break the friction and gravitational pull and allow aerodynamics to take over and cause lift. You have many things to do on takeoff in a short period of time. All of the training is great, but going through the real thing is a different story.

One of the important lessons we are taught in training is that if you have to shut down an engine, once the engine is shut down, you never—*repeat, never*—make a turn toward the bad or "dead" engine. This is because of aerodynamics. The remaining good engine will "overpower" the dead engine side, and as you turn toward the dead engine you will find that the airplane will keep rolling well past where you want it to. The good engine's power will roll the plane completely upside down and keep rolling it because there is no compensating force to stop the roll. In such a case, a crash is practically inevitable.

On this early spring day, the weather was beautiful right over the airport area and to the south down the valley, but to the west of the airport, the Tetons were completely obscured by heavy snow showers. Further to the north, the Black Tail Butte area was also completely obscured by snow showers. Fortunately on this day my copilot was another member of the Church, Gary Winn, who is a very experienced and efficient pilot.

In those days, Jackson Hole didn't have a terminal; they only had a very small building where the passengers would gather. We prepared the flight plan and did the preflight inspections, and soon thereafter the passengers were called to board the flight. We had approximately forty passengers on the plane, and with the fuel required to arrive in Salt Lake City the plane weighed approximately 42,500 pounds.

We started the engines and taxied out to take off to the south. The wind was out of the south at a brisk 18 knots, or about 24 mph. We taxied and went through all the pretakeoff checklists. Everything was checked and scanned and we were ready for another uneventful takeoff.

We had been advised that there was no traffic in the airport area so we taxied onto the runway, lined up with the center line, and I applied full takeoff power, released the brakes, checked the instruments, and began accelerating down the runway for what was soon to be a *very* eventful takeoff.

At about 105 knots Gary called out "V1," which is the speed at which if we had a problem we could pull back the power, apply brakes, and still stop the plane. Almost immediately after V1, Gary called "V2." This is the speed at which you are committed to take off regardless of what happens. You must proceed. Well, we rotated, and I called for "gear up," and at about 200 feet off the ground we heard the sound that makes your heart jump out of your chest and one you hope you will never hear: The left engine fire warning light came on and the fire bell started to ring.

I looked out the window at the left engine to see if there were any visible signs of smoke or fire. We double-checked the fire warning system, and it said we had a fire in the left engine. The manual instructs you to shut the engine down at that point, so Gary grasped hold of the left "E Handle" and asked me to confirm that he had the left one in his hand, which was the procedure we practiced in our training to assure that in the frantic

pace of warning lights and bells going off, the pilot doesn't accidentally shut down the good engine. I was flying the plane and
concentrating on gaining some altitude, but I glanced down and
confirmed he had the correct engine lever, and he pulled it. I
was preparing myself for how the airplane was going to react
and fly with only one engine. The engine shut down immediately and the prop feathered.

We always wondered if the plane could and would be able
to fly well on one engine and now we were going to find out
firsthand. We completed the engine fire checklist and ascer-
tained that everything was as it should be. In the meantime, we
were flying down the valley at about 109 knots at only 200 feet
above the ground. We had our hands full, and I'm sure the local
cows and farmers were wondering what the airliner was doing
"strafing" the local fields.

While all this was going on, the agents back on the ground

heard the engine shut down and saw our precariously low altitude as we lumbered down the valley. They called another Frontier 580 that was taxiing out toward the end of the runway to depart for Denver, and told them to return to the ramp. They had only a few passengers, and the agents told them that they were going to trade airplanes to take all the passengers—"if he makes it back."

As we were headed down the valley at 200 feet the airspeed would not increase and the altitude did not increase. We couldn't turn to the right because the area was completely obscured by snow showers and mountains, and we couldn't turn to the left because the terrain was higher than we were, so I contemplated going down the Snake River and wondered if there were any power lines that we could possibly hit.

Just as I contemplated the decreasing options and said a little prayer in my heart, we suddenly gained about 300 feet, and as I looked out the left window toward the town of Jackson Hole we gained another 200 feet, so I decided to turn toward the town . . . but that meant turning into the "dead engine." I had no other choice. We were surrounded by mountains, but by turning toward Jackson Hole I could possibly make it through the small valley where the town lies and follow that little valley back to the airport.

All I could think of was my multi-engine instructor, many years earlier, specifically stating to "never turn into a dead engine." I thought of the possibility of rolling the aircraft. And I prayed fervently that my decision to discard my training would be the right one.

It was working! We kept the plane under control and made our way back up the small valley and saw the airport. I considered landing straight-in to the north, but that would have given me an 18-knot tailwind, which is *way* above the maximum allowable tailwind for landing. With the plane being so heavy, we might have been able to put the plane down, but wouldn't have been able to stop it before the end of the runway.

In order to land to the south and into the wind, we would proceed north parallel to the runway—and then we would be forced to make another left turn into the dreaded "dead engine." Well, it had worked for us once; we would have to do it again.

The north end of the airport including Black Tail Butte was obscured by snow showers, but we were able to complete all the checklists and make a very steep, left-turning descent over the top of Black Tail Butte toward the runway . . . into the "dead engine."

The other aircraft was waiting for us and we disembarked the passengers, put on the airfreight, signed the paperwork, and took off for Salt Lake City in the second plane. Our one-engine plane was to remain there at Jackson Hole so it could be inspected and fixed. We arrived in Salt Lake City only ten minutes behind schedule.

The agents did a terrific job, Gary Winn did a terrific job, everyone did a terrific job . . . except me: I turned into a dead engine.

PILOT'S BIOGRAPHY

Albert B. Kendell

Service: flew for both the Army Air Corps and the United States Navy before flying for Frontier Airlines (soloed with only two hours of formal instruction); retired from Frontier Airlines with over 30,000 flight hours

Hometown: Uintah, Utah, a small farming community at the mouth of Weber Canyon

Family: married 56 years to Marilyn Summerill Kendell; two sons, Mark and Scott, and one daughter, Jackie Kendell Keyes; thirteen grandchildren; nine great-grandchildren

Church calling: secretary of high priests group

Albert Kendell with a DC-3.

LOCKHEED MARTIN F-16

CHAPTER NINETEEN

"I WILL BE YOUR LIGHT IN THE WILDERNESS"

MICHAEL R. SHEPHERD

Time has long erased many of the specific details of the nearly six months that I spent in Iraq. Nonetheless, there are images in my mind that are as alive and vivid as though I had lived them just yesterday.

I was stationed at Balad Air Base, Iraq (roughly forty miles north of Baghdad). According to the U.S. Air Force, I was an "experienced wingman" (meaning that I had met the required hours to be called "experienced"; by no means did it suggest that I was ready for combat flying). I had been in Iraq for nearly three months when I was scheduled to fly a CAS mission (close air support) with Captain Todd "Thumper" Halverson. Along with being my flight commander and close friend, Thumper also shared my trailer in Iraq. I will always remember him as the person who showed me the chemical boots that we were issued in case of a chemical attack. (They also made great mud boots for the heavy rains that we experienced while we were there.) Thumper would also be my flight lead, as we would spend nearly five hours in the northern area of Iraq, over the city of Mosul. In order to help you fully understand what happened that night, I must explain some things I learned during my training.

The close air support (CAS) mission was the bread and butter of the 34th Fighter Squadron. The pilots who flew the F-16s stationed out of Hill AFB, Utah, had prepared for months for their deployment to Iraq. We had trained for almost every possible scenario. I had flown countless sorties over the Salt Flats in the airspace west of the Great Salt Lake. We had dropped live ordnance of every kind, worked with Army ALOs (air liaison officers), and worked extensively with night vision goggles (NVGs). Flying with NVGs was always an incredible experience! The technology that was provided through the goggles allowed the night to magically transform into day.

I can still recall the first time that I flew with NVGs. I had recently arrived at Hill AFB, having completed the basic qualification course in Phoenix, Arizona. I was a brand-new wingman, and was upgrading in the NVGs. I was scheduled to fly with our squadron commander, Lieutenant Colonel "Bags" Bagnani. It was always intimidating to fly with the boss. He was extremely experienced, he had the power to determine my future assignments, and I was determined to impress him that night. I had received all of the standard academics pertaining to the NVGs. The academics included the most in-depth information, down to the basics . . . how to put them on. In hindsight, I wish I had listened a little more closely.

We had just taken off and had begun our departure toward the Salt Flats. We never departed the runway with the NVGs on; the dangers of ejecting with the NVGs still connected to our helmets was much too high. As a result, we would take off with the NVGs safely stored in a protective case, and then "goggle," or put the NVGs on, when we were safely airborne and on our way to our working airspace. I had already used my radar to lock up my commander, when he told me to goggle. I dug into the case where my NVGs were stored, connected them to the brackets on the top of my helmet, and turned on the goggles. In my anticipation of the wonderful world that would quickly illuminate, the picture that I was given was far less remarkable than what I had expected. In fact, it looked remarkably similar to the darkness that had prevailed moments earlier.

I debated telling my flight lead, the commander, that my goggles were not working. I first tried to change to the backup battery. When that failed I realized that I did not have much of a choice. I spoke out over our interflight radio: "Ram One, Two."

"Go ahead, Two," came the response.

"Ram One, I have the goggles on, but things are still dark. It appears as though the goggles are not working."

"Confirm you tried the backup battery, Two."

I was somewhat insulted that he would doubt my knowledge. Of course I had tried that. However, this was the boss. Therefore, my response was simple: "Affirmative, Ram One, I gave that a shot, but it is still dark."

There were a few seconds of silence before the next call came, "Ram Two, confirm that you have the goggles on correctly."

If I had felt insulted before, I was really insulted now. There were only two ways to put the NVGs on . . . the right way and the wrong way. I quickly recalled the academics that I had received. "When putting the NVGs on, make sure that you put them on correctly. If you put them on the right way, you will be amazed how the night becomes day. However, if you put them on backwards, you'll only get darkness."

I pondered on those words for the next 3.4 seconds (everything in life revolves around the number 34 when you are a member of the 34th Fighter Squadron). In an effort to save face with the commander, I delayed saying anything until I had at least attempted to change around the goggles. As quickly as I could, I took off the NVGs from their bracket, turned them around, and reconnected them in their place. I then turned the goggles on. Incredibly, the dark night that I had previously witnessed changed into a dull green. The mountains, which had previously been invisible to my eyes, now stood out as clearly as they had on the several day sorties I had flown earlier in the week. Most importantly, Bags's jet now stood out two miles in front of me. The only words that came to mind were, "Ram One, disregard. It appears as though the goggles are working fine now." Although I never admitted to Bags that I had put the NVGs on backwards, I know that he must have had a good chuckle in his jet.

As we continued our mission over the Utah desert, we prepared ourselves for a light drill that was part of the NVG upgrade syllabus, as well as something we would do on every future sortie. The F-16 is equipped with special lighting that is only visible while looking thru the NVGs. Ordinarily, we fly with standard lighting so that anyone flying will be able to see us. The red and blue lights, along with the anticollision lights, were mandatory for any airplane flying in common airspace. It was the means by which you could see other jets in order to de-conflict from each other. However, once established in the Military Operating Area (MOA), we would change our lighting to "covert lighting." This allowed the F-16 to virtually disappear to the naked eye, yet still be detectable to anyone with NVGs.

When we were established in the MOA, Bags instructed us to "go covert." I responded with my usual "Two" and made the necessary changes with my switches. As Bags made the changes in his jet, I noticed the change instantly. When I looked underneath the goggles, I was at a total loss as to where my flight lead was. However, as I looked through the goggles, Bags's lights were as bright as before, with only one exception. The lights that were previously displayed in bright red and blue were now just white. Night vision goggles, as amazing as they are, are not capable of displaying color. This would prove to be an important fact in my mission with Thumper over Iraq.

Before I left to Iraq, my parents visited my family and me in Syracuse, Utah. We had just finished Christmas, and I was to leave for Iraq on the 4th of January. As one might expect, I was

nervous! I was nervous to be going to war. I was nervous to complete the assignment at hand. Most of all, I was nervous to be leaving my wife and three kids. As I had done in other important times in my life, I asked my dad if he would give me a father's blessing. I have a strong testimony of the priesthood. I do not doubt that it is truly the authority to act in God's name. From the time I was little, I have always sought a blessing at crucial times in my life. My dad would always give me, along with my brothers and sisters, a blessing before starting each school year. My dad laid his hands on my head before I left on my mission to Chile, and blessed me before I was married. Although I now have a family of my own, and now am able to bless my own children, my father has remained consistent in blessing me at those crossroads in my life. He blessed me prior to my going to pilot training, and blessed me when I made the transition to the F-16. I know that when I receive a blessing from my father, although it is his voice, the words come from my Eternal Father. I cannot remember everything that was pronounced upon me that night. There are some things that I will hold to myself. However, there were two promises that I can share: I was promised that I would be protected as I flew, and I was promised that I would return home safely to my family.

I now return to March 2004 and our flight over Mosul, Iraq. Captain Todd "Thumper" Halverson and I briefed up our sortie in the same fashion that we had briefed countless sorties before this one. We would fly under the call sign of "Ram 41" that night, and "KMART" would be our airborne controllers. We discussed the departure and recovery of the sortie. We reviewed emergency procedures, as well as potential divert airfields. Most important, we discussed the area we would be flying over and the mission that we were to accomplish. That night we would be tasked to support a raid on a terrorist complex. We would provide the "eyes in the sky" as the truly brave soldiers, members of the U.S. Army and Marines, would raid the several farmhouses that doubled as terrorist weapon cells. In the event of anything going wrong, we would be ready to deploy our weapons to ensure the safety of our soldiers. Although the mission was what most weighed on our minds, we also discussed the basics of our sortie, to include the call sign of the tanker we would be receiving gas from and the radio frequencies that we would meet them on. As we left, it seemed like any other mission. We retrieved our 9mm gun, life-support equipment, and pilot aide (a quick guide to radio frequencies, emergency airfields, and so on) and made our way to the jets.

As Thumper and I approached our mighty F-16s, I reflected on the words of my dad. I often thought about the promises that were made to me in that blessing. In countless sorties before, I had come to depend on those promises. Already, during my time flying in Iraq, I had been targeted with small-arms fire, I had experienced aircraft malfunctions, and I had landed in some of the worst weather in my flying career. I knew the promises made to me had indeed been fulfilled.

Our mission that night went extremely well. We made our way to northern Iraq, over the city of Mosul, and supported the troops on the ground as instructed. The mission was a complete success. We had lent our support by advising the troops of the terrorists' movements and ensuring that our side maintained the upper hand in all of their maneuvers. I cannot say enough about the work those young men and women did that night. As they finished their work, Thumper and I had reached our "bingo fuel," a predetermined quantity of fuel that meant it was time to leave the area and rendezvous with the tanker. We checked out with the ground controllers and made our way to the briefed tanker location.

As we made our way to the tanker, we found that the weather was not good over the area we were headed. As we were about to penetrate the clouds, Thumper instructed me to take a radar lock on his aircraft and fly two miles behind him. He also told me to "de-goggle." The NVGs did not work well in the clouds. In fact, it was easy to become spatially disoriented if you flew with the NVGs in the clouds. I quickly stored my goggles and informed him that I had completed the task. To avoid staying in the weather, we requested a lower altitude from KMART. We descended to 5,000 feet, where we found ourselves free from the clouds. Thumper made the decision to keep our lights in the covert setting to avoid being detected by any hostiles on the ground. As such, we were completely invisible to the naked eye. I would maintain my radar lock to ensure that I did not lose track of my flight lead.

As we made our way to the tanker track, we received a call from the air controllers; "Ram 41, KMART."

Thumper replied, "KMART, Ram 41, go ahead."

KMART continued, "Ram 41, your tanker has changed the rejoin area. You need to proceed to track bravo at 25,000 feet. Contact the tanker on Yellow 18."

"Yellow 18" was a code for the frequency we were to use. To prevent potential enemies from jamming our frequencies, we used code names as opposed to actual frequencies. There were nearly 100 different frequencies, all of them located in the pilot aide, which was safely stowed in my flight bag next to me. In order to find out what "Yellow 18" actually meant, you would have to find the right page in the pilot aide, locate the correct color and number, and then associate it with the radio frequency that was listed there.

In an effort to be a good wingman, I decided that I would hurry and find the correct frequency in order to pass it to Thumper, who was still guiding our formation from in front of me. I made a quick check of my instruments. I was straight and level, holding 350 knots, and 2.1 miles behind my flight lead. I decided to add a small amount of power (I was, after all, a tenth of a mile farther behind than I should have been) and began to look in my pilot aide. I have reflected over and over again on the events of the next few minutes.

My memory is that I was only looking down for a matter of seconds. I had some trouble finding the correct page. It took me a few moments longer to find the right column and the corresponding frequency. When I finally found it, I quickly keyed the radio and recited the frequency I had just found. As I finished my transmission, I looked up and saw Thumper's jet directly in front of me, no farther away than 300 feet. I never would have seen his jet if it had not been for the bright red and blue wingtip lights on his jet. I bunted the jet over as hard as I could, and literally could hear the sound of my flight lead's engine as I flew right below it. As I crossed underneath, I lost my radar lock. I zoomed the aircraft in order to slow down and allow Thumper to fly back in front of me. I established myself in two-mile trail once again, and we made our way to the tanker.

I have never been so scared. I was shaking as I connected to the tanker. I could not stop thinking about how close I had come to killing not only myself but also one of my best friends.

I thought about my family, my wife and kids. I said a prayer of thanks that I was still alive and that I had been able to see the lights on my flight lead's jet.

We finished our sortie rather uneventfully. We returned to base and landed without any problems. We got out of our life-support equipment and returned our gun and pilot aide. As we made our way back to our trailer, I once again envisioned the image of Thumper's bright lights that had literally saved my life. It was not until I was in my bed that I finally realized what had happened. I had been saved by those lights. However, I could not possibly have seen them. Thumper had been flying in covert lighting. I had not been able to see him since the time I had taken off my NVGs. Nonetheless, I had seen his lights, red and blue, as clear as day.

I do not doubt what happened that day. In spite of my imperfections as both a pilot and a person, I had been saved by God. I know that it was due to the promises spoken to me in a priesthood blessing given by my earthly father. I know that it was by the mercy of my Heavenly Father that I was able to return home safely to my family, as I was promised. I will never doubt in the power of the priesthood.

PILOT'S BIOGRAPHY

Major Michael R. Shepherd, United States Air Force

Call sign: Frosty

Hometown: born in Salt Lake City, Utah; raised in Albuquerque, New Mexico

Family: married to Jennifer Lea Ford; three children

Church experience: served an LDS mission to Vina Del Mar,
Chile; currently serves as second counselor in the bishopric of the Playa Brava Ward in Iquique, Chile

Current occupation: serving as the first-ever exchange F-16 instructor pilot to the Chilean Air Force

Awards: Air Medal, Air Force Commendation Medal, Global War on Terrorism Service Medal, among others

*Major Michael R. Shepherd
with an F-16.*

CHAPTER TWENTY

A CALM IN THE STORM

DEREK O'MALLEY

The unknown path ahead can be a source of great inner turmoil for many of us. We worry about things in our future that we cannot predict. For some of us, this fear can act as a paralyzing force. Hopefully these fears and anxieties also drive us to our knees, for we must remember that the Lord never gives us this spirit of doubt and fear. His Spirit inspires, encourages, and reminds each of us that no matter what situation we face, we should have tremendous hope. I'd heard this principle taught many times over the years in Sunday School classes. Oddly enough, it was in a dark F-16 cockpit over Iraq that this precept became very real to me. I learned without a shadow of doubt that it was true.

I deployed to Al Udeid Airbase, Qatar, from Spangdahlem Airbase, Germany, on January 16, 2003. The air campaign that would later be titled Operation Iraqi Freedom did not begin until several months later. Our initial tasking was to patrol the southern no-fly zone in Iraq. These no-fly zones dated back to August of 1992. They were actually established to help protect the Iraqi people from Saddam Hussein's aggression. Saddam routinely ordered attacks against the Shi'ite Muslims in southern Iraq and the Kurds in northern Iraq. We were there to protect the innocent.

My unit, the 22nd Fighter Squadron, flew the latest variant of the F-16, the F-16CJ. In contrast to previous versions of the F-16, the capabilities and mission of the CJ were unique. We were tasked with suppression of enemy air defenses (SEAD). Fighters executing the SEAD mission were known as "Wild Weasels." The concept was originally developed during Vietnam to counter the formidable surface-to-air missile (SAM) threat in North Vietnam. Through the years, the mission was proudly conducted by the F-100, F-105, F-4, and now the F-16CJ. Central to the F-16CJ's SEAD capability was the AGM-88 high-speed anti-radiation missile (HARM). When the enemy launches a SAM at a fighter, the missile completes the intercept under radar guidance or illumination from the ground. The HARM detects these radar emissions and targets the source. So, the mission of the Wild Weasel was simple (at least on paper)—bait the enemies into turning on their radar to target our aircraft. When they do, lock onto those signals and fire back.

On March 21, 2003, the coalition forces began the initial "shock and awe" campaign of Operation Iraqi Freedom. Each night I would pull into the arming area at the end of the runway and wait for ground crews to arm the ordnance on my F-16. I'd always take a moment to glance at my instruments to make sure the jet was ready to fly, offer a quick prayer, and then arm my ejection seat as I taxied onto the runway. Although we were launching from a friendly country, there was a credible threat against aircraft on takeoff. During the takeoff phase fighters are relatively slow and require the use of afterburner to gain airspeed for the climb out. This left us vulnerable to certain threats. To minimize threat exposure, after takeoff I would level off at low altitude over the runway and allow the jet to gain speed. The F-16's 30,000 pounds of thrust provided an impressive acceleration. Approaching the end of the runway at 450 knots, I'd aggressively pull the nose of my F-16 into the vertical, while straining to look back over my shoulder for any missile launches. Seconds later I'd rocket through 12,000 feet and reduce my rate of climb for the journey north to Iraq.

The flight to Iraq took about one hour. Typically we'd rendezvous with a tanker over Kuwait to refuel, and then proceed farther north into Iraq. Once we were at a cruising altitude, I would don my night vision goggles (NVGs). NVGs provide an impressive view from the cockpit. You can literally see aircraft more than fifty miles away. Anything that emits light is easily detected by the goggles. The problem with the goggles is they don't provide any real depth perception. You literally see almost everything that is producing light. Naturally, the brain assumes the brighter lights are closer, but this is not always the case. So it is absolutely necessary to cross-check other sensors to truly make sense of the night vision picture.

I'll never forget the sight of downtown Baghdad on those first few nights of the air campaign. I remember watching news footage of the first air strikes of Operation Desert Storm when I was in high school. It was surreal to witness that same picture from my own cockpit. Antiaircraft artillery (AAA) filled the sky. SAMs vaulted into the sky like giant burning telephone poles exploding at altitude. I had trained for combat for my entire flying career. Privately, I wondered how I would measure up in the face of a real threat.

When Joseph Smith went to Carthage, he described himself

as "calm as a summer's morning." I wish I could say I was as "calm as a summer's morning" on my first air strikes into Baghdad. I wasn't. I distinctly remember, despite the roar of my jet engine and constant radio chatter, being able to hear the sound of my own heart thumping in my ears. I prayed at every spare moment. Amidst the chaos of combat, that seemingly small manifestation of faith—a simple prayer—coupled with years of training, suddenly worked. "For God hath not given us the spirit of fear; but of power, and of love, and of a sound mind" (2 Timothy 1:7). Although I certainly didn't forget the stress of the situation, I knew I could handle it and I went to work. Really, this moment was no different from hundreds of other experiences we all face in our lives. To curb our anxieties *we prepare and we pray,* and somewhere along the way we are given the strength to face our fears.

On April 2, 2003, I was tasked to escort a strike package of

F-14s into Baghdad. As we were stepping to our jets we were briefed that the coalition ground forces were pressing very close to Baghdad. If Saddam Hussein was going to use chemical weapons against our forces, this would be the night it would happen. As I proceeded north toward Baghdad to join up with the F-14s, I looked down on the raging ground war between our coalition and Iraqi forces. In the blackness of the night, I could see flashes of small arms and tracers firing south toward the friendly forces. Moments later our forces would retaliate with an impressive arsenal of surface fire. The friendly fire met its mark, and the flashes of Iraqi small-arms fire were replaced with darkness.

As the F-14 strike package released their bombs and turned off target, I heard several fighters call "defending" for SAM launches. The scene was chaotic as jets maneuvered aggressively to defeat inbound missiles. The radio was momentarily saturated with different voices competing to communicate. Nobody in our package was hit. The missile launches had actually been several miles west of the strike package. Moments later, command and control informed me that an F-18 had been hit by a surface-to-air missile. I enlisted the assistance of two other F-16CJs and we proceeded over the location of the downed aircraft to assist in the recovery of the downed pilot and hunt for the SAM that had taken him down. Soon A-10s arrived to conduct further search and rescue efforts. Iraqi AAA was very active in the area, so we did our best to decoy the fire away from the lower and slower flying A-10s.

About forty-five minutes into the search operation, one of the F-16CJs experienced an engine emergency. Since the F-16 only has one engine, we take any engine malfunction very seriously.

He and his wingman made a speedy exit out of Iraq and landed safely just prior to a complete engine failure. This left only my wingman and me to support the search and rescue operation. I made a decision that I would not return to base until command and control secured additional F-16CJs to replace us. We had already lost one fighter to a SAM. We absolutely needed F-16CJs on the scene to engage any other SAMs that might threaten the search and rescue forces. In order to stay airborne, I coordinated several aerial refuelings over Iraq. The tanker pilots were amazingly cooperative in order to keep this critical mission from failing. At one point during the night I was able to convince a tanker to drive farther north into Iraq to expedite the refueling of the A-10 search and rescue forces. As the hours passed and the sun began to rise, we were still not able to locate the downed pilot. After ten hours on the scene, F-16CJs from my own squadron arrived as replacements and we returned to base.

A few days later, I learned the F-18 pilot did not survive the missile impact. I felt a strong desire to learn more about this fallen F-18 pilot. I learned that his name was Lieutenant Nathan "OJ" White. We were the same age. We both had wives and children. We had both attended BYU at the same time, but never met. And we were both over Baghdad on the night of April 2, 2003, in similar performing aircraft, at nearly identical airspeeds and altitudes. Yet his flight path, only a few miles from mine, ended in tragedy.

To those who were privileged to know and love Nate White, from all accounts he was a remarkable man. He was universally respected as a leader, a fighter pilot, and, most important, as a man of God. I know his family will miss him every moment until they are united again. You can feel Nate's testimony in a letter he wrote to members of his ward during Operation Iraqi Freedom:

Greetings from the Kitty Hawk! I hope everyone at home is doing well. All of us out here send our thanks for your unyielding support. Flight operations are near continuous as we work around the clock to support the ground campaign. I don't think many people antici-pated the level of resistance that we have seen. I sincerely hope this ends soon and that the Iraqi people benefit from our endeavors.

When going in on a strike, there is always a lot going on. Here is a brief snapshot: brief for an hour or more to map out the flight, get catapulted from standstill to 140 miles an hour in less than two sec-onds, navigate through a maze of airborne highways that try to de-conflict aircraft and of course steer you clear of the army's patriot batteries, jump from radio frequency to radio frequency at least twelve different times shifting from controller to controller, avoid a sky full of AAA, surface-to-air missiles and ballistic rockets, set up your weapons system, acquire your target, drop on target, fly to an airborne tanker, join up, get gas, and then fly back and land on a boat bobbing around in the middle of a sandstorm. Make it nighttime and throw in some thunderstorms and then it really gets exciting.

Sound a bit overwhelming? Sometimes it feels that way. When it gets really hard, it's like they always say: You fall back on your training. Redundancy in training prepares you for those nights where your legs are shaking and you know that if you don't relax and get your refueling probe into the refueling basket, you are going to flame out and lose the jet.

Life is no different. Success in any endeavor is brought about by personal preparation and training for those inevitable obstacles of life. . . .

In Desert Storm in 1991, several coalition aircraft were lost on low-altitude strikes. Ingressing at 100 feet above the ground near supersonic, they tried to come in under the radar and drop their weapons. They avoided the strategic SAMS but got picked apart by the AAA. We learned from those tragic losses and altered our tactics accordingly.

You will make mistakes. Learn from them. Just don't make the big ones. Don't be the person who finds yourself in a disintegrating fire ball because you thought you could make it in at 100 feet.

Listen to those people who have been there before and use the training that you get here and at home. When you find yourself in a defining situation where a difficult decision has got to be made, you will fall back on your training and come out a survivor.

I wish you all the best.

Love, Nate

The reality of this life is that we truly do not know when we will be called home. For some that call comes at a time that feels painfully soon for those who are left behind. Since we cannot control when the end will come, we must take control of the days we do have. We will all face difficult situations that may try us to the very core. In those moments we should turn to the one Source that will never fail us. Despite the trials, the pain, and the disappointments we may experience, each of us has the capacity to know that our lives are right with God. That knowledge is a vessel of strength that will carry us through. I believe Nate White understood this. I believe he was called home because he passed this test of mortality and his strength was needed elsewhere.

PILOT'S BIOGRAPHY

Major Derek O'Malley, United States Air Force

Call sign: Maestro

Hometown: Albuquerque, New Mexico

Family: married to Samantha Crawford; one son, Conner

Church experience: formerly served as a branch president, Gospel Doctrine teacher, Young Men advisor; currently serves in a stake Young Men's presidency

Current assignment: F-16 instructor pilot, United States Air Force Weapons School

Hobbies: running, snowboarding, radio-controlled airplanes, videography

Awards and recognitions: Distinguished Flying Cross with V Valor Device for Heroism, Distinguished Graduate and Flying Award from United States Air Force Weapons School, Cecil G Foster Outstanding Weapons School Instructor Award (3 times)

Major Derek O'Malley with the F-16.

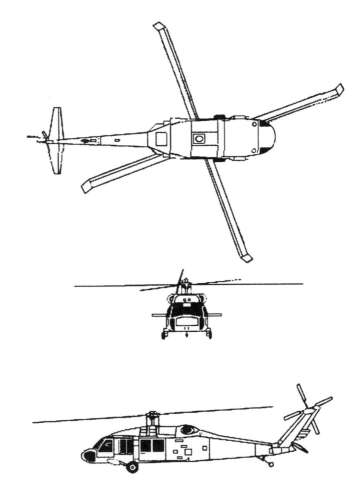

CHAPTER TWENTY-ONE

PRESS FORWARD WITH FAITH

MICHAEL A. YANEZ

It was June 6, 2007, in the middle of the Afghan summer season. This part of the year in this southwestern Asian country is mostly hot, hazy, and very windy at times, and June 6th was very much like this.

As part of a deployment in support of Operation Enduring Freedom, I was sent over to Bagram, Afghanistan, along with a combat aviation brigade supporting elements of the 82nd Airborne Division rotating in for their yearlong tour in the Afghan mountains and deserts. Being a UH-60L Blackhawk helicopter pilot in this mountainous country presents great challenges in a variety of ways. Other than the obvious threat from the enemy, the mountains themselves and the environment they present are enough of a danger to make any pilot take note. These were the surroundings my fellow pilots and I faced day in and day out, as we were asked to fly into some of the most remote areas of this country. Even though this was my second tour of duty to Afghanistan, I had not yet been to the northeastern areas until this second rotation. Among the many missions we were asked to fly as utility helicopter pilots, some required us to spend the day on stand-by duty in order to be ready for any contingency that might arise. These stand-by missions also varied in scope and variety, but the vast majority of them were some sort of emergency response due to enemy fire on friendly forces.

The mission we were called upon to execute on June 6th was in response to an enemy attack on an outpost 150 nautical miles to our east in an area called the Gowardesh Valley. This valley was well known for harboring Taliban and other extremist fighters flowing in from Pakistan, and served as a safe haven for them during certain seasons of the year.

The exchange of fire between the enemy and U.S. forces, located just outside a village named Kamu, was so great that an emergency ammunition resupply request from the friendly forces was sent out to headquarters back at Bagram. Considering the high threat level in the area, we were assigned to rendezvous with an AH-64 Apache gunship as an armed escort for our flight into and out of the valley.

Shortly after departing from Bagram, my wingman and I made a stop in Jalalabad to pick up the ammunition to drop off in Kamu, and also to link up with our Apache escort for the next leg of the trip to our destination. After briefing up the gunship pilots of our situation, we departed to complete our mission. As we neared our destination, we noted that the valley we followed ran extremely close to the border of Pakistan; therefore we had to take extreme care not to cross any borders inadvertently. As we neared the mouth of the valley, we were advised by a nearby firebase that our destination, Landing Zone Kamu, had A-10 Warthog attack aircraft on station. We were further advised of the frequency and call signs with which to gain communication with the A-10 pilots. As we entered the Gowardesh Valley, I established communications with the air force A-10 pilots and advised them of our intentions to land at Kamu. They recommended that we wait until they were done with their "gun runs" and the area had been cleared for any aircraft to enter. As air mission commander of the entire flight, it was my responsibility not only for mission success, but to ensure the safety of my crew and the crews of each aircraft in my flight. Being apprised of this situation, I directed my wingman to lead us back to Firebase Naray, which was the last safe house in which to refuel before heading into the Gowardesh Valley.

While my aircraft and the rest of our flight were momentarily delayed at Naray, we maintained radio contact with the leadership in Kamu, awaiting the "go-ahead" to continue the resupply mission. It was during this time of the delay that I fell into the thoughts of my mind and the uneasiness I had felt in my heart. During all the previous occasions I had flown into and out of this valley, I had always had a sinking feeling in my stomach. I knew that this area of the country was very volatile and dangerous. I'd read about many instances of attacks on our ground forces with devastating and deadly results. But I also knew that our fellow soldiers under attack in Kamu required this ammunition to stay in the fight against the enemy's constant bombardment on their firebase. Every day I had prayed for safety when I flew, and I remember saying prayers in my heart on this day as well that my crew and I would be protected. This day would turn out to be particularly meaningful for each of us, for our prayers would be answered in miraculous ways.

While waiting for the call to continue the mission, I was consumed with anxiety, knowing of the danger that we had to face in the next valley. This thought weighed heavily on my mind, and I had to consciously force myself to put that behind me and let my training and flight experience take over. To do this was essential because the lives of our comrades depended on it. I relied heavily on my faith that our Heavenly Father would protect not only me but also my fellow pilots in our flight of three. It was this faith that allowed me to press forward and direct our flight toward our objective shortly ahead of us. In just a few moments, I would need this faith more than anything else to help sustain us through our experience at Kamu.

After discussing the plan of action with the pilots in command of the other two aircraft, we were given the all-clear to take off. I directed the Apache gunship to "push ahead" a few miles in order to look out for any enemy activity and to possibly clear the objective should any hostilities arise. As we flew ever closer to the Pakistani border, we made the big left turn into the Gowardesh Valley. The terrain below us was unforgiving, with a mixture of evergreen trees along steep, craggy rock faces that rose sharply into the sky. The valley followed the lines of a fast-flowing river moving in a roughly east-west direction. The elevation difference between valley floor and mountaintops varied anywhere from one thousand feet to three thousand feet. Needless to say, the beautiful and expansive terrain relief gave the enemy plenty of places for hiding out. The effort of trying to even spot one person or a group of enemy soldiers congregated on the mountainside would be a fruitless undertaking.

As the Apache gunship neared the objective, we listened out for the radio call giving us the status of the landing zone (LZ). If the objective was designated "hot," then enemy activity was nearby and we would delay and wait until called forward. If the objective was "cold," we would proceed as normal. Since our armed escort wasn't able to raise the fellow ground forces by radio, they made an overhead visual observation and relayed the status back to our awaiting flight. All was quiet for the time being, so I directed my flight lead to take us in. The concentrated green vegetation and tall trees made it difficult to spot the exact landing area, but once we were overhead, the ground forces "popped smoke," highlighting the desired location in which to place the helicopters. I saw the thick, colorful purple hue before my wingman did, so I made a quick, diving, 180-degree turn toward it in order to make my final approach into the LZ. The space available for landing was confined, with trees surrounding us on our front and right sides, and steep mountain cliffs on our left. The land was soft, grassy and terraced, requiring us to position ourselves carefully so as not to land unevenly. Shortly after my "ballet-dancing" landing maneuver to get into the LZ, my wingman landed 100 yards behind me, on a lower

terraced shelf, also carefully positioning himself in order to maintain blade clearance from the trees.

As our crew chiefs and door gunners exited the aircraft to assist in unloading the ammunition, I finally heard the ground force radio controller contact our gunship. The infantry on the ground asked the Apache to "light up" a cave where known enemy activity existed with 30 mm cannon fire and rockets. While the unloading continued, my wingman and I eagerly awaited the engagement that was to take place just a few hundred feet over our heads. What actually happened in the next few moments, however, caught us completely by surprise, and was nothing like what we expected.

As I stretched around in my seat to get a better view of the Apache from my cockpit, I noticed two very loud explosions occur in the tree line just to the right of my helicopter. The thick gray smoke and flying leaves that were left behind definitely caught my attention and gave me pause. I quickly radioed my gunship and asked him if he had witnessed such an engagement toward our direction or if he had indeed seen the explosion himself. The reply I received gave me more cause for concern, for his voice was tensed with uncertainty and nervousness, his answer not in reply to my question, but in questioning the ground forces of an attack. Among all the recent action and changing circumstances, the pilot of the Apache was deeply engaged in coordinating radio calls with the ground controller and may have missed my radio calls. From what I could gather from all the conversations on the radio frequencies, we were indeed under attack. As soon as I came to that determination, two more explosions rocked my aircraft from the left side, this time impacting the cliff face immediately to our left. Time was definitely of the essence at this point and I urged my crew chief and door gunner to speed up the unloading of the ammunition.

As the unloading continued, I heard numerous explosions to the rear of our aircraft. I was quite sure that my wingmen were getting an up-close-and-personal engagement from the enemy and his rocket-propelled grenades, more than what I was getting. Shortly thereafter, my wingman hurriedly called me on the radio to let me know that they were through unloading and ready to go. They noticed that I still had a few hundred more pounds of ammunition left to go, and my fellow crew members were throwing it out at a frantic pace. I requested the assistance of his crew members to help us download the remaining ammunition. It wasn't more than a few seconds after my call when they arrived—I'm sure our Heavenly Father blessed them with lightning speed to run to our aid.

Thanks to the assistance of my wingman's crew members, the unloading was completed and all the crew members strapped in. With rising terrain and obstacles surrounding me on three sides, I frantically searched for an avenue of escape from this landing zone turned kill zone. I quickly determined that the only way out of this place was the way we came in. In light of this fact, I knew I had to hurry, considering the enemy was continuing the attack and zeroing in on our locations with each successive explosion.

I prepared my crew for the departing maneuver I was about to execute and requested assistance from my crew chief and gunner. I advised them that I was going to quickly take off both vertically and flying backwards, and would need their eyes to guide our helicopter clear until I had space to turn our aircraft around to face the direction of flight. By the time they acknowledged what we were doing, we were already in the air, climbing like an elevator on rockets. I summoned as much power as the helicopter could provide in order to expedite our departure. As soon as we were above all obstacles, I finally turned the helicopter to face our direction of flight, and thankfully, it was clear from both the enemy and mountainous terrain. I flew as far and as fast away from the landing zone as time would allow me. We weren't completely out of danger yet, since I still had my wingman down in the LZ and our gunship high above engaging the enemy, covering our avenue of escape.

I quickly turned back around, reversing course, to get a bird's-eye view of the action from afar, and to look for my wingman so we could regroup as a flight. I notified our gunship that we were clear of the objective, with all ammunition "safely" unloaded onto the LZ. He acknowledged my transmission and added that he would be "busy" for a time, actively keeping the enemy at bay and protecting our friendly forces on the ground at Kamu. As we both took up a holding pattern to wait for our Apache to finish up business, I then noticed the many smoke-stack columns of smoke emanating from the north face of the valley due to the many rocket-propelled grenade launches from the enemy on that side of the valley. At that moment I was struck by the sheer amount of firepower and ordnance the enemy had just spent in order to attempt to harm us and our gunship escort. I couldn't help but be in a little bit of awe of the events that had just transpired. But I couldn't let these reflections get in the way of my thought process over our mission, considering we still had to get home before the sun set.

With our gunship now all out of rockets and 30 mm ammunition, they gave us the "Winchester" call and rejoined the flight.

We made a quick refueling stop at Naray and raced the sun westward to make it back to home base before sundown. As my flight of Blackhawks parted ways with our protecting Apache over the skies of Jalalabad, we gave much thanks to the crew of the AH-64 for their courage and bravery in watching over us. They, in turn, reminded us of the courage and bravery required for us to complete our mission. With our good-byes and our mission behind us, my wingman and I turned for home and traveled as fast as our helicopters could take us.

Safely back on the ground, and out of the complexities of the mission we had just accomplished, I had an opportunity to mentally process all the events that had just taken place. Reflecting back on the danger that each of us was in at Kamu, I realized it was truly a miracle that we had all returned safely. Facing the adversity and uncertainty required not only courage but faith: faith that Heavenly Father would watch over us and protect us as we accomplished the tasks that were asked of us. It's situations like these that remind me of the scripture: "Yea, though I walk through the valley of the shadow of death, I will fear no evil: for thou art with me; thy rod and thy staff they comfort me" (Psalm 23:4).

I truly know that God, our Heavenly Father, protected not only me and my crew, but also the crews of the other aircraft that accompanied us. And it was because of our faith to accomplish all that was required of us that we would succeed and that we would be protected by the power of God. I have a strong faith that miracles occur every day, and the events of June 6, 2007, were clear evidence of that.

PILOT'S BIOGRAPHY

CW2 Michael A. Yanez, United States Army

Call sign: Hard Luck 61

Hometown: Hiram, Georgia

Family: married to Mandi Marie Cohn; black Labrador retriever named Georgia

Church experience: ward missionary, Primary teacher, Sunday School teacher; currently serves as ward executive secretary

Current occupation: UH-60 pilot, 3rd Battalion, 82nd Combat Aviation Brigade, 82nd Airborne Division

Michael A. Yanez with the UH-60.

Hobbies: flying, golf, reading, and exercising

Awards and recognitions: Air Medal for Gallantry (3), Air Medal for Valor, Afghanistan Campaign Medal (2), Global War on Terror Expeditionary Medal, Global War on Terror Service Medal, NATO Service Medal, Overseas Service Ribbon, Army Service Ribbon, National Defense Service Medal

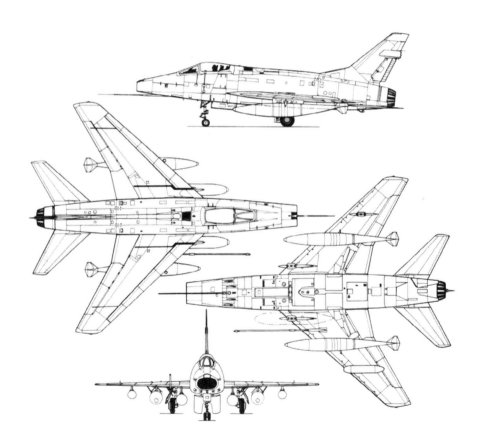

CHAPTER TWENTY-TWO

IN THE BLINK OF AN EYE

MILTON R. SANDERS

In the world of flight, and especially supersonic aircraft, split seconds make a difference. There is no time to open a book, phone a friend, or poll the audience for some advice. At those times, bringing into play all your experience, tips, techniques, experiences of others, plus training and knowledge of your aircraft is essential.

Returning from a bombing mission in South Vietnam, I was the first lieutenant wingman Bobcat 22, flying with Bobcat 21, a captain and one of the flight leads in the 615th Tactical Fighter Squadron out of Phan Rang AB. Our bombing mission had gone well, and we were on a routine RTB (return to base) from the mission. We flew over the runway at 300 knots in our camouflage F-100D, single-seat aircraft, with me tucked in tight formation to look good for anyone watching from the ground.

Bobcat 21 pitched out smartly to the left, with me following three seconds later to get spacing for my landing. The turn to final approach, final, and touchdown with 3,000-foot spacing was totally routine, and I was relaxing from the mission as I reached up and pulled the handle to deploy the drag chute, a small parachute carried in the rear of the aircraft to help slow us down and save wear on the brakes.

Usually we feel a slight tug from the deceleration caused by the drag chute as it billows and catches air. I didn't feel that, and I made a call on my radio to the tower to ask if my chute had deployed, since I couldn't see it from the cockpit. As it happened, the tower was calling me at exactly the same time to tell me that I was a "no chute." The interference from the two radio calls caused me to hear nothing. I had made "no chute" landings before without problems, so I proceeded to test the brakes, knowing that my antiskid braking system would let me slow down without blowing the tires. It was going to be a "no sweat" procedure, although a little out of the ordinary.

As I stepped on the brakes, my heart sank and my pulse began to race because I had no brakes! My mind began to churn into high gear from its previously relaxed state. I was

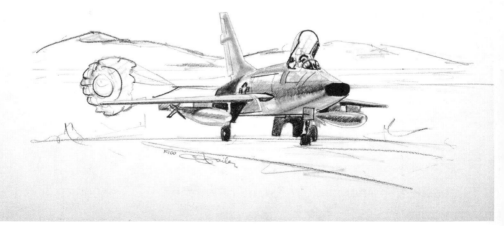

riding a 26,000-pound "tricycle" at 150 knots, with another air-plane in front of me, and no brakes. I knew that I had to get the other airplane to stay on the left as I was going to pass him very soon, so I called on the radio, "Bobcat 21, 22 is passing on your right, no chute, and no brakes! I am taking the barrier."

The barrier is a braided steel cable that crosses the runway near the far end, held a couple of inches off the runway by rub-ber doughnuts. The barrier is designed to allow a tail hook on an aircraft to catch it. The ends of the cable are attached to a very large chain (about 25 pounds for each link of the chain), which is laid parallel to the runway in the direction aircraft are landing. As the tail hook grabs the cable, the cable starts to drag the links with it, dragging more and more of the chain as you go down the runway. This provides a gradually increasing force to slow the airplane instead of one big jerk, which would tear off parts of the airplane!

A few weeks before this, another F-100 had engaged the barrier at high speed and high gross weight while aborting a takeoff. His aircraft had caused the cable to break instead of slowing him to a stop, at which time he ran off the end of the runway, broke up in the rough ground, and was killed in the explosion and fire. This fact was buried in the back of my mind, which was still running at high speed.

My flight lead cleared further to the left and stopped as I passed him so I could engage the barrier in the center of the runway—which is the ideal spot to get equal slowing forces from both left and right to keep you moving straight ahead on the runway. I pressed the tail hook release button at this time and envisioned the big spring—like an old, flat piece of metal spring on a car, but much longer—being released and pressing the tail hook onto the runway.

I wasn't content to completely trust the barrier, so my mind was sifting through other options. Time seemed to go into slow motion as I listened to the Spirit bring thoughts into my mind. I acted almost without thinking as I pulled the drag chute handle again, flipped off the antiskid brake switch, and felt wonderful braking action from the wheel brakes.

I wasn't about to take my feet off the brakes at this time, even though I blew both main tires. The tail hook caught the barrier, and as it was bringing me to a gentle stop, my drag chute popped out for a second, then dropped to the ground as the aircraft stopped. I was delighted to have finally stopped, and was then able to reconstruct the past ten seconds while my heart rate began to slow down. I had to keep the engine running to maintain hydraulic pressure to the landing gear until the ground crew could attach the removable landing gear locks. Then I shut down the aircraft; the ground crew disengaged the barrier cable, then towed me off the runway.

My flight lead told me later that it was comical to see the puff of smoke from the tires when I blew them, to see the drag chute pop out and immediately fall to the ground, and to notice the barrier just stopping the airplane. I told him that I was glad that *he* could get a laugh out of it. I was just happy to be on the ground in one piece, and that I could turn the airplane over to the ground crew, although many people were shaking their heads over the drag chute out, blown tires, and barrier engagement. The ground crew ended up greasing the drag chute deploy mechanism and changing the tires—but it took them two days to find a cracked electrical line in the antiskid brake system before they believed my full story.

I got to thinking about this incident a few days later and wondered what might have happened if the drag chute had deployed normally, lulling me into a false sense of security, then when it was time to use the brakes and they didn't work, the rest of the scenario would have been even more compressed for time and remaining runway. This could have turned out much differently.

About a month later, the company who manufactured the barrier sent me a plaque and a tie clip acknowledging my successful barrier engagement. The plaque hangs on my wall to this day reminding me of this experience.

I am thankful for the Spirit, which "bring[s] all things to your remembrance" (John 14:26). After we have studied and worked hard to put much information into our minds, we can call on the Spirit to help us remember what we need to do.

PILOT'S BIOGRAPHY

Major Milton R. Sanders,
United States Air Force, retired

Call sign: Sandman

Hometown: Orem, Utah

Family: married to Kay G. Sanders (deceased); five children; eleven grandchildren

Church callings: bishop, served in five other bishoprics; high councilor (three times); high priests group leadership four times (twice as group leader); executive secretary four times; currently in high priests group leadership

Current occupation: computer systems engineer, SirsiDynix—a library automation company

Education: command pilot, commercial license (multiengine, instrument); bachelor's in engineering science, United States Air Force Academy; master's in aeronautical engineering, U.S. Air Force Institute of Technology

Milt "Sandman" Sanders with his F-100 at Phan Rang AB, Vietnam.

Hobbies: ham radio, guitar, computers, radio-controlled model airplanes, photography, home video production, singing Elvis karaoke, building a cabin

Awards and recognitions: Distinguished Flying Cross, Meritorious Service Medal (2), Air Medal (16), Air Force Commendation Medal (3), Army Commendation Medal, Outstanding Unit Award (4), Vietnam Service Medal (4 stars), others

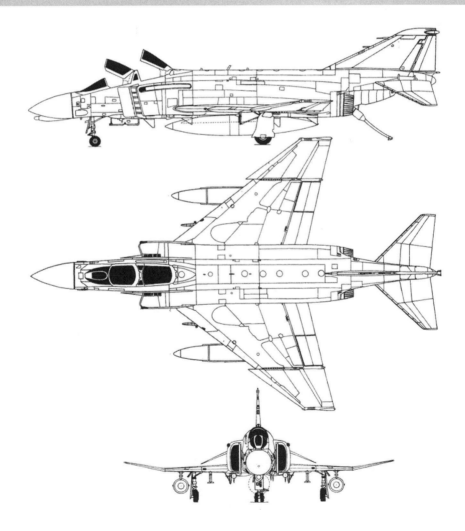

CHAPTER TWENTY-THREE
CHECKLIST FOR LIFE

DOUG ALSTON

I have always liked to fly at night. There's something about the darkness that is more peaceful and calm. The lights give a greater sense of definition and, on a clear night, you can see great distances. Maybe the darkness just helps to filter out a lot of the distractions.

In the F-4 Phantom, there are two of us in the jet. The pilot sitting up front runs the jet. Then there's the guy in back, or "GIB" for short—that was my seat. In the language of the military aviator, I am not a pilot but a WSO, pronounced "wizzo." *WSO* stands for weapon systems officer and, for us fighter guys, differentiates us from all of the other navigators who share the same set of wings but fly in much bigger, blunt-nosed airplanes with more than two engines, have props instead of afterburners, don't sit on ejection seats, or haven't been supersonic before. Although not fighter *pilots,* we definitely share more in common with them, our fellow squadron mates, than with our brother navigators. As the WSO, I run the mission systems, like the radar and, in the case of my jet, the reconnaissance version of the F-4, the camera systems. We do have a stick and throttle and try to snag as much hands-on flying time as we can, but that's not really our job. We like to say, tongue in cheek, that the pilot drives us to work.

As a wizzo, I also back up the operation of the jet by referring to the checklist strapped to my leg and ensure no steps are missed in both normal and emergency procedures. And then there is the second set of eyeballs to look outside and increase the situational awareness that might mean life or death in combat or other dire circumstance. Together we work as a team, each contributing essential elements to accomplish the mission without duplication, competition, or gaps in responsibilities. We try to fly with the same crew as often as possible to get to know each other's capabilities and limitations, how best to communicate to each other, to build on each other's strengths, and to bolster any weakness.

The night I'm writing about was a very nice night on the island of Okinawa. Warm, just a little humid, with a few clouds overhead but nothing really to speak of. The stars were out, but no moon. Assigned to the 15th Tactical Reconnaissance Squadron at Kadena Air Base, I was on my second assignment flying the RF-4C, with over 2,000 hours already in the jet . . . not bad for a young captain. This night's flight was a four-ship mission to go out over the East China Sea and rendezvous with a KC-135 for in-flight refueling, run around the area for a couple of hours, then back home.

As flight lead, we are responsible for the overall planning and execution of the mission. In the flight briefing, we go over the plan with the other flight members and delineate the specific responsibilities each of us will perform to make sure every aspect of normal and contingency procedures is covered. After starting the engines, running through the system checks, and taxiing out to the end of the runway, we check in with the squadron operations supervisor for any mission updates—in this case, the tanker was airborne and would be up there to meet us as planned. After the last-chance check by the ground crew and arming up the jet, we are ready to pull onto the runway for takeoff.

This would be a standard, full afterburner takeoff, with twenty seconds' spacing between each jet to give us a trail departure, in order to allow us more flexibility in getting our jets safely airborne without worrying about bumping into each other in the darkness. We would then join up into formation and head off to the tanker in the night sky. Cleared for takeoff, we pulled onto the runway. The procedure goes something like this: Transponder on . . . engines run up and systems checks normal. We switch the flight to departure control on the radio and check everyone in. Everyone is there and ready to go. We push the throttles up to military power and glance at the tachometers to make sure they're up at 100 percent, then push it up to full afterburner and confirm that we get a good light on both engines. Of course, the kick in the seat from the additional acceleration tells us that they are definitely working. Passing 100 knots, acceleration is good. The nose lifts off the ground and we're airborne. Gear up, flaps up by 250 knots, and the takeoff checklist is complete.

"Departure, Kodak-21 flight of four is airborne, passing four thousand feet."

"Kodak-21 flight, radar contact, climb and maintain one-seven thousand."

What a beautiful night. Over my shoulder I can see the lights from our wingmen following behind us, with number four just rolling down the runway.

Then, passing about 10,000 feet into the climb, darkness . . . quiet . . . nothing. No lights, no instruments, no radar, no inertial navigation system, nothing on the headset. Nothing. We were still flying, however, and the engines and flight controls all seemed to be working okay, but nothing else. Suddenly, the beautiful night was turning ugly.

In abnormal situations like this, we have an ingrained procedure that is almost second nature in our minds from our strict basic flying training and simulator practice:

1. Maintain aircraft control
2. Analyze the situation and take appropriate action
3. Land as soon as practical

First, knowing that the engines and controls seemed to be working, there was no immediate need to reach for the ejection handles. That was some relief. But something was odd. Were those stars or boats I could see out the window? There was no horizon to reference. The dark sea below looked a lot like the dark sky above. No difference between stars and boats to distinguish quickly if we were rolling upside down or whether we remained right side up. Staring too long at a particular light out the window only exacerbated the situation because the light seemed to move and our bodies told us that we should be moving the stick to compensate. More than one perfectly good aircraft and crew have been lost because of this very situational awareness problem that makes the pilot feel like he is somewhere he really isn't.

Finally . . . something. As I looked over my shoulder, there was just enough of the island of Okinawa not covered by the clouds, with the city lights visible, to get some orientation on where the edge of the earth was and which way was up. Working with the pilot to get his orientation fixed on the same reference, we were able to keep the aircraft from going where we didn't want it to go . . . namely, the dark ocean below.

Then, thoughts came of the three wingmen right behind us and starting to close on us into formation. I couldn't see them over my shoulder any longer. We would have to carefully maneuver in a direction that wouldn't present the potential for midair collision. Of course, the wingmen couldn't see us any longer because our external position and formation lights were now dark, matching the sky. I'm sure I could imagine what they would be thinking, as they were closing on us and suddenly their flight leader disappeared into a black hole without so much as a peep on the radio.

Now, we had to figure out what was wrong and how to fix

it. With only about ten minutes having elapsed since takeoff, things were happening quickly. Some emergencies were so severe that immediate action was required without time to reference a checklist. Those procedures were memorized and known as "Bold Face," because they were written in bold type in the emergency procedures (EP) section of our checklist. Since this appeared to be an electrical problem, the first step in the EP checklist was:

Ram Air Turbine—Out

By extending the RAT, we could provide the jet with an emergency source of power to key standby systems in order to allow us to safely recover the jet . . . assuming there weren't other issues to overcome. Of course, the pilot had to find the actuation lever by feel alone. In the case of this dark and lonely night, over the open water of the dark sea, lo and behold, the lever worked as advertised and some of the aircraft came back to life. Essential instruments operated again and one of the radios crackled back in operation with a good deal of conversation between our trailing flight members and departure control trying to figure out what was going on with the flight leader. As we coordinated for an immediate return to the base and declared an emergency situation, the rest of the flight continued on with the mission.

What remained on the EP checklist involved cycling the generators . . . no response . . . and turning off unessential electrical equipment. We tried cycling the generators several more times but nothing changed. The checklist went on to direct us to use the tail hook and do the air force version of a carrier landing by grabbing a cable across the runway to stop us quickly after landing. With only emergency power, the antiskid braking system would not be working, and blowing the tires and losing control while trying to stop the jet on the runway was a real possibility—especially with a heavy jet in the dark. At this point, the night was turning out to be not quite the beautiful picture it had been in the beginning.

The rest of the flight progressed with a heightened sense of anxiety, senses alert to every little bump, sound, and even a few things that we probably only imagined. We burned down fuel to lighten our weight for landing and, between the pilot and I, were doing our best to determine which systems we could get working again and maintain as normal operation of the aircraft as possible. All seemed to be going okay, relatively speaking, as we returned to the base.

As we started our final approach to the runway, we talked about some contingencies should things turn sour. The option of taking the jet around for another try at the landing, missing the cable and blowing the tires and losing control of the jet, and the possibility of using the ejection seat to exit the aircraft, were all quickly reviewed. We could see the red flashing lights from the emergency vehicles lined up on the taxiways to greet us. We hoped they wouldn't be needed but appreciated their presence . . . just in case.

Finally, touchdown. The quick deceleration told us that the hook had indeed caught the cable. Once we had stopped on the runway, the crash crew came out to meet us and chocked the wheels. We shut down the crippled jet and again embraced the darkness and called it a night.

By following the well-defined guidelines that apply to any situation: maintain control, analyze the situation and take proper action, and land as soon as practical, we were able to safely return the jet and ourselves back to the comfort of the base from which we had taken off.

Since my entire life has been centered on flying, coming from a family full of pilots, including my father and all three brothers, I utilize a similar practice of following checklists in dealing with any situation of my life.

1. Hold to the rod

2. Choose the right—or, in Bold Face: **CTR**

3. Reference the checklists of the gospel—the scriptures, conference talks, and so on

I know that by following these procedures, we will be safe with any decision or be able to overcome any situation of adversity. In the end, we will return to the comfort of the base from which we departed, the presence of our Heavenly Father.

PILOT'S BIOGRAPHY

Lieutenant Colonel Doug Alston, United States Air Force

Call sign: Bambi

Hometown: Salt Lake City, Utah

Family: married to Misty Hall; four daughters

Church experience: teaching in the Primary and Sunday School; ward and stake Young Men's president; high council; currently serves as a counselor in the bishopric

Current occupation: administrative officer with the U.S. Department of Veterans Affairs

Hobbies: flying private aircraft, traveling, hunting and fishing, and being with the family

Awards and recognitions: USAF Fighter Weapons School graduate, Meritorious Service Medal (6), Air Medal (4), Aerial Achievement Medal (2), Air Force Commendation Medal (3), Southwest Asia Service Medal with one Service Star, Global War on Terrorism Service Medal, Korean Defense Service Medal; over 3,000 flying hours in the RF-4, F-111, and F-15E, including 28 combat missions over northern Iraq

Doug Alston and an RF-4C Phantom of the 15th Tactical Reconnaissance Squadron, Kadena Air Base, Japan.

MCDONNELL F-15 EAGLE

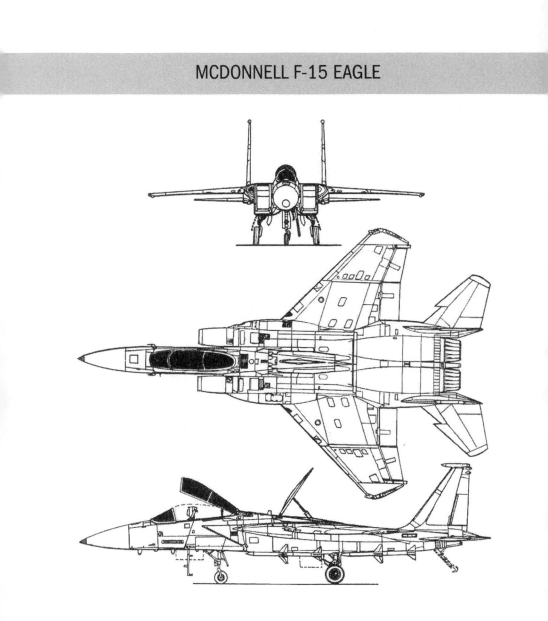

CHAPTER TWENTY-FOUR

EAGLES RULE

DAVID M. NELSON

The mission objective sounded simple enough: Fire the latest model of a live air-to-air missile from an F-15 Eagle at an unmanned drone to verify the missile's performance. To accomplish the mission, a vast team of highly experienced people was assembled, each to perform a specialized task. The team included a dozen engineers to monitor data down-linked in real-time from the shooting aircraft and missile; three expert maintenance crews, one each for the test airplane, the unmanned target drone, and the missile to be fired; and finally the test pilot flying the shooting airplane—me. The mission was so important (and expensive) that we conducted a full-blown dress rehearsal to practice almost every detail. There were only two small, but important, differences between the dress rehearsal and the soon-to-follow live mission. First, the drone had a man in it during the dress rehearsal to make the landing safer (because it was always risky to land the unmanned drones), and second, my airplane would not be carrying the live missile in rehearsal—this part made the man in the drone feel much more comfortable!

With full afterburner selected, and just above Mach 1, I

locked my fighter plane's radar onto the drone and flew the pre-planned ground track beginning a dive at 17,000 feet. Gradually leveling off at 10,000 feet at 1.3 Mach, I paused just long enough to stabilize. Contributing to the feeling of power and speed were the tufts of vapor that were forced to appear by the high Mach number on different parts of the airplane—over the wing, behind the canopy, under the belly. Once stable at 10,000, I simulated the air-to-air missile launch at the target drone. My head-up display (HUD) indicated the target lock and began the simulated countdown for the missile that was not really in flight. The electronic systems on board my jet worked the magic that would be required to support an actual missile launch. But, of course, since there was no missile aboard for this practice run, the missile launcher did not perform its eject function. The drone was flying precisely the profile in this dress rehearsal as we expected it to fly in the live test planned for the following day.

A pilot doesn't really think about it at the time, but pondering later the power required to push this large fighter plane to the high side of 700 knots is remarkable. To say it is "unbelievably powerful" is a good start, but is still lacking as a description of this condition. This is truly one of those cases where "you had to be there." People ask, "Does it get really quiet when you're supersonic?" The answer is, "Anything but." There is a lot of noise in the cockpit but it is a different kind of noise from the cannonlike "BOOM" those in our telemetry-monitoring van experienced as my F-15 flew over them—just ahead of the noise it was making. Later one of the guys in the back of the van (which had no windows) reported to me that he actually saw the sides of the van flex inward and then outward as I "boomed" them when I passed.

EAGLES RULE

The dress rehearsal for this missile shot went very smoothly, with one major exception. One of the panels on the airplane had come slightly ajar during the high-speed runs and just barely caught some of that 700-knot air going past. As a result it was torn from its hinge, leaving an obvious and, might I say, unhelpful hole on the belly of the airplane. I flew home and landed safely, ignorant of the fact that the door was missing, but it would be against regulations and unacceptable for safety reasons to fly the live mission without replacing the panel. After finding the flaw, our mechanics inspected the airplane closely to make sure the departing door had not scarred another part of the airplane after being freed from its assigned spot. Fortunately, the rest of the airplane was untouched.

Then began what turned out to be the *real* challenge: locating a new panel. Our supply folks (actually three brilliant men, all named Tom) started phoning their contacts all over the country. We had to have this part by *tonight* or the live mission for tomorrow would be scrubbed, costing much more than any of us wanted to admit out loud. There were dozens of assets dedicated to this shot already in place and paid for, dozens of team members assembled, range time scheduled, and lots of funding at stake, not to mention the customer for the missile who was in need of the data we would produce from the shot. The pressure was on, but we had no luck. After an exhaustive search, the Toms determined that there were no such doors in the supply system or at any of the F-15 bases in the country. There was one in Japan, but we couldn't get it in time. In frustration, they sat down. I had never seen these three run out of ideas before. They even tried sneaking over to the unflyable F-15 that was on static display near the headquarters building to see if the door from it would fit. It had the door, but, being a different model airplane, it did not fit.

I was back at my desk that afternoon when I got a call from one of the other Toms: "Sir, you gotta come see this."

"What?" I demanded.

"Just come on over," was the reply. I grabbed my wingman and we headed over.

"Now—what?" I requested.

"Have a look," Tom #1 said, pointing under the airplane where the hole had been.

Quietly and without comment, a fourth "Tom" we called Tommy had slipped away from our earlier discussion. In the frantic search for a door, no one noticed he was missing. Tommy was particularly proud to be an F-15 Eagle maintainer. Without asking, he had begun with a sheet of 80-thousandths aircraft aluminum. He cut it to a rough shape, smoothed the

edges, and used some kind of machine that rounded it along its length. Grinding, rolling, and fitting, he matched the sheet to the gaping hole in my airplane. More grinding, more rolling, and more fitting. Then yet more grinding and fitting. When it matched the hole exactly, he drilled and countersunk twenty holes for the screws that would hold the door in place.

What he did that day reminded me of the counsel we receive in D&C 58:26–28: He didn't wait until he was commanded but took the initiative—he did something "of [his] own free will" while "anxiously engaged in a good cause." The power was in him, and he acted as an agent unto himself to solve a nearly impossible problem.

Now, as we viewed his handiwork, Tommy was silent, but grinning like a Cheshire cat. I ducked under the belly of my plane to see a shiny aluminum panel so precisely conformed to the mold line of the airplane as to be completely flush. It fit perfectly. It was secured with twenty countersunk screws. To keep the air out, it was fared in with sealant. The sealant, I was assured, would be cured by takeoff time tomorrow morning. It was a *masterpiece!* The team was exuberant—all smiles— almost giddy! Congratulations were shared. As a joking gesture, my wingman and I got a marker and wrote the name of a popular soda on the fresh aluminum and teased Tommy about having made the new, magnificent panel out of an old soda can.

We retired for the day with light hearts and a sense of having overcome great odds, ready to take on the live fire mission early the next day. We had all tried. Tommy had succeeded. And because he was a part of the team, we had all succeeded.

Before sunrise the next day, I put on my g-suit and harness, grabbed my helmet, and went to the airplane to conduct the preflight. The live missile was loaded. With a great deal of pride in Tommy, I stooped down when I got to the place where he had performed his feat. The sealant was cured. It was ready to fly. But wait. I noticed that the joking scribble I had put there the day before was gone. I climbed all the way under the jet to get a good view. Tommy had replaced the joking words with something that he felt was much more appropriate . . . and we all shared his sentiment. The shiny aluminum panel now bore Tommy's best rendition of an eagle with spread wings and a caption that simply said "EAGLES RULE."

Shortly after takeoff, I accelerated through Mach 1 and began a dive from 17,000 feet. Leveling off at 1.3 Mach, I paused just long enough to stabilize. My HUD indicated the radar lock. Amid the Mach-driven vapor tufts, I hammered down on the pickle button. The launcher briskly accomplished its eject function. My HUD began counting down the time until impact. The electronic systems in my aircraft supported the missile. The result was the THUNK and the WHOOSHing roar of the live missile *rapidly* departing my aircraft. (And I thought *I* was going fast!) The missile obviously knew exactly where it wanted to go. It was not pointing at the drone, but rather was flying to the spot where the target was GOING to be—it was on a collision course. The mission that a day earlier had been written off as dead in the water had now became a complete success.

Landing and some limited celebration followed the successful missile firing. But what sticks with me remains as one of the most memorable experiences of my air force career. That afternoon, the maintenance crew for my airplane showed up at my office. What? This was rare. They always seemed happier to be with flying machines than amidst the red tape of the squadron building. But they had a gift for me and wanted to present it personally. The gift had twenty countersunk holes in it and it was shiny, bright aluminum . . . except for a little sealant around the edges, Tommy's portrait of an eagle, and the signatures of each man on the maintenance crew, including Tommy. Oh, and of course, the caption: "EAGLES RULE."

PILOT'S BIOGRAPHY

Lieutenant Colonel David M. Nelson,
United States Air Force, retired

Call sign: Doc

Hometown: McLean, Virginia

Family: married to Rain Jackson; five children

Church experience: served full-time mission to Columbus, Ohio; has served as bishop, high councilor, and counselor in bishoprics and branch presidencies; currently teaches seminary and serves on the high council

Current occupation: F-35 test pilot for an aeronautics company

Hobbies: Church and family, astronomy, radio-controlled airplanes

Awards and recognitions: Eagle Scout; distinguished graduate from United States Air Force Test Pilot School; A1AA Tester of the Year award, 2001

David Nelson with the F-22 Raptor.

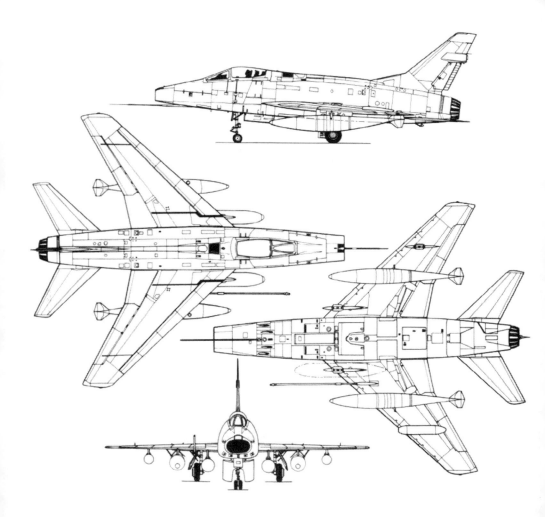

CHAPTER TWENTY-FIVE

THE LONG THREE-DAY TRIP

LEONARD MOON

In April 1970, I was assigned to fly a repaired F-100 Super Sabre jet from the Azores Islands in the Atlantic Ocean back to Cannon Air Force Base, New Mexico. It had broken down several weeks earlier, and a team of maintenance people had repaired it and said it was ready to fly. I was told that I would take an airline flight to the Azores, then meet the air refueling tanker the next day to fly back across the Atlantic Ocean to Florida, and then back to Cannon Air Force Base. I was to be gone only three days. I packed my overnight bag, kissed my wife, Dee, and the kids good-bye, and told them I would see them in three days. I arrived in the Azores Islands the first day and was briefed by the maintenance crew that the air refueling probe on the aircraft had been repaired and an air refueling tanker from Spain would meet me overhead the next day to air refuel me across the Atlantic.

The next morning, after I got the F-100 ready to fly, the KC-135 tanker crew called me and told me they would meet me overhead. I took off and, as soon as we joined up, I hooked up to the air refueling basket with my air refueling probe to take on fuel, but the tanker crew said they could not transfer any fuel because something was wrong with my system. I backed off, disconnected, and reconnected several times, but to no avail. We were now well out over the ocean and about 250 miles west of the Azores. I could not wait any longer to try to solve the problem; I would need what fuel I had to return to the Azores. The KC-135 tanker proceeded on to Florida and I turned around and headed back to the Azores.

I finally made it back to the Azores and told the maintenance crew that I was not too happy because whatever they did had not fixed the problem. They tried to fix it again, but failed. Since I couldn't refuel in the air, I was told to fly to Germany and meet up with a squadron of F-102 jets and we would fly the northern route back to the States. By doing that, we could land at different bases to refuel. The plan was to fly from Germany to Scotland, to Iceland, to Greenland, to Labrador, and finally to the U.S. Overnight stops were planned for each of these bases. I flew my jet to Spain, then on to Germany that day. This was the very first time I had ever been in Europe, so it was rather a stressful experience trying to communicate with the Spanish, French, and German flight controllers. I called my squadron commander and had him call my wife and tell her that I would be a "few more days." The following day, I left Germany with an F-102 squadron of twelve jets. We stayed the first night in Lossemouth, Scotland.

The following day we flew to Keflavik Air Base in Iceland for another overnight stop. The next morning we were briefed on our mission to cross the North Atlantic Ocean. In case one of us had to eject, we were required to wear our rubber anti-exposure suits, which, if we had to eject, would give us a little more survival time in the icy waters of the North Atlantic. Every one of the other pilots had brought their anti-exposure suits with them, but since I had initially been going to cross the Atlantic way down south where the water was much warmer, I had not been required to bring my suit. When they found out that I didn't have one, they almost made me stay there, but I promised I would not jump out of my jet. So that afternoon we flew across the Atlantic to Sondestrom, Greenland. Greenland? Not a tree in sight, nothing but ice and snow! We stayed overnight there and the next day took off for Goose Bay, Labrador. I had my squadron commander call my wife again and tell her that I would be a "few more days."

When we landed, the runway was clear, but in April it still looked like winter. To keep the runway open throughout the winter, snow blowers on the front of snowplows had made fifteen-foot drifts of snow on each side of the runway for the full length of the runway. To help pilots better see the runway in

whiteout conditions, they stuck six-foot green pine trees into these drifts about every 100 feet.

We were supposed to stay that night, but when we landed it was just starting to snow, so they told us to get refueled and get out of there because a big snowstorm was coming. This we did, and by the time we took off it was snowing pretty hard. I was the last to take off, flying on the wing of an F-102. When we got airborne, we put our landing gear up. His went up, but mine stayed down. Because of all the excess drag, I immediately lost sight of my leader in the snowstorm. I tried everything to get my landing gear up, but it wouldn't come up. I told the control tower that I would have to come back and land because of my landing gear problem. They said it was snowing very hard and the runway visibility was now below landing minimums, which was something I did not want to hear. They told me there was another base about 300 miles away and that the weather was good. I did some quick fuel calculations and found I could only fly about 250 miles with my gear down before I ran out of fuel.

I told the radar controllers that my only option was to return and try to land at Goose Bay. They said they would do the best they could to get me down, but the airfield was in whiteout conditions. I asked them to have their most experienced controller help me down. It was snowing so hard, I couldn't see anything. I made three attempts to land; even though each time the radar showed I was over the runway, I never did see the runway, so I didn't land. I was running out of fuel and becoming quite concerned. I told them that I had enough fuel to make one last attempt. I told the radar controller to do the best he had ever done in keeping me on course and on the glide path, because this was my last try. My silent prayers became more audible. I prayed as hard as I ever had to get the help I needed.

The controller did a great job. As I came over the end of the runway on my final attempt, the controller said I was on course and on glide path. By now the runway was covered with six inches of snow, so all I could see was *white.* With the help of someone with much more power than either of us, I pulled the throttle to idle and softly touched down in the soft, white snow, still not knowing exactly where I was. I deployed the drag chute and braked to a stop without hitting anything, so I hoped I was still on the runway. When the ground crew finally found me in that blizzard, I was very happy and thanked Him who guided me to an uneventful landing. Once I climbed down out of the jet, I was very thankful for being on solid ground, even if it was snow-covered. We scraped the snow away from the front tire and found out I was just a few inches off the centerline stripe of the runway.

That was one of the most stressful events of my thirty-year flying career. It took another two weeks to get the part needed to fix my jet. When they called my wife to tell her I'd be home in a "few more days," she said, "Never mind calling me. I'll just see him when he gets home." After three weeks, I finally delivered the jet to Niagara Falls National Guard. So my initial three-day trip became three weeks.

PILOT'S BIOGRAPHY

Colonel Leonard Moon,
United States Air Force, retired

Hometown: Farmington, Utah

Family: married to Delores Cunningham; four children; eight grandchildren

Church experience: served full-time mission to Spanish-American Mission (Texas and New Mexico); served as missionary with wife in Bolivia and Peru; served twice as a bishop and as a counselor in two stake presidencies; served with wife in the Mexico City Mexico Temple and the Villahermosa Mexico Temple

Current occupation: retired from the Air Force and the admissions office at Brigham Young University

Colonel Leonard Moon.

Awards and recognitions: two Distinguished Flying Crosses and numerous other recognitions; more than 4,250 flying hours, including 839 combat hours and 434 combat missions, mostly in the F-4 Phantom and also in the F-100 Super Sabre

E-3 SENTRY

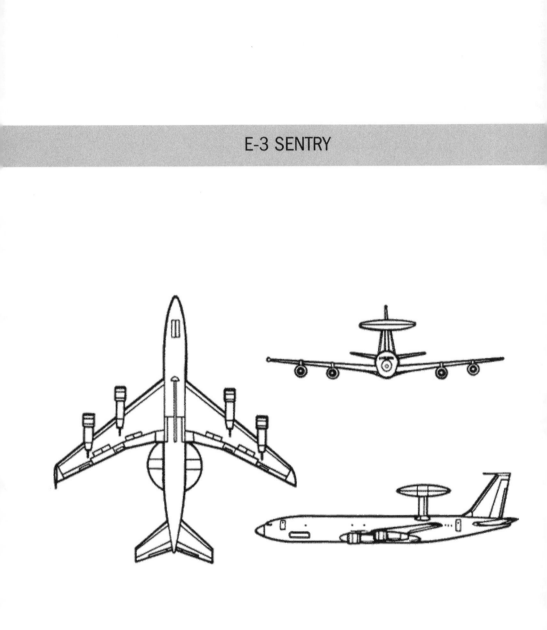

CHAPTER TWENTY-SIX

HELP, ANYONE!

KEVEN P. COYLE

Every good aviator's story must begin with the words "there I was." This story is no different. There I was in the middle of what was shaping up to be an arduous night of operations in Iraq. Significant responsibility had been placed on my shoulders the minute I took over the tactical command and control role as the Senior Radar Element in the area. My primary responsibility was to provide safe deconfliction of aircraft, both manned and unmanned, throughout the entire country. This is a feat of engineering and requires four radars and multiple radio stations throughout the area of operations to be successful. In addition to aircraft deconfliction is the responsibility to provide safe and efficient airspace management, which includes the allocation of some of the most in-demand airspaces in the world.

I am an air battle manager with the burden of making sure that everything—up to the release of a weapon, the deconfliction of that weapon flying through the air, and the effect of that weapon when it strikes its target—is efficiently coordinated and communicated to the persons given the authority to allow for these amazing events to occur. I am not a pilot; however, I am responsible for the safety of all pilots flying in the airspace I have been delegated authority to manage. I consider myself to be the wingman of every aircraft within the sound of my voice.

In Iraq, multiple frequencies are used to communicate with aircraft, ground parties, operations centers, and forward operating locations. This night was shaping up to be one I would never forget. As I was assigning aircraft to work with ground parties around Baghdad, one of my radio receivers picked up a faint voice. Thinking nothing of it, I continued trying to keep up with the feverish pace of operations as they were unfolding that night. Suddenly, we lost power to our system and many of our radios, our lifelines to these fighters, were down. Frantically we reset the system and began loading radio frequencies into our radios to reestablish contact with the aircraft under our control. After tuning the VHF radios I faintly heard the words, "Help, anyone, help."

I was currently listening to three Ultra High Frequency (UHF)

radios, two Very High Frequency (VHF) radios, two satellite communications (SATCOM) radios and three internal net radios and had a hard time determining which radio frequency the sound was coming from. Something inside me told me to look at my communications panel at the VHF radios. Suddenly I saw the "activate" light illuminate as a voice said again, "Help, anyone, we are under attack and my gunny is injured!" You could hear the gunfire in the background and the urgency in the voice of the soldier. I responded on the radio with my call sign and the radio crackled to silence. I began doing what I had been trained to do and immediately coordinated with the Combined Air Operations Center 2,000 miles away to reprioritize nearby fighters to support the "troops in contact" or TIC (pronounced "tick"), as we called it. After getting approval I worked with the Air Support Operations Center to pull the fighters back onto my frequency to initiate the support operations.

Once the fighters checked in and I received their "playtime" information (the amount of time they could support the operation before having to get gas), I realized fuel would be an issue for the jets. Simultaneously I coordinated the airborne refueling aircraft into deconflicted airspace over the operation and the fight commenced. The total time for these actions was less than two minutes and weapons were being released from two F-16 Fighting Falcon aircraft supporting the contingent of marines pinned down by enemy gun, rocket, and mortar fire. Once the F-16s called the situation under control and the area secure, I coordinated with forward operations centers for the immediate launch of the recovery helicopters.

Once the helicopters were overhead and the situation seemed completely under control, I looked at my radios and was amazed to find that neither of my VHF radios were operational according to my system's monitoring functions. I was confused; I knew I had heard something. I dismissed this as a glitch and went on to complete my shift. Once off of the console, I relayed the story to my superiors and they responded that they had heard the UHF traffic and were pleased with my coordination efforts to affect the recovery of these injured warriors. I told them about the VHF radio glitch, and maintenance reported to me that all the VHF radios were down and were expected to be operational again in a couple of hours. I had a comforting sensation engulf my body and I felt that things were right.

The next day I went to volunteer in the makeshift hospital at my deployed location. I came across a young man whose chart reported his status as "injured in combat." He was awake and we began to talk. I don't remember his name but I will never forget the story he relayed to me about how the Lord had answered his prayers the night before. He told me of his marine unit being pinned down by the enemy and how his immediate superior had been hit by a mortar, causing severe injuries to his midsection. He relayed how their vehicle had been damaged and the radio did not appear to be functioning. He conveyed how he had pleaded on the radio for help and heard nothing but a garbled response, then static. He said a prayer, thinking it would be his last, and suddenly there were jets overhead and the sweet sounds of explosions in the distance. He said there was an eerie silence when it was over, and the last thing he remembers was the helicopter landing to transport him and his superior.

The same feeling I had the night before had returned to my body in force. This brave young marine asked me what I was doing in Iraq, so I explained to him my job and told him my radio call sign. He broke into tears and said that was the name he thought he had heard on the radio that night. He introduced me to the man he simply called his "gunny," quite possibly the bravest man I have ever met. I never told him the efforts that went into executing their recovery. The Spirit was strong, and I was humbly happy to have been a special instrument in the Lord's hands that fateful evening.

PILOT'S BIOGRAPHY

Captain Keven P. Coyle, United States Air Force

Call sign: Hitch
Hometown: Cheyenne, Wyoming
Church calling: Marriage and Family Relations instructor
Awards: Air Medal, Meritorious Service Medal

Captain Keven P. Coyle.

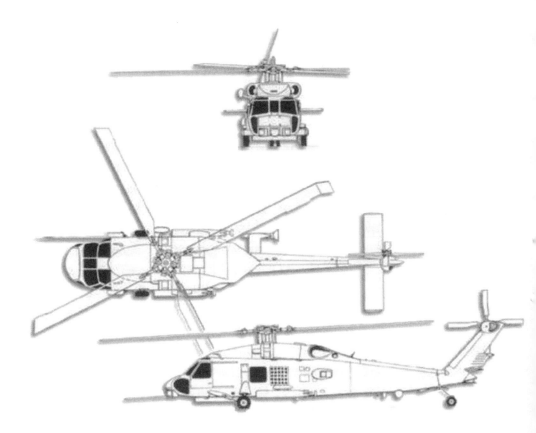

CHAPTER TWENTY-SEVEN

SHOOT!

RANDY VAN HORN

I am a flight engineer on an Air Force HH-60 helicopter known as the Pave Hawk, in a unit that is dedicated to combat search and rescue. We specialize in rescuing pilots who have been shot down, as well as other isolated personnel, which means we train to fly through the battlefield and behind enemy lines to rescue downed aircrew. We train to fly day or night, good weather or bad, at altitudes as low as fifty feet.

The flight crew in each helicopter consists of a pilot, a copilot, an aerial gunner, and a flight engineer. As a flight engineer, some of my in-flight duties consist of scanning for obstacles (terrain, power lines, towers, and so on) as well as scanning for threats—insurgents who shoot at us with everything from AK-47s to antiaircraft artillery (AAA) to rocket-propelled grenades (RPGs) to surface-to-air missiles. In the event that we are fired upon, I direct the pilots on how to maneuver the helicopter to avoid being hit, or return fire with the right-side crew-served weapon.

In the winter of 2006, my unit was deployed to Iraq in support of Operation Iraqi Freedom. As part of a rescue squadron, we flew missions almost every day in support of air force, army, and other coalition forces. Faith, prayer, and relying on the Holy Ghost are important aspects in my life and become even more so when flying in a hostile environment. I truly learned the meaning of constant prayer when I was in Iraq—I prayed before every takeoff, as well as multiple times during every flight. I know that Heavenly Father's protective hand was evident during my rotation in Iraq, and one night in particular in March of 2007.

My crew was flying what appeared to be a normal mission in the vicinity of Baghdad, much like the ones we had been flying almost nightly for several months. We were once again flying low-level, at around one o'clock in the morning on a very dark night. In the middle of the desert, a group of Iraqi trucks were sitting in a large circle that had been modified with heavy machine guns and antiaircraft artillery mounted in the truck beds. Shortly before we were in the area, these trucks had fired on an army helicopter and damaged it.

It was so dark that night that even with night vision goggles, we didn't see this cluster of trucks until we were literally right on top of them. Unfortunately for us, the sound of a helicopter is hard to disguise—they knew we were coming before we knew they were there. To make matters worse, we flew right down the middle of their circle of vehicles—we were surrounded.

My first indication that something was wrong was when I saw a bright flash right outside my door. It seemed that time instantly slowed down. I remember thinking that it must be a 23mm AAA piece because of the rate of fire and size of the tracers. Almost immediately, toward our right front, a second gun opened fire; this time it was a 12.7mm heavy machine gun. I had seen tracers shot before, but this was the first time I had witnessed them coming so close to me. They were so close to our helicopter that I could almost reach out and touch them. In what was a surprise to me, I realized I could hear the sound of the larger caliber guns firing.

At this point, despite the ambient noise of the helicopter and the noise of the incoming fire, I heard a voice that was very calm and clear—yet very distinct—say one word: "Shoot." In proper military fashion, I obeyed the voice and returned fire to defend my aircraft. My returning fire suppressed the heavy machine gun, which was the biggest threat to us—its rounds were no more than twenty feet from our helicopter. In less than a heartbeat's time from when I started shooting, the aerial gunner on the other side of the helicopter started shooting at AAA and heavy machine guns that were on that side of the aircraft.

When I started shooting, the pilots (who were looking inside the helicopter to concentrate on navigating and flying using the instruments) realized we were under fire and started taking

evasive maneuvers. While the engagement lasted only forty-four seconds, that is really a long time to be the center of so much attention from the enemy.

When our aircraft landed in Baghdad, it was my responsibility to inspect the aircraft for damage. I thought that we surely had taken at least a few hits—the sheer volume of fire directed at us stacked the law of averages against us. To my amazement, the insurgents hadn't even scratched the paint on the helicopter. Truly, we were protected.

After we had returned to our base later that night, my crew was reviewing the events that had happened. I asked the other members of my crew who had said "Shoot." The only answer I received was blank stares. No one had said or heard a voice say "Shoot." The pilots said that they had started evasive maneuvers when they heard the aerial gunner and me open fire—they hadn't realized we were under attack until then.

We have a computer on our helicopter that records our communications for review after flight that is used to debrief our intelligence personnel. Later that night I had the opportunity to listen to the communication recording from that flight. I listened to the recording at least ten times, and at no point on the recording is there a voice that tells me to shoot. In fact, the word *shoot* was not even said during the entire flight.

I know that the Spirit was with me that day to protect and warn me so that I could return home to be with my family. That day was another witness to me that our Father in Heaven loves us and is always there to protect us when needed.

PILOT'S BIOGRAPHY

Technical Sergeant Randy Van Horn, United States Air Force

Hometown: Elmira, New York

Family: married 12½ years to Laurence Mezzasalma; three children, Caroline, Ryan, and Megan

Church experience: served in the Belgium Brussels Mission from 1992–1994; has served as a Blazer leader, Primary teacher; currently serves as Young Men's president in Valdosta Second Ward

Randy Van Horn with the HH-60.

ROCKWELL B-1B LANCER

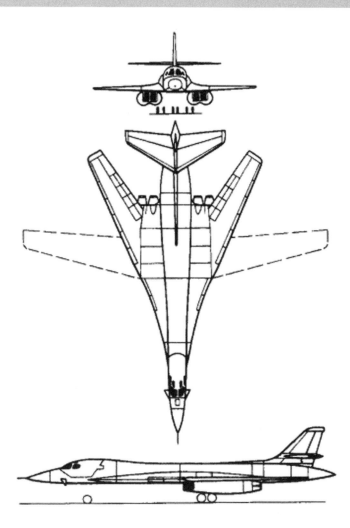

CHAPTER TWENTY-EIGHT

IT'S A SMALL WORLD

CHRIS STEWART

On June 3, 1995, I had the opportunity to attempt to set the world's speed record for the fastest time nonstop around the world. This effort involved three Air Force B-1s (two primary aircraft which would fly in formation around the world, with one airborne spare that would accompany the flight as far as the bomb run over Sicily, then return, if not needed, back to the Azores Islands off the coast of Portugal). The primary purpose of this flight was to test the long-range capabilities of both the B-1 and its aircrews. All of the aircraft carried munitions and accomplished practice bomb runs on military ranges over Sicily, Japan, and the Utah Test and Training Range in the western Utah desert. This flight required almost a year of preparation, 28 air refueling aircraft, hundreds of support personnel, and more than three million pounds of fuel. This was a very important mission for the air force, for it was one of the foundational test beds for the concept of modern global power projection.

What follows are portions of my journal entry that I wrote several days after this flight.

June 11, 1995

It was an extremely busy month. One of the busiest of my life, I think. There was just so much going on, and the round-the-world thing was such a project, it kept me preoccupied all the time. Because I was the guy who came up with the idea and so became, kind of by default, the mission commander, it is all I have thought about for the past four or five months or so. But it was extremely challenging and exciting and rewarding and frustrating and . . . cool. It really was. It was exciting and cool. What can I say?

I want to write about it, to try to remember the details while they are still relatively fresh in my mind. Already, it seems a long time ago. It was funny, even while I was flying it, it seemed almost like it wasn't really happening. Like it was going by fast. For more than 37 hours we sat in the jet, yet it didn't seem near that long and I didn't ever really feel that tired or uncomfortable or sore or bored. Never bored. Always busy. Always working. Always something to do.

There is one overriding impression that I have taken from the whole experience, one that has changed me in a fundamental way, in such a way that I will never look upon the world the same way again. It will sound corny, and it will be impossible to explain, but that one impression is this: The world is so small. It is so little. Not big at all. I think of God, sitting in His heavens, looking down upon this world, and if I consider it so small after flying around it in a little more than a day, imagine how He must feel about it in comparison to His eternal majesty.

I mean, we took off at three in the morning, and within a couple of hours we were off the coast of Canada. Across the Atlantic, an ocean which took the early explorers months to cross, and we did it in three or four hours. Then through the Straits of Gibraltar—the famous rock. From there, I could see into half a dozen different countries. Two continents, the African and European, dozens of different cultures and languages and religions and peoples and histories. And it was all right there, just a few hours after takeoff. (I might add, we were traveling quite fast, about .92 Mach, about 9.2 miles every minute, but we weren't a spaceship or anything, just an airplane cruising around the world.) We passed very close to the Adriatic Sea, about the same time that a U.S. F-16 was shot down over Bosnia. We could almost see it. By then it was getting dark. We went through three periods of night. Note I said three *periods,* since they weren't really nights; traveling east the nights were always cut short and the last one up in Alaska was only about three and a half hours long. That was another cool thing, seeing this constant glow, like a just setting sun, over the North Pole as we traveled up the Russian coast and through the Bering Sea. These were the "White Nights," and they didn't look inviting—not like a sunset or sunrise, which is warm and hints of light and heat. These were different somehow. More pale and cold. You could almost feel the freezing air up over the poles.

Anyway, back to what I was saying: We saw all these countries in Europe, passed over Sicily and Crete. I remember looking down on these vineyards and thinking they might be a thousand years old. And we saw hills that had been terraced in the times of the Romans. After that, it started to get dark again, and we passed over Egypt and Saudi Arabia and Oman, through all these countries that go back thousands of years, to the very beginning of human history. And the distance was all so small. I could see the Nile, and all the cities that lined its banks, and all the lights from the farms that ran along its banks, but away from the river it was nothing but total darkness. It was a very dark night, no moon, and the desert was just so blank. (And I used to think that west Texas was dark.) I remember looking down as we passed over Saudi and seeing nothing but darkness because there was nothing there but desert and thinking, *what makes this land valuable is not what lies on top of the earth but what lies underneath.*

After passing over the Red Sea we flew over Jeddah and by Mecca. (Mecca is a no-overfly zone—they'll shoot you down if you get within ten miles of it.) The lights of Jeddah were unlike anything I'd ever seen before, unlike anything I could ever explain. The sight was like something out of a storybook, out of a fairy tale. It really was. It was just so clear. It was this huge city on the edge of the desert and the Red Sea, and the lights were so perfectly clear. It was like every one of them was

perfect. They all twinkled. Maybe it was because of the clear and dry desert air, but it was almost as if the entire light from every bulb on the ground was able to penetrate the atmosphere to reach us, none of it washed out or faded through the distance. All of us noticed it and we talked about it between the two aircraft. We all wondered why it looked so different but none of us had any explanation. PM: pure magic.

We refueled at night over Saudi (a 205,000-pound onload, at night, without any disconnects, never more than six inches out of position, thank you very much). Then Steve went to sleep and I flew as we went south through the Arabian Sea. I was flying just barely above this cloud deck. It was like our wings were in the clouds, but our cockpit was five feet higher and above the cloud bank so even in the darkness you had this enormous sensation of speed. And it was quiet; people were sleeping and there was no one to talk to on the radio. (We went about three-fourths of the way around the world without ever talking to anyone on the radios . . . an uncomfortable feeling when you are approaching the coast of Egypt and Saudi, both countries with enormous warnings stating DO NOT ENTER their airspace without prior approval and clearance or you will get shot down by one of the dozens of SAMs that were tracking us. How could we go so far and talk to so few people—across the entire Arabic and Indian Oceans without ever being able to get hold of a single air traffic controller? It was weird. But I digress.)

So there I was, listening to Mary Chapin Carpenter in my headset, and it was just one of those times I will always remember. It was this surreal feeling of floating over the clouds, almost weightless, at an unbelievable speed, smooth as foam, and all the while listening to this great music. It was cool.

Soon it was day. I remember watching the eastern sky get light, thinking it had to be the moon rising, that we hadn't been in darkness long enough yet for it to be dawn. But it was the sunrise. Looking down, I could already see these tropical islands. Huge volcanoes rose to just beneath the surface of the sea, then filled in with water. The water was greenish-blue. Very pretty. Not dark or black like I am used to seeing it at 20,000 feet. And here were tropical islands with natives who had spent the first 5,000 years of their existence thinking they were the only people on earth. Yet here we were flying overhead, and only a few hours before we had been passing over the huge deserts of the Middle East. The cultures and climate and history were worlds and worlds apart, yet it was only a few hours' flight.

There were lines of thunderstorms. Huge, never-ending lines. They built up over the chains of islands, which stretched for a thousand miles across the open sea. They rose like perfect anvils. Huge storms, each of them independent, rising from just above the surface of the sea to the upper atmosphere.

We had to deviate south about 300 miles to get through the storms, so by the time we hit Singapore we were very low on gas. (As it turned out, we flew almost 24,000 miles, more than 3,000 miles farther than we planned, all due to weather.) That was our longest leg, and fuel was going to be critical to get to Singapore under the best of conditions, so the storms really hurt us. We only had 27k on gas by the time we hit our tanker. The only divert base was Singapore, 200 miles to the south. If we didn't hit the tanker and start getting gas immediately, we were ready to tell the tankers to turn and head toward Singapore while we still were trying to take on fuel. We just didn't have any time to spare. Plus, the weather at Singapore was not good. Thunderstorms were everywhere. Then they shut down the only airport in Singapore capable of landing a B-1 because of those thunderstorms. Man, glad to have those tankers. It was exciting . . . once it was over. While it was happening, it wasn't as much fun.

Then we headed north. And more storms. Lots of storms. About three hours of constant turning and running to avoid the weather and cutting our way through the worst of it.

I have to inject another note: The St. Elmo's fire on this sortie was unlike any I had ever seen except one time in Montana when the ball of blue fire came into our cockpit and started spinning around like a globe, then exploded. We saw tons of St. Elmo's, mostly because we had to travel through so much weather and because we were flying so fast, which builds up more static energy. Even when we weren't in storms there was a constant sparkling on my side window, and when we were in the weather there were these tiny blue fingers that would stretch up the windscreen, then crackle and disappear.

By then we were in the Orient. Again, another completely different culture and history. It all just seemed so close. Then up the coast of Russia. I have always considered Russia a complete universe away. A million miles. The enemy. Not like me. And yet, there we were, tracking along its coast, and in a few hours we would be over the Alaska Peninsula and then the U.S. What I thought of as so far away was in reality very close.

I don't know if you can understand. I don't know how else to explain it. I just received a strong and never-to-be forgotten impression that the earth is truly His footstool. And if He can create *all this,* surely He can answer my prayers, help me manage my life, perform miracles when I need it, intervene to help my family. It was humbling. And from that humility came gratitude and faith.

A final thought in this regard: The night we took off, when I left home to go to the squadron for the mission, I was excited but a little nervous. Mom and Dad had come down from Utah to be here, and before I left, at about 10:30 at night, I wanted to say a family prayer. I asked Dad to say it and he used the power of the priesthood to bless me with success and safety and protection. As soon as he said the words, "I invoke the power of the priesthood," I had a great amount of faith and a peaceful feeling that everything would be okay. I didn't know that we would be successful, but I knew I would be safe and protected. I thought of that many times on the flight. I know that as Dad said those words, the power of the priesthood rested upon me and it was there always. I felt almost a blanket of peace and protection. It was as real as anything I have ever felt, and I am grateful for that experience.

About the mission itself: It started out as a real thrill. Forty minutes before takeoff, in our final weather brief, Al the weatherguy said there wasn't any weather in the entire state of Texas. Wrong. By the time we got to our jets, twenty minutes later, there was a line of thunderstorms stretching as far as you could see from south to north. It made us all laugh. All of us but Al the weatherguy. The only weather in the whole state, in the entire southwest region, and it was all sitting exactly over the base. It was funny. Kind of.

Turned out to be a good thing for us, though, because when we got to our jet, it didn't have a number-two engine. They had to shut it down for hot oil lights, and then they burned out a generator and couldn't get it started again. Now, the ROE (rules of engagement) stated that if you had a problem with your jet, you were out. There were no bag drags (one of the primary crews snagging one of the spare aircraft.) Remember, we showed at the aircraft only twenty minutes before takeoff. There was simply no time to change jets.

After all that work, and I thought, *I'm not even going to get off the ground.* I had always joked that the chance of completing the mission was inversely proportional to the amount of time spent in preparing for it, thus, as the mission commander, I would probably not get all the way around the world. But I did think that I would at least get airborne. I went to the maintenance supervisor and said to him, "Chief, we need to know right now. We only have a few minutes. Are you going to fix this jet, or should we try to get to the spare?" (Keep in mind, we had about 1,000 pounds of equipment to drag to the next jet. If we had tried to go to the spare, it wouldn't have happened. They would have taken off without us. We would have run out of time.) I will always remember what the chief said. "Sir, I know what I'm doing. We are going to fix this jet. Go get strapped in." Okay, we started loading up our final gear. I got in and started strapping in. By the time I got strapped in, they had it fixed. I cleared the engine to start, pushed the start button, and there she went. It was a truly beautiful thing. By that time lead was checking in the formation on the radios. We checked in and asked for a few minutes, which we needed since the rest of the crew was still packing gear and strapping into their ejection seats, and maintenance guys were still putting access panels back on the number-two engine. It was 0145. Taxi in three minutes. We never even told lead we'd had a problem. We were ready to go. 0148. Ready to taxi. Everything was cool. Let's go.

And then it started to rain. No, it started to pour! Cats and dogs. Goats and sheep. Thunder and lightning. Hail. A bolt of lightning struck one of the light poles across the ramp, which had about ten maintenance trucks sitting under it. They all scattered like scared cows. It was ugly. We listened to Charlie (the wing second in command) talking to the weather guys, looking for holes in the thunderstorms. It was a solid line from north to south. Over the field, west of the field. Wasn't going to be clear of the field for an hour and a half. We told him the radar on our jets showed the main cells were still five miles west of the field and if we took off *immediately* we would have the required three miles clearance from the thunderstorms. Nice try. He didn't buy it. We started listening to guys in the tower working the ALTRV (around the world flight plan) and diplomatic clearance (which are required to fly U.S. air force combat aircraft into another country's airspace) to slip an hour. The amount of work it was going to take to slip all 28 air refueling tankers that were tasked for the mission was simply unbelievable. You have no idea. And if we couldn't take off within an hour, the ALTRV and all our dip clearances would drop out of the system and become immediately invalid. Everything dropped dead exactly one hour past our scheduled takeoff time. It was a real thrill.

At 0245 we taxied. Fifteen minutes before drop-dead. Weather was still calling severe thunderstorms all around us, but they thought there would be a hole to the north, a tiny hole . . . in about 45 minutes. Way too late. Charlie told us to taxi anyway. We held on the hammerhead. 0255. Five minutes till all the clearances dropped out. Suddenly, weather shop called a hole in the storms. "Bats, you are cleared for an immediate takeoff. Go baby, go." Blue afterburners and lots of noise. We took off at 0259. Mere seconds to spare.

What a way to start the mission. It was good to be airborne. I didn't think we were going to make it. Everything went pretty uneventfully for us until we got through our second air refueling over the Straits of Gibraltar and in the Med (five tankers, three bombers, what a sight). Then we got an oil hot light. Number-two engine. Same one they had to shut down before.

Now, here's the problem. At that time, we still had three aircraft in the formation: us, lead, and an airborne spare that would be with us until Sicily. Our mission ROE was clear: if one of the two main aircraft had to divert, we had to divert as a formation. That ROE cut the chances of actually setting the world record by about 70 percent, because I figured there was a very good chance that somewhere, someone was going to have a problem, and since we had to stay together, if one aircraft aborted, the other aircraft had to abort as well.

So there we were with an oil hot light. We could have aborted and directed the airborne spare into the number-two position to take our place. But if we continued past Sicily and had a serious problem with the number-two engine later on, we would have to abort when there was no spare to take our place, and that would have messed up the whole mission. And all because we had made a bad decision and hadn't let the airborne spare slip into our spot. That would have been unforgivable. But were we really ready to turn around? Not yet. We decided to watch it, monitor the temp on CITS (the central computer), and see how it was doing through the bomb run in Sicily, then decide.

After the bomb run (all three airplanes hit within fifteen feet of the target!), the temp went down and stayed down, so we went for it. The quantity was reading 100 percent, so the oil quantity was obviously over-serviced. The question was, would we blow a seal? That was one of the real crunch points, one of the times that I thought we might not make it. All those four-star generals waiting on us, betting the reputation of the B-1 on this mission. It was extremely important that we get these jets around the world. If neither of us made it, especially when they said we would have to divert as a formation—well, there was just a lot of pressure to continue. To get the job done.

The number-two engine was okay until about Singapore. Then it suddenly dropped to 65 percent and kept dropping. We had to power back the engine, which really didn't hurt us since the other aircraft had powered back one of his engines already because of excessive oil consumption. Anyway, I figured we would have enough oil to make it through the bomb run in Japan, then we would have to divert into Kedina. But for some reason, the oil dropped to 45 percent, then stabilized. In fact, when we landed we had about 50 percent of our oil in all our engines. But it was another crunch point. More excitement. There we were, twenty-six hours into the sortie, over the Pacific Ocean, out in the middle of nowhere, and running out of oil. What I needed at that time was less excitement and more sleep.

A couple of other things to say: It was way too cool to see the priority that the whole thing got, once the four-star generals all got on board. For example, the Wednesday before we were to take off, Saudi canceled our clearances. Said they wouldn't allow any more military overflights of their country. None. Nada. HQ Air Combat Command worked the issue for a couple of hours, going through all of the military channels. The three-star air force guy in Riyadh went to the Saudis to talk to them, and they wouldn't even see him. They left him waiting outside their office for over an hour, and he finally just left. So the Chief of Staff called the crown prince of Saudi, and within a few minutes we had permission for a one-time overfly, providing we didn't release to the press the fact that we overflew their country.

Another time, just a few days before takeoff, we lost a bunch of our tankers on the first refueling due to some real-world commitments. Within six hours, they had deployed six tankers from Malstrom and Rickenbacher AFB to Bangor, Maine, to refuel us. Those guys were on the ground and in crew rest for the mission within twelve hours . . . that would have been on Thursday afternoon. Or the KC-10s out of UAE. The runway there was under construction, so they actually got a waiver to take off on a taxiway, yes a taxiway, so that we could have the KC-10s for the third air refueling that we needed. In addition to the three KC-10s, they also had six KC-135s on alert for us, waiting at the end of the runway in Riyadh, in case the 10s couldn't take off. (If it was too hot, and their takeoff data was too close to the limit, they weren't going to let them take off on the taxiway.)

Basically, we had every tanker in the region committed to our mission. The same thing happened in Japan. We had all these tankers, plus all these backups. The tanker task force was told that there was no higher priority mission than this one. It was great. We would have had to cancel the mission a dozen times if we didn't get the priority that we needed.

And when it came down to it, it was a beautiful plan that all came together. What a beautiful thing. I remember when we came back to the States. The air traffic control guys were vectoring other airplanes out of our way, trying to help us with the record. (At that time, we were within about two minutes of the around-the-world speed record and still had two hours to go.) I remember one guy saying, "Delta 345, you've got two B-1s coming up your tail and they are SMOKIN'." He was telling all the other aircraft what we were doing, how we were trying to set the world record and that we were two minutes behind, and they all got on their radios to wish us luck. It was cool. It was morning then and we had set up our little portable grill and were making pancakes.

It was cool. What more can I say?

We did end up setting the world's record for the fastest non-stop flight around the world—36 hours and 13 minutes—as certified by the International Aeronautical Association. Later that year, both aircrews were awarded the Air Force MacKay Trophy for the "Most Meritorious Aerial Achievement of the Year."

PILOT'S BIOGRAPHY

Major Chris Stewart,
United States Air Force

Call sign: Stewbabe

Hometown: Logan, Utah

Family: wife, Evie; six children

Church experience: various teaching and leadership positions; currently serving as high priests group leader

Current occupation: president and CEO, The Shipley Group; author of bestselling national-market techno-thrillers and LDS fiction series *The Great and Terrible*

Awards and recognitions: Distinguished Graduate, Officer Training School; Distinguished Graduate, Pilot Training; Air Crew of Distinction Award; Air Force Air Medal; MacKay Trophy, "Most Meritorious Aerial Achievement of the Year"

Major Chris Stewart with the B-1B.

INDEX

INDEX

INDEX

LEARNINGAMES
for
THREES AND FOURS

A GUIDE TO
ADULT/CHILD PLAY

Joseph Sparling and Isabelle Lewis

**Frank Porter Graham Child Development Center
University of North Carolina at Chapel Hill**

WALKER AND COMPANY • NEW YORK

Photography coordinated by Isabelle Lewis
Photographs by Joseph Sparling

First published in the United States of America in 1984 by the Walker Publishing Company, Inc.

Published simultaneously in Canada by John Wiley & Sons Canada, Limited, Rexdale, Ontario.

ISBN: 0-8027-0748-3

Library of Congress Catalog Card Number: 83-7038

Printed in the United States of America

10 9 8 7 6 5 4 3 2 1

Library of Congress Cataloging in Publication Data

Sparling, Joseph.
  Learningames for threes and fours.

  Sequel to: Learningames for the first three years.
  Bibliography: p.
  1. Children. 2. Child development. 3. Play.
4. Educational games. I. Lewis, Isabelle. II. Title.
HQ774.5.S6 1983   649'.5   83-7038
ISBN 0-8027-0748-3

for Halbert Robinson—
who dreamed of a good life for all young children

ACKNOWLEDGMENTS

Are the ideas and activities suggested in the Learningames new? Some are; some aren't. We have tried to collect good practices that have been used for years by thoughtful parents and teachers, so some of the ideas will be very familiar to you. We've taken the trouble to write them down because they are important—even though most of them are simple and some are familiar. We hope to have contributed by making all the ideas conveniently available and by revealing the important goals hidden in these everyday activities.

The Learningames were produced in the Frank Porter Graham Child Development Center of the University of North Carolina at Chapel Hill. This center has been providing day care for infants and preschool children since 1966. The parents and children taught us a lot during this time. The staff in our center have also contributed many excellent ideas, and we gratefully acknowledge these individuals:

Sally Nussbaumer, Day Care Director
Carrie Bynum, Home Visit Supervisor

Day Care and Home Visit Staff

Phylinda Baldwin
Mary Bogues
Bettye Burnette
Eva Caldwell
Johnnie Cates
Helen Edmonds

Ruth Farrington
Sherman Fogg
Fannie Harrington
Annie Johnson
Toni Joyner
Eva Minor

Aloha Peyton
Josephine Riggsbee
Phyllis Royster
Dorothy Siler
Jean Whicker

In addition, we want to recognize the special contribution of Gael McGinness whose ideas about language development influenced many of the games. And, thanks to the intelligent work of Brenda Bergeron, the manuscript went swiftly through many complex revisions on the word processor.

During the time that we were working on *Learningames for Threes and Fours* we had grants on related topics from these federal and state agencies:

Administration for Children, Youth and Families
(U.S. Office of Human Development Services)
Special Education Programs
(U.S. Department of Education)
Day Care Section
(North Carolina Department of Human Resources)

We wish to acknowledge this vital support that indirectly made our curriculum development work possible.

Contents

Introduction

The early years of life are important. They are not just a time for waiting around to get big enough to do serious things like go to school. Many of the important things of life are learned before kindergarten. But they are learned gently and easily as the adult and child play together.

This is where the Learningames come in. The games are two hundred experiences a child can enjoy from birth through age four. The first volume, *Learningames for the First Three Years* (Walker, 1979), contains games 1 through 100. This second volume is for three- and four-year-olds and contains games 101 through 200.

In most of the Learningames a child and adult are interacting—and learning as they have fun. Yes, they *both* learn. For example, while the child is learning to follow directions, the adult may be learning to give directions more wisely. Some readers will wish to select just a few games for their own use. Others will choose to use the activities systematically and frequently—making the games a curriculum or educational program. The Learningames are a resource for child development. Hopefully, the uses that parents and day care centers make of this resource will reflect the healthy variety that exists and should exist in parental goals.

Using the Learningames

These games are for parents, the natural teachers of their children. They are also for people who are preparing for parenthood and for professionals who have responsibility for young children in preschool, day care, or other types of child and family programs. Each game is presented on a double-page spread so that it can be found quickly and used easily. Some of the activities won't seem much like "games" at first sight, but we've called all of them games to emphasize the fact that they go best in a playful, back-and-forth exchange. The most important thing you can do to make these games succeed is to adopt the child's attitude that playing is the best way to learn.

What kinds of information are provided in each game?[*]
The double-page description of the game provides information in

---

[*]For the sake of equity, the pronouns in the games that refer to the gender of the child and the adult have been varied between male and female. In this introduction the female pronoun has been used for the child.

brief, ready-reference style on the right-hand page and in greater detail on the left. Each side is divided into two main sections. The first section on each side tells how to play the game and the second section tells why.

The HOW section first describes what the adult does. The right-hand page will help you get a brief idea of the game's contents before going to the left for a closer reading. (This is not the usual sequence or direction for reading, but it puts all the "quick reading" on the convenient right-hand side.) Also on the right are one or two photographs of people engaged in playing the game. These photos were chosen to help you understand a particular action more clearly or to show appropriate materials or toys.

On the left-hand page the how section describes, also, the responses children usually make to the adult's action. The adult will want to give encouragement and praise when he sees these expected behaviors in the child. The response written for the young child is based on our experiences and is more a prediction of what your child may do than a promise that she will. Children have individual likes and dislikes. If your child does not like a particular game, it makes sense to either change the game so that it interests her more, or else to go on to another one.

The WHY section on each side of the double-page spread tries to give reasons for playing the game. We believe that if you know the reasoning behind a particular game, you'll be able to invent other games or variations. And some games seem so simple that their importance may be underestimated—so we have tried to say why we think they're worth playing. On the right-hand page the why section gives the goal for your own behavior. This information is expanded on the left, and the uses of the child's new skill are given. By knowing how the child can put a new skill to use to master an even more difficult skill (sometimes one that is only weeks away and sometimes one that won't be learned for years to come), we can appreciate each simple bit of learning as a building block for the future.

Of course, whether your child masters skills in the future depends on many more things than these games. But when a preschool child has been given many opportunities to stretch and explore through Learningames, the parents or careteachers can feel that they've used one systematic method for laying the foundation for the child's future learning.

How are the games arranged?
Each of the book's four sections spans about a half-year of develop-

mental age and begins with a short description of what to expect during this time. The games are arranged within each section in approximate order of increasing difficulty. This is meant to make it possible for the child and you to move easily through the games—not using every one but choosing those that are interesting to the two of you. You will be experiencing a developmental progression as you move along. Even with picking and choosing on the basis of interest, you are likely to select games for a variety of skills. If you are interested or concerned about particular types, each section's table of contents classifies the major child skill of each game under some aspect of social/emotional or intellectual/ creative development. Of course, these classifications or themes don't tell the whole story because each game teaches more than one major skill. (For example, a game may be classified under the reasoning theme but may also teach language and independence.) Still, the major classification will help those parents who seek certain types of games or who wish to keep track of their random choices.

Which children will benefit from the games?

Learningames are for any child who is developmentally between 36 and 60 months of age. This includes most three- and four-year-old children and some normal and developmentally delayed children who are a little older. These games are not specifically designed for poor kids or rich kids, fast kids or slow kids—they can work for *any* child whose parents value the games and adapt them to the particular needs of the child. The games are not complete enough perhaps for some handicapped children, but they may provide a good starting place. If the child is not developmentally average, the adult should ignore the "month age" in the titles of the four sections. Indeed, none of us should be too impressed with the "average" ages given for the activities, but should simply use them as they become appropriate for the individual child.

Another aspect of individualization has to do with where you start in the books. It's simplest if you started when your child was a newborn and you are moving together through the entire set of 200 games. However, you can begin at any point. For example, if you are the parent of a four-year-old or the teacher of an age four day care group, you might consider starting slightly before the forty-eight-month section. Many of the earlier games are challenging enough for fours who haven't had the preparation of the entire sequence. Also many games such as "See and Show" have variations that are challenging enough for someone of developmental age four and even older. Be sure not to let the early placement of a game cause you to miss its more advanced variations.

How do I get started?

If you are a parent, you've probably been observing your child from the start. That is the first step—having a general idea of what your child can do already. For day care professionals who may be just getting to know a child, this observation period may be a bit more structured.

The checklist at the beginning of each section is a useful tool for identifying a behavior which should be observed before a given Learningame is taught—that is, a child behavior that will be used in the game. You will want to try to notice "new" behaviors or skills as soon as the youngster begins to show them. Each emerging skill will be a starting place for a Learningame. The games will then take the child to a deeper level or to a more advanced skill.

How do I match an emerging behavior with the right game?

Once you have noticed a child behavior or skill that might be used as a starting place for a game, find it in the checklist, make a check by it, and note the number beside it. This number will identify a particular game activity that is probably right for the youngster.

You may not always find on the checklist the exact behavior you are looking for, so look for one that seems similar. Don't expect to make a perfect match every time between your observation and a Learningame. Sometimes you may find that your child can play a game so well from the start that it bores her. Other times, you may find that a game is still too advanced for her. You can then go back to the table of contents or the checklist or thumb through the neighboring games in the book for a slightly harder or easier game.

How do I play the game?

Remember that for the young child, playing and learning can be the same thing. In playing, she's exercising her curiosity about the world. By helping her satisfy that curiosity and get enjoyment from learning, you are helping to build positive attitudes for that later time when she has much more learning to do on her own.

The first step is to read the game description. Notice that the goal of the game is always a goal for the adult. That is, we reach the goal of the game by doing something with our behavior—not the child's. We hope the child will respond in a particular way, but we can't be sure, and we have no right to insist on it (or any reason to be disappointed if she doesn't).

After you have gathered whatever materials are needed for a particular game, sit down with your child and enjoy. There is no pressure for the child to do these games in a hurry or to get them exactly "right." Usually, you begin by showing her something and then letting her take over. Give her lots of chances to experiment with the activity.

The experience may last only a minute or two, or if the child enjoys the game, she may want to go at it longer than you would prefer. If you begin to tire of it, perhaps you can introduce a new element into the game. But remember, she's enjoying success, and that's one reason she likes to repeat it. If she doesn't catch on to the game right away or gets fussy, give her a little extra help. Or reach a good stopping place and change the game to something you know she can do. It's important to let her get plenty of fun out of your time together; she can always come back some other time to the game that didn't go well.

When and where can I use the games?

The games are varied so that, with a little common sense, some of them can be used just about anytime and anywhere. Some of the language games are good to use when you are driving in the car or doing household chores. A few of the games the child can play alone, if you have gotten ready the things she needs. Other games require that you and the child give your full attention to each other, and some you can play with a small group of children.

Keep in mind that some games require you to have simple materials on hand when you start to play. This takes only the same foresight as making sure you have all the ingredients before you begin to prepare a recipe. The materials are usually in italic print on the left-hand page so you can locate them at a glance. Some of the games tell you when they are best used, but most are flexible enough that deciding when and where is really up to you.

Should I stick to the letter of each game, or can I make changes?

The most important part of these Learningames is you. Your observations should be your best guide to choosing games, and to varying them to keep your child's interest. The game description puts you in the ball park, but you call the plays.

Do these games have any side effects?

Yes. Both adult and child learn to work and play as a team and to have fun doing it. The adults sharpen their ability to take note of needs and to contribute to the growth of the child as her teacher. The adults become more aware of the importance of their role in the child's future. And they develop feelings for the child—especially respect—that are deepened by the game interactions. In addition to her new skills, the youngster gains confidence in herself and in adults. She learns that people are responsive and helpful and that her actions have a predictable effect on the exciting physical world around her. She continues to build a curiosity and persistence that make her unafraid of new challenges.

The child approaches kindergarten having had experience in cooperating with playmates, following directions, answering questions, listening for letter sounds, solving problems, and using art materials. Such a background makes the demands of school seem familiar and manageable. And gaining this experience will have been enjoyable for both the adult and the preschool child.

In both volumes of Learningames, a lot of attention has been given to needs and feelings. Parents today are sensing how important it is for the child to accept and understand her own feelings. Indeed, a recent national survey* found that a positive self-image (feeling confident and good about oneself) was the thing most desired by parents for their children. For these parents and other adults, the Learningames can provide ways to help the child to make choices, name her feelings, notice and understand others' feelings, see herself as a unique individual, define her own progress, and express freely her likes and dislikes. As time passes the child necessarily spends more and more time away from her parents and familiar caregivers. The child's security in her own ability to function well in these situations will have been strengthened by the time spent in the loving, learning activity of the Learningames.

---

*Sparling, J., and Lowman, B. Parent information needs as revealed through interests, problems, attitudes, and preferences. In *Parent Education and Public Policy*, by R. Haskins (ed.), Norwood, N.J.: Ablex, 1983.

LEARNINGAMES
for
THREES AND FOURS

36–42 Months

The young three-year-old has good control of the large muscles of his arms and legs. Now that he's walking really well, he tries to perfect many variations of this means of locomotion, such as skipping, hopping on one foot, and walking a balance beam. In the first half of the year as his coordination improves, he begins to enjoy activities that use equipment. Jungle gyms, tricycles, and balls become important to his play.

As his play expands, the words you say to him naturally become more explicit. A word like "up" used to be sufficient as a direction, but now you find you're using phrases such as "up higher than." The child is beginning to practice subtle differences in language, too. For example, he no longer uses the word "no" only as a refusal. He uses it in negative concepts, such as "Can't find it." He is beginning to use a variety of kinds of sentences. He asks simple questions: "Can I go?"

Most of this early language is learned from the family. But another group of behaviors will be learned from outside, from society. Children of ages three to four usually like to play with others. Perhaps because of this, and the fact that their attention span is longer, many children begin regular group experiences now. Often this is the first time the child has had the opportunity to learn social concepts different from those of his family. A desire for these broader experiences may even be a major reason for enrolling him in a preschool group now. Some families find, however, that their child is learning a few ideas and behaviors they cannot approve of. They will need to stay calm and take time to decide which unacceptable ideas to make an issue of (by correcting them), which to ignore (until they lose their shock value and go away from lack of reinforcement), and which they should just laugh about.

Parents would indeed be wise to begin thinking before they enroll their child in a group about how they plan to react when he comes home with statements like, "Boys don't cook" or, "I fell and hurt my damn knee." They must become comfortable with their own feelings about these things before they can help the child deal with them.

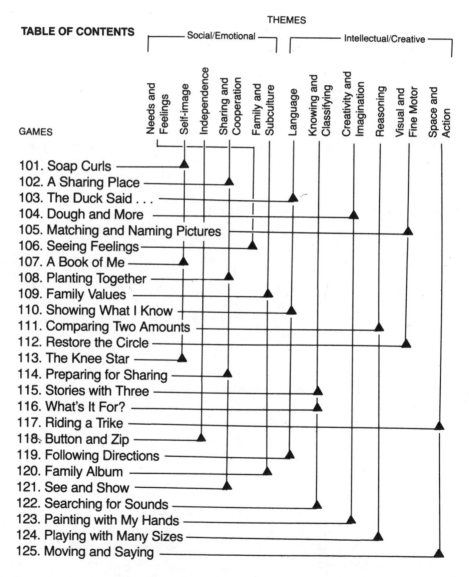
2

Checklist: 36–42 Months
(Developmental Age)

NEW BEHAVIORS	SUGGESTED GAMES	NEW BEHAVIORS	SUGGESTED GAMES
☐ Takes a shampoo willingly	101	☐ Pays attention to another child who is playing nearby	114
☐ Says a few words when showing something	102	☐ Holds up fingers to show age	115
☐ Mouths some familiar words as they are read	103	☐ Names pictures of common items	116
☐ Shows an interest in mud play	104	☐ Knows a number of directional words	117
☐ Recognizes some road signs and trademarks	105	☐ Puts on most clothing; has difficulty with fasteners	118
☐ Recognizes some of his own basic feelings	106	☐ Follows instructions containing one step	119
☐ Has a variety of favorites	107	☐ Maintains interest in a project for several days	120
☐ Is interested in doing things with others	108		
☐ Understands the idea of preparation	109	☐ Follows two-step instructions	121
☐ Says at least 200 words but understands many more	110	☐ Comments about environmental sounds	122
☐ Recognizes words such as "big" and "little"	111	☐ Scribbles with controlled movements	123
☐ Sees differences in squares, circles, triangles	112	☐ With two objects, identifies which is larger	124
☐ Recognizes the names of some body parts	113	☐ Follows a simple obstacle course	125

101. Soap Curls

HOW ADULT: Your child can get a little more out of a shampoo than clean hair. Make the *lather* especially thick and let her sit in front of a *mirror*. Then shape the lather to let the child see herself in several "new hair styles." Pull everything up to a tall peak and step back to let her inspect the results. Watch to see how she responds, and take your cue from her. If her expression is serious, say something mysterious like, "It makes you look like a moon princess." If her expression is humorous, join the amusement with something like, "What funny, tall hair you have!" □ Continue by creating many hair shapes or adding a beard or side burns. Pause after each for an inspection. The child is getting used to seeing herself in new, often startling, ways, so give her as much time as she needs. She may have special interest in one of the styles and want to touch it or keep it for a while. This might be an occasion to show the child how to hold a second, smaller mirror in order to see the back of her head. It's a tricky business so don't expect instant success. □ The soap curls game will be played mainly by the parent. But occasionally a caregiver may play when the parent agrees. □ After the shampoo is all rinsed away be sure to give her a special hug and let her know, "The suds were fun, but it's you I love."

CHILD: Both boys and girls like to see the unusual shapes their sudsy hair can make. They may just stare quietly at themselves or break out laughing—sometimes switching from one to the other in the same play session. The child will enjoy coming back to this activity and may, in fact, ask to have a shampoo just to see the soap curls.

WHY GOAL: To give the child a new reason for looking at herself in the mirror. To laugh a little.

USES: We all have a visual image of ourselves that both stays the same and changes throughout our lives. Experiences such as this game are useful to help make the child comfortable and familiar with her image even while some details (such as hair) change.

4

101. Soap Curls

HOW Make the child's shampoo lather into some shapes: a tall peak, wide butterfly wings, bug buns over the ears, a Santa beard. After each let the child decide what she thinks about herself as she looks in the mirror. Match your response to hers. She may be anything from a dignified princess to a silly giggler.

WHY To let the child see herself in some new ways.

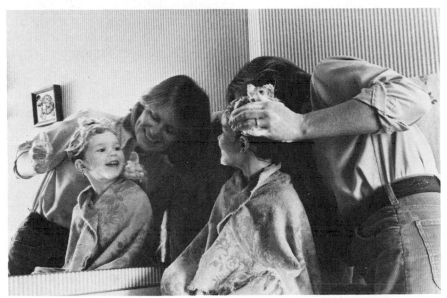

102. A Sharing Place

HOW ADULT: A three-year-old likes to share. The adult can encourage and expand this pleasant behavior by providing a family sharing place. It will need two things: a flat surface for laying things on and an upright surface for hanging things up. And it must, of course, be low enough for the child to reach and see easily. A *low box* or *shelf* with a *cork board* or *cloth* hanging behind it will be fine. □ The adult puts on the sharing place something he wishes to share with the child. When the child has a minute he draws her attention to it. "Look, Anna, here is a letter. See the stamp? It's from Grandmother. She sent us a new picture." After a few minutes of looking, they pin the picture on the cloth. He asks, "When Mommy comes home would you like to tell her it's here?" He may need to prompt a little but the child will be able to share it with Mommy. □ When the child has an object or drawing she's showing, the adult might first thank her for sharing it with him and then suggest it be displayed on the sharing place. She will be able to share it with Mommy. □ When the child has an object or drawing she's showing, the adult might first thank her for sharing it with him and then suggest it be displayed on the sharing place. She will be able to use a few words to tell about it when someone else notices and asks about it. □ Children in preschool or in group care can have a similiar sharing place. In that situation, perhaps the adult will want to take a more active role in arranging a chance for the children to use the sharing place.

CHILD: The child may have only a brief interest in the early days. But she will feel good about the time spent together in talking about the object. Later she will begin to remember for a day or so the story of the object. She will sometimes handle the objects in passing or maybe even ask a question to remind herself. Gradually she will begin to contribute things to the sharing place.

WHY GOAL: To encourage sharing behavior by providing a convenient place for the child and others to display things they want to share. To talk together about the things.

USES: Words will become the principal way of sharing as the child grows and her experiences occur in many environments. She will not be able to take home the spaces and experiences but can share them through her words, drawings, and later even with her own letters and snapshots.

102. A Sharing Place

HOW Make a place to put objects the family wants to share with each other. Have a low flat space for laying things on. And behind it have a surface for hanging things up. Take time to look at the child's memento. Thank her for sharing it with you. Leave some interesting object there you want to share with her.

WHY To provide a place for everyone to put things they want to share.

103. The Duck Said . . .

HOW ADULT: When you read stories aloud to children they hear many new words used in many different ways. In this story game you give the child a chance to say words also. Choose a familiar story, such as *The Little Red Hen*, which has repeated situations and repeated words. As you read let him say the repetitive lines. For example, when the Hen asks who will plant the wheat, you can read, "The Duck said . . ." Then, let him fill in the words, "Not I." You read, "The Cat said . . ." Again he says, "Not I." Another time you read the answer and have him fill in the name of the animal. □ When he's very familiar with the story leave out a word that shows the sequence of the story. Read, "Who will help me . . . this wheat." He will need to choose from several words (plant, water, cut, eat) remembering what has already happened. Stay tuned to his interest and don't pause so often that the story gets lost. □ For three-year-olds choose funny stories that have repeated noises and sounds. And if you choose books with big pictures and only a few words on each page the child will be able to "read" these alone later. Stories about animals, or machines that act like people, or stories about families and other familiar things and situations, usually provide good opportunities for children to chime in.

CHILD: The child who has been read to a lot is probably already saying a word or two with the reader while listening to a familiar story. In this game, he may find that naming the animals a little more difficult than just saying "Not I." He has to remember both the name and the right order. He enjoys the sound of a "big" word sometimes, even though he has no idea of its meaning. He seems to be rolling it around, trying it out for sound. The combined pleasures of the adult's attention and lap, and hearing the story make reading one of the favorite activities for this age child.

WHY GOAL: To increase the child's understanding, memory, and use of words. To provide experiences that will help him learn to love reading.

USES: Completing or filling in a familiar statement is an easy way to use words correctly. Our culture often judges the competency of an individual by the way he uses words.

103. The Duck Said . . .

HOW Read *The Little Red Hen* to your child. Let him fill in some words. You say, "The Duck said . . ." The child says, "Not I." Look for other words in the story the child can "read." Find other stories where words or noises are repeated. You'll enjoy reading them with his help.

WHY To encourage the child to use words by filling in blanks in a familiar story.

104. Dough and More

HOW ADULT: Give the youngsters some opportunities to press and mold some soft materials without too much direction. Outdoors help the children dampen a clay or dirt area that will make good *mud*. The adult needs to do nothing but watch the fun, after making sure the kids are wearing old clothes that are less important than the learning experience. (Hopefully she can choose a time for the mud activity when a little messiness doesn't matter.) □ For a more extended, indoor experience, give each child a lump of *play dough*. You may again observe the children experiment to find out all the things the dough will do. Your occasional comments can add descriptions to their creativity. "You've made something flat and round." "What a long coil!" "You pushed your thumb all the way through the middle." □ After many sessions with the dough the children's interest may begin to wane. Renew their interest by making available some tools to press or shape the play dough. Good tools include popsicle sticks, sea shells, and pipe cleaners. □ Below is a recipe for a play dough which will retain its softness for several weeks.

2 cups flour	2 cups water
1 cup salt	1 tablespoon cooking oil
2 teaspoons cream of tartar	food coloring

Cook over low heat, stirring until it forms into one big ball. Put the ball on a board and knead for 2 or 3 minutes. Store in an airtight container between play sessions.

CHILD: Most children will confidently shape the dough or mud. A few will be concerned about cleanliness. But having the adult's aid and approval will soon have them enjoying this most natural activity.

WHY GOAL: To provide materials that will enable the child to learn how three-dimensional shapes are formed.

USES: Experiences gained directly through the fingers leave us with a special and lasting awareness of our physical world. Early art explorations can give us confidence for later creative expressions.

104. Dough and More

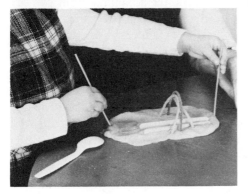

HOW Give the children something to mold and explore with their hands. Outdoors let them explore mud; indoors let them explore homemade play dough. You don't need to give them any direction, but when they shape something, describe it. Later, renew their enjoyment by giving them some popsicle sticks and other tools to use with the dough.

WHY To give the child a chance to mold and shape something.

105. Matching and Naming Pictures

HOW ADULT: Play a game in which the child matches some pictures using visual clues and then hears the adult say the name of the matched pictures. You will need *two identical copies of ten or more pictures*. These could be lotto cards, old maid cards, or pictures cut from two same-month copies of a magazine. Place four picture cards (two of them identical) face up in front of the child. Invite the child to find the two that are the same. (He may either point to or pick up the cards.) If he immediately finds the correct ones, congratulate him and say, "Yes these two are just alike." Then, help build the child's vocabulary by labeling the matched pictures, "These are called tomatoes." □ Do not bother to label the other pictures. They will be labeled in future turns. When you are finished with that set of pictures, they can be shuffled back into the rest and four more chosen for the next turn. □ After you've played the game enough times that the child no longer hesitates in finding each pair, let the child do the labeling. When he finds a pair, ask, "And what are these called?" If he can't think of the word (for example, banana) you might say, "Is it a bana____?" If this hint doesn't help you might say, "You know what it looks like to me? It looks like a banana. Can *you* say banana?" Congratulate him when he does. □ Keep the game cheerful and lively as the child identifies each pair of pictures. For each pair he names, hand him the two to keep in "his" pile. At the end of the game all the pictures will be his and you will have none.

CHILD: From a three-year-old point of view, handling of the cards or pictures may seem like a "grown-up" thing to do, and he will probably take it quite seriously. His ability to recognize and match will be well ahead of his ability to say the names of pictures.

WHY GOAL: To give the child a chance to look at pictures carefully and to recognize those that are alike. To let the child first hear and then say the names of pictures he recognizes.

USES: We get information from two-dimensional pictures and print throughout our lives. In the early years we need lots of practice with recognizing the flat forms and linking them up with ideas and language.

105. Matching and Naming Pictures

HOW Put four pictures (two of them alike) in front of the child. Ask him to find the two that are the same. When he does, praise him and then give the name for the matched pictures. When he's good at matching the pictures, let him be the one to say the name. The child may win the pairs that he matches and names. In the end he will be proud to have them all.

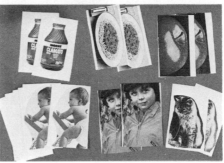

WHY To help the child look at, recognize, and finally, name pictures.

106. Seeing Feelings

HOW ADULT: For some time now you've probably been talking to the child about his feelings and about your own. The next step is to talk about the feelings of other children. The parent can point out the feelings of neighborhood children, and the teacher can point out feelings of classmates in the day care center. □ When another child near your child displays a strong emotional expression, draw it to your child's attention. Lean down and say something like, "I think Matt looks very happy now, don't you?" That may be all of the conversation, or the two of you may talk for a moment about what made Matt so happy. Continue from time to time to point out feelings and to name them. If your child independently notices someone else's feelings, he deserves a compliment, such as, "You're paying good attention to other people. You know a lot about how they feel." □ It's especially helpful for the adult to comment on feelings that can be frightening to everyone. With your arm reassuringly around your child, explain, "Chris is so angry right now. That's called a tantrum. I think he will be over it soon." Sadness is not likely to be so threatening but it can be puzzling. You might try saying, "Harry looks kind of sad—with tears in his eyes. I wonder if that's because he dropped his cupcake. I think I'll see if he needs some help. Would you like to come with me?"

CHILD: Children "see" people around them expressing feelings. But they will need a lot of experience to accurately interpret them. Most children will not begin to use the names for other's emotions (happy, angry, sad) until the adult has used them for many months. Other names (joyous, suspicious, etc.) will take much longer. And just as with adults the child will sometimes interpret incorrectly but he's becoming aware.

WHY GOAL: To point out and name emotions when they occur in the child's peers. To help the child feel comfortable with frightening emotions in others.

USES: The better we can "read" the emotional state of the people around us, the more successfully we can interact. Recognizing another's emotion is one step in the difficult task of taking another's point of view.

106. Seeing Feelings

HOW Tell your child what feelings others are expressing. Point out the feeling when a nearby child is happy or angry or sad. If he's interested, help your child understand what caused the feelings he sees. You'll recognize his slowly increasing awareness of others' feelings as a sign of his maturity.

WHY To name the emotions the child sees.

107. A Book of Me

HOW ADULT: The child knows many individual facts about himself. Help him bring some of these together in an *album*. Begin with something like a favorite food. Suggest, "You like peaches so well. Let's save the *label* from this can of peaches." Put it aside. Both of you can continue to collect mementos that are special to the child. These might include a *leaf* from his favorite climbing tree, one of his scribble *drawings*, a *postcard* he received from Grandma, and the *dust cover* from his favorite book. □ When the two of you have a small collection of items, fasten together a dozen or so sheets of construction paper to make an album. On the cover you can add a title, such as "A Book About Edwin," and he might then trace around his hand for a decoration. Let him attach the mementos to the pages in any order or arrangement he likes. As you admire his handiwork talk about what each page tells you. Say, "Oh, this reminds me that your Grandma loves you and writes to you. And this shows how much you like to draw with your crayons." □ As the days go by add other things to the empty pages. Some can be *cutout magazine pictures* that show a favorite activity, a pet, or another food. As the album develops, make opportunities for him to show and explain it to other interested people, including his day care group.

CHILD: The child begins to recognize himself as a complex person. He will probably come back to the album many times to pore over it and ask, "What's that?" as he reviews the things. And he may surprise the adults with his level of concentration. He may not be able to tell a lot about it with words but he will enjoy showing it.

WHY GOAL: To help the child collect things that tell about himself. To let the child feel pride in himself.

USES: A rich, detailed image of himself is a source of confidence for the child.

107. A Book of Me

HOW With the child, save things that are special to him. They might be boxtops, pictures, or scraps of cloth, etc. Help him put them in a book. Give him chances to show the book to others. He will be telling them what his favorite foods, activities, and pets are. From the faces of the viewers the child will get the important message that he is an interesting person.

WHY To help the child tell about himself.

108. Planting Together

HOW ADULT: Choose a sunny windowsill to grow a family "garden" cooperatively. Each member of the family collects one type of item from the list of needed things: *seeds, potting soil,* a *pitcher* of water, styrofoam *cups,* and plastic snap *lids* to use as saucers. Then the items are shared all around. The person who has collected the cups passes one to each person, and so forth. When the cups are filled with potting soil and the seeds planted, each cup is marked by its planter so it's easy to recognize. □ Choose seeds that sprout and grow quickly. Green peas, or almost any kind of bean, are good. Explain to the child that once the seed is in the ground it must be left to grow. Talk about three things the plant will need: soil, light, and water. □ When the seeds are planted, work out a simple schedule for watering. A paper with one (or two) names for each day's watering can be kept near the window. Watering in pairs allows the child to participate more often. Each day the names can be checked off when the responsibility is complete. Say what happened: "You watered the plants in your turn. When we all remember our turn, the plants get what they need to grow." □ With cooperation and some luck the plants will grow big enough to need *sticks* to climb. The family can then have a "stick planting" session. □ Friendly competition creates a sustained interest in what is happening to the seeds. Only the simplest explanations need be given for questions about how the plants in "our" garden grow.

CHILD: The young three-year-old cooperates by imitating and repeating what is demonstrated. Though peas grow very quickly, before the sprout appears, a child may want to dig up the seeds to see how they're growing. But, since the rest of the family is waiting too, the child will manage to wait. The child is not aware of a great cooperative effort, just of having fun with the family.

WHY GOAL: To use the child's curiosity to develop interest in a cooperative family project.

USES: Doing things together is an early form of cooperation. The child is learning to be a follower, a contributor, and a partner: all of which are roles frequently played in school and later in adult life.

108. Planting Together

HOW Someone collects a styrofoam cup for each member of the family. Others collect the remaining items needed for planting. Each person can then fill her own cup with soil and plant a pea in it. Put the cups in a window and all can take turns watering the seeds. Talk about how everyone worked together to make the window garden grow.

WHY To give the child a chance to cooperate in growing a windowsill garden.

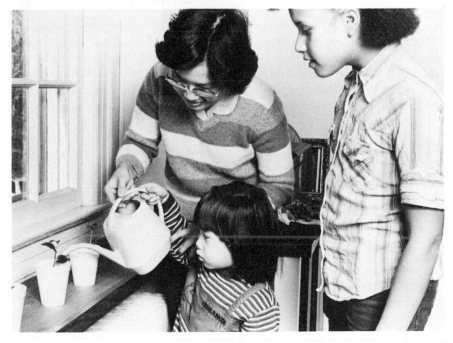

109. Family Values

HOW ADULT: Include your children in plans and events that convey the family's values. For example, when you feed birds let three-year-olds use their hands to mix the *seeds* you've poured in a *large container*. Talk to them about big and little seeds for big and little birds. Give the youngsters a spoonful of *peanut butter* to mix with some seeds. Have them tuck pinches of the mixture into *pine cones* and twist *cord* around them to hang for the birds to eat. Or make a ball of the mixture and tie into the corner of a mesh *fruit bag*. □ Later, when you fill the feeder box, the three-year-old can fill the *scoop* with seeds and hand it up to you or choose the branch for you to tie the peanut-butter-and-seed balls to. Say things like, "I know the birds are going to be happy to get these seeds. I can't see many seeds on these bushes for them. Can you?" □ When you are finished feeding, spend a few quiet minutes watching and sharing the sights. "That bright red one is called a cardinal." "See the spry little hops the brown one makes?" □ You and your child can share with the play group your concern for other creatures. Volunteer to help the group make peanut butter and seed balls, or to show the caregiver how. You might help the children make a shrub or tree in the play yard into a bird-tree with the cones and bags. Or use a Christmas tree when it's time to take it down. □ Think what parts your child might play in other valued family activities.

CHILD: The children won't remember all the bird lore right now, but they will understand that they are a part of something the family thinks is important. Mixing the seed is even more fun than sand play. Having a specific job like filling the scoop lets the child feel needed. It will be very satisfying to the children to watch the birds eating the seeds they've supplied. Soon they will be surprising the adults with a reminder that the feeder's empty.

WHY GOAL: To include the young child in activities or hobbies that the family feels have value in their culture.

USES: Children will value those things that make them feel good. They are likely to gain more understanding of why the family values an activity if they participate in it.

109. Family Values

HOW Show children they are important members of the family. Let them be involved in valued family activities. For example, if you feed birds let the children help get the food to the birds. Watch together as the birds eat it. Talk with the children of the pleasure it gives you. Help them find ways to share such family activities with their play group.

WHY To let the child act out family values.

110. Showing What I Know

HOW ADULT: This game will give the young child a chance to proudly show you some of the many words she understands but cannot yet say. When you'd like to have a pleasant time together, say, "Let's sit down with a book so you can show me all the things you're learning." Then thumb through a *household magazine* or a *children's book,* pausing on pages that interest you both. The adult's job is to ask questions that will let the child demonstrate her knowledge—especially knowledge that goes beyond her current spoken vocabulary. The child's job is to think and to point. □ Ask questions that you feel she can answer. If there are only one or two pictures on the page, her task will be easier. If there are many pictures it will be harder. Here are the kinds of things you might say:

> Point to the spaghetti.
> Show me the frog.
> Put your finger on the open window.
> Point to the monkey's toes.
> Which one is the grandmother?
> Show me something to wear.
> Point to a thing that's round.
> Can you find something that goes fast?

□ When you come to something that you know the child is able to say, let her give its name and ask you to point.

CHILD: Sitting in your lap, a child or two can have a quiet, secure time as they confidently answer questions by pointing. They will especially enjoy going through the grown-up's magazines and finding that they recognize many of the pictures.

WHY GOAL: To let the child practice using her ability to understand words. To use books in a comfortable adult-child partnership.

USES: All of us understand more words than we actually use in our speech. This gives us a big "cushion" for understanding conversation. This game can help children be aware of all of the unexpressed knowledge inside themselves.

110. Showing What I Know

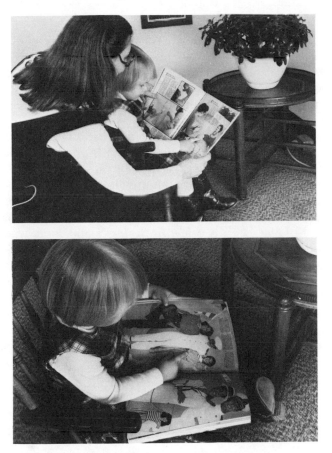

HOW Thumb through a magazine with the child. On a page with several pictured items, name one and invite the child to point to it. This can be a cozy time together while she shows you how many words she understands.

WHY To let the child practice hearing and understanding words.

111. Comparing Two Amounts

HOW ADULT: When the child intentionally or accidentally divides her *play dough*, say, "You made this into two different parts. Look, this ball has more play dough and this ball has less." Then move the two balls around and say, "Point to the one that has more. Point to the one that has less. Good! I couldn't fool you." □ Continue the game by pressing the dough back together and then making a new ball from part of it. Suggest, "This can be the ball with more dough. Could you make one with less? How much dough do you need?" When she finishes, label each as having more or less. Then change their positions and ask the child to label them. Pointing, say, "How much does this one have? How much does this other one have?" If the child doesn't use the word, help her as much as necessary. □ Later, with two *identical glasses* and some water you can continue to work on the concepts and words for "more" and "less." Let the child move through several levels of understanding as you did with the play dough: 1) The child (accidentally?) makes unequal parts, the adult labels them, and the child demonstrates her understanding by pointing as asked. 2) The adult makes a new model, and the child makes one of a different amount as requested. 3) The adult reviews the labels, and the child finally says the labels as requested. This is a nice plan for the adult to have in his or her head, but for the child we can make the whole thing a relaxed time of messing around with some interesting materials.

CHILD: Children are born manipulators. Given things that can be grouped or divided or poured, they will begin acting on them.

WHY GOAL: To let the child create some amounts that she can then describe with words such as "more" or "less."

USES: Recognizing the difference in two amounts is the basis for almost all math concepts that will follow. For example, this skill is necessary before game 124 makes much sense.

111. Comparing Two Amounts

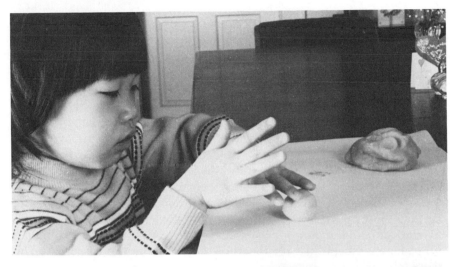

HOW Give the child something to play with (such as play dough or water) that can be divided into two parts. Label the amounts she creates. Use the words "more" and "less." The child first shows that she understands these words by pointing to the amount you name. Later, you point and the child says the words. It's a pleasant experience for the adult to see these words and concepts being fixed in the child's mind.

WHY To let the child experience and talk about amounts and sizes.

112. Restore the Circle

HOW ADULT: Sharpen the child's understanding of the differences in shapes. Cut out some large (typing paper size) *circles*. When the child is finishing a game at her play table, sit down with her and invite her to play something new for a minute. Show her the circle. Tell her, "This is a circle. See, it goes around like a circle's supposed to do." Hold the shape up and let her run her finger around the whole edge. Lay it on the table and let her piggyback her finger on yours as you trace around it. Both of you can find words like "moon," "ball," and "circle" to talk about it. □ Tell her you're going to play tricks on the circle. Cut the paper in half. Show her that it's no longer a circle but point out that the curves are still there. Ask her, "Can you make it a circle again?" When she fits it together, repeat the earlier tracings and tell her, "You made it a circle again." □ Another time cut a smaller segment off the circle and later cut out a pie shaped piece. Keep the game short and don't try to make more of it than just a minute of learning fun with circles. □ Other shapes such as *triangles* and *squares* are harder to restore. But if the child is immediately successful with the circle, it might be fun to move on to these others.

CHILD: The child will be participating in a moment of interesting play with the adult and will enjoy that. She will also be pleased to restore the circle to its original shape and may show it by clapping for her own achievement. She will use the word "circle" as a natural part of her game.

WHY GOAL: To help the child recognize that actions such as dividing a circle can be reversed. To help the child use words for shapes in a meaningful way.

USES: Being able to visualize the whole from its parts is necessary for many things the child will do. Letters and numbers are typically made from parts such as lines and circles.

112. Restore the Circle

HOW Take a minute to play a "magic" game with the child. Show her a large paper circle. Have her trace the edge with her finger. Think of words like "ball" and "moon" to say. Cut the paper in half. She will be pleased when she's fitted it into a circle again.

WHY To help her see the shape of a circle can be restored after it's divided.

113. The Knee Star

HOW ADULT: Play a quick review game to find out which body parts your child doesn't know. Say, "Touch your neck; touch your elbow; touch your ankle; etc." Then teach one of the parts the child is not aware of. If you decide to teach "knee," make it clear where the knee is by putting a *stick-on star* on it. While the child is wearing the star, refer to knees often. Say, "I see that you're bending your knees." Or, "Your knees are under the table when you sit in that chair." At the end of the day check the child's understanding. Say, "Put your hands on your knees." For some children you might ask for words, saying, "What is your star on?" □ Continue teaching as many parts as you think are appropriate for the child. Think about some that are not used every day and so may be a little more difficult, such as shin, knuckle, and sole. □ Find an interesting way to mark each one you teach. Stickers are best for some, but for wrist and ankle a loose *rubber band* is a clearer marker. For larger parts a line or a circle drawn with *washable paint* or *lipstick* may be best. □ Each time a new part is learned, go back and check all the ones taught earlier. Soon you'll be able to say with justifiable pride, "You know so many parts of your body!"

CHILD: Most children learn to recognize words such as nose, eye, tummy, hand, or foot very early in the first year of life. However, their progress is not entirely predictable from there. That may be because adults use so many overlapping and confusing names for the body. And they don't take time to sort the names out for the child. When someone makes them clear, the child will learn to recognize the names, and later to say them.

WHY GOAL: To give the child some markers to help locate body parts and connect them with their names.

USES: Knowing the words for body parts helps the child understand when other people use them. Adults use the words frequently in instructions to children, such as "Hold your shoulders straight," or "Tilt your chin."

113. The Knee Star

HOW Put a stick-on star on a part of the body the child doesn't recognize when named. Talk about that part as the two of you go about your daily activities. Each day give a new body part the "special treatment." At the end of the day the child may proudly point to all the parts as you name them. You'll have the pleasure of giving praise.

WHY To help the child locate body parts and recognize their names.

114. Preparing for Sharing

HOW ADULT: No one expects the three-year-old child to be an expert at sharing. But, neither is he totally self-centered. He's begun the slow process of learning that things go better if you think about others as well as yourself. That process will continue into adulthood. For right now, here are a few things that you can do to help with the first faltering steps of sharing:

INDOORS	Arrange a special play corner where children can play together. Two is a good number of children at first. Later, the number might go up to four. Have some *duplicate toys* in the space, so sharing won't always be an issue. Have some toys like *puppets* or *blocks* that stimulate interaction between children.
OUTDOORS	Put out some toys such as *wagons* so one child can pull while another rides. Put out some *short ropes* that can be used for a game of "horsie" with one child being the horse and the other the driver. Attach some rope handles to each side of a large *cardboard box* so two children can carry it.
TIMED TRADING	If there is a problem knowing when to trade toys, put out an *egg timer* or a portable *oven timer* with a bell. The adult can start the timer at first to determine the length of turns. Soon the children will use it themselves.

Don't expect lots of sharing or cooperation, even after making all these arrangements. But when it does happen, show your pleasure by describing the event. "Ed, you hopped right out of the wagon and gave Josh a turn before he even said he was tired of pulling. You boys must feel happy to have such good friends."

CHILD: Progress toward sharing is neither steady nor sure. Two children may do something loving and thoughtful for each other and five minutes later be fighting over a toy. This simply means that the skill is not yet firmly established. But it will slowly increase in frequency and the fighting will decrease—if these values are communicated to the children.

WHY GOAL: To arrange a play space that will make sharing and cooperation more likely. To compliment children for their early efforts at taking turns and trading.

USES: From home, to day care, to school, to college, to work—all these times of life involve getting along with other people. Good social skills help the individual move smoothly into each new situation.

114. Preparing for Sharing

HOW Put out some toys such as puppets and wagons that make more sense if they are shared by two children. Give a sincere compliment when you see them getting along well together. If they have trouble deciding when to trade or take turns, give them an egg timer as a guide.

WHY To give toys and to say things that encourage sharing.

115. Stories with Three

HOW ADULT: Now is the time to encourage the child to talk about and fully experience a special number: three. After all, she's three years old and is interested in that number. But it will take a lot of experience before she fully understands the concept of three. ☐ You can repeatedly bring the number to the child's attention by telling or reading stories with threes. Fortunately, there are many of these, including such classics as *The Three Bears, The Three Little Pigs,* and *The Three Billy Goats Gruff.* (In addition there are stories with three wishes, three tasks, or three fairies, etc.) As you get out the book, emphasize the number three in the title, "Let's read the story of the **Three** Bears. Look, here are their pictures: one, two, three." During the story when you come to the bowls, or chairs, or beds, you or the child could count them. ☐ When the story is over it might be useful to get out some counters (such as poker chips, blocks, or clothes pins) and practice handling some groups of three. Say, "Count out some more blocks to show how many bears there were. Yes! Let's put that group over here. Now can you count out some more blocks to show how many bowls there were?" All this practice will eventually help the child learn that "three" is an idea that is not limited to story bears and beds but can be used to describe all sorts of items.

CHILD: The young child is proud of being three years old. She may hold up three fingers when asked about her age. She will probably enjoy all the emphasis these stories give to "her" special number. If the stories are used in a day care center perhaps three children will be listening. If so, they may want to pretend to be the Bears and to count themselves. Perhaps they could also count their three chairs, cots, etc.

WHY GOAL: To strengthen the child's concept of three by telling traditional stories that are built around the number three.

USES: Numbers help us think abstractly. We use numbers with money, time, and other things that are measured in quantity.

115. Stories with Three

HOW When you read, often choose stories with threes. Stop and let the child count items that come in threes; "Here are the Bears' chairs: one, two three." Afterward, sometimes have the child think about parts of the story by using counters. Ask, "Can you count out some blocks to show me how many Bears there were?"

WHY To let the child hear the number three in stories.

116. What's It For?

HOW ADULT: In this game the child will try to decide what lots of familiar things are used for. These may be *real objects, cutout pictures,* or a combination of both. Spread out about ten things and/or pictures and say, "Some of these are things we can wear. Let's find out which ones." Let the child examine each one while you ask some questions and make comments. The very young child may not be able to say the names of all the items, but he can answer "yes" or "no" to your question, "Is this something to wear?" Confirm his answer by saying something like, "You're right, I can't imagine anyone wearing a crayon! Let's put that over here in the pile of things you can't wear." If the child's answer is "yes" to the next item, elaborate with a comment such as, "Yes, that's a cap and you can wear it on your head. Let's put it in the pile of things to wear." Continue until all the items are classified. ☐ Sometimes it's rather fun to wonder if certain items could be used in another way. The child may want to try wearing a book on his head before concluding it's not really for wearing. Take time to enjoy the humor of these things. ☐ On another day change some of the items, and one by one ask if each is "something we can use to help us eat" (for example: *spoon, straw, cup, chopsticks, knife*). And on yet another day sort items into groups of "things we ride" and "things we can't ride." By guiding the child to focus on items one at a time, you are showing him how to deal with big tasks slowly and systematically.

CHILD: The child may pick over the items, choosing first the ones that are most attractive to him. Most children will want to hold or touch the item they are considering. This should be encouraged. For children who need a little more action in the game, it might help to have the separate piles at opposite ends of the table. Then, when he classifies an item, the child can get up to place it where it belongs or at least stretch to reach the pile.

WHY GOAL: To give the child practice in thinking about categories and hearing the names of categories that tell the functions of objects.

USES: Classification into groups is one way to organize our knowledge.

116. What's It For?

HOW With the child, look at some things and/or pictures. For each one ask, "Is this something to wear?" Let the child decide. Then he can place the item in one of two piles: "things to wear" and "things you can't wear." Later, with another set of pictures, let the child decide which ones are "things we ride."

WHY To help the child group objects by thinking about what each one is for.

"Which ones are things to wear?"

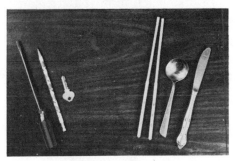

"Which ones can we use to help us eat?"

117. Riding a Trike

HOW ADULT: A *tricycle* can provide the child with a new way of getting about. It is quite different from anything he has used before. He must simultaneously provide the power to move, turn, and make decisions about using the brakes while riding something that often moves faster than he can walk. And when he fails to do any one of these things right, he can be hurt. □ The adult helps by giving him special words to understand what's happening.

for direction:	turn, ahead, path, guide
for movement:	slow, fast, stop, go
for tricycle:	pedal, handlebars, wheels, seat

The adult uses these to help the child control his own actions by saying, for example, "The path between the chairs isn't wide enough for your wheels to go through," or, "When you're ready to make that turn you'll need to slow down." Some special words, such as "stop" and "go," might make nice *signs* for the riding area. □ At this age trike riding is not a group activity. The adult supervises closely each child who is beginning to ride and allows time for each to learn full control. Only after he gains such skill should he pedal with another in the same space.

CHILD: Not all children are interested in riding yet. But if a safe, right-size trike is left in the child's play space, he may play with it as a non-riding toy for a while. He may turn it upside down and spin the wheels or pedal with his hands to make the big wheel turn. Later he will climb on the seat and, turning the handlebars a little back and forth, pretend to ride. Allowed his own schedule, he will begin to move about on the trike. Learning words for controlling could help him avoid the hurts that might discourage him.

WHY GOAL: To give the child a chance for a new physical activity that allows him to move his body through space in a new way. To protect him while he gains control.

USES: The child lives in a culture that moves on wheels. He will need to know how to operate vehicles. Learning, understanding, and respecting the rules that produce safe driving habits could begin with tricycle riding and may be the start of an attitude toward safety that is responsible for saving his life when he drives a car.

36

117. Riding a Trike

HOW Choose the right time and right tricycle for the child to ride. Give him new words for this new experience. Talk about "slow," "fast," "ahead," "turn," "pedal," "guide," and "path." Stay with him and don't ask him to share the experience with friends just yet. This will show him how special his new learning is.

WHY To help the child learn to ride a tricycle in a safe situation.

118. Button and Zip

HOW   ADULT: Independent dressing means mastering the fasteners. Give your cleaning smock to your child for a lesson in buttoning. Show her the big *buttons* and the *buttonholes*. Explain it's the job of the button to go through the hole. Show her how to push the button halfway through the hole, then hold that part as she pulls the cloth over the other half. (Before you show her take a few minutes to refresh your own memory by buttoning something intentionally. You've been doing it without thinking for so long you probably don't really know how you do it.) Keep several things handy with easy buttons. Let her practice on a long car ride or waiting at the doctor's office. When she's ready, encourage her to button her own clothes. □ On your own jacket hold the bottom of the *zipper* while she pulls up the tab. Then have her try it on her jacket while you hold the bottom. Next she will be ready to hold and zip it by herself. □ Using her outgrown diaper *pins*, let her practice pinning two of Daddy's handkerchiefs together. When she's skillful, let her try it on her own shirt-front. □ Think carefully about what steps are necessary to master the skills involved in dressing. Observe her and see what she's ready for. Once she's been shown how, the rest is just practice. Or let her figure out how for herself—when it's possible and desirable. Your biggest job might be to control your own need to do it for her.

CHILD: "I'll do it myself" is the battle cry of this age. Children who are struggling to be independent are often unwilling to accept the help they need. They require understanding and patience from the adult while they practice. Sometimes a child doesn't seem to want to dress independently. If she's given just one small step to do and is praised for that effort before she's given assistance, she will very likely move step by slow step to independent dressing.

WHY   GOAL: To guide the child in learning to button, zip, and do the other skills that are needed for dressing. To make dressing herself a good thing to do.

USES: Independence in self-care is desirable social behavior. By learning the more difficult steps like buttoning and zipping, she will be able to take care of her own dressing whether at home or in school.

118. Button and Zip

HOW Give the child a piece of clothing with big buttons and buttonholes. Let her practice buttoning and unbuttoning. Show her how to zip your jacket as you hold the bottom of the zipper. Let her practice on her own zippers. She will be able to dress herself when she learns the hard parts. And you'll be as happy as she is when she says, "I dressed myself."

WHY To lead the child through the steps of buttoning and zipping.

119. Following Directions

ADULT: Use this game over a long period of time, perhaps a year or more, to give the child an opportunity to practice following directions in many situations. Begin with directions that ask for two actions, but increase the number of steps in the directions to three or more as the child shows she can handle them. Spread your requests throughout the day. □ Some of the directions can help the child accomplish ordinary chores. "Please find your boots and then put them in your cubbie." Others can have an element of surprise. "Look in the grocery bag, then take what you find there to the table for our snack." □ Many of your practice directions should refer to the objects that are common in school: *crayons, scissors, books, tables, chairs*. Have fun with the instructions even though they have the serious, direct purpose of helping the child prepare for school work. Here are a few ideas:

> Put some newspaper down before you begin to paint.
>
> When you get up, push your chair in.
>
> Take a book from the shelf, then go and sit where we can read a story.

CHILD: The child will enjoy pleasing you by following your directions. If she gets mixed up, it will be helpful if you repeat the full set of directions so she can get the whole idea rather than just a part.

WHY GOAL: To give some clear, multi-step directions that the child can follow.

USES: People follow verbal and written directions throughout their lives. The first place that will demand a lot of direction-following is kindergarten.

119. Following Directions

HOW Give some friendly directions that ask for two or more actions. Some of the directions can use things like paper, crayons, and books. These will help the child listen as she will need to do later in elementary school. "Good listening! You did both things I asked you. You didn't forget anything." Praise such as this makes it clear why you are pleased.

WHY To give the child practice in following directions.

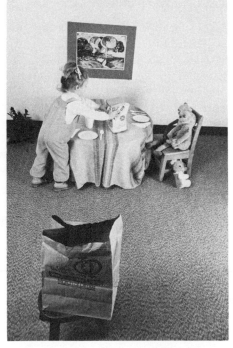

120. Family Album

HOW ADULT: Take a week or more to help the child create an album that tells something about her family. It can be about her natural family at home or about her day care or preschool "family." When it's finished, the album should contain a separate page for each member of the group—including any important animal members. Each page should begin with the name of the person (printed by you) and the person's *photograph*, glued or taped down by the child. ☐ Each day help the child think about one of the family members. Ask questions such as, "What is this person's favorite food? Favorite color? An activity he or she likes?" The child may not know the answer to some of the questions and may need to go and ask that family member. Using the answers, help her search through *magazines* to find pictures that illustrate the food, color, activity, etc. (A few children want to draw their own instead of using picture cutouts.) The child may attach the magazine pictures or her own drawings on the page with the appropriate family member photo. ☐ Build the story of the family, one member at a time, until all pages are completed. Then help the child fasten the pages together and decorate the *cover* of the album. ☐ You, the child, and other members of the family will spend many happy moments together "reading" this album—and perhaps adding to it.

CHILD: If the child has seen other photograph albums or scrapbooks, she will be glad to make one of her own. This is a fairly long project. The child may seem to forget about it between days, and the adult's enthusiasm and questions will probably renew her interest. When she's invited to she may explain her finished album to a visitor. You will be pleasantly surprised at how well-informed and talkative the album helps her be.

WHY GOAL: To let the child make an album that will help her think about the members of the family and what they do.

USES: It is helpful to summarize and record our knowledge on any topic. Usually we find that we know more than we had previously thought. A simple album can remind very young children of their substantial family knowledge and family ties.

120. Family Album

HOW Help the child attach photos of members of her family to individual sheets of paper. Each day let her think about one of the family members . . . their favorite food, favorite color, or typical activity. Help the child cut out pictures of these things. Put them on the page beside the photo. When all the pages have been put together, the opportunities for talking and pleasant sharing have just begun.

WHY To help the child think about the family by making an album.

121. See and Show

HOW ADULT: When several friends are together take one child aside and invite him to watch you do a straw painting. As you demonstrate, let him know that later he will have the important job of showing a friend how. Organize your instructions into three main parts, so they will be easy to remember. First, put your *painting paper* down on some *newspapers*. Second, pick up some paint in a drinking *straw* and drip it on your paper. (To do this dip the straw into a jar of *thin paint*, put your thumb tightly over the straw's top, move the straw over the paper and lift your thumb to release the paint.) Third, blow gently through the straw to scatter the paint around, making an interesting shape on the paper. □ Let the child enjoy making his straw painting immediately after your demonstration. When it's clear that he understands the process, decide with him who he'll show how to do a straw painting. Do a quick review with him. Ask, "Now what is the first thing you will show?" Continue to "talk through" the remaining steps. □ When the child tries his wings as a teacher, be near but "occupied" with another task. If the two of them call you over to see the new painting, you can praise the painter for his art and the teacher for his instruction. Naturally, the second child may now want to teach someone. Be sure to give that child the benefit of a verbal review before he starts. □ Other processes the child might "see and show" are making a peanut butter banana, or planting seeds in a garden.

CHILD: Young children are usually confident with art projects. Most will readily take on the responsibility of showing someone else. Some children will teach by showing or acting out the process while others will add words to the demonstration. Either way the child is accomplishing the main goal of this activity: sharing.

WHY GOAL: To demonstrate a process for the child so he can demonstrate it to a second child.

USES: As we grow, we often receive information and with it the responsibility of passing it along. The more accurately we transmit information, the more others trust us.

121. See and Show

HOW Privately show one child how to make a straw painting. When he's finished let him show another child how. He'll feel good that you trusted him to pass useful information along. You'll be glad that he's experiencing the mature pleasure that comes with helping someone else.

WHY To give the child a chance to share information.

1

2

3

4

5

6

122. Searching for Sounds

HOW ADULT: A surprising variety of sounds occur around the house or day care center. Make a game out of "finding" sounds and talking about them. Ask, "Are there any sounds hiding around here? Let's search and see if we can find some." □ Then walk around the room and stop near various objects while wondering aloud, "What kind of a sound could this make?" Encourage the children to experiment and find out. When they make a sound, describe it. If they hit a *pan* with a *spoon*, say, "Listen to the loud clang, clang, clang!" If they drop a plastic *toy* into the *sink*, say, "I hear a soft splash." □ After finding a half dozen or more sounds, help the child review them and classify each as either loud or soft. Suggest, "Let's think about the sounds that we just made and decide which ones were loud and which ones were soft. First we heard the sound the pan made. Was it loud or soft?" Continue through all the sounds—returning to listen again to any that the child can't remember or classify. □ On another day search for sounds outdoors. This time listen for sounds that occur by themselves, such as sounds from crickets or automobiles. Let the child find the sounds. You describe them. Be sure to praise the child for careful listening. Each day the sound search will be different, so you and the child will enjoy returning to it many times.

CHILD: The game may start slowly, but once the children catch on, they will enjoy making or finding a sound and then hurrying on to the next one. A group of children may scatter, as on a scavanger hunt!

WHY GOAL: To expose children to a variety of sounds so that they will recognize their labels and begin to classify them.

USES: Sounds are one of the elements of our environment. Knowing and classifying them is a part of the child's growing awareness of the world. Since sounds occur and are then gone, they demand a different kind of thinking than do objects that will remain in front of you.

122. Searching for Sounds

HOW Find various objects and see what kind of sound the child can make with each. Describe the sound as it is made. At the end of the game the adult can name the sounds one by one. The child can say whether each sound was loud or soft. Three-year-olds will do some careful listening. Praise them warmly for it.

WHY To let the child hear and classify sounds.

123. Painting with My Hands

HOW ADULT: Let the children get into some paint. Protect their clothes by taking off shirts or putting on smocks. Use *fingerpaint* directly on a formica or varnished wood *table top*. Dampen the table surface with a *sponge*. Then put a big spoonful of color in front of each child. Two or three can paint at opposite sides of a table. □ As the children move the paint around, stand back and enjoy yourself. The adult's role is to notice what happens and to draw the child's attention to something that happened. You might say, "Jana moved her arm in a big circle and now there's a circle in her red paint." □ Let the children paint with one color at a time in the beginning when they're discovering how the paint can be marked. Then try two colors. Start them with a light color such as yellow. When they've spread it well, add a dollop of red or blue. As these mix together everyone will enjoy seeing the new colors. □ For a nice change from commercial fingerpaint, whip a cup of Ivory soap flakes, a little water and some food coloring to a thick cream consistency. Use on the table top or as body paint on a warm day. Even the clean-up will be fun if the children are sprayed off with the hose outdoors.

CHILD: The children won't need much prompting. They will enthusiastically spread the paint around on the table and experiment to find all the things the paint can do. Since large movements of the arms and shoulders are used, the children will do better when they're allowed to stand rather than sit at the table. Most children are interested only in the joy of the fingerpainting process. If the adult wants to "save" a painting, she can press a sheet of newsprint on it and lift off a copy.

WHY GOAL: To let the child fully explore a new art medium. To encourage the child to notice the relationship between her movements and the marks that are made.

USES: Fingerpaint gives a "direct contact" experience that helps release tension. It is satisfying as an art medium because the child's actions have an immediate effect. The relaxed, free approach the child develops here can be carried over to expression in other media.

123. Painting with My Hands

HOW Put a large spoonful of fingerpaint on the table in front of each child. Let them spread it around and make marks in it with their hands. Do this on many days. Then use two colors, starting with yellow and adding red or blue. Use some whipped up Ivory soap flakes for a change. If they paint their bodies it will wash off—it's just soap!

WHY To let children learn how to make something happen with their hands.

124. Playing with Many Sizes

HOW ADULT: Find some household things the child can handle that are graduated in size. Some already-made series are: *measuring spoons, cannisters, nesting toys, a set of graduated wrenches.* (You can also create some series by gathering items such as *shoes* or *jar lids* of graduated sizes.) □ Show the children one of these sets of items and invite them to play. Say, "Here are some interesting things. See what you can do with them." You want them to handle the objects so that they will eventually notice the relative sizes and begin to compare them. Don't be so anxious that you "tell" a child about the sizes. Let the children have plenty of time to play with the things and begin to think about their sizes. This may take a number of play sessions with several different sets of materials. □ When the children do something that shows they've discovered size relationship, talk about it. "You put them all in a row. They look great! Let's see, this is the littlest one at this end. And what about this one down at the other end?" After they can readily arrange a set in order, they might enjoy making a record of this accomplishment, placing the row on a large sheet of paper and tracing around each one. □ A half dozen *identical glasses* filled to varying levels makes another kind of series. When a child has arranged them correctly, add some more water to one or two of the glasses to allow the fun of finding the new order.

CHILD: Children like to play with all sorts of things whether or not they are toys. Children will stack the objects, push them around as if they were vehicles, and sometimes experiment with arranging them by size. This is just play to the children, but they are doing some important mathematical thinking and reasoning.

WHY GOAL: To let children play with several things that differ only in size so they will begin to compare. To encourage the child to arrange things in order by sizes or amounts (seriation).

USES: We need to be able to tell the differences between two sizes but also among a whole series of sizes since clothing, food, tools, and many other things come in graduated sizes. It helps in making choices when we are able to understand where any one item fits in a series.

124. Playing with Many Sizes

HOW Give children some "toys" that are graduated in size—perhaps a cannister set. Let them have plenty of time for free play with them. When they arrange the things by size, tell them how clever they are. Say, "They look great! And it was you who made them look that way."

WHY To let the child learn about graduated sizes through experience.

125. Moving and Saying

HOW ADULT: You may have used a fun path to give you an opportunity to tell the child words for positions in space. Now it's time for him to say the words. Use a *garden hose* or a *rope* to mark an interesting *path*, and as he follows it describe his moves: **through** the box tunnel, **under** the bench, **over** the block. Have him say the words first with you and later by himself. ☐ Then entice the child to new skills by adding new challenges to the fun path. Add a small plastic lid for standing on one foot, an inch-wide tape for walking-the-line and parallel lines to begin and end a 24–inch broad jump. Reposition the things occasionally to provide for new actions and to help him learn new positions. Now use more subtle position words as he moves: walk **next to** the box, jump **away from** the paper, in the **middle of** the loop, **around** the puddle, **along** the line. Walk him through it the first time you use the new position words. Then tell him as he goes again. When he's familiar with the actions encourage him to say the words. ☐ Invent a game with one rule, "You say the word while you do the action." Failure to do so means you must repeat that action. See if you can go the whole course without any repeats. He can play this with a friend if they each move one challenge at a time, in turn.

CHILD: The child likes to invent new actions for himself, so when the path is rearranged he may have some suggestions of his own. He likes challenge but if he doesn't feel sure of a new action he may avoid it for a while. To learn the words best he will need to hear and say them just at the moment he's engaged in doing them. If several children are playing he might get confused unless the adult names actions for just one player at a time.

WHY GOAL: To increase the child's understanding of positions in space. To provide a pleasant and safe situation for physical development.

USES: On-going physical development is essential to healthy growth of the child. Knowing the words for space relationships increases his understanding of situations and of instructions. "Go around the puddle to the car" is quite different from "Go to the car."

125. Moving and Saying

HOW Add new challenge to the child's fun path by adding new objects. Arrange them so he can try new positions and movements: next to, away from, around, and along. Say the words to tell him what he's doing—as he does it. Then have him say the words. Sometimes enjoy playing together with this simple rule: Say what you're doing as you do it.

WHY To provide a path that gives experience with positions and position words.

42–48 Months

Concepts (that is, ideas that cover many specific examples) are beginning to grow in the child's mind. Some groupings the child must learn for herself by trying them out; like what breaks, moves, bounces, or flows. Other ordering or grouping she understands by listening and watching; like big, little, next, later, heavy, or red.

Give her lots of safe opportunities for experimenting with and observing many kinds of things so she can reason out these concepts for herself. That's the most basic way for her to learn them, by reasoning them out of her own direct action. And art experiences such as painting and block building are a perfect laboratory for the child who is building concepts. Your role can be to help her verbalize what she discovers.

Children of this age also like to look into books, hear stories, and talk about pictures. Interest in books leads the child naturally to curiosity about the letters and words that surround her in this society of printed materials. But as always parents should be guided by the child's behavior and help her to learn what she shows interest in. At this age it is usually the spelling or writing of a few letters of her own name, although some want to know more. Adults must guard against "pushing" the reading development of their child to satisfy a parental goal that may be unrealistic.

An excellent alternative goal to teaching early reading is to stimulate the child's oral language. (After all, this is the foundation that reading later is built on.) It is appropriate to encourage the older three to ask and answer questions, describe things and events, talk about plans, and express feelings. Such activities not only contribute to the child's development but will draw the adult and child together in a positive relationship.

TABLE OF CONTENTS

THEMES

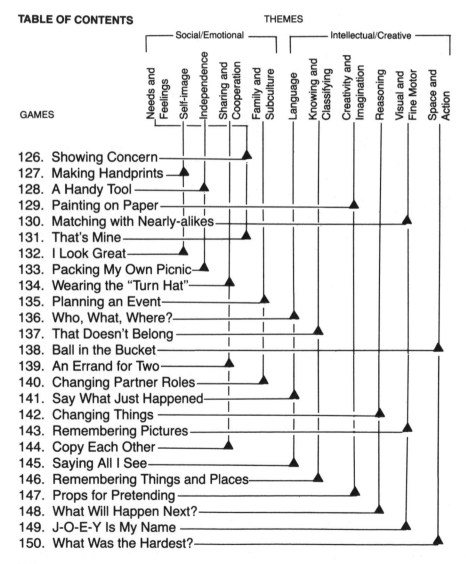

Social/Emotional

Intellectual/Creative

- Needs and Feelings
- Self-image
- Independence
- Sharing and Cooperation
- Family and Subculture
- Language
- Knowing and Classifying
- Creativity and Imagination
- Reasoning
- Visual and Fine Motor
- Space and Action

GAMES

126. Showing Concern
127. Making Handprints
128. A Handy Tool
129. Painting on Paper
130. Matching with Nearly-alikes
131. That's Mine
132. I Look Great
133. Packing My Own Picnic
134. Wearing the "Turn Hat"
135. Planning an Event
136. Who, What, Where?
137. That Doesn't Belong
138. Ball in the Bucket
139. An Errand for Two
140. Changing Partner Roles
141. Say What Just Happened
142. Changing Things
143. Remembering Pictures
144. Copy Each Other
145. Saying All I See
146. Remembering Things and Places
147. Props for Pretending
148. What Will Happen Next?
149. J-O-E-Y Is My Name
150. What Was the Hardest?

56

Checklist: 42–48 Months
(Developmental Age)

NEW BEHAVIORS	SUGGESTED GAMES	NEW BEHAVIORS	SUGGESTED GAMES
☐ Asks about the feelings of other people	126	☐ Throws a ball over hand	138
☐ Is familiar with the use of fingerpaints	127	☐ Is interested in helping adults	139
☐ Uses a tool with adult help	128	☐ Sometimes cooperates with another person	140
☐ Competently uses crayons and fingerpaints	129	☐ Uses many action words	141
☐ Finds a pair of pictures in a group of four	130	☐ Notices changes in things	142
☐ Sometimes tells wants and needs	131	☐ Matches two pictures in a group of eight	143
☐ Is beginning to use a comb and brush	132	☐ Skips, hops on one foot; says short sentences	144
☐ Likes to try doing things by himself	133	☐ Uses many descriptive words	145
☐ Plays follow the leader	134	☐ Hunts for misplaced toys	146
☐ Enjoys participating in family activities	135	☐ Asks questions about the work people do	147
☐ Answers questions with specific information	136	☐ Shows curiosity about surprises	148
☐ Classifies things by the way they are used	137	☐ Points to letters and asks their names	149
		☐ Says words for a number of space relationships	150

126. Showing Concern

HOW ADULT: You've already been helping the children notice the feelings of others (game 106). After one of the children has noticed another's strong emotion, invite the one who noticed to do some *doll play*. Say, "This doll just fell down and skinned his knee—just like Jimmy did a few minutes ago. What can we do for this dolly?" Hopefully, the child will suggest something like a *bandage* or a *wet cloth*. Then, if the child holds the doll for a minute, say, "Oh, I see that you're going to give him some comfort. I think the doll needed that as much as the bandage." □ At another time the doll might be sad and the child could practice cheering him up. At yet another time there might be an angry doll for someone to try to calm down. □ After the children have had a number of opportunities to respond to the doll's "emotions," begin to encourage them to respond helpfully to the feelings of their playmates. Say, "Jimmy looks a little sad right now. Do you think you might be able to cheer him up?" These efforts won't always be successful, but when they are, everyone's feelings will soar.

CHILD: Sometimes children treat dolls with disregard, even apparent .cruelty. So they may need some chances to make an adjustment to using the doll for role playing feelings of sympathy or concern. Most children will have noticed adults comforting other children and will model their behaviors on these observations. When it comes to responding to another child, some will be able to do little more than give a hug. But with a prompt from the adult, such as, "Maybe he'd like a drink of water," the child may move on to deeper levels of understanding.

WHY GOAL: To let the children use a doll to practice feelings of concern or sympathy. To guide the children to sometimes express concern in real problem situations.

USES: Our tendency to help others in time of trouble is one of the qualities that keeps any group strong and united. Learning effective ways of providing help makes it possible for the child to show personal concern more readily.

126. Showing Concern

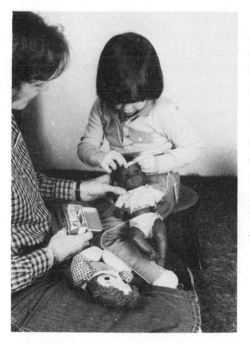

HOW Ask the child what can be done about the poor dolly's hurt knee. Maybe a bandage will be suggested. And if the child rocks or pats the doll, say, "That is the best comfort of all." With this encouragement, the child may sometime comfort a playmate in the same way.

WHY To guide children to practice sympathy.

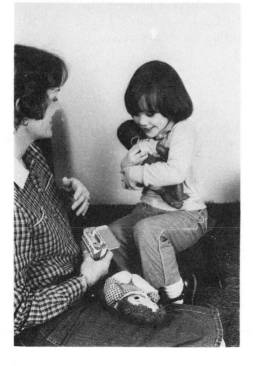

127. Making Handprints

HOW ADULT: Toward the end of a fingerpainting experience give the child a new *sheet of paper*. Ask her to press her hand lightly into the *paint*, then firmly onto the paper. Wait for her reaction to the design. Is she surprised? Does she recognize that it's a picture of her hand? Does she try it again? Does she want to do the other hand? Does she look to you to share what she just did? Use her behaviors to help her see the handprints are one kind of picture of herself. □ At her day care center the child can hang her paper on the wall beside the prints of the other children. She can count the fingers on her hand and on the other prints and discover they all have the same number. You can also point out that just as each print is different, so is each child special. □ At home the child might be allowed to decorate the refrigerator with her handprints, maybe with Daddy's and Mother's beside them. (They will easily wash away later.) Or, they can be printed on paper and hung. Or, she may press her hand on a paper for the next letter to Grandmother . . . so her handprint can show Grandmother how big she's getting.

CHILD: The child will be delighted to see that she can actually make a picture of her hand. She may want to fill many sheets with them. And she will think it was fun to make red and green and blue hands. If she's outside she will enjoy making prints on the walk or fence or any other washable surface. There's something satisfying about seeing prints of herself. It's like saying to the world, "Look at me; here I am." After all, adults feel this, too. Look at their initials carved on trees!

WHY GOAL: To use handprints to help the child become a little more aware of herself as a unique person.

USES: Feeling you're somebody is necessary to human happiness. Seeing her own handprint helps the child begin to define and know herself a little more surely, and knowing ourselves is what we spend our life time doing.

127. Making Handprints

HOW Show the child how to make a picture of her hand with fingerpaints. Have her press lightly on the paint, then firmly on the paper. See how many ways you can use the handprints to make her feel good about herself. See how many things she can tell you about her handprints. Let her make the prints inside and out on places that can be washed off later. She's telling the world she's here!

WHY To have fun making her own handprints.

128. A Handy Tool

HOW ADULT: A principal distinction between human and lower animals is the ability to use tools. Adults at home and in group care can encourage a child to use objects in creative ways—as tools, for doing things independently. *Paper cups*, for example, are useful for many things besides drinking. Help the child think of ways by making the cups easily available to her. Mount *dispensers* of various sizes in places where the child works. She can use them as a dish for her dolls, as a scoop in the sand box, a watering can for her potted plant or a temporary cage for a snail she's studying. Tell her how cleverly she used it. "Using the cup to hold the snail was good thinking." When she uses it unwisely, to stand on to reach higher, for example, try to restrain yourself from stopping her. She'll learn best if she tries it for herself. And, after all, she can't hurt herself falling off a paper cup! □ Take a few days to observe your own behavior. See how many things you do for a child that she could do by herself if the tools were handy. Then make them available. A few to get you started are: *tape*, a collection of *boxes*, safe *scissors*, a small *wheelbarrow*, a small step *stool*, a washable *marker*, or a *bucket*. Don't restrict her using them in a new way because it's different—only if it's damaging or unsafe.

CHILD: The child will use equipment in the way that is helpful to her needs. If she gets the attention she needs in other ways, she will not demand that the adult do things for her that she can do for herself. The adult's specific statements of approval give her the guidance she needs to do what she most wants, to do it herself.

WHY GOAL: To help the child independently use the objects around her for her needs. To allow creative and different use of ordinary objects.

USES: Early and varied opportunities to use tools help the child think creatively about objects and how she can use them to help herself. Available bicycle parts and a creative mind gave the world the airplane.

128. A Handy Tool

HOW Mount paper cup dispensers in several places handy to where the child works. Let her use them for tools in ways she thinks up—as scoops in the sandbox, cages for snails, or dishes for dolls. She will like being able to do it for herself. You like knowing she can do it. Watch her carefully for a day or two to see what other things you can leave handy for her.

WHY To make objects available that will help the child act independently.

63

129. Painting on Paper

HOW ADULT: Children's early painting experiences require a good bit of preparation by the adult. As a result, we sometimes skimp on giving children opportunities to paint. As often as you can manage the bother, put out the painting materials. A low, flat table surface protected with *newspapers* is easy for the child to stand at and work. An adult shirt worn backwards and gathered with a clothespin in the back makes a fine *smock*. □ At first put out just a couple of jars of *tempera paint*, with a *brush* in each. Let the child have plenty of sessions just exploring with the paint and brushes. You need to say or do little during the painting time, but it's nice to end it with a descriptive compliment that shows your genuine interest in what he has done, "You made a big red shape and some long blue lines. That's a wonderful painting!" □ After a half dozen experiences when the child has gained some painting skill, begin to offer him choices. First, increase the number of colors he can use at one time. Then offer two different *colors of paper* or put out *large paper* and *small paper*. On other days provide *several sized brushes* as well as *sponges* to paint with. □ Making choices and experimenting until you find out how each thing works is the heart of creativity. To give this opportunity requires extra effort from the adult, but provides a valuable gift to the child's growing-up experience.

CHILD: The child will paint spontaneously and without instruction. He takes this experience quite seriously and is usually deeply involved in what he is doing. At first he is more interested in the process than the product. Sometimes he won't even recognize his own picture a half-hour after finishing it. That's why comments on the painting should come just as it is being finished.

WHY GOAL: To give the child many opportunities to express himself with paint. To let him make many choices.

USES: These early painting experiences come at a time when the child is by nature spontaneous and intuitive. (Many adult artists work hard to recapture these qualities.) An early creative outpouring can provide a style and momentum that may enrich the later, more cautious stages of art development.

129. Painting on Paper

HOW Provide paper, brushes, and two colors of paint. Stand back and watch the creativity! After a number of days increase to three or four colors. Later still, offer some choices in size and color of paper and type of brushes. When you offer a compliment, let it describe the painting, "I like that big red shape and those long blue lines."

WHY To give the child a variety of painting experiences.

130. Matching with Nearly-alikes

HOW ADULT: Earlier you played a game (105) where the child found two identical pictures in a group of four. Now, make that game harder by increasing the number of pictures in the group and by choosing pictures with smaller differences between them. Two copies of last year's mail-order catalog can provide the necessary *pictures*. Cut out *two copies each* of about eight winter coats, of eight shoes, of eight tools, etc. Don't worry that some of the pictures aren't perfect or are of slightly different sizes. □ Begin playing by putting out a group of pictures. (You might begin with four and later work up to eight.) The pictures you put out should all be similar (perhaps coats) but with only two that are identical. Ask, "Can you find the two coats that are just alike?" When she succeeds, say something like, "Good, you looked very carefully and didn't let any of those other coats fool you." □ To continue, have the child hide her eyes while you switch positions of the cutouts and bring out another to create a new pair. After a few turns with the coat pictures, go on to a second group of pictures, such as tools. □ When it's clear that the child can find each pair, even when there are similar ones nearby, have a "wild" game. Put as many of the pictures on the table as you wish—maybe all of them. The child will have fun searching through them for pairs.

CHILD: Some children will immediately zero in on the identical pictures. Others will need to search more slowly and systematically, perhaps pointing at each picture as it is inspected. At age four, children enjoy a "big" challenge. The wild game may be the part they like best.

WHY GOAL: To challenge the child to observe and to make careful choices from among items that are similar.

USES: As we grow, the distinctions life requires us to make become finer and finer. Soon the child will need to be able to quickly and accurately see the differences between all the letters of the alphabet, even those that are very similar to others.

130. Matching with Nearly-alikes

HOW Show about eight similar pictures (cut from catalogs) but with only two that are just alike. It takes careful looking for the child to find the two, so compliment her by saying,"Good, you looked very carefully and didn't let any of those other pictures fool you." Continue to play by changing the pictures while the child hides her eyes. Each time there should be just one pair.

WHY To help the child notice which pictures are nearly alike and which are exactly alike.

131. That's Mine

HOW ADULT: You can guide the child to use his developing language skill for expressing his own needs and wants. You may already be helping him say what some of his needs are. But also help him know when to say it assertively. You can help him use particular phrases to tell in words instead of actions.

-a personal choice:	"I want a . . . (banana)"
-an ordinary need:	"I need my . . . (potty)"
-an alternative to physical aggression:	"That's my . . . (toy)"
-a self protective statement:	"I don't like . . . (to be hit)"

☐ Experts call this self-maintaining language. The adult needs to observe carefully the child's need for such statements and to specifically praise him for using them. "I'm glad you told me that was your car. I'm sorry she took it from you." Or, "I'm glad you used words to tell her you don't like to be hit. That's so much better than hitting her back." ☐ You are helping the child use the main tools of survival in his culture: words. They can be used in positive and socially acceptable ways to express how he feels. You can tell him also, "Please don't take that away. It's mine."

CHILD: The child may slip back into physical assertion because his vocabulary is limited. He will depend more and more on words as he discovers their power. Indeed he may become "bossy" for a time, but he will balance out his pleasant and unpleasant behavior as he receives encouragement for what the adult considers appropriate.

WHY GOAL: To help the child express himself in appropriately assertive ways to practice a pleasant style of "self-maintaining" language.

USES: The child needs to be able to protect his rights and feelings with words rather than actions, to "stand up" for himself verbally rather than "hitting back." Otherwise he will have rights only when he's dealing with someone physically weaker than he.

131. That's Mine

HOW Encourage your child to protect his rights and express his needs with words. Tell him, "I'm glad you used words to tell her you don't like to be hit." Use pleasant words to assert your rights to him, "That's mine. Don't take it away, please." He will learn that words can help him satisfy his needs in positive ways.

WHY To help the child use words to satisfy his needs and rights.

132. I Look Great

HOW ADULT: The adult provides *a full-length mirror* as a way of helping children know themselves better. After they help to get themselves dressed, she says, "You did a good job. You look great! Look at yourself." □ When the children look directly at their own body, they see it in bits and pieces: their hands or feet, their tummy, or toes. In the mirror they are a whole person, all complete like those they see around them. □ After the bath the adult can suggest dressing in front of the mirror sometimes. When the child has dressed, the adult can stand beside the mirror and point out what a good job of dressing that was. □ The adult might think of ways to keep the child's *comb* or *brush* nearby. Three-year-olds can usually do a pretty good job of brushing their hair. And when it's done the adult should respect their handiwork and not try to improve on it. □ When we adults groom ourselves we usually insist on having a mirror and some privacy. The child who's interested in learning good grooming may often need the same consideration. □ At other times, just for fun, the adult can arrange for children to share the mirror at the same time. They can see how they're alike but different.

CHILD: For the child, the "feel" of dressing is different from the sight. They will probably find it fun to see the image following their lead in putting on the clothes piece by piece. They will be able to see that buttons marching down a shirt look different from when they are seen one by one. Sometimes the child will just like staring and smiling at the image.

WHY GOAL: To help children know, more wholly, what their own bodies look like. To provide a way for them to see the results when they groom themselves.

USES: Children need a mirror to see what their hair looks like as they comb it, to know the color of their own eyes, and what their face looks like—clean and dirty. They take the confidence of this positive self image out to meet the world.

132. I Look Great

HOW Make a full-length mirror available to children. They will see who "me" is. They can see how to comb their hair and how it looks. They can know what they look like after they've dressed themselves. They will feel the same pleasure you feel when the mirror reflects a satisfying image.

WHY To help children feel good about the way they look.

133. Packing My Own Picnic

HOW ADULT: When the child seems to be ready for an adventure, suggest he pack a picnic for *lunch*. Go with him to the kitchen and point out what is available to him for packing. Talk a little about where he will be going to eat and what might be convenient to eat there. Lay out the things as you talk, along with several *sandwich bags* for him to use, and help him remember where his *lunch box* or *picnic basket* is. Offer your expertise, "I'll be here in the kitchen for a few minutes. Let me know if you need some help." Then let him do it. □ Don't try to balance his day's diet with this one meal. This is an exercise in independence, not in proper diet. You have some control over what's reasonable when you first say what's available. Just be sure he has several choices, among them things he likes. If he insists on a particular thing you feel is unreasonable but not actually harmful, you might want to let him pack it. □ In his day care group the same game can be enjoyed. The choices will necessarily have to be more limited, but the preparation can be independent. It might be fun to have a by-myself picnic with the children preparing it together, but with each one eating in his or her own little special place— they'll probably be giggling and eating together before they're through.

CHILD: Threes like to do things for themselves. Within limits they can get and wrap the things they need. The bags will help him limit the size but some things are best learned by experience. How else will he learn ice cream doesn't travel well in baggies? He will begin to discriminate more carefully, letting his experience guide his decision. Some reminders like, "Last time the pudding leaked out, remember?" can help him to choose the banana instead.

WHY GOAL: To help the child do something independently. To set up a pleasant experience where the risk of failure has minimal consequences.

USES: An important part of independence is knowing that sometimes you fail. Handling the problems of a mispacked lunch is a gentle introduction to the risk of failure in later responsibilities, like getting all the homework collected into the school bag.

133. Packing My Own Picnic

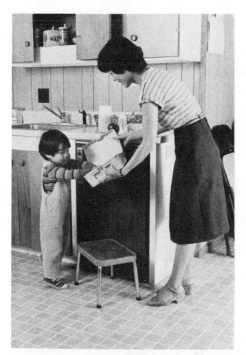

HOW Go with your three-year-old to the kitchen. Show him a number of things he might pack in his special picnic basket for a picnic. Give him a few sandwich bags to help and let him pack with his own style. He will like doing it all by himself. He will learn the fun is worth the risk of a bad choice. Take a special treat along and join him for dessert.

WHY To let the child act independently with minimal risks for failure.

134. Wearing the "Turn Hat"

HOW ADULT: The adult finds a colorful *hat* and three children who would like to play together. He says, "Let's play follow the leader. This hat will tell us whose turn it is to be the leader." Choosing one child, he says, "Jon, will you be the leader? You can put on the hat so we'll all know it's your turn." When they have repeated several times the action Jon suggested the adult finds another leader. "It's Davie's turn now. Jon please give him the hat." They continue until all have had turns. □ The adult puts the hat away and says, "We'll wear the hat again when we play a game together. It's fun to wear the turn hat isn't it?" □ Moving the hat from one child to the other makes it easier for the children to get the idea of the leadership role passing from one to another. Children really do like to share with each other as long as it stays fun. It isn't fun to wait a long time for your turn, so the adult keeps the group to just three at this age. □ When the turn hat has served its purpose, you'll want to encourage the children to take turns without this symbol.

CHILD: The idea of wearing a special hat appeals to most children. They may not always understand what a "turn" is, but wearing the hat lets them know quite plainly they are "it." The children are just having a good time playing a game with a hat, but they're learning about cooperation in the process. And passing the turn on with the hat somehow seems easier than just "giving up" your turn.

WHY Goal: To help the children understand the concept of cooperation by sharing a physical symbol of the concept.

USES: Symbols often express expected behaviors in our culture. The child will begin to know the role of the one who wears the hat just as later he will know the roles of those who have crowns or gavels or plastic helmets.

74

134. Wearing the "Turn Hat"

HOW Play a follow-the-leader game with three children. Let each child wear a special hat for a turn to lead. After you've all followed that leader three times, pass the hat and the turn to the next child. The children will be pleased with the funny "turn hat" game. And you will be pleased they're learning to take turns.

WHY To help the children feel good about taking turns in a game.

135. Planning an Event

HOW ADULT: Include the three-year-old in planning for some family event, perhaps baking a grandparent's birthday cake. When the family's together you might present the idea, "Next week is Grandaddy's birthday. Do you think he might like a birthday cake?" Everyone gets a chance to answer. If it's agreed, say, "Let's plan the kind to make." They all talk about what's needed for the cake and make a list: cake mix, icing mix, candle holders, and candles. □ After collecting a *magazine, scissors, paper* and *glue*, the family gathers for the next stage of planning, making the shopping memos. Each person chooses an item to shop for, finds a picture of it, and glues it on his or her own memo card. While this is happening they agree on a shopping time. □ At the store each person carries the memo. The three-year-old is given guidance in finding the item but is encouraged to take it from the shelf alone. The adult helps the child match the memo to the package picture to be sure it's right. □ The last stage of planning is evaluation. When the items are taken from the bag at home, an adult calls out the things on the list and the child holds them up to check. The adult evaluates with words. "We were smart to plan. We have everything for Grandaddy's cake." □ Such simple planning can also be done at the child's care center for the jack-o-lantern, a child's birthday, or a special cultural celebration.

CHILD: The child may at the beginning of the planning be surprised that other people have birthdays too. To the child the grandfather will become a person, with likes and dislikes. The child will find shopping with a purpose and a list more satisfying than just going along with the adult. Seeing Grandaddy with the cake the child is likely to tell him, "I did it."

WHY GOAL: To provide an opportunity for the child to participate in a family event as an equal member. To help the child begin to see the process of planning.

USES: As children's activities become more complex they will need to plan for what they need and what they need to do first. Even such an everyday event as bathing requires planning for soap, cloth, and towel before getting wet.

135. Planning an Event

HOW Plan for the family to make a cake for Grandaddy's birthday. Together, decide what you need. Let each person make a picture-memo of what he will buy for the cake. Take the family and their memos shopping. When you're back, check off the items to see if you got what you planned. Talk about the fun you had and the fun Grandaddy's going to have.

WHY To help the child participate with the family.

136. Who, What, Where?

HOW ADULT: The three types of questions in this game will give the child a reason for using the many words he has learned to describe people, things, and places. Throughout the day the adult can include questions of the following kinds.

Who?	Who has on blue sneakers?
	Who works at the hospital?
	Who's coming to visit us?
What?	What sound do you hear?
	What's Mary bringing us?
	What's the matter?
Where?	Where are your socks?
	Where's a good place to hide?
	Where do airplanes land?

You'll enjoy asking these appropriate questions because without them, the young child will not have as many opportunities to make short, useful statements using the many words now in his vocabulary.

CHILD: Children like to answer if the questions are not too insistent. Answers of children to "who, what, or where?" will be brief. Appropriate answers may be no longer than these: "My friend . . . doctors and nurses . . . thunder . . . I dropped it . . . at the airport." These wonderfully short and accurate answers provide clear communication from child to adult. They are an excellent starting point for further back and forth conversation on the same topic.

WHY GOAL: To ask questions that will help the child use many of the words he knows. To follow up the child's answer with some more conversation on the same topic.

USES: The answers to these basic questions help the child describe a particular situation—to report what he knows about it. It is no accident that these are some of the same questions journalists use to guide them in telling a clear story.

136. Who, What, Where?

HOW At various times in the day ask a question the child can answer in a word or two. "Who works at the hospital?" or "What sound do you hear?" or "Where's a good place to hide?" When you get the child's answer, try to build some more comments on it to carry the topic of conversation forward.

WHY To pose questions that the child can answer in a word or two and that will encourage more conversation.

137. That Doesn't Belong

HOW ADULT: When the child is playing near and you're setting the table, put something on one place mat that doesn't belong. A *tiny truck* or a *book* will do. Say to the child, "Something doesn't look right. Can you please come and help me see what doesn't belong?" Show her the setting and tell her, "I was putting the things on that we need to eat with. But something is there that shouldn't be. Can you see what it is?" When she finds it, show how pleased you are she noticed it. Tell her that your little trick didn't fool her because she looks and thinks so carefully. □ If she doesn't discover it right away, draw her attention to it by touching the other things and making remarks like, "To eat we need the spoon, and the cup, and this napkin." If she doesn't anticipate you and see the truck doesn't belong add, "And look at this truck. Do trucks belong on tables at dinnertime?" □ When she notices well, put on two odd things or play with several children and several things that don't belong. Limit the number of children in the interest of the table setting! □ Think of other ways to tempt the child into the reasoning process: a toothbrush stuck in the crayon box and a slipper in the washcloth drawer are only two of the foolishnesses you can try. Each time you must make sure there is a clear group of things that have a logical reason for being together and one that has no reason for being there.

CHILD: The child feels important and needed when the adult enlists her help, but she probably knows it's a game. It tickles her sense of humor to see things that aren't right. She may try to tell why it shouldn't be there, "Don't eat books!" Or if she is very imaginative, "Milk can't go in a book, silly!"

WHY GOAL: To put some things where they don't belong so the child will notice. To let the child learn to express reasons why something belongs or does not.

USES: Classifying is a principal way of making knowledge manageable. Noticing the thing that is not a part of the class or group helps the child clarify her understanding of group membership.

137. That Doesn't Belong

HOW When you're setting the table add something that shouldn't be there, perhaps a small toy truck. Enlist the child's help in finding what doesn't belong. When she picks up the truck tell her the reason, "We don't use trucks to eat, do we?" Have fun finding other groups of things where you can tuck one thing that doesn't belong. You'll have some shared laughter when she notices the odd thing.

WHY To encourage the child to notice the thing that doesn't belong in the group.

138. Ball in the Bucket

HOW ADULT: Help the child learn new control of an old skill. Provide a bucket, ball for the child, and a ball for yourself. Both of you stand back a few feet and each throw your ball into the bucket. If he misses move up a foot closer and try again. If he's successful reward him for accuracy. Say, "You're getting it right where you want it." When he gets it in every time increase the challenge. Stand further back from the bucket. □ To expand the game, use several *buckets, balls,* and children. Space the buckets on a line that allows each child to see what's happening but not interfere with the others. Or once in a while use only one bucket in the middle of a circle of kids. Each kind of experience will have its own special fun. □ Outside on a warm day try partly filling the bucket with water and using a heavier rubber ball. The water splashes when the child's aim is good. □ The child's been rolling, kicking, and throwing balls before his first birthday. Now he can polish his control. He'll have his own style of throwing, and with plenty of time to do it his way he will increase his accuracy.

CHILD: Just throwing is fun for most children, but to be good at a game, some control is needed. Having a stable object to aim at may be easier for him than tossing to another person. The bucket stays right there and waits for his ball. Having a target also helps the child become more discriminating about where he throws. He will become aware that throwing is usually done for a reason.

WHY GOAL: To help the child learn to control and direct his own body movements in order to aim at a target in space.

USES: To be functional to the child, his body actions must be under control. Tossing paper into the trash or clothes into the hamper become efficient arts only after a certain amount of skill is developed.

138. Ball in the Bucket

HOW Give the child a bucket and a ball. Let him practice control by throwing the ball into the bucket. Outside, fill the bucket with water so the splashes reward his good throws. For more practice use three children, three balls, and a bucket. Stand back!

WHY To help the child gain more control In throwing.

139. An Errand for Two

HOW ADULT: When your child has a friend in to play, it might be a nice experience to let them go on an errand together. Call the children to help you out. Ask them, "Will you do an errand for me?" (Giving them the name for the task helps to make it important.) Explain that you need them to go next door to get something. Think how you might give each a specific responsibility. One may take the *note* that tells what's needed. The other may carry back the item, perhaps in a *basket*. See if they can determine which for themselves. Make sure they know their parts and send them off. □ When they're back, review what happened, "You two did a great job together. Jackie, it was important for you to get the note there. And Leslie, you did a good job carrying. Thanks for coming back so promptly." □ In group care two children can go to the director's office as messengers or to an adjoining room for supplies. Perhaps the errand could be to the kitchen to bring back the snacks, one carrying the milk and one the apples. Send two together for safety and for cooperation but also because it takes two to giggle together and create moments of comradeship. □ Whenever the children are sent out of sight you will want to make arrangements beforehand so they will be expected.

CHILD: For most three-year-olds it's a big step to go off without an adult. But having a friend along gives the child a sense of adventure. Having the duties spelled out allows the child to be relaxed about it. For children in group care it's exciting to have just one friend to relate to for a few minutes. It forms the kind of relationship that is hard to have when groups of others are always around. The children are likely to take this responsibility seriously and may not even need the reminder of the second adult to go carefully, and go "straight back."

WHY GOAL: To help the child learn that cooperation is each doing his expected part in an activity; to have fun doing an errand with a friend.

USES: Companionship is important to humans. Taking pleasure in needed activities done cooperatively is a small building block for sound mental health.

139. An Errand for Two

HOW Let two children go on a short errand together. Make sure that each has a specific duty in the process. One might carry the note going, the other might bring the item back. Let them help to work it out so they will know their part. Be sure the other adult knows all about it. The two will have a buddy-buddy time as they go. And they'll be very proud to have helped!

WHY To help the child enjoy taking part in a cooperative activity.

140. Changing Partner Roles

HOW ADULT: Setting the table for the family meal is often the job of the children. The wise adult can use this simple task to lead the children through several partnership roles. □ When the child was quite young the adult assigned her the **junior partner** role. She cooperated by placing *things on the table* but it was the adult who decided and directed. □ Now the adult can move partnership along to the **equal partner** stage. Together they decide who will put what on the table and they each independently do what they've agreed upon. The adult, of course, does those things that might be unhandy for the child. But he does not tell the child what to do. He can say, "I'll be responsible for the plates. What do you plan to put on?" This makes it possible for the child to have an equal share in the decision making. □ By school age the child will be able to take the full responsibility for getting the table ready. She will place most of the things herself and direct the placement of the others by the adult. She will then have become the **senior partner.** □ You can plan other activities that will let the child move more rapidly through the three levels of partnership. For example, the two of you might make some paper mosaics. On the first day you could direct the cutting and placement of the *paper pieces*. On the next day the two of you could make a second mosaic and share equal responsibility. On the final day the child could be in charge of a third mosaic while the adult follows directions. When you admire the finished mosaics, you will want also to admire the increasing responsibility she took.

CHILD: Some children seem more comfortable in the junior partner role (and some adults are content to keep them there). But most children will enjoy the comradeship of equal partners and the responsibility of being the senior partner. Sometimes in a game the child will slip from one to the other with little distinction. The role the child finds most satisfying varies from time to time.

WHY GOAL: To let the child experience family responsibility in various partnership roles.

USES: Different situations require differing balances of cooperation and leadership. Children need experience in all three partnership roles if they are to function well in group situations.

140. Changing Partner Roles

HOW Think of setting the table as an opportunity for trying different cooperative roles. First the child is a junior partner helping the adult who is directing. Later the child is an equal partner with both deciding together who does what. By school age the child can be the senior partner taking most of the responsibility and directing the adult who is helping. All this cooperation lets you get to know and respect each other.

WHY To help the child learn to lead as well as follow.

141. Say What Just Happened

HOW ADULT: This game gives the child a reason to use her growing vocabulary to report events accurately. Several times during the day draw her attention to something you're doing. Then ask, "What did I do?" Her first answer may be as simple as, "Jump." You can respond, "Yes, that's one way to say it. Now watch again. Can you see more?" Repeat your action and your question. This time she may add to the description. "You hopped on one foot." If she doesn't add information, model a sentence for her. The next time she'll probably be able to tell you more. □ To help her get ready to watch carefully in school, some of the actions you describe should use school materials. *Crayon* an "X" on a *sheet of paper*, put the crayon away, and then fold the paper in half. If her description of your action is imperfect, praise her for the part she got, "Yes! I did fold the paper. I'm glad you saw that. Now I'll pretend to repeat what I did so you can see if you can remember what happened before I folded the paper." Gentle questioning will lead her to talk about writing the "X" and putting away the crayon. □ With many opportunities like this, the child will begin to watch carefully and to describe accurately. □ If you and the child would like to add some motivation to the game, give her a *token* such as a popsicle stick for each correct, complete description. When she has five tokens, she may have a special treat such as a tickle session or a story of her choice.

CHILD: It may take a number of trials in this game before the child begins to understand that you want the clearest description she can make. But she will be proud to communicate well and will try hard to meet the adult's high standards if she is not criticized when she falls short. The child can tell that her efforts are accepted by the patience in the adult's voice and the willingness to give many second and third tries.

WHY GOAL: To invite the child to use words to report an event that just happened. To stimulate the accuracy of the child's reporting.

USES: We can gain a lot of information by watching carefully. Describing what we saw further fixes it in our minds and enables us to communicate what we know to others.

141. Say What Just Happened

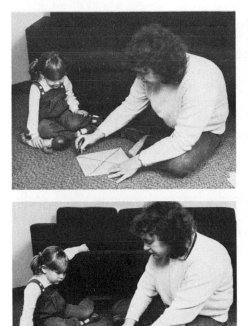

HOW Get the child's attention with a sentence like, "Watch me, Martha." Then do something such as hopping on one foot. Ask her to say what you just did. Try to help her give the best description she is able to give. Use plenty of praise, "You watched everything I did, and you told the whole story!"

WHY To let the child report what she just saw.

142. Changing Things

HOW Adult: An adult can have fun with three-year-olds by showing them that some things that seem to be two are really one. The adult has carefully labeled "ice" and "water" for the children. Now he can show them they're the same thing. He lets the children fill an *empty ice cube tray*. Then to identify it in its other state he suggests they add a *raisin* to each section. He puts the tray into the freezer section of the refrigerator in a space they've chosen. They notify everyone not to move it for two hours. ☐ After play, or a nap, or an errand, they come back. When the tray is removed from its identified space, the adult asks, "Where's our water? This doesn't look like water. What's this cold, cold stuff?" The children can verify it's theirs by the raisins. They can label it ice and talk about what happened, using the words "change" and "same." ☐ The adult may also use a *balloon* to show how things change. Before he blows it up he takes a minute to help the children predict the new look of the balloon. He can talk about the flat, floppy object. He asks them, "How do you think it will change if you blow into it?" Or, "What will it look like when it changes?" ☐ The adult is hoping to make the children aware that the condition of things can change. He lets the reason stay a mystery. Technical explanations at this age are unnecessary and will probably lose him his audience.

Child: The children can have great fun with the changes. They see these as interesting events but usually have no particular curiosity about why. They will later on begin calling the adult's attention to changes they have noticed—the ice changing back to water as it's stirred in a bowl, for example.

WHY Goal: To make the child aware that things are not always the same, that often things can change and then return to their original state.

Uses: Recognizing that things can change is an important aspect of reasoning. Creating a change and then reversing it (conservation) is one way of mathematically checking things.

142. Changing Things

HOW Fill an ice cube tray with water. Let the children drop a raisin in each section so they can tell it from the other trays. Put it in the refrigerator while you do something else for a while together. When you take it out talk about what happened. Use the words "same," "water," "change" and "ice." Enjoy the mystery of this and other changes with them.

WHY To help the child see change.

143. Remembering Pictures

HOW ADULT: Show the child a picture. Then ask her to find it in a group of related pictures. You can do this easily with *two copies* of last year's mail-order *catalog*. From one catalog cut out a variety of items such as a shoe, a lawn mower, and a piece of furniture. In the other copy of the catalog, put a paper clip on the pages that shows the items selected. □ Sit on the floor with the child, the paper-clipped catalog, and the cutouts. Give her one cutout to hold, and explain, "Here's something to take a good look at. Be sure you've tucked it away in your memory before you hand the picture back to me." When she returns the picture, put it out of sight behind your back. Then open the catalog to the page that contains that picture. Say, "Point to the one you just saw." If she's not sure, close the catalog, show the cutout again, and finally return to the catalog. Congratulate her when she finds the picture, no matter how much help she needed. □ Now that she has the idea, you can play this game with many variations and increasing challenge. For example, show several cutouts, put them all away, and search for them on several pages. Or show five cutouts but search for them through ten pages, some of which are decoy pages. Sometimes show her the cutouts, stop and do something else, and then return to search for them in the catalog. □ Notice how she goes about this task and give special praise when she works carefully and systematically.

CHILD: Some children will pounce on the matching item. Others will take plenty of time to examine the whole page and give careful consideration before deciding. A "pouncer" who lands on the wrong item might be guided by the adult to be a little more systematic, inspecting each picture until her memory tells her she's come to the right one.

WHY GOAL: To give the child practice in recalling a picture she has seen (visual memory). To encourage systematic searching when the task is difficult.

USES: We carry around many memories of sounds, sights, and motions. But they don't do us much good unless we are able to recall them. The ability to recall visual memories is especially important to our using the books and printed materials that are so much a part of our world.

143. Remembering Pictures

HOW Show the child a cutout picture. Then hide it and let her see a catalog page that contains the same and many other pictures. When she finds it, say, "Good for you! You held it in your mind and didn't let any of these others get you mixed up." When she's got this game down pat, show her several cutouts all at once to find on a page. As you make the game harder, you'll be able to see her ability to remember grow.

WHY To show the child pictures she can later recall.

144. Copy Each Other

HOW ADULT: Children like to try new ways to move and they like to do what you do. You can combine these two pleasures in a game that is fun for you both. When you're about to do some routine task say (or sing) this little verse:

> I can, You can
> Hop, hop, hop.

You then perform that action as you go. A trip to the bathtub is a lot more fun if you change your song to "slide, slide, slide," and both go sideways. Try motions you have noticed the child learning to do, like hop on one foot, or skip a step, or jump up with both feet. But try some silliness, too. That may make you both laugh. So she can easily repeat it with you, use a single word to say what you do (tap; clap; nod; jump; bend; march) and make it clearer with your actions. □ When she knows the game, invite her to be the leader sometimes. Or when you see her involved in some action on her own, sing the song naming her action and copy her. This is a perfect game for her to play with a friend her own age or even a small group. The children are sharing in the activity, but are not dependent on each other for the success of it. □ Sometimes, of course, she may get an idea all by herself and start the song. You will want to follow excitedly.

CHILD: The child likes imitating and saying new words, so she'll soon pick up the song, though at first she may only join in saying the action words. Using lots of different motions (and muscles) is fun for her, but of course her imitation won't always be perfect. And if she's with a group she may intentionally do the motions wrong. That tickles her developing sense of humor.

WHY GOAL: To make it fun to practice the following and leading skills that grow into cooperation.

USES: Knowing the names for her actions allows the child to better explain what is happening. When she can say what she's doing she can play the leader's role in some games.

144. Copy Each Other

HOW Play a do-like-me game with your child. Make up a simple song about hopping. You and the child hop as you sing the word "hop." Sometimes let the child choose an action. Then you both can sing the song with her action as she leads the game.

WHY To give the child a chance to say words that help her lead or follow.

145. Saying All I See

HOW ADULT: Play this game when you come to an interesting page in a household magazine or a children's book. The page should have a *picture with lots of details* or should have several pictures so there will be plenty to talk about. It's important not to rush. Ask the child to tell you what is on the page; then give her plenty of time to look and think. □ You are hoping the children will use all the language they have to describe the pictures. Listen for names of things, descriptions of actions, and words that tell details such as size and shape. Enjoy all the things the children spontaneously come up with. If they run out of ideas, but you are sure they have the ability to say more, gently probe with a few questions such as, "What size is the gorilla?" or "How many apples are there?" or "Is there something outside the window?" or "What is the little boy doing?" or "Could you tell me more about the things at the bottom of the page?" And while you don't want to take so much time that it becomes boring, looking at the picture can give you and a child an opportunity for a relaxed time of sharing. The attention of both is focused on the same place—and this draws you together. While the children are stretching their powers of description, they can snuggle in your lap, and receive warm encouragement.

CHILD: The children may begin by talking about the few things that immediately attract them. They are more likely at first to identify people and things rather than actions and details. After having been asked about actions in several pictures, they may look for actions in the next. In this way, the total number or variety of things the child labels should increase through many play sessions with this game.

WHY GOAL: To help children notice all they can in a complex picture and to report in words what they see.

USES: Reporting is one of the basic ways language is used. Reporting visible information correctly is a prerequisite to some of the more difficult forms of thinking such as reasoning, empathizing, or evaluating.

145. Saying All I See

HOW Invite children to tell you all they see in a detailed picture. Give them plenty of time. Compliment them when they talk about things, people, actions, and details such as size or shape. If they miss something, ask a friendly question to draw their attention to it.

WHY To let children report all they can.

146. Remembering Things and Places

HOW ADULT: Let the child warm up for this game by telling you "what's gone." Put three familiar things on the table and have the child name them. While she turns her back, take one away. Now she can turn around and tell you what's gone. ☐ When it's clear that the child remembers removed items, go on to a more challenging memory game. With the child, find and name two *common objects* that you will use in the game. For instance, these might be a ball and a cup. Now put each in a particular place. Say, "Let's put the ball right here in this chair, and where shall we put the cup? How about under the table!" ☐ Have the child review where each thing is and then hide her eyes or go out of the room while you change something. On this first turn simply remove one of the items. When the child returns, let her discover what happened and tell it in her own way. She may say something like, "Cup's not under table anymore." ☐ This game can be either easy or hard. Here are some of the ways you can slowly increase the difficulty: 1) increase to three, four, or more items; 2) begin by removing one item, but on later turns remove two; 3) instead of removing items, interchange their locations; 4) remove one item **and** change the location of another; 5) play with a group of children so there is gentle (but not urgent) competition to find the changes.

CHILD: The child will enjoy the increasing challenge to her memory if you move ahead so that she's successful most all of the time, but not quite every time. She'll probably do better if she names the things and places before hiding her eyes and then again while she searches. Also, learning the locations in a particular order and then searching in that same order can help. She may learn these tricks on her own. If not, the adult can suggest them when things get difficult.

WHY GOAL: To give the child an enjoyable way of first linking pairs of things and places and then calling them back from her memory.

USES: People are able to recall information because of the many links between the things that are stored in memory. When you are reminded of one idea, another one often comes along with it out of your memory. Places are especially easy to remember and form a good "handle" for retrieving other things that have been linked to them.

146. Remembering Things and Places

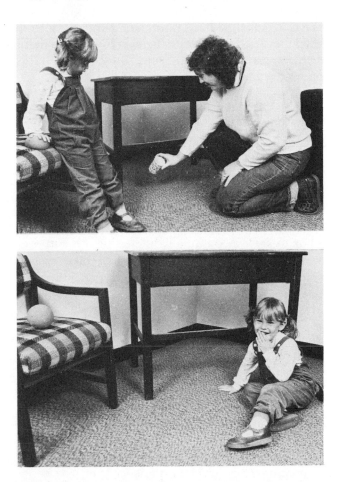

HOW With the child, choose two or three objects. Let her name them as you put each in a special place, "The ball is in the chair; the cup is under the table." While the child hides her eyes, remove one object or trade the positions of the two. Let her guess what's changed. When she tells you, praise her for using her memory. Think of other ways to vary this game—making it gradually harder so the two of you can have fun with it over and over.

WHY To help the child practice linking places and things as a way or organizing her memory.

147. Props for Pretending

HOW ADULT: Make some *prop boxes* to encourage pretend play. Help children collect and store the props they need to play different roles. Begin one day when they have finished a game of pretending. Suggest they put what they used in a box for the next time. Help them find a place they can reach to store the box. □ Spend some time with them setting up more boxes. A few possibilities are:

A BOX WITH	TO BE A
dolls, cloths, a baby bottle	parent
aprons, pans, spoons	cook
book satchel, notepad, keys	office worker
a record, umbrella, flashlight	space visitor
blocks, dump truck	builder

It doesn't take much to get a child's imagination going so you don't need to overload the boxes. As you notice appropriate objects around, add them to a box to keep it continually interesting. Or surprise them with a box of unrelated things and see what their own creativity can do. Children in a group can sometimes work out cooperative use of the boxes since the alternatives are visible and ready.

CHILD: Finding the needed equipment handy makes it easy for children to get started. (Otherwise an idea can be lost in the preparation.) They may not always use the objects in the way the adult would, and as creativity increases they may borrow from one box to supplement another. The adult will find some of the substitutions amusing. In a group, when several boxes have been used at the same time, getting the right things back in the right box becomes a game with its own merit.

WHY GOAL: To encourage children to use pretending as a way of trying out situations they haven't experienced yet.

USES: Pretending lets one rehearse situations and make decisions. Adults call it considering the alternatives. Children need physical things to supplement their mental imaginings.

147. Props for Pretending

HOW Collect the props children need to pretend to be somebody. An apron, pans, and spoons make a cook. Put these in a box the children can get when they need to. Let them become a cook at will. Appreciate their creativity as you help them collect props to stock boxes for being a space visitor, a parent, or whatever.

WHY To supply props that will give a child ideas for imaginative play.

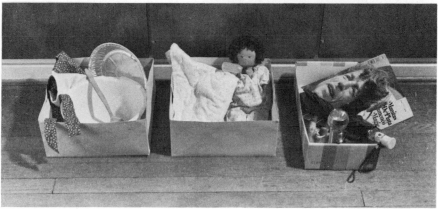

148. What Will Happen Next?

HOW ADULT: When there is an event that is going to involve a change in something, the adult can pause in the action to let the child predict what will happen. □ A *small empty box* might be left after storing away things from a shopping trip. The adult turns it over in his hand and shakes it for the child to see, observing to her, "This is a mighty quiet box. It doesn't make any noise at all when I shake it." He hands it to her to try. Discovering a *marble* in his pocket, he drops it in the box, acts as if he's going to shake the box again, but pauses and asks, "If I shake this box, what will happen next?" He waits to give the child a chance to find some words for what she believes will happen. After the child makes her prediction he continues his interrupted action. □ As the box is shaken again the adult reviews the prediction. "You thought it would make a noise. You were right! Listen to it now." If she predicted an unrealistic action the adult makes little comment, simply stating what does happen. "Putting something inside makes it rattle when we shake it." □ Stirring *chocolate* into *milk*, sitting on a *balloon*, lowering an *orange* into a full *cup* of water, are other events that afford an opportunity for the child to predict. The adult needs only to pause and ask, "What will happen next?" □ What other opportunities for prediction occur to you?

CHILD: Children of this age experiment and make things happen. This more formal activity helps them to learn that words can describe an event before it happens. The child's words may not be perfectly organized. (She may say, "It bounces" and mean it will roll around inside and make a noise.) But she's doing some clear thinking about the results. The game also gives the child just a plain old, fun time with her favorite adult.

WHY GOAL: To help the child begin to predict what will happen next. To encourage the child to experiment with objects to see if her predictions are correct.

USES: Thinking ahead about changes is an early step in reasoning. Predicting is an essential skill in adapting specific knowledge to your own needs. For example, a hammer that can drive nails, can be predicted to also crack nutshells.

148. What Will Happen Next?

HOW Change the color, size, and weight of things. Stir some chocolate into milk. Pop a balloon. Put an orange into a full cup of water. Just before you do each thing, pause a second. Ask the child, "What will happen next?" She will learn to predict about what she'll see happen. And you'll have fun together watching it happen.

WHY To give the child a reason to begin to think ahead.

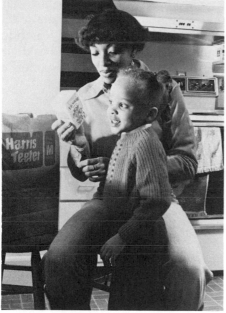

149. J-O-E-Y Is My Name

HOW ADULT: The letters of the child's name provide a good beginning place for learning letters. You've always made a point of saying his name to him. Now you will want to spell it to him. When you call him chant, "Joey, J-O-E-Y. Can you come, please?" He will begin to associate the letters with his name. When you have done this a few times, try getting his attention by using just the letters. □ After he responds to the sounds of his name-letters, help him know what they look like. Present one at a time. Point them out in many places during the day. *Cereal boxes, magazines, sign boards, toys,* and *labels* provide good sources for big, colorful letters. Ignore the fancy ones unless **he** recognizes them. When it's possible, both of you trace them with your fingers as you share their sound. □ Use his knowledge of circles, lines, and crosses when you're acquainting him with the letter. (An O is a circle, an E is four straight lines, a J is curved at the bottom, etc.) If he makes an association, "It's like a candy cane," go with it. He's using a memory aid. □ As he begins to form the letters with his crayon, use these same descriptive words to remind him of the shapes.

CHILD: A child will usually learn to recognize his name by the sound of the letters if he hears them frequently. But, recognizing the written letters is a very individual thing and does not always occur so quickly. (The child who is forced beyond his interest may indeed learn more letters initially, but soon will be turned off.) When he does begin to search for familiar letters, he will be greatly reinforced by finding them. His desire to form letters will develop on a timetable established by his experiences in seeing others use letters and by his own urging.

WHY GOAL: To help the child become aware of letters as symbols and to recognize the sound and sight of the letters of his name.

USES: The alphabet is the basis of reading in most languages. Learning to recognize the letters of his written name is a very early step toward reading.

149. J-O-E-Y Is My Name

HOW Chant the letters of your child's name to him, "J-O-E-Y." When he knows the sound of the letters, let him know what they look like. Together find them on cereal boxes, signs, ads, and in books. Trace their shapes with your fingers. Let him set the pace so the two of you will be happy together about each letter he learns.

WHY To say and show the letters in his name so the child will learn them.

150. What Was the Hardest?

HOW ADULT: After an active session of exciting play with a game such as 125, the adult sits quietly for a minute with the child. She asks, "Can you tell me what was the hardest thing you did?" She waits for the child to remember and tell her. When the child answers, "Jump away from the box," she repeats his words emphasizing "away from" and adding, "But you did it well didn't you?" □ If the child doesn't remember, the adult suggests some choices, "Was it walking along the tape? Or perhaps going around the circle?" The adult is trying to encourage the child to remember and report, so if he isn't interested, she doesn't press for an answer. □ She can ask the child other questions to help him recount the experience. "What was the first thing you did, the easiest, the scariest, the favorite?" Not, of course, all at once. When he has trouble thinking of the words, the adult always clues with those they've been using in the game. □ The next time the adult waits until a little later in the day. She helps by reminding, "Remember how it felt when you went on the fun path? What was the hardest . . . ?" □ Other action experiences like nature walks or circle games provide similiar chances for reporting with position words. Sometimes share your own feelings. "I always like to run around and around things, too." "Climbing high would a little difficult for me to do."

CHILD: Whenever he hears the question that's been asked immediately after the experience, the child receives the double clues of physical feeling and words to help him remember. The words of the question also provide him with the tools for reporting the event. He is not able to remember all the things he did. So without the clues his answer to your questions might be, "Nothing" or "I played."

WHY GOAL: To ask questions in a way that will help the child recall and tell about play experiences. To help him by using words about space relationships.

USES: For a little child a physical action is easier to report than an idea. The remembrance of a sensory feeling helps to recall the word for it. As the child's world enlarges it becomes increasingly important to his safety and learning that he be able to report recent actions.

150. What Was the Hardest?

HOW After an active game on the fun path (see 125), share a minute of quiet with the child. Help him remember and tell what he's just done. Ask, "What was the hardest thing you did?" Give him time to remember the action, and help him remember the words. Share what was hard for you. Sometimes ask things like, "What did you do first?" or "What was the easiest?"

WHY To help the child recall and tell what he's experienced.

48–54 Months

Many parents find four a delightful age, calmer than a year ago when constant short-term exploration of everything sometimes made life tempestuous. Last year the child asked "Why?" at every turn. Now these questions are more likely to be reserved for serious concerns, and some of his "whys" are just to reassure himself of something he already knows. He's learning so much right now, with the aid of new language, that he finds it hard to keep it all straight.

Fine motor skills also contribute to a calmer year since they have developed to an extent that allows the young four-year-old to enjoy using crayons, scissors, paste, and pencils. Hand and finger skills will continue to develop so that the child will be ready for many independent art activities by the second half of the year.

Most fours have decided which hand they will use for these activities, though some are still alternating. The natural next step is for the child to experiment with different ways of using these skills and materials. Observant parents will see that now less help is needed and, instead of help, will provide the materials and opportunities for free experimentation. The resulting creations will be treasured for their beauty or originality. The child who is expected to use these wonderful new skills for narrow pre-planned projects (such as cutting out patterns and coloring in the lines) is being denied his precious right to create.

The four-year-old is losing some of his fears of the unknown as he becomes more able to express and question, and so is a rather happy creature most of the time.

TABLE OF CONTENTS

THEMES

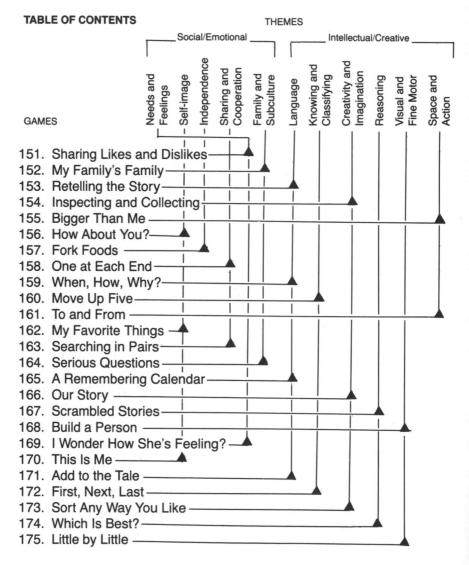

Social/Emotional — Intellectual/Creative

GAMES	Needs and Feelings	Self-image	Independence	Sharing and Cooperation	Family and Subculture	Language	Knowing and Classifying	Creativity and Imagination	Reasoning	Visual and Fine Motor	Space and Action
151. Sharing Likes and Dislikes				▲							
152. My Family's Family					▲						
153. Retelling the Story						▲					
154. Inspecting and Collecting								▲			
155. Bigger Than Me											▲
156. How About You?	▲										
157. Fork Foods		▲									
158. One at Each End				▲							
159. When, How, Why?						▲					
160. Move Up Five							▲				
161. To and From											▲
162. My Favorite Things	▲										
163. Searching in Pairs				▲							
164. Serious Questions					▲						
165. A Remembering Calendar						▲					
166. Our Story								▲			
167. Scrambled Stories									▲		
168. Build a Person										▲	
169. I Wonder How She's Feeling?	▲										
170. This Is Me		▲									
171. Add to the Tale						▲					
172. First, Next, Last						▲					
173. Sort Any Way You Like								▲			
174. Which Is Best?										▲	
175. Little by Little											▲

Checklist: 48–54 Months
(Developmental Age)

NEW BEHAVIORS	SUGGESTED GAMES	NEW BEHAVIORS	SUGGESTED GAMES
☐ Uses the phrases "I like . . .," "I don't like . . ."	151	☐ Asks many "why" questions	164
☐ Knows words for several family relationships	152	☐ Uses short sentences to recall events	165
☐ Answers questions about a story he's just heard	153	☐ Recounts parts of familiar stories	166
☐ Looks at small objects when he goes for a walk	154	☐ Retells three events from a fairy tale	167
☐ Asks about sizes	155	☐ Occasionally draws a simple human figure	168
☐ Often uses three-word sentences	156	☐ Says words for some feelings	169
☐ Feeds himself well with a spoon	157	☐ Is interested in mail and in using the phone	170
☐ Plays for a time with another in the same activity	158	☐ At the end of a story, asks for more	171
☐ Dependably answers who, what, and where	159	☐ Knows which of two events happened first	172
☐ Counts by rote to five	160	☐ Recognizes words for basic colors, shapes, and sizes	173
☐ Combines some words for actions and space	161		
☐ Begins to talk about preferences	162	☐ Holds two or three alternative ideas in mind	174
☐ Matches things that are used in a like way	163	☐ Names many pictures in household magazines	175

151. Sharing Likes and Dislikes

HOW ADULT: While you're on the way to the doctor, play an "I like . . . I don't like" game. Say, "I like going to the doctor. The plants in the waiting room are so beautiful. What do you like about going to the doctor?" Give him time to think. And accept anything he says—it's his opinion. Then say, "I don't like going to the doctor because sometimes we have to wait. What do you not like about going to the doctor?" When he answers again, just accept his feelings with a calm comment, "So that's what you don't like." □ You are making it possible for the child to talk about his feelings and to be more aware of them. Trying to change his feelings or making him feel guilty about them will discourage him from expressing them again. You can correct misinformation at a later date. Right now you're just helping him put into words some of what he is feeling. □ This game has endless topics: birthday parties, big sisters, long car rides, etc. But it should be used with discretion, taking cues from the child to start and stop. The place to play can be anywhere you can give the child your full attention for a minute or two.

CHILD: A few words will be all that most children can say now. "Don't like shots" will express a lot to the adult. The important thing for the child is that feelings have names and can be talked about. Gradually he will learn to express his likes in reasonable terms without prompting.

WHY GOAL: To model for the child a way to express what he likes and dislikes about a situation.

USES: Expressing one's feelings and dislikes without having to justify them is important to mental health. As children grow and develop their own values, it will be easier for parents to respond to the child's point of view if they are in the habit of accepting his expressed feelings.

151. Sharing Likes and Dislikes

HOW When you're on the way to the doctor you can say, "I like . . . about going to the doctor." Then say, "I don't like . . . about going to the doctor." Encourage the child to say what he likes or doesn't like. Accept the answers he gives. You will each know more about the other when the trip is finished.

WHY To let the child say what he likes or doesn't like.

152. My Family's Family

HOW ADULT: Your child knows enough members of her extended family to begin to see their relationships to each other and to her. Put on the wall two pieces of *poster board* or *construction paper*. Label one MOMMY'S FAMILY and the other DADDY'S FAMILY. Put a *photo* of each parent on the right poster and have the child put a *picture of herself* on each. □ When a letter comes from a family member (Aunt Marie, for example) put her *picture* on the board. Explain, "Aunt Marie was Daddy's little sister when he was a little boy. Grandpapa was their daddy." This will lead to some questions. Answer with simple, direct explanations using the words brother, sister, uncle, etc. Point out Uncle John's place in the family (Grandmother's little boy, Mommy's brother) before he visits. □ If she is isolated from her biological family, make one of the posters a "love family" of the friends who play the roles of aunt and uncle and grandparents to her. Say things like, "She was a little girl when I was little." Or, "His children are grown-up like me now." □ At her day care center there could be a small poster for each child with mother, father, and grandparents.

CHILD: The child will enjoy seeing and talking about the pictures and will begin to associate each fairly early with the real person. She will not fully understand the relationships for many years, but she is getting the sense of a family. Her questions, such as, "Did Daddy have a dog, too?" will give the adult clues to how much she's understanding.

WHY GOAL: To give the child a visible reminder of family relationships. To let her know that grown-ups were once children.

USES: At an age when children try to understand things by sorting them into groups and categories it is helpful for them to gain some knowledge of the relationships among family members. Words like aunt and uncle will gain more meaning for the children as they begin to understand that one person can be many things (old, young, sister, mother) and cannot be easily categorized.

152. My Family's Family

HOW Put two poster boards on the wall. Label one MOMMY'S FAMILY and the other DADDY'S FAMILY. When a letter comes from an aunt put her picture on the board and talk about her relationship. "She is Daddy's sister. They were little children in Grandpapa's house." On other occasions add other family members. Over many months your child will come to know family relationships. You'll enjoy her observations as she sorts it all out.

WHY To help the child understand simple family relationships like aunt and uncle.

153. Retelling the Story

HOW ADULT: Explain to the children that Charlie *Puppet* loves to hear stories, but that he likes to hear them only from children and that he likes only new stories. □ While the puppet takes a nap, take a child aside and suggest, "You could tell Charlie a story. I'll tell you a brand new one he's never heard. You listen carefully so later you'll be able to tell the story to him." □ If your story is about a raccoon, begin by describing him, then tell what happened in three clear events. For example, first, he went looking for someone to play with. Then, he met a scary lion who chased him home. At last, inside his own house he found his friend rabbit who had come to play. Of course, add a few details at each stage of the story. □ Now, together go and wake up Charlie so the child can tell him the story. You can make the puppet a wonderfully enthusiastic audience (frightened of the lion and greatly relieved when the friends are safe at home together) who compliments the child for good storytelling. □ The first stories have only three main events, but later ones may be increased gradually to six or seven events. □ After many different stories on many days, the puppet may get "brave" enough to retell one of the stories he has heard. Be sure Charlie make some mistakes so the child who taught him the story will have the pleasure of coming to the faltering puppet's rescue.

CHILD: The children will probably figure out that this is a make-believe device to allow them to practice storytelling. But this won't detract from the fun if the adult keeps it light or even silly. Occasionally a child may not want to talk to a puppet, but will tell another child or another adult the story.

WHY GOAL: To encourage the child to retell the main events of some new stories.

USES: Sometimes we can hear lots of details and still miss the events. But these main events are important because they act like a clothesline on which the details are hung. Without them everything else is a jumble.

153. Retelling the Story

HOW Secretly tell a child a short, original story. Then let that child tell the story to a puppet. The puppet can listen enthusiastically and say what a good storyteller the child is. Then the puppet may try to tell the story to someone else. If the forgetful puppet gets the story mixed up, the child will be delighted to help him out.

WHY To give the child a reason to remember and retell stories.

154. Inspecting and Collecting

HOW ADULT: When you notice the child fingering and admiring small objects he's found, try to help his interest grow. First, talk about his new discovery. If it's a rock say, for instance, "Oh, that one has gray and white specks in it. It would be fun to save it. I wonder if there are any more pretty rocks around here." □ When you go back indoors, discuss how these and· other rocks could be saved as a collection. A creative display idea adds importance and pleasure to the collection and will make the child want to add more items. Here are a few ideas that have been used successfully: 1) display rocks or shells in a *jar* of water—it makes their colors brighter; 2) display fragile items in the individual sections of an *egg carton*; 3) display bird feathers by sticking them one-by-one in a block of *styrofoam*. □ Use these ideas if they seem appropriate, but of course the best ideas will be the ones you and your four-year-old discover together. However you display it, come back and admire the collection often and wonder aloud whether something else might be added to it. Enjoy it for as long as it lasts, but you shouldn't be surprised (or disappointed) if what was a burning interest last week is forgotten or replaced this week.

CHILD: The child's interest may be quite fleeting at first. The length of his interest can't be predicted. But, as he gets older he is more likely to inspect things more carefully and remain interested in them over a longer period, maybe several days or weeks. He will appreciate having an adult partner who takes an interest in his collection and helps him solve the problem of displaying it. The child may want to renew the collection from time to time by throwing some things out and replacing them with new items.

WHY GOAL: To encourage the child to notice interesting things in his environment, and then to help him stretch out that interest by keeping the found items available as a collection.

USES: Collecting is an activity that begins in childhood but is still fun in adulthood. It gives each person a chance to make choices, to develop his own personal tastes, and to stick with an idea for a period of time.

154. Inspecting and Collecting

HOW When the child finds things, share some talk about their interesting shapes and colors. The two of you will want to plan a way to save the found items. Displaying them nicely helps make them important. The child has the fun of choosing what goes into the collection. The adult has the pleasure of admiring it.

WHY To help the child see and collect interesting things.

155. Bigger Than Me

HOW ADULT: Help the child see that big and little are relative. They change in different places and situations. In the beginning, let him use his body as the measure to understand this idea. ☐ Stand with him in the middle of a large room. Say something like, "Without moving from our spot let's try to touch the walls. Now the ceiling!" When you've tried unsuccessfully, point out, "The room is **big** . . . bigger than we are." ☐ Go into a closet or a very small room and do the same thing. Point out, "This room is **smaller** than the other." Move back and forth between the two several times (while it's still fun). Listen carefully to his comments so you'll know he's getting the right impression of big and little. ☐ At another time bring together *two cardboard boxes*. One should be big enough for him to sit inside, the other too small to get into. Suggest he get into the smaller one. When he can put only a foot in, ask him why he can't get in. The two of you may have a good laugh, but you can still help him use the words "smaller than me," to explain. If he doesn't try then to get into the bigger box suggest it to him. Hand him the smaller box to hold while he's in the big one. Again, affirm what he notices about the sizes by helping him use the words bigger and littler. ☐ Outside, make a big circle of *rope*. Let him march around it. Then make a very small circle. It will be easy for him to compare the sizes. You can think of other interesting ways he can use his body to compare or experience two sizes.

CHILD: The child will enjoy the activities as games. He will also be learning the words "big" and "little" are used for comparison. They are not just names, like Big Bear. At first he may use "small" or "smaller," "little" or "littler," etc. indiscriminately. That's not important. He will correct that later as he hears them used correctly. He's learning the idea of relating one thing to another to judge size.

WHY GOAL: To help the child understand that objects are big and little by comparison to something else. To give the child greater experience in using size words.

USES: Learning to consider an object or space as it is related to another is an early step in evaluating and comparing.

155. Bigger Than Me

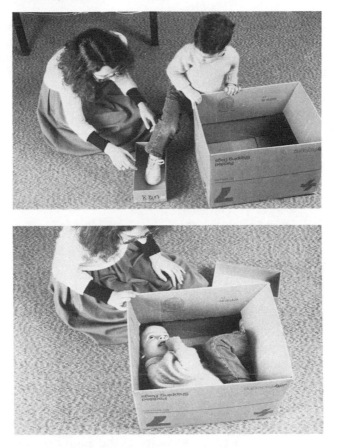

HOW Find a very big box for the child to climb in. Use the words, "bigger than you." Give him a shoe box to try to get into. Enjoy the joke while you both use the words, "smaller than you." Find other ways he can be the measure. He will learn that big and little can be different things at different times.

WHY To help the child understand that the words "big" and "little" compare things.

156. How About You?

HOW ADULT: A *puppet* can help the child express her own concept of herself. You will want to make sure the puppet's questions can be answered in the young child's limited vocabulary and are about things she is proud to reveal. A conversation might go like this.

PUPPET:	CHILD:
"Hi, my name is Calvin. What's your name?"	"Ann"
"Ohhh, Ann is a pretty name! I'm two, how old are you?"	"Three."
"That sounds sooo big! I can't wait 'til I'm three. Do you like cats?"	"Uh huh."
"Me too. They're so soft. I wonder who has a cat at home . . ."	"Me! I do."
"Oh, how lucky you are. Do you help feed your cat?"	"Sometimes."
"I bet your mommy's glad to have you as a helper."	

☐ If the child doesn't have enough words to talk about a topic, the puppet can always phrase his questions so they can be answered with a "yes" or "no." When the child develops a new skill or interest, the puppet might come back for another interview.

CHILD: Even if the child answers only in single syllables and with nods of the head, this game gives her a chance to think about and talk about herself. Most children will look right at the puppet when talking. Of course, they'll steal an occasional glance at the adult because they know it's all pretend. But they'll still enjoy the fun just as an adult does at a play or movie—which is also pretend.

WHY GOAL: To provide some easy questions about herself that the child can proudly answer. To make talking about oneself fun.

USES: As the child answers questions about herself, she is slowly forming her present and future self-image.

156. How About You?

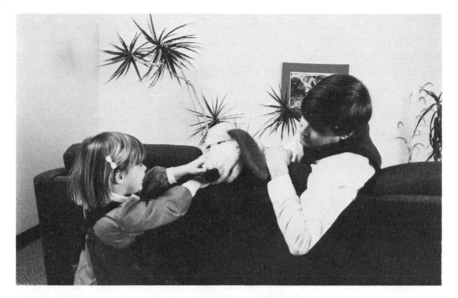

HOW Let a puppet tell something about itself ("I'm two years old,") and then ask the child about the same things ("How about you?"). Make sure the conversation gives the child a chance to share new things she's learning or doing. It would be nice if the puppet went overboard in its enthusiasm and admiration for the child's accomplishments. Then the adult could calmly agree.

WHY To let the child talk about herself to "someone new."

157. Fork Foods

HOW ADULT: The adult makes using a *fork* a special new thing to do. On a *big piece of paper* she draws a fork. She and the child look at the empty page and talk about filling it with pictures of foods that he might eat with a fork. Then hang it in a low place. When she prepares the next meal, she spreads out the foods and draws the child's attention to them. She asks which of the foods are usually eaten with a fork, and if the child is unsure, help by saying, "Remember how Daddy eats his greenbeans with a fork? Let's put the label from the greenbeans on your fork chart." □ As they paste the beans label on, the adult makes a promise. "When we serve beans tonight, you may have a fork to use, too." When mealtime comes, the adult makes sure the fork she gives the child is a proper tool. (Most salad forks are a comfortable size for this age child.) She expresses her pleasure about his using the fork but is not too concerned, now, about how it's held. □ In a group where a number of children become ready at the same time to handle a fork, a similar game can be played. However, when the first few fork foods are introduced, the adult might serve them in *small dishes* and remove the dishes and the forks before continuing the meal. As the children's skills increase this will no longer be necessary.

CHILD: The four-year-old is pretty good at using his hands and he likes doing grown-up things. So most fours learn easily with a fork. Comments from the adult help. "You put your fork under the mashed potatoes, didn't you," or "Just stick the fork into the carrot slice gently," will give him the kind of reassurance he needs. If things get difficult he may revert to a spoon or his fingers temporarily. That's okay; he will return to the challenge of the fork soon.

WHY GOAL: To help the child know the names of fork foods and use tableware efficiently. To make using a fork a special thing to do.

USES: Using tableware properly is a part of being able to handle the ritual of eating in culturally acceptable ways. In school, peers are intolerant of the child who "eats like a baby." They do not willingly share their table with him.

157. Fork Foods

HOW Draw a fork on a big sheet of paper. As you prepare the next meal, ask your child which one of these foods is eaten with a fork. Put the food label on the fork chart. Then at the meal he can have a small fork for this food. Tell him you're happy he's learning to use a fork like grown-ups do. He will be happy, too.

WHY To give the child experience with the fork.

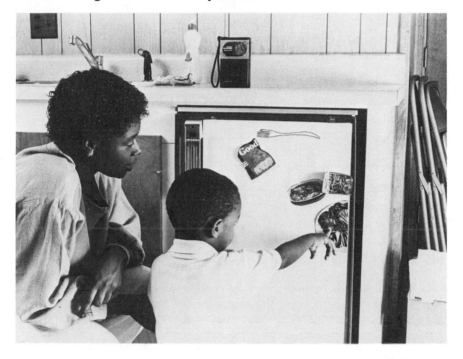

158. One at Each End

HOW ADULT: When two children are playing separately in the same space the adult might provide a way for them to share an activity. She can give them a *yardstick* and *sand bucket* and suggest they act out, "fetch a pail of water" while she sings "Jack and Jill." First she shows them how to hang the bucket from the yardstick with each child holding an end. They act out what will happen if one lets go, or what will happen if one end is held too high. "Look, it slides right down to the low end." Outdoors on a warm day, a little water in the bucket helps them see how cooperation keeps them dry. The adult adds the words, "You're both being very careful to help the other. You're cooperating." Or, "You're sharing the weight of the bucket by carrying it together." □ When one child gets tired or really uncooperative, end the game. There will be more opportunities other times. □ Group care provides endless opportunities for the child to share in doing a task one could not do alone. Two children can help each other carry lightweight *cots* (too cumbersome for one child to manage) to the sleeping place. They can put the *sheet* on with one holding an end while the other spreads it. Two children can share the fun of jumping over a *rope* if one end is tied to a tree. They take turns alternately holding the other end and jumping over the rope.

CHILD: The children enjoy cooperating for short periods of time. They're still in a mostly self-centered stage, so sharing time is short. Often the activity dissolves in laughter. That's okay. They're learning that cooperating is really fun and games. If one child seems still to prefer parallel play, the second child may enjoy playing the game with the adult as a partner.

WHY GOAL: To help children learn that cooperation can help solve some problems. To provide situations for cooperating that are brief and enjoyable.

USES: Many things in life are achieved by several people lending their skills to the task. Using another person as a resource is one adaptive way to solve a problem.

158. One at Each End

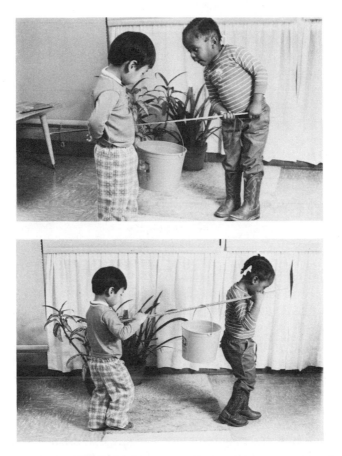

HOW Help two children play a cooperative game. Give them a yardstick and a sand bucket. Let them carry the bucket on the stick with each holding one end. Help them see how they must work together to keep the bucket from sliding. Sing "Jack and Jill" as they pretend to fetch a pail of water. Laugh along with them when it all falls apart.

WHY To help them see that cooperation helps them do something they can't do alone.

159. When, How, Why?

HOW ADULT: The child has been answering questions (game 136) that have had to do with things seen and understood directly. But the questions in this game are harder. To answer them the child will need to talk about time, about process, and about reasons.

When?	(concerns time—which can't be seen)
	When do we eat breakfast?
	When does it snow?

How?	(reports two or three steps of a process)
	How did you dig that deep hole?
	How do you feel?

Why?	(asks for reasons to support the idea)
	Why is this water so cold?
	Why do you like this one best?

☐ Give the child plenty of time to think about her answer to these questions. And don't demand an answer if she doesn't seem to want to try. That may be a signal to go back to some of the easier "who, what, where" questions for a little while. But be sure to return to this more exciting level of thought. And continue to feel gently with a question for the growing edge of the child's reasoning ability. She will benefit from the mental challenge an you will benefit by having more interesting conversations with your child or children.

CHILD: At first the child may answer only part of "How can we fix the broken toy?" But, she may be able to suggest additional steps if the adult uses some skillful follow-up questions. A question about why water is cold may at first receive the answer, "Just because." Simpler follow-up questions such as, "Who did something to it?" or "What's in it?" may lead the child to the answer of the original "why" question.

WHY GOAL: To ask questions that will deepen the level of the child's thinking. To encourage the child to give longer answers with several parts.

USES: Thinking about how and why are some of the hardest tasks we do throughout life. This early practice can give the child a pattern of successful thinking to follow and to build on as she grows older.

159. When, How, Why?

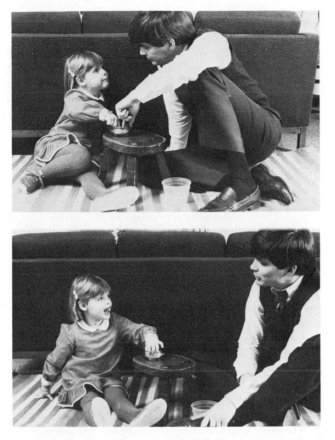

HOW Occasionally ask a question that requires the child to talk about time or about the ideas of how or why. "When does it snow?" or "How did you dig that deep hole?" or "Why do you like this one best?" If the child has trouble answering, use some simpler questions to help her along. You will enjoy hearing the child's serious ideas.

WHY To give the child experience with deeper questions.

160. Move Up Five

HOW ADULT: Invite the child to play a counting game. Using a simple path *gameboard* and a *die* to determine the count, the two of you will take turns moving *markers*. Explain, "We'll toss the cube and see which side comes up. The dots on top will tell us how many spaces to move." Practice a few times just tossing the cube and counting. (The cube is a die with one dot on the first side, two on the second, etc. with the sixth side having a happy face or a design instead of dots. The die should be large enough for the child to touch each dot with her finger as she counts it.) Point to the top the first time or two to help her know which side to count. Touch each dot as you count aloud. Take turns with tossing and touching but always count together. ☐ If she's still interested, go on to the gameboard. If not, play with it at the next session. Let the special sixth side be a reward, perhaps an extra couple of tosses or two free spaces. Use a path with large enough spaces to accommodate touching down easily. Encourage the child to move the marker in a hopping motion instead of sliding so each block can be counted as it is touched. ☐ As you play, emphasize differences in numbers by saying things like, "Five! That's a lot"; "You moved four, that's more than three"; "Two is a quick hop." The object of the game is to understand the meaning of five, not to be the winner, so stop when her (or your) interest ends.

CHILD: Moving the counter exactly one step for each count may be difficult at first. But touching each space as it's counted makes the process visible. The fun of the game is the counting and moving, which she does with vigor. The special moves earned when the happy face turns up make it exciting and continually rewarding, so she squirms and claps with excitement. An older brother or sister might be her partner in the game. But the adult should stay by to see that she gets to move her own marker.

WHY GOAL: To help the child understand that the numbers from one to five each stand for a definite quantity. To practice words for numbers to five.

USES: Numbers are used every day by the child beginning when she holds up two fingers for "two years old."

160. Move Up Five

HOW Show the child a simple path gameboard, two markers, and a cube with dots on each side. Point out that each side of the cube has a different number of dots, from one to five. The sixth side has a happy face and gives you a couple of extra turns. Sit with her to play. Show her how to get a number by tossing the block. Help her count out that number of spaces to move along the path. Take turns with her, cheer her when she gets the extra-turns side, and enjoy!

WHY To make it fun to learn and use numbers to five.

161. To and From

HOW ADULT: Use the child's natural joy in active play to help him learn more about the meaning of "to" and "from." When he's playing, name what he's doing (running) and in what direction (from or to). Invite him to repeat the action but in a different place.

> You're running to the tree.
> Can you run to the fence? It's farther.
>
> You're skipping from the swings to the sandbox.
> Can you skip from the sandbox to the slide?
> It's uphill.

☐ You are giving names to his actions. By asking him to repeat that action in a different space, you are broadening his understanding of "to," "from," etc. Labeling it "uphill" or "farther" adds to the challenge (and also starts him on some new concepts). ☐ Sometimes, have him assign an action to you. He will love playing the senior partner. ☐ Later, expand this game by using words such as "behind," "between," and "beside."

CHILD: Making his body do what he wants is just fun for the child. His desire to try new things is catered to when he repeats an old action in a new way. And he knows he's repeating because he hears the same words. He might enjoy sharing this activity with a friend (or several, now that he understands a little about taking turns). One runs to a far place, while the other runs to a near place. Then they trade. Seeing his friend take a different amount of time adds another clue for his understanding.

WHY GOAL: To increase the child's understanding of what some basic prepositions tell him and to help him learn how to use the words.

USES: Little words like "to" and "from" show specific relationships between actions and objects. They carry essential information in verbal directions. "To the table" conveys a quite different idea than "from the table."

161. To and From

HOW When the child is skipping, tell him a new place to skip from. As he runs, suggest a new goal to run to. With his fun he will be gaining a little clearer idea of what "to" and "from" each mean.

WHY To help the child know and use words like "to" and "from."

162. My Favorite Things

HOW ADULT: To help the child develop her own personal tastes, the adult plays a word game with her. The adult makes a statement about the child's favorite things leaving the last word for the child to complete. To give her a stronger sense of how important her own tastes are, the child's name is used in each statement. The adult says:

"Jennie's favorite person is . . . "
"Jennie's favorite hat is . . ."
"Jennie's favorite story is . . ."
"Jennie's favorite food is . . "

□ No judgment is made. The adult simply affirms the statement, "I like green, too," or "That *is* a pretty color." Making a game of it helps the child to confirm and express an opinion from her feelings. □ If this game is played with more than one child at a time, the adult is careful to honor each opinion without trying to change it. She also sees to it that others do not belittle it.

CHILD: Hearing her name helps the child know her opinion is valued. In this early stage of exploring her own feelings she may say "ice cream" is her favorite today, and tomorrow say "hamburger." On some days she may not be able to decide and will have two or more favorites. Though her tastes change, the good feelings she gets from having them respected stays with her.

WHY GOAL: To support the child in her choices. To help the child deliberately consider what her personal and esthetic tastes are; to encourage her own belief in them.

USES: It is important to a mentally healthy life that people feel good about themselves. Having one's feelings and tastes respected helps this happen.

162. My Favorite Things

HOW Ask your child to express her opinions about things. Put her own name in a sentence she can finish. Say, "Jennie's favorite person is . . ." Let her give you the last word. At other odd moments let her name favorite clothes, food, stories, etc. She is gaining confidence in herself as you respect her choices.

WHY To help the child develop personal, esthetic tastes.

163. Searching in Pairs

HOW ADULT: You and your child have played games in which you matched things that were alike. Now go a step further and match things that are related by use. Introduce the game to your child and a friend by naming an object *(key)*. Then ask, "What goes with a key? What does a key need in order to work?" If they don't remember, ask, "Where do we put the key to turn it?" If they say door (or lock, or car), ask further, "Where in the door?" Then, let them use the key in the *keyhole*. Now explain that you're going to play a game where the children work together, too. ☐ The three of you think of a pair of related objects (like a lock and key) and decide which one of the pair each child is to go and find. Tell the children, "Bring it back here," or "Think of a way to show it to us." Then call, "Go!" When both objects have been located, talk about how they need each other to function. Talk about how the children played together to find them. Some possible pairs are:

light and *switch*	*shoe* and *sock*
brush and *comb*	*hammer* and *nail*
soap and *water*	*paper* and *pencil*

You and the children will have many of your own to add.

CHILD: The children will enjoy this as just a new version of their old finding games, but they are learning about cooperation. They'll find it fun to figure out how to "bring" the keyhole or the ceiling light. Switching the light or hammering the nail after finding take time, so they will probably be ready for a new game after searching for only one or two pairs. They might "trick" the adult by making silly combinations of their own like soap and a spoon. And they will find it very funny when she shows they've "fooled" her.

WHY GOAL: To help the child learn that things and people sometimes need a partner to do a complete job. To learn which things in the world function in pairs.

USES: Awareness of partnerships gives the child a beginning understanding of the interdependence which exists throughout the world.

163. Searching in Pairs

HOW Let two children be a pair and find a pair. Talk about things (like a key) that have a partner object. Let the children name what goes with it (a lock). Have each child find one part of the pair. Take turns using the objects. Talk about each thing needing the other. Talk about each child helping the other.

WHY To help children cooperate in finding objects that work in pairs.

164. Serious Questions

HOW ADULT: Three- and four-year-olds ask "How?" and "Why?" many times each day. Sometimes the questions are so frequent that they are irritating. What parent or teacher can give dozens of good answers daily and still get anything else accomplished? □ But good, scientifically complete answers are not always what's needed. A brief, sincere response to the questions will do. It's probably better to risk being too brief than too long. An answer that goes beyond the child's intent will only be confusing. If more information is needed, the child will ask for it. □ Even if questions are on serious topics (such as sex, death, or divorce) simplicity is still the best course. As with all other "why" questions, the child is particularly concerned with the adult's belief or attitude about the topic. So it's important that the answer have the ring of sincerity about it. This is an age when children are checking, always checking. It makes sense for the adult to assume that the spoken question "Why did our turtle die?" includes the implied question ". . . and what do **you** feel about pets and death?" □ Each generation must pass things on to the next. Knowledge and skills are the easiest to transmit. But along with these we must pass on some attitudes. Our answers to serious questions (including the **way** we answer) will communicate important attitudes and values to our children.

CHILD: The number of questions the child asks increases dramatically now in these late preschool years. They ask about many topics, but sometimes they come back to one over and over. They may have heard a perfectly good answer from the adult earlier, but if they are for some reason anxious about a topic, they will check it many times.

WHY GOAL: To answer children's serious questions with brief, honest replies that reflect something of yourself. To remain patiently open to questions.

USES: Asking questions is a way for a child to get information on facts and attitudes. Children build their value system on what they learn from this information and their own experience.

164. Serious Questions

HOW When your children ask a "How?" or "Why?" question, give a brief answer. Tell just one or two facts. But let the way you answer express your attitude, belief, or feeling about the topic. Children really want to know how family adults and how teachers feel about serious things.

WHY To give honest answers to serious questions.

165. A Remembering Calendar

HOW ADULT: Use a large *calendar* to help the child remember a special event for a few days. Find (or make) one with day spaces large enough to paste a small picture on. When an event occurs which is special to the child, record it on the calendar. Have him paste a picture of the event on the square as you recall and describe what happened. Explain, "Here is a *little picture* of shoes like your new ones. Let's cut it out and stick it on your calendar. That will help you remember the day you bought them." Or if your talents are in drawing, sketch in a picture. □ A few hours later, maybe just before lunchtime, look at the calendar with the child. See if he can tell you why today's picture is there. If other family members are around maybe he can tell them also. His report will not be long. "Got new shoes," might be the extent of his language. A day later look at the calendar again and see if he can tell what the picture represents. □ Limit the number of events marked by the child and follow his lead about what's important to him. Putting up the reminder should not be more important than the event. Keep a bit of *tape* or *glue* handy and perhaps a *catalog* for pictures so the excitement of the event is not lost in the search for a proper picture. Each time a new one is added, review the others.

CHILD: The child recalls most events better if he has a visual reminder. An immediate review followed by one the next day also strengthens his memory. On a later day when he's adding a new cutout he may not recall the old ones without help from the adult. As the remembering calendar becomes part of his life, the child begins to decide for himself which particular events are worthy of his calendar. The adult may be surprised to learn that finding the odd stone at the zoo was more important to him that seeing the animals.

WHY GOAL: To provide a reminder that will help the child recall an event and tell about it in a few words.

USES: Memory is necessary for all learning. Using records to jog the memory is an effective plan. Using words to express memory gives the child the pleasure of sharing.

165. A Remembering Calendar

HOW Use a large calendar to help the child remember and tell what happened. After a special event put a small cutout picture on that day's space on the calendar. Invite the child to talk about it as he pastes the picture. The next day let him look, remember, and tell again. You'll be surprised at what he considers important enough to record on his special calendar.

WHY To help the child remember and tell about an event.

166. Our Story

HOW ADULT: Invite the child to join in a game of creative storytelling. Say, "Let's make a story together!" For the first few times the adult may need to be the major storyteller, occasionally pausing to encourage the child to add a word or a sentence. □ The first story might go something like this. "Once, a little rabbit was hopping down the forest path. He looked up in an oak tree, and who did he see but . . . (pause for the child's idea, for example, a squirrel). Down came the squirrel and said, "Let's go to the . . . (another pause for the child)." □ Of course the adult continues in a different direction if the child suggests that a hungry mountain lion were in the tree! The fun of this kind of story is that no one knows where it will go, since the adult happily accommodates all the suggestions the child makes. The first stories may be quite short. That doesn't matter as long as the child is learning that her ideas are an important part of these creative ventures. □ When the child is skillful and comfortable in adding a word or two, see if you can enlarge her participation by leaving longer pauses. When you stop for her to tell who was around the corner, don't be in a hurry to pick the story up again. Wait, and maybe she will add a paragraph rather than a sentence. If not, you might ask her, "Did anything else happen?" Soon, you will be giving only the introduction and then listening proudly to your budding storyteller.

CHILD: Children will vary greatly in their contributions to this type of storytelling. Some will give very brief responses. Others will weave detailed episodes. And experience will help every child increase his own contribution. Although children enjoy the one-to-one attention of story time, they also appreciate the unpredictable nature of a group-made story and enjoy the pleasure of creating something with their friends.

WHY GOAL: To let the child add ideas to a story. Later, to give the child just the beginning of a story so she can use her imagination to finish it. To encourage creative storytelling.

USES: Creative storytelling provides a safe opportunity for the child to try out ideas—even wild ideas. Telling a story is good preparation for the later task of creative writing.

166. Our Story

HOW Let the child help you make up a story. Pause in the story so the child can fill in things such as who came around the corner or where the bunny hid. When she finishes, tell her how interesting it was. Sometimes play this game with a group of children. Let each one add an idea to the story while you tell the in-between parts.

WHY To make up the beginning of a story so the children can join in to finish it.

167. Scrambled Stories

HOW ADULT: "I've made up some stories to tell. They've gotten a bit mixed up, but I think you can help me straighten them out." This might be the adult's introduction for a Learningame that teaches the children to look for logical order. Say, "The first story's short. It has just two parts. This is one part: At the end of the day Jim came home tired but happy. And here's the other part: All day Jim helped his father carry bricks in a wheelbarrow." Ask the child which part of the story should be first and which last. That will be fairly easy for her. What you do next is very important. Ask how she knew which part should be first. Hopefully, the discussion will get around to clues such as "first he helped carry bricks; then he was tired" and "he worked all day; then he came home." □ When she can easily arrange the parts of a two-part story, tell a story with three parts. And if that goes well, move on to a four-part story. As a variation on this game, you might break familiar fairy tales down into parts. Each time, your most important task will be to help the children notice the words that reveal the story's order. Over a number of days or weeks you'll see the children gain more skill at this task. Your praise will be sincere when you say, "You're beginning to listen carefully and understand how stories are put together."

CHILD: The children will recognize that you know the sequence of the stories. But since their effort seems to please you, they'll be anxious to try to figure the stories out. Children who have a shorter memory span will need to have the parts repeated while they are puzzling over them. Other children will promptly master the four-part stories and enjoy the challenge of going on to stories with even more parts. It may be best if these long stories are done with the adult and one child alone rather than with a group of children.

WHY GOAL: To give the children practice in mentally arranging stories in logical order.

USES: Information doesn't always reach us in perfect order. For example, in writing a report, information must be gathered from various places and then organized in the most understandable sequence.

167. Scrambled Stories

HOW: Tell a story with just two parts, but tell the last part first. Ask the child to straighten the story out. When she does, ask how she knew which part should come first. Help her remember the words that told what happened first. Then go on to longer stories. You'll enjoy seeing her ability grow.

WHY To let the child organize some stories.

A few ideas for stories:

Two parts
1. A cat sat on a soft pillow
2. Soon the cat was fast asleep

Three parts
1. Ed went fishing
2. Ed fell in the water
3. Ed built a fire to dry off

Four parts
1. Mary woke up
2. Mary got dressed and ate breakfast
3. Mary rode on the school bus
4. Mary said "Good morning" to her teacher

168. Build a Person

HOW ADULT: One day when the children are playing with their *play dough*, say, "I think you could make a person if you had some more things to use." Show them a box with *popsicle sticks, toothpicks, thumbtacks*, and a variety of other *small items*. Ask, "Which of these would you need to make a person?" And if they are unsure, add, "What could you use for the legs?" ☐ Soon the children will be selecting items and attaching them in various ways. Most will use a dough body to stick other things into. The toothpicks may need to be broken in half so they won't be too long as fingers. But, who knows, after E.T., long fingers may be popular. ☐ The adult's role is to provide the materials and to make encouraging comments. "Those thumbtacks make nice round eyes" and "I see you're using popsicle sticks for legs. Do you plan to add feet and toes?" and "What a nice way to make buttons!" ☐ Come back to this game often, and perhaps they'll make animals or more exotic creatures sometimes.

CHILD: Children who have only rolled and shaped the dough without thinking about "making anything" may be slow to get into this activity. That's why it's nice to have a small group of children working around a table together. They will get ideas from each other, and a little copying is okay to get you going. A few children may add parts that reveal the "person's" gender. This is not too surprising since they've been encouraged to think about detail and to notice differences.

WHY GOAL: To encourage the children to gain skill with their fingers. To help them remember what parts make up a whole.

USES: Throughout life we are called upon to use our fingers skillfully to assemble things. This Learningame makes a small contribution to that skill while increasing the children's awareness of how the body is put together.

168. Build a Person

HOW Provide some sticks and other small things when the children are using play dough. Ask them if they can put together a person. If they can't think how to get started, ask questions about the arms or legs to help them see what they need to add. Then sit back and enjoy their creativity.

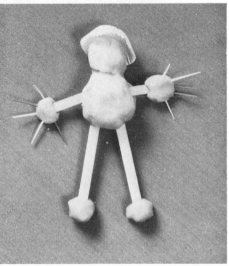

WHY To let the children use their fingers to put together a toy person.

147

169. I Wonder How She's Feeling?

HOW ADULT: When you read a story, pause occasionally to let the child wonder about the feelings or needs of one of the characters. In the story of *The Three Bears*, pause when Goldilocks is tasting the bowls of soup. Say, "I wonder how she's feeling. What do *you* think?" If the child suggests any emotion or need, graciously accept his answer and go on with the story. If the child is unable to come up with a feeling, encourage him to use clues from the illustrations or, give him some choices. Ask, "Do you think Goldilocks is full or hungry?" As the story goes on, confirm his answer, "You were right! She was hungry—she ate the little bowl of soup all up!" □ There are many places in a story where you can wonder about feelings, but one or two questions per story time may be enough. Most good stories reveal the feelings of their characters, so it will be easy to come back to this game many times. (For example, the classic *Cinderella* and the modern *Where the Wild Things Are* contain many feelings.) □ At first in this game, accept any answer as long as it represents a feeling or a need. Later, encourage a little more accuracy by asking the child to tell what the characters did to show the feeling, or how he would feel in the situation. For example, "How would *you* feel if someone broke your favorite chair?" In these discussions you will be able to admire the child's gradually growing ability to understand others' feelings.

CHILD: When you get beyond the most familiar feelings (happy, sad, angry, scared), the young child may vaguely recognize the feeling but be unable to name it readily. When this happens he will appreciate having the question rephrased as a yes-no or multiple-choice question.

WHY GOAL: To guide the child to think and talk about the needs and feelings of characters in stories. To increase the child's vocabulary by giving him the names of many feelings.

USES: We understand the feelings of others by mentally projecting ourselves into their situation. This skill will help him begin to be more sympathetic and understanding of his peers' behaviors.

169. I Wonder How She's Feeling?

HOW Pause in a story and ask about a character's feelings. The easiest questions can be answered with a yes or no. ("Is she feeling hungry?") Questions that give two or three choices are a little harder. ("Is she happy or sad?") Open-ended questions are the hardest. ("How is she feeling?") You'll enjoy guiding the child to think about deeper levels of feelings.

WHY To help the child name the feelings of story characters.

170. This Is Me

HOW ADULT: Help the child begin to learn some facts that define her as a person. Play word games that help her learn the facts. Sing, "I am Eva Black. Daddy is Adam Black. Who are You?" Help her answer with her whole name. When you pick up the phone, answer clearly, "This is 942–1017." As you pull in the drive or get off the bus, say, "Here we are at 310 Pine Street." When you're giving her a hug on her way out to play, ask her, "Do you live on Oak Street or on Pine Street?" Be sure you speak clearly and slowly as you give her information. Listen carefully as she gives it back to you. □ Show her the *identity cards* of the family members. Point out they tell the full name, address, and telephone number of the person. Talk about how this lets people know "who Daddy is." Make her a card with abbreviated information so she can show it sometimes, too. Expect some time to pass before she knows all the information. But continue to make her aware of it.

CHILD: The child will enjoy answering questions about herself when they are made a part of what she's doing. She is probably already able to say her whole name. But she'll take longer with the street address and phone number. She may have learned to say hello into her play phone when she could hardly say another word. She will learn her telephone number just as readily if she hears it as frequently. Her practice in dialing it (with the adult's prompting of the numbers) will help, too. She will continue to gain a sense of importance as she adds these things to what she already knows of herself.

WHY GOAL: To say things and ask questions that will help the child know her family name, address, and telephone number to identify herself.

USES: Names, addresses, and telephone numbers provide ways for children to be identified with their protective adults. They are the way she will identify herself to other people, especially in case of an emergency.

170. This Is Me

HOW Help your child learn who she is. Find times to ask her whole name. Answer your phone with the number instead of "hello." She'll learn the number when she hears you use it over and over. She will like knowing her street has a name. And she'll learn that, too. Both of you will be glad she has this information.

WHY To help the child learn her name, phone number, and street.

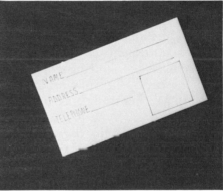

171. Add to the Tale

HOW ADULT: When finishing a favorite story, take a minute to reflect on the ending with the child. After *Jack and the Beanstalk*, for example, talk about the fact that Jack now has the treasures and the giant is dead. Ask a question that will help her take the story a logical step forward. "What did Jack do the next morning?" Pause and give her time to think and come to a conclusion. □ When she answers, just listen and she may tell you how she came to her conclusion. For example she may say, "Nothing." That may seem like she's not giving it much thought, but if you wait she may add, "He has lots of gold. He doesn't have to go to work." □ If you sense her answer really doesn't imply any thinking on her part, encourage her with a question she can answer with a word. Ask, "Did he get up?" and after a "yes," ask, "What did he see out his window?" Sometimes repeat her words to her and pause. "Oh, so he saw the giant again?" If you repeat her words with the tone of a question and an expression of interest, she may add more information. □ But don't burden her with questions if she isn't interested. Instead try the game another time. □ By helping her reflect on the past events of the story your leading questions will help her to draw logical conclusions about the next event.

CHILD: The child might say something that seems to have no logic to the adult. Questions can sometimes clear up the reasoning but not always. The child's experience and language is so limited that she may not be able to make her thinking clear. This doesn't mean it isn't logical. (How clear is Picasso's logic to most of us?) Time and repeated opportunities for talk will give her confidence in her own ability to express ideas.

WHY GOAL: To give the child an opportunity to verbalize an idea that is a logical next step and to talk through the decision.

USES: By asking the child to verbalize you are helping her to establish a new or future idea based on previous events. Throughout life we wonder about the future and try to project our ideas into it.

171. Add to the Tale

HOW After a story is finished, ask the child, "What do you think he did next?" Give her time to think before she answers. You'll be helping her to put her ideas into words. And her ideas may inspire you to explore some new conclusions yourself.

WHY To give the child a chance to think about things that haven't happened yet.

172. First, Next, Last

HOW ADULT: In this game, Dad and the child can make Jell-O to surprise Mom. While the water heats, show your child *three index cards.* Tell her that as you work you're going to draw pictures of what you did. Pick up one card and say, "This card is for what we do first. First, we collect the things we need." As you name the things *(Jell-O, bowl, spoon, measuring cup,* and *hot water),* make a very simple outline drawing of each on the card. Together you find the things. □ Then review, holding up the card, "First we found the things. Next, we have to put the Jell-O and the hot water together. How could we do that?" Wait for her suggestion. Agree, "Right, we put them into the bowl and mix them. That's the next step. Let me put that on the card." Draw the spoon and bowl with things poured in. Ask, "While I get the hot water can you dump the Jell-O in?" □ As she stirs you can review with her what you just did. Then say, "The last thing we do is put it into the refrigerator to cool and get hard. Isn't Mommy going to like this red Jell-O?" When that's done, draw the refrigerator on the last card as she watches. Put all three cards together, out of order. As you gather up the cooking things ask her to look at the cards and remember which came first, then next, then last. □ The following day look at the cards again to remember the order and to use the words. Suggest that she can make Jell-O with Mother next time and can use the cards to show her how (game 187). In day care or preschool, the children can plan to show a neighboring teacher how.

CHILD: The child may not immediately get the words that describe the order of the steps. She may, however, very quickly get the idea of the steps. If she sees the cards drawn as the actions happen, she will remember what the pictures show. She is likely to combine gestures with her words when she explains what happened.

WHY GOAL: To provide a pleasant situation for learning a fuller concept of sequence. To help the child see that some things happen in a given order.

USES: This game builds concepts that will help the child remember the order of events. Many tasks such as bathing, dressing, or driving a car must be done in a particular order to be successful.

172. First, Next, Last

HOW Dad can use Jell-O making to help the child learn what happens first. Divide the process into three steps. First, get the things ready. Next, mix and stir the Jell-O and water. Last, set the bowl in the refrigerator. Draw a picture of each step on a different card. Let the child make a game of putting the cards in order as you both use the words "first," "next," "last."

WHY To provide an experience of "first," "next," and "last" so the child learns the meanings of the words.

173. Sort Any Way You Like

HOW ADULT: Cut two big circles and two little circles from construction paper in each of three colors: red, blue, and yellow. Spread out the *12 circles* and say something like, "There are lots of ways we can put these into groups. Will you show me one way?" The child may go right to work grouping the shapes. If so, observe quietly and when the child is finished, say something like, "I like to see how carefully you worked with the shapes. Tell me about this group." And after you've expressed appreciation for his answer, you might then say, "Let's spread them out again and see if you can think of another way of sorting them. You may make as many or as few piles as you wish." □ The most expected grouping will be by like color and size, or a combination of these. But we should be especially accepting of classifications that the child makes that do not fit these patterns. The adult should make it clear that finding lots of ways to do something is an important skill. □ At the end of each turn, the adult player should summarize the reasons the child gave for his classification, "Here are all the large blue circles and these are the little yellow and blue circles together, and here are all the red circles." You might say, "You took **four** turns grouping the circles! What a lot of ideas you have." □ This is just the tip of the iceberg. You can expand this game by adding *multi-colored wrapping paper, more sizes, other shapes*.

CHILD: Some children will start immediately and will seem to understand the task. Others may not seem to know how to get started. They may be helped if the adult takes a turn first, talking out loud about her own actions. Some will group to no apparent pattern and others will not be able to find the words to explain. Many opportunities to play will give them these skills.

WHY GOAL: To encourage the child to think of many ways that shapes may be grouped. To give the child confidence in his own solutions.

USES: This gives the child experience in considering several possible solutions (divergent thinking). There are no correct answers in this game. Most of the important decisions in life are like that.

173. Sort Any Way You Like

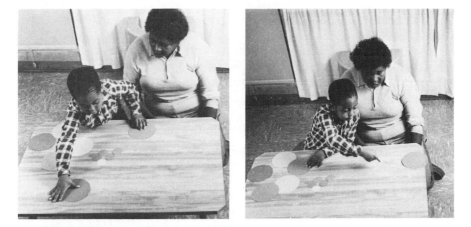

HOW This is a game for special fun—because it has no "right" answers. Let the child sort 12 colored circles (of two sizes and three colors) any way he likes. Show how interested you are in his work by making a few pleasant comments: "You worked carefully! Tell me about this group." Let the child know there are lots of ways to sort the circles; give him some more turns and some new materials.

WHY To let the child try several ways to do something.

174. Which Is Best?

HOW ADULT: This Learningame is a way of dealing with problems and conflicts that inevitably come along. The adult's role is two-fold. First, to encourage the child who is in a problem situation to pause; and second, during this pause to suggest two options for the child to think about. □ Perhaps a tower of blocks fell over and the child is upset. The adult might begin comfortingly, "That tower keeps falling, it's made you so unhappy." Talking quietly, with your arm around the child, continue, "There are some things that could be done, let's talk about a couple of them." The adult's goal for now is to get the child to consider just two options. Say something like, "You could build the next tower wider and stronger at the bottom, **or** you could decide to build something else—maybe a long train. Which of these ideas would be best for you?" Encourage the child to consider the two options. Accept any decision the child reaches, after thinking about both alternatives. □ Use this process also for problems between two children. When two are arguing (or worse), put a gentle hand on the shoulder of each and calmly say, "Come sit over here with me for just a minute and let's talk about this problem." Suggest two courses of action and say, "Can you pick one that will make **both** of you happy?"

CHILD: Skill in this area progresses slowly. The child is being asked to do some hard thinking just at the time when things are not going well. Seeing (over a period of time) that this thinking pays off, children will gradually learn to respond to problems by considering rather than blindly pursuing the first thing that pops into their head. Fours will need the assistance of an adult for some time yet.

WHY GOAL: To guide the child in a problem situation, to weigh some adult-suggested alternative actions. To provide enough practice so that considering alternatives will eventually become a habit for the child.

USES: Weighing of alternatives is a key step in solving problems. It's not the first step, but later the child will be able to link this skill with others that will complete the complex chain of behaviors we call problem solving.

174. Which Is Best?

HOW When the children face a problem, encourage them to pause for a moment. During the pause, suggest two possible things that could be done. Let them decide which one is best. Then they can try it out. Use this "stop and think" approach with many kinds of problems. Try it with a block tower that fell, a broken toy, an argument between two children, or a disagreement over ownership.

WHY To give the child practice in choosing between two possible actions.

175. Little by Little

HOW ADULT: Here's a game that uses a book in a different way—you hide the pictures. Begin with a *familiar book* that has large, clear pictures. Insert a *piece of construction paper* so that the first picture is covered when the book is opened. Explain, "I'm going to hide some of these pictures from you. But I bet you'll be able to guess what they are. Here's just a little peek." As you say this, reveal a part of the picture by slipping the covering paper part way down. Show as much of the picture as necessary for him to guess successfully. Compliment him, "Right you are! You named the picture without seeing all of it." □ Go from page to page, moving the construction paper ahead each time before turning the page. Try to get him to guess after seeing as little of the picture as possible. If the book is familiar enough he may recall the next page without seeing it at all! That's all right; this is just a warmup session. □ The next time you play, use a book or magazine he is less familiar with. Soon you will want to search out some books you know he has never seen before. Make sure the *unfamiliar books* have clear pictures so his job won't be too hard. To vary the game you might want to cut three hinged "doors" in the construction paper. Instead of moving the paper down, let the child open the doors one by one.

CHILD: The child is used to sitting with the adult to read a book. Covering the pictures may be quite a puzzling idea at first. But he'll catch the spirit of fun as the adult s-l-o-w-l-y uncovers part of the picture, then recovers it in a swish. He will experience a lot of satisfaction when he finds that he can identify an entirely new picture after seeing only a part of it. Two or three children might enjoy playing together if the adult does not foster competition among them.

WHY GOAL: To reveal some pictures a little at a time so the child will have a chance to mentally complete the picture (visual closure) and name it before he sees it all.

USES: Often a person gets only a glimpse of a word or picture (for example, while driving in a car). With good visual closure, a child will be able to read the word or understand the picture, though only part of it is visible.

175. Little by Little

HOW Use a paper to cover a picture in a book. Encourage the child to guess what it is when you show only a little of the picture. Slip the paper down a little, and then a little more, until he guesses what the picture is. Do this with lots of pictures. Let him know he's developing sharp eyes!

WHY To let the child guess at some partly shown pictures.

54–60 Months

Imagination is delightful to observe in the older four-year-old. For some time she has been pretending with objects, people, and situations. But now she's also beginning to pretend without props, to imagine as a purely mental exercise. It is a privilege of the adults to nurture this new growth.

When she puts on boots and a fire chief's hat and carries a piece of hose, she is a firefighter in her own mind. When she imagines something to exist or happen, then for that moment it does. Of course she will need to separate reality and imagination in days to come . . . and she will. Many parents will be almost sorry when it happens!

Other parents have difficulty with this period because they feel the child is telling lies and needs to know what is real and not real. It is well to remember that through imagination, children learn to manipulate ideas and grow intellectually. But it's also okay for parents to let the child know how they feel. Tell her, "That's a lovely idea. I wish it were real." Or, "Isn't it fun to imagine things to be just the way we want them to be." You'll be helping her understand without belittling.

It helps to remember too that this is a stage and children pass through it in various ways. Some even acquire an imaginary playmate with a name and definite personality. The friend usually fades away as the child gains real friends in her group activities.

Encouraging the child to "try out" new situations through her imagination is excellent preparation for the actual new experiences of kindergarten. Your support and praise of her attempts at independence, your respect for the feelings she's beginning to express, and your acceptance of her likes and dislikes all make her feel worthy and important. Who could have better preparation for the future?

164

Checklist: 54–60 Months
(Developmental Age)

NEW BEHAVIORS	SUGGESTED GAMES	NEW BEHAVIORS	SUGGESTED GAMES
☐ Recognizes when others show their feelings	176	☐ Plays games with imaginary people	189
☐ Handles small things well; likes trying new skills	177	☐ Asks why something happened	190
☐ Follows directions in supervised art activities	178	☐ Gets dressed with little help	191
☐ Likes to use a pencil and pretend to write	179	☐ Waits for own turn and usually follows directions	192
☐ Classifies things by one characteristic	180	☐ Anticipates the major holidays	193
☐ Sometimes pretends she's someone else	181	☐ Knows the concepts of same and different	194
☐ Uses scissors to cut snips in edge of paper	182	☐ Sometimes says words for numbers to ten	195
☐ Cooperates with another person in throwing a ball	183	☐ Can think several steps ahead before acting	196
☐ Recognizes some needs of self and others	184	☐ Understands the rules of Simon Says	197
☐ Asks about earlier days	185	☐ Follows directions that require precise action	198
☐ Dependably follows simple adult-made rules	186	☐ Notices "errors" adult makes in nursery rhymes	199
☐ Uses the words "first" and "last"	187	☐ Names the opposite of a word on request	200
☐ Uses names of many colors; says numbers to five	188		

176. Show Me How It Feels

HOW ADULT: In earlier games the child was encouraged to understand feelings by looking at pictures of happy or sad faces. Continue helping her to accept and sort out feelings by playing a different kind of game. Practice acting out feelings instead of searching for pictures of them. Start with a familiar feeling. Say, "Show me how it feels to be happy." Pick up on her behavior in your reply. If she gives a big smile mention that, "Your big smile shows me." If she dances around say, "That certainly is a happy dance. It shows me you really feel good." Offer to show how **you** look when you feel happy. Recall some times each of you were happy and how you looked. □ Another time say, "Show me how it feels to be afraid." After she's shown you, try to recall together a time in the recent past when she was afraid and how you recognized she was afraid. "I noticed you stood very still and watched." Ask her how it feels to be angry, excited, or left out. □ Take your cues from her as you continue the game. Acting out just one emotion may be enough for now. Trying out two or three feelings may be the way you play the game another time. □ Accept whatever posture and expression she uses. But give your own feelings, too. "I'm glad you showed me. Now when you look like that I'll know you're annoyed. Want me to show how I feel annoyed?"

CHILD: At first the child may not be sure how to begin. Support from the adult for any motion she makes will encourage her. She may tell the adult instead of showing, "I stamp my feet." When prompted, "That seems like a good way, show me what you mean," she will begin. She may act silly or exaggerate her movements. That could be a way of showing another feeling . . . uncertainty. She may begin to use this game as a way to express feelings she doesn't have words for and may ask the adult, "Want to see how I feel?"

WHY GOAL: To guide the child to further recognize feelings in herself and others. To let her try new ways of expressing them.

USES: Acting out feelings provides a way of expression beyond the child's limited words. It helps her sort and define her own feelings in a comfortable, accepting atmosphere.

176. Show Me How It Feels

HOW Say to the child, "Show me how it feels to be happy." Tell her what you notice. "Your big smile shows me that you're happy." Play "show me" with other feelings such as afraid or excited. Help her remember a time she felt that way and how she showed it then. Talk about a time you were excited; show her how you felt.

WHY To help the child define and recognize many feelings.

177. Today I Can

HOW ADULT: Prepare a *box* with a number of *cloth squares* about 12″ × 12″ for the child to practice using a needle and thread. Keep with it *spools* of several colors and some *needles* with a large eye (like embroidery needles) and *scissors*. Sit with your child the first time and help him with the process and with the words. Unwind some thread from the spool and cut it. Thread it through the needle and knot the two ends together. Stick the needle in and out of the cloth until the thread is all used up. Then cut the needle loose. Say what you're doing at each step. □ Invite the child to try. Do what's necessary to help him, but be sure to point out each step he did for himself. At first he will do only one or two steps, maybe the cutting or stitching. Each time you get the box out, help him remember what he was able to do last time. "Can you remember if you threaded the needle before? No? Well perhaps you can practice that today." When the box is put away, review what he did. "I didn't need to help you much today. Can you remember all the things you did all by yourself?" □ Any task that can be broken into short, manageable steps can be used to do this. Other examples are tying shoes, fastening the seatbelt, or taking a bath. Your role is to help him see the steps and catalog his learning of them.

CHILD: Just sticking the needle in and out, in and out is a fun thing to do. But learning each step in the process is also very satisfying. Once the adult has pointed it out, it's easy for the child to tell about his own progress. "Yesterday I couldn't put the thread through the hole. Today I did it. See. I did it all by myself." That's a big boost for his good feelings about himself! The many skills involved allow him to choose a realistic goal for himself each step of the way. For the child who hesitates to use a standard needle, a large plastic needle is available in some craft stores.

WHY GOAL: To see for himself how he can do what he couldn't do before. To provide a game that has a series of simple skills so he can see his progress.

USES: Almost no adult activity involves just one action or skill. Learning to see progress in a series of steps makes it possible to set realistic goals for oneself that can meet with success.

177. Today I Can

HOW Give the child a box with a cloth, a needle, thread, and scissors. Give him a chance to learn each step in the task of sewing, how to: 1) unwind and snip the thread; 2) thread the needle; 3) make a knot; 4) stitch the cloth; and finally, 5) cut the thread loose. As he learns each step, help him review so he will be able to say, "Yesterday I couldn't. Today I can."

WHY To point out the child's own progress in learning a skill.

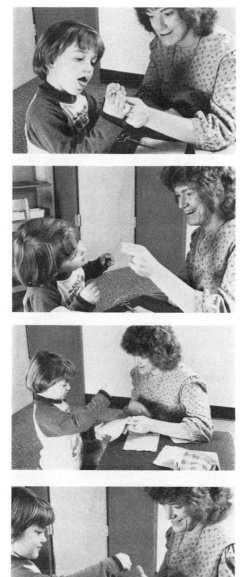

178. I'll Get It Myself

HOW ADULT: With your help the children have done many art projects and are familiar with a variety of art and craft materials. Now you can allow them freedom for some confident exploration on their own. Start by planning a "drawing center" with them. Some things the adults and children may need to decide are:

> Where is a handy storage place where the children can reach a small
>   stack of *paper* and boxes of *pens, pencils,* and *crayons?*
> During what part of the day may the drawing center be used freely?
> May more than one child at a time work in the center?
> Is there a trash can handy?
> Who will help with tacking up finished work?

Once these decisions have been reached (using the problem-solving techniques in game 174), the center can be set up. □ The adult's main challenge is to be available but to avoid hovering as the children try out their new freedom. You have arranged it so that natural consequences can be the best teacher. □ When the children have had the satisfaction of using the drawing materials independently for a few weeks, create a "cut and paste center." You and the children can repeat the process, thinking now about *scissors, scrap box, paste,* and handling the problems of cleanup. □ The satisfactions of independent art activity are so great that you will all want to gradually plan other centers for modeling, printmaking, and painting.

CHILD: The children may come to you often at first with questions or problems. That's to make sure you're still interested and haven't "abandoned" them. Warm assurance from the adult and a reminder of the procedures that were agreed on will help. Soon they will begin to prefer this uninterrupted, independent way of working. Sometimes a child will enjoy keeping a project secret as a surprise.

WHY GOAL: To arrange art materials in a way that will let the child independently get, use, and return them.

USES: As we grow, most of us prefer the freedom of doing things for ourselves. Independence means we have to work a little harder, but it opens up the fascinating choices of when to do work, how to do it, how long to take, etc.

178. I'll Get It Myself

HOW Plan with your children where the art materials will be kept and how they may be used. Then give them the opportunity to do "projects" when they have some free time.

WHY To make it easy for the child to use art materials without help.

179. Mailing a Letter

HOW ADULT: Every family has its own special celebration days. With some it's birthdays, with others it's achievement days or religious holidays. These special times provide you with chances to make your young child aware of the members of her family who live in other places. Use these times to send letters. The "message" can be a *picture* the child draws, her *photo*, *scribbles* she calls writing, a card you buy together, or whatever else you both agree to send. □ You provide an *envelope* and she can stamp it. Then show her the three things that must be on the envelope. Tell her, "These words and numbers tell who it will go to. This tells that you sent it. The stamp pays the mail carrier." Don't expect her to learn the address yet, although she'll enjoy hearing the lovely names of strange towns and states. Bigger brothers and sisters are often willing partners in this activity. If they're old enough you may need only to make sure of correct addresses; they can be responsible for writing them and collecting the letter contents. When it's time to mail the letter, you and the child will want to do it together, whether it's picked up at the door, the corner letter box, or the post office. You can explain, "The mail carrier will get it, and his helpers will take it to Grandmother." You might clue the relative that a return message is much more effective if sent quickly while the child still remembers mailing her letter.

CHILD: The child will not be able to really comprehend the whole process of mailing. But as she receives a response from Grandmother or Aunt Jane sends her a card in thanks, she will begin to understand. She probably thinks the mail carrier will literally take the envelope to its destination. That's okay. For now it's enough that every time she mails a letter or receives one she's building up the image of her family.

WHY GOAL: To help the child become aware of people in her larger family or group and to provide a reason for writing and reading.

USES: Having a reason for writing and reading will increase her interest in learning how. The child takes her sense of group membership with her as she approaches new experiences. Her awareness of a strong group backing her up is an important source of confidence.

172

179. Mailing a Letter

HOW Help your child send a letter to a relative who's far away. Tell her what must be written on the envelope. Write it on for her. Let her lick the stamp and put it on. Put her message inside. Then go together to let her drop it in the mail box.

WHY To help the child make contact with distant family members.

180. Double Treasure

HOW ADULT: In this treasure hunt the children search for things that have two characteristics. Say, "Let's look all around the room for some 'double treasures.' The things we find must be red and they must be toys." When a child finds something, check by saying out loud, "Let's see. This is a toy **and** this part of it's red—so it's a double treasure! We'll put all the treasures here on this table." □ As each thing is found, ask about the two characteristics. "Is it a toy? Is it red?" If necessary, say, "That's a pretty toy, but it doesn't seem to be red. Let's keep looking until we find something that's both." Compliment the children on their sharp eyes when they find an item and again when you review the pile of things on the table at the end of the game. □ This Learningame can be made new on many different days by changing the definition of the treasure. You might look for things that are: blue and running shoes, round and a container, or canned and a vegetable. For variety, search for pictures of double treasures in a book.

CHILD: Most preschool children do not find it simple to focus on two features at the same time. Typically they will zero in on one feature that seems most important to them. Playing the game gives them practice in shifting their attention back and forth between chosen features. Some children may take a little time to develop this skill but when they catch on they make rapid progress. Once they get going, some may even ask for "triple treasure."

WHY GOAL: To help the children create groups that are based on more than one characteristic. To encourage them to think carefully and systematically.

USES: In most situations it is necessary to consider more than one aspect of an object. In choosing a cup to use, the child may have to think about whether he can hold it easily and whether it is breakable. Later, as an adult, it is necessary to consider taste, preparation needed, and nutritional value when choosing items for a menu.

180. Double Treasure

HOW Have a treasure hunt for things that are round and are containers. Each time the children find something, ask, "Is it round? Is it a container?" If both answers are yes, say, "You found a double treasure!" On other days let two other features define the treasure.

WHY To encourage the children to classify using two features of the object.

181. Walking Lost

HOW ADULT: Walk a crazy way past the child. Be sure she sees you. When she asks (or looks like she'd like to ask) what you're doing, tell her, "I'm walking like I'm dizzy." See if she'd like to play a game about walking. Tell her you'll ask about a new way to walk and she will answer by walking that way. Ask the question the same way each time: How do you walk when you're: lost?

> —in a hurry?
> —tired?
> —cold?
> —carrying a heavy bag?

☐ If she can't think how, ask her to close her eyes and think how she might feel and then walk that way. If she still can't do it, sympathize. "Yes, it is hard to imagine some things isn't it? Can you imagine . . . instead?" and move to a new idea. Use the word "imagine" as you talk to let her know it's fine to "make things up" and to say that this is an acceptable situation for doing it in. ☐ After she's played several times you might join in as she acts out her ideas. But don't do it too soon or she might imitate rather than imagine. If you play with more than one child, be sure that each one's ideas are respected so that the children won't be tempted to copy. ☐ Later, ask how a bird might walk when it's lost. This requires two ideas ("bird" and "lost") to be combined.

CHILD: Her walks may seem much alike at first. But when she gets into the spirit of the game, she will add all kinds of individual touches. She might explain some. "I walk like this when I'm cold 'cause it helps me get warm." She might have other interesting ideas. "I know how I walk when I'm wet. Up on my toes so I won't get drips on the rug." If she doesn't have enough experience to imagine an action, she may act very silly instead. This is a sign for the adult to move on to more familiar examples.

WHY GOAL: To help the child act out what she imagines. To let her know that imagining is acceptable behavior.

USES: This imagining is actually an early step in manipulating ideas rather than manipulating things. Later her imagination will carry her beyond her familiar world and allow her to think about places she's never been to and solutions to problems that haven't even occurred yet.

181. Walking Lost

HOW Play a game that lets the child try her imagination. Say, "How do you walk when you're lost?" Let her show you her own way. Play again with: in a hurry, tired, cold, etc. Laugh at her comic actions. Tell her she has a good imagination. She's learning to separate pretend from real.

WHY To be a good audience as the child acts out what she imagines.

182. Cutting New Lines

HOW ADULT: When the child makes lots of irregular snips with *scissors*, he's ready for more challenge. Prepare a series of *sheets with lines* that help him develop direction in his cutting. On firm paper 6 or 7 inches wide (pieces from grocery bags are just right), make some thick lines straight across. When he's learned to cut on those, make thinner lines. The next stage is a slightly curved line. Later, curve a strong diagonal across a *magazine cover* picture so he creates a puzzle when he cuts it. Point out, "You can fit it back together. You made a puzzle." □ Curving the line around to make a circle is next. You need to make it at least 8 or 10 inches across at first. He still may be closing the scissors the length of the blade so he needs plenty of space. At first his result may not greatly resemble a circle! But as his snips become shorter he will stay more on the curve. Talk about "not straight" and "curved." As he moves to cutting large squares add a new word, "corners." □ It will take some months to go through all these stages. Some he will master sooner than others, so it's good to have new lines handy when you notice he's ready. As he becomes more skilled, describe what has happened, "I see you're using shorter cuts now. That makes it easier to stay on the line, doesn't it?" □ A child who insists on snipping everything within reach can be given limits. "For now, you can use the scissors only when you're seated at your table and I am with you."

CHILD: The child enjoys the process of cutting. He's on the lookout for new things to use his scissors on. An available supply of attractive practice sheets keeps the cutting under control. The child is excited about making something new and will usually not be upset if he goes "off the line." He would be happy to keep the family supplied with scraps for notes, lists, and bookmarks if he's given a box to put them in.

WHY GOALS: To provide an acceptable and safe way for the child to improve his scissor skills. To help him be more independent in choosing his activities.

USES: Tools that use the "scissor principle" are an integral part of this culture. A child skilled in the use of such tools has a greater capacity for independence and creativity in his life.

182. Cutting New Lines

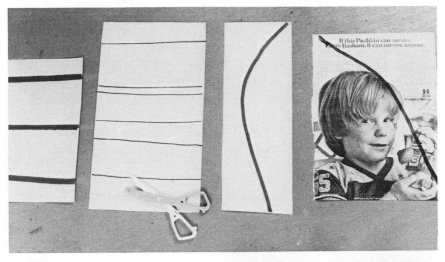

HOW Help your child use scissors in new ways. Prepare some paper with simple lines for him to cut along. Start with wide straight lines. Go to thinner straight lines. Later give him gentle curves to follow. Watch and be interested in how he does. Let him know he's in control by saying, "You made the scissors go just where you wanted them to!"

WHY To encourage the child to follow a line with his scissors.

183. Three-Corner Catch

HOW ADULT: With one child the adult tosses a large *lightweight ball* back and forth a few times. He then suggests an expanded game. "Brett, let's ask Anita if she wants to toss and catch with us." When Anita joins, the adult introduces the new game. "We have three people. We can play three-corner catch. Each of us will be a corner." He then explains the rules. "Brett will throw to Anita. Anita will throw to me, and I will throw to Brett." Walk through it first, holding the ball in front of the thrower, then walking it to the catcher, and so on. Then, begin the game. □ The adult encourages success in catching by praising those who helped it to happen. "Brett you threw that **so** carefully to Anita. That helped her to catch, didn't it?" Or the adult might say what he is doing. "I'll step a little closer to you Brett. It will be easier for you to catch." □ If another child is watching, the adult offers his place to that child. "David would like to play. He can take my corner." The adult stays with them because they cannot manage the whole responsibility of turns yet. The name of the game limits the number of players to a reasonable group that doesn't require a long wait for turns.

CHILD: The children may miss the ball a lot at first. Hearing the words "toss" and "catch" helps them to realize they are engaged in two separate activities. The fun of playing with several friends makes up for the short wait for turns. A child who thinks it fun to throw so the catcher misses will begin to change his mind and feel good about helping when he is praised and approved for doing so. Practice in a pleasant three-corner game soon improves catching skills.

WHY GOAL: To give the child a chance to catch a ball thrown from 4 or 5 feet, in a cooperative game requiring several children to take turns.

USES: Tossing and catching is a universal game in all children's cultures. Children who are skilled have an easier time finding a place in their group to learn further social skills.

183. Three-Corner Catch

HOW Toss and catch a large lightweight ball with a child. Invite a second child to join to make three-corner catch. Toss from one person to the other in turn around the triangle. Praise for cooperation, "Brett, you threw that carefully so Anita could easily catch it. Good player!" Limit to three so the wait for turns is not long.

WHY To let the child catch and throw a ball in turn.

184. I'd Like Help

HOW ADULT: Provide the child with a simple statement he can use to express his need for help. Begin by using the statement yourself when you need help from him. Say, "I'd like some help!" Then ask, "Would you like to know how you can help me?" When he agrees, tell him how. Later, when you see him in need, ask, "Would you like some help? Can you tell me 'I'd like some help?' " Don't demand that he repeat it before you help him. You are simply giving him a tool for expressing his need as you might give him a spoon for satisfying his hunger. He won't be skilled at using it right away. □ After the need for help is made known the adult can follow with a question (or several) to the child to help him say just what the need is. After his plea "I'd like some help," you then say, "What would you like me to do?" Following the same pattern of question and response each time helps him to organize his thinking and gives him clues for finding the right words to use. Often a child who whines or pulls at the adult for help simply has learned no other way for getting it.

CHILD: As the child hears you repeat the same statement in many situations, he will begin to use it also. Since real help usually follows the words, he will be more likely to know and use the words the next time. He will be more willing to tackle new tasks as he feels confident of help when he needs it. And he will enjoy that comfortable feeling that comes when someone understands his needs.

WHY GOAL: To provide the child with an acceptable method of enlisting help from others. To set up a situation that is likely to give him positive feelings about turning to others for help.

USES: Learning how to determine need for help and how to ask for it becomes more important as the child's tasks become more complex. Few tasks are accomplished completely by oneself.

184. I'd Like Help

HOW Provide the child with a way to ask for the help he needs. When you need his help say, "I'd like some help." Then tell what he can do for you. Soon he will say it to you. It will be easier for him to try new things if he has a way to ask for help if he needs it. And knowing you'll understand if he asks makes him feel good.

WHY To help the child learn an effective way to ask for what he needs.

185. My History in Clothes

HOW ADULT: When one of the children asks what he or she was like as a baby, use this opening to stimulate some serious thought about the children's personal histories. A parent might say, "Let's look in this suitcase. I've kept some of your *clothes* in it that you've outgrown." Spread the clothing out and together decide which were from the earliest time and which were more recent. If enough have been saved, the children will be able to see a progression from babyhood to the present. □ Let the clothes be a guide to discussing what each age was like. "See how the knees are worn on these overalls; you were still crawling when you wore them. And see the legs of these can unsnap. That's because you weren't toilet trained then." Let the conversation be a pleasant reminiscence. But conclude with a positive assurance about today. "You've grown so much. I like the age you are right now because we can do so many interesting things together that we couldn't do before." □ At another time you might remember with *photographs* or *toys* that have been saved. At the day care center each child might bring two or three items of clothing to share and discuss with the group. And, by saving examples of *art work* and other *mementos*, the caregiver can help the children look back on their past year together.

CHILD: It's hard to predict when it will occur, but sooner or later most children develop an interest in their own past. Usually the task of thinking back is taken very seriously, but most children have to repeat the process many times before they are convinced that this is really their history. Some will want to dress a doll with the clothes and pretend they are the parent.

WHY GOAL: To help the children use their old clothes or toys as memory aids. Together, to think fondly of other times.

USES: Each of us knows we have grown and changed when we compare the present to the past. Since children's early memories are rather sketchy, they need some help in recognizing the tremendous growth they are undergoing.

185. My History in Clothes

HOW Get out some clothes the children have outgrown. Talk about what it was like when they wore the clothes. "You were still crawling then." Finish by reminding the children that they can do many new things now they couldn't do then. Say, "I like what you can do today!"

WHY To help the children see how much they've grown.

186. Rules to Grow On

HOW ADULT: By the time the children are ready for more independence, the adult is usually tired of participating in so many child decisions. This is a good time to establish some rules that will lead to new ways of doing things. Begin by letting the children know that new rules are to make them free to do some things on their own. □ Suggest that it would be nice, for example, if they could safely go outdoors without having to wait for you each time. Ask what each person could do to make this possible. Could the child tell the parents before going out? Could he play in a space near the house? Could the adult stay near the window to watch and be handy in case of an emergency? After some discussion, jointly make a rule. It should clearly state the conditions under which the children may independently choose to go out and play. After the rule has been used a time or two it may prove to have some bugs in it. Working them out is a part of the learning. □ Tell the child you're proud he's growing up enough to make rules and stick with them. Many other aspects of the daily routine can be the subject of new mutually agreed upon rules, such as when and how he could choose and prepare a snack. It's unimportant which rules are chosen as long as they open up safe, new areas of decision-making for each child.

CHILD: A child may rush into making a rule before he thinks it through, but by the second conference the discussion gets serious. Given repeated opportunities, most children this age will actively try to create realistic rules. Sometimes new freedom is a little scary, so the child playing outdoors may need to see Mom and blow her a kiss or come to the door for a reassuring hug.

WHY GOAL: To let the children participate in making some rules that enable them to be more independent. To think about what everyone needs for independence.

USES: By making and following rules, children learn that independence is based on responsibility. Later they will need to participate in the responsibility of making rules for a club and still later in deciding on their own personal guidelines such as how late to stay out at night.

186. Rules to Grow On

HOW With your children make some rules. The rules might allow them to independently get a snack or go out and play. Thinking about the rules and agreeing on them are the important parts of this Learningame. Adult and child will benefit from the experience because both have to adjust their earlier behaviors.

WHY To grant more independence to the child.

187. Telling How

HOW ADULT: Let the child take a new role in a familiar, cooperative project. A few days after she has participated in making *Jell-O* (game 172), let her help another adult make Jell-O. In her new role she will be the one who directs the activity. The adult must of course support her efforts (and provide some quiet guidance if needed). □ After the water is hot the child gets the *cards* that were made in the first game. The adult asks, "Now, what do I do first. What did you and Daddy do first when you made Jell-O? Do the cards tell you?" If she has difficulty, help her by reviewing the drawings and by asking questions like, "What do I need to put the Jell-O in?" or "If we're making Jell-O do I get the package first?" This will jog her memory of what went first. □ After the first step, ask for the "next." Continue in this way through the three steps. Then take a minute to sit down and talk about how she guided you. Be honest with her and don't imply that she did it all . . . she knows she didn't. Instead say how it made you feel. "I'm so happy you're getting big enough to help by telling me what comes next" or perhaps, "It's fun to have you as my partner."

CHILD: The child is taking an unfamiliar role in this activity. In most cooperative games with an adult she is the junior partner or at most shares an equal role with the adult. Now she's in the director's chair. She will be gaining a sense of trust in her own ability to make decisions in a sharing experience and will begin to think cooperating is a good thing to do. If the steps are chosen for her or her choice is called wrong, she won't feel as good about sharing in a future activity. With a little subtle guidance the child will be able to choose the first, next, and last steps—to direct the activity. By the next session she will probably be able to do it without the cards!

WHY GOAL: To help the child take a more important role in a cooperative activity. To practice doing things in order from first to last.

USES: Learning to take a more directive and responsible role leads to new kinds of partnerships. Changing one's role in a familiar situation is a first step for taking on the risk of a new role in a new situation.

187. Telling How

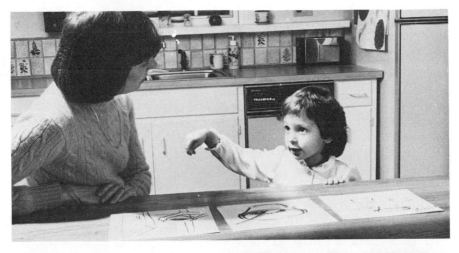

HOW Practice cooperation by making Jell-O with the child. Let her lead the game by telling what must be done first, next, and last. Let her use some cards that will help her remember what came first when she made Jell-O before with another adult. Then she can tell you. You'll want to tell her how much fun it was to share the activity with her.

WHY To cooperate with the child when she is the leader.

188. Playing School

HOW ADULT: Invite a couple of children to play school with you. Tell them they'll need to have sharp ears and remember their colors and numbers. Give each child a set of 2″ × 2″ cards to spread out on the table. Start with just three colors and five numbers. □ Make what follows into a lively time. You should move quickly from one question to the next with enthusiastic punctuations of praise such as, "Good listening. You heard all three parts of that direction!" Move from simpler directions to harder ones. If you're at the right level of difficulty the child will make only an occasional error. Here are samples of the many things you could say:

Put your finger on the number two.
Pick up the red card.
Put the number three on top of yellow.
Put two, four, and five in a row.
What is the middle number in your row?

Touch your favorite color.
Hand me two colors.
Pick up all but two numbers.
Pick up the smallest number that's still on the table.
Touch, in order: red, three, blue, one.

You'll be able to tell when the children are ready to play with six colors and ten number cards.

CHILD: By now, four-year-old children recognize most color and number words and probably use some of them in daily conversation. However, they'll need some practice to understand these same words when they are sandwiched into a hard set of school-like directions.

WHY GOAL: To let the child hear instructions that contain the names of colors and numbers. To give directions that have more than one part and so are like school directions.

USES: This game tunes the child's ears to hearing the precise directions that are typical of school.

188. Playing School

HOW Give the children some color cards and some number cards. Play school by giving directions about the cards. Say things that will have the children point to the cards or move them around. This can be a fast-paced game that will give the adult many pleasant opportunities to say, "Good listening!"

WHY To give instructions that require careful listening.

189. Let's Imagine

HOW ADULT: In an earlier activity (147), you helped the child pretend by setting up prop boxes to help her play a role. Now use a purely mental exercise to help her imagination grow. Create a quiet time for the two of you by sitting together or taking her in your lap and rocking her as you do for a story. Recall a character or situation from a recently read story. Have the child extend the earlier story by asking her questions she must imagine the answers to. For example, "When the bear was on the ice floe how do you think he felt?" "If you had been there how would you have felt?" □ Pretend a situation, "If you were going to visit Red Fox what would you pack in your bag?" "If you had an invitation to a dinosaur's birthday what present would you take?" □ Make sure that your questions refer to something she has some knowledge of—either from a book, a reported event, a T.V. program, or her own experience. Then you can expect her to project at least one or two feelings or behaviors that might be possible, and to imagine reactions for both herself and other people. □ With encouragement, children of this age develop such delightfully creative ideas that many adults keep journals to note them for a later time.

CHILD: The child is so busy playing with objects she doesn't often take time to stop and just imagine. When the adult makes it possible by enclosing this little minute of time, she usually responds well. Her ideas, of course, are based on her own knowledge and experience. But she imagines them into her own creation. For example she might say, "I'd be so sad. I'd fly away." Her emotion is real but the behavior unrealistic—although, admittedly, exciting to think about. She will begin slowly with an idea or two but later be able to imagine sequential events.

WHY GOAL: To create a specific time to play a game of pretending using just the mind and no props.

USES: Imagining is a way of experiencing without physical participation. A child uses this method to enrich her own creativity and later to write school papers on topics like "My Visit to the Moon."

189. Let's Imagine

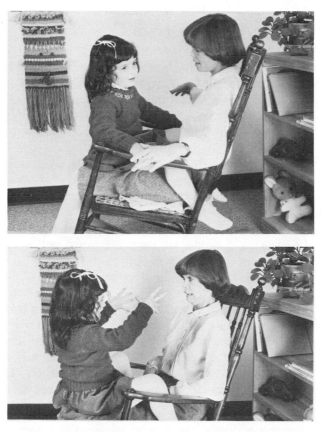

HOW Create a world where you and the child can pretend with just your minds for a minute or two. Sit with her or hold her on your lap. Think with her about a question that only her imagination can answer. "If you were invited to a dinosaur's birthday what present would you take?" "How will the man feel when he gets to the top of the telephone pole?" Listen to her answers with respect. You'll feel joy in what you're nurturing.

WHY To help the child play a mental game of pretending.

190. Wondering What Caused It

HOW ADULT: Many events during the day may momentarily puzzle a child. At these times, guide the child in wondering about cause and effect. Add some excitement by saying, "We're going to have to do some detective work to find out what caused that!" The adult can often help by asking questions that help the child recount what just happened, "Now let's see, you were painting with *two jars of color*. What were the colors? Yes, that's right, red and yellow. And then you saw what? Yes, orange paint. Where was it? Uh huh, here in the middle. Well, where do you think it came from?" □ By asking questions about what occurred before the puzzling event you are helping the child learn that causes usually precede effects. You might help the child focus on who was there and what things were involved. □ The child's conclusion about "what caused it" may not be entirely accurate by adult standards, but he is getting the valuable experience of trying his wings at reasoning. (If you are worried about an incorrect conclusion, don't correct it, but say you have a different idea which is . . .) □ If you're lucky, in addition to answering the adult's leading questions, the child may take off on his own avenue of speculation. Even if these ideas are rather farfetched, they should be generously accepted as long as they stay on the topic. All the attempts the child makes are worthy of your praise and encouragement. If older siblings and friends learn to accept the child's attempts, they can be wonderful partners in this detective game.

CHILD: Children are naturally curious about what caused things. However, they may be perfectly happy with the idea that the paint turned orange, "because it wants to be pretty." Children may in one situation believe that inanimate objects act with a will and in another situation come up with a very logical explanation of events.

WHY GOAL: To ask questions that will guide the child in thinking about cause and effect. To use the ordinary events of the day for learning.

USES: The puzzles we attempt get harder as we grow, but the method of thinking back to what happened before continues to be an effective way to try to solve them.

190. Wondering What Caused It

HOW Ask questions that will help the child do some mental detective work. If you guide him he may be able to figure out where the orange paint on his paper came from. He may be able to make the connection between other things like cold weather and frozen water in a bucket outdoors. Don't be surprised if he has some fanciful explanations as well as logical ones.

WHY To help the child think back to the causes of events.

Examples of other situations to wonder about:

tricycle seat is wet in the morning
water comes out of the drain pipe
paste dries up in open paste jar
fish in the aquarium dies

191. Clothes for Tomorrow

HOW ADULT: Before bedtime talk with your child about what she's going to do tomorrow. Invite her to choose some *clothes* that will be suitable. As she chooses, help her lay them out so can put them on in the morning. Guide her to see what's reasonable so you won't have to veto her choices. "If you're going on a field trip, will you want your comfortable running shoes?" Help her think about how much dressing she can do by herself. "That shirt's a good choice. You can pull it over your head . . . no buttons." Remind her why you're doing this. "In the morning you can get dressed all by yourself. I'll be anxious to see how nice you look." □ Think with her about alternatives in case of rain or changed weather. Sometimes lay out the raincoat or boots. She can decide in the morning if she needs them. □ Later, instead of actually laying out the clothes, verbally agree on the kind of clothing she might wear. Together you might just peek in the closet or drawer to see what she will wear, without needing to handle each piece. □ At first you may find the choice-making takes more time than dressing her yourself. But as she gains confidence, through the planning that gets her started and the praise that maintains her interest, she will become quite independent about dressing.

CHILD: The child who is not criticized for lack of perfection likes to do things for herself. Once she has learned the buttoning and zipping skills, she needs plenty of time and occasionally a reminder of what comes next. Dawdling is a common part of the activity. It doesn't mean she's less independent—just that time has little meaning.

WHY GOAL: To provide a series of experiences that will help the child become more independent in choosing her own clothes appropriately and dressing herself.

USES: We can be more independent and successful in many activities if we give them some prior thought and planning. Examples in life include preparing a meal, taking a test, and spending money.

191. Clothes for Tomorrow

HOW Help the child choose her clothes for tomorrow. Together, lay them out the night before so she can dress herself in the morning. Later, let her decide by looking in the closet but without handling the clothes. This activity at night helps her to act independently in the morning.

WHY To give the child practice in being independent by planning ahead.

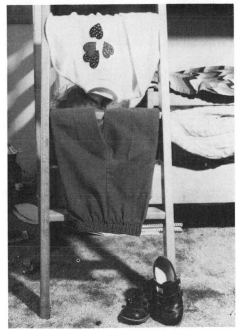

192. We Play Relay

HOW ADULT: Create a little fun with a relay that accomplishes some ordinary task. For example, let several children cooperate in transporting some toys to the outdoor sandbox. The adult's instructions might go something like this, "Let's pretend these *sandbox toys* are very big and we can carry just one at a time. Jeri, you be the starter. But let's pretend Jeri can go only from here to the indoor slide. So, Maria you stand here at the slide to take the toys when Jeri gets them here. And let's pretend Maria can't go any further than the door. So Jose you stand by the door so you can take the toys from there and leave them in the sandbox. It will take several trips back and forth for everyone. When the last toy is in the sandbox, Jose can call us and we'll all go there to play." □ Let your comments tell about cooperation. Perhaps, "Jeri, it was nice to see you wait for Maria until she got back to the slide." Or, "Maria, you handed that one carefully so Jose wouldn't drop it." Later, when everyone is playing happily in the sandbox, talk about the funny rules in the relay. Explain that they allowed everyone to have a special job and to cooperate by doing his or her share. You and the children could plan similar relay games to practice cooperation: taking the *snack* out for a picnic, putting away the *indoor toys,* or moving the *tricycles* to the shed.

CHILD: The children will probably "go along" with almost any set of relay rules for a time or two. Their interest does not last unless the adult is wise enough to devise a new relay for them. The more the children are involved in inventing the rules ("Let's pretend that . . ."), the more enthusiasm they will have for the relay. And they will catch the spirit of the adult who cheers them on toward their group goal.

WHY GOAL: To give a group of children a chance to accomplish something cooperatively. To experience the fun of doing something together.

USES: Many enjoyable activities, (team sports, for example) are accomplished only by groups of people working together. Non-pressured experiences in group effort at age four can help create a positive, confident attitude toward later cooperative activities.

192. We Play Relay

HOW Take an ordinary job and turn it into a relay. Let the children take toys one at a time to the sandbox. The first child takes a toy to the slide; the second child takes it from the slide to the door; and the last child takes it from the door to the sandbox. Afterward, everybody gets to play together in the sandbox. And you might casually mention how nice it was to see everybody cooperating to get a job done.

WHY To let children have fun cooperating.

193. Let's Celebrate

HOW ADULT: Now that your children are well aware of the major holidays observed by almost everyone, add some celebrations that may be special to your family. Before the chosen holiday comes, talk about it as a family group. Let the younger child participate by asking questions and helping with the preparations. Usually a special task can be found for him in getting ready the *food* or *decorations* that go along with the celebration. Explain that not everyone observes this holiday but that your family or group will because it means something special to them. The meaning, of course, is usually from your own religion or national history. □ Sometimes, however, it's nice to venture outside your own experience and "borrow" a holiday from another culture. Searching for answers to the four-year-old's constant questions may give you some ideas for celebration. The parent can answer, "Gee, I'm not sure why the Japanese make kites like fish. Let's go to the library and see if we can find out." □ Your research might help you decide to celebrate the Girls' Festival on March 3 or the Boys' Festival on May 5. And your child would learn that an important part of the first is a fine display of dolls and of the second is the flying of fish kites on bamboo poles from the rooftop!

CHILD: Ordinary things become special on a holiday. A decorated cookie, a kite, a small present, a hat—all have more meaning for children who have been preparing and looking forward to them. And, for preschool children, getting ready is probably the most important part of a holiday. An event that simply appears unexpectedly may have much less meaning than an anticipated celebration.

WHY GOAL: To introduce the children to holidays that have particular meaning to your family or subculture. To broaden the family's experience by celebrating holidays of other cultures.

USES: Holidays are usually connected to the history of the group. They remind us of certain values. Because holidays are repeated every year they give children a way to mark the passage of time and the security of knowing a familiar event will return.

193. Let's Celebrate

HOW Celebrate some special holidays. Some of these might have important meaning to your own ethnic group. Others might be holidays chosen from another culture. Involve the children in lots of the preparations ahead of time, and you'll see a happy explosion of enthusiasm when the special day arrives.

WHY To spread joy and learning through holidays.

194. Same Sounds

HOW ADULT: This game gives the child a reason to listen to the sounds that come at the beginning of words. At any time during a day say, "Listen to these words. Do they sound the same at the beginning? Or do they sound different? Mouse, mat." If the child is puzzled or unsure, you can repeat, "Listen again: mmmouse, mmmat." Exaggerate the m-sound or your lip movements or whatever is needed to help the child understand the game. When he succeeds, be very enthusiastic in your praise because the child is doing a difficult task. □ You can do a few pairs of words many times during the day: while driving in the car, shopping, cooking, walking down the stairs. On the first day it might be a good idea to stay with "m" words so the child can gain confidence with this sound. Soon you can start mixing up pairs and including some that don't match. Moving rapidly from one pair to another is a way of getting in a lot of practice and making the game exciting. □ When the child is almost always correct with word pairs, go on to groups of three. Say, "Listen: bus, bake, hat." Ask the child to repeat the word that begins differently. The two of you can enjoy playing this challenging game for many days, even months.

CHILD: At first the child will have difficulty and may not understand what he is being asked to listen for. On the first few trials it helps when the adult repeats and exaggerates. It may help also if the child repeats the word pairs. There will be a point at which the child "catches on" and things will go smoother. The child may begin to initiate the game himself after that. Until then, a lot of adult patience is needed.

WHY GOAL: To say words in twos and threes that call attention to the beginning sounds. To let the child use the words "same" and "different" in describing the beginning sounds of words.

USES: Hearing the beginning sounds of words is a first step in understanding that a word is made up of a series of sounds. The skill of hearing the individual sounds in words will be used later by the child in spelling and reading.

194. Same Sounds

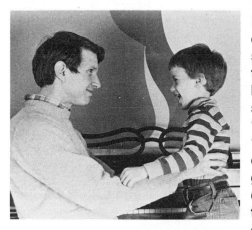

HOW While you're doing everyday activities, say some pairs of words. Let the child tell you if the beginning sounds are the same (as in "mouse" and "mat") or different (as in "tall" and "put"). After lots of practice, say words in groups of three. Let the child tell which one of the three begins with a different sound. Let your praise tell the child how carefully he's listening.

WHY To give the child words that help him pay attention to beginning sounds.

195. Counting to Ten

HOW ADULT: Use a finger play song to help the children practice their numbers to ten.

SING	PLAY
one, two, three, four, five	close up the fingers of one hand, one at a time to make a fist
I caught a fox alive.	enclose the first fist with the second hand
six, seven, eight, nine, ten,	open up the fingers of the second hand, one at a time
I let him go again.	separate the hands, with the fingers making running-away motions

Sometimes practice with *counters* (such as pegs, or crayons, or clothes-pins-in-the-basket) or with motions (like steps going up the stairs, hops on one foot, or hand claps). Always say the number clearly as you touch the counter or perform the action. □ Use words like "more than" or "less than" or "most" when you talk about groups of things. □ You will think of many ways to introduce counting into your day's activities and still keep counting a fresh and fun thing to do.

CHILD: The child will be able to count accurately to ten before fully understanding the quantity of each number. Some children understand concepts of numbers very quickly. Others learn the words long before they understand quantity. Both are normal developmental behaviors.

WHY GOAL: To help the child practice using the words from one to ten in sequence. To play with numbers.

USES: The numerical system of our culture is based on ten. When a child masters tens, it will be a good start on the whole system. The child will live in the "computer age" and will need to be comfortable with numbers.

195. Counting to Ten

HOW Sing a song with your children about numbers up to ten. Act it out on your fingers. They will learn how to count to ten. And they will begin to understand what numbers mean. Your pleasure will be in watching them learn.

Sing: 1,2,3,4,5; I caught a
         fox alive
         6,7,8,9,10; I let him
         go again

WHY To give the children experience counting from one to ten.

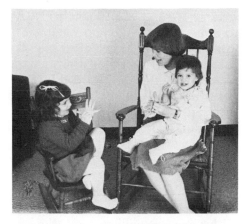

196. Thinking It Through

HOW ADULT: Earlier you helped the child gain skill by deciding which one of several solutions to a problem was best (game 174). Now, build on that skill by adding two other problem-solving steps that come before it. In these steps he will learn to name the problem and then to think of several possible solutions. □ If Ed's truck damaged Amy's sand castle, the steps might go like this. 1) **Name the problem.** Begin, "Amy seems unhappy. I wonder what the problem is." After this statement of concern, the adult should listen for some description of the problem from the children. Almost anything that goes beyond "He's mean," or "I didn't see it" can be a statement of the problem. If you hear something like "My castle's flat," or "There's not enough room in this sandbox," accept one of these and go on to the next problem-solving step. Say, "That sounds like the problem: not enough room." 2) **Think of some solutions.** Continue, "I bet you can think of some things to do about our problem of too little room." In earlier problems you suggested some solutions, but this time you want the children to try. Give them as much time as they need. But if no solutions occur to them, try a few more questions. "Do all these activities have to be in this one small sandbox?" or, "Could we play one game instead of two?" 3) **Choose the best and try it.** Now let the children do the thing they learned in the earlier game. Say, "Which of these ideas do you like best? Which one will make both of you happy?" As soon as a decision is reached, the children will be anxious to get busy and try it. You will want to stay nearby for a moment or two to see that the new plan gets off to a good start.

CHILD: When a typical problem comes along, the children may tend to argue with each other or to appeal to the adult for help. If the adult doesn't take sides in the argument, but rather asks questions that will help them think through the situation step by step, the children are likely to discover that they have good ideas and a growing ability for solving problems.

WHY GOAL: To ask questions that will enable the child to identify a problem, name two alternative solutions, and evaluate these alternatives before acting.

USES: Systematic problem-solving can be used simply (and with outside help as in this game) or it can be used at a very complex and independent level in adult life.

196. Thinking It Through

HOW When a problem happens, ask the child (or children) some helpful questions. First ask, "What's the problem." Then, "What are two or three things we could do?" And finally, "Which idea is best?" When the child chooses an idea and trles It out, congratulate hlm. "You thought through that problem carefully and now you have an idea that works!"

WHY To ask questions that lead the child through the steps of problem solving.

197. Silly Simon

HOW ADULT: Play a Learningame that will be fun for a small group of children. Use this new rule for Simon Says: "Always do what you hear, not what you see." Then explain to the children that sometimes you will say and do the same thing, but at other times you will say one thing and do another! □ Then, slowly at first but gaining speed, give a series of directions such as these:

> Simon says touch your nose
> Simon says jump up and down
> Simon says stand on tip-toe

Make your actions match the words until the third direction. Then as you say "stand on tip-toe," bend over instead. If some of the children bend over too, laugh about it together and then remind them of the new rule. □ Continue to play, giving directions that contain all the action and space words that the children know. When they successfully ignore your distracting actions, say, "You listen so carefully. Silly Simon did the wrong thing, but not you!"

CHILD: At first the children may confuse this game with the traditional Simon Says. But soon they'll sort out the rules. Some children will be able to play correctly as long as the game goes slowly but will get confused if the directions are fast. They'll get the most enjoyment from a pace that causes them to make a few funny errors—but not too many.

WHY GOAL: To give two conflicting messages together (verbal and visual) so the children will have a chance to practice paying attention to the right one. To let the children move their bodies according to verbal directions.

USES: Seldom are the messages we receive perfectly clear. Sounds or actions often intrude to take attention away from what is most important. Children in school will need to be able to attend to the message from the teacher while other children are talking, or interesting things are happening outside the window.

197. Silly Simon

HOW Invite the children to follow your direction. Say "Sometimes Silly Simon does the wrong thing, so don't be fooled by what he does. Your ears will tell you what to do." Then give lots of directions. For some, say one thing (like stand on tip-toe) but do another (like bend over.) Enjoy the funny mistakes that happen then. And when they catch your "mistakes," you'll want to let them know what a hard thing they did to notice and not be fooled.

WHY To help children focus on verbal instructions.

198. Playing More School

HOW ADULT: After the child is comfortable with the *color cards* (from game 188) through many sessions of "school," add a *sheet of paper* that has been folded into four parts called squares. Number the squares one to four. Now give directions that call for actions. Also ask questions that call for words. For example:

Put a color in each square.	Put colors in the bottom squares only
What color is in the third square?	See what color is in the fourth square, then raise
Where is the color orange?	your hand before telling me.

□ When the child responds by arranging the color cards or by pointing, say, "Good! I can **see** your answer." When he responds by speaking, say, "Yes! You **said** the right thing." □ For a change, some days give the children crayons instead of cards to use with the folded paper. Give directions like these:

Draw a green circle in the second square.	Make an "X" in each of the bottom squares.
Turn the circle into a happy face.	Put a red wiggly line in the empty square.

□ For some children the words "left" and "right" can be added to the instructions. And any youngster will enjoy being the teacher while you sit down with the cards.

CHILD: A child who knows the word "red" may be temporarily stumped by a complex question that has the simple answer "red." But, the child will improve as he gets used to the form and the sound of the questions.

WHY GOAL: To give directions that can be carried out on paper. To ask questions that can be answered with color words.

USES: This game gets the child accustomed to one of the most common items in school: a piece of paper.

210

198. Playing More School

HOW Give each child a paper that's been folded into four parts. Ask them to put their color cards on various parts of the paper. Sometimes the children can answer with words or can mark with crayons. You'll have a lot to praise them for.

WHY To let the child use paper, cards, words, and crayons to follow directions.

199. Rhyming

HOW ADULT: An earlier game (194) called attention to the beginnings of words. Let rhymes help the child notice how words end. Begin by repeating some words the child has heard in a nursery rhyme such as "Old King Cole." Say to the child, "Cole, soul, bowl, all those words rhyme. Now I'm going to say some more words. But **one** won't rhyme with the others. When you hear that words tell me to **stop**. Are you ready? Listen: book, hook, cook, took, look, apple." If the child doesn't shout "Stop!" when you reach apple, patiently invite her to listen as you say the words again. □ You can repeat this game many times by using the various events of the day: words that rhyme with lunch, words that rhyme with nap, words that rhyme with ride, etc. Sometimes put the non-rhyming word early in the series, and sometimes put it at the end of a long string of words. For fun, toss in an unexpected word such as applesauce or halloween as the non-rhymer. Nonsense words make good rhymes, too. In this game the child and you can share some of the delight language holds.

CHILD: At first the child may identify the non-rhyming word only because you hesitate on it. But soon she will get her ears in tune to the rhymes and will gleefully pounce on the word that doesn't fit. □ It's much easier to hear rhymes than to make them, so a child is unlikely to spontaneously make up many rhyming words. If she does, the wise adult will enthusiastically echo them back to her and perhaps add to "her" rhymes.

WHY GOAL: To give the child practice in hearing rhyme patterns and eliminating words that don't fit. To enjoy the sounds in language.

USES: Recognizing rhymes is another step in understanding how words are put together. Most ear training games develop skills that will be useful in learning to spell and read.

199. Rhyming

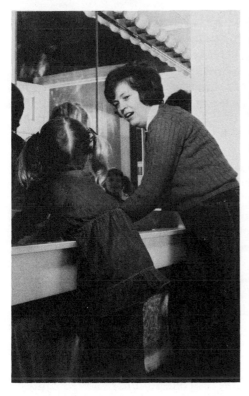

HOW At any time during the day, say a series of words. Let all of them rhyme but one. When you say that one, the child calls "Stop!" Put in some unexpected words or nonsense words for a little spice. And wouldn't it be nice for you both if once in a while you cuddled the child in your arms and whispered the words in her ear?

WHY To use rhymes to help the child listen more carefully to word sounds.

200. Beginning Analogies

HOW ADULT: Introduce the word-fun of analogies. For the first one you might want to have some props ready (a sock and a mitten) in case these are needed to dramatize the explanation. But then try to get away from props because the main idea of analogies is that they are pure word play—a time for searching in your mind for relationships. Begin by saying, "Listen to these words: 'sock-foot'. How do they go together?" "Yes, the sock goes on the foot. Now, remembering that the sock goes on the foot, where does the mitten go?" If the child says "hand" congratulate him for careful thinking. If he doesn't understand, get out the sock and mitten and see their relationships to the foot and hand. Restate the analogy, "The sock goes on the foot; the mitten goes on the hand." Then, while the pattern of this analogy is still fresh, go on to several more. Say, "A horse stays in a stable; a car stays in a . . .?" By using the words "stays in" you are emphasizing the relationship that the child is supposed to notice. □ For the first few play sessions try to let your choice of words give the relationships away. As soon as the child is familiar with the analogy pattern of thinking, try dropping out the give away words. Instead, use a less revealing word such as "is." For instance, "an apple is red; a banana is . . .?" The next page contains a few suggested analogies. Of course you will need many more than these, and your everyday experiences with the child will suggest them to you.

CHILD: The child will know the word "hot" long before he is able to complete an analogy such as, "Winter is cold; summer is . . .?" In the analogy he's having to search out a relationship and then apply it. That's pretty difficult even though the answer is a word the child has known for a long time. The wise adult will give the child plenty of practice before expecting much progress on this difficult task.

WHY GOAL: To talk about some pairs of words so that the child will see the relationships among words. To familiarize the child with the analogy as a way of thinking.

USES: Analogies help you look for patterns and teach that a clue to the answer is often found in the question.

200. Beginning Analogies

HOW Introduce your older four-year-old to the pure word play of analogies. Say, "An apple is red; a banana is . . .?" If the child doesn't get it, go back and use some give away words. Say, "The apple's color is red, the banana's color is . . ." Do all you have to do to make the pattern of analogy-thinking clear.
Demonstrate it with props or talk it through. Soon you and the child will be free of the props. You will have a fine time playing with words in the car, at the playground, at the laundromat, or anywhere at all.

WHY To help the child find and apply relationships.

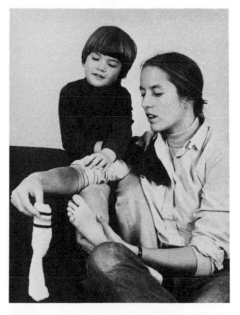

With give away words:
the sun shines in the day
the moon shines at __ (night)

a car travels on the road
a plane travels in the __ (sky)

a calf is a baby cow
a kitten is a baby __ (cat)

Without give away words:
sand is dry
water is __ (wet)

an elephant is big
a mouse is __ (little)

we ice skate in winter
we swim in __ (summer)

215

BIBLIOGRAPHY

1. References on Child Development and Activities

Braga, Laurie and Joseph. *Learning and Growing: A Guide to Child Development.* Englewood Cliffs, N.J.: Prentice-Hall, 1975.

Comer, James, and Poussaint, Alvin. *Black Child Care.* New York: Pocket Books, 1976.

Gordon, Ira, Guinagh, Barry, and Jester, Emile. *Child Learning Through Child Play: Learning Activities for Two- and Three-Year-Olds.* New York: St. Martin's Press, 1972.

Granger, Richard. *Your Child from One to Six.* Washington: U.S. Dept. of Health and Human Services, 1980. (DHHS Publication No. OHDS 80-30026)

Spock, Benjamin. *Baby and Child Care.* New York: Pocket Books, 1976.

Leach, Penelope, *Your Baby and Child from Birth to Age Five.* New York: Alfred A. Knopf, 1978.

2. General Topics for the Family Library

Green, Martin, A *Sigh of Relief: The First-Aid Handbook for Childhood Emergencies.* New York: Bantam Books, 1977.

Jones, Sandy. *Learning for Little Kids: A Parents' Sourcebook for the Years 3 to 8.* Boston: Houghton Mifflin Company, 1979.

Kelly, Marguerite, and Parsons, Elia. *The Mother's Almanac.* Garden City, N.Y.: Doubleday and Company, 1975.

Knight, Bryan. *Enjoying Single Parenthood.* New York: Van-Nostrand Reinhold, Ltd., 1980.

Showers, Paul. *The Moon Walker.* Garden City, N.Y.: Doubleday and Co., 1975.

Stein, Sara Bonnett. *About Dying, An Open Family Book for Parents and Children Together.* New York: Walker and Company, 1974.

Stein, Sara Bonnett. *About Handicaps, An Open Family Book for Parents and Children Together.* New York: Walker and Company, 1974.

Stein, Sara Bonnett. *On Divorce, An Open Family Book for Parents and Children Together.* New York: Walker and Company, 1974.

Stein, Sara Bonnett. *That New Baby, An Open Family Book for Parents and Children Together.* New York: Walker and Company, 1974.

Stoddard, Alexandra. *A Child's Place: How to Create a Living Environment for Your Children.* Garden City, N.Y.: Doubleday and Co., 1977.

3. References on Day Care

Provence, Sally, Naylor, Audrey, and Patterson, June. *The Challenge of Daycare.* Binghamton, N.Y.: Vail-Ballou Press, Inc., 1977.

Robinson, Nancy, Robinson, Halbert, Darling, Martha, and Holms, Gretchen. *A World of Children.* Monterey, California: Brooks/Cole Publishing Company, 1979.

4. Especially for Younger Ages

Ross, Cathy, and Beggs, Denise. *The Whole Baby Catalog.* New York: Drake Publishers, Inc., 1977.

Sparling, Joseph, and Lewis, Isabelle. *Learningames for the First Three Years: A Guide to Parent-Child Play.* New York: Walker and Company, 1979.

Sparling, Joseph, and Lewis, Isabelle. *Learningames for the First Three Years: A Program for Parent/Center Partnership.* New York: Walker Educational Book Corp., 1981.

217

Final Acts

A NOVEL

Alex Abella

SIMON & SCHUSTER
NEW YORK LONDON TORONTO
SYDNEY SINGAPORE

SIMON & SCHUSTER
Rockefeller Center
1230 Avenue of the Americas
New York, NY 10020

SIMON & SCHUSTER and colophon are registered trademarks of Simon & Schuster, Inc.
Designed by Karolina Harris
Manufactured in the United States of America

10 9 8 7 6 5 4 3 2 1

Library of Congress Cataloging-in-Publication Data
Abella, Alex.
Final Acts : a novel / Alex Abella.
p. cm.
1. Mexican American women—Fiction. 2. Los Angeles (Calif.)—Fiction. I. Title.
PS3551.B3394 F5 2000
813'.54—dc21   00-057406
ISBN 0-684-85989-0

ACKNOWLEDGMENTS

AS ALWAYS, I wish to thank all the learned members of the legal profession who have given me guidance and encouragement in my pursuit of true fiction. I am particularly indebted to Los Angeles Deputy District Attorneys Eric Lavine, Joseph Esposito, and Scott Gordon and, of course, to Judge Gregory Alarcon for his keen insights on the law. I would be remiss if I didn't also remember my agent, Joe Regal, and my friend, brother, and adviser, L. Travis Clark.

To Armeen, Nicolas, and Veronica,
who have made me happier than I ever dreamed

Final Acts

1

"*DISS   ISS* what salsa is all about, baby!"

Raúl's words were swallowed up by the lilt of the wild *descarga* of Makina Loca, a riff on a classic *son montuno* that got everybody on the floor eager to shake their fanny.

Like always when they play L.A., the Makina had packed the Rumba Room with Chicanos, *salvadoreños, peruanos, cubanos,* all kinds of Latinos as well as the Latino wannabes, the ladies with their skirts up to here and the guys with their clingy shirts open to the breastbone. If only they had some hair on those chests, *pobrecitos!* But I'll say this for those white guys, they sure keep trying, don't they?

Of course I should talk. Sometimes I'm the only white girl in a room full of sweating *papacitos* and *mamacitas,* all shimmying and shaking and swaying to that beat. In fact if it weren't for salsa I wouldn't have learned the little Spanish that I know. I wouldn't have met Raúl either, but that's a different story. The point is, after the wild *descarga*, after the crazy jam session ended and the floor cleared, I went back to our table while Raúl excused himself to the men's room. The waitress was having trouble navigating the crowd—and believe me, there's nothing worse than a bunch of thirsty patrons wanting their drink right now, if you please, I should know, that's how I put myself through law school—so I decided to get my own at the bar. I waded through the mass of sweating bodies and had just put in my order when he finally approached me.

"Can I buy you a drink?" he asked, using those words like nobody else had said them before.

He was a tall white guy, about six feet or so—which is gigantic for a little bit like me who's five one in her pantyhose. He had deep hazel eyes and a full head of gray hair, very nice even features, almost like a model's, except for a scar right under his left eye socket. I would have pegged him for one of those wannabes that hit on you by asking if you dance on the two or the three in salsa but he was way better dressed than that, wearing a smart black Donna Karan suit and a discreet gray shirt, a Piaget watch, and shoes that did not look like the duck's feet everyone was wearing that year. Besides, I could tell by his expression that he wasn't really interested in my musical opinions. This was a man after bigger prey.

"No, thank you, I don't drink alcohol," I said, turning away from him.

I certainly didn't want to start a conversation with some stranger at the Rumba Room. The last time I'd done that I'd met Raúl and I was not in the market for a substitute. But this guy at my elbow was not so easily discouraged.

"I've been watching you on the floor," he went on, in a nicely modulated voice that carried a slight twang. Where was this guy from? Georgia? Mississippi? New Orleans? Somewhere down South.

"You're a fabulous dancer," he added.

"Thank you," I said, looking around for the bartender to bring my order.

I caught a glimpse of myself in the bar mirror, looking like a floozy with my mass of curls falling all over my shoulders, so I proceeded to quickly put them up. I could have walked away right then but there was something about this stranger that was ringing all kinds of alarm, not all of them unpleasant. So I stayed in place, I guess unconsciously waiting for his next overture.

"You're Rita Carr, aren't you? The public defender?"

Oh God, that's it, another former client.

"Ex–public defender, please. I started my own firm last year."

The man gave me a full, very pleasing smile, basking in the knowledge he was about to share.

"That's what I heard. And that's what I want to talk to you about. My name is Charlie. Charlie Morell."

Well, duh! No wonder he looked so familiar. This guy had just managed to turn upside down all the usual conventions of law and legal practice in Los Angeles, thrown the District Attorney's office into a million conniptions, and made himself the most controversial defendant in Southern California since O.J. Simpson.

I turned around to face him head-on, no more hiding behind girlish moves like fixing my hair—which has a mind of its own, anyhow—or looking for another drink. This was serious. This was business. I hoped.

"Mr. Morell, what a pleasure," I said, putting on the kind of

smile I usually display behind closed doors in chambers when
the judge is supposedly deciding whether to appoint me 987—
that's court appointed counsel—but is really just checking out
how high my skirt will ride when I sit down.

"I've read all about you. How's your case going? I asked.

He shrugged and I swear that for a moment there I thought he
looked just like that actor I'd seen in one of those French New
Wave movies of the 1960s my ex-husband, Greg, used to drag
me to.

"I'm in Department 100 next month," said Morell. "I get a feeling Judge Strummer is going to send me to Norwalk to face the
music."

"God, that's terrible! Norwalk, you mean like in no deal, no
walk, go straight to jail?"

"That's about the gist of it. He denied my change of venue.
They're all in on this. They know they'll get reamed if I win. From
Wheeler to Pérez to Polonsky, a lot of people are fixing to put me
away for life. It's a conspiracy."

"I see. But you're still walking. I don't know of too many murder suspects out on their own recognizance."

A sparkle went off in his eyes, which for a moment changed
from hazel to brilliant green.

"I'm glad to see you're so well informed."

"Like I said, I've read practically everything about your case. I
mean, the *Daily Journal* has been going to town on you," I blustered, then I stopped, to gauge his reaction. He didn't seem to
mind the Manolo sticking out of my mouth.

"That's great. So why don't we talk about it tomorrow in your
office at ten-thirty. You're still at that place in West Hollywood?"

"How do you know? I just moved from downtown."

Once again the smile—charming, debonair, a roué, a man of
the world. A total act, I suddenly realized. The man is terrified
and he doesn't care to show it.

"Let's just say I've done my due diligence. Good night."

He started to walk away when I grabbed him by the arm—I felt well-defined muscles under the soft fabric of the jacket sleeve.

"Before you go, what is it that you want to talk about? I have my clients to take care of."

He looked down, pressed my hand, then bent and whispered in my ear the words that forever changed my life, even as an old La Soli song came over the sound system: "I want you to represent me."

"Co-counsel?" I snapped back.

"No, no. Sole counsel. Top banana. You're in the driver's seat, I'm riding." He smiled again. "I know you know from hot rides. Good night."

And with that he slipped out of my grasp and blended so quickly into the crowd that I lost all sight of him, as though I had imagined him and his proposition. That's when I recalled who he reminded me of—Belmondo in that movie where he falls in love with the American chick in Paris. What was it? *Breathless.*

That's funny, I thought. He doesn't look like Belmondo, but he still gives off that air. I wonder what that means.

Needless to say Raúl was not amused by my encounter. He sidled up to the bar just as Charlie was vanishing in the crowd like a guy used to pulling disappearing acts when it suited him.

"Who was that you was talkin' to?" snapped Raúl, his little pug nose up in the air, a wire terrier smelling out a brawl.

"A new client." I sipped the San Pellegrino the bartender finally plopped on the counter.

"Uhm!" snapped back Raúl with the utmost eloquence. He was about to give me another lecture on socializing with strangers—the kind my dad used to give me when I was an overheated fourteen-year-old—when I yanked Raúl back to the dance floor.

"C'mon, baby, let's dance. I've got to think."

I'll say this for Raúl—he is a fabulous dancer. He's so good he grows when he's on the floor. He's no longer five five in three-

inch Cuban heels with arms as thick as my thighs, he's Gene
Kelly rhapsodizing with a chair, he's Fred Astaire dancing on the
ceiling, he's a demigod flying low over the dance floor.

And dancing was just what I needed right then. I wanted to
keep my body in motion as long as I could so my mind could
concentrate on the offer Morell had just proposed. See, some
people go pump iron at Gold's, others go for five-mile runs
around Lake Hollywood. Me, I put on Tito Puente and I swing
my hips and lift my arms and step and spin and everything is as
clear as could be—salsa as a road to enlightenment. What a slo-
gan, huh? Not exactly what a Mexican-Irish girl like myself
would be expected to like but there it is.

Only that night, it wasn't.

My brain was not connecting, the switches were off and all I
accomplished with my dancing was to work up a sweat. Even
when we went home and Raúl and I made baby happy, I still
wasn't all there, my mind worried but yet refusing to concentrate
on the problem, as though some barrier were holding me back. It
was a very unsettling sensation.

Even Raúl, who ordinarily just rolls over after making love
with the excuse that his security guard schedule has screwed up
his sleeping patterns, even he noticed something was wrong.

"You worry too much, baby," he said, brushing his teeth vigor-
ously, standing at the door to the bathroom, wearing the Joe
Boxer shorts with the red hearts I'd bought him for Valentine's
Day that year.

"You should try and get into another kind of practice that don't
get you wrapped up tight like that."

"Like what?" I asked, staring at the ceiling above our bed,
noticing how the crack in it looked like a rabbit's head.

"You should think about bankruptcy law. There's a ton of
money to be made in that. My cousin Jaime, he just filed for BK
the other day? He had to pay seventeen hundred dollars to some
fool in Tarzana just to fill out some papers. And the fool's waiting

room was packed with people. That's easy money, baby, not this sweating bullets stuff of yours all the time."

I patted the pillow next to mine.

"Raúl, honey, please shut up and come to bed."

He looked at me for a moment, shrugged.

"Okay," he said, then returned to the bathroom to rinse. He was snoring within five minutes.

I tried my best to join him in the land of nod but sleep would not come. So after tossing and turning for a half hour, I got up, went to my desk, and turned on the computer. As I waited for the screen to come on I glanced out my window at the reflection of the full moon on the reservoir.

I live in a two-bedroom Spanish bungalow in the hills of Silverlake. The house needed a ton of sweat equity when I bought it and the yard is no bigger than a postage stamp but the view of the water and the backdrop of the hazy San Gabriel Mountains at times make me feel like I'm in Europe, Como or Lugano or Zurich or somewhere where it's always spring and there's always another thing of beauty just around the corner. Then the smog rolls in and I'm reminded once more that I'm still in my hometown, Los Angeles, where you can see the air and chew the water.

I wouldn't have it any other way.

Just then my Windows 98 kicked on and I connected to the Internet. I typed in on Alta Vista, "Find Charlie Morell"—and within seconds I had enough information to keep me up all night. And that was without dipping into the Lexis legal files.

The upshot was that when Raúl finally rolled out of bed, around eight in a warm autumn morning, I was still going at the computer, reading, downloading, and plotting. I gave him a kiss, fixed him his coffee, then sent him on his way as I took a shower, put on a Richard Tyler lilac dress and Chanel slingbacks, and drove out to my office in West Hollywood to meet the rest of my life.

· · ·

MY OFFICE is on the second floor of a strip mall off La
Cienega, just up the hill from Yamushi's, the hottest sushi place in
L.A. right now, where you can court death by eating $300-a-pop
orders of blowfish. I'm also two blocks from the official start of
Boys Town, the heart of the gay ghetto on Santa Monica Boulevard. For a while, right after I left the Public Defender's, I shared
an office downtown with three other ex-champions of the public
innocence, but between the late rent payments (theirs) and the
compulsive need to tidy up messes (mine), I realized I was not
primo partner material. So when this little office became available, I moved all my files, my Herman Miller desk and Eames
chair and John Baldessari prints. Unlike downtown, here I don't
have to worry about being pounced on by the perverts or the
homeless when I work late; the boys on the street give me plenty
of company without competition, which is fabulous (although
sometimes I'm a little sad when I see all the wasted talent). And
then there's that incredible rent payment—none. My aunt Flora
owns the mall and she gladly leases me the office in exchange for
keeping her legal affairs in order. Besides, on a clear day you can
see all the way to paradise from the railing outside my door—or
at least all the way down to Palos Verdes, which is a damn close
second.

I parked in the basement garage, then hustled up the stairs to
the Dietrich's on the first floor to pick up a tall latte. My assistant,
Jon, was on vacation down in Cabo so the office was still closed
and I wanted to make sure I looked like I had a thriving practice
instead of the usual one-person billing agony.

I should have asked myself why I was trying to make a good
impression on Charlie Morell. I mean, I'd just had the best year of
my professional career, won three murder cases in a row and negotiated great pleas for all the others. I was making twice as much
as I'd ever brought home from the county and was calling my
own shots. In short, I had accomplished everything I'd set out to
do. I had no need to impress anybody. Yet here I was, hustling

like some law school intern trying to impress the deputy in charge.

I was ten minutes early but Charlie had beat me to it. He was idly leaning on the railing, dressed as though for court, in a smart dark blue pinstripe suit with a crisp white shirt and a gold tie and gleaming wingtips. Très *GQ*.

"Nice view up here," he said good-naturedly.

"I'm glad you enjoy it," I said, a little peeved at getting caught off guard. "Please come in."

I fiddled with the lock until the sliding glass door opened.

"I hope you don't mind I'm early. I didn't sleep much last night."

"You should stay away from dance clubs then, Mr. Morell," I said. "Loud music is not conducive to sound sleep."

"I wish it were that easy. Was that you in the yellow Alfa Spyder? You came blasting in."

"That it was," I said, placing my briefcase on the desk. "She's my pride and joy."

"They don't make them anymore, do they?" he said, sitting down, crossing the dangerously creased legs of his suit pants.

Churchill & Churchill shoes, I noticed, and some fine hose with little clocks stitched on. A very fancy dresser, Charlie Morell. But why is he so careful about his appearance?

"That's right, it's out of production. I got the last new one a couple of years ago at Alfa Motors. She's as temperamental as a diva but she makes a beautiful noise. I can give you all the specs, if you want. I tune her myself. Or we can talk about why you want to hire me."

Charlie wiped the smile off his face, tugged at the French cuffs of his shirt.

"Okay, fine. Let's talk turkey."

He leaned over, placed his big boxy leather lawyer's case on my desk, took out two three-ring binders and several folders held together by blue rubber bands and frayed string.

"As you know, the District Attorney's office rushed the preliminary hearing. I'm out on OR because I agreed to return voluntarily to the country, since there's no extradition treaty between Cuba and the U.S.

"Now, we'll be going to Department 100 the 14th next month, that gives us approximately three weeks. I've been representing myself so here's a copy of the murder book, copies of the discovery motions, and all the rest, as well as appropriate newspaper clippings and material that might impact on the investigation."

He shoved the pile toward me with great relief, one fewer millstone around his lean, elegant neck. I flipped quickly through the files as he spoke, fiddling with his onyx and gold cuff links, looking like a man who could use a cigarette but would never allow himself the weakness.

"Excuse me, let me get this straight. You're telling me that you want me to be your attorney and that I'm going to have three weeks to read, digest, interpret, and research all the material covering the murders and still be ready to announce ready for trial when we show up in Department 100?"

He smiled again, amused, no, charmed by my vexation. He was beginning to get on my nerves and I hadn't even agreed to take on the case yet.

"That's the long and the short of it. I was told if anybody could handle it you could."

"Who?"

"Friends. Colleagues. Dale Rubin. Roger Rosen. Chuck Lindner."

"I know those guys. They're solid. Why not any of them?"

"I need a woman. You know what this case is about. The jury might think I'm some kind of monster unless there's a pretty lady like you in their face telling them hey, this guy's human, how can you think that. I also need somebody like me out there, someone who can really understand the case. I'm ready to hire Jo-Ellen Dimitrius as our jury consultant."

"The lady from the O.J. trial?"

He nodded. "She's a friend too. She's already started preparing the prospective juror's questionnaire to weed out the ones that—"

I raised my hand and stopped him in mid-sentence.

"Let's not get ahead of ourselves, all right?"

I took out a yellow legal pad, wrote his name in capital letters at the top of the first page.

"I don't know how much money you have tucked away but this is not going to be low-cost. It might not look like it but I have a lot of overhead—my investigator, the time I'll be spending away from other cases, not to mention the psychic toll the trial will take on me personally. Because, you know, I will have to be living, breathing, and sleeping this case for the next three weeks if you hope to stand any chance of victory. Because when I take on a case I give it my one hundred ten percent. Because I'll have to reassign everything . . . what is this?"

He pushed a pale ivory linen envelope across the desk. I opened it. Inside was a cashier's check in my name for one hundred thousand dollars.

"That's your retainer. The publicity I've gotten lately has done wonders for my standing in Hollywood, so I've been able to re-option my books. Are you all right with that figure?"

I glanced down, felt myself blushing with greed.

"For the next three weeks? I can live with it."

"Good."

I couldn't help myself, it came out almost automatic.

"There will be expenses."

"That's all right. I'll pick those up. I wouldn't want Judge Carr's daughter to go begging."

"So you know about my dad."

"Who doesn't?"

"Is that the reason you're hiring me, because he's at the Court of Appeal? If so, you better take this back because he always re-cuses himself."

"Please, Rita, if my only hope of getting out of this is by winning it on appeal, I am in so deep I'll never get out."

"You are in deep. What else would you call it? You are facing two counts of murder with special circs, one here and another in Alameda. And if I'm not mistaken, the L.A. District Attorney's office will be alleging the death penalty—no L-wop for you."

"El wop?" he repeated, his expression like that of a man listening to a celestial whisper in his ear.

"You know, life without parole. Have you been out of the practice so long that you've forgotten?"

"No, no," he blustered, "I was just thinking how much that sounds like *el guapo*."

"Sorry. I don't speak Spanish. Dad never spoke it at home."

"*Guapo* usually means handsome in Spanish but in Cuba it's sort of like, the tough guy, the bully. Like in that Ray Barretto song from 1963, 'El Watusi,' you know? *Ahí viene el guapo del barrio, yo no le tengo miedo a nadie, Watusi!*"

"Which means?"

"Here comes the neighborhood bully, I'm not afraid of anybody, Watusi!"

"That's nice but I'm sure I don't have a clue."

Of course I did but I wasn't about to admit I'd been dancing to a song for years without knowing what it meant.

"Let's get back to your case, all right?" I pressed on. "If I take this case I'm going to want you to waive time so I can prepare."

He shook his head emphatically.

"No. That's the only condition I'm asking. I'm not waiving any time. This has to be resolved right away. Don't even try to argue 'cause I won't do it."

I stared at him for a beat, noticed the jaw set firmly, the crossed arms, all his body language screaming forget it, lady. I decided it was best to save that battle for later. I pulled out a double folder full of computer printouts.

"Fine then. Look, I have tons of information about you, your books, your family, this case, previous cases. But I still haven't been able to figure out what you're going to do about this case."

Something resembling grief, or a very deep loss, came over his features, his lips turning down at the corners, his eyes clouding dark and sinking deep into their sockets.

"If you've read all about me, then you know I was involved in a real bloody case a few years ago . . ."

"The Ricardo Díaz cult murders?"

"That's right. Some things were left unresolved from that case."

"Such as?"

"Such as the death of a state senator named Tom Decker. His daughter, Miranda, was involved with Díaz's cult. I think that would be a good point of departure for looking into this one."

"What makes you think that?"

"I asked Miranda. I went and interviewed her at Vacaville. She didn't tell me much, just that a lot of people were still gunning for me. People who had been running around with Díaz."

"What kind of people?"

"Well-placed people. Powerful people."

"Great. I love a good fight. So we'll start with her. I can send my investigator—"

"You needn't bother."

"Why not?"

"She was stabbed to death by her cellmate the day after I talked to her. Look."

He leaned over, extracted a box of typing paper with the title "Acts of Mercy." He threw it upon the table.

"I wrote down an account of what has happened to me over the last few months. It's sort of a first draft for a novel. I want you to read it. And finish it."

"What do you mean?"

"Whatever happens to me, that will be the end of the story."

"And if the jury finds you guilty and gives you the lethal injection?"

He stood, breathed in deeply.

"Then I guess we'll have a problem selling the film rights, won't we? Let's talk soon. My number's on the envelope."

He shook my hand and then exited quickly, as though afraid I would open his manuscript right then and start reading something that was not meant for other people's eyes—or for daytime consideration.

What kind of trip have I signed on for here? I wondered.

2

FINGERS OF fog wrapped themselves around the Italian cypresses by my house in Kensington, refusing to acknowledge the coming of the blazing sun out of Contra Costa County.

Looking out my window at the vast expanse of San Francisco Bay down below, I saw that the fog bank which had draped the Berkeley shoreline overnight was beginning to break up. At the far end of the bay, the graceful lines of the Golden Gate Bridge emerged from the retreating gossamer fog like a sleeper tossing off blankets, while next door the city on the hill, still cloaked in a cold mist, looked on expectantly through sleepy eyes, wondering what her next move should be.

I opened the shutters. The air smelled of hopes and many things, of damp earth from the newly planted garden, of fresh plaster from the renovation of our Spanish Revival house, of the pot of coffee my son, Julian, was brewing in the kitchen downstairs.

I smiled. All was right in the world at last.

Whistling an old show tune, I laced up my running shoes and took off for a brisk run down my new neighborhood, still trying to accustom myself to its dewy freshness, so different from the furnacelike desert air that had greeted my mornings in Los Angeles for so long.

I ran down past the Tudors and the Queen Annes, winding alleys soon giving way to straight wide avenues in the flats. By the UC campus, alongside the myriad storefronts of copy places, bookstores, and school memorabilia, I spotted the first students of the day heading for the vast coffeehouse located inside a former gas station. In slouchy jeans and baggy sweaters, they carried backpacks stuffed with books and term papers, tossing long locks carelessly over their shoulders. Involuntarily, I recalled my own glory days at Brown, twenty-something years before.

Back then the Ivy League seemed to this misplaced Cuban refugee the perfect escape from the Grand Guignol of abuse at my parents' apartment in Miami. I firmly believed you could run away from your past, reshape yourself into a new man with a new profession, a new language, a new outlook on life. I didn't know that we always carry the past with us, its awesome shadow falling on everything we touch, regardless of our intentions.

I raced back home, leaning into the hill to propel myself up the slope. My sore quadriceps screamed in unaccustomed agony, my lungs swelled like an accordion of pain, while my forehead was ringed by a crown of burning sweat, but I pressed on, wheezing and gasping, refusing to surrender. Finally, thankfully, I reached our cul-de-sac and the handful of identical Spanish houses at its summit, ours distinguishable only by the blue banner that hailed a listless welcome by the door.

In the middle of the cul-de-sac sat a black and white police cruiser from Oakland, our neighboring town.

Gulping down as much of the moist air as I could, I jogged around the street, trying to guess which of my neighbors' houses was being graced by Oakland's finest. I glanced inside the squad car. Empty, windows rolled down, radio transmitter chattering about a 459 near College Avenue.

I stopped, wiped the sweat off my face with my T-shirt. The sun broke through, splaying pale lemon rays through the mist, which gathered like curtains on a stage. A bird somewhere cawed, another one trilled, a far-off ambulance wailed in the lowlands.

Julian appeared at the doorway, ruddy face as flushed as if he'd been the one running four miles at a seven-minute clip. Tommy Hilfiger sweater over his broad shoulders, his long hair framed his lanky face like that of some minor, pimpled rock star.

"Dad, you better come in quick. There's some officers here to see you."

THE COP who greeted me was young and raw-faced, still in that odd stage of a man's life where blustery bravado hides a fundamental fear of everything new. He stood up the moment I walked in, shoulders hunched forward, left hand resting on his weapon.

"Mr. Morell? John Fowler. Sorry to bother you so early but we have a case that requires your attention."

I grabbed a hand towel off the guest bathroom by the door, wiped my dripping perspiration before shaking his hand.

"Sit down," I said. "Would you like some Cuban coffee? My son made some a little while ago."

"No, thank you. Just had a latte down on College."

Fowler sat back down with perfect posture on the overstuffed salmon-colored couch I'd bought in a moment of weakness near my office in Jackson Square (Cubans cannot resist colors).

"Well, this is kind of unusual, Officer. I don't ordinarily work with police. I'm private counsel. I defend the people you put away. Or at least try to."

I smiled, leaving the last phrase deliberately ambiguous. He nodded, his face all business. I always forget that subtlety, like a sense of humor, is a sign of weakness in law enforcement.

"I understand, sir. But we were informed you have the background knowledge that might assist us in an investigation."

"Are you the investigating officer on the case?"

Fowler cleared his throat, looked awkwardly around, glancing at the open French doors to the garden. I smelled the faint whiff of cigarette smoke and briefly wondered when my neighbor, Mrs. Gates, had taken up smoking.

"No, sir, but I did find the body. The case is being handled by our homicide unit."

"I see. So you're hoping I might be able to help you get in on the case. I didn't know they let you do that kind of thing in the Bay Area. This place is even more unorthodox than I remembered."

Fowler again looked out the doors at the yard, as though waiting for the gnarled olive tree to help him. I went on.

"I would think there's some kind of departmental rule about this kind of thing. Whatever. What was the body you found, Officer?"

"A thirty-year-old female. Name is Elsa Martin. A former teacher. She was wrapped in some kind of African cloth."

Fowler tilted his head, the professional observer at work.

"Is there something wrong? You seem distracted," he said.

"No, no, I'm still out of breath, that's all," I replied, taking in a gulp of air. I was afraid I knew exactly where the conversation was going and it was a place I didn't want to go back to ever again.

"Where and when did this happen?" I asked, trying to control myself.

"Joaquín Miller Park, by the Mormon Temple. About five days ago. Do you know the area?"

I nodded. Joaquín Miller Park is a few miles down Highway 13 on the border between Berkeley and Oakland, a place full of high pines, old eucalyptus, and miles of hidden, leafy trails.

"Have you heard about this?" asked Fowler. "It was all over the papers."

"Sorry, I've been busy. I haven't been paying much attention to the news. What else?"

"The head was severed. The body was mutilated with some strange markings we assume were *santería* symbols."

SANTERÍA.

The marriage of Catholicism and African cults. The much maligned and misunderstood religion of the dispossessed, of poor Hispanics, blacks, and desperate people everywhere, with more followers now in this country than the Episcopal and Methodist churches combined. The faith of garrulous saints that possessed their followers, making them capable of superhuman feats of strength and daring when in their thrall. The cult of a pitiless killer who had slaughtered my friend and almost murdered my son and myself. The reason why I'd left Los Angeles and sought shelter in the Bay Area. Obviously to no avail.

"And who told you I might be able to assist you in this investigation?"

"I did, Charlie," said Michael Kelsey, stepping in from the garden. "I'll take it from here, Johnny."

Kelsey's curly reddish hair was turning gray and his gold-rimmed eyeglasses had been replaced by contacts, but he was still the same deliberate caricature of the slovenly detective—ill-fitting suit, big brass belt buckle, scuffed cowboy boots. He dropped his cigarette on the flagstone, stamped it out with his heel. At least he had graduated from generic to brand smokes. Marlboros, it looked like.

"Michael. I thought you'd retired."

Kelsey showed no sign of discomfiture at my less than friendly greeting and with three long-legged steps heaved himself into an armchair, which groaned from the sudden weight. The image of a bear in the parlor flashed in my mind, quickly followed by the memory of a skinless body in a Los Angeles basement.

"No, buddy," he said, shifting uncomfortably in the Palazzetti. "Thanks to you I had to quit before the LAPD fired me. I was lucky the Sheriff needed bodies out in Palmdale."

"Gee, guy, I'm sorry," I replied, not feeling regretful in the least. "Is that why you came all the way up here, not enough crime in L.A.? 'Cause of course there's no crime a great detective like you can't solve."

He cracked a smile. Some counselor somewhere had taught him how to break the tension.

"Boy, you still know how to get a rise out of me, don't you? Johnny here's my nephew. I was up visiting his folks in Richmond when he mentioned the case. The brass wants to keep this hush-hush, it's not PC."

"I still don't understand. Why are you tagging along on this?"

Kelsey took a letter envelope from the inside pocket of his jacket, threw it on the beechwood coffee table.

"We had the same thing down south last week. Take a look."

I opened the envelope. Out tumbled four Polaroid pictures of a dead female, her neck like a bloody stump in the absence of her head. Caucasian, her chest was covered with wriggly symbols that looked like they had been drawn with markers but were actually scored into the tender flesh itself.

A wave of enormous sadness engulfed me.

How can there be such madness on earth? What justice is there that allows such abominations? Someday, when I'm up before the Creator, I will hold Him accountable for His deeds.

"We haven't ID'd her yet but by the looks of her the coroner says she wasn't even fifteen years old. Probably a runaway, maybe even a strawberry, you know, hooker does it for drugs? You don't see it here but the guy who did her apparently also kept all her toes. Sliced off to the bone."

Julian, who had come in and taken a look at the pictures, now shook his head in disgust, muttered Cuban curses under his breath.

"We found her out on Avenue J, behind a subdivision in Lancaster."

Kelsey stuffed the pictures in the envelope, which he stuck back in his pocket.

"I was second unit on the scene. She was wrapped in this kind of serape, with little dolls all pinned to it. They left a silver dollar with it. No prints. I knew right away what it was. I tried to talk some sense into the IO but he wouldn't hear it. Especially after what I went through. Thanks to you, asshole."

"So you're not a detective anymore."

Kelsey chuckled, took out yet another smoke, lit it with his old Zippo, engraved with his Marine Corps regiment insignia.

"Right now I'm just another deputy cruising for donuts in the high desert, Charlie. But I can still put two and two together. To me this is very much like Ricardo Díaz. If I'm correct, you know what that means?"

I stared at him, as chilled by the implication of what he had just shown me as if I had jumped into the gleaming bay shining outside my window.

"Let me throw some clothes on," I said, getting up. I turned to Kelsey's nephew. "I want you to take me where you found the girl's body."

THE PATH wound around a grove of tall pines and through an overgrown thicket of madrones which seemed impenetrable at first sight. We'd parked our cars at a turnout on Highway 13 and were now about a quarter mile off the paved road.

The chilly breeze blowing off the bay was left behind as we dipped into a gulch, the warmth of the April sun stinging our unseasoned skin. A few tattered cumulus clouds drifted by above; a red-tailed hawk swept down from the treetops to pluck its morning meal. We pushed into the thicket through an opening of broken branches on the muddy trail, which smelled of warming compost and eucalyptus.

I followed Fowler, who broke through the brush, leading our ragged group Indian file into the gulch. Behind me came Kelsey and then my son, Julian, who out of perverse curiosity had cut his morning class to tag along, claiming he could use the experience as the basis for a term paper.

"Guy searching for mushrooms found it about a week ago," said Fowler, ducking under a redwood's cracked branch.

"'Shrooms? Psilocybin?" asked Julian, displaying more knowledge of psychedelics than I wanted him to.

"No. Your namesake, morels, and boletus, for Chez Panisse," said Fowler, breaking through a veil of vegetation down to a narrow brook, running clear over a granite gravel bed.

"Hey, Johnny, where you learn so much about all this gourmet shit?" blared Kelsey behind me.

"It's in the report," said Fowler defensively. "Just because I'm a cop doesn't mean I don't know about fine cuisine."

"Take it easy, just wondering," replied Kelsey.

Fowler stopped, pointed some fifty yards up ahead.

"Over there," he said.

The lush ferns and gurgling water lent an otherworldly air to the hidden grove, the yellow police tape around a bush almost like streamers left behind after a raucous birthday party.

I ducked under the tape, walked up to a massive Douglas fir. White flecks of molding compound, left behind after investigators lifted the tracks of shoe prints, were scattered on the muddy ground like so much confetti.

I walked around the site. Behind a rock about ten yards from the tree I spotted the smashed remains of a pint-sized bottle of *aguardiente*, the rough firewater that fathered modern rum. I took a twig, inserted it into the broken neck of the bottle, returned to the group.

"I found the body right here," said Fowler, standing in front of the tree.

"What about the head?"

"Over there," he said, pointing at the shelf of a large granite boulder. "It was all covered with red ants. Looked like somebody had spilled some kind of honey on her."

"Molasses," I muttered. "It was a good *ebbó*."

"What's that?" asked Kelsey, lighting up a cigarette in between hoarse breaths.

"A sacrifice," I answered. "The bugs all over means the gods accepted the offering."

"No, what you got," said Kelsey.

"Take prints off this. Most likely whoever brought her here drank from the bottle and sprayed her with the rum. Part of the ritual."

Fowler took out a handkerchief, which had been fastidiously ironed and folded, to grab the bottle. His long tapered hands were perfectly manicured, matching the general air of careful neatness about him, like that of a man who spends a great deal of time worrying about his appearance every morning.

"So what bloodthirsty son of a bitch voodoo jungle bunny did this?" asked Kelsey.

I bent down, groped carefully around the site, picking up four purple and white beads deliberately hidden under a spreading cyclamen.

"C'mon, Michael, you know the routine, it's not voodoo—"

"It's *santería*," he said, in unison. "But it's still bullshit bloody witchcraft."

I turned over the beads to Fowler, dropping them in his up-turned palm.

"These are the colors of Ossain, the doctor god, the curer of diseases."

"Why would a doctor god want a human sacrifice?"

I stood, looked around again, searching for more clues that an ordinary investigator, not in tune with the requirements of the religion, might have missed.

"That's a good question. Ordinarily Ossain wants only offerings of fruit. The coin doesn't add up either. This doesn't make sense unless—"

"Hey, Dad, over here! I found something!"

Julian was about fifty feet away, under the outspread branches of a white fir. We hurried over, then stopped in our tracks. Perched on the lower branches lay the freshly decapitated body of a white goat, still dripping fat globs of blood on the ground.

THIS TIME the police perimeter was much broader, a good five hundred yards instead of the original twenty feet when the woman's body was found. Although the slaughtered animal was not technically anything other than a misdemeanor, the fact that it had been found so soon after the original death and just a stone's throw away proved conclusively that the woman's death was part of a religious ritual.

And that whoever was responsible might go for another human sacrifice the next time.

At least that's what I was trying to get the assigned homicide investigator in the case to accept. But Detective González, who had done the initial evidence gathering, was not particularly happy to hear my theory. He nodded, his bushy salt-and-pepper mustache bristling, as I went over the details of a ritual sacrifice, the prayers, the location, the time of day, the spiritual intentions. He listened absentmindedly, his head bent close to the ground, beady weary eyes searching for the clues he had missed the first time around. Some distance away, next to the fateful branch, Julian stood posing for the *Oakland Tribune* photographer.

"Any particular read on why here, in this place?" asked González, glaring at the small offerings left near the goat—the cowbells with roosters, the spent bullet casings, the cement and cowrie shell–encrusted heads of the trickster saint, Eleguá.

"The woods. The brook, the pines. They had to do it in a place where the divinity would be sure to find it, to come feed. Not everyplace will do."

"Okay, fine. I see that."

González stood, looked back toward the highway.

"We're about a quarter mile from the road so we're accessible. But what makes you think this goat thing is related to the other? How do you know it wasn't just two random acts, some weirdo who read about the murder in the paper and decided to pee in the pot as well?"

"That's very sensitive of you, Detective."

"The city doesn't pay me to be sensitive, Charlie. It pays me to catch killers. So what about it?"

"Well, I don't think this is a copycat, if that's what you mean. How would the second guy have known where to come? It's a pretty big park. Plus add the fact that both the murder and the sacrifice bear *santería* ritual details and it all becomes pretty obvious."

"I don't think it's so obvious at all," said a voice at my elbow.

I turned to face a black woman in boots, dark slacks and leather jacket, police badge and pistol holster hanging from a thick belt. Aviator glasses covered her eyes, showing my own unshaven reflection.

"It's an unwarranted assumption that lends itself to shoddy investigation. It's what happens when civilians get mixed up in police work."

"Captain Cynthia Rawls," said González with a slight shake of the head, resignedly acknowledging his superior's opinion, as though he had been forced to do so many times before.

"You're Morell?" she asked, moving her head to scan the site. She didn't bother to shake hands.

"That's right."

"You're out of here. Take Junior and your paparazzi with you."

"You don't believe this murder was related to *santería,* is that your problem?"

Rawls took off her sunglasses, revealing large protuberant eyes with the yellow coloring of the early stages of cirrhosis. She rubbed the bridge of her nose, like someone who hasn't slept in days—or someone repeatedly trying to latch on to her few remaining strands of patience.

"I don't have a problem, *Señor* Morell. I know what I'm doing. But you're going to have a big *problema* unless you get your Cuban ass out of here. I'm familiar with your work and I don't see a need for you. First off, we have enough cult experts from law enforcement agencies working on this so we don't need you. So far they haven't told me this murder had anything to do with *santería.*"

"You mean they haven't ruled it out," I blurted.

"They haven't ruled it in either, okay? Second, not all the followers of *santería* are into the grisly kind of human sacrifice you seem to love writing about."

"I have never said such a thing," I protested but she went on.

"And third, and most important, you have no business being on the site of an ongoing investigation. Nobody with authority invited you. This is an Oakland police matter and I would appreciate it if you kept out of it. Now beat it before I have you arrested. *Entiendes, Mendes?* Where's Fowler? Hey, you, Fowler!"

She stalked off, peeling Fowler away from the *Oakland Trib* cameraman to a bough under a fir tree where she laid into him with such fury we could hear practically every choice curse word.

"She's been under a lot of stress lately," said González by way of apology. "We're breaking homicide records for the nation, a hundred forty-six this year so far and we're only into April. We're down three detectives on the squad and City Hall's been beefing us like crazy over this murder."

"Why? They think it's a serial killer?" I asked. González chuckled.

"We got so many dead people around here nobody would notice if we had a serial killer. The victim was related to a city councilman. He claims we're not digging deep enough because she was Mexican instead of African-American. You know how it is, nobody's ever happy no matter what we do. We get it going and we get it coming. I tell you, I'm moving up to Idaho with Mark Fuhrman when my turn is up."

"When's that going to be?"

"Another three years, four months, ten days, and . . ." He stole a look at his watch. " . . . forty-eight minutes."

Kelsey, who had wandered away down a trail into the park, now returned, observing with growing disbelief the tongue-lashing his nephew was getting from Rawls.

"Who the fuck is that bitch? Nobody treats my people like that."

Kelsey lumbered away, covering the fifty-foot distance in a matter of seconds, a large and furious grizzly about to defend his cub.

González and I bolted after him but it was too late; he had

already reached Rawls, grabbed her by the shoulder, spinning her around.

"Hey, sister, who the fuck are you?" he bellowed, rearing above her as though to swat her down with his large paw. Rawls stepped right into his face, their noses practically touching.

"And who the fuck are you to stick your sorry butt in this?"

"I'm with the L.A. Sheriff's and I can tell when someone has stepped into a pile of shit and doesn't want to smell it."

Rawls glared back, not about to give an inch in this confrontation.

"What's your name?"

"Michael Kelsey."

"Well, listen, Michael Bozo Kelley, why don't you get the fuck back down to Wayside and leave real cops alone? You're out of your jurisdiction. I'm commanding officer here!"

"You might be calling the shots now, girlfriend, but you have no right to talk to people like that. I have a mind to report you to the chief for screwing up an investigation, missing evidence right under your nose, contaminating a crime scene, and harassment of civilians. Am I making myself clear or do I need to bring out a tambourine and sing you chapter and verse?"

The two looked daggers at each other, hands on their respective weapons, and for a brief moment I was wondering who I'd have to rush first. Fortunately Fowler interposed himself between them, gently pushing Kelsey back.

"That's okay, Uncle Mike. Let's just get going."

That was González's cue to grab ahold of Rawls by the arm.

"Could I have a word with you, Captain?" said González, also gently, very gently, leading Rawls away from the confrontation.

Rawls glared at Kelsey, took a few steps away, then wheeled back around, unable to resist the last jibe even as the *Trib* photographer snapped away at her display of indignation.

"Next time I see you on my turf you're under arrest, Kelsey!"

"You do what you gotta do, girlie!" shouted back Kelsey,

grunting and hitching up his pants as he swaggered away.

Julian came up to me, shaking his shaggy surfer locks.

"Are cops always like this?"

"Only when they're scared. We better get going too."

SANTERÍA.

The things of the saints.

That was the contemptuous name Spaniards gave to the devotion of their slaves for the plaster saints of the Catholic Church, ignoring that those saints were stand-ins for powerful deities the slaves worshipped back in Africa. The word *santería* is an insult that endures like a badge of honor—much like the Christian cross, itself a mark of shame as a death fit only for thieves and traitors under the Roman empire.

Nowadays *santería* might have millions of followers, from Alaska to Tierra del Fuego, but like all religions it had started small, its few members chased down by authorities who feared the empowerment faith brings to the oppressed. And, as with all minority religions—the Christians under Diocletian, the Jews in Constantinople—there were blood legends to *santería*, tales of unspeakable horrors carried out by the believers in the name of their mysterious deities.

Many of the blood legends blamed on *santería* were actually a misreading of the rites of a related cult, *palo mayombé*, the perverted black magic that occupies in West African religions the place Satan worship holds in the Christian pantheon.

But unfortunately, the two murders that had just occurred did not bear the imprint of either religion.

The words etched on the corpses were neither the flowery praises of Yoruba, the language of the Nigerians who brought forth *santería*, nor were they the elaborate curses of the Kongo people who created *palo*. They were something different, phrases and formulas belonging to a sect which supposedly had been extinguished for a hundred years, a sect hunted down mercilessly by the Spaniards as the most bloodthirsty of all the African cults.

They were the words of the Abakuá, followers of the god who lives in a bottomless well and craves human life for reincarnation.

I had thought it was all behind me, this nightmare of fear and horror, that the evil that men do unto others and themselves had been interred, never to trouble my sleep again. But the beast had awakened, demanding its measure of blood again.

I thought I could escape my past.

How foolish of me.

LATER THAT day I dropped Julian at his Statistical Analysis class and drove down to the main library on the Berkeley campus. The slender tower of the campanile stood proud and confident in the window frame as the young clerk ordered up my books from the bowels of the research stacks. While waiting I watched the usual crowd of students, reading, writing, and, more often than not, nodding off in the vast room under the coffered ceiling. Many years ago, more than I thought possible, I too had fought boredom and sleep under the yellow library lamps at Brown as an undergraduate. Later, as a law student in Gainesville, I had felt the sand under my eyelids at three in the morning from the lashing of the methamphetamine I'd taken to cram for tort law. It all seemed so far away, so innocent.

MY NUMBER flared up in the huge light board above the desk. I turned in my stub. The diminutive Asian student with wide eyes and porcelain skin could barely lift the old vellum-covered volumes up to the counter. She smiled awkwardly, embarrassed by her burden. I grabbed the first two volumes before they fell to the floor.

"Thanks," she muttered, shaking her head. "What are these for, anyhow? Your thesis?"

"You might say that."

"Oh. What is it on? Anthropology? Comparative religion?"

"Good and evil in the modern world."

"Good luck," she snickered. "You'll never reach the end of that project."

"You're probably right," I said, taking the books to a distant corner of the hall.

IN 1898 the once ever-faithful island of Cuba, Spain's last colony in this hemisphere, was convulsed by an uprising that cleft the country into two camps, each waging war on the other with the viciousness only close kinship can spawn. In the middle of that final chapter of the Spanish empire, the colonial authorities found themselves with a new kind of crime on their hands, even more dangerous than the rebellion itself.

It began with the odd discovery of a Valencian girl, fresh from Formentera, gone to draw water from a public fountain at Galiano and Neptuno streets.

The rosy-cheeked peasant, unused to the late-rising customs of her adopted country where no one except butchers and bakers got up before eight, had walked down with her *cántaro*, her earthenware jar, at the earliest light. Her shock at her find was so great that she dropped the jar, which shattered into pieces around the lifeless body of a beheaded woman wrapped in African cloth, a silver coin in her hand.

Horrifying as it was, had the incident ended there it would have been just another piece of news fodder in a country where fifteen daily papers vied for the attention of the half of the population that knew how to read. But the following morning there was another find out in the Luyanó neighborhood—a second beheaded woman, also wrapped in African bunting, with yet another real in her hand.

Havana's attention, riven up to that moment by the steady progress of the rebels, the *insurrectos,* out in the eastern half of the island, now was captured by these two ghastly discoveries. Worse, enterprising reporters soon found out that the second woman was the Spanish wife of a Spanish merchant. It was later discovered that said merchant was actually an itinerant peddler often gone for long stretches of time from home and that the forlorn wife had been entertaining male friends on the side for suitable compensation. But at that moment all of Cuban colonial society was stirred up by a holy fear—*peninsulares,* Spaniards, were being attacked in their most vulnerable spot, the virtue of their women.

When two other white women were also found beheaded in the same manner, a black neighbor of the first victim was taken into custody by the authorities. He died after two days of torture, but not before implicating a secret society of former slaves like himself, who drew the blood of white women for their dusky rituals of witchcraft and possession. They called themselves *ñáñigos,* the sons of Abakuá. The sect, made up mostly of the Efoks and Efiks tribes from the estuary of the river Niger, claimed to be the chosen people of Africa. The women's blood, confessed the man, gave the Abakuá miraculous powers—to fly in the darkness, to lift a horse and buggy with one hand—and it would be used to destroy the white population of Cuba.

This news brought back the old fears of the revolt of the blacks, an awful thing in a country where at least sixty percent of the population was of pure or barely mixed African blood. The slaughter of the whites which had happened in Haiti almost a hundred years before was about to be repeated in Cuba!

From one end of the island to the other white voices of fear and indignation rose up in a chorus of self-righteousness. My own great-grand-uncle, Archbishop Morell of the Archdiocese of La Habana, excoriated the heathen blacks from his pulpit at the cathedral. Squads of *vigilantes,* newly arrived, poor and ignorant Spaniards fighting for the little they had lately come to possess by virtue of the color of their skin, scoured the streets, chasing down blacks, burning their shacks, lynching anyone even remotely suspected of belonging to the dreaded Abakuá. The entire structure of colonial authority devoted all its resources to eliminating the sect from society.

Then came the explosion of the USS *Maine* in Havana harbor. Within weeks, the start of the Spanish-American War. Suddenly, just as mysteriously as it had begun, the rash of beheaded bodies by the fountains of the capital stopped, swept away by the stronger currents of a conflict that forever destroyed the old way of life. It was the last time the Abakuá sect was ever heard from.

I CLOSED the old book, puzzled, and stared out the window at the slender campanile, sounding the five o'clock bell while western clouds lowered into a darkening sky.

None of it made sense.

The murders had happened a little over a hundred years ago. As far as anyone knew, the Abakuá had been wiped out. Yet now these two women had been killed in Los Angeles and Oakland, like ghastly mementos of another time and another culture, in the same identical fashion, down to the writings etched on their skin, an invocation to the spirit of the mysterious god Ekué.

Suddenly I remembered the frightful message I'd tried to erase from my mind: Ricardo Díaz, my half-brother, drawing the *nkisi* figures in blood in the note he sent me after skinning alive my old friend.

Ricardo promised me he would not rest until I and all my dear ones were dead. Could this be his revenge beyond the grave? Had he enlisted someone else to help him with this ghastly purpose?

All the unanswered questions of that case, which I had written about in my last book, appeared again before me like some foul spirit from beyond.

Were these tragedies just the alarm bell for a far greater horror about to unfold?

I returned the books to the counter, walked out to the patio to place a call on my cell phone.

"Kelsey? This is Morell. We have to talk. The sooner, the better."

3

IN LEGAL circles in Los Angeles, where you go to lunch is almost as important as who you go to lunch with. The attorneys with the most savvy try to find a place that's simpatico to their persona, as they see it, like the Pacific Dining Car with its steaks for the O'Melveny and Myers crowd; the Water Club for the Wells Fargo counsel crowd; Enterterman's at MacArthur Park, with its pastrami sandwiches and fat knishes, for the underpaid and overburdened public defenders.

Judges, on the other hand, want somewhere bland, safe, predictable, that will tell folks yes they have to eat but no, they're not
some kind of radical that takes more pleasure from food and
wine than from the law. In their eyes pleasure should be reserved
for briefs, golf, and back-stabbing in the judges' lounge. That's
why so many judges favor a certain Indian tandoori chicken
palace on Spring Street, as a sign of their conventional cosmopol-
itan spirit. I mean, who's going to object to curry or lentils and
rice?

Fortunately I don't have to play that kind of head game with
my dad. He, after all, is Mexican—even if he never changed the
family name back to Carranza from Carr—so it didn't take me
long to talk him into meeting me for *mole* day at Lucinda's, a
Mexican dive on Adams that I grew to love while going to law
school at USC.

As usual Dad carried on for most of the meal about his latest,
and third wife, Kathleen—twenty years younger and twenty
times as socially ambitious as my poor late mom or even the
chickie he married after divorcing Mom. Kathleen's latest scheme
is to start a book-reading circle among the wives of the top L.A.
politicians she's met at the Jonathon Club. She sees herself as sort
of latter-day Mme. de Staël, with a literary boudoir and a gaggle
of writers writing down her witticisms. If only she had some wit.

In any case, I couldn't get a word in edgewise until the end of
the meal, when Dad had his *arroz con leche* and I was able to ask
him about a certain State Senator Tom Decker whom Charlie had
mentioned during our conversations.

"You mean the gentleman whose daughter got involved with
Morell's brother, that Raúl Díaz character? No, wait, that wasn't
his name. It was Ricardo Díaz. Sorry, Freudian slip."

"If you say so, Dad. Anyways, Charlie claims there's a conspiracy of cult members out to get him and that the senator, who's
now dead, was heavily involved. I know Decker was a big political honcho back in the 1980s when you were in the U.S. Attor-

ney's office so I wanted to know if you ever heard anything like that. It sounds funny but then, think of those Starburst people, the ones who committed suicide in Switzerland a few years ago? Thinking they were going to be transported to a new life?"

"Or the Heaven's Gate people," added Dad.

"That's right. Or the Branch Davidians or a number of other cults, who had followers who seemed perfectly normal until one day, bingo, off the deep end. So I'm wondering, from your experience, does Charlie's theory hold water? Do you think there was some kind of, I don't know, some conspiracy connection to Decker?"

Dad leaned back, stirred the cinnamon stick in his coffee, let his large brown eyes rest about midway down the Tecate girl poster. He's aged a lot, I thought. But it suits him somehow, this beige-colored English professor type, even if it's all made up. I mean, his dad was just a pipefitter from Torreón who hit it big during the 1920s L.A. oil boom. I guess that makes us real Americans.

"I've always thought that the role of the devil is highly exaggerated in cases like this," he said finally, chagrined. "People look for a scapegoat to pin it all on; Satan or Charlie Manson or even this character Díaz instead of looking in their own hearts. I realize people nowadays believe in vast conspiracies of evil but I don't. In any case, his theory of the case will be hard to prove."

"Or to contradict," I countered, waving at the waitress for the check. One of Dad's least endearing habits is that he never picks up the tab. He says he gives great advice and I ought to pay for the privilege of picking his brain. I do, but it does put a little distance between the two of us.

"It is totally useless and if your prosecutor is worth his salt, he will totally destroy it," continued Dad. "What are you alleging? That a vast, nameless cabal of shady characters, for reasons that they have kept to themselves—because if I'm not mistaken, even Morell doesn't know why this happened—for reasons best known to themselves have decided to make Charlie the fall guy? So you have crimes and you have witnesses but unfortunately for your client you have no proven conspirators. I mean, who else can you name? No one, right? Well, like Mr. Sinatra said, this is like love and marriage, or horse and carriage, you can't get the one without the other. Richard Ramirez, the Nightstalker, tried that faceless conspiracy of evil as his defense. It didn't fly then and it isn't going to fly now either, kiddo."

I hate it when my father calls me kiddo. It makes me feel like I'm still a babbling seven-year-old trying to prove water shrinks when frozen. But I know how to get my digs in. It takes one to know one.

"But, *papacito*," I said, in a loud Mexican voice, making him squirm with ethnic displeasure, "just think O.J. Simpson! Johnnie Cochran and his crew were able to turn the whole case into one vast conspiracy to destroy not just O.J. but every black man who became too successful in the white man's world. Never mind the facts, the conspiracy said, we all know police lie and cheat, manufacture and plant incriminating evidence. How can we trust anything they tell us when we know what they're really like?"

Dad sat stiffly, his lips turned down in a professorial chagrin of disdain.

"What is your point, counsel?" he said, dripping with condescension.

"That conspiracies do fly—they fly under the radar of the prosecution because, like in the Simpson case, prosecutors can't believe people are actually so gullible as to believe them. But people are. Do. Are. Whatever."

Dad sniffed, glanced around at the shirtsleeved office workers digging into their painted rice and gooey chocolate *mole* lunches, then he stood and signaled for me to follow him. I left the money on the table, took a last sip of my iced tea, and scooted behind him to the wide burning sidewalk on a Santa Ana afternoon. Across the street the green and yellow tiles of the Aztec Theater writhed in the sun's cutting brightness. He stooped to whisper in my ear.

"Simpson succeeded because of black racism. A lot of blacks simply cannot stand whites and will go out of their way to screw them. Plus, you had a Fuhrman, who justified their fears of a secret Klan in the force. Who do you have so far?"

"I guess I'll have to find somebody," I said.

He gave me his most patronizing look, then walked stiffly to the parking lot. He was climbing into his Cadillac when, after the ritual invitation to dinner and my ritual refusal (he knows how much I loathe Kathleen), he added one last detail.

"Sweetheart, if I were you I'd do well to remember the story in the Bible, since your client seems so obsessed with religion. When the soldiers came to get Jesus, Peter raised his sword and cut off the ear of one of the soldiers. Jesus healed it and told Peter to sheathe his sword because he who lives by the sword dies by the sword."

I stared at him, momentarily dumbfounded. My father is a life-long atheist; his Bible is the California penal code. I never knew he could quote Scripture.

"Meaning what, *papi?*" I kissed him goodbye.

"That the conspiracy thing works the other way too. Look into how Charlie Morell was able to get back into the country and remain free on his own recognizance in spite of having a capital case. A good prosecutor will turn that around and hint that maybe it's Charlie who heads a conspiracy of cultists, out to protect him."

"In the District Attorney's office? That would be a kick. Although I don't think any deputy D.A. would go so far as to malign his own."

"You'd be surprised at what people will do to win a case. *Te quiero mucho,*" he said then, the only words of Spanish that ever came out of his mouth, a vestigial Mexican trait even he could not eradicate.

I stared at the shining taillights of his DeVille, his words sinking slowly into my consciousness.

"*Te quiero mucho* too," I muttered to myself, and then realized he hadn't said a word about the senator.

I hopped in my Alfa, picked up the cellular from the glove compartment, hooking the plug into the lighter, then turned on the engine and let her idle, the soft roar of her pipes like the growl of a lioness waking in the afternoon. The hot black leather seat almost scorched the back of my thighs. I reached Danny after the second try.

"Danny López Investigations, how can I help you?" he said over the sound of the jigsaw in the background. That was good. That meant he was in his workshop making yet another toy for one of his twelve grandkids. Or was that eleven? In any case, that meant he was available.

"Danny, it's me, Rita," I said, slipping into first and easing out onto Hill Street.

"Hey, *m'hija,* what's going on?" he asked, the buzz of the saw ever louder.

"Got a job for you," I said, squeezing into the one lane of traffic allowed on Broadway now that Metro Rail is tearing up the street for its subway. A red-faced cop blew his whistle at a dump truck, stopping traffic to let me pass. I scooted around and threw him a kiss. He actually smiled, imagine that!

"What is it this time, Rita, another gangbanger out of East Los?" said Danny in my ear. "Last time I had to run so fast my old legs hurt me for a week."

"C'mon, Danny, you know you're looking good," I said. Danny is seventy-seven years old, a retired Sheriff's detective who's known more criminals than a jailhouse block.

"Yeah, I look good for a toad. I'm fat, squat, half blind, and three-quarters bald. I look good for someone fixing to die."

"Stop it, Danny, don't go playing old man on me," I said, finally easing out to Pico, heading west past the Salvadoran bakeries, the Guatemalan markets, and Cuban *botánicas* of Pico-Union.

"I'm not your father, Margarita," he said, having finally roused him from his self-pity. "What do you have for me?"

"You coming out to the West Side today?"

Danny lives in Montebello, among the dusty casuarinas and 1950s tract houses of the Mexican middle class. By the way, my father lives in Pacific Palisades, next door to Ronald Reagan's old house.

"Well, *m'hija,* I was going to see my granddaughter perform at the Plaza de la Raza this evening at six. They're into Mexican dances, you know? That Chicano pride thing."

"I wouldn't know, I'm a white girl myself."

"Sure you are, *m'hija.* You look in the mirror lately?"

I pulled down the vanity mirror in the sun visor—a russet-curled, green-eyed woman with a spray of freckles on a pert Irish nose stared back at me.

"I'm looking now. What am I supposed to see?"

"Your soul, *m'hija.* You look in the mirror and tell me what your soul is."

"Hundred percent Latina, Danny, you're right. You want the job?"

"Who am I supposed to be investigating?"

"Former State Senator Tom Decker."

"Oh!" was the slow, cadenced reply. I could picture Danny turning off his jigsaw, taking a deep breath, scratching the scar on his bald pate where a 39 Streeter tried to whack his skull open with a bolt cutter fifteen years ago.

"Him with the daughter into voodoo and all that stuff?"

"*Santería,* I think it's called."

"*Drujería,* is what you mean."

"Whatever. I want you to find out everything you can about the old man. Especially whether he was into the cults, like his daughter."

"Let me see what I can find. You know he killed himself, don't you?"

I came to a stop at a red light next to a storefront church, La Piedra Cardenal de Jesús, the Cornerstone of the Lord. Inside the congregation was rehearsing for that evening's service.

"So I heard."

"You know how?"

"No. Pills? Gun in the mouth?"

"*Se colgó*. He hanged himself in his ranch a couple of years ago. My buddy Rafael Rojas was in that investigation, let me see what I can find out. *Ahí te wacho*."

He hung up. The light turned green, the chorus of "Closer to Thee My Lord" in Spanish drifted out to the bustling street, with its tamale and corn on the cob sidewalk vendors, its rock cocaine dealers, its humble people bustling to and fro, scrambling to make a living in the heedless City of the Angels. I drove on to Alvarado, then swung up, past MacArthur Park all the way to Vermont, then headed north, through crowded Koreatown with its garish furniture store sale signs that only Koreans can read, past the cartoonish Kentucky Fried Chicken outlet and the equally modern Lighthouse for the Blind, both buildings wasted on people who can't appreciate them, past the young, brown, and yellow faces streaming hopeful out of City College, and past the worried mothers dragging their ailing brood to Children's Hospital, Queen of Angels Hospital, and that old standby of the working poor, Kaiser Hospital, as I headed north to the hills to pick up my new and also ailing client, Charlie Morell.

Charlie had leased a house in his old neighborhood of Los Feliz, the Beverly Hills of Los Angeles seventy years ago, lately hip again for being home to Madonna, Brad Pitt, and other stars, starlets, and their lovers. I rumbled down the nice downslope on the boulevard from Vermont, past the Moorish castle fantasies, the remodeled Mediterranean mansions and Tudor piles lining the wide street, a testament to the endless possibilities that California has always inspired in clients who want new houses to go along with their new lives, as long as it's something like they knew back home, whether back home happened to be Italy, Tehran, or Tegucigalpa.

A stretch limo eased out of the gated entrance to Laughlin Park, where Chaplin and DeMille once, briefly, held court. The limo blocked the entire boulevard as it straightened and headed east, and through the driver's rolled-down window I thought I recognized the pudgy cheeks of Mariah Carey.

If the music people are now moving in, the property values are really going to shoot through the roof, I thought, in typical Angelino obsession with the price of real estate, instantly regretting I hadn't ponied up a little more money and bought here instead of Silverlake.

I swung right past the bronze statue of the Bruin, next to the wide stretch of lawn that on a sunny day becomes the gay Hollywood Hills version of Fire Island, then trundled up the hill to the low-slung, neo-Bauhaus ranch house Charlie had picked as his temporary residence. I pulled up into the carport, next to a kidney-shaped pool that sparkled aqua blue in the lemony afternoon light. Charlie was waiting at the door, dressed in Zoran black sweats and black sneakers, looking like a cat burglar lounging in his work clothes.

"I'm so glad you got here," he said, throwing the door open wide. "I just found the place."

I stepped inside the house. It sported an open floor plan, the kitchen to one side and the big room/dining room on the other, with just the requisite number of postmodern chrome and steel chairs, a dining table, and black leather couch. Not my kind of place, that's for sure. Chintz and cabbage roses are sacred words to me, but in this house that would have been grounds for conviction not to mention eviction. In any event, the barren decoration didn't seem to faze Charlie; if anything I thought it matched the isolation I perceived in the man. Where was his family? Who were his friends? Did he have a lover? I knew he had once all those things but now it seemed as though he was the most bereft man in the world, with the self-referential air of hermits and monks. But I wasn't there to improve his social graces, I was there to try and save his neck.

My eyes hurt from the glare of the view at the far end. Through a floor-to-ceiling wall of glass you could make out the hills and valleys of Hollywood and beyond, to the flats of the West Side out to Century City and even past that, all the way to the gray cloud-rimmed Pacific in the horizon. I grimaced, felt my stomach heaving. I hate these weird heights in Los Angeles, with the houses set on pylons and sticking out like flat matchboxes in the air. This one literally seemed to be flying, set on the lip of a steep rocky hill. Still, I made nice.

"That is some view," I offered, stepping away from the wall of glass onto the, I hoped, more solid flooring of the living room.

"It's a real pain in the ass," said Charlie. "Half the time you can't see anything from the smog. Then, by four o'clock in the afternoon, since it's facing west, the sun heats it up like a friggin' oven. I should have never rented this place. Come, let me show you something," he said, hurrying down the circular staircase to the living level below.

"Well, why did you rent it then?" I asked, following him as best I could in my three-inch heels—one of the hazards of being a short woman.

"I knew I'd be here for a while and I didn't want to stay in some soulless hotel. This place has a history. Jerry Rubin owned it for a while."

"Rubin, the hippie?"

He opened the door to a small, cool den, with two filing cabinets and a child's plain school desk. On the desk, an IBM laptop with a color image of a tunnel entrance.

"The Yippie. He stayed here when he was working for Keating."

"Jack Keating, the convicted financier? I never knew that."

"That's what the Realtor who leased the place swore to me. Recognize this picture?"

He pointed at the image on the screen—an entrance to some sort of mine shaft, decorated with the stylized glyphs of Los Angeles gangs in a rainbow of colors. I counted at least ten different groups I'd had dealings with, from the Royals to the Crazy Eights to the always memorable Mara Salva Trucha.

"*Placas,*" I said, using the barrio term for gang graffiti. I grabbed a chair, sat down to examine the image closer. The entrance was built of stone, set into a rocky cliff littered with trash. On the fringes of the image you could see a ragtag chain link fence from which dangled a banged-up NO TRESPASSING sign.

"Sure, they're *placas,*" said Charlie, all excited, "but do you know what that is?"

I looked at the grass-covered railroad tracks leading to the entrance, the date 1919 etched on the lintel, and then, of course, at the Microsoft Explorer site identifier, Los Angeles.

"I've never been to this one but I'd say this is an entrance to the tunnels of the old electric cars that used to run here in Los Angeles."

Charlie beamed with happiness at my response. I had passed his test.

"Exactamundo. That's the entrance near Echo Park. I'm sure you noticed all the different gang graffiti. That's because it's set in a no-man's-land, so all those different gangs have been fighting over it for years. I found this as a link to my Web site, would you believe it?"

"What's your point?"

I swiveled to look back at Charlie, his hazel eyes glaring wildly, as though he'd finally found the meandering path to his salvation.

"That's where they killed the girl they found in Palmdale."

4

THE SUN rises blue in the wastelands north of Los Angeles.

Up in the high desert, past the burgeoning spread of strip malls, housing developments, and ramshackle schools of Palmdale and Lancaster, deep into the still dunes of the Mojave, the wilderness greets the new day in astounded silence. Out of the thin mist at the far horizon, against the eastern flank of the mountain ridges encircling the area, a flurry of something will suddenly stir, struggling to be born.

The high clouds will move, the earth will turn with the burrowing of the myriad insects digging deep to escape the coming daytime heat, and the prickly Joshua trees will again hoist their branches as though heralding the daily miracle. Then a blue glow will shine forth out of the mountains and for what may seem like the longest time, all of creation will hang in the balance, as though Nature or the Creator could not decide whether to go through with it or just revert back to the scarlet night of yore.

Then, as though finally catching its breath, the sun strides forward, its yellow rays piercing the blue veil that covered its arrival.

As if on cue, all over the area commuters will begin to pull out of their driveways and head down to Metro Rail or to the cliff-hugging Antelope Freeway on their way to their jobs down in the San Fernando Valley or L.A. forty and sixty miles away; griddles will light up under the fat to cook eggs and pancakes in homes and cheap diners; the massive air-conditioning units of the malls will kick on in preparation for the scorching temperatures; school custodians will open the doors for the first children to be dropped off; post offices will clamor with the arrival of eighteen-wheel trucks bearing letters and parcels; and everywhere in the vast plain the bulldozers will roar to life, readying to churn some more sand and dirt to build yet another housing tract in the far reaches of Los Angeles County.

IT WAS by one such tract at the end of Avenue J, a long ribbon of asphalt tying the folds of the surrounding Antelope Valley desert, that the body of the second victim of the Abakuá cult was found. Beheaded, her nakedness covered only by a scanty piece of fabric, she was lying a few hundred yards away from a construction site rollout Dumpster. The Oaxacan Indian who discovered the dead woman had only recently joined the drywallers crew and he always liked to be the first one on the job to show how grateful he was for the work. Isidorio Guzmán was his name and when he saw the lump on the ground he thought at first that it was the work of the coyotes that had broken again into the lockers searching for food. Oftentimes on arriving at the site Isidorio would see the packs of rangy beasts scouring the area, digging into trash containers, hungrily rooting for easy pickings. But on approaching the bundle he realized it was not something a four-legged beast had dragged out, but a deliberate offering to a deity.

Isidorio had seen things like this back in Oaxaca, the spoor of desperate people who trafficked with *brujos* and *curanderos* to secure the success their own enterprise could not achieve. The brightly colored bundle was set on a straw basket, surrounded by offerings of fruit, feathers, and blood in tiny earthenware containers.

Isidorio grabbed a stick, poked at the bundle. He uncovered the body, then saw a snake wrapped around the corpse. The snake uncoiled to its full ten-foot length and sounded its rattle, annoyed at the worker for disturbing her sleep. To Isidorio's terror, the reptile turned and spoke in Oaxacan, then slithered across the dry, littered ground. Isidorio dropped his stick and ran in the opposite direction as fast as his legs would take him. He stopped running only long enough to alert his supervisor, who was just pulling into the site; then Isidorio climbed into his beat-up Toyota pickup and raced down to the San Fernando Valley and the safe crowds of Van Nuys, never to be heard from again.

THE MORNING Kelsey and I showed up to talk to the supervisor, the site was buzzing with activity, the crew struggling mightily to put the finishing touches on the first of four model houses for the subdivision. Down the street, the dug-up dirt rose in mounds around the concrete foundations of the future homes like so many footprints headed into the desert. The sound of Mexican *ranchera* music drifted from the workers' radios, turning the place into a California version of the *colonias* of Tijuana.

Kelsey parked in the twenty-by-forty parking lot next to the showcase house, the blacktop so new it still glistened like some dark jewel. Kelsey slammed open the door of his Caprice, wrinkling his nose and sniffing the air, as though smelling something foul.

"You know, we busted this place two years ago," he said, stretching his massive arms.

We had met at seven in the Sheriff's station after he'd put in his graveyard shift. He looked rumpled and bone-weary, his big brass belt buckle riding even lower than usual under his rounded belly.

"Really, what happened?" I asked, as a catering truck drove into view, sounding "La Cucaracha" to alert the workers to their morning break. The truck pulled up alongside us and all at once the men put down their tools and swarmed around the truck's open windows, from which wafted the aroma of *machaca, burritos,* and *tortillas* on the griddle.

"We busted these *muchachos* running a meth lab in a house trailer up here," he said as he dove into the crowd, the laborers looking askance at the lawman and his sidekick—me.

"Whole place was lined with barrels of ether, they had Bunsen burners and pill presses and all the rest of the stuff. The guys denied they knew anything about it, they were just taking care of the ranch. They had a bunch of ponies and *paso finos* up here. Christ, the guys were practically sleeping on the stuff, they'd set their sleeping bags next to the barrels and all, but they didn't know. Yeah, right."

"So, what became of those fine Latin gentlemen?"

Kelsey spotted a tall, muscular man in a chambray shirt and

black leather vest, his long, flowing ponytail flying from the wind blowing into the hollow frame of a new house. The man shook his head at the work left undone, picked up a paint bucket and a paint gun, peering at them as though expecting some wondrous clue to reveal itself to his eyes. Kelsey waved at him, the man waved back.

"The boys got twenty years each up in Tehachapi," said Kelsey, as we advanced toward the man. "The place was confiscated and sold at auction to an outfit out of Newport Beach. Didn't catch the big cheese, though. He was a Peruvian national and got on the next plane to Lima when he got word of the bust. Never thought the developers would build up this fast. Hey, Gil!"

The big man shook Kelsey's hand vigorously, rippling biceps writhing like snakes under his skin. Standing about six foot five in cowboy boots, with hooked nose and pockmarked face, he looked like the crazed killer of every bad Hollywood movie.

"Gil Luján," he said. I shook his hand, thick like a foundryman's glove.

"Luján. Mexican?"

"Aguascaliente Indian."

"That's a Spanish name."

"One more thing the padres gave us we can't get rid of. I'd change it to Lewis but it's the same difference, know what I mean? It's what *they* call us. Let me show you where we found the body."

Luján led us to a small brick-lined pit in a hollow some distance behind the last of the showcase houses. Surrounded by rows of dried-out peach trees, it was the kind of place where field workers long ago gathered for barbecues and beer, back when the Antelope Valley was a wilderness dotted here and there with oases of fruit trees.

"The little brown brother who found it is now somewhere south of Oaxaca," said Luján standing astride the last steps leading to the pit. "Son of a gun was so spooked, if I hadn't run into him when I was coming to work, I would have never known."

I looked at the semicircle, where so many fires had been lit, so many meals consumed. There was not a trace of anything at all, just sand blowing in to cover the mistakes the world had made and kept on making.

"So this was a ranch years ago?" I said, looking for a source of the water that might have fed the dying trees.

"Squatters. Just around the bend out there . . ."

Luján pointed beyond a low-lying ridge, where the remains of a structure showed through the sand. "That was Plano. Founded by commies back in the 1920s."

"Socialist utopians," I said. "They wanted to set up the perfect society up here. No individual property rights, free love, communal housing. I didn't know we were so close."

Both Luján and Kelsey stared down at me, as though surprised for their own reasons that I would know about that forgotten relic of brotherhood. I caught their look, shrugged.

"I have a thing about Southern California. I love its history. There were a lot of experiments in living down here. It wasn't always Mr. Businessman trying to make a buck. Lots of people tried new things, even way back a hundred years ago. There was another housing settlement like this in Los Angeles, down in Sunland."

"Isn't that where old bikers go to die?" cracked Kelsey. I ignored the remark.

"Back at the turn of the century a bunch of socialists set up a community called Las Casitas. Little stone houses with their own rose gardens and stuff. It's now the headquarters of the Hell's Angels."

"See, I was right," said Kelsey to Luján.

I walked down to the middle of the pit. I could not imagine why anyone associated with *santería* or Abakuá would want to leave a body in the middle of the vast, unforgiving desert that had seen so many hopes wither and die.

This had nothing in common with the murder up in Northern California, except for the same markings and odd mutilations. There were no glades, no trees, no streams. All at once it came to me.

The water. It was always the water.

In Havana the bodies had always been found by a *pozo*, the communal well that served the needs of the people until the Americans laid down the water and sewer lines during their occupation of the island. In Berkeley the woman's body had been discovered just a few hundred yards from a gurgling creek in Joaquín Miller Park. But here? In the Mojave?

I walked across the pit and down a slope barely visible from the end of the road. About ten feet down, a mantle of gray rocks lay across a twenty-foot-wide gully, a gash in the land that snaked sinuously as far as the eye could see into the sere mountains in the distance. I picked up a pebble, smooth, round, warm, as close to the feel of human flesh as something lifeless could be.

The little mute children of the desert. I tossed it clear across to the other side, dinging a prickly Joshua tree, then climbed back up the embankment.

"What you looking at?" said Kelsey, carefully observing me with the pasted-on half smile of someone who can't decide if you're a serious threat to life and limb or just mentally defective.

"Aren't you going to have problems with flooding in these houses?" I said, pointing with my chin at the half-built models. Luján shrugged his hefty shoulders, giving me the wide shaman grin of indifference.

"I only build them, I don't site them. Not my fault if the developers set them on a floodplain. That's between them and the Planning Department."

"Flooding? What kind of flooding are you talking about?" blustered Kelsey. "We're in the middle of the desert, for Christ's sake."

"You remember the old song, 'It Never Rains in California but Man, it Pours'? That's what you get here, Michael," I replied, waving my hand at the dried-out gully and the seemingly endless expanse of sand and dreams.

"This is a classic desert arroyo formation. It looks dry as a bone and it usually is, for years. A perfect wasteland, not a blade of grass will grow. Until you get a fifty- or a hundred-year storm. Then this here becomes a rushing torrent. This whole area is like a little lake. In fact, I'd say that at one point this must have been a year-round stream until they drilled wells upstream and tapped the water table. That's how come you can have those stunted peach trees over there."

"Pears," said Luján. "I used to pick in this valley when I was a kid."

"Pears, then. Point is, lack of water was probably the reason why the farmer sold it to the drug dealer, who then passed it on to the developers. Who of course just pass it on to the unsuspecting homeowners."

"That's why they had the cookout over here, it used to be by the side of the creek," said Kelsey.

"You bet," I replied. "Kicking it with a few brews, a *carne asada*, and the old lady in the shade by the stream of the desert. A little oasis of felicity. Till progress came around."

"That's why they built that commune out here," added Luján. "They tapped the water."

I nodded. "Let's head on back, I want to check out the medical examiner's report."

By the time we reached the parking lot, the catering truck was trundling down the grade, quilted metal sides flapping as it negotiated the bumps, playing "La Cucaracha" like some plaintive love song. Luján looked at the workers, still milling around with their *tortas* and breakfast *burritos* in hand, and ordered them back to work. I stepped on an errant brown bug, which splattered under the lug sole of my desert boots.

"I forgot to ask you," I said to Luján as we shook hands good-bye, "what was it that drove your worker out of here?"

Luján reset his flowing ponytail, his eyes opaque from recollection, then he looked down at me, amused by what memory had whispered in his ear.

"You're going to like this. He said that when he found the body there was a snake wrapped around it. He grabbed ahold of a stick to whack it when the snake told him in Indian to go back home to Mexico, his mother was dying. Imagine that, a talking rattler!"

The sounds of Juan Gabriel echoed in the models as we drove away, Luján rousting his reluctant workers like a basketball coach twenty points behind in the third quarter. The sun burned down, the air smelled of sage, the clouds wheeled around and disclosed a sparkling burning sky. Kelsey chuckled to himself.

"What's so funny?" I asked. He gripped the steering wheel, cut in front of a Vons semi.

"Just thinking about that Mexican who ran away when he saw the talking snake."

"What about him?"

"That he's obviously never dealt with L.A. lawyers before."

THE POLICE car radio squawked. We were on Highway 14 past Pearblossom, the blank walls of the new malls by the freeway rising like the brown overhangs of the mountains in the distance. Kelsey picked up the mike.

"This is C-2180. What's up?"

A woman let out a peal of laughter in response to an unheard joke out in the dispatch room.

"Hey, Mike," she said, barely containing herself, "we just got a wit to the 187 out on Avenue J. Deputy Marshall is holding him at the Unocal station on Márquez Drive. Just thought you'd like to know."

Kelsey blinked repeatedly, as if his commanding officer had called him honey during roll call.

"Ten-four, Alicia. We'll check it out."

"How far is that?" I asked, as he hung up the mike, gripping the steering wheel with more than his usual intensity.

"Next exit."

TWO CRUISERS were parked at intersecting angles by the service bay when we pulled into the gas station, blocking the way for the other vehicles, which streamed out in single file onto the avenue. A chubby Hispanic man, the name Jorge stitched on the label of his station uniform, wiped his hands with a greasy rag as he walked up to us.

"Fill it up, mister?" he asked in a sorrowful tone, almost abjectly devoted.

"*Pues no, Jorge,*" I said, getting out while Kelsey traipsed off inside the station's office without bothering to say a word.

"We're with the Sheriff's. We wanted to ask some questions," I continued in Spanish.

"You too?" asked Jorge, in Spanish as well, a sly grin lifting up his broad features, coarsened by a lifetime of burning sun, rich food, and manual labor.

"*Seguro que sí,*" of course, I replied, sensing that Jorge probably had not been quite forthcoming in his answers to the detectives—assuming they'd bothered to ask him any questions at all.

"So tell me, why the line of cars?" I continued in Spanish.

"Oh well, that's the promotion," he said, with a grand shrug that lifted his shoulders almost to his ears, as though saying what fools these Anglos be.

"The gas, she's selling at ninety-nine cents, and all these *gabachos* from Palmdale come here wanting to save the extra twenty cents a gallon. They don't realize how much they burn up on the drive out here, or waiting to fill up. They don't think through things, these *gringos,* don't you agree? All you got to do is put a sign saying 'special discount' and they all fall over themselves to get to it. They think they're so smart."

"You have all the reason," I replied, nodding at the long line of idling cars, the odor of their exhausts fouling the morning air.

"Excuse me, *señor.*"

"You go ahead, please."

Jorge walked to a nearby pump, jiggled the handle for a woman customer whose gas was not coming out. I leaned on our unmarked patrol car. I could see through the glass walls of the small station's office a worried-looking stocky man being questioned by a potbellied white detective, while Kelsey and another, thinner, more elegant man in a buttoned-up yellow linen shirt looked on with analytical detachment.

Jorge returned with his amiable smile, eager to share something but not knowing how to do so. I nodded at him.

"Have you been many years in this country?" I asked him, still in Spanish.

"All my fucking life," he replied in effortless, unaccented English. "But you know how it is, people expect you to talk a certain way, so you give them what they want."

"I'm sorry. I didn't mean to insult you."

"No offense, you didn't mean anything by it. It's these racist people up here get on my nerves. They think you're not really human if you got a Spanish last name. So I say to myself, you know what, why fight it? Give them what they want, maybe that way you'll make more money. That's what this country's all about anyhow. So where you from? Argentina? España?"

"Cuba, originally," I replied.

"Celia Cruz! *Azúcar!*" said Jorge, suddenly wiggling his hips. "I take it you like Cuban music."

"Like it? Man, I love it, no, take that back, I adore it! Beny Moré, Vicentico Valdés, Fajardo and his Estrellas, Sonora Matancera, Orquesta Aragón, man, the list of great musicians that little island has given the world just goes on and on. I know, I mean, I used to have my own salsa outfit back in the 1970s, the Antelope Valley Sound Machine. That was before I got my kids. When they came around I had to put down my trumpet and get a steady gig. So I bought this place instead. Now instead of tuning horns I'm tuning engines. But it's all an art, you know? I can listen to an engine and tell you by the way it kicks and hums what's wrong with it. Nine times out of ten I'm right on the money. Mechanics with a salsa beat!"

"Wait a minute," I asked. "You're the owner? So who's that they're questioning in there?"

"That's Vartan, my night clerk. He was working the graveyard shift when that guy showed up, the one they're looking for for the killing of that girl up in Avenue J? Now, Vartan's English," he briefly lapsed into an imitation of an Armenian accent, "she is not too good, you know? But they want to talk to him all the same instead of me on account he's white. Fine by me, *pendejos.* By the way, you say you're with the Sheriff's?"

"In a manner of speaking. I'm an attorney, but I know a little about the case. You mean the investigators didn't ask you anything?"

"Oh, yeah, sure, who was working here and all that but not enough. I guess I could have told them I saw the suspect too but they never got around to asking me. I mean, I know who the dude is."

I stepped away from the car, still capable of surprise at the stupid mistakes racial prejudice can make.

"Wait a minute. What exactly are you talking about?"

"I'm saying the man they're all interested in, who came here to get his tire fixed after it blew out on him out on the desert, I saw him when I was parking. It was around seven-thirty that morning. His left front tire was bald and he probably hit the curb or something so it blew on him."

"Well, who was he?" I asked, determined not to make the same mistake.

"Dude's Max Prado. Maximiliano José Prado. He used to be a big-time record producer in New York. He discovered La Soli and cut all kinds of albums with the Fania All Stars, Johnny Pacheco, all those salsa guys way back when twenty years ago. But I'll be damned if I'm going to volunteer any information to people treat me like I was some *mojado,* some wetback, like I wasn't human."

Jorge stopped, gave me his most servile grin and nodded in the direction of his office.

"And now if you'll excuse me, I better get back to my customers. By the way, I do believe they're calling you in there, *amigo.*"

Kelsey was waving at me to join the group inside the glass-walled cubicle. I nodded goodbye to Jorge, who went to make change at the register in the service bay.

THE OXYGEN seemed to have been sucked out of the office when I walked in, the small room reeking of smoldering cigarettes, motor oil, cheap cologne, and nerves. Kelsey dropped a heavy hand on my shoulders, gripping my bones as though he never wanted to let go.

"This here's the man I was telling you about. Do you know Mr. Morell, Vartan?"

I pushed Kelsey's hand away. "Excuse me," I said, "but I've never met this man before. How could he know me?"

Vartan, sweat ringing his receding hairline, large saucer eyes popping out from his sallow face, shook his head.

"No, no," he muttered, "like him but not same. Thinner. Long hair."

"I meant if he'd maybe read your books or something like that," begged Kelsey.

"As far as I know my books haven't been translated into Armenian, so I don't see how."

"There's no need to indulge in ethnic prejudice, Mr. Morell," said the thin man in the yellow shirt, looking at me down his long aquiline nose. "We're not all slaves to our origins."

I turned to Kelsey, pointing my chin at the interloper.

"Would you mind telling me who Mr. Bones is? What's going on here?"

Kelsey exchanged glances with the paunchy investigator, the sunburned, light-haired, blue-eyed kind that seems to have vanished from Los Angeles after the Rodney King beating. Or, as in the case here, migrated en masse to the high desert after the '92 riots.

"I'm Captain Voinovich with the Sheriff's detectives. This is Officer Ted Núñez, special adviser to the Miami PD."

"Long way off from the mangroves," I said in Spanish at Núñez, moving closer to the door, away from the trio of lawmen, who instinctively closed ranks around poor puzzled Vartan.

"Officer Núñez is here on loan," said Voinovich, choosing to ignore my outburst in a language he also chose to ignore. He hooked his sausage-thick fingers on a big brass buckle stamped with the image of a racing stagecoach. "His speciality is—"

"Cult murders?" I ventured. "Particularly as regards *santería*, voodoo, and other West Indian magic?"

"That is correct," said Núñez.

"You were in charge of the investigation of the *obeah* murders in Lake Okeechobee last year, bunch of white kids wanting to be bad-ass rastas."

Núñez smiled, the glow of conceit lighting up his spare features.

"I see you've done your homework."

"And I hope you've done yours, Officer. What's going on here should be very apparent."

"You mind if we step outside?" he asked.

We walked out of the stinking booth into the garage, where a green Explorer was being noisily hoisted by the gleaming hydraulic lift while Jorge and a browner, fatter man also in mechanic's uniform crouched underneath, wrenches in hand.

"Mira," said Núñez, slipping into rapid-fire Cuban Spanish. "I hope you're not going to start telling all these *americanos* that this was committed by some sort of *ñáñigo* sect."

"Your research into the paranormal is paying off, Officer," I replied in English. "It's amazing how you can read my mind."

Núñez chose to argue on in Spanish, as though by drawing me into the same language we became more than experts but accomplices.

"Coño, chico, you and I both know the Abakuá sect disappeared, that it hasn't been heard from in its original form since the Spanish left Cuba."

"So what? It's now come back."

"Carajo," he said, growing more agitated. "You don't want to understand. This has got to be some sort of copycat. Cults don't just show up out of the air, like that. They have to grow, they need a fertile soil, adherents. You say anything else these guys are going to nail you."

I looked aghast at Núñez. It's true, I said, repeating to myself the most worrisome saying of the Spanish language, there is no worse blind man than he who does not want to see.

The hydraulic lift reached its end, the Explorer jolting to a standstill. Jorge's wrench clattered as it hit the floor. He took up the service light and hooked it to the undercarriage, the better to look at the innards of the vehicle.

"Just like I thought. Rear differential's got a leak," he told the worried customer in Spanish.

The door to the office opened. Voinovich and Kelsey lumbered out.

"Mr. Morell, we'd like you to come down to the station for a talk," said Voinovich.

The stifling heat of the garage disappeared and all I could sense was the slow wail of an alarm somewhere and the distant buzzing of a light airplane overhead.

"Am I under arrest? Or actually, let me put it this way, so there won't be any doubts in court, am I free to leave?"

"Let's just say that you're being detained for further investigation."

"Into?"

"What do you mean, into?" asked Voinovich, distorting his face, unable to believe someone somewhere could not understand everything he said.

"I meant further investigation into what?"

"Let's cut the crap," said Kelsey. "He means you're a possible suspect in this murder. You want us to make it formal or you want to come talk to us?"

I stared at the three lawmen for a second, then glanced at Jorge, who'd stopped his repair work long enough to contemplate the scene, his smile seeming to say I warned you never to trust the *gringos*.

"Let's go," I said.

5

THEIR CHARGES were laughable—if the facts, in some perverted way, didn't justify their conclusion.

But perhaps it wasn't Voinovich and Kelsey who had dreamed
this up. Perhaps this was all the brainchild of Captain Rawls,
who had come all the way down from Oakland to join in the
grilling fun.

"I'm hurt, Kelsey," I said, tapping my fingers on the rickety
card table, trying to feel as cocky as I hoped I sounded. "I open

my heart to you and you go and pin this whole thing on me. You know there's no jury in any civilized country—not even in California—that will convict on a cockamamie scheme like this."

"Kelsey is staying out of this," snapped Voinovich, his freckled face mottled with surging pride. "This is my case!"

Rawls, sitting at his right, threw him a dirty look.

"All right, all right, I'll admit it, my colleague here has a stake in this as well," conceded Voinovich.

"A stake?" Rawls yanked off her mirrored aviator glasses, her beaded tresses clattering as they swung agitatedly back and forth. "Goddamnit, sonofabitch, we found the body!"

"It's Voinovich. And we have a body here too."

"Whatever. If it hadn't been been for me tipping off you guys you would have never known he was coming here."

"Kelsey is working for us, it's our jurisdiction and he's here now!" blared Voinovich, his cheeks getting rosier by the minute. "You want him, you charge him when we're done with him!"

"Guys, guys. I'm flattered you think so much of me," I said. "But I still haven't heard any charges. Now you mind telling me the theory of the case first and fight over my body later?"

But Rawls couldn't leave well enough alone.

"Racist motherfucker," she muttered.

"That's it!" exclaimed Voinovich, slamming a hammerhead fist on the table, which bent and twisted from the force of the impact. "This interrogation is over. You're out of here, sister."

"What do you mean I'm outta here?" said Rawls, getting to her feet. Voinovich stomped to the door, jerked it open.

"You mind stepping outside to discuss this, Captain?" asked Voinovich, biting off every word.

"I'll be happy to discuss this with you anyplace, anytime," snapped Rawls, who kicked her chair to the ground and stalked out to the hallway, cinching her belt with the most clichéd macho swagger she could muster.

Rawls slammed the door behind her. The hum of the AC unit

filled the cinder block room, and a great fear fell on me. I pushed it away.

"A fine show, guys!" I hollered at the glass wall, knowing the two officers would be standing there, huddling in the shadows, watching. I turned to Kelsey.

"Why didn't you talk to me before?"

"This wasn't my idea, kid," countered Kelsey, taking out a cigarette pack, shaking one loose, lighting it with his old Marine Corps Zippo. "You gotta understand, the whole thing has got to be looking suspicious for somebody on the outside."

He puffed a few clouds, then brought down his red eyebrows, now beginning to be tinged with the gray that had already infected my own temples.

"Anyhows, I sure don't know what the hell you're talking about," he added. "You've never let anyone into your life. You're as closed as Magic Mountain on a Sunday morning."

"Not true. I've always been straight with you."

He batted his almost invisible lashes, took another hit from his cigarette.

"C'mon, Charlie, come clean. You can probably use a diminished-capacity defense again. Just like in the Valdéz case."

"Whoa, whoa. Hold it right there a minute. Am I being charged here? 'Cause I sure haven't heard that Miranda tune."

Kelsey sighed, took out his plastic-coated Miranda rights card from the hand-tooled leather wallet he'd picked up on a fishing trip to Baja many moons ago. He glanced at the card, raised an admonitory finger, then let it drop again.

"I don't know why I'm doing this. Force of habit, I suppose. The truth is you are not being charged with a thing. Not even a parking ticket, although you are delinquent on that expired meter ticket on Melrose last Christmas. I'm warning you, unless you pay up they're going to jack you with a Denver boot next time you're in L.A. Better make sure you take care of it when you get back to Bezerkeley."

"And when is that going to be?"

He grinned once again, hoping for once to have me exactly where he'd always wanted to have me.

"That's up to you. You cooperate, tell us how this all happened, and you'll be on your way in no time."

"Oh, puhleeze!" I blurted out. "This is such a load of bullshit, Michael. You're dancing around the issue. You will tell me anything, you will lie through your teeth to get me to 'fess up to the murders."

He grew stern, as serious as though I'd just maligned his dear old Irish mama.

"I would never tell you anything but the truth."

"That's all right, Michael. Even the Supreme Court says you can lie while questioning a suspect. But that's only if I'm a suspect. Now, you're going to have to make up your mind, because you're not getting any extemporaneous admissions out of me. You going to read me my rights or not?"

He hesitated, glanced back at the mirror lining the far side of the room, then he began to recite the fateful words known to all crime aficionados around the world, courtesy of the farmworker roughed up one time too many by the mean *hombres* in uniform of Arizona: "You have the right to remain silent . . ."

I answered yes to all of Kelsey's questions and gave up all my rights to have them prove their case, instead of dumping it all on me. But that's all right, I thought. I have strong shoulders. Call me Atlas. But can I really hold up my world all by myself? Does anybody today know any more who Atlas was? Do they care? Does anybody really know what time it is?

Kelsey seemed befuddled by my sudden conversion. I pressed my advantage.

"Anything I'm going to say I want it tape-recorded. And I want Rawls present. No more playacting for my benefit, okay?"

"Okay. Sure. Anything you say, Charlie. I'll be right back."

He got up, walked out of the room, leaving me alone to stew in my misery for a few minutes, a procedure some cops call soaking the suspect.

In the silence of that suddenly frigid room I thought back to my first client about twenty years before, back in Miami, a clerk charged with regularly skimming ten percent of all the money bags he'd handled in the Crockett Bank vault, how he'd been found guilty because of his confession under pressure at the station house even though he'd had a perfectly legitimate explanation for the missing funds. I remembered how many times I'd told students at law courses that most criminal cases are solved when the defendant opens his mouth and that if criminals kept it shut there would be such a crime wave the country would go under martial law. I thought of Julian, back at the Biltmore in downtown L.A., who'd already paged me four times that morning and who I had not been allowed to call. I thought of everything and everybody except what I was going to tell these people because that was not planned.

Some things you don't think about, you just do them.

The door opened. Kelsey returned with Núñez, the cult expert, still calm and collected in his buttoned-up yellow linen shirt. I caught a glimpse of two brown-shirted deputies dragging a handcuffed Mexican down the floor to the fingerprint rolling station before the door slammed shut again.

"There's your tape recorder, Charlie," said Kelsey, setting the tiny Sony on the rickety card table.

"What's he here for, Spanish translation?" I asked, jerking my head at Núñez. "Where's Rawls? Where's Voinovich?"

"They're still . . . discussing police procedure," said Kelsey. "Officer Núñez asked to be present during the questioning. Is that a problem?"

The recorder's tiny wheels were spinning already—Kelsey was hoping to catch any off-the-cuff incriminating remarks I might blurt out.

"Your dime, your time," I said. "Bring down the whole goddamn station to the show if you want. I have no say on that."

Núñez sat quietly, with the stern seriousness of one of the courtiers in an El Greco burial canvas.

"You're right about that, Charlie," said Kelsey. "So. Here we are. March 28, 2000, at the Antelope Valley station at . . ." He rolled up his shirtsleeve, glanced at his Seiko. "Eleven hundred hours, with Carlos Morell and Officer Ted Núñez re the Olive Lane, Peach Blossom murder."

"What's this about Olive Lane and Peach Blossom?" I asked. "We're opening a farm in the San Joaquin Valley?"

"That's the name of the victim and the name of the subdivision where her body was found. You want to tell us about it, Charlie?"

I glanced at Kelsey, then at Núñez, both poker-faced, waiting for the words that would slip a noose around my neck.

"Once there was a way . . ." I started, following the lyrics as best as I could remember.

"Yeah?" prodded Kelsey. "What way?"

I proceeded, now hearing the violins and the horns and the full orchestra opening up in the back of my head, as if John and Paul and George and Ringo were there in the room with me and the string section of the London Symphony Orchestra was sawing away in the background.

"To get back homeward . . ." I sang, in my most deliberately off-key pitch, then I stood and let her totally rip even as Kelsey and Núñez looked at each other and wondered if I was just putting on an act or if I wasn't really truly and unequivocally going insane after all:

> *Once there was a way*
> *To get back home.*
> *Sleep, pretty darling,*
> *Do not cry,*
> *And I will sing a lullaby.*
> *Boy, you're going to carry that weight*
> *Carry that weight*
> *A long time.*

And I sang all the instrumental portions, the French horn, the violin, the guitars, the piano, and the tympani, jumping up and down, until the whole majesty of the song poured out of me down to the very last note and I sat down again.

Kelsey was speechless. Núñez clapped. Slowly. He knew from Cuban song and dance.

"Very nice," he said. "Give us your funny papers."

"Don't mind if I do," I replied. "Tell me, gentlemen, have you ever felt the need, the desire to conquer, to leave your mark on this world so that everyone a thousand years from now will still remember your name, so that you will live forever?"

"Okay, Charlie," said Núñez, undoing just the top button of his shirt, "first you sing the Beatles now it's 'Fame.' What's next, *K-Tel's Greatest Hits of the 1970s*?"

"That's the point, you see," I answered, pushing my face forward over the table. "We're talking eternity here, we're talking strange phenomena, we're talking about the sun and the moon and the stars up above . . ."

"And a thing called love," concluded Núñez. "Will you stop this!"

"I don't get it," said Kelsey, looking totally at sea as Núñez and I glared at each other. I knew Kelsey couldn't understand the references but I had a feeling, no, I was a hundred and ten percent certain that Núñez was following me every step of the way, perhaps even looking down the road at where I was heading, and not liking it one bit.

"Let me explain," I said, finally feeling reason return her sweet smile. "All these lyrics can be seen as keys to another life. They all talk about death and resurrection and the eternal return of the soul. Richard, you remember Charlie Manson and Helter-Skelter. Charlie thought the lyrics were telling him to go out and kill LaBianca and Sharon Tate and who knows how many others. It's the same thing here."

"Excuse me, but there's no mention of any songs in those two murders," said Kelsey, eyebrows raised almost to his vanishing hairline.

"You are too literal. It doesn't matter that they're not written out, quoted, or sung in any of those murders. Or like with Manson, drawn in blood on the walls. These murders—and many more we don't know about, I'm sure—were carried out by people who want to live forever, who believe in the transmigration of souls, who think that by making human sacrifices they will achieve immortality and gain power here on earth."

"That whole show for this?" said Kelsey, putting out his cigarette on the sole of his boot. "That's a pretty pedestrian argument, Charlie."

"I'm surprised you know the word."

"I know more than you think, kid. Let me tell you something. This cult, this, what do you call it, the A-B-Q cult?"

"Abakuá," put in Núñez.

"Whatever. Let me give you my opinion. I think this is all about one writer whose sales are down and who wants to make sure his next book is a best-seller and he will do anything to get that. So he's gotten involved with some people who came up to him and said let's make a deal. When we get rid of these people and we get off on them, cutting them up and shit, you can dress them up and say they're victims of this weirdo cult shit and you can make a name for yourself and sell a ton of books of shit. Huh? What do you think of my theory?"

"It stinks," I said. "Why would your writer go along with it? If they can prove he's tied in to those murders, he's as guilty as the people who killed the girls."

"Why? Man, that's a stupid question. To sell more books, of course. Why maybe this writer was looking for a crime that he could solve that would put him on the front pages of the paper and get the free publicity he deserves. Failing that, this was the next-best thing. Hey, the ride is sweet! Oprah, TV interviews, Lifestyle Section features, all the rest of the gravy train if you are the one who broke the story and supposedly solved the murders. Shit, you could ride this baby to the top of the *New York Times* best-seller list.

"Now, let me tell you, I've been doing some research. These guys, like, what's his name, Goorsham and Thoreau and even Patty Cromwell, they all rake it in. It's like a golden shower of money people pee on these guys once they're on top. And it never stops coming. When you're on top people buy you because you're a brand name, it doesn't matter what kind of shit you put out. You're in for life."

"In for life is right," I answered. "That is the most bogus line of reasoning I've heard in a long time. Even from you, Richard."

"Well, that's my story and I'm sticking to it," said Kelsey. "See, I can quote lyrics too."

"Groovy, man, you're the bomb. Six months from now nobody will know what you're talking about. But that's okay. I just want to know, what evidence do you have that I'm the writer involved in all this?"

"Hey, you said it, not me. Hope that's clear."

"I'm sure it's clear enough on the tape."

"But if you were and you could help us find the people who actually did these girls, maybe we could cut a deal."

"A deal, huh?"

"Yeah, sure. A real sweet deal. You interested?"

Kelsey lit another cigarette as I stared back at him in silence. The AC unit wheezed feebly and I could feel the heat irradiating from the gray walls as the sun pinwheeled above the high desert. My stomach growled, I looked at my watch. One in the afternoon and we were still playing games. I just hoped Julian was out of harm's way.

"You want time to think about it?" added Kelsey. Núñez coughed from the smoke.

"Richard, do you mind?"

"I fucking mind," snapped Kelsey. "You be quiet and watch.

I'll tell you when I need you. You want fresh air, leave the room."

Núñez opened his mouth to protest, then thought better of it and leaned back in his folding metal chair. Kelsey contemplated my silence for all of a minute; then he couldn't resist, he had to gloat, just as I'd hoped he would.

"While you're thinking about it, you want to know when I suspected something was fishy, counselor? When I found the body out on Avenue J."

"So it was you," I countered.

"Of course. Why else would I be so interested?"

"That baby officer up north is as related to you as I am."

"Well, we're all part of the human family, aren't we? When I came upon the victim I said to myself, not again, I mean, it's like déjà voodoo time. So this time I called Núñez here, who told me he had just heard of a similar murder up in the Bay Area. That's when it clicked. You had just moved up there and bingo, lo and behold, another stiff. Núñez then told me they found a couple of bodies in the Everglades too, where the jet crashed a couple of years ago. The victims turned up more or less at the same time that you were out there touring for your last book. I got the schedule off your Web site. You should update it more often, you know."

"I had no idea you were into the Internet," I said, lamely, regretting that I had ever listened to my publicist, who touted the World Wide Web as the best place to create a buzz for my works.

"You kidding? After I got shit-canned out of LAPD and I transferred up here that's all I did for months, surfing the Web for a way out. That's when I stumbled on your site. As I recall you were one of the first commercial writers to use the Web. I was trying to learn as much as I could about *santería* and ritual murders and I found your site was linked all over the place. To Cuba this, Cuban that, Afro-Caribbean magic, other writers' sites, bookstores, blah, blah. That's when I came up with this."

Kelsey opened his file, pulled out a grainy eight-by-ten glossy of the front of a speeding vehicle at an intersection somewhere in the desert.

"Mercedes C230. Look familiar?"

The front plates of the Mercedes were partially obscured by a black mass of vegetation that grew out of the left corner; even so, the first few numbers were still recognizable enough: 41A82 . . . But what drew my eye was the telltale ding in the left fender, an incongruous sight in an otherwise new car. I twitched, involuntarily, hoping Kelsey had not noticed.

"This picture was taken by a speed trap the morning of the murder up on Avenue J. This is about half a mile from where the body was found. Using the timeline given by the coroner, we conclude the picture was taken more or less fifteen minutes after the girl was killed. This vehicle also matches a description given by a guy riding his mountain bike out on the trails that go around the subdivision. He was coming out onto the street when he was almost run over by this car and fell, breaking his elbow. He filled out a police report. There's more, of course, but we'll get to that in a minute. Do you recognize the vehicle?"

I stared at him in dumbfounded silence. For once I had no quick repartee, no sassy comeback. Hulking, bulking, stumbling Richard Kelsey of the Sheriff's department in Antelope Valley no less had come up with a damning piece of evidence—a photograph of my own car. I knew that from having a photo to proving my involvement in the crime was a huge leap indeed, but I had a feeling Richard had been planning this confrontation now for the longest time, building his edifice brick by bloody brick, and this was only the first room.

"You don't have to answer right away, Charlie," said Kelsey, putting the paper bag on the table. "I've got something else I want to show you."

"Wait up," I said, finally awake. "What exactly are you telling me?"

Kelsey brightened at my desperation.

"C'mon, I know that's your car, Charlie. DMV doesn't send out the picture and the ticket unless all the numbers are nice and clear but you and I know that's what it is. I pulled your DMV record, you bought it in '98, Buena Park, House of Imports. Paid twenty-eight five. Good deal."

"Okay," I countered, "let's assume that is me, which I am not conceding but let's suppose it is me. So what?"

This was the part Kelsey had been waiting for. I could almost touch his happiness, so palpable was the feeling of joy that possessed him.

"Well, Charlie, you figure it out. You're a pretty smart guy. Let's see. You got an author with plummeting sales—"

"They are not," I barked.

"Okay, they've crash-dived. You didn't earn out your advance, a hundred grand I think it was, and your publisher turned down your next book."

"How do you know that?"

"Charlie, you'd be surprised how much information a publisher gives you if you dangle a subpoena in front of him. Anyway, your practice in the Bay Area is going nowhere but you just bought that beautiful house up in the Berkeley Hills."

"Kensington," I muttered, knowing it was just another piece of hanging rope collected by the whirring Panasonic.

"Right. It was half a million dollars, if I recall correctly from the County Registrar's office. You got a kid in Berkeley and an office and a lifestyle and you're thinking, how the hell am I going to come up with the cash?"

"You're not making any sense if you're saying what I think you are."

"It makes perfect sense. This is what I really think went down. You picked up some fucked-up chickie down on Hollywood Boulevard, brought her up here, killed her, dressed her up in all that weirdo ritual stuff then dropped off the body. Now you've come up with this shadowy group of cult killers, which happens to be the subject of your next book. Like I said, great publicity, sell the movie rights, make a million or two, end of problem. And hey, the bitch had it coming, she shouldn't have been in the life, right? What do you say? Or are you going to tell me somebody else did it and you're just along for the ride? That's what your fellow Cuban here, Officer Núñez, thinks. But then he doesn't know you like I do."

He put his cigarette out on the floor, wiggled his eyebrows again. The AC unit developed a strange thumping—my heart, I decided. Núñez crossed his arms expectantly.

"Do you like me repeating myself?" I said. "I already told you that kind of thinking is the most stupid theory I've ever heard. You forgot one thing, Richard. One obvious thing if you're a writer, which you're obviously not. Who's the bad guy? Who's the heavy? 'Cause you can't have a thriller without a bad guy, it's against the rules. Evil has to be personified. You need a villain that's larger than life if you want to have the kind of best-seller you're talking about. Who's the killer in the book?"

Kelsey shrugged, lifted his palms outward, as though holding up the world.

"You tell me, Charlie. Who were you going to pin it on?"

"This is ridiculous. Look, this interview is over. I want that attorney after all."

"Before you do that, Charlie, let me show you something else."

Kelsey bent down, retrieved something from the depth of a hamper, then threw it on the table. A long, thin cotton tissue stamped with the wriggling black and brown design of West Africa, which Kelsey folded over and over until it lay clumped on the table, a yellow evidence sticker stuck to a corner.

"Recognize this?"

"Yeah, it's a Kuban cloth. Senegal, Liberian origin. So?"

Núñez lifted his chin, glancing down at the fabric.

"That's what Núñez here told me," replied Kelsey. "Kuban. With a K. Isn't that cute? He says this kind of fabric is usually part of a baby's swaddling cloth, when a newborn is wrapped around for the first time. Only this piece of fabric was wrapped around the body out in the pit. Rust marks are the chickie's blood. And this . . ."

He pulled out another rag, this one stained with what seemed to be oil and heavy grease.

"This is . . . well, I don't have to tell you, you recognize it."

I was not going to add another word, for I realized every utterance would be another nail in my coffin.

"I want that attorney, Richard."

"Sure, you'll get your shyster, hold on a minute. You don't have to say anything, just listen. This rag was left behind by the driver of that Mercedes I showed you the picture of. That was at that gas station we were at earlier. The guy was in hurry after he changed his tire, he had a flat and needed help. Service station guy got a fairly good look at him, was even going to help him but he got tied up with another customer and by the time he returned the guy was gone, leaving behind this rag and a can of that inflatable stuff for tires. The station attendant threw away the can, unfortunately, which would have been helpful, since it probably had the suspect's fingerprints. But that's okay too because this rag also has drops of the chickie's blood. So. Are you going to tell us why you did it or are we going to be playing this game all day?"

"I want an attorney," I repeated. "And if you keep going on like this, you know this whole tape will be thrown out of court."

"We'll see about that. Lancaster judges are not like those pussies downtown."

Kelsey's hand flew to a pager on his belt. He grabbed at it, glared at the number display. He stood up, pushed his chair away.

"I've got to make a call. Ted here will keep you company."

Kelsey walked to the door, knocked. Someone opened it, he stepped out. Núñez looked at me blankly, deliberately discarding all emotion from his expression to try to get me to open up. I folded my arms, closed my eyes, and, of all things, promptly fell asleep.

That is, I believe I must have drifted off—raptured is more like it—for all at once I found myself back in the desert, by the pit where the body was found, under a surreal sun, the light turning everything into a black and white of fierce intensity. Somewhere in the background Mozart's Clarinet Concerto played as I watched a dusty car drive up to the pit, my own Mercedes, which I had banged up in a minor accident in Oakland. An iguana slithered down an olive tree and stopped in its tracks next to me, also watching the approaching vehicle.

The Mercedes halted, raising a cloud of dust and sand. The driver exited so fast I failed to see him. He went to the trunk, opened it, lifted a body wrapped in a bloody cloth, which he carried in his arms. The iguana at my feet turned its purple head and spoke to me.

"*El movimiento se demuestra andando,*" it said, then glanced back at the approaching stranger carrying the corpse. Like in a movie I looked at the stranger up from his lizard skin boots to his leather pants to his broad chest and shoulders to the long flowing hair and to his face, which was covered by his flowing long locks, which he now shook and revealed himself to be—

"Wake up, Charlie, wake up! Will you get a medic, see if this guy's on drugs!" shouted Kelsey, shaking me by the shoulders.

"I'm okay, I'm okay," I muttered, opening up my eyes.

I had slipped out of the chair and fallen to the ground, splitting my lip. I sat up, my hands braced on the warm concrete floor, the drops of blood dripping in between my fingers.

"Give me a hand," I said, then sat down slowly again, the tiny interrogation room coming back into focus.

Núñez came out of nowhere, gave me a glass of water. I gulped it down. Kelsey eyed me suspiciously. Voinovich and Rawls were standing close by, watching me with the apprehensive look of a shopper who's last in line for a special that's going fast with no rain checks.

"You're not going to claim we did that, now are you?" said Kelsey.

"Not if you get me my attorney," I croaked.

"He's on his way. What happened to you?"

"The stress, I guess. I'm exhausted, I don't know. I haven't eaten all day. I guess I just passed out."

"Really?" asked Voinovich, all sweetness and concern, knowing this could conceivably be used to invalidate anything I might confess. "You want something to eat? One of the deputies can bring you a Whopper."

"That's all right, I don't eat meat anymore. I'll be fine in a minute. Just get me that attorney."

Kelsey glanced at Voinovich and Rawls, who shook his head no, then signaled at Kelsey to step outside. I sat, gasping for air, examining the possibilities in my mind like a dog searches for fleas, thinking it must have been high blood pressure just like my father and reminding myself to have it checked and that I'd probably had a minor stroke but that now I knew who the killer was when Kelsey came huffing back.

"Get up, we gotta go," he said, helping me to my feet.

"Richard, how many times I have to tell you, I want my attorney."

"In a min. Anyhow, we're not asking you any more questions so let's skedaddle."

"Where the fuck we going now?"

"Turns out the guy we talked to at the gas station was not the right guy after all. Somebody else was there that morning and you're going to see him for a field ID."

• • •

OVER THE mountain ridge, large masses of inky black clouds were swooping in with the swiftness of a monsoon. Kelsey drove on in silence, the rolling of the tires on the pitted pavement like the rolling of drumheads before an execution.

My execution.

"You're wasting your time," I told Kelsey through the plastic partition from the back seat of the car. "You're not talking, I can understand that. But think about this, Richard. If I killed this girl down here, then why would I do the girl by my own house? What's in it for me?"

Kelsey drove on, still not responding. A few fat drops of moisture pinged off the hood of the car. I glanced back, Rawls and Voinovich rode close behind in an unmarked squad car. They'd left me without handcuffs, so the identification by the service station attendant would not be marred by the evidence of my presumed guilt under arrest. I stopped my mind from thinking down its usual judicial track.

"Will you please listen to me, Richard. It makes no sense. I have no history of violence, there's no connection between me and the girls, you are wasting taxpayers' money. And our time."

Kelsey still refused to acknowledge my arguments, driving through the congested traffic on Pearblossom Highway. The rain began to pelt the car steadily, then the skies opened up in great black sheets.

Kelsey turned on the wipers, which barely coped with the onslaught pouring down. In the right lane, a car skidded on the slippery pavement forcing a van to cut in front of us, missing our bumper by scant inches. Kelsey braked, our car wiggled its tail but Kelsey muscled the steering wheel back under control. The rain lay down like a shroud all around us.

"This is all going to be kicked by the court and you will look even more like a fool than before," I went on. Up ahead, a line of chugging semis sounded their horns, demanding local traffic let them through.

"You know you have no authority to take me anywhere once I

have asked for an attorney. One has to be provided ASAP or this ID shit, even if it's positive, will be thrown out. You are wasting your time. Turn back, Richard. You are digging your own grave, man. You're going to be pulling DUIs for the rest of your time in Barstow if you don't put an end to this. How much more scandal can your career take, man? Don't you think the courts will see this as police misconduct? We have a history, Richard, this is only going to prove it. Turn back."

Kelsey looked over his shoulder, taking his eyes off the road for the first time. He smiled, enjoying every word he was about to spit at me.

"What are you so afraid of, Charlie? That we'll finally nail you to the wall like you deserve, *ese*?"

"Watch out!" I shouted, as up ahead an eighteen-wheeler jackknifed when it tried to avoid crushing a Pioneer Bread van. The truck fell over the traffic divider, jostling cars out of the way like a bull swatting flies.

Kelsey jammed on the brakes but the patrol car slid down the pavement, screeching and wailing as it bounced off the other cars hurtled our way, bumping against the back of the rig's trailer, then spinning around like a top, the car finally coming to a halt with its nose pointing at the oncoming traffic.

I pulled myself off the floorboard and glanced to my right— the force of the impact had popped the passenger door open.

"Don't run, Charlie, don't do it!" shouted Kelsey.

It was too late, I had already dashed out of the car and onto the freeway and was running on the pavement, getting drenched by the squall as I headed into traffic, the cars blaring their horns as they moved to avoid me and I jumped around the rushing bumpers like a swordless matador and then I hustled down to the sandy gully of the arroyo by the road and I looked over my shoulder and saw Rawls and Voinovich get out of their vehicle and watch me disappear down into the embankment and into the soggy sands of the expectant, forgiving desert.

6

A ROOSTER went cock-a-doodle-doo when we reached the end of Glendale Avenue, half a block from the Temple Street overpass. I wedged my yellow Alfa in between two banged-up tow trucks and killed the engine, feeling more skeptical about the whole enterprise by the second.

All around us, neon-colored gang signs had been sprayed on houses, walls, fences, sidewalks; even a truck parked up the street was lit up with *placas*. To our right, a rusty chain link fence surrounded what had been the entry yard to the Los Angeles street car system. A huge real estate sign offered the entire street-car site for six million dollars. I wouldn't have given six dollars for that dump.

Charlie jumped out of the car, walked across the street to an old lady watering a handful of sorry tomato plants in her front yard. He spoke quickly to her in Spanish, pointed at my Alfa and then at me. I smiled, waved. Might as well be gracious about this, I thought.

I crossed the street after Charlie, who laughed at something the old lady said. He dug into his pocket and tried to hand her a twenty but the woman shook her head vigorously and actually wished us, in a voice loud enough for me to overhear, *"Vaya con Dios,"* like in some old Western movie.

Charlie took me by the elbow, moved me back across the street.

"Hasta la bye-bye," I said to the woman, who waved back.

"What was all that about?" I then asked Charlie, who was following the length of the fence to the steps at the bottom of the hill.

"I told her we're tourists looking at the old L.A. subways. She says there's a whole bunch of us coming out here every day, in tour buses."

"What about my car? I didn't put the top up."

"That's okay, she said she'll keep an eye on it for us. Anyhow, and this is where we were laughing, she says it's safe now, all the *cholos* are sleeping off their hangovers. They won't be out till three or four."

We hustled up the steps, past piles of trash with clothing, empty bottles, torn plastic bags. A kitty ran through the grass, then I saw its long thin tail and I realized that was no cat, it was a rat.

"How does she know that?"

"Easy. There's one of them inside her house."

"Like who?"

"Like her son. He was peeping out the window at us. Funny, she thought we were Germans. She was surprised to hear me speak Spanish."

"Does that happen to you a lot?"

"People telling me I don't look Cuban? I've been hearing it at least once a week since I came to the States. People think we all look like Desi Arnaz."

"You mean you don't?"

"No, some of us look like Cesar Romero. Duck through here and be careful."

Charlie squeezed in through a hole in the fence broken open by generations of trespassers. I shook my head no, walked up to the next landing, then dodged in between two railings, treading carefully on the dirt path circling atop the entrance to the tunnel.

"This way," said Charlie, leading down the path to the north slope. Fearing a broken ankle more than a torn pair of hose, I took off my Manolos and walked barefoot the last fifty yards or so. I gasped as I jumped down in front of the burned-out toll house.

The courtyard walls were plastered with giant cartoon characters—like outtakes from some bizarro Disney movie, they were bopping down the walls to some funky barrio rhythm. Charlie walked across the yard to the tunnel entrance. I slipped on my shoes and hurried after him. The fencing that once blocked the way was torn down, dangling from a metal rod.

Charlie entered the shadowy mouth of the tunnel. To our left, the menacing face of a man-sized horned toad painted in vivid green was grinning silly at us. Charlie felt the wall, then he bent down to look closer.

"See this?" He pointed at a small painting of a vat or a bucket, water flowing out of it, an inverted cross floating above it.

"What is it?"

"It's to tell the followers of the Abakuá that they're on the right track."

He straightened up, laughed at himself.

"The right track. Get it?"

"I got it," I said, not finding it funny in the least. Behind us, in the yard, a couple of scruffy men in shorts and sweatshirts straggled out of the toll house, sniffing around like coyotes looking for something warm to eat.

"Can we please get going?" I asked Charlie. He turned on his Maglite, bowed like asking me to dance.

"After you, madame."

We walked on in; I don't want to exaggerate but I know I smelled death in that place. A chill went through me and I wished I hadn't left my wrap in the car.

"Tell me again why you think the girl was murdered in here," I said.

"The accumulation of evidence," answered Charlie, his words echoing down the tunnel. The sounds of the outside traffic receded with every step we took.

"The girl had been dragged through the dirt, leaving abrasions on her back. The dirt and pebbles ground into the skin of her lower back and shoulders, even into the base of the skull, according to the coroner's report. The burn marks on her ankles suggested she had been dragged by her feet, naked, over dirt for some distance."

He stopped, took out a drawing from his sweatpants pocket.

"And what might that be in your hands?"

"Copy of the engineer's plan for the train system that used to run down here."

His flashlight shone on a photocopy of an old drawing with the ornate lettering of a turn-of-the-century document. Charlie glanced up at the ceiling, shining his light on the electrical wiring still dangling overhead, then brought the light down to a marker on the wall.

"Like the miner's daughter said, Eureka," muttered Charlie, taking the left tunnel at the first fork in the road. We walked on, the darkness only broken here and there by beams of light streaming through cracks in the ceiling.

"All right," I said, trying to sound courageous, "so the girl was dragged on the ground, what of it?"

"Well, during the autopsy the examiner found a small piece of wire wedged in between the girl's buttocks. Now, my good friends at the Sheriff's didn't think much of that, but fortunately I was able to have the wire analyzed, as well as the dirt that was embedded in her skin. Isn't it great what you can do when you have the money to pay for your own lab work? That's what made the difference with O.J., you know. Money is the great equalizer."

"Skip the lecture," I said, surrounded by a dusty gloom that was starting to feel like one of my worst nightmares. "What did you find?"

"Well, the lab told me that the dirt most likely would not have come from the desert. Then we looked again at the piece of wire. I lucked out—it had a marking. The manufacturer back in Ohio confirmed it was an electrical wire, used by the streetcars that ran down here."

The sound of our footsteps echoed ominously down the empty tunnels—or were they really empty?

"Did anybody ever tell you the story of these tunnels?" I asked him. Charlie shook his head no, looking around for who knows what hidden track.

"What story? They were built for the electric cars."

"Maybe so, but I once read this book back in college, about how these tunnels were dug under downtown by this race of, like, Indians or aliens, and how they'd hidden all this gold here."

"You didn't really believe that, did you?" he asked, condescendingly.

"I'm telling you, it wasn't me who believed this. It all happened back in the 1930s. For years people were digging up holes, trying to find the gold. Then there's also the legend of the CCB spook."

"Is that like the *Blair Witch Project?*"

"So you don't know everything under the sun. Some of the people I worked with at the CCB said there's like this Sasquatch-like creature that lives under the Civic Center. He kidnaps people and then—"

I stopped walking. From somewhere near we could hear muffled cries, the hurried patter of people running away, then the ground shuddered to the throbbing and heaving of a train going by us. The ghost of streetcars past?

"The new Metro Rail. The line is about one hundred yards on the other side of the wall," said Charlie, shining his beam on the tunnel wall. "They built it right alongside it but never tapped this one. That would have been too easy. Anyway, that means we must have walked about a quarter mile by now, which is perfect."

"What do you mean perfect? How do you know you'll find what you want down here?"

"Patience is a virtue," said Charlie.

"In my book, it's a vice. Nobody ever got anywhere by waiting."

"Ah, ye of little faith. Look at that."

Charlie crouched next to the wall, shining his light on yet another vat drawing. But this one had a stick figure stuck to the inverted cross, with the stylized head of a snake next to it, its pointed tongue pointing further down the tunnel. If the place hadn't been so creepy, I would have had to laugh at the whole thing.

"We're almost there," he said, straightening up, then hurrying nervously further into the tunnel, as though eager to face up to the evil that had put him in this position.

"All right," I said, trying my best to keep up with him, "let's assume everything you said is true. How do you know it would be in this tunnel, and not somewhere else, let's say at the El Monte yards, for instance?"

"Because of the confession," he said, moving even faster, then stopping somewhere in the middle of the gallery.

"What confession? You never told me about any confession!" I said, catching my breath as I caught up with him. Charlie scowled, glaring all around, his flashlight darting crazily all over the walls.

"I know it's here somewhere, it's got to be— There!"

He found a rusty iron ladder leading up to the ceiling. Two large red smears had been painted next to the bottom rung.

"I didn't want to tell you because I couldn't corroborate it until I got here. But I think I just got my confirmation. This way."

I could feel my frustration rising. An enormous desire to scream and throw a fit almost overtook me. My own client was playing games, leading me down shadowy hallways—literally— and coming up with crucial pieces of evidence at the last minute like I was some kind of final-year law student. For a moment I debated whether to have it out with him right there and then. I had to preserve some kind of client control, after all.

Charlie stood on the last rung of the ladder, looked down at me, as though reading my mind and waiting for the ensuing explosion.

"Are you coming?"

I looked around the dusty, grimy gallery, moisture dripping from the ceiling out of God knows where, the sound of hollering and a pounding steam drill in the distance. Then, as if to spur me along, a flurry of six or seven sewer rats came scraping along, running in between my legs. I jumped on the ladder. The arguing could wait.

"You win. Let's go."

Charlie nodded pleasantly, climbed up.

"I got a confession on tape from one of the cult members. I'd chased him down to Cuba," he said, working his way up. He stopped at a large round metal cover, put his shoulder against it, strained to move it. The cover rattled as he rolled it aside.

"When did you get this tape?" I asked, wishing I'd brought my .38 Colt Special after all.

"Yesterday," he said, grunting, as he lifted himself into some kind of room up above. "A guy from the Cuban Interest Section in Washington was on business in the Bay Area and he flew down to drop it off. Jesus K. Rist!" he added, his voice registering all kinds of surprise.

"What is it? Is it safe to come up?"

"It's safe. Come on in."

I clambered all the way to the top, then eased into a small room that led to another, larger area. The rooms, which probably had been a storage depot at some point, gave off an odd odor. A large and bare makeshift altar was set in the middle of the larger room, rusty brown streaks leading down from it to the linoleum floor. The walls, illuminated by Charlie's roving flashlight, were all covered with drawings. But it wasn't the usual gang stripes we'd seen out on the courtyard; these were actual jungle scenes, as though we had set foot into darkest Africa itself.

I stood there, taking in the strange setting, while Charlie waved his flashlight on scenes of lions in the jungle, antelopes grazing by a pond, cheetahs running in tall grass, until the light stopped on the source of the stench—a woman's head pinned to the walls from one long blond tress of her hair.

A caption in what I hoped was red marker underneath it read: "2 L8 4U, CHARLIE!"

It was signed, again in red, with a flourish script, "Payaso."

"Some clown," muttered Charlie.

I N   A L L my years as attorney and public defender I'd never been in such a scene of wanton cruelty. I'd gone to your normal autopsy where the coroner slices up the body like some side of beef and I'd only felt a little queasy when the drill opened up the skull to expose the cranial cavity. I'd been to a number of murder scenes, sometimes when the corpses were still warm in the gutter of some South Central sidewalk. But I'd never been exposed to this kind of deliberate violation of the sanctity of life.

Charlie shone the light on the head, walking up closer to examine it. He shook his head; even he couldn't believe it.

"Look at this," he said, "they must have hacked at the neck with some serrated knife, you can see the gouge marks."

He took out a Swiss army knife, opened it, prodded open the jaws.

"It looks like they severed the tongue and—"

"I've had enough," I said. "I went to school to dissect the law, not corpses. Let's get the police."

"Yes, of course. I'm sorry."

He stepped back, looking like the Prince of Denmark before the skull.

"Still. Poor girl, I wonder who she was." Then the final flourish, unable to restrain himself: "They took out her eyes, did you see that?"

A large black bug suddenly eased out of the head, crawling up the brittle yellow hair, its antennae quivering under the bright light.

I felt my stomach heaving, doing all kinds of dances to my breakfast. Mercifully Charlie moved the light, shining it on the rest of the room. The floor was littered with beer cans, plastic store bags, pages of old newspapers. Charlie slipped two latex gloves out of his pocket, handed me a pair.

"Better wear these. You don't want to leave any prints."

I jammed my fingers inside the gloves, not knowing which was going to explode first, my stomach or my head.

"We've seen enough," I repeated. "I think we should go call the police." I moved back to the manhole. Even cat-sized rats in gloomy tunnels were better than this.

"No, please, don't go. I'm sure we're not that far," said Charlie.

"Far from where? Do you know where the hell we are?" I snapped.

"I have a pretty good idea," he said, stepping around a couch I hadn't seen before, thrown against a wall.

"You mind letting me in on it?"

"In a minute," he said.

I was about to argue when I slipped and almost fell to the floor. I glanced down at my shoe. The tip of my heel had stepped into a used condom, piercing it. I grabbed the prophylactic from a corner and held it up to Charlie's light.

"Look at this."

Charlie came over. I showed him the glistening sac, still holding sperm, then I removed one glove, dropped the condom inside, and tied the glove into a knot.

"Why don't you hold this," I said, sticking the glove in his jacket pocket. "The DNA should still be good."

He shone the light on the floor, picking up the glint of another three or four condom wrappers.

"These people are sick," I said.

"No, Rita," answered Charlie, sounding as sorry as though his own son had died in that room, "they're evil. They laugh at our pain, it makes them warm inside. Will you come this way?"

I hesitated for a moment, then decided I might as well check out the crime scene before the police came blundering in.

"Lead on."

We walked through a doorless doorway into a filthy kitchen with a 1920s stove and icebox and into a shuttered, empty living room. Our footsteps echoed as we hurried down the long, wooden floor.

He crossed the foyer, slid open a metal accordion gate, walked up to a peeling wooden door. He tried opening it. It wouldn't give. Charlie took a step back, lifted his right foot, and with a loud yell stomped on the old door. The top hinge broke out of the frame, the rusty lock flew to the ground. He gave another kick and the door and its equally ancient frame fell out onto a sunny sidewalk. I followed him outside.

We were standing in the middle of Chinatown, next to the Hueng Sung Bakery on Hill Street. We looked back at the house we had just exited. A large sign on the outside announced, COMING SOON—RED DEVIL BURGER! I whipped out my Ericsson.

"Let's call in Homicide."

7

THE CRICKETS were raising their cloud of musical calls
when I rounded the last curve of the running path on the north
side of Lake Hollywood. Past the six-foot-high chain link fence
and through the cypress and the Monterey pines, the green waters of the reservoir glinted from the last rays of the sun. A
brace of ducks paddling out from shore left a rippling wake behind them while overhead a red-tailed hawk wheeled and
canted, searching for the last morsel of the day.

The stillness of the Swiss Alpine scene was broken only by the chugging and huffing of joggers completing the last painful leg of the three-mile run around the lake. Up in the hills flanking the path, expensive vegetation grew around stately homes. From some open window the Anvil Chorus of *Il Trovatore* floated out, then the sky turned a violent pink and the spider's web of streetlights flared on. My motorbike chugged on, tut, tut, tut. I braked and stopped on the near side of the safety fence behind the narrow entrance.

I was to meet my son, Julian, at the corner of Mountlake and Lake Hollywood Drive. Over the past forty-eight hours I had put together all the details needed for our getaway—I was innocent and he was going to help me prove it.

Together we would beat the world.

It had all seemed so harmless at first.

I was going to be the investigator and he was going to be my assistant, his first time out in the field. Two days after Kelsey's visit, my house was quiet in the stillness of an overcast sky; even the birds had put away their chatter—only the quarrelsome squirrels in the huge Monterey pine in the side yard were still clucking and scrambling up and down the branches.

I walked into the den, the hum of the refrigerator from the kitchen down the hall following me like an old dog. Seven o'clock and still no sign of Julian. I walked up the stairs to my son's room, knocked, entered.

A single lamp shone on my son's desk, where a book had been left open, surrounded by empty cans of diet soda plopped across from the computer, whose screen showed schools of flying toasters sailing into cyberspace. A rustle from the bed and a tousled brunette with round blue eyes sat up, yawned, smiled.

"Hi! You must be Julie's dad. I'm Monique," she said, pulling down her rumpled Cal sweatshirt. Julie? I thought. That's new. I walked up to her, shook her soft, small hand.

"Pleased to meet you, Monique. Any idea where my son might be?"

She pointed her dimpled chin at the floor next to the bed. Julian had fallen asleep with a book on his chest—*Shamanism and the Cult of the Divided Self.*

"We were cramming for Anthropology, got a final this morning. I couldn't go past one but Julie insisted. You know how he can be, he just talks people into anything."

Maybe I don't know, I thought, with some admiration for my son's powers of persuasion. Monique leaned over, whispered in the tone of someone who's been very close very often before.

"Julie! Julian, honey, time to wake up. Your dad's here!"

Julian stirred, pushed the thick honey blond hair out of his eyes, smiled with the tender expectation of those for whom life is a series of welcome discoveries and every next day promises to be better than the last.

"Juventud, divino tesoro, que te vas para no volver," I muttered under my breath.

"Hey, *Papi.* Quoting Rubén Darío again?"

"Better than Che Guevara."

Julian sat up, shook the cobwebs from his head.

"Yeah, well I've always thought youth is way overrated. Just a bunch of hard work, if you ask me. What's up?"

"Come on down and have some coffee with me after your shower. I'll tell you all about it."

By the time Julian made it down to the kitchen I too had showered, shaved, and changed into the lawyer's protective armor of a gray pinstripe suit. Julian had slipped on jeans and an oversize CK sweatshirt, his wet hair clinging to the back of his neck. He poured himself a *café con leche,* and served himself one of my *torrejas,* the cinnamon-spiced Cuban version of French toast I'd made the day before.

"Where's Monique?" I asked, putting down the *Chronicle.*

"She's taking a shower, she'll be right down. What do you think?"

"I'm jealous. French?"

"Nah. From San Diego. Any more news on that murder up in

the park?" he asked, speaking through a mouthful of food like all young guys do, as though bad manners was synonymous with maleness.

I took one last spoonful of my Raisin Bran, remembering for some reason my aunt in Jacksonville, who would not allow any sweets in her house except for the stale homemade bran cookies she kept in a glass jar in the kitchen.

"No. And I've got a feeling I won't find out until I get down to L.A. and check out the other body down there. I wanted to talk to you about that. Something wrong?"

Julian looked down at his *café con leche,* shook his head no, his damp hair flying out in a cloud of coconut-smelling conditioner.

"I was thinking, I don't like to stay here all by myself and—"

"What? Since when does a nineteen-year-old object to having the run of the house all to himself? C'mere, you must be feverish."

He grinned, he knew I had him.

"Let me try this. How about you get some help in this investigation, huh?"

"You mean like, you?"

"Sort of."

"What about your finals?"

"Today's the last one. Then I've got spring break. We haven't been down to L.A. since last year and I thought Monique and I could go check out Hollywood while you go and—"

I raised my hand. "Done. That's exactly what I wanted to tell you. We're leaving this afternoon. But without your girlfriend."

"Pop!"

N O W   I   saw Julian, leaning on a peeling green lamppost. He was waiting for me, just like I had asked him to.

I don't think that I'll ever find the words that can describe the mountainous waves of feeling that crashed within me the moment he came into view. In a flash, in mere nanoseconds, I saw him again when he was born, crying and shitting in my arms just moments out of his mother's womb, then when he took his first steps chasing a runaway ball in our backyard in Miami, then his first day at school, waving tentatively at me before dashing off to class, then his first karate championship, then that night at my father's grave during a tropical thunderstorm when I exchanged my life for his and saw him race away to safety behind the palm trees.

It had all come down to this, to this one instant, this indivisible particle of time when he and I were separated by a seven-foot-high chain link fence, twenty feet of pavement, and a world of betrayal. Because I'd already seen the telltale flashing of blue nylon jackets barely hidden in the bushes, and the beat-up Crown Victorias with two antennas parked some distance up the steep hill.

I peered through the fence. Julian glanced in my direction but did not recognize me until I whistled low the two-note call of childhood. Like a well-trained son he turned his head, wide hazel eyes opening even wider. I trembled, thinking at first it was from the cold but realizing it was from fear of losing him. But I had already lost him, even if I was trying still to catch him before he sank out of view.

"Julie! *Es el viejo!* I whispered urgently in Spanish, taking off my helmet so he would recognize me. "C'mon, let's go before they come out!"

I waved at him, urging him to enter the pedestrian walkway and hop on my bike.

"Dad!" said Julian, his hands outstretched to show me he bore no weapons—or to signal to the cops, who began to pour out of the bush.

"C'mon out here, Dad, we have to talk!" he said now, flipping his long hair back in his eternal gesture of nervousness. "You can't run away, *Papi,* it's impossible. You have nowhere to go!"

Julian, strapping, handsome, six-foot-tall Julian, with the surfer build and the mellow voice, the child I'd tried so hard to please and bring up right, Julian, for whom I'd give my life in a second, shuffled toward me, prodding me to accept a crime he knew I could not have committed. I trembled again, from fear and pain.

"Son, don't do this," I said, revving up the bike. "Tell me I'm wrong, tell me they forced you, I beg you!"

Julian's features folded into a frown. He took another step forward, arms outstretched, still beseeching me to surrender.

"Pop, you have to come in! There's no place to run to now. They know all about it. They showed me the evidence, Pop. Your fingerprints, your blood. They even found the knife, Dad, buried in our backyard. It all matches, there was nobody else. It was always you."

I heard two car doors slam shut and in the distance the loathsome whirring of helicopter blades.

"Come in, Dad, please! You'll get treatment. You're not well, they know that. It's not your fault. Please!"

Tears began to slide down his cheeks, his arms shaking from grief.

Kelsey finally stepped out from behind a bush of overgrown oleanders, gripping his Beretta in front of him.

"The kid's right, Charlie," shouted Kelsey, over the growing noise of the chopper. "You probably don't even remember what you did. Come on in and we'll talk about it."

"*Adiós, mi hijo,*" I shouted, revving up the bike's motor, then spinning and racing away.

THE BIKE screamed between my legs as I opened up the throttle and headed south on the running path. A couple of shots whizzed by, raising plumes of gravel on either side of me, even as I headed straight for a pack of red-faced overweight men trying to complete their run before total darkness set in. They made way like a flock of flapping geese, flailing at me as I went by. I knew the cops wouldn't shoot if the joggers were in between. I felt terrible, but then I had not asked for this either. And, awful as it sounds, I did not care. My own son had betrayed me and the only way to get him back was by proving my innocence—which I definitely would not be able to do while in the tender care of the LAPD.

By the time I'd cleared the group, I was out of firing range— even a cop on horseback could not catch me. I headed south, knowing the path was obstructed at either end of the path and that the LAPD patrol cars could not negotiate their way in. Just then I heard the chopper, louder than ever, the blinding beam of white light from its fifty thousand watts of illumination beaming down on me, turning my surroundings into the eerie black and white of Batman cartoons.

"Stop your bike now!" hollered the officer over the loudspeaker. "Pull over and surrender!"

He ordered me around time and again, like all LAPD officers, thinking that because they willed something it would be so. I raised my left hand and gave them the finger, knowing that that solitary act of defiance would probably be picked up by the media helicopters, which now drew near like green flies to carrion. But I wasn't dead yet. If I could just reach the south gate at Lake Hollywood Drive, I'd be able to lose myself in the maze of streets and alleys dotting the Hollywood Hills like capillaries on a drunkard's nose.

Now the pathway became straighter, the last inlet of the lake behind me. Less than five hundred feet ahead of me, the exit gate and freedom.

"Stop your bike now!" bellowed the helicopter again, a mad angel of revenge.

I opened up the throttle, determined to grab my last chance

at freedom, when a sudden squeal of tires and headlights put an end to my illusions. Three black and white patrol cars came out of Georgius Way, jumping the curb and slamming into the exit, their doors slapping open almost simultaneously as six officers took immediate position behind their vehicles, aiming their guns at me.

I slammed the brakes so hard the engine died. I fell sideways, sliding to within forty feet of the officers.

"Lay down on the ground, face down!" shouted the one nearest me.

I caught my breath for a second, feeling the blood beginning to ooze out of my left leg, badly burned during the slide. My hands were still on the handlebars and for the briefest moment I hesitated, then realized that way lay certain death. I wheeled around and finding strength from I don't know where straightened out the bike, kicked it into life, and jumped back on, screeching away while a couple of bullets dinged my back mud flap.

Again I roared up the path, the helicopter still hovering above me, its high-intensity beam illuminating the pavement and the sloping hillside like a spotlight on a darkened stage. The other exit was still blocked by Kelsey and his minions. Then I spotted it, the same seventy-degree grade I had come down on from the street overlooking the lake.

I plowed straight into the hillside. The wheels of the Suzuki slipped at first on the loose dirt but then the tires gripped and I flew up, hurtling through masses of oleander, ficus, and agapanthus, veering wildly left before losing my balance, then zigging back to the right to muscle my way up to the top of the three-hundred-foot slope, finally making it onto the flat lot of a spec house, timber and tiles stacked on the side of the half-built frame.

I surged out onto the street, the neighborhood dogs barking at the deranged lone cyclist. My only way out now was to lose the choppers in Griffith Park, its long verdant finger curling around the imposing homes on the hills.

I raced down Mirror Lake Drive, jumped the curb, cut across an open backyard and exited on Canyon Lake, then on to Innsdale and up a fire road snaking all the way around the steep hillsides of the park.

At the summit I hit old Mulholland Highway, here just a broadened dirt road on which I had run when I lived in Los Feliz so many eons before. At one point I went off the highway and down another trail, heading for the safety of familiar territory by Vermont, when I found myself behind the Hollywood sign, its thirty-foot letters shining brightly down on the madness of Los Angeles while the LAPD helicopter still bore down on me.

I had one final weapon, one final trick to escape, but the time wasn't right yet. I knew that as long as I kept running they would keep following but would not shoot, and that they would not take their eyes off me for a moment, unwilling to give me the leeway I needed to get away. Exiting from behind the letters I spotted a figure moving quickly right into my path. I braked as hard as I could, my left leg scraping the ground like a third brake on the gravel road.

I came to a halt. Before me stood the biggest coyote I'd ever seen, spindly legs, narrow body, and bushy tail, wise old eyes staring at me even as its jaws were clamped on someone's pet shih tzu, white and furry, trembling and yelping. I hollered but the trickster only growled back, shook the dog as though claiming ownership, and dashed away into the bushes. Poor pup, I commiserated, and hurled myself down yet another dirt road.

I reached Mount Hollywood Drive, the police helicopter still in pursuit; to my right rose the Griffith Park Observatory. Then I saw the light I had been searching for—the tunnel linking Hollywood Drive and Vermont Canyon Road, leading down to the Greek Theater. I checked my gas gauge. Still a quarter tank left. I went for my last hope.

The pilot saw the red streak shining eerily in the night sky, then took evasive action to dodge the boat flare I'd bought at the army surplus store. The chopper canted to the left as the projectile exploded in a shower of red, gold, and blue at the precise moment that I entered the tunnel. I braked, got quickly off the bike, stuck a stick to hold the throttle open, and sent the bike racing down the road for another five hundred yards or so.

The bike followed a straight line, then dropped in the far side of the canyon, down the deep ravine facing the tennis courts, the golf course, and the twinkling lights of the stream of vehicles on the Golden State Freeway. I ran to the bushes behind the tunnel and slid down the bare hillside on my butt for five hundred feet, pushing aside with my boots all sorts of rocks and gravel and empty beer cans until I fell, with a heave and a grunt, on the fields behind the Greek. I raced around the shuttered building, climbed a chain link fence, and dropped down to the nicely paved, quiet streets of Los Feliz.

I took a deep breath, checked my pocket to make sure I had not dropped my wallet, then hustled at a spirited clip to the Old Brown Derby bar on Hillhurst. I had only one lead and I was going to have to chase it down to Cuba. There was no other choice. For me or my son.

"Where to?" asked the leather-jacketed female taxi driver, thinking she had another scruffy swinger out for a musical good time.

"How does Tijuana sound?"

I flashed her a wad of hundreds.

"Buddy, you're on."

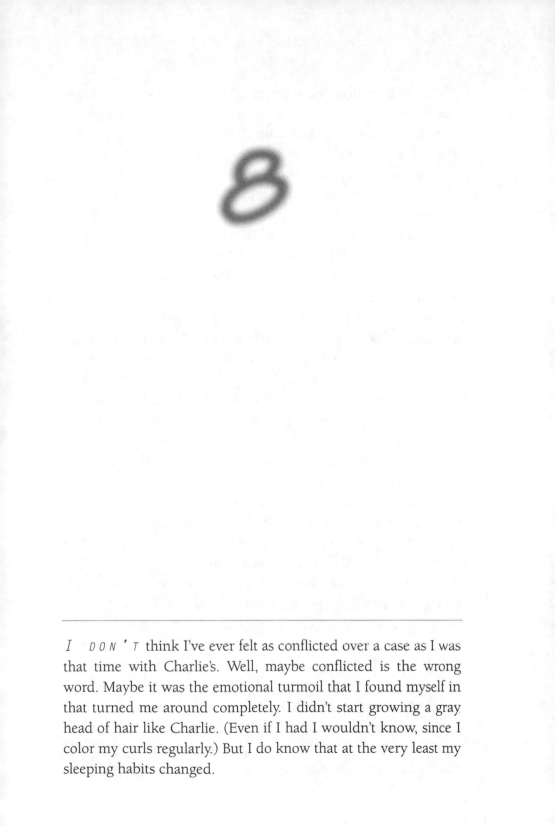

_8_

_I_ _DON'T_ think I've ever felt as conflicted over a case as I was that time with Charlie's. Well, maybe conflicted is the wrong word. Maybe it was the emotional turmoil that I found myself in that turned me around completely. I didn't start growing a gray head of hair like Charlie. (Even if I had I wouldn't know, since I color my curls regularly.) But I do know that at the very least my sleeping habits changed.

Even Raúl noticed, poor darling, fixing me all kinds of weird teas to bring me down; finally some guys at his gym suggested Saint-John's-wort and that seemed to do the trick somewhat. That, plus nonstop dancing to Tito Puente and Celia Cruz the next couple of days after finding the severed head. I mean, I played "Oye Como Va" so many times my neighbors thought I'd opened up a dance studio.

The point is, I was scared. And the fear I felt could not be faced down by Raúl, with his Glock, or by any kind of muscle or fire-power. It was all in my mind, like a chill that had sneaked inside of me and wouldn't let go until I sweated it out. I was jittery, high-strung, defensive, and combative, lashing out at the slightest hint of criticism from anyone. The perfect litigator, in other words.

I also developed a morbid fear of insects, and when I found a little silverfish in my bathtub that had crawled in from the lilac bush outside the window, I called in Western Exterminator to have them fumigate the entire property with as much Diazinon as the man would let me and then I had him make the house ro-dent-proof as well. I didn't have nightmares about the head but I sure have hated all vermin from there on.

Here's what I mean. I never thought much of the occult or the dark arts until I met Charlie. Black magic and all that stuff was for losers, stoners, Goths who didn't have a life so they invented their death. But after that day in the tunnel, and after reading more of Charlie's manuscript, I became convinced someone was tailing me, watching me. Raúl did his best not to laugh at my fears, especially since I could never catch anyone watching me. Until one time at the Beverly Center parking lot, when I thought I'd left my wallet in my car and I suddenly spun on my heels. Fi-nally I caught sight of him, a little elfin-looking, brown-skinned guy with a big head and a bigger smile, looking like an over-grown kid, who waved at me, then moved behind a Ford Expedi-tion. I ran after him but he had simply vanished from sight. I told Charlie about my sighting but he wasn't fazed by it at all.

"That's Eleguá, he's checking up on you."

"Ellie who? What are you talking about?"

That's when Charlie sat me down and gave me his spiel, his explanation of the different deities of *santería* and how this particularly repugnant cult that we had stumbled upon was a variation of the religion of the saints.

"Eleguá is the patron saint, or god, if you will, of lawyers, salesmen, all those who make their living by spinning tales. He's represented by Saint Anthony in the Catholic Church, but in *santería* he's said to have twenty-one manifestations, sort of like the avatars of Krishna in India. I wouldn't worry if I were you. It just means you have been granted protection. I just wish he'd been on my side; none of this would have happened. But like a *santero* friend of mine said, we all have our own paths to the pumpkin patch. I guess mine is just full of rocks and thorns."

I don't know that I would have said thorns—perhaps poisoned man traps would have been more fitting in his case. For even when things seemed to be going right for Charlie, they were really going wrong. But you had to hand it to him, he always struggled on, trying to keep his heart and soul together, no matter what.

Take our finding of the cult's sacrificial headquarters, for instance. The media, like he would say in one of his books, had a field day. The *Daily News* splattered all over the next morning's edition, "Cult Deathtrap Under Chinatown." We even made the Metro Section of the Times, "MTA Tunnels Lead to Grisly Find—Heads Roll."

The house that we came out of became the site of countless stand-ups by local and network TV reporters; our story made it into *Time, Newsweek,* the *New York Times,* and *The Wall Street Journal.* Some punks, ever on the alert for a new thrill, made a little shrine of the location, quickly covering the outside with pentagrams, inverted crosses, and the rest of that nonsense. Eventually even the hamburger chain withdrew its offer to build an outlet and donated the land to the Southeast Asian Battered Women's Shelter.

Fortunately, for once the LAPD had its act together. Within twenty-four hours of our discovery investigators had pinned down the identity of the victim—Sarah Chase, a seventeen-year-old runaway from Ohio who'd last been seen hustling for fries at an Oki Dog in the Glendale Galleria. Her parents, a couple of college professors who'd been searching for her for months, flew in from Dayton to pick up the head, which they carried home in a box. The body was never found.

Awful as this all was, you would think it would have vindicated Charlie's contention that there was a conspiracy of cultists who were trying to pin it all on him. But for Charlie nothing was ever easy. Or for me, either, as long as I was with him.

I found out about this the hard way, when I returned to the CCB to have what I thought would be a friendly, dispository conversation with Mike Cleary, the deputy district attorney assigned to Charlie's case. When he told me he had a nine o'clock calendar call in his court and could only see me at eight-thirty, I should have guessed something was up. But unlike Charlie, I am always ready to believe the best of people, so I agreed to see him in his office on the eighteenth floor at the time he wanted.

Strangely, I hadn't made an appearance at the Criminal Courts Building since I'd opened my office the year before, so stepping back into the old gray monolith at Broadway and Temple was like a high school reunion. From the moment I parked at the lot next to the building, paying twenty dollars for what once I got for free, to the moment I walked around the sidewalk and down the pedestrian entry on the south side of the building to stand in line to go through the metal detector, I was accosted by old friends and colleagues, each and every one green with envy at my success.

I thoroughly enjoyed it.

The presiding judge had cajoled some extra money out of the county supervisors to hire more security guards, so entry to the building had speeded up considerably since my last appearance. As I stood in line to place my case on the conveyor belt through the X-ray machine, I thought of my own little darling Raúl. I could see him standing there with his handheld metal detector, telling people to please go through the gate again or to please empty out their pockets of all metals, keys, and coins, strutting his hard little tush around the lobby in his stacked heels. I thought he would be perfect for the job and made myself a mental note to look into the hiring of personnel down there.

The elevators were as cranky as ever. A very pregnant black lady, who must have been just a week shy of her due date, let out such a whoop when we flew up to the fifteenth floor that I was afraid I'd welcome her little one to the arms of the law already.

Our elevator opened its doors and then promptly shut them before anyone could step out and returned to the ground floor. Everyone trudged out, telling the other visitors in the lobby that the unit was broken. Me, I stayed in, knowing how unpredictable these machines are. Sure enough, within two seconds the doors slammed shut again and I was transported, all by my lonesome, to the District Attorney's lair.

I waited inside the reception area for ten minutes, sitting in chintzy chairs under placards honoring past DAs of the year, charity marathons, and all the other civic stuff that law enforcement awards itself as pats on the back for a job well done regardless of results. It reminded me of the time the District Attorney held a press conference to congratulate the losers after the not guilty verdict was in on the O.J. Simpson case. Of course, that particular DA was now gone, replaced by the fulsome Phil Fuentes, who by the grace of his photogenic smile, big shoulders, and even bigger ambition had stomped his old-line Anglo competition for the job.

After a fifteen-minute wait I asked Vivian, the receptionist, to try Mike again. Ever gracious, Vivian called for the third time. She smiled as she hung up.

"Mr. Cleary says for you to come into the conference room."

Vivian got up from her desk and opened up the gate, showing off the kind of svelte body I want to have when I'm a fifty-six-year-old grandmother of four like she is. I followed her into the inner sanctum of the District Attorney's office, past the two administrative secretaries posted by the plush chair and couches by Phil's office.

"Are you still running 10Ks?" I asked Vivian.

"*Ay no, m'hija,*" she said, her speech still carrying the intonation of her native Puerto Rico. "I'm training for the Long Beach Marathon next month so I got to take it easy on the old knees. I figure if I finish, I'll be happy."

"I'm sure you'll leave them eating your dust," I said absentmindedly, my mind leaping to overdrive when I saw the bodyguards by the door to the conference room. What's going on in here, I wondered.

"Thank you, dear, you're as sweet as always."

Vivian opened up the door to the oak-paneled conference room. Sitting at the head of the table was Phil Fuentes himself, flanked by Mike Cleary to one side and Ronnie Brightman, the deputy in charge of Central Trials, on the other. Ronnie was the kindest woman you would ever meet, with her hippie dresses and hemp farmer boots, until you ran across her in court; then she became a killer shark. They all smiled brightly, no doubt smelling blood in the water.

"Thank you, Vivian," said Phil, "please close the door behind you."

He stood up, shook my hand languidly across the shiny fruit-wood table.

"Thank you for coming so early, Rita," he purred. "I remember when we were together in Compton you were always late to court so I appreciate the effort. Still dancing at Rudolfo's?"

And that was the essence of Phil Fuentes—a combination of charm, disdain, and instinct for the jugular. In one sentence he had remembered not only my professional weakness but my per-

sonal predilection, reminded me of our past together and under-
lined the fact that now he was in charge and that people like myself had to come begging for favors. But I can't stand
condescension, even if it's only implied.

"Well, you know me, born to dance. But really, Phil, I had no
idea you still spent so much time worrying about Charlie
Morell," I said, sitting down before I was asked. "I came here to
talk discovery with Mike and here you are. I'm sure you have
many other important cases, so I am sincerely flattered."

Phil took it well, I must say. In fact, that was always Phil's forte;
no matter how unexpected the event, how unforeseen the twist,
he always kept that smile glued on, never losing his temper,
never letting on that the latest debacle was anything other than
what he had planned. A dyed-in-the-wool politico.

Now he chuckled, jerked his head at his underlings to sit
down, while he remained standing.

"Charlie is an old friend. Like you, Rita. I always keep a place
in my heart for guys like you. You know I wouldn't pass up a
chance to work with you again," he added ambiguously. He signaled another flunky, who came out of a side door pushing a
courthouse-issue TV and VCR.

"I take it Mike has given you all the paperwork, the police report, coroner's interrogatories?"

"Sure, sure, but let me get one thing straight. Is Mike prosecuting the case? Is Ronnie? Or are you? I mean, what's the deal here?
Why the big powwow?"

Mike's pale cheeks flushed with embarrassment at being up-
staged by his boss, bowing his head so low I could see the glow-
ing skin of his spreading pate. Ronnie stared at me with the blank
smile reserved for cops, cashiers, and other bearers of bad news.

"I haven't decided yet," said Phil in his burnished baritone, as
smooth as any soap opera thespian. "Maybe we won't have to go
to trial. Maybe your client will plead guilty."

"And maybe the sun will rise out of Malibu. I don't think so,
Phil. My client is not just not guilty, he is absolutely innocent of

these charges. This is all a conspiracy by people who feel threatened by his works, who know he could find out who they are and who want to put him out of commission."

"I see," said Phil smoothly. He nodded, as though contemplating the immense wisdom of my observations, and sat down in his black-leather upholstered chair.

Ronnie took me on, snapping, "You have any names for us as to who these people might be? We'd sure like to check them out. We're entitled to discovery too, you know. It's not just a one-way street to be used by one-way lawyers."

"Excuse me, Phil, but will you please call off your attack dog? I'm a dues-paying member of the bar. I know my legal responsibilities. I don't have to talk to her. In fact, I don't have to talk to any of you. I'm here to try to resolve this amicably. My client didn't want me to; he wants to pursue this all the way. He wants a trial to air all this out. But I figure his interests would be better served by a swift and discreet dismissal of all the felony charges. He'll plead no contest to a misdemeanor evading police and we'll call it quits. Like I said, I'm ready to talk disposition but I don't need the farmer's wife here to tell me how to do my job."

I guess it was the farmer's wife that really bit Ronnie, since her lesbianism was an open secret in the courthouse. She swatted the table, her jowly cheeks trembling, livid with anger.

"I am not going to put up with this kind of name calling!" she blared, glaring at me like she wanted to spring across the table and grab me by the throat.

Phil let out one of his carefully modulated sighs, as though reminding himself they paid him for this too.

"We are doing the people's business here!" continued Ronnie.

"Ronnie, bring it down a notch, will you?"

"Phil, I'm not going to put up with any of these ad hominem attacks!"

"Ad feminam," I retorted.

Ronnie returned a blank, contemptuous stare.

"It can't be ad hominem, it has to be feminam, that's Latin for—"

"Thank you, Rita, you can skip the tutoring," said Phil.

"Boss, if you don't mind," said Mike, looking longingly at the door, "I have an appearance in Judge Clavel's court at nine. You know how she gets if you're late."

"That's fine," said Phil warmly. "You go ahead. And take Miss Brightman with you, please."

"Phil!" exclaimed Ronnie, turning her wide round eyes on her boss.

"Yes, Miss Brightman?"

Silence fell in the room as Ronnie considered her options, then she got up as well, her collection of Mexican silver bracelets jangling loudly as they slid down her chubby arms.

"We'll talk later?" she pleaded.

"Of course."

Phil waited until his underlings had closed the gleaming oak door behind them, then he turned to me with his toothiest grin, the steady thumping of the air-conditioning acting like a sonic wall behind us.

"That was quite a performance."

"You know me, Phil, it's always brass tacks. Life's too short to waste on pretense. *I* am too short to waste on pretense."

Phil raised his tapered, perfectly plucked eyebrows, as though toying with the idea of replying in kind, then a cloud settled over his face, a certain sadness creeping in, like this too was one of the burdens of his great office. In other words, an act, just like always with Phil; with him it was hard to tell where the pretense ended and the real fakery started.

"It's a really sad case and it's one we'd rather not be prosecuting at all. That's why we gave him that break and let him stay out OR instead of locking him up."

"Really? I thought that had something to do with his agreeing to be extradited from Cuba—where he could have stayed the rest of his life. He has dual citizenship, you know. And the Cubans believe him."

"They'll believe anybody with money."

"I tell you what. If you're really all worked up about poor Charlie, drop the charges."

"You know I can't do that. It wouldn't be seemly. Not when there are three bodies and accusations of wide-ranging conspiracies, witchcraft, and all that. For all I know people might think Charlie's weirdo theories are true and we hold black masses here in the office every Friday."

"You mean you don't?"

That was meant as a joke but it took Phil a couple of beats to see the humor in it, strained as it was. Finally he chuckled, shook his head, and, ever careful to defend his turf, turned the argument around.

"Yes, and Charlie is saying them. How is Charlie, by the way? How is he taking this?"

"I'm surprised you show any concern for someone you're trying to put away for life."

"No, no, death," he corrected me, sternly. "We'll be asking for the death penalty. But don't get me wrong. I've always liked Charlie. He's a charming guy whenever he wants to be and he doesn't get on his high horse. But I also think he's seriously deranged. Schizoid. Not enough to meet the definition because he's cognizant of his own acts but he's certainly one step beyond the borderline. He's got this obsession. He sees the devil everywhere and is always trying to fight the darkness, which I think is admirable but really, in the final analysis, silly."

"So you think evil doesn't exist, that people don't sell their souls and do all kinds of nasty things to get power and money?"

Phil shook his well-coiffed head none too convincingly.

"You know, this kind of argument is exactly what I want to avoid. He's done it twice before. I don't want the jury to start hearing all his disquisitions on the nature of evil in modern society, how the so-called powers of darkness thrive among us, taking hold of so many impressionable minds. It's not germane. There's nothing in our law books that says devil worship is an indictable offense. That is why Anton LaVey founded his Church of Satan. That is why we have a separation of church and state. We deal with facts, things, the tangible, and we consider the mind— or the spirit, if you will—only as to how it informs the act."

He leaned in closer, his Armani suit wafting clouds of cologne as sweet and tart as a key lime pie. I know it sounds weird but my stomach grumbled. I felt like taking a bite out of him. I pushed the thought out of my mind and did my best to concentrate.

"We are talking three murders, maybe more. Victims hacked to death in some sort of sacrificial pattern. Victims who didn't know anything about this weird cult Charlie espouses, victims who didn't want to be plucked and quartered like the chickens they put on those *santería* altars. We have got to stop it. I have a sworn responsibility to do so and I intend to carry it out."

"Phil, don't take this personally but it sounds like you're trying to make a mountain of evidence from a pile of garbage."

"Bullshit, Rita. We've got the bodies, the witnesses."

"Give me a break, Felipe. The only reason you're still prosecuting is because of the political repercussions. You don't want to be seen as giving Charlie a free ticket to walk because you once worked together. I know what you're about to say, political considerations don't affect the operations of this office, blah, blah, blah. Cut the crap, okay? We're here alone, this doesn't go outside these four walls, and I know you pulled out the recording equipment, right?"

"Why, counsel, recording this conversation would be illegal," he said, recoiling in mock horror into his leather chair.

"Not really but hey, it sounds good. Okay, let's review the evidence. Two female victims, one up in Oakland, the other here in Palmdale. No witnesses or physical evidence to the first one, just an MO that suggests cult slaying. Nothing linking Charlie directly except for that."

"Don't forget the knife on his property."

"If I'm not mistaken, there was no conclusive DNA on the knife, correct?"

"Maybe, but how many people bury bloodstained knives under their lemon tree?"

"Three inches deep? How convenient. Let's go on. There's nothing else linking him to the murder up north. In any case, that's outside your jurisdiction. And they still haven't filed. Gee, I wonder why.

"Now let's look at what we have down here. Girl slaughtered in the desert under similar circumstances, granted. But there is no clear-cut ID of Charlie. Moreover, we have a statement from the gas station owner that he had seen someone else in a vehicle similar to the one allegedly used by the perpetrator and he clearly ID's that person as being other than Charlie. We already gave you that statement. You've read it, right?"

Phil nodded, waiting for me to finish. He crossed his arms over his head, completely at ease. That gesture should have told me volumes about what was going to happen. But sometimes I get carried away by my own convictions—just like Charlie. I guess it's a Latin thing.

But if Phil had a surprise for me, I was springing my own as well. I took the tape out of my purse.

"Okay, now, I'm so glad that you brought out that VCR because I have here a taped statement from that man, giving you details about the true perpetrators of the crime. They are all members of a cult, the same that killed the girl whose head we found in Chinatown. Here."

I flung the tape at him. He caught it midair, looked at it clinically.

"I mean, lookit, Phil, what do you have against Charlie? You're not alleging there's any connection between him and that Ohio girl—he wasn't even in town at the time of death. He was in Cuba and we can prove it. So what's your point? Get out of it, keep your nose clean. Otherwise people *will* think you guys are holding black masses in here."

Phil examined the tape, holding it against the light, as though to detect the unseen fingerprints on it.

"Label's in Spanish. Where was this shot and what does it say?"

"It was taken in Cuba. Guy basically confesses to the murder, says he was there when the Palmdale girl was killed. He didn't do her in but he was involved."

"Declaration against self-interest? How are you going to get that one in?"

"It's an exception to the hearsay rule. Read the code, Phil, we can get it in."

"We'll see about that. I don't know what the circumstances were behind this. As regards the weight of the evidence against Charlie, you're forgetting how things have played out since he came back. Charlie now has a book deal worth four hundred thousand dollars, he sold his movie rights to Universal for seven hundred thousand, and he's filed a false imprisonment suit for five million against the L.A. Sheriff's department, so we have some heavy money riding on this pony. He has profited handsomely and stands to profit even more if he prevails."

"I don't see how his intellectual properties or his business acumen have anything to do with the crimes alleged. He's a noted author; he could have come up with this whole thing as a novel and he would have made just as much money off it."

"Are you kidding? He was down to his last thirty grand when this all happened—thirty grand, I hasten to add, he got from tapping the equity in his house up in Berkeley. And now he's cleared over a million bucks. You tell me this isn't mighty coincidental."

"You try and bring all that in and I'll fight you to the death, Felipe."

"Lay off the Felipe stuff. My name is Philip. Philip José Fuentes," he replied, his feathers finally ruffled. Score one for me, I thought.

"Whatever. I'm just telling you proceed with this case and I'll have you tied down in such a 402 hearing you'll wish you'd never taken Law 101. And if you think I'll back off because I work alone and you can bring in your whole department, I'll have you know my phone's been ringing off the hook with lawyers who want in on this case."

"I bet they all want to be the next Johnnie Cochran."

He smirked. I relaxed a bit. That meant he wasn't going to call in the heavyweights—for now.

"You bet. They want to whip your ass and get their show on Court TV and MSNBC and write for *Vanity Fair.* It's the way of the world."

"So it is," said Phil, playing with his Mont Blanc, passing it from finger to finger as though a baton. He clenched his right hand and then opened it to show me it was empty. Then he produced the pen from his left hand.

"Stop it, Phil. I know about your pen tricks. We worked together, remember? You told me how you always wanted to be like Johnny Carson and how you studied magic just like him. You forgot already?"

"I told you that?" he said. "I don't remember being so upfront with you."

"You should try it more often. It's very becoming. Telling the whole truth for a change."

"Oh, I always tell the whole truth. Eventually. Which reminds me. There's something we forgot to turn over in discovery."

"And what might that be?"

Phil moved to the VCR, pressed the play button. The screen flashed on and the handsome face of a young man, sandy hair and hazel eyes, looking like a cleaned-up surf rat, came on. The rolling numbers of the tape's time code flashed at the bottom of the screen. The boy looked at the camera and an offscreen voice asked him to state his name.

"My name is Julian Michael Morell. I'm here to testify my father murdered those girls in Oakland and Los Angeles."

El bobo de la yuca
Se quiere casar
Invita todo el mundo
A la capital
Va a pasar
La luna de miel
Comiendo trapo
Comiendo papel.

A   DIRTY,   crowded jet pierces white clouds at daybreak.

I sit by the window as the fat woman next to me speaks in-terminably in Spanish. So thick is her Cuban accent that I can-not understand a single word she's saying . . .

Peering out the window as the plane flies low over the green keys and islands of the archipelago that is Cuba, shimmering azure and aqua bathing blindingly white sand beaches . . .

Stepping off the rollaway ladder at José Martí Airport in Ha-vana, greeted by an enormous poster of Che Guevara, proclaim-ing the revolution will not die (though he did) . . .

A guitar trio playing guarachas to Italian tourists disembark-ing from a nearby Alitalia jet, a young man holding a platter serving complimentary samples of Cuban rum . . .

The ebony-skinned customs agent in a cotton suit the color of a ripe lemon ostentatiously stamping a preprinted visa slip which he inserts in my U.S. passport, saying with an equally yellow grin, "Bienvenido" . . .

Crowds of island relatives at the baggage depot swarming over the avalanche of packages the returning exiles have brought back on the plane, the fat lady talking nonstop to a small, swarthy man who huffs and strains as he hoists the box of a thirty-two-inch Zenith TV on his shoulder . . .

Sitting in the worn leather back seat of a '54 De Soto, a mu-seum piece anywhere but in Cuba, rolling out of the airport past weed-choked fields and canting apartment buildings held up by long wooden braces . . .

A sea of bicycles parting before us near the Plaza de la Rev-olución, the gigantic plaza where Castro regularly harangues the people, now taken over by some modeling photo shoot . . .

Rolling into the long forecourt of the Spanish colonial Hotel Nacionál, an ornate palace a stone's throw from the concrete and glass slab that once housed the American embassy . . .

My vaultlike room, with magnificent Moorish tile work, original 1920s plumbing, and threadbare 1970s Russian curtains, looking out on a courtyard and a gurgling fountain, the strains of "Malagueña" drifting from the piano bar downstairs . . .

The old Malecón, the seawall that girths the old city, with its smell of sea spray and rotten fish, its shirtless fishermen trolling for porgy from the reefs, its roving couples, its teen prostitutes and gaggles of the eternally underemployed, all lolling about in the ramshackle paradise that is Cuba while across the bay the El Morro lighthouse stands like the defiant phallus of a regime that will not breed but will not die either, the revolution as a sterile mule . . .

My mind devoid of all conscious thought, I amble from the mausoleum that is my hotel to the monument for the USS *Maine,* sunk in Havana harbor one hundred years ago in a mysterious explosion that triggered the Spanish-American War, or, as the old Marist brothers who taught me called it, the War of Independence of 1898 (there were officially three, all of them aborted).

I sit on one of the benches surrounding the mounument.

Havana, city of my dreams and my nightmares, my pole star and my Hades, my inspiration and my torment. I have a vague recollection of seeing a frenzied crowd tear down the proud American eagle that once surmounted the column but I know I was too young to have been there and I realize I'm remembering newsreels as reality; my revolution is a media memory.

In my mind's eye I see the child I was or that I dreamed I was (there is little difference between the invented and the factual, for the real imaginary is the essence of Cuba).

I'm walking around the park with my father, he dressed in his Sunday *guayabera,* me in shorts and orthopedic shoes, and he's teaching me how to wrap the string and throw the old wooden top, which spins hypnotically on the limestone pavers, a thousand revolutions dancing on that patch of symbolic ground. My father picks up the top and lets it spin in the palm of his hand, then sets it back on the ground. I try to pull off the trick but fail—the moment I touch the toy it falls listless on the ground. I will never have my father's gift to hold the revolving top in my hand but now, in this remembrance, I am the one holding it up forever, the top still spinning in my memory through these words.

The seagulls and ospreys of yesterday still fly overhead, crash-diving into the bay for food. Across the curving avenue, the crumbling facades of nineteenth-century mansions eroded from the constant siege of sea spray and neglect; pieces of cornices, moldings, and roofs have fallen to the ground, where they lay uncollected, split open in coats of fine-grain dust like rotten fruit, like the body parts of a leper.

I have been here so many times in my dreams, have sat at this very bench, have stared at this same headless monument, walked down these very same streets so often—sometimes naked and looking for my lost family, other times fully clothed but in flight from an unseen terror that always captures me before the dream ends—now I don't know where the dreams end and the reality begins. Am I the child dreaming that he left and has returned? Or am I the adult dreaming of the child that never left? Like the Chinese poet wondered, am I the man who dreamed he was a butterfly or am I the butterfly dreaming he is a man?

But what is it that I am? What do I stand for? Where am I going? Why have I been chased, shot, beaten, kicked, pursued, and accused?

Why am I here?

If the inherited faith of my ancestors, that incense-burning, cross-wielding religion that served as the spiritual backbone of my family dating back to the Moors, is of any use, I must believe there is a reason for all this, that the universe is not a random act, that it does have a purpose and a plan and that if I apply myself, I will find the answer.

So I sit on the bench and let the sun burn down on me until

my jangled nerves calm down. A few passersby stare at me oddly when I cry, and an old, rail-thin man in stained pants and laceless shoes comes up and whispers, "Don't you worry anymore, the eagle will return soon," pats me on the shoulder, then ambles down the Malecón, sidling down the street like a man expecting to be blown away by a strong wind.

I stare at him until he turns a corner, then I get up and journey on into the past.

I WALK into the heart of Old Havana, the historical center coveted by so many nations over the centuries. The long wide avenues are only occasionally occupied by cruising taxis and crammed buses, passengers hanging out of windows and latching on to the bumpers like fleas on a dog's tail. I walk up the Prado and stare at the Art Nouveau buildings, the gracious iron grillwork in the windows and balconies corroded like the gaps in a starving beauty's smile. In the inner courtyards of the tenements and in the empty-shelved bodegas and cafés, the underweight and underworked population, wearing threadbare shorts and T-shirts and cheap shoes, wait patiently, trudging up the colonnades, piling up at the bus stops, furrows of frustration etched deeply on their faces. La Habana feels like a theater of war in a temporary truce, the *habaneros* survivors of a blitzkrieg of some sort, resigned to waiting for the next battle in an endless conflict whose start has been forgotten and whose end is nowhere in sight.

Are these the laughing people of Cuba, the avatars of *el son*, the hosts of ten thousand rhythms, the most musically prolix people on the face of the earth? Where is the joy of revolution Cuban style? Where are the songs? Where is the soul of this country?

•   •   •

"IT'S THE Special Period," Scott Blane, the local stringer for the *Los Angeles Times*, said over a plate of smoked pork chops and *tostones* at a *paladar,* one of the privately owned restaurants that have sprouted throughout the city.

"When the Soviet Union collapsed, the subsidies that allowed this show to go on all of a sudden dried up. Four billion dollars a year, poof, gone like that."

Scott snapped his fingers as he sank his small, irregular teeth into the flat discs of refried plantain, little yellow crumbs sticking to his salt-and-pepper beard.

"Doesn't the country have any resources?" I asked, taking another sip of the Marqués de Caceres I'd ordered with my chicken fricassee. The owner, standing guard over the serving cart, flicked an African swatter at a fat fly buzzing our table.

"None. These guys were living on handouts. It was pretty touch-and-go there for a while for Fidel and his boys too, let me tell you. A few years ago, in the middle of all the boat people, you remember, the rafters taking off from everywhere in the island? People actually rose up against the government. For the first time in thirty years, there were riots in Havana. Unheard of. In the interior, the army had to be called in to crush the revolts in some cities. This was big-time. Some people in the government were very scared. They thought the Marines were about to land."

"We'd never send troops here, not after the Bay of Pigs."

"I know that. You know that. But the top honchos in this place, they don't know that. They are positively terrified of another U.S. invasion. They know they couldn't hold out if it happened."

Scott paused, swilled some of his Miami-brewed Hatuey beer. Gaunt, with a receding hairline that he uselessly tried to offset with a long ponytail, he reminded me of some sort of Puritan preacher, a Dimmesdale waiting for his Hester Prynne to come along.

"That's why your boy Max Prado is so important to the government," he went on. "Prado, with his recording contracts, brings in greenbacks. People like him are what's holding up this regime. That, European tourism, and last but definitely not least, money the exiles send from Florida. Oh, the *gusanos* may rant and rave about not trading with Castro, but when push comes to shove they'll turn around and send money to the *viejos,* to the *tíos,* to the cousins, all that. Without exile money, this country wouldn't last six months. Entropy. In any case."

He grinned, let out a discreet belch.

"Did I tell you I'm really looking forward to your confrontation?"

"So am I," I said, downing another glass of wine, disbelieving my own words.

I'd called Scott the moment I'd checked into the Nacional, betting on the reporter's greedy heart; sensing a good story in the making, he'd be more concerned about getting a scoop than being a good scout and turning me into the authorities. So far I'd proven right. Besides which, this wasn't his country; it was mine, even if I was coming back to claim it thirty years later.

At a nearby table a vast black man, a tropical version of the slain rap star Biggie Smalls, was speaking rapid-fire Cuban into a cell phone.

"I hope you know, my man, that you are *numero uno* on the FBI most wanted list. I'm surprised they let you into this country," Scott went on. "Although, knowing how disorganized the *muchachos* are nowadays, nothing surprises me anymore."

I nodded. Getting to Cuba had been easier for me than getting out of Los Angeles. Once at the Mexican border, I walked across without incident, hailed another taxi to the Tijuana airport, and waited for the daily Mexicana Airlines midnight flight to Havana. Throughout it no one questioned me, or even looked at my passport—as long as I paid cash, I was welcome by the mercenary governments of Mexico and Cuba. I still had ten thousand dollars left of the twenty I'd withdrawn the week before in Los Angeles and the wind was blowing my way, for once.

Scott smiled, took out a panatela from his shirt pocket, fondling the cigar like it were the breast of a beautiful blonde. Or perhaps I should say a beautiful *mulata.* As Scott had told me over the meal, he'd first come to Cuba in the late 1980s chasing a dancer in the Cuban National Ballet Corps he'd met in Spain who wouldn't defect. Eventually the fling wore off and the dancer married an agronomist and moved to Oriente province but by then Scott had a new love—Cuba itself. At first he'd had a hard time, but lately, with the heralded upcoming demise of Castrocommunism, Scott was making a very nice living churning out political analysis pieces, which were paid for in dollars. I was hoping I was not going to be his major breaking new story before Castro kicked the bucket.

"One thing I have to say about your people," he said over his *cafecito,* "they know how to make the three most important things in a reporter's life—women, coffee, and cigars." He inserted a toothpick into the rolled end, then lit the cigar, pulling with the glee of a connoisseur.

"Quality has improved enormously since the Special Period began. Before, when the cigars were going to the socialist brotherhood, the government never cared much about quality. They didn't have to depend on exports. But now that they have to sell to the imperialists, the country is very sensitive about its *tabacos.*"

He exhaled a great cloud of spicy smoke. "Of course their politics stink. But they always have. Now, tell me again, what exactly are you going to tell Prado when I take you to him?"

"That's a very good question," I said, "which I thought I already answered."

I drained the last of the wine, the welcome buzz of the alcohol starting to numb my nerves. Was I becoming a lush? I certainly hoped so; that would take care of all my problems.

"I just want to know if you've changed your mind over the

last hour," said Scott, regaling me with a whaler's open-mouthed smile. "Just kidding. So. You really think that dropping a couple of names will be enough to get you what you want. But, what is it you want? Surely you don't expect him to confess."

"No, I expect him to tell me who else is in on this with him."

"Charlie, how could you be so naive? Why should he? You're the fugitive, while he's a special friend of the revolution. He can have you arrested on the spot. Given that you're Cuban born, there's nothing the U.S. can do to save you from the comforts of the Combinado del Este prison. So I hope you'll excuse me for saying this, my friend, but if what you claim is true, why the hell are you down here? *Estás tostado,* major wacko, pal."

I shrugged. An old-fashioned klaxon resounded down the empty Vedado street beyond the cinder block wall of the restaurant. All at once a hummingbird appeared at our table, fluttering its wings so fast it seemed to stand still before us. Scott stared at the visitor, its green and yellow feathers resplendent like some exotic airborne jewel.

"What the hell is that doing here?"

The bird flew twice around my head, as though to inspect me, the beating of its tiny wings the whisper of a song I heard as a child and then forgot. I moved my hand to shoo it away but the bird insisted on staying. It darted to my wine glass, took a sip, then flew up again, standing perfectly still in midair in front of me, gazing into my eyes as though meaning to impart some urgent message. Then, with the same swiftness with which it flew to our table, the hummingbird flittered away, losing itself among the branches of the huge dusty ceiba tree growing in the yard.

The black man at the table nearby was slackjawed, put his cellular down. His companion, a fine-featured *mulata* wearing an imitation Chanel suit and a towering silk turban, crossed herself. The man rose, came over to our table.

"*Tú sabes quién es ese?*" he asked in Spanish, then in broken German, "*Du ist . . .*" I stopped him before he further slaughtered Goethe's glory.

"*No, quién es?*"

"That's Eleguá, the messenger of the gods, *asere,*" buddy, he said, awe burnishing his deep baritone. "He's trying to tell you something for sure. You're from Miami?"

"You could say that."

"I thought so, white people like you look just like these *gringos. Cómo tú te llamas?*"

"Morell. Charlie Morell."

"Okay. *Soy Davíd.*"

We shook hands, he nodded at Scott.

"*Qué tal, Escot?*" Scott grunted in acknowledgment.

"*Qué tal, David.*"

The corpulent man named David nodded energetically.

"Tonight in Guanabo we're having an *encuentro* at my godfather's house. Please come. You have been greeted by the saints, *asere*. You better find out what they have to tell you or you will come to great harm."

"I understand. I'll try to make it."

"*Muy bien.* What hotel are you at?"

"Nacional."

"I'll pick you up. Midnight. You'll like it."

"Sure."

"*Chévere.*"

He winked at Scott, then ambled off, waving goodbye at the other diners in the yard. He climbed into a bright red Toyota convertible and drove off with his curvy companion.

"That was David Ichaso, lead singer of Los Nuevos Tártaros, the New Barbarians."

"Who are they?" I asked.

"The latest sensation in Cuban music. They play *timba* music. You know what that is?"

"*Timba?* Like the slang word for guava jam?"

"Right. It's the hottest sound in Havana today. Salsa, with rap lyrics. David's a great man to know. Even the CBs have been known to go to his concerts."

"The CBs?"

"The Castro Brothers. As in Warner?"

"I get it."

"He's playing tonight at the Palace. I'm sure your boy Max would love to sign him. Hey, maybe you can tell Max the gods want you to put him in contact with David."

"Maybe I should."

I pulled away from the table, laid down sixty dollars for the meal—a year's wages for the average worker in Cuba.

"Thanks for lunch. You're going to enjoy the *bembé* with David," said Scott as we walked out. "You know, *santería* has become a major revenue earner for the government. Everybody's into it down here and the tourists love it. You never know when some fine little girl is going to get possessed and start stripping. Want a ride?"

The fawning proprietor flicked her swatter once more and opened the door to the lonesome street.

"If you don't mind."

"Not at all. Where to?"

"My childhood nightmares."

OUR HOUSE was where I remembered it, some distance down from the Brazilian embassy in the Miramar district; it still proudly displayed, below the pitted tile roof, the coat of arms of my Catalan ancestors. The house next door, a two-story modernist fantasy built in the 1930s for the owner of the island's Mercedes-Benz dealership, had been left to decay. Its front lawn had turned into crabgrass ripped by foot traffic; the graceful railings that once made it ressemble a sleek cruise ship or a fleet space vehicle had been torn away; the windows were shattered; the exterior stucco was peeling off in large flakes. The upper half of the building, blackened by a fire, was shut down; the bottom was inhabited by a collection of families, half-naked children running on the cracked and warped driveway, lines of tattered laundry hanging from the pillars of the porte cochere.

But our ancestral home, the twenty-one-room manse patterned after a Florentine palazzo, the site of countless political intrigues since the time of the Spanish governors, host of a thousand balls, witness to one family's helpless struggle against the perilous pull of history, the Morell estate, was still intact.

Scott parked his Nissan at the curb, next to the sign that proclaimed the reason why time and revolutionary fervor had spared the old home—it had become the Instituto Técnico César Sandino.

I stood on the front lawn, hemmed in by its twin arms of boxwood hedges, the deep silky green of the Kentucky bluegrass unrolling toward the structure like a welcome mat, broken only by the enormous lilac jacaranda tree on the left and the row of old-fashioned tree roses on the right.

It was all bigger than I remembered.

Now I understood what was so obvious to everyone but me, the visceral attraction I always felt for the estates of San Marino, the works of George Washington Smith, and the Spanish cul-de-sacs of Los Feliz and Berkeley, all vain unconscious attempts to recapture that brief moment when I lived in the center of the universe called Havana.

I heard the click of a shutter. I turned to see Scott aiming his pocket Olympus at me. I wiped my eyes with the back of my hand and walked up the incline to the house.

"What was it like living here, Charlie?" asked Scott, turning on his tape recorder. I shrugged, felt the sting of the afternoon sun.

"This was my grandfather's house. I lived here from the time

I was born until I was six, when we moved to a house my dad built over in Marianao."

"You want to go there later?"

"We don't have to bother. It was torn down the year we left for the States. The government built a sports stadium on the site. This is all I have left."

Going up the flagstone entrance I kept hearing the cries of children over the faint, remembered voice of my grandfather, my father's father, who had studied in Paris, New York, and Salamanca, who had the affectation of pronouncing his Spanish Zs like a Castilian and his English vowels like a plummy lord, to distinguish himself from his fractious countrymen who mangled both languages the Cuban way. Abuelo's deep rumble of a voice surged up in the back of my mind but for some reason I could not quite recall why he was arguing so violently with my father—or what about.

I knocked at the studded oak doors, welcomed by the intoxicating smell of jasmine and orange blossoms. A slim black teenage girl in a brown and white uniform answered the door.

"Normally for visits you have to apply for permission with the ministry but you're in luck, the superintendent is visiting us today. I'll take you to him."

She opened wide the door to the marble foyer, with its swooping staircase leading grandly up to the second floor; peals of laughter rang out from somewhere in the back, where the au pair's room had been. The girl walked us down the groin-vaulted corridor to the wood-paneled library and introduced us to Compañero Villa, a small, gray man who looked up from an old ledger.

"You are a Morell? Why of course, *chico,* go right ahead and take a look around. The government has taken care of the property while you were gone. It's now a vocational school for children from the provinces. This library has been transformed into our main office, as you can see. Do you mind if I accompany you?"

I stood by the eight-foot-high limestone fireplace from Flanders, letting my eyes run along the inlaid, coffered ceiling, the Cuban mahogany floor planks, the rose marble pavers. The sixty-by-thirty room was taken up with desks and cheap metal bookcases instead of the heavy Spanish tables and tasseled sofas of my childhood but otherwise there had been little structural change. Then I heard my grandfather's voice, loud as a bell:

"What this country needs is a Franco, to teach these people how to respect authority."

My father, a liberal Democrat then, and, unbeknownst to us, already involved with the revolutionary underground and the 26 of July movement, replies: "And just what do you call Batista?"

"Bah, he's just a mulatico lindo, *a pretty little* mulato *boy. A weakling. He'll turn this country over to the reds to save his own skin. He doesn't have the balls to fight this like it should be fought."*

"Then we'll go to the Isle of Pines, we'll set up our own government over there, like the Chinese in Taiwan."

"It'll never work. This country is doomed to repeat its past. We never learn. We never learn."

I STOOD outside what had once been my room, at the end of the corridor in the east wing. I hesitated, as if once I stepped through the threshold I would be returning to those years when I was Carlitos, the engineer's son, bearing lightly the weight of our history on the island. I walked in, half expecting to see myself in blue shorts and white shirt, struggling with the tie that the Marist brothers required we wear to school. The room was crammed with six bunk beds, the peeling wallpaper covered with torn-out pictures from girls' magazines. I recognized the Hispanic singers—Ricky Martin, Chayanne, Enrique Iglesias—peering proudly from the walls as though the revolution never happened. The few girls in the room stood at attention when the superintendent entered. He gestured at them to return to their books. A toilet flushed and another girl, about fourteen years old, came out drying her hands. She looked around, asked who we were and what we were doing. She came up to me, fixed her round brown eyes on me.

"*Ah, bueno, usted debe de saber,*" you must know.

"What must I know?" I replied in Spanish.

"*Lo que signfican las letras VF ahí en el marco de la ventana.*"

She showed me the letters etched in the windowsill, right next to her bed.

"Sometimes I think it was a lover's message, then I think, who was she? Can you tell me?"

I glanced out the window at the inner courtyard, its fountain gone dry, the orange trees growing unruly and unkempt in tropical exuberance, ivy spreading wildly from its planter. What hath we wrought?

"That means Viva Fidel. I was six years old. My grandfather hated him and this was his house so that was all I dared to write."

The girl turned proudly to her roommates.

"See, I told you even the *gusanos* loved the old man back then. That's why this house survives."

I nodded as graciously as I could, then walked out, followed by Scott and the superintendent. Only when I was outside the door and I glanced back did I realize all the girls in the room were black.

The rest of the rooms in my family's house were even less recognizable. My father's bedroom was turned into a laboratory, while, perversely, my father's den had become yet another crowded dormitory, this time for boys. The kitchen had become a workshop, while the garage was a makeshift gym, with weights made out of poured concrete and benches of old splintered wood. Everything had been turned upside down, with a logic that was not our own, pressed by need and improvisation during the long pauperization of the country.

At the end of the tour, by the well in the yard where my sister, Celia, and I had loved to play hide and seek, the Compañero approached me. Speaking softly, so as not to be overheard by his staff crisscrossing the patio, he asked if by any chance I was contemplating returning to Cuba.

On a permanent basis.

Anytime soon.

"As you know, once *he* goes . . ."—here he stroked an imaginary beard that could only be Castro's—"a lot of things will change in Cuba. Why, if you look at our former socialist brothers in Eastern Europe, some of the properties there have been returned to their former owners under the law of return."

"And how do you suppose one could do that here?" I asked, disingenuously.

"*Bueno, tú sabes,* the proper paperwork should be filed right around now with the proper authorities."

"Really? And how much do you think one would need, should one decide that is the path to follow in this matter, of course?"

"Of course, you must realize that all this is strictly voluntary, we would never desire anyone to feel even the slightest amount of coercion or anything other than a warm welcome to the long-gone brother who is returning to the welcoming arms of his *patria,* his ancestral homeland. But a move such as we have been contemplating could have handsome returns when the moment presents itself. Personally, nothing guaranteed, of course, because the exigencies are such that the immediate situation could change unexpectedly, but at this point, I, personally, would surmise that if one were to make a donation of, let's say, fifty thousand dollars to the appropriate authorities, to demonstrate a desire to return and claim the property, and were one to state such funds were to be considered compensation for the support and maintenance that the revolution has bestowed on this building all these years, I would surmise that the government then might let one regain possession at the appropriate moment. Cases such as this are being handled in this fashion throughout the country even as we speak, you should know. In this particular instance, my research indicates that the family who owned the estate never formally renounced it, just like the government never formally expropriated the house. The building was merely deemed abandoned after the grandfather's death of a heart attack during the invasion of Playa Girón. So the way is paved for the eventual return of this wonderful mansion to the scion of the family that built it."

"I take it that would be me."

"If you are interested, yes, of course, that could be you. That would be you."

"I see. And I assume you would be handling all the requisite paperwork, yes?"

The superintendent nodded.

"What about the children? Where would they go?"

"Oh, room will be found for them elsewhere. There are plenty of suitable houses in Havana."

I nodded, stroked my chin, pretended to mull his offer as I looked back at the old manse, now rightly taken over by those who needed it. To them, soiled and blemished as it was, the house was a future; to me it would never mean anything other than the painful past. I was not in Cuba willingly and I would not willingly return to a life that had rightfully ended.

"Carpe diem," I said.

"Excuse me?" said the superintendent, batting his eyelashes.

"I am not interested. I am also certain that the revolution would not wish to be compensated at the expense of its most vulnerable, its children."

The superintendent took off his steel frame glasses and wiped them with a wrinkled handkerchief.

"As you wish. It is your decision. But you should know that

the revolution is for those who know how to advance the cause of the people. And that there are many, many ways to advance that cause. Sometimes even in ways that seem, shall we say, the most antithetical to the purported aims of the revolution. The revolution is a living thing and, as such, it is full of paradoxes."

"Well, then, put me down as one of those paradoxes—a capitalist with a conscience. Thank you for the tour."

"You are most welcome."

SCOTT WAS waiting for me out by his car.

"You want a ride back to the Nacional?"

"If you don't mind."

All at once a bevy of small banged-up European cars—Fiats, Renaults, Seats—converged on the driveway, surrounding us, screeching and throbbing with the squeal of bad brakes and faltering engines. Half a dozen men in civilian clothes jumped out of the vehicles, guns of different makes in their hands, all pointing straight at us.

The man closest to me, a small wiry redhead, wore a Hard Rock Las Vegas T-shirt several sizes too small even for his scrawny chest; the Walther PPK he held in his two-handed grip was half the size of his skull.

I slowly raised my hands up in the air, waiting for a command or an explanation. Scott snapped at the men, demanding to talk to whoever was in authority, insisting that he was a legitimate foreign journalist covering a story and that the Minint had no right to intervene. The men stood their ground, weapons pointed perfectly still, as though daring Scott to make a run for it. Scott continued to berate them, but he did not budge. He was loud, not suicidal.

Finally, after about a minute of our standoff, a spanking-new Toyota Camry rolled slowly into the scene. A tall, lanky white man, looking incongruously like the young Peter O'Toole, eased himself out of the car. The crease in his white linen pants could have sliced bananas, his starched *guayabera* giving off the old pre-revolutionary smell of lavender cologne and cordite. He rolled a small cigar between thin lips, which spread into a sardonic grin.

"Dr. Morell, I presume?" he said in perfect Spanish, using the honorific title once reserved for physicians and attorneys in Cuba.

"I am he," I replied, also in Spanish. "But I know you're not Stanley." He let his bad-boy grin expand some more.

"I am not. If you will please accompany us."

"Do I have a choice?"

"Not in reality."

The tall man shook his cigar at the men surrounding Scott.

"Him, house detention. After you seize his notes and tapes."

The skinny agent in the Hard Rock T-shirt stuck his gun in his waistband, grabbed me by the arm, shoved me inside his rusted Fiat.

"Where are we going?"

"What do you think this is, *NYPD Blue*?" screamed the gunman. "Shut up and get in the fucking car!"

He pushed me inside. I ducked and fell in, propelled by the man's booted foot, landing in the back seat of the overheated, gasoline-reeking junker. The Hard Rocker sat next to me, while a second goon opened the other door and sandwiched me in between like some piece of imported meat. Two other gunmen sat in the front. The driver kicked on the engine, which hacked to life, the cassette deck blaring a Gipsy Kings tune.

The car sputtered away. I turned and looked out the rear window. Scott was spread-eagled on the hood of his car, being searched by the remaining gunmen, who were laughing as they played with the unraveled cassette tape, throwing it up in the air like excelsior at a children's party.

10

THE OLD jalopy whisked us through the worn-out streets of Miramar and into the Vedado, the car rattling so loudly it threatened to break down into a shower of nuts and bolts at every pothole. On the corner of F and Tercera Avenida, the sputtering tin can scrambled down a service ramp to the parking lot in the basement of a tall building. We pulled to a stop a few feet from the elevator shaft. Other equally beaten-up vehicles were parked nearby; beyond them, reaching back as far as I could see in the dingy lot, lay the hulking, gouged-out remains of cars of every make and model since the 1950s. In this shadowy grave-yard, a couple of mechanics with acetylene torches were weld-ing yet another cannibalized part.

The agents hustled me out, took me up to the twelfth floor in a cargo elevator painted in black, and dropped me in a little waiting room.

I tried the door handle. The door was bolted from the out-side. I took in the contents of my cell. A metal desk, an easy chair, an empty bookcase and drawers, a folding metal chair across from the desk. I opened the top desk drawer. Empty. I tried the door in the back of the room, which at one time proba-bly led to yet another waiting room. Locked. No windows or means of exit. No way out.

So I sat in the folding chair and stared for a half hour at the peeling 1950s wallpaper, with its dancing bears and toy drums marching gaily to some frozen snippet of a children's march last heard at the time I was born, until my laconic captor opened the door, cheroot still in hand. He stepped inside, nodded, sat be-hind the desk.

"Do you know where you are?" he asked, in perfect English this time.

"Oh, that I do, but what I don't know is who you are. That is, I don't know exactly, although I have a pretty good idea. I know I'm not going to like it but all the same I would appreciate some specific information, like name, title, reason for my detention, and do you still believe in bail in this country and if that's the case where do I post it. Little things like that. If you don't mind. I have this terrible habit, you see. I like to know the name of the people who kick me in the ass."

He grinned ever wider, showing off perfectly even, sparkling white teeth. Odd, I thought, someone so young wearing full dentures.

"You are just like your characters, aren't you, Charlie? Opinionated. Wisecracking. Always got to have the last word in."

"That's how the readers like it."

"I disagree. I think readers nowadays crave sincerity. Earnestness. Guilelessness. Cornwell, not Chandler. Cynicism is out, devotion is in."

"Oh brother. *The Havana Review of Books.* Fine, so why don't you sincerely tell me what the fuck I'm doing here?"

"We'll get to that in a minute. But I hope you will indulge me first. Do you really know where you are?"

I leaned back in my chair. This was going to take longer than I expected—maybe years. Just then I heard a loud moan, followed by the sound of a chair or some such large object thrown against the other side of the far wall, which rattled from the impact. My captor grinned once more.

"That was not planned."

"That's okay. This place was built with pain in mind."

"How so?"

"All right, all right, I'll play along. This building is the former Clínica Antonetti. It was owned by a maternal uncle of mine who turned it into the largest private hospital in Havana before the revolution. When I was a kid my mom used to bring me here to have my ears cleaned out. Some things never change, I suppose. Happy now? Your turn."

My answer pleased him no end. He shook his head with the self-satisfied smile of a man settling in for a long entertainment.

"Yes, *plus ça change.* As you'll see when we let you out. Because we will let you out, I want you to know. I don't know if right now you are dreaming of any heroics, that you're going to languish in one of our famous penal establishments where you'll wear striped boxer shorts and clang your tin cup on the bars and shout *libertad* for the next twenty years. We've put an end to that."

"I hate to ask how," I replied. "In any case, it's good to know because I would never make it as a political prisoner. I'm American now. I believe in the almighty dollar and that's all. Although maybe that does make me very Cuban after all. Funny business, history, all its twists and turns."

"I don't know, Charlie," said my captor, extracting a small metal case from his *guayabera* pocket. "You're more idealistic than you let on. Cigar?"

He lit my cheroot with a Colibrí butane, which he flicked on with great ostentation.

"Thank you," I said, feeling, as I exhaled that mouthful of spicy smoke, that I was reliving some dark ceremony, some last rite or final act that was once common knowledge to Cubans like me but that I had forgotten after we breached that other, Anglo shore. After all, other than romancing a *muchacha* or dancing the rumba, what could be more typically Cuban than to be questioned by some cynical government minion for a crime you did not commit? Or maybe I had done something, after all. Only, like Joseph K., I didn't know I had done it but was about to be punished for it all the same.

"You play at the cynic," continued the blond man in the white shirt. "I detect a certain idealism in your works and in your life. And a great deal of naïveté as well. You seem to think God takes care of children, drunks, and Charlie Morell."

"Not really. I would say I believe in *la divina providencia*, something I'm sure your government has outlawed. But, excuse me, and I certainly don't mean any disrespect, since I'm sure you can have my balls on a silver platter by lifting your left pinkie anytime you want, but, who the hell are you and why are we playing charades here?"

He stood, pushed his chair away. I winced, expecting the blow from the secreted blackjack. He took out a leather wallet, threw it on the desk, showed me a picture ID from the Ministry of the Interior.

"I am Captain Lee Gutiérrez. I am the Interior Ministry's

deputy head of security for the greater La Habana region. I have been waiting for you for about two weeks now, ever since the news broke in San Francisco. We figured sooner or later you'd have to come down here to solve the murders."

He put his wallet back in his rear pocket.

"So, on behalf of the revolutionary government of Cuba," he added, biting off every word as though it pained him as much as that other suspect was hurting in the room next to ours, "I welcome you to the fatherland. *Bievenido a la patria.*"

"Where have you guys been? I've been expecting you since I got here!"

Gutiérrez sighed. "Our security forces are not quite what they used to be. The Special Period. Everybody's too busy driving cabs and pouring drinks for the almighty dollar, like you say."

He put out his cigar, obviously upset at the thought.

"That's why I'm glad I have you here. I know you've come after Max Prado. And you are hoping to find a way to somehow get him up north and have him tried for the crimes. Or at least have his associates face justice with whatever information you might glean from him. And clear yourself in the process, of course."

"Sounds about right."

"That's a big job, even for you. But maybe there is something to that *divina providencia* you just mentioned. I want you to take a look at a couple of things."

He walked up to the door, knocked three times. The door slid open. We stepped into the hallway, where sat the same scrawny redhead with the Hard Rock T-shirt, an AK-47 on his lap. Gutiérrez nodded at the guard, who frowned and pointed his chin down the hall. I followed Gutiérrez past the shuttered doctor's offices and waiting rooms for what had once been the ward for infectious diseases.

"What's with the guns?" I asked, noticing the submachine-gun-toting guards stationed every few hundred feet.

"We've had some problems in the past few weeks," said Gutiérrez unworriedly, patting his guards on the shoulder as he passed by.

"What kind of problems?"

"Internal opposition," said Gutiérrez, pressing the call button for the elevator, a gleaming 1950s chrome and steel relic lifted straight from the Mayo Clinic. The door slammed open and we stepped inside. He swung the control lever to the close position and the elevator began a dizzying drop to the bowels of the building, past the numbered floors and the parking floor all the way down to the SS level.

"I didn't know internal opposition was allowed in Cuba. Or that it counted for much."

"It counts when higher-ups in the government feel threatened and want to make sure things go on the way they have been."

"Which means what exactly?"

Gutiérrez nervously swept back his hair again.

"I am sure you studied political science back in college. Perhaps you remember what happens in the final stages of a, let's say, an authoritarian regime. Factions develop, differing interests struggle to position themselves in a restricted reality so as to reassert control and expand their particular spheres of influence. Moves are made to eliminate competing factions, which answer in kind, which leads to even greater instability, the whole thing being ultimately solved by either the hegemonic triumph of one factor or the imposition of a new extraneous order which takes advantage of all the infighting among the competing power centers, you see?"

"As the day is long," I answered.

The elevator clanged to a halt. The doors opened onto a damp corridor lit by ancient fluorescent lights. We walked out. The walls were lined with tall steel filing cabinets, all alphabetized, the tabs in old typewriter script. The last cabinet I could see was dated back to 1952, the long shadow of other cabinets fading into the serpentine hallway.

"Why are you giving me a textbook answer?"

Gutiérrez traipsed down the corridor, stepping around the occasional puddles of water leaking from the overhead pipes.

"Because this is a textbook case. The old man is dying, there are people who want to cut up the country for their own benefit, and they resent us for trying to stop them."

"Resent you?"

He stopped at a door still bearing the skull and bones sign warning that infectious wastes were stored inside.

"That's a kind way of putting it," said Gutiérrez. He took out a key, inserted it into the ancient lock.

"A delegation from the army came in here three weeks ago and tried to wipe us out. We had a shoot-out in this building. Raúl himself had to intervene."

The tumblers fell into place, the lock slid open.

"That's Raúl Castro, Fidel's own brother, the head of the army?"

"Yes."

"That's not a political disagreement, that's a civil war!"

"That's what I'm talking about. They resent us to the death. Over this."

He opened the door wide. Arranged on tables and cabinets, strewn in no particular order around the floor, were a collection of ancient African artifacts. Masks, buckets, spears, hammers, rusted sickles; statuettes of long-legged figures with shields for faces, limbs pierced by rusty nails, chests covered with chicken feathers, faces smeared with blood.

I stepped closer to the pile. In one box I saw stacked more than a dozen animal masks made out of coconut shells, bedecked with beads, feathers, colored pebbles, and other kinds of ornaments. In a corner a wondrous leopard skin costume lay all crumpled up, waiting only for someone to step into it and become the mighty killer of the lair.

"You know what these are, of course," said Gutiérrez, picking up one of the masks.

"This is not my specialty," I said. "They are not Yoruba. But judging by the markings on the mask and the ornaments I'd say these are from the Fon people of the Ivory Coast. Ceremonial costumes."

"Benin. But you're right, costumes is just what they are. These are some of the things we've seized on raids on the Abakuá sect."

The Abakuá.

I'd finally made the contact. I was one step closer to solving the murderous puzzle that had brought me so far, that had taken so much from me.

GUTIÉRREZ WALKED amid the strewn paraphernalia of ancient strivings, picked up a cat's mask.

"When we first heard of these people and we raided them, I was expecting something horrible, not these toys," he said, examining closely the iridescent beadwork of the object.

"I thought that they'd have people's heads shrunken up like the Jivaros of Colombia, or penises pickled in brine, or maybe even a *caldero* or two, you know, like the followers of *palo mayombé*?"

I nodded. I recalled all too well my own two dreadful encounters with the adherents of that most bloody of cults.

"Like your half-brother, Díaz," said Gutiérrez, as though reading my mind. "You said so in your book, *Slipping into Darkness*, Cuba has always been a place for things like that, this meeting point of Western and African barbarity. The Spanish started ethnic cleansing in Andalucía and we, their brilliant children, carried it one step further by inventing the whole notion of concentration camps, with General Weyler last century. The Boers picked it up for their war and then the Nazis. Who knows. Maybe in a way we're responsible for Treblinka and Dachau."

Gutiérrez put the mask down on a *timbal*, the sawed-off half of an oil drum converted into the musical kettle of Trinidad and Jamaica.

"Funny. People make the mistake of thinking Cuba is all about music, rum, and a good time—even the Castro revolution was done to a rumba beat. They really don't know us, do they?"

"So what was it you found?"

Gutiérrez glared at me, annoyed I'd cut him off at some intellectual pass before he hustled down the slippery slope of rhetoric.

"Do you know what we found? Do you know what their most sacred object was?"

He made a broad sweeping gesture, encompassing all the gathered artifacts, then uprighted an old splintered whiskey vat, the name Ballantine's burned into the old gray wood.

"This! Those fools think there is a god at the bottom of this barrel. They claim when they fill it with water, their god comes out and tells them what to do. *Comemierdas!*"

He hurled the bucket against the wall. It may have been my imagination but for a moment I thought I heard a moan coming from the discarded barrel, as though bewailing its painful fate. But if there was such a lamentation Gutiérrez chose not to hear it, for now he picked up a smaller vat, shaking it like a stubborn suspect or an errant fool.

"This is another one of their sacred objects, the god and the goddess. You know what I say to that?"

He heaved it against the wall, the bucket cracking open into two halves. This time the moan was unmistakable. Gutiérrez looked at me with a fierce expression, his cheeks flushed.

"Yeah, I heard it too. You know what it is? Goddamn worms in the wood ate through it so the air makes a whistling sound. It's rotten wood making noises and these murderers think it's the godhead."

He pushed back his hair, flared his nostrils, glaring at the objects as though defying the divinity to rise up and smite him.

"In the last raid they had skinned four people alive. Three

were dead when we got there. The survivor was a five-year-old girl. They'd taken off her scalp and yanked off her fingernails, then pulled her skin out like she was some sort of rabbit. She howled for three days in the hospital before dying of cardiac arrest. A five-year-old with heart failure, you tell me."

He looked around, his eyes ablaze. "This is the kind of thing that brings out the Stalinist in me. If I could kill them all I would, if I could have a mass purge in this country—"

He stopped, took a deep breath, reining in the horses of his outrage, then he whirled around, headed for the door.

"Let's go. You've seen enough."

We didn't speak again until we were back in the elevator, the indignity of the horror he had recalled finally flowing out of his features. He patted his pockets, searching for something lost.

"I left the cigars in the office. No matter, we'll get some later," he said, apropos of nothing, as though wanting to offer some excuse for a wrath that might be righteous but not professional.

"Aren't you making this too personal?" I asked finally.

The elevator shuddered to a halt, its doors thumping open to a hall jammed with desks, office clerks at each station laboriously stamping piles of internal security passports. Gutiérrez raised his finger, puncturing the air as we walked through and down the hall.

"Let me tell you something. I believe in the revolution."

He said this with such emphasis that several workers at their desks raised their heads in surprise, then quickly resumed their labors.

"I may be the last revolutionary left on this island but I do not care. I believe we have a responsibility to improve the life of our fellow Cubans. I believe that socialism is the correct path to justice and equality—that all men are equal. Like Marx said, from each according to his skills, to each according to his needs. This, this horror you just saw, is the product of capitalism. We never had it before this . . ."

He lingered over the phrase, then he spat it out too, as though banishing it from his mouth and history at the same time . . .

". . . this Special Period. Follow me."

We had come to a large wide anodized aluminum frame door, pitted by rust and salt air, which opened to a vast terrace. We walked through, all the way out to the railing. Twenty-five stories below us, Havana spread out with its soft hills and shimmering bay, its crumbling buildings and desolate streets, like an old courtesan forced by hunger to show her faded charms in cruel sunlight, using flour for powder and biting her lips for color, hoping for the last customer that would show her the way out, be it with a clean passport or a dirty knife.

"You should see this at night," said Gutiérrez, his voice tinged with longing. "When the lights come on, it's like a fairy tale come true, the last act of the last socialist paradise on earth. Until we get a power failure. But even then, the stars never disappoint me. When all else fails, we still have the million stars of our Cuban heavens. Incomparable."

"You're not from Havana, are you?" I asked, unable to believe his odd mixture of sincerity and cynicism.

"No, I'm from the countryside. Sancti Spíritus."

"Was your mother American, you know, one of those SDS people who came here in the 1960s?"

He smiled, used to the question, no doubt.

"No. We're *gallegos* on both sides of the family. El Ferrol, like Franco. My grandparents came here after the republic fell."

"And the name Lee?"

"That was my mother's idea. She named me after Robert E. Lee. You know, the Confederate general. He was a rebel against the U.S. government and so was she. A faithful party member until the day she died. Look over there."

He pointed vaguely north, at the rippling shoreline and the vast blue-gray harbor that opened like a hungry mouth by the enclosures of Morro Castle and the Malecón.

"What are you pointing at?"

"Regla, on the other side of the bay. See it?"

He waved his long index finger at a collection of white houses splattered against the rising hillsides girthing the bay.

"That's where it all began, in the black quarters of Regla. When the government decided to loosen up on *santería,* to put on the *bembés* and the other rituals to bring in the tourist dollar, we opened up the *casas de santos,* the meeting places in Regla. We never should have done it. It was like rolling away the lid and letting the vampires out. The Abakuá, which had been dormant for almost a hundred years, was revived. This is the price we're paying. Over there you can see the reason."

He signaled to the west, past the spreading suburbs, to a string of tall new skyscrapers lining the white sandy shores.

"Tourist palaces. The Melia, the Sol, all the others. Capitalists come and spread their diseases like a vector, with their money and their women. That's how Prado made it happen. Now we need you to stop it."

"And if I choose not to?"

Gutiérrez shrugged, leaned so far back on the railing I thought he might drop off.

"What makes you think you have a choice?"

11

THE MUSIC comes at you from all sides, a sonic wave that envelops you in the enfolding arms of tropical rhythms from the time you walk into the dismal, raggedy hall that bills itself El Palacio de la Salsa.

Italian tourists, Canadian tourists, French and British tourists, even the occasional gringo tourist in shorts, loud shirt, and seared pink flesh, stand around, drink in hand, stupefied by the throbbing, pounding blare of the horn and the electric piano and the violins and the four conga players all in a row, playing with the fervor of the blessed and the rancor of the damned, the cascading trills and thrills and chills of the music making a tonal medley of all they had been led to expect.

It's as though in this tiny recondite corner of the universe all laws, musical and otherwise, have been turned upside down and all that exists is the moment, the joyous moment of transport. This used to be the Riviera owned by Sam Giancana and his mobster pals but all that is the gory past not the gory present but the past all the same and all that matters to the couples on the floor is the pulsing, twirling, entrancing shouting of the band that gives the message of song and dance to all the young lissome honey-colored girls in all their slinky black dresses and all the buffed young men who sneak in past the bouncer pretending to be all-Italian or all-Sardinian or even all-Spanish, anything but Cuban because Cubans have no place in here.

But now the music comes and lifts them and tells us in bright brassy notes to play for today, to love for today, to dance for today for tomorrow never comes and he may have been dying for thirty years but his heart still pumps strong and the music unlike his revolution will not let you down and the blood that burns feverish in your veins will not let you down either even if everything else will and so you persuade yourself you're a Cuban too and you join the ballroom madness and you let the music sweep you away and you get some young girl with hungry brown eyes and cheekbones honed by want who's poured herself into a hot red dress that lets you count every rib and appreciate every curve of her little body and the two of you swing and sway to the bleating music as the other tourists, the ones who know nothing of Africa or soul or the longing for lands never known, stand around rum drink in hand, and wonder wide-eyed if they will ever get that Cuban beat, that Cuban rhythm, that Cuban thing going.

Of course they never will and you don't care you don't even want

to think about them or even yourself for all that matters is the mu-
sic, the brass, the beat, the call and response of the band and the
players and the crowd and then the music ends jolting you as sud-
denly as the last car in the roller coaster, the montaña rusa *that*
now has become the montaña cubana *and she offers herself to you*
but you turn her down and you buy her a drink instead and you
ask her what she would do with the hundred dollars she would
charge you to spend the night with her and she answers with
misty-eyed wonder that she'd buy herself soap and towels and bed-
sheets and maybe even an iron if she can find one for Cuba is now
the place where the only forbidden pleasures are those you find
every day in Kmart, Sears, and Wal-Mart back home.

So even though you're sorely tempted you give up and hand over
the hundred dollar bill and wish her all the best that capitalism can
buy, for there, at that corner table, surrounded by equally young,
nubile beauties, quaffing Absolut like a princeling, a fat Cohiba
plugged into his round face, sits the man you've been looking for,
the man who holds the key to your life and your salvation, the man
you've been sent here to kill.

A L L   A T once the reverie ended and the detached, other-
wordly feeling that had haunted me since I'd set foot inside the
Palacio lifted from me. I was concentrating again—I had focus, I
had a mission.

In the lull of the band break, I made my way through the still
swirling crowd, dancers standing on the dance floor, reluctant
to leave the place of their recent ecstasy. My eyes were firmly
set on that corner table occupied by Max Prado and three girl-
friends in miniskirts that seemed to ride all the way to their
waist. His black and white Versace shirt was open to the breastbone, showing a thick golden medallion of the Virgin of El Co-
bre dangling on a hairy chest. Between puffs of his cigar he
compulsively downed spoonfuls of caviar from a small tin on

ice, as though afraid someone might walk up and snatch it away.

"Sevruga is the best contribution the Soviets ever made to world welfare," he said to another, thinner, darker man at the end of the table. The man nodded in paid assent.

Prado let his gaze sweep the room until he noticed me approaching. Like in a silent movie, his caviar spoon stopped at his mouth the moment he caught sight of me, wide green eyes bulging with surprise. The dark man at the end of the table put his hand to his waistband.

"Max? Max Prado?" I said now, only a handful of steps from his table.

"I've been looking for you all night, *coño!*" said a voice at my side, a heavy hand dropping on my shoulder.

I turned quickly, trying to brush the giant paw off my shoulder but now the other one landed on my left and the hulking giant that was David Ichaso squeezed and hugged me, putting his face next to mine as though I were a newly discovered member of his tribe.

"Max," he rasped out, "this is the guy I told you about, the one that Eleguá visited in the *paladar. Asere,* what's your name, I forgot."

The dark man at Prado's table still eyed me warily but Prado waved his hand at him to calm down, then he put down his caviar spoon.

"Charlie Morell," he said, with the broken voice of the ringmaster who's been barking orders all day long. "*Es un placer.*"

"The pleasure is mine," I retorted, grasping his square, damp hand.

"I've been looking forward to this," he continued in Spanish, his round eyes gleaming in the club's half light. On the stage behind us I could hear the musicians coming out to tune their instruments.

Ichaso glanced at him, then at me, then shrugged his shoulders, like a good Cuban, accepting the unforeseen without surprise.

"I have to do one more set but after this we're all going to Guanabo, okay? You remember that *bembé* I told you about, Charlie? I definitely think the saints are burning up the wires to talk to you, *asere*."

David moved to the stage with amazing fleetness. Prado smiled knowingly, pointed at an empty chair.

"Please join us," he commanded in English. I took a seat.

"Absolut?" he asked, offering the bottle. "It's a wonderful commodity in Cuba. Better than money, sometimes. But most people are still chasing Washingtons around here."

"Washingtons?"

"As in dollar bills."

I nodded at the three teenage girls, who giggled and whispered at each other, their breasts barely held inside their skimpy tops.

"So how much are you paying these kids? Hundred a pop?"

"Not even. These cuties are *jineteras,* riders of good times. A hot meal, a CD, and a pair of jeans and they'll fuck your eyeballs out. Want one? Take your pick. Teresa, Magalys, Nubia, *saluden al Señor Morell.*"

A pleasant, high-pitched euphony of hellos flowed from the girls' glistening lips. I smiled, shook my head no at Prado.

"Don't take this wrong but it's you I'm looking for."

Prado looked fixedly at me, as though considering a particularly poignant problem, then he bent across the bosoms of the girls and whispered in the ear of the dark man. The gunman raised his razor-sharp eyebrows in surprise, nodded, and walked away. He walked across the dance floor past the stage to the bar at the back, where he accosted Gutiérrez, who had been sitting on a stool. The two conferred quickly, then exited the bar.

"Now that Captain Courageous True Believer Lee Gutiérrez has left, maybe you and I can talk more freely, my friend."

My heart began to race. If he could get rid of Gutiérrez so quickly, what hope did I have of ensnaring him?

"I don't know what you're talking about."

"Of course you do. Look, Charlie, Cuba is a small country. Here in Havana it's incestuous. Everybody knows each other's business. You've heard of the Stasi, in East Germany, how they kept files on everyone?"

"The secret police, yeah."

"The Cubans were trained by them, but they eventually outdid their mentors. Not even the Germans had a paid informer on every block like they do in Cuba, with the Committees for the Defense of the Revolution. The government here knows everything. Do they choose to do something about what they know? That's something else altogether. I should tell you, though, I didn't know you were in town until CNN picked up the story."

"You get CNN down here?"

"At all the major hotels. CBS and HBO too. Cuba is a time warp, Charlie. Nineteen fifty-nine and 1999 coexist right next to each other. Anytime you turn the corner, you never know which time zone you're going to walk into. Just like the people. Some of them talk like Fidel rolled down from the mountains yesterday, while others can't wait to open up their Charles Schwab online investment account. Any minute now Rod Serling is going to walk onstage and introduce us to the audience."

The loud riff of a trumpet broke through the din of the club, as the organ and the congas picked up the beat and Ichaso strutted on stage, mike in hand, delivering rapid-fire raps in Spanish about the loves of a little housewife.

"This guy's going to make a mint back in the States once I get him over," said Prado, nodding pleasantly at the dollar signs in the flesh on stage. "He'll have to tour, naturally, but he's got a brilliant future ahead of him."

I saw then the same statuesque *mulata* with the turban who had been sitting with Ichaso at the *paladar* earlier in the day regally make her way through the floor. She came up to our table, looked disdainfully at Prado's harem.

"Really, *Papi*, don't you think they're a little young for you?"

"Ah, *beba*, but don't you know it's youth eternal that we crave?"

"There are better ways to find it," said the woman, who now with an imperious wave dismissed the little *horizontales*, who got up and went down to the floor to dance with themselves.

Max kissed the woman on the cheek, then beamed as he introduced us.

"Charlie Morell, my daughter, Gertrudis."

The woman nodded with a half smile, as sure of herself as any aristocrat, then turned her loving gaze on the big, loud spectacle of Ichaso on stage. Prado moved closer to my chair, his body reeking of lime cologne and antiperspirant.

"So tell me, Charlie, how did you do it? I want to know. Is it true the *ebbó* also talk to you?"

"Excuse me?"

"The ceremony. When you sacrificed the girls. What did the voices tell you?"

I looked at him, flabbergasted, my head reeling from the implications of his statement: I'd been chasing the wrong man all along.

"The funny thing is, I was up there not too long ago. I was in Vegas, and on my way back to Los Angeles I cut through Palmdale, there had been a major accident on the 15. I was going through that desert, thinking how lucky I was to be away from that jam, how the gods don't live in all that sand. So when I heard about you I thought, there you go. You were wrong. So, what did the gods tell you?"

I leaned closer, whispered in his ear: "The gods said to come get you."

12

"*YA EMPEZÓ la misma mierda*," same shit starting all over again, muttered lchaso.

"*Jodío país.*"

Four in the morning.

We're on our way to the small seaside town of Guanabo and one of the island's recurrent power outages has struck. The Carretera Central, the two-lane highway that runs from one end of the island to the other, has become a darkened country road. Ours seems to be the only vehicle still moving.

Spectral clouds stretch their gauze fingers across the yellow moon.

I ride in the back of the speeding Land Cruiser next to Gertrudis, who sits quietly throughout holding Ichaso's hand. Prado sits up front, his henchman at the wheel. Unfazed by the pitch-black night, the gunman drives at breakneck speed with his brights on. I suppose we're all tired or worried or perhaps just anticipating our arrival, for on the way over there has been little conversation, a strange thing among Cubans, who feel a minute without conversation is a minute not worth living.

When we got into the Cruiser Ichaso was still keyed up about his two-hour performance; a chatterbox, he rhapsodized endlessly on his favorite topic, himself. He imagined himself playing the Orange Bowl or maybe even Dodger Stadium, like Ricky Martin, as thousands of brown, black, and white people swayed to the beat of his *timba,* the newest Caribbean sensation that would make reggae and rap *cosas chiquitas,* little things that wouldn't compare. Prado mostly just assented to Ichaso's ravings, promising little and encouraging everything. But soon the post-performance high crashed and David slumped silently in the back seat, giving off a smell of sour oranges, tobacco, and black sweat.

Now, at the top of the hill outside Guanabo, the Land Cruiser took the dip into town at full speed, hurtling down at a forty-five-degree angle. A few buildings whooshed past—crumbling 1950s style motels, boarded-up gas stations, summer homes turned into everyday residences, all illuminated by the lights of the Cruiser, which rattled over the potholes.

Prado rolled his window down and pointed with his cigar at a vacant sand lot, lit up by the strong rays of the waxing moon over the ridge.

"You know, I saw El Duque playing in that field three years

ago," he said, indulging in Cuba's third national obsession, after sex and Castro's demise.

"You mean Orlando Hernández, the Yankee pitcher?" I asked.

"The same. This was a couple of years before he climbed on the raft," he said, looking longingly, if such a thing is possible, at the weathered benches, gouged fences, the darkened spotlights.

"He pitched a perfect game. For four hours he struck out each and every batter, it was embarrassing. Thirty-six runs his team scored. And this was after he'd spent a full day working at the sugar mill. He was *fenomenal*."

Prado turned, his fat cigar now like an extension protruding from his face.

"This country is full of talent, Charlie. Like David here. They just need people like me to show them the way out."

"Con la ayuda de los dioses," muttered Ichaso, with the help of the gods.

"A eso vamos," that's where we're going, assured Prado, turning back to face the front.

THE LAND Cruiser swept through the ramshackle town, then headed further east, along the winding roadway parallel to the shimmering sea. After ten minutes of rolling through the lush countryside, under darkened canopies of spreading tropical trees, we pulled off the pavement and onto a dirt and sand trail leading down a peninsula. A quarter mile in, we were stopped at a barbed wire fence by two army officers in full olive drab gear, Kalashnikovs in hand. They shone lights at us and ordered the Cruiser to a halt. Prado's bodyguard stopped the vehicle. The soldiers, black and gaunt, walked up to the driver.

"En nombre de Ekué," said the driver. The soldier, a large knobby scar on his left cheek, nodded a silent go-ahead to his partner, who moved the concertina wire gate out of the way. We passed through.

I looked back at the soldiers as we pushed on down the road. If ever I harbored any hope of being rescued by Gutiérrez, that hope was now long gone. I didn't know what Prado's bodyguard had told Gutiérrez back at the club, but from the time the gunman returned to Prado's table, all the Minint plainclothesmen I'd asked for seemed to have vanished. I did not see them at the parking lot, nor following us on the road, nor anywhere at all. All of which meant I'd been left to my own devices, which would have been fine ordinarily but this time I kept getting the nagging notion that I was an expendable element in his scheme.

If Gutiérrez was so keen on getting rid of Prado but couldn't do so until he captured him in the middle of something, that meant that I was going to be in the middle of that something. And if I was killed while trying to solve that something, then that simply meant another expatriate fugitive from justice had met his timely end in the Land of the Revolution. It was up to me to deliver the goods and get out of the line of fire. Which should prove as easy as cutting off an LAPD cruiser without getting a ticket.

Soon we came up to a white house at the end of the road, a plain stucco and cinder block structure facing the dark, vast Caribbean. A makeshift jetty of massive black boulders lay a few hundred feet beyond the house; anchored incongruously, bobbing in the choppy swell, was an old wooden speedboat, the kind seen statewide in maritime museums and rich men's lakeside lodges, all gleaming mahogany and teak and shiny brass. The usual collection of ancient American automobiles and newer Japanese cars were parked on the paved side yard of the house, which was all lit up as though for a birthday party or a wedding reception. Other soldiers in mufti directed us to park alongside a hefty Russian Lada.

"Are we expecting the Marines too?" I asked Prado as we stepped out.

A few clouds scuttled across the giant yellow moon, a night-bird warbled its throaty cry, the air spread heavy with the smell of jasmine and molasses.

"Protection. Some top people in the government have joined our group. I know they'll all be happy to meet you."

We walked up a path bordered with white flagstones and potted red geraniums.

"Whose place was this?" I asked Prado.

Prado waddled ahead of me, still puffing on his cigar.

"The property originally was owned by the Hedges family. Textiles and sugar. Fidel took it over in '59."

"So this used to be Castro's own pad?" I asked.

"One of them. He's got about a hundred of them scattered around the island. That way his enemies never know where he's going to spend the night. *Comandante! Comandante Fayos, qué tal!*"

Prado hurried with Gertrudis across the garden to ostentatiously embrace a paunchy, bearded man in tailored fatigues who stood under the branches of a flowering flame tree, smoking a cigar the size of a small torpedo. The three exchanged hugs, whispers, glanced in my direction with famished smiles, then Gertrudis walked away, melting into the surrounding darkness.

I walked with Ichaso and the bodyguard, who knew better than to press on without Prado's protective presence. The portly producer returned, slapping me on the back as he joined us.

"Who was that?" I asked.

"Former head of the Treasury. Says he's looking forward to seeing you by the altar."

"And your daughter?"

"You'll see her later. She has to get ready."

"She lives here?"

"All her life. Refuses to leave, says there's nothing up north that could tear her away from Cuba."

"She looks like a model."

"She is. But not the kind you're thinking. We should hurry, the ceremony is about to begin."

I nodded, saying nothing, and moved on to the house.

I T   I S here, dear reader, that I find myself confronting the ineffable, the undescribable, the unspeakable, that noumenon of which Kant wrote, that unknowable, abject depravity known as evil.

I know, it sounds absurd, that in a battered beachside house in a run-down country lorded over by run-down revolutionaries I would find the locus of all that is the opposite of life, of that thing that extends its grip on us further every day, from the caves of Tibet to the island of Manhattan, from the banks of the Seine to the trickle of the Los Angeles River, but as a matter of fact that is precisely where evil was to be found that night.

Not that the locus of evil is there anymore.

Evil, like Yahweh in His Ark, travels everywhere. For all we know, its epicenter today might be next door to you, in the apartment across the hall or in the house halfway down the block, in the office suite covered by peaceful ivy or even, especially, in the brightly lit statehouse domes and sterile television studios of our fair land.

What melodrama, you say.

Evil is banal. Evil is a benighted civil servant carrying out murderous orders for the greater good of party, country, or race.

Evil is lurid deviation, not willful depravity.

Or, as Saint Augustine wrote, evil is the absence of good, the vacuum that follows in the wake of God's departure.

I disagree.

Perhaps hell—which I now believe in—perhaps hell is the absence of the divine spark that animates everything on this earth. But evil itself is personified; evil has taken human form not just once but many times, and that night its sad, blighted countenance paraded itself before the assembled guests in the former lair of one Fidel Castro.

No, Fidel wasn't there. But his presence loomed over everything, from the veterans of his guerrilla days and his wars in Africa to the latest emissaries from the different ministries, all gathered to feast on the blood of the innocent for the consecration.

One last note, to my Jewish family and friends—deliberate evil need not be a Holocaust. It doesn't even need a Goebbels or a Mengele drawing the sharp knife of prejudice.

Evil is the sheer disregard for fellow humans, captured and tortured in the spurious hope of success. The Aztecs knew this and practiced it, which is why I always defend the conquistadors for storming the watery pyramids of Tenochtitlán. The Spanish were often wrong and the Spanish were always brutal but the Spanish were never evil.

INCONGRUOUSLY, IN a country shaped by salsa and mambo, I heard the flaccid strains of Barry White's Love Unlimited Orchestra on our way up the flagstones, as though his paeans to lust were stand-ins for another, darker kind of love. But a sudden silence greeted our arrival; so great was the stillness that I could hear the slapping of the waves against the rocky shore hundreds of yards away.

I stepped inside.

ALL AT once, as though awaiting our arrival, came a clatter of drums, the rasping singsong of a guiro and a gourd, a strange cluster of out-of-tune guitar chords as an unseen choral master raised his high, plaintive voice in a cascade of open vowels strewn with exploding consonants in a language I knew was African but I knew not where from and all the people who had been outside now rushed inside the house and all the doors were locked, the loud rattle of the bolts drawn close as all the lights went out and one great candle was lit before a painted landscape surmounted by a pair of animal eyes and all the people in the house answered the choral master with a cry that sounded like

> Anumé, anumé,
>
> go loi hai,
>
> anumé, kanto,
>
> anumé

and they all kneeled, the *comandantes* in their olive green fatigues and the roly-poly civil servants in their polyester shirts and cotton pants and the women in their tight dresses and the handful of foreigners, their sunburned skin sprinkled throughout the mass of sallow and black and brown faces.

All at once I realized why Gertrudis had left us, for she came into the front of the room by the altar dressed in the flowing white and purple robes of Ossain, the healing god, wearing a crown on her dreadlocked hair and carrying aloft a saw-toothed blade and she called out for the presence of someone or something of Ekué Yamba O like a high priestess, which is what she was, and from the sides men appeared with baskets full of masks, animal masks in crude papier-mâché, lions, foxes, gazelles, cheetahs, murderous birds, and stage monkeys. I was presented with the mask of a rat and Prado beside me, donning his gorilla mask, asked me to put my mask on quickly as the priestess in her white raiments raised a wooden basket which she swung around violently and the sacred drums began their pounding and the music reached its cackling crescendo and we all fell under its spell so that time ceased to exist and the heat and the smoke and the pounding of the drums carried us along so far that we knew not how long we were there or even who and why we were there living in the present in the heat of the moment and the exhaustion and the fear and then from somewhere in the back of the house an obviously drugged naked *mulatica* was brought in by two muscular guards. The prisoner was barely pubescent, her breasts still swelling into womanhood, and the men forced her to kneel before the basket and then I felt strong hands grabbing me and pulling me up and two guards dragged me to the front of the room and Gertrudis intoned, Our visitor from abroad will conduct the ceremony tonight, and she handed me the knife and ordered that I slice the throat of the sacrifice so the blood would pour in the vat and the goddess would slake her thirst, and the guards pulled their knives and the congregation lowered their heads to the ground, wailing and lowing like animals for the kill.

I took the knife and held it high, realizing this was the end of the line, the very end I had long feared from which there was no escape, and I drove the knife into my arm and the blood flowed out into the vat as I turned and said the goddess is satisfied and the vat gave a great sigh as though belching with satisfaction and Gertrudis stared at me wide-eyed, unbelieving, when the shots were finally heard and the loudspeaker ordered everyone to surrender and the loud report of a chopper rattled the air. Everyone panicked and rose to their feet and burst open the doors and ran from the building, rushing like roaches from a glass trap, into the bright white klieg lights of a dozen army vehicles posted outside.

Prado raced down the hallway against the crowd and I followed him, shoving everyone else aside, knowing he was my last hope for survival. He sprinted through the kitchen and jumped through the glass louver windows and fell outside and got up and I followed him out of the house and down to the jetty even as out of nowhere a sudden rainstorm rose and the moon was covered with clouds and a great thudding boom rent the air as he joined two other people in the launch casting off the ties. I jumped on the boat after him, knife still in hand. The two other men in the boat raised their guns and fired but missed from the sudden rocking of the boat as it raced onto the choppy waters even as the whirring of a helicopter flew overhead and a great white light shone down on the waters and someone shouted for us to surrender and the men jumped in the water but Prado still drove on, one hand on the wheel and the other forcing the engine to fly even faster and I inched my way up to him and ordered him to stop and he turned and took out a small gun from the waist and fired at my chest and I jumped on him and we struggled as the great white light kept shining down on us and the boat struggled out of control and plowed into a buoy and capsized as we both fell into the water, still struggling for control, and we sank deeper into the black waters even as the light receded from me and I heard a sweet music as I dropped deeper into the water and Prado slipped from my grip and swam away and a great white light appeared at the bottom of the ocean and a woman's voice rang out saying fear not Carlos my son fear not fear not fear not . . .

PERHAPS IT was just as well that I gave Charlie the news about his son being a witness for the prosecution at the Court-yard of Tranquillity, over in the big Theosophical Temple in Los Feliz.

He listened quietly to my recounting of Julian's accusations, staring off into the distance, beyond the carefully trimmed euca-lyptus and olive trees surrounding the place. He was pale and noticeably thinner than the last time I'd seen him, long lines now etched on both sides of his face. His gray hair was cut short, Caesar style, his wide hazel eyes filled with what looked like grave resignation.

"How's your health? You look like you've lost a lot of weight," I asked after a silent pause that stretched for minutes.

A bird chirruped up in the olive trees; in reply, two turtledoves cooed their mournful two-note song from their cote on the building's roof.

"I've been fasting," he said, exhaling as if the mere act of breathing was physically painful.

"Really?" I said, wondering if he'd be up to the demands of the trial. "How is that?"

"I'm on a liquid diet. Fruit juices and water. No solids, coffee, tea, or alcohol. Kind of makes it hard when you're running ten miles a day too."

Now I was really concerned. At that rate I wouldn't have a client in a week.

"Why are you doing this?"

"I'm trying to clear my mind. I don't want to sound too mystical but I want to open up my inner eye. Develop my inner vision. I don't know if you understand what I'm talking about."

"I think I do," I replied, even though the only mystics I'd ever seen were buried in Spanish cathedrals centuries ago. Now Charlie turned around on the stone bench, staring blankly at the nearby fountain.

"I've always loved the sound of running water," he began, his words coming out softly, as though trying to remember a reality vanished long ago.

"My family had a fountain in our courtyard back in Cuba. When I got married my wife, Livvie, and I bought a house in Coral Gables, and practically the first thing I did was install a fountain we'd bought in Rome in our backyard. I remember it took forever to get a plumber who knew how to install the damn thing; the Italian pipes were a different grade or some such. By the time it was put up, Julian was already born. That was a fine fountain we had, you know. A lion's head. A true king of fountains."

He stopped, his voice eerily calm, as though he were trying to haul back into reality the thing he'd cast out so long ago.

"Do you know José Martí?"

"Sort of. Cuban poet? Fought the Spanish?"

Charlie smiled, the beaming professor, the proud papa he must once have been.

"Very good. That's more than ninety-nine percent of all Americans know. Castro uses his writings a lot. Martí was sort of like a combination George Washington and Walt Whitman, if you can imagine that. Well, he wrote a very famous poem called 'La Mora,' the Moorish girl.

"It's all about this Moorish princess a long time ago who owned a priceless pearl but she grew to hate this pearl because she was a flighty and senseless girl. So one day she went to the ocean and threw the pearl back into the water. But she was instantly remorseful, horrified at what she had done, and so every day from there on she would go to the shore and sit on a rock weeping, saying, '*O mar, devuélveme mi perla!*' O sea, return my pearl to me! Which of course it never did. The point is obvious, I guess."

"That sometimes we throw away, out of anger, that which we'll miss for the rest of our life?"

"You see my point. I should have never walked away from my family. I should have never—"

Charlie stopped, closed his eyes to control himself.

"Well," he said. Then he repeated, "Well, well, well," as though tantric repetition would bring him the wellness he desired. We fell silent; a couple of monks in saffron robes walked down the path, nodded in greeting. We nodded back, they glided away.

"Have you ever wanted something really, really, really bad?" asked Charlie, softly.

"Of course. Who hasn't?"

"Well, I really, really, really wanted to make up to Julian. I really wanted to be a good father to him. But I don't know. Sometimes I wonder if we should ever desire something so fervently, if we should desire anything at all. Maybe the best way to achieve peace is like the Buddha says, through renunciation, giving up all our earthly desires. For every time I've really wanted something, that thing has always been denied me. So I ask myself, why want at all? Why have any desire? Just take life as it comes, *corta y traicionera*, brief and treacherous, and be done with it."

I looked at Charlie, took his hand, long, rough, and dry.

"Do you want me to negotiate a deal for you?"

He jerked his hand away, then, almost as if regretful for his acts, he draped his arm around my shoulder, whispered in my ear.

"Nothing would please me more than to be done with all this. I'm not afraid of dying, you know. Not anymore, not since Cuba. And even if I go to prison, it really wouldn't matter. This . . ." he said, gesturing at the yard, the buildings, the world, "all this is a prison too, from which there is no escape. But the answer is no. I cannot authorize you to cut a deal."

"Why not?"

Charlie got up, dusted some invisible motes off his trousers, tugged at the ends of his sleeves.

"For Julian," he said, calmly. "I have realized my prison but he has not. I need to be a father to him, teach him. This is not a legacy I wish to bestow on him. In other words, we're fighting this sucker. And we're going to win it."

He bent down, kissed me lightly on the cheek.

"I'll see you Monday at the CCB. Eight-thirty sharp. Judge Strummer loves to impose sanctions if you're one minute late."

He turned and then he stole away, a brave man with nothing but his will and his desire to clear his name.

•   •   •

DANNY WAS ladling steaming bowls of soup at his son's restaurant on Whittier Boulevard when I walked in. It was the lunch hour and all the workers from the Welfare Building across the street were standing in line for the special of the day—*caldo de albóndiga.*

"Hey, *m'hija,*" said Danny, when he noticed me elbowing my way through the crowd behind the people hovering over the handful of stools at the counter. "Are you hungry? You came at just the right time."

He set a bowl of the spicy broth with three floating meatballs before a tiny, poker-faced old woman. She inhaled fiercely the clouds of steam floating off the bowl, ran her purple tongue over her lips and toothless gums, then she hacked at the meat with the edge of her spoon, loading the pieces onto a warm corn tortilla, adding chopped raw onions, cilantro, and jalapeño, making an improvised, fiery taco that she gummed in three swallows.

"Thank you, Danny. I gave up meat for Lent."

"Lent ended last month!"

"I guess I'm behind the times. Can we talk?"

He nodded, ambled to the back of the restaurant. I followed him through the swinging doors into the tiny kitchen, where four people managed to chop, cook, and clean in a space no bigger than my hallway closet. I said hello to Danny's son, Ray, busy chopping up tomatoes for the *salsa fresca,* even as his father told him to hurry up and serve the *enchiladas suizas* already.

I don't know how they did it but their kitchen was annoyingly spotless, not an onion skin or a leaf of lettuce on the floor; theirs had been the only restaurant in the neighborhood to sport on their door the coveted A from the Health Department the first time out. You might think they were trying to disprove the old image of the greasy Mexican dive but the truth is, I don't think it ever occurred to Danny, Ray, their cousin Rick, or anyone else in their clan to be anything other than what they and what millions of Mexicans always have been—clean, honest, hardworking people. I know it sounds forced coming from me but somebody's got to say it and it might as well be me right now.

Danny led the way out to the service alley, behind the parking lot of the auto body shop next door. He sat on a low wooden bench, adjusting his stained white apron in between his legs, took out a pack of Lucky Strikes from his shirt pocket.

"You know, you really ought to quit that dirty habit," I said as he lit up, his broad nose flaring with delight at the enveloping clouds of nicotine.

"*M'hija,* when this is about the only pleasure you have left, it's hard to give it up."

He wiggled his bushy eyebrows to make sure I understood his meaning but I wasn't about to let him off so easy.

"You should try Viagra then."

"*Uy, la Viagra!*" He shook his head in dismay. "I tried that once and that was the other problem, the little fellow wouldn't go to sleep no matter how much I rubbed him. And then, who's going to kiss him for me now that Adelita's gone? We're not all like Bob Dole, with a nice little white wife who wants to ride the *burrito* all night. But I know you didn't come here to talk about my sex life. What can I do for you?"

He untied the strings of his apron, which fell all around the round protuberance in his middle—his belly, that is.

"I just had a talk with Charlie. We were reviewing his case."

"And how do you see it?"

"It's bad for him, Danny. His own son is turning state's evidence."

He spat out a few odd pieces of tobacco leaf, making me think that perhaps he still smoked his unfiltered cigarettes for the excuse of being able to spit out his displeasure at regular intervals.

"The boy is a *rata?* On his own *papi?* What kind of son would do that to his father? No matter how bad your dad is, he's always your *papi,* you can't turn him in. What kind of Latino would do that?"

I nodded, seconding his observations.

"That's part of the problem. Cubans are not really Latinos."

"Oh, I know, I know, I've heard it all before. I've been dealing with Cubans since they first started coming out in 1960, right after Fidel took over. The first ones moved out here to Montebello, the Aramendis. They moved next door, I remember, you were just a little girl then or maybe you weren't even born then. How old are you now?"

"Thirty-one."

"Oh, *m'hija,* one of these days you're going to get married again, right? You can't be living in sin all your life. I hope you'll invite me to the wedding."

"Not if you keep bugging me like this, Danny. What's your point about the Cubans?"

"Well, what I was saying is, they're not *gringos,* that's for sure. They worry too much about nonmaterial things to be regular white people. They're always thinking about the spirit, the soul, honor, things like that. It's like losing their homeland made them like pilgrims, you know? Like the *Judío Errante,* you know that story? The Wandering Jew. Always saying I'll be back someday and meantime they never fit in anywhere. They're not from here, they're not from there, they're from nowhere and from everywhere. Now, we Mexicans, we have it different, you and I, little girl. We know this is our land. Even if the *pinche gringos* stole it from us, they couldn't get rid of all of us."

He stomped his heavy foot for effect, his penny loafers stretched tight by his swollen feet, lifting a little cloud of dirt and debris.

"Even the mighty *gringos* with all their science and knowledge, they can't stop people from making whoopee. Know what I mean, jellybean? Men and women always get together and always make babies and it's a simple fact, there's eventually going to be more of us than of them and when that happens, we'll be on top. Because that's what happened originally, you know. The first illegal aliens here were the *gringos,* they snuck into Mexico, then they took it away. But that's ancient history. I don't know why but the older I get the more I look to the future, you know? I just know it's going to be better than anything else we had so far, for us brown people. Chicanos, Mexican-Americans, Latinos, whatever you want to call us. Just look at Sacramento right now. The Speaker is a Chicano, so's the GOP leader."

"So is the County Sheriff and so is Phil Fuentes, neither of whom is going to help my client, Danny."

"Huy, girl, there you go again, it's that *gringo* blood in you, always to the point."

"Well, what about it?"

Danny shook his head side to side, debating the unfairness of it all.

"Now, your client, I don't know about that Charlie. So his own son says he saw him do it?"

"Thankfully no. But he did say Charlie was dating one of the victims, the one up in Oakland. Charlie confirmed it to me today."

"*Uy!* That is bad."

"Very. Makes him look guilty as hell and gives him a link to the victim. The boy also says his dad had become obsessed with finding this secret cult, this society of devil worshippers."

"So that helps him."

"If we can find that so-called secret society. What did you learn about Senator Decker?"

Danny tossed away his cigarette, looking disgusted with himself and with the world. He tied the strings of his apron around his waist again.

"I'm kind of disappointed because I can't find out anything. I called my buddy who did the investigation, Rafael Rojas, he's now retired, I think I told you? He won't return my calls, I finally go out to his house in Brea and he won't even say hello to me or anything. And I saved his butt so many times when we were riding together out in La Puente too! So finally when I go out to his house, like I said, he answers the door, he won't even invite me inside his house, the *cochino*. Says he don't remember and anyhow it's all classified. Classified, what do you mean? I ask him. What is this, the CIA or something? So he turns to me and he says, it's worse than that, Danny. Leave it alone. Then he slams the door on me, would you believe it? So I truck down to Records and wouldn't you know it, the *cabrón* was right!"

Danny got up, scratched his belly as though he had all the time in the world, then jerked his head up when he heard the first few bars of "Wooly Bully."

"There goes Anacleto again, playing those old songs real loud. I told him the customers don't like that, they all want to hear Enrique Iglesias, none of that old Chicano stuff. I'm going to have to shut down that Victrola."

He moved to return to the restaurant but I stopped him.

"Wait up. What happened with the case file?"

"That? It's under court order, sealed. They say it's still under investigation, an ongoing investigation, couldn't give me any details. But I'll find out about it, don't you worry, gimme a couple of days."

"But the senator died two years ago! How can it still be ongoing?"

"Like I said, let me see what I can find out. Call me back on Friday, okay? Now I've got to stop that music before it drives away my customers."

Danny slammed the door behind him and entered the restaurant, as next door the body shop's paint oven door opened and a newly painted '57 Chevy was eased out into the parking lot to finish drying out in the warm California sun.

14

I USUALLY don't do this, that's what I have an investigator for, but this one time I went down myself to Sheriff's headquarters on Ramona in East L.A., a beer bottle throw away from the 710 Long Beach Freeway.

The grim reaction I got out of the deputy in charge of records set the tone. At first he wouldn't even confirm that there had been an investigation and I had to threaten him with a court order before he came back with the empty folder bearing the name of Senator Decker and the URN file number on the tab.

Sergeant Hansen, paunchy, weary, blond, and blue-eyed, slapped it down on the Formica counter, turned his back on me to pull some other form from some other basket even though I was the only party in the room.

I opened the folder. Aside from the face sheet of the complaint report, the entire contents had been removed. In its stead there lay a second page reading, "Subpoenaed by the Grand Jury" with a date stamp of November 8, 1998.

"What happened here, Sergeant?"

Hansen sneered, digging deeper into a basket of forms.

"I told you already, counsel, that's all we have on that case."

"But this is just the incident report. There must have been a supplemental report, that's SOP, standard operating procedure."

Now Hansen glanced up, stuck a piece of chewing gum in his mouth.

"I know what SOP means, counsel."

He then rummaged through the file drawer in his desk, as though a bright idea had just dawned on him.

"I know what," he said sarcastically, "let me go through my things, maybe I accidentally misplaced it with my handcuffs."

He made a whole show out of his search, then slammed the metal drawer shut, tsk-tsking at his failure.

"Not there. I guess you're shit plain out of luck. You want the rest, you go to the grand jury, okay? I just work here. Now if you'll excuse me, it's time for my coffee break."

Hansen then walked back into his filing room and left me standing at the counter feeling like the biggest fool. I guess I could have told him Sheriff Baca would have his ass in a sling if he heard about this but judging by his age and his stripes and his attitude, he wouldn't have cared if I did haul him before the board. He was just another dinosaur marking time until his pension came up and he could retire to Idaho with the rest of the dinosaurs.

Now, this is where a little education on our country's wonderful legal system is in order. By their very nature, grand jury proceedings are secret, Special Prosecutor Ken Starr notwithstanding. In principle this is so the grand jury can freely investigate the circumstances behind a particular set of facts without undue pressure and obtain indictments in an equitable fashion. The truth is that, as every prosecutor knows, you can get a grand jury to indict a ham sandwich. It really is a Star (Starr?) Chamber, where the usual nice distinctions of law and constitutional due process are thrown out the window.

But the intriguing part of this missing file was that, as far as I could tell, no one had been indicted. I knew because I'd pulled a Lexis legal search on the computer and had failed to run up any hits. That meant that presumably, for whatever reason, the grand jury had done its job but nothing had come of it. Which meant either the crime had not been committed or there wasn't sufficient evidence to merit an indictment. Either way, the results were now sealed, which probably was the reason why the whole thing had been done this way to start with. Which made me even more eager to find out just what was there that somebody would want to hide.

I thought about all this as I tooled down Eastern Avenue to the 10 freeway, heading westbound that afternoon, with the traffic already stacked up all the way past the four-level interchange downtown out to Crenshaw. I was staring at a billboard telling me the Doobies were playing at that very moment on some classic rock station when I decided it might be wise to swing by the Coroner's and pull the death certificate, just to be on the safe side.

I drove past the white wedding cake of unhappiness known as the USC Medical Center and parked a couple of blocks away, by the brick structure housing the County Coroner's, the only place of its kind with a souvenir shop in these United States.

At the front desk I asked for Keith Noyer, a medical examiner

I'd had some dealings with in the past, but that week he was at a conference in San Francisco so instead I just asked the clerk for Decker's information. She was not very helpful either but at least she wasn't surly as she pushed me a couple of pages under the plexiglass barrier.

"Where's the rest of the report?"

"Sorry, subpoenaed by the grand jury," she replied, as though I couldn't guess.

I sat on one of the rickety plastic chairs outside the gift shop and tried my best to disregard the beach towels, T-shirts, and sun visors bearing the outline of a dead body with the words "Property of the L.A. County Coroner." Even a Mexican like myself finds this year-long Day of the Dead celebration a bit excessive. But the money supposedly goes to charity so what the hell.

I opened my copy of *Vanity Fair,* ripped open the scratch and sniff strip of the latest fancy perfume ad and held it under my nose as I read the pages. To this day I can't look at a picture of Elizabeth Taylor or a bottle of a certain brand of perfume without seeing visions of tiny dancing skeletons and smiling death's-heads.

At least the coroner's report, although sketchy, gave me a clearer idea of how the late, great Sacramento powerhouse that was Tom Decker had met his untimely end. The examiner, working from officers' notes and conversations with the detectives on the scene, Rojas and Mankewicz, had quickly come to the conclusion that the deceased had indeed died by his own hand. Rope burns were evident around his neck, death apparently having been caused by a combination of a broken trachea and a dislocated vertebra, which had cut off the supply of blood to the brain. There were no apparent signs of any other injury, although the specialist did report noticing an animal tattoo etched in the left thigh of the deceased. How funny, I thought, the senator was a secret punker.

Apparently Decker had been found by his housekeeper, who on a Monday morning stumbled onto the body swinging from a thick horsehair rope tied to the main cross beam of the living room. Must be a Spanish estate, I thought, before reading on. No suicide notes were found. The housekeeper, Encarnación Ramírez, stated that the senator had lately taken to drink, as they say, and would spend days in his den, listening to strange music, downing Ballantine's while staring at the fire.

The senator had climbed on a chair, which was found on its side on the floor near the body. He had worn a dress shirt, bolo tie, jeans, and fine leather boots to his demise.

I paid the clerk the fee for the copy, stuck it in my purse, and glanced at my watch. Two-forty-five. With any luck I could make it to the senator's ranch before dark, leaving me enough time to take a look around and see if there was anything of interest that could prove useful. I walked briskly to my Alfa, climbed in, and after double-checking the address in my trusty Thomas Bros. guide, I turned on the engine. I felt the throaty *varroom* of the Italian aluminum engine vibrate all the way to my funny bone. I raced out of the parking lot and headed north on the Santa Ana Freeway, past the abandoned factories and overpasses of East Los Angeles through downtown, zigzagging at sixty, clocking eighty on the straightaways, leaving behind Griffith Park, Glendale, Burbank, and Sylmar until I turned north by northeast on the Antelope Valley Freeway, racing the sun to the late senator's horse ranch.

G R O W I N G   U P   half Irish and half Mexican, I was always aware of Senator Decker's colorful career. For more than twenty years he represented a district that had gradually been transformed from lily-white upper class to lower-middle-class brown. Irish like my mom, he too had a Mexican spouse, and he reportedly mangled the Spanish language with the largesse that only those who live with a native speaker would dare. Known as the *compadre güero,* the fair-skinned *compadre,* he controlled his fiefdom with an iron fist. He was, in essence, the last of that small group of Anglos who ran Southern California until the 1970s, when Tom Bradley and his black-Jewish coalition defeated Sam Yorty and brought the century-long reign of the white man to a close.

Not that the Anglos were all bad, mind you. They gave us the California Aqueduct, the San Fernando Valley, the Progressive era, the San Pedro Harbor, and the freeways, remaking this little cactus patch peopled by feckless Mexicans into the biggest powerhouse west of Chicago. Besides which, they were our parents, literally and otherwise. But their time had run out, just as it happened to the Californios, whose land they stole; only a few Anglos, like the senator, were smart enough to call it quits years before the ugly strains of Proposition 187 woke up the Sleeping Brown Giant.

Senator Decker became lobbyist Decker after his district was reconfigured by the U.S. Justice Department to encourage more minority representation. By all accounts he became then even more powerful, and certainly wealthier, once he plied his undeniable eloquence backstage on the newly minted assemblymen and senators of color. But when Decker's daughter, Miranda, became involved in Ricardo Díaz's satanic cult, the ex-senator cut off all his ties to Sacramento. Whether shunned or on his own accord, he withdrew to his horse ranch up in Agua Dulce, halfway between Santa Clarita and Palmdale. There he was said to be writing his memoirs, according to the few political writers who came to listen to the nuggets of political wisdom from the exiled prince of a disappearing class.

THE ROAD up to the senator's ranch was behind the old Agua Dulce airport, now for sale by its private owner as advertised in the *L.A. Sunday Times* and *Daily Variety*. A half mile down from the airport I located the access road, which circled up and around the mountainside, leading me to another barren valley, smaller and even more isolated than Agua Dulce itself, so that now, even though I was less than sixty miles from downtown L.A., I might well have been in the Badlands of North Dakota.

I swung right at the gravel driveway leading to the twin masonry pillars holding up the double D brand of the senator's ranch. I stopped the car, asked myself if I really wanted to go through all this trouble after all and even if it was worth it.

The oval emblem with the winged Ds was askew, one of its support bars dangling like the arm of a corpse from a stretcher. The pillars themselves had been pockmarked by bullet holes from passing potshots and smeared with the graffiti of the local white gang, Aryan Posse. A sign for McGroarty Realty declared the availability of the property. The unlocked fence gate had been left ajar; from the entrance I could see the red-tile roof of a building.

I got out, pushed open the gate while taking care not to ruin my Valentino pumps with the red mud of the property, got back in my Alfa, and drove on in.

The winding allée must have been planned with great care once upon a time, probably modeled after the entrance to some Mediterranean estate. But now the trees looked scraggly and dried out, weeds growing malevolently around the trunks. The road debouched on a roundabout in front of a long, two-story building that looked like a fantastic mishmash of Andalucía and Provence, with turrets, balconies, shutters, and more balconies, the architect obviously believing, the way most people did back then, that more is more.

I parked next to the dry fountain, littered with beer cans and McDonald's wrappers. In the silence of the late afternoon, with a mauve sun setting behind the khaki mountains, the cold wind blew and I felt like I was in an L.A. version of *Citizen Kane,* in that odd shot of the old Charles Foster Kane estate. Or maybe it was more like *Rebecca,* where she says, at the start of the movie, "Last night I dreamed I was back in Manderley."

• • •

BUT THIS was not a Hollywood fantasy at all, even if the building could easily have been sited on the Universal backlot, right next to Norman Bates's sweet hilltop home. I opened my glove compartment, took out my flashlight and my .38 Colt Special. I once got a concealed weapon permit from the Sheriff's after one of my clients threatened to put a hit on me because I couldn't beat the mandatory three-strike twenty-five-to-life rap. Although usually I don't like to carry my weapon, in this instance I thought it would be the wisest thing to do. I grabbed my Ericsson cellular and then, like a good failed Catholic, made the sign of the cross and went in.

The front door was locked, but it was a fairly simple thing to enter through the kitchen door. Was it Raymond Chandler or Ross MacDonald who once said this was typical of California, an impenetrable front door and a paper-thin back door? In any event, I was not the first one there. Debris from a number of parties was scattered all around, beer cans and cigarette packs, odd articles of clothing discarded in pursuit of who knows what natural or artificial paradise.

I made my way through the huge kitchen, past the butler's pantry still bearing the handwritten signs on the china cabinet reading Daily, Occasional, State Function, and Royal Visit, next to a series of pull strings with labels for Senator's Chamber, Madame's Boudoir, Great Suite, and Royal Room.

Everything about the house looked as though it had been lived in continuously without any renovation since its construction back in the 1920s. In the living room the old flecked wallpaper so popular in the flapper era still hung on the walls, while the wide wooden floorboards bore the scuffmarks of decades of use.

I walked through a set of large sliding doors into the hallway, looked into a den with built-in bookcases and a fireplace that would have been at home in Bluebeard's castle. Then I entered the elegant living room, with picture windows looking out on the fields sloping away from the house.

Something made me look up. Above my head was the large wooden beam, stenciled and painted in the Spanish manner, from which the senator had hanged himself. I walked over to where the report said he had been found and I stood there for a moment, trying to conceive of what had driven him to leave everything behind, what crimes he felt guilty of or what torments assailed him with such force that he saw no way out but the rope.

I don't know why I did this, I'm usually not so morbid, but for some reason I can't explain I wanted to see exactly what it was the senator had seen in his last moments on earth, as though I could then explain to myself what had driven him to suicide. I grabbed hold of a large bookcase, dragged it to the middle of the floor, threw it on its side and stood on it at approximately the last position of the body. From my perspective I could see a cross in one of the west-facing stained glass windows shining against the last rays of the sun, a field of yellow and red flames against the divine tree, and I swear to you that for a moment I heard voices and laughter and felt the cold, rough noose around my own neck. I got down as fast as I could.

That's when I heard the voices again. This time I knew I was not imagining them. I slipped off the safety of my Colt and turned on the flashlight to illuminate the vast volume of the house, which seemed to grow larger and emptier, daring me to come and explore its darkness. I followed the sound of the voices silently, retracing my steps to the kitchen.

I stood outside for a moment, getting up my nerve, then I swung into the room, with my gun in my hand.

"Who's there?" I shouted.

To my surprise, I saw two Chinese men in their early twenties huddling around the old fireplace. They dropped their bags of charcoal briquettes and their hibachi and rose up slowly, hands in the air, their gaunt faces blank with fear.

"Please, no shoot!" said the short, wirier one of the two, his hair cut in an outmoded spiky punk style. The other wore his hair in a long braided ponytail that seemed like something out of Fu Manchu China. They didn't look like much of a threat but I kept my gun trained on them all the same.

"Who are you? What are you doing here?"

"We from China," said the one with the spike cut, his hands trembling. "We stay here, house back."

"Who said you could stay here?" I barked, beginning to feel the jittery nerves of a near miss. "How did you find this place?"

The wiry one spoke to the long-haired one in Chinese, then he answered, "My friend find place. We look for gold, we no have work. No shoot, please!"

I smelled the sour aroma of urine and saw that the second man, still trembling, had a large dark spot spreading from his crotch.

"Oh, for Christ's sake, you're illegals?"

"Yeah, yeah!" answered the one who spoke English, obviously willing to agree to anything just to get me to put my gun down. Which I did, but still held it in my hand.

"Let's go outside."

We walked out to the porte cochere, the wind rustling up tumbleweeds like in some old Western.

"What's your name?" I asked the first one.

"Erik," he said. "Erik Hong."

"Where are you guys staying, Erik?"

He pointed at a guest apartment over the garage, out in the northeast corner of the property.

"We no have kitchen, come cook in big house. We go now, okay?"

"No, no, it's okay. I'm going. It's none of my business what you guys do here. But I should tell you this is private property."

Erik's face lit up, proud to show off his knowledge of his new country.

"Oh yeah. This house of movie cowboy. Tom Mix fellow, he ride Tom Mix, Hopalong Cassidy too, you know?"

I glanced at the two of them, dreamers like all of us, aliens like all of us.

"Is that a fact. So what are you going to do?"

"We from China. We go look for gold tomorrow, promise."

"Hey, you guys, I don't care. Just don't let the Migra catch you," I said, walking to my car.

"What Migra?" asked Erik.

"The INS," I said, easing into my seat.

"So, what are you?" asked Erik from afar, standing perplexed after a quick conference with his fellow immigrant.

"I'm an attorney," I said, almost to myself. "I defend people."

Erik came running over, stretched out his hand.

"I don't have any change. Anyhow, you said you were going to go mining."

"No, no. Your card, please. Never know when need attorney," he said, grinning. I just had to grin back. I opened my purse, handed him my business card.

"Here you go, guy. Just don't let them catch you until you strike it rich."

"I won't," he said confidently, then he hurried back to his fellow explorer.

They both waved at me as I drove off down the allée, never having asked me what I was doing there. They were true Americans already, I thought, as I drove down to the Antelope Valley Freeway, the long lines of commuters' cars stretching all the way down to Santa Clarita.

They don't care who I am, they just want to get rich and cover their ass. Even if they don't find their gold mine, they'll do fine in Los Angeles, I decided. Just fine.

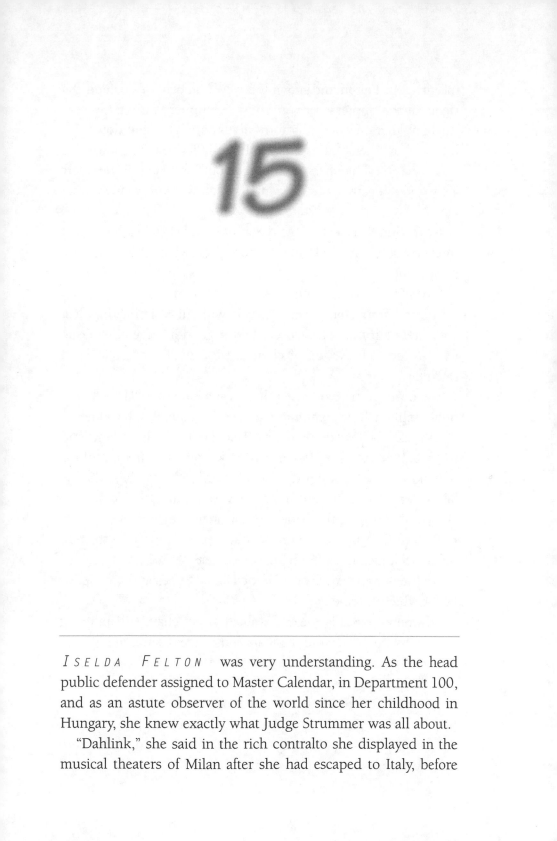

15

ISELDA FELTON was very understanding. As the head public defender assigned to Master Calendar, in Department 100, and as an astute observer of the world since her childhood in Hungary, she knew exactly what Judge Strummer was all about.

"Dahlink," she said in the rich contralto she displayed in the musical theaters of Milan after she had escaped to Italy, before meeting Mr. Felton and moving out to California to defend the rights of the oppressed, "you know Strummer is a total queen. Anybody that questions his authority is a threat to put down. He hit the roof when you subpoenaed him last week. You know, he called me into chambers to inquire about you! He said he knew we worked together and he wanted to know if you were competent."

Iselda fingered the large gold Star of David she always dangled from her still firm neck, raising her eyebrows as though to say, what a putz.

"So what did you tell him?"

"I said, 'Your Honor, Miss Carr is without a doubt the most competent attorney I have ever had the good fortune of working with. After Your Honor, of course.' He actually smiled when I said that."

She dropped her voice to a theatrical sotto voce, "He is so full of himself any little compliment makes his day. Here he comes."

"All rise," bellowed the deputy. The handful of defendants and the usual collection of lawyers in dark suits and dresses folded their newspapers, stopped their chatter, and hid their double lattes. Jennie Corbin, Strummer's favorite bailiff, stuck her flat chest out, gripped the wide bandolier around her even wider hips, and tilted up her pug nose, like a palooka defying the title holder to knock that chip off her shoulder.

"In the presence of the flag of the United States and the republic for which it stands . . ."

Strummer took his cue and walked out of chambers, mincing quickly to a place next to the Stars and Stripes, bending his head down to indicate the solemnity of his duties—or the sanctions he was about to impose on me.

". . . Department 100 of the Superior Court of the State of California in the County of Los Angeles is now open, Judge Arnold Strummer presiding. You may be seated. No drinking allowed in the courtroom. Please put away all your reading material."

Strummer hopped to his bench, sat down with the gusto of a man about to impart his own brand of justice, God help us.

"Who wants priority?"

At that the Ralph Lauren and Ermenegildo Zegna–clad private attorneys, bucking to have their cases heard first so they could be out by nine but charge a full morning session, raised their hands, waving their fancy French cuffs in the air like so many Century City flags.

I glanced around, past the two front rows crammed with counsel, then out to the sparse audience, where a handful of relatives watched the proceedings, not understanding what was said but knowing that the fate of their loved ones was being decided in that bleak room. I was waiting for Charlie, who had not returned any of my messages over the last forty-eight hours.

"C'mon, Charlie, don't do this to me!" I muttered, gritting my teeth. Strummer, who must have been planning this moment all weekend long, waved aside the clamoring counsel and reeled me in from his polished bench.

"Miss Carr," he said benignly, his reading glasses on the tip of his long narrow nose, "what a pleasure to see you again. You bring back such fond memories of battles litigated before my elevation."

"Likewise, Your Honor. Those memories are . . ."

I hesitated momentarily, then found the right word: "Unforgettable."

"Indeed," said Strummer, nodding vigorously, "Just like this case promises to be. I have reviewed the documents that you have requested in your subpoena duces tecum on behalf of your client, Mr. Morell—who, by the way, is nowhere to be seen. He knows the sanctions this court imposes for tardiness. Do you know where he is?"

The game was up. There was little I could do to save Charlie from being hauled into jail for contempt of court—which was funny, considering he was the one who had warned me about

Strummer's wrath for late arrivals. But Iselda, bless her, rescued us.

"Your Honor, if it please the court, we now have defendant Domínguez from Friday afternoon. He's been waiting to plead for the last three days, and the District Attorney has graciously agreed to sever his case and allow him to plead open to the court. It would be cruel and unusual punishment to prolong his agony anymore, Judge."

That distracted Strummer for a beat, just like the smell of a fresh carcass draws the attention of a hammerhead.

"Plead open, Ms. Fulton, before this court? Do you dare?"

"He dares, Your Honor," she said, pointing at a brown stub of a man in county blues, burdened with chains, flanked by two deputies who crossed their ham-sized arms, waiting for the wrong move. "Against my advice, he is willing to throw himself on the mercy of the court."

The Spanish interpreter, a gray-haired woman with a wandering eye, all of a sudden conferred with the defendant, who seemed to be arguing furiously with her interpretation.

"Well, how lucky do you feel today, Mr. Domínguez?"

The interpreter spoke up in pure New Yorkese, which I guess is another kind of foreign language out here.

"Yaw Honor, I wuz born a lucky guy, but Judge, I want to fire my attorney. I wanna state attorney."

A groan through the courtroom. That meant a Marsden motion, which would necessitate asking the District Attorney and all law enforcement personnel to step outside while the judge questioned the defendant on the supposed misdeeds or incompetence of the defense. Probably some of his fellow homies in lockup had told the defendant to ask for one of those other state attorneys, because everyone knows the PDs are really working for the system. It was all a waste of time, but of course the defendant didn't know that. In all my years I've yet to see counsel being substituted out on a Marsden. The courts hate to give the accused the idea they can control their own destiny.

Just then, Charlie walked in—but if I hadn't been looking out for him, I would not have recognized him. He was dressed all in white and had shaved his head; his scalp glistened in the yellowish light of the courtroom. He came up to me, nodded at the battery of lawyers present—I'm sure he knew them all—and he whispered in my ear: "Sorry I'm late. A truck overturned on the 10 right outside Pomona this morning."

"What were you doing out there? What are you doing to yourself?"

"I'll tell you later, let's just get out of here ASAP."

I turned and seized the moment.

"Your Honor, my client is now here and we're announcing ready."

"The people are also ready, Your Honor," said Mike Cleary, who had been sitting quietly at the far end of the jury box, working discreetly on the *New York Times* crossword puzzle he'd cut out and stuck in his Day Runner.

Strummer let his narrowed eyes fall not so gently on Charlie.

"Mr. Morell, about time. I never thought I'd see you in your position, sir."

"To paraphrase Thoreau, I never thought I'd see you in yours either, sir," replied Charlie.

"Hush!" I urged, elbowing him. Charlie grinned. He knew too many people and too many secrets for his own good.

"I'll take that to mean you will be pleasantly surprised by my selection of judge to hear your case, Mr. Morell. This matter is transferred to Department 247 forthwith."

I picked up my things and was heading out the door when Strummer thundered, "By the way, Miss Carr. I'm sending the papers you requested to Department 247. At the conclusion of your trial I expect you to show cause why you should not be held in contempt for wasting the court's time with your SDT when such a subpoena could have been handled elsewhere."

"Your Honor, that will matter only if I lose, which I don't intend to do," I answered, walking backward, Charlie by my side. "But I'll be here."

The judge hooked his finger, signaled for us to approach. He bent over, his reading glasses almost sliding off his long aquiline nose.

"You don't seriously think you're going to win this case, now do you?" he whispered.

"Judge, stranger things have happened." Like you on the bench, I thought.

"Not during my watch," he said, chuckling, then, done with me, he waved at me to return to my rightful place, which in his mind was somewhere licking his boots, no doubt. He made a show out of turning to Iselda.

"Now, Miss Felton, let's see if we can talk some sense into your client."

"I got plenty of cents, Your Highness," were the words of the interpreter, which drifted outside to the thirteenth-floor hallway. I joined Charlie at the elevators.

"Who's the judge in 247 nowadays?" he asked.

"Ray Mathews. He was up for assistant supervising judge but he lost out to Sandino. Look, I've got to get a cup of coffee. I got three hours sleep last night and I practically camped out in front of 100, I was so afraid I'd be late."

Charlie followed me into the snack bar at the far end of the hall, the fresh smell of popcorn and aerosol whipped cream on cappuc-cino as tempting as Raúl's kisses on a Sunday night. But I was good, I served myself a medium regular coffee, poured just enough non-fat milk into it to take away the bitter sting. Charlie, looking even thinner than before, had apparently given up on his diet; he grabbed a large bag of popcorn, which he munched on like he was at the front row of the multiplex watching the latest horror movie.

"This place has gone through so many hands," he said, walk-ing with me to the side room where the sugar and condiments are kept. "See that?"

He pointed at a sign reading SAL'S FRIENDS inside an empty display case on the freshly painted wall.

"Sal was the blind guy who ran the place years ago when I started, back in the Reagan-Wilson dark ages."

"I don't think I ever met him, that was before my time."

"Yeah, well, it was like open warfare back then. Judges would sign off on everything the prosecution wanted. Defense people like me, we saw ourselves as guerrillas, waiting for the day the North Vietnamese regulars would roll down from the DMZ."

"Excuse me?"

"That's all right, you wouldn't understand. In any case, the funny thing was that Sal used to go around with a Polaroid taking pictures of all the courthouse regulars to pin them up on that wall. He couldn't see what he was shooting but everybody gave him a real smile so they all came out looking great. You would come in here and it would be like the pictures of your school yearbook, watching all your friends and foes on the wall."

He pointed out the picture window at the looming gray building across the street, the old Hall of Justice, its copper roof tarnished and gouged, the many window air conditioners, smudged white from pigeon droppings, sticking out like carbuncles on concrete.

"Back then the HOJ was still being used, instead of being just a boarded-up white elephant. Sheriff's headquarters in the lower floor and a county jail on top. Looked like something out of Dickens. Many's the time I was grilled by some detective up on the sixth floor for the job I did on behalf of my clients. They hated to lose. Even if it was only one case out of a hundred, that was one too many. This is when I was a PI and I was trying to run away from myself. Now look at it, another dinosaur stuck in the mire of downtown with nothing to do, nowhere to go. They won't even put it out of its misery and tear it down."

"I heard it was the asbestos on the heating pipes, that removing it would cost a fortune."

"Bullshit. That's just the way L.A. is, it doesn't know what to do with its past. See that other building over there?"

He pointed at yet another shuttered structure two blocks away, a six-story-high mural of the Virgin of Guadalupe on one of its walls.

"That was known as the Whitebread Building, it also housed some courtrooms. The county shut it down for being structurally unsound after the Whittier Quake of '87. Now even the illegals from the Placita church won't go inside."

"Why not?"

"Guys who spend the night there say it's haunted. They hear chanting, chains rattling, the usual spook stuff."

"You believe that?"

Charlie shook his head emphatically, his lips curled in a sneer.

"I sure don't. I don't believe in any of this stuff. *Santería, palo mayombé,* voodoo, this weird *ñáñigo* shit we're dealing with. It's all fake. Human attempts to put a face on the unknowable, which, by definition, cannot be understood and, if ever you get a glimpse of it, is undescribable. If there's any haunting to be done around here, it should be right at that parking lot next to the Whitebread but I've never heard of anything there."

"Why? What happened there?"

"That would be the original *camposanto* of Los Angeles."

"You forget I don't do Spanish."

"In plain English, that was the first cemetery for the pueblo of Los Angeles after it finally settled down away from the banks of the Los Angeles River. That's why it's practically next door to La Placita Church. Our good town fathers paved it over sometime at the turn of the century but I'll bet you there's still a whole bunch of old Mexicans just a few feet under the pavement there. This place is like Rome. We're walking on bones all the time. The difference is here nobody knows."

"Or cares."

"Or cares. Anyhow, let's go back to 100."

He mouthed the last handful of popcorn, scrunched up the bag, and tossed it into the garbage can across the room in a perfect basket.

"Charlie, are you okay? Didn't you hear? We've been assigned to 247!"

"Yeah, and I want you to paper the judge. Mathews had me banned from his courtroom years ago. Said I was a disgrace to my profession and an insult to my race, whatever that is. He didn't like my comments about him in the *Daily Journal.*"

"That good?"

"I just said he was fixated on the sex life of young girls. It was a child prostitution case and I was defending the pimp. Mathews wouldn't recuse himself even though his own granddaughter had been one of the original MacMartin child abuse kids. Let me tell you, he really hated it when the jury came back after twenty minutes with a not guilty on all counts. Let's see where His Majesty sends us next."

Charlie was right; Strummer glared at me balefully when I told him I'd be filing a motion to seek another magistrate. Luckily for Charlie, Strummer was kowtowing to County Supervisor María Medina, who had walked in during a break in her jury service to see how the county's funds were being expended. Strummer barked a few words at Gil, his senior clerk, then continued talking with the diminutive Medina, as wide as she was tall, dressed in a red as fiery as her diatribes against the white man's establishment.

Gil, ever the picture of fastidious efficiency, never a paper clip out of order on his pristine desk, returned promptly with the fateful file.

"Have fun," he said, handing me the discovery papers I'd been fighting for. "You can walk this yourself to Judge Winger in Department 230."

I looked at the envelope, stamped "Sealed Grand Jury Proceedings—Do Not Open," stunned by Gil's casualness.

"I know you won't open it, right, counsel?" said Gil, winking, then he turned his back to us and glided into Strummer's chambers. I never knew he hated the judge so much.

Charlie grabbed me by the elbow, steered me outside.

"Let's go kid, *para luego es tarde,*" he whispered.

"There you go again."

"Put it another way, keep your head down and your butt low when the shit is flying," he replied, opening the door.

This time the media was ready and the glare of the news cameras blinded me as the reporters surrounded me, waving their mikes like so many fishing poles, angling for a bite.

"Rita, what's going on with Charlie's case?" asked the Channel 9 bimbo, who planted herself in front of me, sticking out her elbows like bat wings, blocking the view for all the other cameras. "Is it true he's been making animal sacrifices to win the case?"

I must have looked aghast, for she whispered, apologetically, "My news director insisted I ask you the question."

"Well, is it true?" she pressed on, in a louder voice.

I looked down the hall at Charlie, who again had slipped away unnoticed and was entering the exit stairwell. He waved the case file in the air, then jerked his thumb upstairs to let me know he'd join me in Department 230. I composed myself, hoping the circles under my eyes would not show through my makeup, and stood as straight as I could in my heels, every inch the offended princess of the law.

"I don't think I will dignify that question with an answer. My client is not on trial for his religious practices, if that's what you're asking and assuming those are his religious beliefs. I don't practice *santería*. Neither does Mr. Morell. We believe the evidence will show Mr. Morell is completely innocent of the charges, which are baseless and without a scintilla of credibility—as regards Mr. Morell. Now, if you will excuse me, I have a case to try."

I moved outside the circle, hoping someone would pick up the lead. KTLA's Stan Chambers asked the question I wanted to hear:

"Miss Carr, does that mean you believe the evidence points to someone else in particular?"

I stopped in my tracks—dramatically, I hoped.

"Well, three people, perhaps more, have died as a consequence of the activities of a nefarious cult that has taken hold in the highest levels of government. I believe there is a conspiracy to make my client the scapegoat, the sacrificial victim, if you will, and I will not allow that to happen."

Now the hubbub really broke; they all smelled blood and their questions came barking out:

"What sort of conspiracy are you talking about?"

"Who's involved in that conspiracy?"

"What is this cult?"

"Why is everybody after Charlie?"

But again it was Chambers who asked the question I most wanted to leave hanging in the air: "Does that mean you believe the prosecution is involved in a conspiracy against your client?"

This was my turn and I wrung every little drop of juice out of it.

"You are the reporters. You ask yourselves, who stands the most to gain from this connection? This is an auto-da-fé, a political lynching, and I will not let my client be slaughtered on the altar of District Attorney Phil Fuentes. Now, if you'll excuse me, I have a client to defend."

The questions kept popping but if there's something I've learned from Hollywood it's always leave them begging for more. So I pushed my way through and out to the stairwell, the lights of the cameras following me into the stairs. I hustled up, then stopped at the fourteenth-floor landing to catch my breath, hoping it had all worked.

"What do you want, counsel?" came a voice from above.

I looked around frightened, then located the source—a speaker and video camera perched in the corner above the security door to the inmates' interview room.

"I beg your pardon?"

"You're leaning on the doorbell. Please step away, counsel," said the deputy's voice. "You're interfering with our operation."

"Sorry," I said, walking up the other flight of stairs to the fifteenth floor, readying myself to really gum up the works.

"S o   T E L L me, Mr. Morell, how did you manage to convince the District Attorney's office to grant you OR status? When I was a DA we would have never done that."

We were sitting in Judge Winger's chambers, a utilitarian office with built-in bookcases and city view. Two marble busts, the kind sold at garage sales and museum shops, were set at opposite ends of Winger's desk, as though to give a hint of his personality: John Milton, his blank eyes still dreaming of paradise lost; and an owlish William Shakespeare.

"I can answer that, Judge," said Mike Cleary, shifting in his seat, fiddling with his thick horn-rimmed glasses.

"Our office felt that given Mr. Morell's lack of a criminal record, and the distinct possibility that this case might not go to trial otherwise, that justice would be best served by allowing Mr. Morell to remain free on his own recognizance pending the outcome of the trial. I should add that this kind of situation is unusual but certainly not unheard of."

"Humph," garrumphed Winger, his tiny body rocking inside the large, padded chair. "I suppose it's none of my beeswax what kind of deals the prosecution cuts with an accused murderer outside the courtroom. But in my courtroom everything goes through me, is that understood?"

We all nodded. He might have been frail, his hands occasionally trembling from the onset of Parkinson's disease, but Winger was still a bench officer to beware of. As a prosecutor back in the 1960s he had handled the Bobby Kennedy assassination, putting Sirhan Sirhan away in record time; as a Superior Court judge in the 1970s he had subpoenaed President Nixon to testify about his knowledge of break-ins at the L.A. Democratic party office; in the 1980s he'd won a mano-a-mano with Chief Daryl Gates over a rash of police brutality cases in South Central. Winger had handled more capital cases than any sitting judge in the county and he was beyond the reach of political pressure because he was dying and he knew it. He handled only one or two cases a day but those had his full and awesome attention.

"Yes, Judge," said Mike, "but in this case—"

"I would still like you to answer my question, Mr. Morell," interrupted Winger, his soft voice barely audible over the racket of a clerk pushing a cartful of files down the hall. "Had not the District Attorney's office offered you this deal, would you have come back to the jurisdiction?"

This was a trick question—for if Charlie said the wrong thing or crossed Winger in any way, as the judge assigned to the case, he could instantly revoke the OR status and remand Charlie.

But Charlie grinned, ran his hand over his head as though he still had hair, then he leaned forward to the edge of his chair.

"Judge, you're asking me if I would have remained a fugitive in Cuba for the rest of my life, since there is no extradition treaty between the two countries, and, in such a case, would I have flouted the laws of the United States and my sworn duties as an officer of the court?"

Winger nodded his egg-shaped head in assent, picked at a scab on his face.

"Yes, I guess I am asking you that."

"That is a hypothetical, sir, that might tend to incriminate me but I will answer all the same: I would have tried to find a compromise that would have allowed me to return to this country and mount the most vigorous defense possible to these scurrilous, baseless accusations, as I am completely innocent of these charges."

Winger peered hard at Charlie for a moment over the rim of his glasses, his outsized doll eyes made even larger by the ampli-

fication of the lenses. I am sure he was troubled, like I was, by
Charlie's way of phrasing things, so that you never knew what
was real and what was not, the funny and the ironic always
marching hand in hand with the serious and the earnest, like
some weirdo Zen master telling people to describe the sound of
one hand clapping.

"Well, I'm glad to hear that, sir," Winger finally drawled out.
"No matter what the charge, there's nothing worse than a man
who refuses to acknowledge his responsibilities, who runs away
rather than face his accusers. Ours is not a perfect system, God
knows, but we do impart our modicum of justice."

"Amen to that," I said.

All three men looked at me. I laughed nervously, threw up my
hands. "I mean, that's what we're here for, Judge. Mr. Morell has
denied all the charges and we believe he is the subject of a political vendetta on the part of the prosecution—"

"Judge, I object strenuously to that!" thundered Mike, his
cheeks flushing, moving as awkwardly as if he'd sat on a thumb-
nail. "That is un-germane, unproven, and unfair and I—"

"Enough!" bellowed Winger. We all fell silent. He removed his
glasses, wiped his lenses with his ample flower print tie, the kind
last seen on men's chests sometime back in the Jimmy Carter era.

"We are not here to investigate political conspiracies," he said,
so softly we all craned forward to hear better. "I will not turn this
into another legal disaster like a certain celebrity trial that shall
go nameless. If an allegation is made, it better be relevant and
corroborated by the facts. I do not allow speculation the smallest
toehold in my courtroom and I hope everyone understands because I hate to repeat myself."

We all nodded again. Winger slipped his glasses back on, the
better to see his quarry.

"That being said, I do believe there is something spacious
about the allegations of impropriety based on the grand jury investigation . . ."

He mumbled a few more words.

"Excuse me, Judge, did you say spacious?" asked the court reporter, Francesca Monet, bent over her steno machine, shaking her feather cut out of her face. Winger glared at her, annoyed.

"I said suspicious," his voice barely a decibel louder. "Because there might be a connection between the cases Mr. Morell has previously handled, specifically the Díaz matter, and the instant case, I will go over the transcript of the grand jury proceedings and I will make those parts available to the defense that I deem relevant."

He looked at his watch, then back at us.

"You can all go get a coffee or something. Be back in a half hour."

"Judge, the transcript of the proceedings is over four hundred pages!" complained Mike.

Winger shrugged.

"I took Evelyn Wood's speed reading course before I passed the bar, young man, and it has served me well all these years. I can sift through the shit pretty quickly, if you get my drift."

"Excuse me again, Judge," said Francesca, is that 'sift through the swill' what you said?"

Winger's eyes fell on the glyphs spewing out of the machine which would one day become the official record of this conference.

"That is exactly what I said, Miss Monet. Thank you. So I will see you all here at eleven."

"¡*MISTER CHARLIE*! *¿Cómo ha estado?*" blared the short, henna-haired woman at the steam table in the CCB cafeteria, putting down her ladleful of grits to shake Charlie's hand. They indulged in long, loud squawks of Spanish while I stood there, tray in hand, trying to get some breakfast.

"Excuse me but my eggs are burning!" I finally exclaimed,

forcing her to turn back to the griddle and flip my scorched eggs onto a clean plate, scooping up a pile of hash browns, sausages, and bacon strips, which she piled on top.

"I didn't ask for this."

"You Charlie friend, no problem," she said, then shouted something at the cashier, who let out a little yelp of joy when she spotted Charlie and came running from behind her register, giving Charlie a killer Latin bear hug. Charlie beamed and hugged her back, then rattled off even more Spanish. I picked up my tray and took it to the counter but the cashier, running back, waved us through.

"No charge today, Charlie friend," she said.

While Charlie finished his lengthy hellos, I walked to the last table in the L-shaped elbow of the room, facing the cinder block retaining walls around the corner of Broadway and Temple, a poster of a Southern veranda hanging askew over our little Formica table.

I was happily inhaling the side dish of grits when I thought, Oh, how cute, the artist who did this drawing put in a bug on the porch, one of those palmettos the South is famous for. Then I realized that was a real live roach I was staring at. Before I could grab a napkin to crush it, the roach scuttled away around and then under the gleaming chrome frame of the picture. Suddenly I lost my appetite. But Charlie took one of my strips of bacon, straightened out the picture frame and sat down opposite me.

"Why the reception?" I asked him. "You get them out of jail?"

"Better. I got them all green cards when the previous manager tried to run them all off, saying they were illegals. They were only trying to unionize, so we put an end to that real soon. Now they're dues-paying members of the SEIU and proud of it."

He leaned back against the wall, seeming to stare at the dying potted ficus dropping its leaves in the corner.

"It never changes, does it, this pattern of exploitation? Nobody cares that there's always someone out to screw somebody else."

"It's the way of all flesh, Charlie," I said. "What's that saying, every time a friend of mine does well I hurt a little? Imagine with strangers."

"I don't know. This is going to sound naïve but I always ask myself why is that? Why must it be so? Why is there injustice in this world? Especially when it's within our reach to stop it. Why?"

I shrugged, sipped my weak coffee. "What can I say, Charlie. Why is the earth round, why is the sky blue? That's just the way it is. First let's solve our own problems and then we'll tackle humanity's."

Charlie shook his head, popped another piece of bacon in his mouth.

"Did you hear about that study they did on the foods people crave? They found out it's not true that women all over the world crave chocolate, like American women. In Spain and Italy, for instance, women are immune to chocomania. It's all culturally conditioned."

"Great, Charlie, I'll bring that up at my next Jenny Craig session. Now let's talk about what we are going to do if Winger rules against us. I was thinking of bringing up the Cotton Club case. As I recall, there was a declaration against self-interest there as well that—"

Charlie stood up, brought his face right next to mine.

"Don't you see?"

"What? Your big nose?"

"I'll admit it's not the prettiest but that's not what I'm talking about. I'm saying forget legal maneuvers. If we play by their rules, we'll lose."

"Are you trying to get me disbarred?"

"No, but I am saying that we've been conditioned to stay inside the box and now we have to go outside it."

"That's a nice thought, Charlie, but it doesn't mean a thing. We don't know what's inside the report."

"You're going to like this. I took a peek at the grand jury transcript. I couldn't open it because of the red tape sealing it. But I saw who the adviser was."

"Who?"

"Phil Fuentes."

Lucidity fell around me like a bell jar, vibrating with the full blast of the truth.

It all made perfect sense. That's why Fuentes had been playing games with us, that's why he had allowed Charlie to come back and stay OR, that's why he wasn't going to let him off the hook. At least not yet.

"So that's the reason he got a grand jury convened," I said. "It was an investigative grand jury, not an indicting grand jury. That's why there was no indictment!"

"Bingo."

"Well. That's good to know. Unfortunately, we're still flying in the dark since we don't know what's inside the report. Too bad you couldn't open it."

"I did the next best thing."

"What's the deal?"

"I read the jacket. Fuentes had a law clerk who helped him run the grand jury. I figured she would be practicing by now and lo and behold, a couple of calls to the State Bar while you were arguing in court and I confirmed she has indeed joined our wonderful fraternity."

He handed me his business card, his handwriting a chicken scratch fit for a med student.

"Jill what?" I asked.

"Jill Greene. She's at Crutcher, Dunnings & Blain. I took the liberty of pretending I was your assistant Jon and I rang her up. She's only a junior associate so she's delighted to know you're thinking of her as partner material."

"You told her what?"

"Hey, I had to say something to get her attention. It's only a lunch. Bill me. Twelve-thirty at Café Pinot."

I pushed my plate away, got up.

"This is one hell of a way to fight a case."

"Don't look at me. I've always said grand juries are unconstitutional. Go ask Bill Clinton."

"I'll pass on that."

We walked out the back exit, past the potbellied security guard at her card table by the door, reading *Telenovelas en Español*. Charlie shook hands with me by the elevators.

"I think it's better if I face Winger alone," I said. "I'll tell him you had to go home and take your medication. Prozac okay?"

"Oh, Zoloft, Prozac, whatever suits your fancy. They all think I'm crazy anyhow."

"That's why I'm doing this. You know. Always use your opponent's misreading of the situation to your advantage."

"I've been there."

The clothes on his body seemed to hang as loosely as an inmate's garb as he waved goodbye, and I thought maybe his enemies were not so wrong about his condition after all. I had to ask him.

"Listen, I know you told me about the running and the fasting and stuff but, you don't have AIDS, do you?"

"Don't think. Not according to the last test I took."

Just then the elevator doors opened and Charlie's expression froze into the saddest mien I had ever seen on a man—not like he had seen a ghost but like he had seen a sin.

Standing, equally frozen inside the empty elevator, was his son, Julian. They stared at each other in silent shock, their equally hazel eyes locked on each other, like they were expecting the other to raise his hand and they were already bracing for the blow.

The doors began to close, but Charlie ran his hand in front of the photo sensors and they slid open again.

"Come on out, son," said Charlie, finally. "There's nothing to be afraid of."

Julian stepped out into the foyer. A handful of harried passengers walked around him and climbed in, the doors slamming shut like a guillotine snap. The two men still stared at each other,

Julian's face taut with tension, Charlie's burdened with pain.

"How have you been, Julie? I've tried calling you a couple of times in Berkeley but you weren't home."

Julian glanced down at his shoes, shrugged.

"I went back to stay with Mom for a while until they asked me to testify here." He glanced up, made a face.

"What's with the hair, Dad?"

"I needed a change. Lots of things are different now."

"It's not you."

"What is. So, how are the DAs treating you? They put you up in a nice hotel?"

Julian's face lit up. "Yeah, Shutters, by the beach, I can go surfing now every morning."

"Well, make sure they pick up the tab for everything."

A grunt of assent.

"Listen, Jules, if there's one thing I've taught you is that you have to do what you think is right."

"That's what I'm doing, Dad."

"I understand. You're wrong in what you think of me and I intend to prove it to you. But I know how this looks from the outside. That time when I was up in Palmdale—"

"Charlie, I really don't think you should talk to him anymore," I said, pulling Charlie by the arm. "He's the people's witness and they might see this as harassment."

"Harassment? Talking to my own son?"

Charlie was suddenly indignant, playing the sorry father instead of the canny lawyer. "Since when is that against the law? I'm not harassing you, Jules, am I? Am I?"

Charlie reached out, touched Julian on the shoulder but the boy recoiled from the touch, as if horrified.

"Get your fucking hands off me, Dad! You're a murderer!"

Charlie stood still, shuddered, breathing hard, as Julian lurched backward, his backpack dropping off his shoulder.

"I don't want to be caught up in this! You're a homicidal maniac! You're evil, Dad, I never want to see you again! Get away from me!"

Julian's screams drew the attention of the guards and deputies by the registration desk, who hurried in our direction.

"What's going on here? What's the commotion about, Rita?" asked Deputy Brightly, rushing over. "Do we have a situation?"

"It's okay," I said, trying to control the scene. "It's the kid, he got excited."

Charlie stepped back, raised his hands up in the air as though to show everyone he had no weapon and meant no harm. Julian reeled, trembling from fear, then he spun on his heels and raced to the glass doors at the south side of the building and ran out, away from his father. Charlie stared at him until he could no longer see him, then he turned and walked out the north door, to the Temple Street side, putting the whole CCB between him and the frightened boy who saw the light of death in his father's eyes.

16

"THE WHOLE thing was a travesty, if you ask me."

Jill Greene pierced the chicken wing with the tines of her fork, playing with the remains of her meal. All around us, in the courtyard full of round, white-draped tables, executives from downtown firms sipped their espressos, swigged the last drops of their San Pellegrino, tossed their last wisecrack before returning to the tyranny of their desks.

Short, zaftig, with her brown hair in a bob cut, Jill suffered
from the usual delusion of young associates at big downtown law
firms—that if they had the right connections they could make
partner by the time they turned thirty. Partnership in an outfit
like mine, though, just might be the kind of lateral move that
would place her ahead of the pack a few years down the line
when she rejoined the universe of big law firms. In other words,
she thought she was using me, while, of course, it was she who
was being used.

Not a pretty world, this law business.

"Why do you call it a travesty?" I asked, sipping my jasmine
iced tea, trying not to think of the untouched mound of crispy,
ultra-thin fries which had come with my grilled salmon.

"Because it seemed like Phil didn't really care about getting a
consistent narrative, or even finding out much about the senator's
last days. Look, can I be frank here?"

She leaned on the table, round cheeks flushed.

"Sure, this is just between us." I couldn't bring myself to say
girls.

"Here's the scoop. I think Phil was actually trying to cover his
own ass."

She sat back, nodded at her own sagacity. I shook my head,
playing my part to the utmost.

"No! What makes you say that?"

"Simple. When one of the grand jurors passed a note saying she
wanted to know more about how Fuentes had handled the Díaz
case and if he had any information linking the senator directly to
Díaz, Fuentes shut her down but fast. He told her they were just to
look into a possible murder but that there was nothing to indicate
the senator ever knew Díaz personally and that he, the adviser,
would tell them what was a proper question or not. Never mind
that Decker's daughter was still fighting extradition over those murders. That wasn't even mentioned, much less alleged."

"So what did you find out?"

All of a sudden Jill turned coy, swizzling the tea in its frosty glass.

"You know that's confidential."

"C'mon, partner, you won't talk to me?"

That did the trick. Nothing like a blatant appeal to self-interest to breach the walls of secrecy.

"We had testimony from his psychiatrist, and he'd been interviewed by the detectives on the case. This is where it gets mighty interesting, if you know what I mean."

"Go ahead."

"Well, it seems the doctor, Dr. Kevin Schwartz, I think it was, he advertises in *Los Angeles* magazine, he's got an office out in the Marina? Well, he'd been treating the senator for bouts of severe depression. It had gotten so bad Schwartz had called the police to report him."

"That explains his suicide, he was a danger to himself."

"No, no, no. It was the other part of the warning."

"You mean he was a danger to the community?" I asked, referring to the clause that allows psychiatric authorities in California to hold somebody in custody for observation against their will for forty-eight hours when they pose a threat of suicide . . . or homicide.

"Bingo. You know a doctor only does that as a last resort, when they think their own tush is going to get burned."

"Like the Menéndez brothers, what's-his-face."

"Exactly. Schwartz had been treating Senator Decker for five years too, so that had some credibility. Well, it turns out that the doctor called 911 from his home, which is in an unincorporated area out in the Marina, which is covered by the County Sheriff's. They sat on his report for two weeks before finally sending it on to their people up in Lancaster. So what happened? By the time it finally registered, the senator had hung himself."

"Hanged," I said, mindlessly correcting her.

"That too. Turns out the Sheriff's report mentioned that the senator was delusional, but that he was also afraid someone was

going to kill him. Listen to this. He told the doctor he had participated in some weird religious rite and he couldn't get the
screams of the victims out of his head."

"Whoa," I said, but Jill needed no further encouragement, she
was off and running.

"I thought, great, this'll really make for something. Because the
case had been pretty dull up to then, usual coroner, witness,
blah, blah. But you know what? Phil never even wants to call the
doctor, says he wasn't going to legitimize a sick man's ravings. In
the end when the doctor did testify, all he was allowed to talk
about was the drug treatment the senator was under and how depressed he'd been in his final days. That was it. Phil never asked
him what he was depressed about, never called the detectives
who took the report."

"You saw the report?"

"Hell, yeah, it was right there in the narrative. Oh, there's our
waiter. Gianni!"

Jill ordered a crème brûlée while flirting with our Mexican-
passing-for-Italian server. I smiled and pondered what she'd just
told me. If the report was sealed along with the rest of the grand
jury proceedings that meant I'd never be able to see it unless
Winger ordered it released. Even then, it was highly unlikely that
any court would let me introduce it into evidence without more
corroboration. It was all pretty useless hearsay, but it did point to
other interesting avenues of investigation. Only I didn't have time
to start digging up any new information, I was due back at
Winger's courtroom by three o'clock. Whatever I was going to
find out, I had to get it now.

"Do you remember the name of the officer who took the report?" I asked Jill.

"Gee, I don't know. Red, rojo, something like that in Spanish."

"Rojas?"

"Yeah, that's it. Phil wouldn't let him talk either, kept him waiting outside in the hall for two weeks until he finally got fed up
and walked. He never returned."

I nodded, trying not to disclose my cards. Rojas was the name of the detective who wouldn't even come to the door when Danny called. What was going on here? Who was behind all this? And most important, how could this conceivably save Charlie's ass?

"So tell me, Rita," said Jill, wringing the lemon peel into her demitasse, "what kind of salary are we talking about?"

"In my outfit?"

"That's right."

"Well, if you come in as partner, obviously fifty percent of net proceeds. Last year I billed four hundred fifty, netted three seventy-five, so you do the math."

Jill nodded, her lower lip sticking out and her eyebrows raised in approval—or so I thought.

"That's nice. But what about a 401K? You gotta have a 401K, ride this stock market right now. You do offer one, don't you?"

Damn if that's not when I recalled that old saying on Wall Street: Bears make money, bulls make money, pigs get slaughtered.

"Of course, Jill, I'm working on it."

"That's good to know," said Jill, stirring the six dollar cup of double espresso Charlie was going to get billed for.

She added, almost but not quite as an afterthought, "By the way, you did know that Phil called your dad as a witness before this grand jury?"

DAD WAS on his throne. Maybe I should say in his pulpit, since every time I entered his courtroom I always felt like I should genuflect. Or at the very least cross myself for protection.

That was the intention, originally, of the architects: to make us mere humans, with our foibles and our foolishness, stand or sit, as the case might be, in awe of the majesty and grandeur of the federal government as represented in its imposing halls of justice. Thus the fifty-foot-high ceilings, the three-hundred-foot-wide courtroom, the friezes, Doric pillars, humongous federal seal with its hungry eagle gripping arrows by its talons.

It's a cheap trick, done since time immemorial by all civilizations: the Assyrians in Nineveh, the Egyptians in Luxor; the Romans and the Greeks with their temples and mausoleums, the Christians with their cathedrals, and most recently, the Nazis at Heidelberg. The worst part is that I was aware of all this but I still felt an overwhelming desire to kneel after sitting for a few minutes at the high-backed pews in my daddy's courtroom. I guess you can't take the Catholic out of this girl, after all.

"I'm not going to rule on that now," said my father, addressing the two teams of attorneys fighting over the penalty enhancement the U.S. Attorney's office was seeking for a trio of alien smugglers captured near San Diego.

"This has to be charged conduct, which it is not. And even if it were, though the facts surrounding the death of María Cordón are unusual, it would have to be proven that she died as a result of the smuggling. I'm not inclined to rule that if somebody dies during the course of a smuggling operation, under other than usual circumstances, that such death is an enhancement to the smuggling regardless of the degree of involvement of the accused."

I'll say this for my dad, he always knows how to play the judge. Dressed in his robe, sitting up straight in his padded chair, formulating his sentences in long and complex yet entirely lucid and logical structures, with a nuance for language and precedent, he could have been a proconsul or some minor official of a colonial power. I know that sounds like admiration mingled with resentment, but that has always been my relationship with my father. He is not a cold man but he is deliberately aloof, expecting a certain dignity of treatment from the world. And this was even before he became God's own prophet, i.e., a federal judge.

"That's a pretty strong tentative," said my father, who now let his majestic eyes swoop down and spotted me sitting in the last row. He glanced at the clock above the red-leather-lined courtroom doors.

"And now, if there are no further questions, we will be in recess for the rest of the afternoon."

The clerk at the desk below the bench closed his book, the reporter took off his mouth the funnel he used to repeat every word said in the courtroom into his tape recorder, the attorneys scooped up their ostrich skin briefcases, and my daddy waved me over.

I followed him down the hall into his chambers, an ornate, wainscoted place the size of my bungalow that would have done Mussolini proud. He carefully took off his robe, perched it precisely on the mahogany coat rack, then gave me the perfunctory peck on the cheek, after which he sat down at his pristine, immaculately arranged desk.

I sat on the Chesterfield leather couch while he turned on KUSC. A Saint-Saëns symphony played, safely and tastefully under control.

I wanted to scream.

I again asked myself what I was doing there, how I could be such a glutton for emotional punishment and what my mother had seen in him. Maybe when he was young . . . I calmed myself down by remembering I at least had Raúl, while all he had was Kathleen.

"We missed you on Easter Sunday," he said, taking out his carefully folded brown paper bag containing the tuna-on-rye sandwich he made himself every day before setting off for work.

"Did you guys have turkey again?"

He shook his head no, took another measured bite of nourishment.

"Ham this time. We thought we should do something more befitting Kathleen's roots, since her parents were visiting. I must say they were mighty surprised to know that my only daughter did not show up for Easter supper."

"Well, Dad, you know I've never been big on rituals."

"I had noticed but one keeps hoping."

"Anyhow, you're an atheist. I still don't understand why you pay so much attention to these religious holidays."

"They're more than religious holidays, Rita. They are tradition, customs that bind us together, no matter what God we pray to."

"Or not."

"Or not, agreed."

Kathleen's folks are originally from Virginia and although they have lived in San Marino for the past forty years, they still can't seem to shake off the habits of the Hunt Country. Dad couldn't have found a more alien culture to marry into. High Episco palians, with their snooty sense of quiet refinement and blessed entitlement, are light-years away from Dad's raucous Mexican-American relations in Montebello—or Mom's equally boisterous New York Hell's Kitchen Irish.

But that was precisely the way Dad willed it. He wanted to evolve into some stilted, repressed version of what he imagined as a child the ruling class was like. He tried to shape me into his little ice princess, sending me to Miss Day's private school, Sacred Heart High School, and then on to Vassar. But I was too aware of the gap between our worlds to make that change. Besides, I like to feel my heart beat without the benefit of alcohol. That's the thing Dad chooses to ignore, that all that Waspish hauteur is made tolerable only through the wide and frequent use of the Anglo confessor, a bottle of booze. Wasps need alcohol to feel; that is why at their parties hardly anybody dances—they'd rather drink themselves into a sentimental stupor. Dad's problem, it seems to me, had always been the opposite—he is afraid of his surfeit of feelings.

"So now you're here to tell me you will grace us with your presence at next Sunday's supper, I take it."

He took his final bite, folded the foil into a square packet, then placed it back in his brown paper bag for reuse sometime later. I stared at the silver-framed picture of Dad, Kathleen, and their twin boys, Mark and Philip, with their mother's vanilla pallor and Dad's dark Mexican eyes, Dad sticking out in the middle like the gardener posing with the lady of the manor.

"I don't know, Dad. I'll see if I can make it. But that's not the reason I'm here."

"Excellent. So you are concerned about the health of your half-brothers and how they are dealing with this awful strep throat that kept them unable to eat for two days. They're much better now, thank you. It was very kind of you to ask. Antibiotics are a wonderful invention."

"I'm happy to hear that, Dad, but I'm really here to ask you why you never told me you testified before the grand jury investigating Senator Decker's suicide. It would have saved me a lot of trouble."

Dad forced himself to finish drinking his ginger ale before he finally gave me his slow, studied reply.

"I'm not going to ask you how you knew that, since it's confidential information. I only would like to know why you believe I should have broken my vow of silence and told you."

"Because I trusted you, Dad. I told you I was looking into Senator Decker's suicide because that might tie into our theory of the case, namely, that there was a conspiracy to falsely accuse Charlie of the murders. People tied in with Díaz and Decker's daughter and Decker himself. You heard me out but you didn't say peep. You could have told me you yourself gave evidence on the case. But you didn't. How deep in his pocket were you?"

Dad crossed his arms, then opened them again, played with his chrome pen and pencil desk set.

"You kids nowadays have no idea what we went through," he said, resentment coloring his words, even though his expression was as controlled as ever. "Sometimes I think we did our job much too well."

"How deep, Dad?"

He shifted in his seat, bobbing up and down as though he wanted to get up, then changing his mind again, finally settling in with a sigh that was half anger and half regret. I don't think I'd seen my father so nonplussed since the day he picked me up at the airport after Mom had died.

He looked away at the window, like guys do when they're trying to talk and deal with something emotional, as if talking at the vision before their eyes makes it easier to unload.

"Tom never got to me. But he tried. Every week he'd call me, wanting to sound me out, asking for my read on different things. How the federal government would handle whatever project he was working on, if it had any federal ramifications."

He swiveled his chair and faced me, making sure I'd hear clearly what he was about to say.

"I owed Tom Decker. He was the one who recommended me for this job. I was just a Muni judge in Pomona when he got Senator Wilson to put my name up with President Reagan."

"But I thought Decker was a Democrat?"

Dad laughed, barking almost, the contemptuous scraping sound he reserved for hyperventilating actors at Oscar time.

"My dear child, at a certain level, there is no difference between the parties. There's no real animosity between the Democrats and the Republicans, unless they're extremists like Tom Hayden or Ralph Reed and even they have learned to get along. For the record, I am a registered Independent—with Republican leanings, of course. And with this face . . ."

He gestured at his sepia skin, the shade of light caramel or watery café au lait.

"This was before Wilson became governor and started hating us Mexicans, of course. But getting back to Tom. Own me? No, he didn't. But then he didn't have to. People like him, all they want is a friendly ear, so they can pour their polished suasion. They want the number to your private line, or to be off with you at the first tee in whatever godawful golf course it is powerful people play in. But since I don't golf and I married my mistress . . ."

He paused, to let me know he was aware of the source of my resentment.

"Tom had nothing on me. But I heard him out all the same."

"That's touching, Dad, your impartiality and all, but what about the fact that Senator Decker's daughter was in federal custody, didn't that kind of smell funny to you?"

"I never discussed the matter with him. He knew my position, that I'd have to recuse myself if I was ever involved in anything regarding the case and that I would state on the record my reasons why."

"So he just talked and you listened, right?"

Dad nodded and I wondered if he was regretting the firebrand daughter he had brought into this world.

"Sometimes that's the best course of action. I'm sure you'll find out about it someday, when you grow up."

"Dad, I'm not sure when I'll ever be an adult in your eyes."

"When you begin to act like one, instead of a petulant child."

We glared at each other, repeating the same behavior that had always prompted my mom to intervene between her stubborn husband and her equally pigheaded daughter. Next on the script would have been me screaming and throwing a temper tantrum and him leaving the room with an acid remark that would sting for weeks. But now we both stepped back, dreading the confrontation.

I guess I had done some growing up after all.

"Whatever you say, Dad. I can't control your feelings but I can control mine. My apologies."

"Nothing to apologize for."

"Good. Then suppose you please tell me what you discussed with Phil Fuentes before the grand jury?"

Dad laid his long slender hands on the desk, running his fingers up and down as though he was playing the piano, then pushed himself off the desk, and walked over to his library. He pulled down a reference tome, looked something up, and re-turned to his desk, somewhat relieved.

"I had to check and make sure. Sometimes state law is slightly different. I can tell you what I said but I cannot disclose his questions."

"That will do fine. What happened?"

"Tom called me a week before he passed. Our conversation was different from previous ones, no longer about politics or culture, the kind of thing he relished. He sounded very nervous, his thoughts kept drifting. Then he said he'd found a religion. I thought he had become a born-again Christian—he was a Jew, you know—so I congratulated him for receiving Jesus. But that wasn't what he was talking about. He said he'd come across this sect of spirit worshippers, like the Zoroastrians who worship the sun, only these people worship the water.

"I asked him if this had anything to do with his daughter, who had just been extradited from Mexico. He said no but he hemmed and hawed and then he asked if I would like to come to one of their ceremonies, that a lot of people I knew would be there."

"Did he say who?"

"No. I asked him but he said if I wanted to know I should come, that I would find it supremely interesting, in his words."

"So what did you tell him?"

"I cut him off and told him I was a practicing Christian. He hung up a couple of minutes later. He seemed peeved but I wasn't about to get involved in that kind of thing. Down that road lies perdition and the devil."

I laughed. It was absurd, a man who does not believe in God believes in the personification of evil.

"That must be a figure of speech," I said.

Dad was deadly serious.

"I'm telling you, the devil does exist. I've seen him."

"What, a defendant? I would think that would make your job easier."

"Oh, no, he's never been a defendant. He's too smart to be caught like that. Criminals are just the devil's minions, the poor souls of the damned. No, the devil is always a lawyer."

"Really, Dad? You don't say. Defense or prosecution?"

He stared at me blankly. "Prosecution, I'm sorry to say. That is why I love my job—to do justice in spite of the devil."

"But you're being illogical, Dad. God and the devil go together, as you said, like horse and carriage and love and marriage. How can you have one without the other?"

"I don't know. It's a mystery to me. But it's true."

"Okay, that's my cue," I said, getting up, straightening my skirt, picking up my purse. "Well, Dad, it's been very enlightening. I take it that was all you told Fuentes about your relationship to Decker?"

Dad returned to his usual cheerful, safely ironic manner.

"Naturally. Now, you know I might not answer your subpoena, if you serve me."

"Don't worry, Dad, I don't think I'll call you. Thanks for everything."

"You're welcome, dear. Please try and come this Sunday?" he said, kissing me on the cheek by his door.

"I'll see you, Dad," I said, noncommittal to the end.

I was halfway down the hall to the elevator when I realized I'd left my pager behind. Dad's law clerk, Paul, waved me back in.

Inside, I saw the door to the bathroom open and my father's legs sticking out as he kneeled in front of the toilet, vomiting his lunch into the white porcelain bowl.

I grabbed my pager off the side table and hurried, almost running, out of my father's chambers.

"ARE YOU feeling better now, sir?"

We were the last case of the day in Winger's courtroom. It was four o'clock, the time when clerks disappear, district attorneys turn on their answering machines, and public defenders pick up their golf clubs, telling the receptionist they're out to interview witnesses at County Jail.

In ten minutes the security guards downstairs would close off all exits but one on Temple Street and, their shift ending, would be substituted by genuine Sheriff's deputies. In a half hour the elevators would refuse to lurch up past the fifth floor and the entire Superior Court would shut down for the night. But there we were, the five of us—judge, prosecutor, defense attorney, client, and court reporter—holding down the fort. Winger's court trial had just concluded and the unlucky defendant, still in civilian clothes, had been hauled off to lockup after handing his tie, belt, wallet, and keys to his simpering attorney, who'd been unable to get him off.

"Much better, Your Honor," said Charlie. "I find I have a sunnier disposition when I remember my medication."

"I know what you mean, sir," replied Winger, his voice raspy and mumbled. "When my wife passed away last year I too had to resort to some of the products of pharmacopoeia to stabilize my grip on life."

The judge stopped talking for a moment, then hung his head low, almost whispering to himself.

"God knows how I would have coped if not for that."

The reporter strained to hear and did not write that down.

"But the past is another country, like the Bard said," continued Winger, bobbing his head up and down to signal that although he might be down he certainly was by no means out.

"Let us now deal with our present and the headaches of the day. Which are certainly abundant in number for you, Mr. Morell. It's a good thing I had a court trial ready so I wouldn't waste the court's time, otherwise I would have imposed some sanctions, medication or no. Hear me well now, for I hate repeating myself. My name is not Ito. I will not have that kind of gamesmanship in my court. The next person who tries that better pack a toothbrush for he—or she—will need it in County Jail."

He waved the transcript of the grand jury proceedings in the air like it was a smelly sock.

"As regards this evidence, I have reviewed the record and I am ready for arguments."

Charlie and I looked at each other, surprised. Ordinarily judges issue their rulings on sealed material without hearing from the defense attorneys or even without explaining their reasons, other than the perfunctory reason of confidentiality. But Winger went one step beyond.

"I'd particularly like to hear again from the District Attorney's office as to why this transcript should not be unsealed and if so, which are the sections that should be redacted to preserve the presumed confidentiality of the document."

Mike Cleary blinked repeatedly, pulled on his glasses like they were hurting the bridge of his nose.

"Well, Your Honor," he stammered, getting to his feet. "If it please the court, I would like to make my arguments in chambers to preserve the confidentiality."

"Nothing doing," snapped Winger. "I want this on the record. The public record, sir, so speak up."

Mike turned this way and that, as though expecting help from some unseen or invisible quarter. Charlie cocked his head, leaned back casually in his chair, like a man about to witness a nice cockfight or a walking circus dog.

"Well, sir, the reason is simple. There is no proven nexus between the findings of the grand jury and this case. It's not relevant."

"That grand jury didn't make any findings, counsel," whispered Winger. "As to the relevancy, that's what I would advise you to argue right now. I should say I find it odd that your office would have gone to all this trouble to keep under wraps the particular information that these proceedings contain."

But then Mike found his stride: "With all due respect, sir, the proceedings are sealed and not a part of them is to be disclosed. There is a court order to that effect and I will be glad to explain the reasons why in camera, if Your Honor doesn't understand."

I shook my head. That was a bad move. Condescension, a common weakness of prosecutors, doesn't play well with judges with nothing to lose.

"Oh, I understand plenty what you have done here, sir. Under the thin pretext of looking into the deplorable death of a prominent member of our community one gets the impression you have made disappear certain evidence that might not be in the best interests of your office."

"You Honor, please, this is an open record!" whined Mike.

I had to stand up. "Your Honor, I would now petition the court to disclose what the evidence is that was concealed, so that proper sanctions be imposed for prosecutorial misconduct. I again ask the court to release the transcript so we know what we are dealing with. If there is evidence that is material to the case, my client has a constitutional right to know—and the prosecution the obligation to disclose the exculpatory material."

Winger spun his chair around, staring at me like I was some sort of curious insect that had just flown into his court. I sat down. Winger searched for his microphone, turned it on, blew into it to make sure it was indeed on, then spoke as forcefully as he knew how, his words echoing in the deserted courtroom.

"Counsel, let the record be perfectly clear that I never said there was exculpatory material in this transcript. I said *certain* material. If I knew it would absolve your client, I would release it on my own motion. But I haven't reached that degree of certainty about the character of the evidence."

This was getting on my nerves. I shot up again. It was time to lay all the cards on the table or risk losing everything out of misguided caution.

"Judge, what exactly are you talking about here? We already know that the grand jury interviewed not only the investigators on the case but also the senator's personal physician, servants, and friends, all of whom might have given information that would help Mr. Morell. Granted, we could interview these people ourselves, perhaps even compel their testimony. But our point is, we are sailing in the dark without a compass, trying to reach harbor and we don't know if ahead lies a safe port or reefs that will shatter our craft."

Winger blinked. Even I was surprised at my sudden rapture. The last time I was on a boat I was ten and I got sick to my stomach, so I don't know where the sailing analogy came from.

"Meaning?" asked Winger.

"How can I possibly guide my client if I don't know where we're going? Release the information and let the ultimate trier of fact, the jury, decide if the evidence is exculpatory or not."

"Your Honor, Miss Carr is forgetting we have rules of evidence in this state," countered Mike. "She is requesting privileged information."

"Which could exonerate my client."

"Hardly," sniffed Mike.

"Then let us see it, let us touch it, let us smell it. What kind of proceeding is this where one side holds all the cards and the other none?"

"I tell you what I'm going to do, counsel," said Winger, a glimmer of a smile for the first time on his thin, peeling lips. "I want to hear from the man who advised this grand jury proceeding, I want to hear his reasons why he requested it be sealed."

"But Your Honor, you know who that is!" squealed Mike.

Winger sneezed, blew his nose in a yellow handkerchief he took from his shirt pocket.

"I'm aware of that, Mr. Cleary. But in the eyes of the law we are all equal. And I am the law in this courtroom. So tell District Attorney Fuentes to make himself available for sworn testimony tomorrow morning at ten. That will be all for today. This court is adjourned."

Mike threw his files into his leather case and stormed out. Charlie for once was quiet when we walked to the elevators. Mike, still waiting for his ride up, turned his back to us.

"Is Phil going to show up, Mikey?" I asked Cleary, rubbing it in.

The elevator bell tinkled. Mike strode away.

"It'll be a cold day in hell," he blurted, pushing the button to slam the elevator doors shut.

"Bundle up tomorrow, Rita," Charlie told me, squeezing my shoulder by way of goodbye, before sprinting for the stairwell, a thin sad man in white.

"Where are you going? It's eleven floors down!"

"I need the exercise. Don't forget, bring your overcoat!" he shouted, then darted out the door.

"Hell's bells!" I replied and all the elevator doors opened at once.

THAT NIGHT, even the veal scallopini at Mario's was off. The Chardonnay tasted sour, the San Pellegrino flat, the gnocchi salty and gooey. I sent my entire dinner back, sipping instead some of that wonderfully metallic L.A. tap water while I watched Raúl dig with quiet gusto into his green lasagna. He knew better than to try to talk me out of my moods. He was the total opposite of my ex-husband, Greg, who would always compound my problematic state by practically coercing me into disclosing the reasons for my mood, then dissecting them with the skill of a veteran surgeon, only to tell me in the end that I was being overly emotional over things that could easily be kept under control. That's what you get when you marry a litigator, cross questioning over your pasta.

You might think that at times like these I would want some loving affection, some understanding, a shoulder to lean on, a sympathetic face to tell my troubles to.

Wrong.

I have to work things out myself or I will not be happy. In fact, I would consider it a slight that my partner would not have enough confidence in me to let me handle my own crisis by myself. Grown-ups have to take care of grown-up problems, not go rushing to some big daddy to clean up the mess you made.

Now, I don't know if Raúl had ever thought all this through like I did, or, as I suspected, he was just one of those people with the unerring instinct for the right reaction at the right time. People like that have an uncanny empathy quotient that tells them just when to be lovey-dovey and when to stand back and say you mix it, you fix it.

That's why now Raúl attacked his pasta with such concentrated delight, occasionally bobbing his head to Bobby Darin singing "Somewhere." Nowadays every other restaurant in Silverlake is into the Swingers scene, waiting only for Frankie and the Rat Pack to step out of their graves and groove the town once more.

But eventually even Raúl had to speak, which he did sometime after his double cappuccino.

"Man, I tell you, working out makes me so hungry I could eat a cow," he said.

"It's eat a horse, Raúl. In English we eat a horse."

"That doesn't make any sense," said Raúl, who might be from Guatemala but is certainly no fool. "We don't eat horses, we eat cows."

"I don't know, that's the point, I guess."

Mario himself brought the check, placing the tray equidistant between Raúl and me. Raúl grabbed for it first.

"No, please, you just had a glass of wine and you are going to pay? I can handle this."

He peeled off a couple of fifties from a roll he carried that, yes, would have choked that horse he could have eaten that night. I giggled.

"What's so funny?" he asked defensively.

"Nothing. I was just thinking about cultures and my case."

"That's all you think about, baby."

He called Mario over with great flair and told him to keep the change. I wouldn't have given him the extra twenty but I know better than to argue with Raúl's macho tipping. It's a Hispanic thing and besides, it buys a lot of goodwill. Raúl laid his hand on mine.

"Honey," he said, oozing with sincerity, "if there's something I can do . . ."

"I know, thanks." I squeezed his hand. "It's just that I'm worried how this is all going to end. I don't know who the players are but I have a feeling they're much bigger than I imagine."

"You think Fuentes is in on this?"

"People bigger than Fuentes."

"Who? The governor? Really rich people?"

"I don't know. Could be."

"And you think these people are going to do what?"

"I don't know, that's the thing. Of course they can't do anything now because that would lend credibility to our conspiracy theory. Their best hope is that Charlie will lose and this whole case will go away."

"You're not going to let them do that, are you?"

"I thought you knew me better than that by now."

Raúl grabbed my hand with both of his, kissed it.

"I know you are the girl with the biggest heart I ever know. I'm behind you a million percent."

"Now why do you have to talk like that?" I said, smiling. I wiped the stray tear with my sleeve. Raúl moved back in his chair, his face taking on the puppy dog expression he puts on whenever I reproach him.

"I'm sorry," he said.

"You can make it up to me."

His eyes brightened, the old sparkle coming back.

"Yeah?"

"Yeah. Let's go dancing!"

• • •

S O W E paid our bill and we sailed off in my Alfa and we wound up at La Conga, where one of Tito Puente's old sidemen was playing with his new crew and the place was packed and the music was loud and I had to elbow my way to the dance floor but I didn't care. I knew I should be home preparing my questions for Fuentes but I didn't care. And I still didn't care when two o'clock rolled around and we drove down Wilshire and then to Beverly and up to my house up in Silverlake and we parked in the driveway and we made out like a couple of kids while the moon beamed down on the silvery reservoir and a handful of stars twinkled behind the great San Gabriels in the distance. And I only cared when finally we made it inside the house and we ran to our bedroom and Raúl fell on top of me, as though to drown me, licking every inch of me for his delayed dessert and then he entered me and I rocked in his arms with the spell of lust and love and hurtful need, feeling the world finally ease out of my consciousness and there was just the two of us, me and my handsome tiny titan who never seemed to tire of me until we both did tire and we fell asleep.

I T W A S about four-thirty in the morning. I had woken up after a couple of hours sleep and I was preparing the questions for Fuentes after all, sitting naked on the living room couch, as though being free of clothing would let me get to the heart of the matter and rid me of the awful anguish this case was bringing on. That's when I heard a thump. At first I thought it was my cat, Nicky, turning over the food dish again. Then I saw the lights go on in my den.

I should have woken up Raúl but it was as if something bigger than me was pushing me forward to my den—still without a stitch of clothing on, as if I were in that half dream world where you're flying over skyscrapers in your car, which then suddenly plummets.

I stood at the doorway and looked in.

A man was busy rifling through my cabinets, throwing the files around as though in a great hurry but without any concern about the noise he was making. I ran back to the living room and returned with a poker from the fireplace, waving it in front of the man.

"Who the hell are you?" I screamed at the top of my lungs. "Get out of here!"

The man, tall, dressed all in black, turned at the sound of my voice. I gasped when I saw his face—it was like a cat's, with pointed ears, fangs, and whiskers, but with eerie green eyes, a beast about to pounce. He let out a scratchy growl from his throat, then he lunged at me, leaping almost six feet across the room. I swung the poker, striking him on the shoulder with all my might. He landed on all fours, then he turned and was about to jump on me again when a shot rang out.

"Get the fuck outta here!" screamed Raúl, who fired again at the intruder.

The creature growled, then leapt out the window, crashing into the glass and landing about twenty feet below in my neighbor's yard down the hill, next to the blooming orange tree. The catman turned and snarled again, then took off running, as Raúl aimed and fired, still missing, the creature leaping across the thirty-foot yard in two bounds and disappearing into the darkened alleyways at the bottom of the hill.

17

ARE YOU sure it wasn't a mask?"

Charlie did not laugh when I told him what happened, like the cops had done when they came to my house. He did not even hint at a grin, as Raúl himself had done over coffee at Astroburgers when I insisted on my story before he left for work.

"I don't know. Raúl said he never saw the guy's face and that it all went by too fast. I realize it sounds wacky but I'm sure it wasn't a mask, it was like he was some kind of monster from some old B movie."

"Jacques Tourneur's *Cat People*. But even in that you never saw the beast."

"Well, I saw him, Charlie. I know I did. Look, I don't want to be in a Stephen King novel or a Dean Koontz story. I don't even want to be in one of your books. I'm just a Latina lawyer from L.A. I don't do this kind of witchcraft, evil spirit stuff. And I don't like it."

Charlie fixed his large eyes on me, the hazel now a bright, shiny green—like the eyes of a cat too, I thought, shuddering.

"Do you want off the case?"

I slumped in my chair. We were back in Winger's courtroom, Mike at the far left corner of counsel table, his files spread out before him. Winger's female deputy, at her desk behind us, strapped on her Beretta; the clerk hung up the phone; the judge painfully walked out of chambers with his robe open, his tie half undone.

This is the time to do it, I told myself. Charlie is out on his own recognizance, the 402 motion has not begun, the trial is probably weeks away at this rate. I am getting too personally involved. My father was a witness, my house has been broken into, my sanity is beginning to crack.

So I lose the money. I can always find another client.

"I think—"

The back doors swung open and Phil Fuentes waltzed in, flanked by his two bodyguards, with Special Counsel Tom Weinberg by his side. Like always, Phil was a dark star, sucking all the life out of the room into himself, which he then cast out from his beaming, handsome expression. Jimmy Smits as DA.

He waved at us, like a politician looking for a baby to kiss. Just then I changed my mind. No way he was going to get away with it. I was in the fight to the bitter end.

". . . I'm all right," I said, finishing my sentence. "Just nerves. Probably dreamed the whole thing. Let's get down to business, shall we?"

Charlie looked quizzically at me for a moment. He must have recognized some of the mettle I was so desperately trying to show, for he nodded, then wheeled his chair around to smile knowingly at the prosecutor's end of the table.

"Hey, Mike, I understand it's snowing outside!"

Mike sneered at us, then shook Phil's hand. The two conferred briefly and Phil swept through the gate to come shake my hand.

"Rita, pleasure to see you again," he said, pumping away.

"No, no, Phil, the pleasure *will* be mine."

Phil glanced at Charlie and for a moment you could hear the whirring in his brain, the calculations of the practiced politician: Do I shake this hand or not? What will it cost me if someone sometime finds out I was friendly to the defendant? Will I look like a sellout or a firm defender of the law who bears no personal animus? What the fuck do I do?

Fortunately for him Deputy García just then put down her phone and intoned, "Department 230 is now in session, the Honorable Irving Winger, judge presiding. Please remain seated."

Phil looked at Winger, then at Charlie, regret furrowing his brow, I believe is the expression, then he went to sit next to Mike. The judge eased into his outsized chair. Mike stood up.

"Good morning, Your Honor. As you requested, District Attorney Philip Fuentes has made himself available for the in camera on the disclosure of the grand jury proceedings. Ready when you are."

"Your Honor," I began, but Winger raised a bony hand, his pale skin almost translucent.

"Sit, counsel, I'll handle this," he said in a raspy voice. He coughed, spoke into his mike.

"Mr. Cleary, you must have misunderstood me. I have not granted nor am I going to grant an in camera on this matter. I want this on the record, not sealed again. This motion to disclose would be ill served by not being out in the open air, even if the odor of exhumation has rendered it into a witches' brew. As the

Bard would say, fair is foul and foul is fair. So, Mr. Fuentes, if you would be so kind . . ."

Winger pointed at the witness stand.

"Your Honor, I object—" began Mike but Phil shushed him, whispered in his ear, then rose with a gracious smile. Mike turned around in his seat to look at the back of the courtroom, where tall, gangly Bruce Bern of the *L.A. Times* had taken his seat, alongside Michael Harris of the *Daily Journal*.

"Certainly, Your Honor," said Phil. "After all, we're all here to do justice."

"I certainly hope so, sir," rasped Winger. Fuentes stood, walked to behind the court reporter as the clerk administered him the oath. How can he be so self-assured, I wondered. How can someone's persona be so impermeable? Just what does he have for breakfast?

"*Menudo,*" whispered Charlie.

"Excuse me?"

"I said *menudo.* I happen to know for a fact that he eats tripe soup every morning for breakfast."

"How did you know that's what I was thinking about?"

He shrugged, fluttered his thin eyelashes.

"Lucky guess."

I pushed my chair away from him, concentrating on Phil.

"My name is Philip José Fuentes. I am the District Attorney for the County of Los Angeles. I was elected to office on—"

"That's fine, Mr. Fuentes," interrupted Winger. "We recall your election. Now, Miss Carr, I realize this is a part of your 402 motion but I trust you won't be terribly disappointed if I ask a few questions first."

"Not at all, Your Honor, especially if you rule in my favor."

Winger took me seriously for a moment, then he granted himself a pained expression that lifted the corners of his lips, almost a smile, but not quite.

"We'll see. Now, Mr. Fuentes, were you advisory counsel to the grand jury charged with investigating the death by suicide of Senator Thomas Decker?"

"For the record, Your Honor, we object," Mike said perfunctorily, looking down at his notes, then at his watch, as though already we were taking too much time off his schedule elsewhere.

"This is privileged information," Mike continued. "Even disclosing the identity of the adviser is a breach of the privilege."

"Your objection is noted and overruled, counsel. Mr. Fuentes?"

"Yes, I was."

"Then, Your Honor, we would like to make a continuing objection to this entire proceeding."

"Fine. It's noted, it's overruled, and when this is done you can take it to the Court of Appeal," snapped Winger, peeved by the interruption. "Now, Mr. Fuentes, please tell us, why did you ask for this grand jury to be convened?"

"We had received information from the investigators that the senator's death might not have been a suicide. Specifically the lead detective on the case, Rafael Rojas, as I recall, suggested that there might be a connection between Senator Decker's demise and a previous case this office had handled."

"Why did you call the grand jury, when all this could have been handled by a regular coroner's inquiry?"

This is when Phil finally showed a crack, even if slight, in his façade. He shifted in his seat, hesitated, raised his right index finger to his mouth for a moment of photogenic contemplation, then he answered: "Because we were not completely confident that the information would be kept secret."

"In spite of the confidentiality of ongoing police investigations?" asked Winger.

"Well, this was County Sheriff's, sir, and yes, we were not certain that the information would not be revealed to the media or even to possible defendants. We felt a grand jury would be the best way to keep a lid on this case in a way that would allow us to investigate the death and not compromise any of our sources."

Winger, his face wrinkled by skepticism, looked at Fuentes, then he swirled his chair in my direction.

"Your witness, Miss Carr."

Just then the back doors of the courtroom opened. Charlie's son, Julian, walked in, looking sunburnt and unkempt, a day's growth of beard on him. He sat at the very last row, some distance from the reporters, slinging his backpack to the floor with a thud.

Charlie's eyes grew wide when he saw Julian, but Julian ignored him, devoting his attention to the proceedings. Mike waved at Julian, Julian waved back.

"You have to stop this," Charlie whispered urgently.

"What?"

"I said stop this motion right now!"

The others stared at us. I grinned nervously at the judge.

"May I have a moment with my client, Your Honor?"

"Certainly."

I whipped around, my nerves and my anger surging forth. I had overcome my own doubts, I was not going to allow him to surrender to his.

"Charles, you hired me, you let me do my job! I'll handle the questions."

"You don't understand—"

"I understand perfectly. I see your son back there. It's you who has to understand. They're blackmailing you. If you're innocent, like I know you are, you have to go through with this!"

Charlie grimaced, his face hardening, and for a moment I asked myself if perhaps I'd been wrong all along about him.

"I'll give you ten minutes," he said.

I stood, tried to concentrate as best I could on my questions.

"Are you ready, Miss Carr, or do you need more time?"

Phil looked superciliously at me from behind the pull-out microphone while Mike chortled into his notepad.

"Thank you, Your Honor. I am ready. Good morning, Mr. Fuentes."

"Good morning to you, Miss Carr," came the earnest reply, as though Phil had nothing better to do than answer my inane questions.

"Did your office call in my client's son, Julian Morell, to intimidate us? Is that why he's sitting in the back?"

"What?"

"To coerce us into making a deal?"

All at once a hubbub broke out—Charlie screaming at me to shut up, Mike objecting that this was irrelevant, Julian shouting he was nobody's puppet, he was there of his own accord. Winger grabbed his mike.

"Everybody, shut up!"

We all fell silent. Winger raised his chin, jerked it twice at Julian.

"What is your name, young man?"

"Julian Morell," he said, throwing himself back into his bench, crossing his arms.

"Stand up when I speak to you, sir!" warned Winger. Julian sullenly got to his feet, as Deputy García moved closer to him, her hands on her cuffs.

"Are you the defendant's son?"

"Yeah."

"Did the prosecution subpoena you to come here today?"

"I don't understand," said Julian. "Do you mean if they ordered me here? No. I'm here because I want to testify."

"Your Honor, I can explain," interrupted Mike. "Julian Morell is a witness for the prosecution. We anticipate we will use his testimony, depending on the outcome of this hearing."

"Regarding?" snapped Winger.

"Regarding the continuing investigation into the death of Senator Decker and its connection to the instant case, the murder of Olive Lane."

Winger frowned, shook his head disapprovingly.

"Counsel, I already warned you not to play these games with

the court during the pendency of this hearing. If you have him as a witness, he can certainly wait in your office without bringing him here. This gives the impression of coercion. Not to mention that his listening to any of this might taint his future testimony. Young man, please report immediately to the District Attorney's office on the eighteenth floor. Deputy García will escort you out of the courtroom. As regards you, Mr. Cleary, take out your checkbook and write out a check for five hundred dollars for contempt of court. You too, Mr. Morell. I will not have this kind of outburst in my courtroom."

"Your Honor, I wish to give notice that we will be appealing these sanctions," said Mike, even as he searched his wallet with barely restrained fury.

"Fine. But right now you are paying, sir, or your office will have to get a replacement for you, as you will be going into lockup otherwise."

Charlie pulled out a wad of hundreds, peeled off five, and handed them to the clerk. Mike examined his anemic wallet, raised his palm upward at Fuentes, who shook his head, then took out his own wallet, flashing his AmEx card.

"Plastic, Your Honor?"

Winger snatched it from his hand, tossed it at the clerk.

"It'll do. Go on with your questions, Miss Carr."

A second deputy came and occupied García's desk as she escorted Julian out.

"Thank you, Your Honor. Now, Mr. Fuentes, previously you told us there might be a connection between this case, the senator's death, and another case you'd previously handled. What was that other one called?"

"*People v. Díaz*. I don't think that's a secret; your client wrote about it in *Slipping into Darkness*."

"Please try just to answer the question, sir. Don't volunteer information. In that case of *People v. Díaz*, who was the prosecutor?"

"Ultimately the State Attorney General's office because of a conflict for our office."

"Well, before the State Attorney General's office got involved, weren't you the deputy district attorney assigned to the case?"

"Objection, assumes facts not in evidence," interjected Mike.

"Overruled. You may answer, Mr. Fuentes."

"No, I was not. Lisa Churchill was the lead prosecutor."

"But you were her immediate supervisor, were you not?"

"Yes, but I was also supervising about twenty other trials going on at the same time."

"But this Lisa Churchill was more than just another underling at the time, she was also your girlfriend, wasn't she?"

"Objection, Your Honor. Irrelevant," exclaimed Mike.

"Counsel has a point. Where are you driving with this, Miss Carr?" asked the judge.

"What I'm driving at, Judge, is that by virtue of his involvement in the Díaz case, Mr. Fuentes was aware of all the particulars of the case. And that as a result of that knowledge, he chose to convene the grand jury, to keep secret not the existence of sources or information but links that could impact on his own political career."

"Your Honor, this is totally unfounded," said Mike. "We're here to determine if a grand jury proceeding should be disclosed or not, but we are not here to assassinate the character of Mr. Fuentes. What kind of hearing is this where first we are sanctioned for having a witness in court and then we are calumnied for wanting to preserve confidentiality and privilege?"

"Last I checked this was a 402 hearing on the admissibility of the evidence," wisecracked Winger. "But counsel has a point, Miss Carr. Even assuming, arguendo, that everything you allege is true, what of it?"

"Well, if there is such a link as Mr. Fuentes alleges, then he should disclose the information and unseal the proceedings."

"Or not," deadpanned Winger. "I'll tell you what I'll do. Let me review the transcript right now in chambers in light of the information we have just received. We are in recess."

And with that Winger jumped down with more alacrity than I would have thought possible, rushing back to chambers and shutting the door behind him.

"Your Honor, is it okay if I step down?" asked Fuentes of the empty judge's chair. "Yes, of course," he replied to himself. "You're very kind."

He strolled down the stand to counsel table.

"Let's go out to my office," said Charlie, practically hoisting me off my chair, grabbing me by the elbow.

"Nice try, Rita," said Phil, waving all five fingers of his right hand at me.

C H A R L I E   A N D   I walked out of the main hallway to the emergency exit corridor and down to the emergency stairwell, where the floor's unrepentant smokers gathered for their furtive, verboten, against-county-ordinance cigarettes. Bearded public defender Frank Lehar and his *compadre,* prosecutor Ralph Williams—both jazz musicians in San Pedro in their off-hours—threw down their butts when they saw us coming.

"Fellows, if you don't mind," said Charlie.

"No problema, Charlie. How's the trial?" asked Ralph.

"That's what we have to talk about."

"It's bogus, man. Fuentes has a hard-on for you. But don't tell anybody I told you," added Ralph with a wink.

"Hey, it's confidential with me. No, stop, it's privileged information with me."

"That's the ticket," said Lehar with a chuckle as the frustrated beboppers walked out.

Charlie waited until they had closed the door behind them before he wheeled around and let me have it: "You have to stop this nonsense! I told you I'm doing all this to spare Julian. If they are going to put him on, I am pleading, you hear?"

"Charlie, control yourself!" I snapped back. "I have no intention of letting your son get on the stand. I understand your emotions but you have to give me the elbow room I need to maneuver. Don't second-guess me, otherwise, just go in right now and throw yourself on the mercy of the court. You know how much he'd be forced to give you—minimum twenty-five to life. And just look at you. You're a wreck. You wouldn't last a year in the joint."

Charlie grabbed at the rusty iron bars separating the end of the hallway from the ledge running all around the building. At the far corner I saw the carcass of a pigeon, ravaged by the marauding falcons nesting in the Civic Center.

"Don't be so sure, I'm tougher than I look. But my son is the third rail, you hear me? You've made your point with Winger, now drop the whole subject. Or you're fired."

"Is that a threat?"

"No, it's a loving promise."

He flew off, racing down the emergency stairs, the sound of his footsteps echoing like a bad dream in the stairwell, until I heard the distant blast of the street door closing. I spotted him walking at a clip, almost running, furiously down Spring, heading for the Federal Building. One of the falcons swept down from an overhang, suspended on a thermal, wheeling around, over and under the scraggly palm trees. In the distance, the Hollywood sign was barely visible through the smoggy haze. A door opened behind me.

A pale, thin, defense attorney walked out to join me.

"Is it safe here?" he said, taking out a pack of Marlboros.

"Brother, it's never safe in this building, don't you forget it."

I walked out to the hallway and sat down on the stone bench with the next jury panel, waiting for Winger's bailiff to come get me. Bruce from the *Times* had already gone, probably to have another morning beer, but hardworking Michael from the *Journal* came up to the bench, towering over me, his notepad at the ready.

"Not now, Michael, let me think things over. I'll give you a call."

"Okay, but I'm on deadline. I got to put this out by three."

"We'll talk by then."

He nodded, then scuttled away, in search of yet another piece of legal dross he could spin into headline gold. My cellular buzzed. I picked it up.

"Hey, Rita Chiquita," came the voice of my investigator. "I have good news, girl. I hit pay dirt!"

"What do you have?"

"Well, *m'hija*, you're not going to believe this but the other day I got an invitation to go to another one of those old-timers' parties, you know, an old fart like myself retiring from the Sheriff's. *No, Joel, no más chile!*"

Danny put the phone down. By the sound of it he was in his kitchen with his grandson. The phone clattered against the tile counter as Danny's stream of Spanish rose against the whirring noise of his old Osterizer blender. I looked aghast around me; across the hall, a short blond juror from the trial next door sat down on the bench, opened her shiny Coach leather bag, the kind that costs you five hundred dollars but looks like a twenty peso item from a Tijuana market, then extracted her *Daily Variety*, hiding her tanned, bored face from the crowd thronging into the courtroom. "X-EX NIX F-X" read the puzzling headline. I wondered for a moment what that meant, then Danny came back on the line.

"You're still there?"

"I'm waiting for you to tell me how we struck gold."

"Sorry, but Joel was helping me fix a *salsa chipotle* and he fixed it so hot we'd have to call in the fire department if anybody touched it. So anyways. I went to this party at Candilejas the other night, you know the place?"

In my mind's eye I saw the old watering hole on a hillside by Cal State, the venue de rigueur for those who once flirted with calling themselves Chicanos but now are safely Mexican-Americans, none of that newfangled we-are-all-Latinos stuff.

"Get to the point, Danny."

"Rita, you keep going so fast you're going to have a heart attack. Life is too short, which is what I was telling my *compadre*
Pedro Huerta, he's' now the watch commander at the East L.A.
station. So he tells me, I hear you're wanting to know what Rojas
found out about the senator's suicide. So I asked him like a *pen-
dejo,* who, me? Just to see what he would tell me. So he takes me
out back and makes me promise not to tell and all that and I say,
sure, sure, and that's when he spills the *frijoles, m'hijita.* He said
Rojas was really scared because when he got to the senator's
house and was looking around, he goes downstairs to the basement and he hears a voice. He turns on his flashlight because it
was pretty dark already and out of the shadows comes this big
cat, like a mountain lion or something. Rojas doesn't have time to
take out his weapon but he notices that this cat is mighty big and
mighty peculiar and then the damn animal stands up and he's a
man with the face of a cat! What the hell, Rojas is thinking, and
he goes for his gun and then the creature jumps out the window
and runs away in the night."

I felt chills, my stomach rose to my throat, I was in a diving
capsule plummeting into a caldera.

"I don't see how that helps us any," I heard myself say to
Danny, my voice cracking, my throat suddenly parched. "It was
just something he saw, who's going to believe it?"

"That's just what I was telling my *compadre.* I said that Rojas
should have laid off the sauce a long time ago before he retired.
But then he told me the real good news. It seems when they cut
the senator down, you know, he had peed on himself from hanging? So when the criminalist gets there, he takes off the man's
pants."

"I hope you're not going to start talking about circumcision or
penis size."

"No, no, he was normal, circumcised. Well hung. For an Anglo, I guess. But the thing is this, *m'hija,* he had a tattoo on his

inner thigh. It was the head of the same animal that Rojas saw, like a cat or something. So I thought, that's strange. I can see some youngster doing that to himself to get the ladies excited, you know, he's a beast and all that, but an old guy like that? And the next day I checked out the coroner's report—the victim in Charlie's case, she had the same thing. And you know what? The girl up in Oakland too, the one by Charlie's house, she had one too. You know, nobody pays attention to that because nowadays everybody has a tattoo. Butterflies, roses. I even saw this cute deputy with a lizard tattooed on her ankle, so—"

I cut him short. "I'm already aware of the tattoo. What's so important about it?"

"It's a white jaguar. Very rare, they tell me."

"What do you think it means?"

"Well, I know this. That's a very distinctive sign, and to have it all in the same location? *Ajuuy, m'hija,* your boy is right. There is a conspiracy, but I don't know if it's going to do him any good because—"

"Thanks, Danny, let me look into it," I said.

I cut off the call even as Danny said, "Hold it, Rita, I got more to tell you!"

I turned off the phone. I couldn't face that reality anymore. I sat there, numb, dumbfounded, exhausted. Just then the exit door to the smoking alcove opened a crack—and for an instant I saw the same feline mask, the same feral creature now lurking in that corridor, waiting for me to make a mistake.

I jumped to my feet and the door slammed closed. I ran into the corridor with my purse, taking out my gun as I ran. Something or someone was ahead of me, I could hear the footsteps, then he or she raced through the exit door and leaped up the stairs. I raced up, hearing the steps thumping ahead of me, my gun firmly gripped in both hands—past the last exit door to the nineteenth floor and then to the roof. But on the last landing the thumping disappeared and when I reached the padlocked exit door, only a black and orange cat stood in front of me, its back arched, fangs bared, snarling, then the animal sprung away and landed on the ledge around the building, through a widened opening in the bars and out to the freedom of the padlocked roof.

I slid down to the landing, shaken, drenched in sweat, panting from running up six floors, my shoes discarded somewhere along the way, my hose torn, my skirt ripped at the seam. I sat there feeling the world spin slowly by, until I finally got up and slowly made my way down. I picked up my Manolos, grabbed my purse, dragged myself out to the hallway, now empty and quiet.

The door to Winger's courtroom opened and Deputy García dashed out.

"Counsel! We've been looking for you! Everybody's here, the judge is ready to rule!"

WINGER FAILED to admonish me or even to comment on my tardiness. He merely nodded as I walked in, starting to talk even before I cleared the gate to counsel table. Phil and Mike huddled at their end, the two bodyguards slouching in the blue-felt-covered juror's chairs.

"I was starting to think you'd fled the jurisdiction too. Any idea where your client is, Miss Carr?"

"I'm 987 for the rest of today's proceedings, Judge. He . . . had a doctor's appointment."

I sat down, wiped my sweaty brow with a lipstick-smudged tissue, my last.

"Humh! You're not declaring a doubt about his condition, are you? Peculiar, yes. Eccentric, perhaps, but then who isn't? However, he seems perfectly capable of aiding in his defense."

"Oh, believe me, Judge, he is doing just that."

"That's good. In any event, I have reviewed the transcript again and in light of the information imparted to us by District Attorney Fuentes I have decided—"

"Your Honor, before we proceed, you should know we are

withdrawing our request for the transcript of the grand jury proceedings," I said.

"Excuse me?"

Winger craned forward, his beaked nose even more hawklike
than usual. Even Phil seemed astonished for once.

"This is not gamesmanship, Your Honor, but after the statements made by Mr. Fuentes and the fact that this grand jury concluded only that Senator Decker died by his own hand, I
presume?"

I looked at Phil, who nodded, no doubt puzzled by my change
of heart and wondering where I was going with all this—as I was,
for I was improvising, staked out at the far end of a branch I'd
never seen, much less walked on.

"Therefore whatever information the transcript might contain
is irrelevant to this case, since it has no bearing on the charges."

"Well, that's mighty—" began Winger. I interrupted at the risk
of contempt.

"Instead we're asking that the coroner's report be unsealed, as
well as all the other appropriate documentation surrounding the
senator's demise."

"I don't see why not, it should all be public, anyway," answered
Winger. But Mike, who'd been in a huddle with Phil, stood up.

"Your Honor, this begs the question. If the senator's death is irrelevant to the case, how then is the death certificate relevant?"

I stood up too, barefoot this time. My big toe had swollen after
stubbing it against the stairwell railing, and it was beginning to
throb painfully.

"Your Honor, my argument is that how the senator died is not
material to this case—but information contained in the coroner's
report is relevant, as I intend to show."

"And how are you going to do that?" asked Winger, who then
was racked by a convulsion of coughing, which lasted almost a
minute, before he finally took a sip of water.

"How?" he croaked.

"With this tape, Your Honor," I said, taking out the video from

Cuba that Charlie had handed me. "I have here a taped confession by one Max Prado, who says he was present when the victim was slain. Information he gives on this tape will, we believe, conclusively link Senator Decker to a wider conspiracy of secret cult members."

"What? Your Honor, this is unheard of!" howled Mike, who realized he had walked into a trap. "Why hasn't this information been given to the police? Where has this tape come from? Who is this character who now is going to provide an alibi?"

"Your Honor, I turned over a copy of this tape as discovery material to Mr. Fuentes last week."

Mike turned to his boss, who smiled, shrugged.

"I sent it along, Mike." He then whispered, "Just tell them we haven't had time to examine it."

"Have you looked at this yet, Mr. Cleary?"

"No, Your Honor, there seems to have been some sort of miscommunication. I never received my copy."

"Well, I'll tell you what," said Winger. "I have a VCR in chambers. How's about I make some popcorn and we can all watch it there?"

I KNOW that elsewhere Charlie refers to Max Prado as an imposing man, the kind that loves to chew on cigars, fondle babes, and drink Absolut by the gallon. But the Max Prado we saw on that tape was not that man. True, he seemed tall, although he was lying in a hospital bed, and while his arms were still thicker than a man's neck, the tubes sprouting from him and the pallor on his face made it clear he was not long for this world.

The video had the grainy quality of a third- or fourth-generation dupe; only the sound came through loud and clear, as if Prado were right there in chambers with us.

Now, I am not going to go into all the details. Perhaps Charlie would, but I've never been into blood. Besides, his story was not only horrific, it was revolting. Even as I heard his tale and watched the stunned reaction of the judge, Phil, and Mike, in the back of my mind I kept thinking of the strange creature I'd just seen in the stairwell. Was I imagining everything, had I gone psycho from tension and overwork, mistaking a feral cat for a messenger of evil? Or had all these detestable, disgusting people in Prado's cult stumbled onto a magic secret that actually worked—but at the price of their life and soul? And had anybody in this room made that pact with the devil?

At the head of the tape a lanky blond man, looking sort of like the actor Patrick Swayze, was bending over Prado's bed, clipping a tiny mike on Prado's ratty hospital nightgown. They exchanged a few words in Spanish for a sound check, then the blond man crossed his arms and nodded at Prado.

"We better speak English," he said. "This is for the American courts."

"Okay," was Prado's painful reply. Two other men, dressed in green uniforms, hovered at the edge of the frame, as though watching out for someone or something.

"Please tell us your name, where you live, and where you are now."

"My name is Max Prado," wheezed the patient. "I live in New York City."

Prado gasped for breath with a hoarse sound, as though air was being let out of his lungs elsewhere than from his windpipe. He would do this throughout the interview, always answering in short phrases and long breaths.

"I am in Havana right now, at some hospital. I don't know the name. What's it called?"

Off camera, someone gave an inaudible reply, which Prado repeated.

"I am told I am at the Hospital Coronel Enrique Lister, whoever he was."

"Why are you here? What do you have to say?" asked the unseen interrogator.

Prado looked blankly at the lens, then he shrugged and

sneered disdainfully as though he was still calling the shots. But then, acknowledging the gravity of his situation, Prado abruptly transformed his expression to that of confessional concern.

"Why am I here? *Bueno,* I came to Cuba to sign up more people for my music label. I'm a record producer. I have made many records in my time. I cut Beny Moré's last disc with Tropicuba, I've worked with people like Tito Puente, Celia Cruz, Hector Lavoe, Cheo Feliciano, Tito Rodríguez, Olga Guillot, La Soli. Many."

He stopped, out of breath, his face a shade of gentian, then he spoke on, deliberately.

"Specifically, I came here to get a record contract with David Ichaso. You know him. He's the king of timba music. I thought his tunes would be really popular in the States, what with the Ricky Martin craze and all that."

"Tell us about your religion," came the disembodied voice.

"You mean . . . the two societies?" whispered Prado.

"That's right."

A deep breath. Then: "The secret societies. They go by the name of Abakuá. Our religion. We believe in the transmigration of souls."

He stopped, again out of breath, blinked repeatedly. He went on.

"We believe in one god, all powerful, creator of heaven and earth. Ekué. Her spirit is found in the waters of the sacred rivers and streams. In our ceremonies she dies, like Christ on the cross. Every month her blood taints the waters, and we drink her spirit and eat her flesh."

Winger stopped the tape.

"Miss Carr, what is the relevance of all this mumbo jumbo?" he said, wheezing, echoing Prado's own labored breathing.

"Judge, if you just let it roll a couple of minutes more, I think we're almost there."

"We better be. You have two minutes otherwise I will sustain my own objection and exclude the tape from this hearing."

"Thank you, Your Honor."

Winger pressed the play button of the remote. We were back in the Havana hospital room, the unseen interrogator asking Prado, "And how does her spirit enter the water?"

"With blood from the sacrifice."

"What *is* the sacrifice?"

"Usually a young person, a girl, about sixteen to eighteen years old."

"You mean you kill them."

"Well, I don't, I just . . . it's symbolic, you see. You take a little of the flesh, that is all. It's not like you make a meal out of it or anything. Just a bite. The main thing is the blood."

"These girls. Who are they?"

"They are nothing. Nobodies. They become something when they are chosen. Then they become the goddess. They live forever. Like us."

"Jesus Christ," muttered Mike. Fuentes glared silently at the screen, Winger also staring in dumb disbelief.

Prado went on, in between great gulps of air, to give a detailed description of how the cult picked out its sacrifices, how they were drugged and slaughtered. Their bodies were then ceremoniously wrapped in African blankets to await the coming Apocalypse, when all the victims' bodies will rise and join their creator in heaven, as part of her living body, in one large multisoul, multibody organism that I found hard to understand or to think about.

"Why are they called the secret societies?" went on the voice.

"Well, obviously, because people don't understand these things. In fact, if I wasn't about to die, I wouldn't be saying anything."

"Is anybody forcing you to do this?"

"No, no, it's just—"

Prado stopped, looked straight at the cameras, then his eyes rolled back and his tongue seemed to implode, his words swallowed by the rattle in his throat.

"I have to talk or—"

He seemed to black out, his head rolling to the side of the bed. All at once several men rushed toward him from outside to inside the frame: the blond man, a nurse, a man in a doctor's coat. The physician shoved the others aside, pummeled Prado's chest, began mouth-to-mouth resuscitation even as the blond man stuck his face in front of the lens and ran a finger horizontally on his neck. The screen went dark but the white letters and numbers of the time code rolled on.

"Is there more?" asked Mike, his face drained of color.

"It's coming back, hold on," I said. After a few seconds the screen came alive again. This time Prado was propped up; someone had raised the bed's headboard and oxygen tubes were piped into his nostrils, a saliva vacuum dangling from his jaw.

"How are you feeling?" asked the voice again.

"Better, better. I think I fainted."

"Do you want to go on with this?"

Prado again stared at the camera silently for a few seconds, as though pondering his fate, then he nodded.

"We were talking about the ceremonies of your religion. So you drain the blood from their bodies, then you eat some of their flesh. You, and the priest that carries out the sacrifice, all the faithful too?"

"It depends. Sometimes everyone participates."

"How?"

"You stick in the knife so as to make sure the victim is over to the next world. It's symbolic, you see."

A silence fell in the hospital room and also in the judge's chambers. No longer was anyone wanting to know how long this would go on. Everyone was transfixed by the ghastly story that had been spewing out like some poison from the mouth of this obviously dying man.

"Have you ever seen or heard of a man named Charlie Morell?" asked the interrogator.

"When?" came the ghostly reply.

"Before this last visit of yours here to Cuba had you ever met Charlie Morell?"

"Met him? No."

"But you had heard of him?"

"That, yes."

"Why? In what context?"

"Because for some time people in our church have been discussing ways to get rid of him. They said he is a threat because of his knowledge of our religion. He could stop our outreach efforts. But others said they had found a way to get to him. They never said how but I assumed—"

"Do you know if he's ever been to one of your ceremonies?"

"Our rites, yes, he has," answered Prado. Even in Winger's chambers I could smell the stench of Prado's medication. "He did not know about it . . . my idea."

"You're saying it was your idea?"

Prado nodded.

"That sounds pretty incriminating to me," said Mike, almost relieved.

"Hold on," I warned.

"Where was this?" asked the interrogator.

"Aquí," whispered Prado. ". . . here, in Cuanabo."

Prado's voice dipped, and his face again began turning purplish. Almost as if realizing he had little time to waste, the interrogator raised his voice, full of urgency.

"Had you ever met with Mr. Morell before?"

Prado shook his head no.

"Do you know if he's a member of your religion?"

"He is not."

"In March of 1999 were you at a ceremony of your religion in Los Angeles, where a young girl named Olive Lane was sacrificed?"

Prado nodded, his strength fading.

"Is that a yes?"

"Yes," croaked Prado.

"Was Morell there?"

Prado shook his head slowly.

"No, Charlie Morell was not there."

"Did you dispose of the body of the sacrifice later?"

"Yes, we did, we left her body to be taken to Palmdale . . ." His head hung loosely, his eyes closed.

Then a jump cut, and again the same scene of flurrying and hurrying and doctors and nurses gathering at the bedside.

This time the blond man stared straight at the camera: "My name is Lee Gutiérrez of the Ministry of the Interior of the government of Cuba." He then went on to certify that all we saw was true, happening in Havana, Cuba, and so forth. He concluded with: "Good luck, Charlie."

Time code frozen, the screen went to black.

A STUNNED silence filled the room, as we all gathered our thoughts, the banality of evil once more confirmed. What could be more ordinary than a man about to die wanting to confess? What could be more haunting and awful than the matter-of-fact telling of torture and slaughter for an unfathomable cause, a deeply repugnant religion?

"You realize that is not true," murmured Fuentes.

"Excuse me?" I asked. Phil seemed almost embarrassed, picked up a paper clip, twisted it into odd shapes.

"The Abakuá," he added. "I did a little research on this myself when I was on the Díaz case. It's a legitimate religion, none of this blood sacrifice stuff. This guy is talking about a secret society."

"It's Charlie's people again," said Winger, almost to himself, staring at the black screen as though still unable to believe what he'd just witnessed. He took off his glasses, looked at his hawk-like nose reflected in the lenses.

"I'm sorry, Your Honor, but you just heard Mr. Prado, the deponent, state that my client had nothing—"

Winger cut me off. "I meant Manson, young lady. Another Charlie. Before your time."

Mike wheeled around in his chair. "I'm sorry, Judge, but that tape we just saw is inadmissible. It's all hearsay."

"Whoa, hold on a minute," I said, knowing I had to rip his argument into shreds right away. "This is a clear exception to the hearsay rule and it can be admitted into evidence. Look, the man is in a coma and he's not available as a witness and we have no way of forcing him here, since there's no extradition with Cuba."

"How do you know that?" asked Mike.

"Come off it. Why do you think we have convicted Cuban felons sitting in IRS detention in El Centro for years after serving their sentence? Because Castro won't take them back."

"She's right, Mike," said Fuentes, for once following my lead. "We have a couple of hundred Cubans up in Mira Loma cooling their heels right now."

"No, I meant how does she know that the witness is in a coma," argued Mike.

"Weren't you watching? That guy had a stroke right in front of us. But regardless. Let's say now he's dancing up a storm in the pink of health. As long as he's in Cuba we can't get to him. You know the rules. The declarant also has knowledge of the subject, since he's a member of the cult. And he wouldn't have made the statement unless he thought it was time for him to die, because it's going to subject him to criminal prosecution if he comes back to the U.S."

"Judge, this is all so convenient," bickered Mike. "At the last minute, before trial, counsel comes up with this tape that has never been seen before that magically exculpates Mr. Morell. At the very least, since we can't certify its origin or reliability, it should be excluded. For all we know, this was shot in some soundstage in North Hollywood, just like the moon landing."

"Oh, please! Let's get real here!" I wailed.

Winger nodded, leaned back in his creaking chair, then shaped his hands into the triangular position of princes of the church. And ornery judges.

"'Take then thy bond, take thou thy pound of flesh; /But in the cutting it if thou dost shed /One drop of Christian blood, thy lands and goods /Are by the laws of Venice confiscate /Unto the state of Venice.'"

We benighted attorneys looked at each other, puzzled. Only the court reporter allowed herself a smile.

"I'm sorry, Judge, I don't understand," I admitted.

"Shakespeare, Miss Carr. The master jurist. The one man who truly could read men's hearts."

"I'm sure, sir, but I'm still not following."

"I mean we cannot tell if this tape has been fabricated or not."

"Your Honor, Mr. Morell could testify—"

"Sure he could but who's going to believe him? Not I. But I don't want to be unreasonable. I tell you what I will do. If you can get independent confirmation of the existence of this man and this seeming declaration against interest, I will allow it."

Winger looked down at his red-leather-bound calendar book, then opened up his desk drawer and took out a Palm Pilot, which he proceeded to use deftly. He glanced up.

"You have until Thursday. I guess I could busy myself with another couple of court trials in the meantime. If you come up with something by then, well, who knows? Meantime, Mr. Cleary, what about young Mr. Morell? Will he be one of your witnesses and is defense going to object?"

"We most certainly will," I said. "Julian Morell is a minor."

"Not anymore," countered Mike. "He turned eighteen three months ago."

"That may well be true, but at the time of the purported crime he was still a minor and the people did not obtain the proper parental consent to enlist his cooperation—and they subjected him to undue pressure, coercion in fact, to build the case against his father."

"You really think Morell would authorize his own son to give testimony against him? That is preposterous! No consent was needed."

"So it looks like we'll be handling that issue too," said Winger. "Fine. So I will see you all on Thursday. Including your client, Miss Carr. Is that clear?"

"Your meaning is transparent, sir," I replied, as Winger was suddenly racked by another fit of coughing.

I FOUND Charlie at his aerie in Los Feliz, sitting out on the balcony, watching the prismatic sunset while sipping an orange Mexican soda.

"Gorgeous, isn't it?"

He pointed at the wild display of colors beyond the towers of Century City and Santa Monica, the shoreline a smoky frame for the sinking sun.

"That is one of the few known advantages of pollution. You can see the beauty of our chemical death in the air. See, we are all one in the end. There is great beauty in death, if you open yourself to the universe."

I was exasperated. I didn't have time for Kahlil Gibran.

"Charlie, I would really appreciate it if you would please pay attention. Your head is about to be handed to you on a platter and you're rattling on about the sunset? Who cares? We have to think about your trial, how you can get your evidence in. Make up your mind. You're either Raskolnikov or you're Krishnamurti but you can't be both at the same time. This act of yours is truly driving me nuts."

Charlie eyed me up and down. I had my shoes in my hand, my right big toe still swollen, my hair falling all over my face. The wind blew in a scent of orange blossoms, car exhaust, and lilies, like the day I accompanied my mother to Forest Lawn for the last time.

"He got to you, didn't he?"

"Who?" I snapped. "Fuentes? The judge? Your son?"

"The catman."

I stood there glaring at him for a few seconds, asking myself how he could have known, then I remembered I had told him about the break-in at my house the night before. It seemed like years already. I collapsed on the chair next to him, my shoes clattering on the slate tiles.

"Yes," I said, dumbly, relieved to finally admit it. "He came back. I think. I chased him but he wasn't there. I'm starting to think I'm losing my mind too."

Charlie shook his head no. "You're suffering from sleep deprivation. It rattles everyone. Also makes you more spiritually attuned, your nerves are so sensitive then. That's how coffee was discovered—the Sufis wanted to stay awake and dance all night."

He may have been right but that was definitely not what I wanted to hear at that moment.

"Charlie, back to basics. I'm not ready for satori. Everything has turned out just as we expected. The tape is in but it has to be authenticated. I take it the chances of us getting cooperation from the Cuban government are zilch. Right?"

I glanced at Charlie, who stared away, still scanning the horizon as though it alone could supply him the answers.

"Hello, Charlie, are you there?"

"I hear you."

"Fine, then listen to me. There is a way around this. If we can firmly establish that the tape came from a government source, it can be admitted into evidence as an official document. Especially if we can prove that in the normal course of business, the Cuban government videotapes confessions of this sort. Now I have a couple of professor friends at USC Law School who can testify that—"

"It won't work," was Charlie's somber reply. "The exception would be denied due to the lack of normal diplomatic relations between the two countries."

"You mean because there is no way to properly certify the origins of the document the testimony of the professors would be speculation?" I said.

"Correct."

"Well, in that case you are going to have to go back," I said.

For the longest moment Charlie just sat there quietly, watching the flaming ball of the sun sink into the far horizon, then he turned and nodded, his features already draped by the shadows lengthening around us.

"I'm afraid you're right."

18

B L U E . B L U E . B L U E .

The tanginess of salt air, mist rising from the vast, glittering pool that is the ocean off Varadero. The flatness of the water merges in the horizon with the equally blue, cloudless sky, so that the powdery white sands I stand on are the only solid thing is this blue universe, where everything is liquid, everything is shifting, there is nothing to hang on to, nothing that is real.

I turn my head.

At the far end of the bay that opens like a crooked smile at the docile Caribbean I can see the white rhomboids, spheres, and cylinders of the other Cuba, the one where tourists flock, the country of domesticated communism, syrupy ballads, and spicy *guarachas,* fabricated for foreign consumption out of the hopes of a starving revolution. I can almost smell the suntan lotion spread thickly on the charring white tourists.

But I am here, in the other Cuba, at the tip of a verdant peninsula that was once the property of an American industrialist and now a very private hospital, a refuge—or is it a prison?—for those whose health problems are commensurate with their bank accounts. Robert Vesco, Eldridge Cleaver, Timothy Leary, all the wild-eyed subversive debris of the U.S. floated down here and spent their season or two in this tropical purgatory. From the wide terraces of the Georgian colonial behind me, straddling the dazzling white sands like some misplaced antebellum fancy, sundry American rogues, adventurers, and revolutionaries contemplated their fate, gazing blindly north at their own feckless homeland. Max Prado, sitting in his wheelchair next to me, is only the latest in a long line of captured cons.

"We're different, you and me," he says, the ending of his words swallowed up by the lingering effects of his stroke. "We're nowhere people, Charlie."

He shakes his head as though to free the errant thought, then sinks again into the old wood and cane contraption lifted from a turn-of-the-century nursing home. Turn of the nineteenth century, that is; in Cuba the ancient articles of daily existence live on, much like the people, refusing to surrender to a graceful end.

I nod silently at Prado. Now he's the captive and I am the free man, I'm the favorite and he's the outcast. The occasional Minint officer strolling the grounds with his submachine gun slung from his shoulder only confirms our reversal of fortune. But for how long?

As long as I am in Cuba I'm just another player being jerked around by the matchless puppeteer behind the red screen, the one with the graying beard and the insatiable lust for power. For all I know in the next scene it'll be my turn to sit in Prado's chair. Or maybe we'll both have our heads chopped off, to the laughter and jeers of the world's peanut gallery.

I have to move on. Returning to Cuba was the easy part, returning to America with my prize, my prey, will be the hard part. He, after all, has to want to return.

"Who is behind the Abakuá?" I ask him.

Prado chortles, a spray of spittle flying out in an arc from his thick lips, amused that even after all that happened, I still don't understand.

"You mean is there a Pope, a head of the Abakuá that lays down the law for the religion? Maybe that plays in your books, Charlie, but that's not the way it goes. We're like the Protestants, different preachers set up their own congregations. Or, if you want, like Africa before the white man. Back then each village chief was a king and wherever he peed, that was his kingdom. In answer to your next question—"

"I haven't asked it yet."

"I can read you like a poem, *asere*. You're all worry and duty and brotherhood. You're like those knights in the tales of chivalry, like Amadis of Gaul, Sir Lancelot, all those white idiots. You should try being Cuban and surrender to the moment. Don't fight it."

"I can only be what I am. In any case, look where being Cuban has gotten you."

I gesture at the wheelchair, at the guard strolling the grounds.

"This is temporary," he whispers hoarsely. "We're too strong. That's why they still haven't killed me. Even Lee Gutiérrez and his *blanquitos* can't stop us. So in answer to your question, there is no Stalin. Only a vague Politburo."

"I just want to know one thing. Do you really believe?"

He beams a warped smile, lighting up the half of his face that he still controls.

"I go with what works, Charlie. All my life the Abakuá has worked. So I follow."

"But these are people you slaughter, they're not chickens."

He shrugs his one free shoulder.

"Don't be so squeamish. Think of the Aztecs, of Neanderthal man. Think of Jesus Christ. Don't you eat His flesh and blood every week when you go to Mass? So what are you complaining about? Man has always eaten his own kind. And these *chiquitas*, the sacrifices, they become a better person for it. They will join the goddess at the end. You should see it. Here in Cuba sometimes the families bring the sacrifices to us. It's better than this endless round of hunger and prostitution they endure. They know we'll compensate them too, that's why we always leave a coin with the remains, to pay off the debt."

He pauses, whisks his hand at a dragonfly, which buzzes noisily around his head.

"I don't have to tell you that not everyone is equal. The blacks, the Mexicans, the Puerto Ricans, the Chinese. Every society has somebody at the bottom. For the Romans, it was the blond, blue-eyed Germans who were the favorite slaves. For the Japanese, it's the Koreans. For the Aztecs, it was the Toltecs, and so on. We of the Abakuá give all these wretched of the earth, like Frantz Fanon would have said, we give them a chance to break free, to fly all the way to the top of the chain. In one fell swoop, as it were."

He laughs again, his wattled neck shaking with joy. I feel something like righteous wrath rising inside of me, I feel like taking his fat, hulking body, throwing it in the water, and holding his head down until he cannot breathe anymore and his cries are swallowed up by the shiny blue sea . . .

"But what about Jesus?" I cry out, almost in spite of myself, digging up the old catechism like the peasant brandishing the cross and garlic wreath before the monster. "That is why Jesus came, to offer us a way out, to bring love."

"Love? Jesus?" he snarls. "The Western world has been Christian for two thousand years now. Can you really say we are better people than when the Roman emperors were gods? Has this faith of yours stopped the slaughter? Just now, look at Bosnia and Kosovo, those good Christians maiming, chopping, and slicing their Muslim neighbors. You call that an improvement? No, my friend, mankind will always need to make blood sacrifices. It is the nature of the beast."

"We were not put on earth to kill one another, Max," I answer somberly.

"Fine. Then, why are we here, Charlie?"

His eyes grow wide, his words drip with cold self-righteousness. I shake my head, sit on the sand next to his chair. I cannot hate him, hatred is too heavy a burden to bear. A sunbeam breaks through the pine branches, falls warm and lustrous on my open hands. How do I answer him?

"We're here to do good. To love one another, like the Lord has loved us."

"Right. How much good have you done in your life?"

I turn, I grab his arm. He flinches, as though I'd burned him with a hot poker.

"We are better than animals. We are much more than the birds and the lilies of the field. Perhaps there shouldn't be war, perhaps there shouldn't be the exploitation of man by man, perhaps we should all live in an earthly paradise. But even though that isn't the case now that doesn't mean we should give up trying. We are past the time when war and human sacrifice could be accepted. We can change. There used to be slavery, we no longer have it. It's a small step, I grant you, but it's a step we have taken in the right direction. We cannot go back to the bloody altars of the Aztecs and the Druids and Neanderthal man. I don't care how corny you think this is but I believe it with all my heart: our destiny is to build peace and harmony here on earth."

A sweat breaks out on his forehead, he breathes heavily, waves his good arm at me to fend off my bothersome beliefs. He slobbers while trying to find the words.

"You go ahead with your fairy tales, I know the heart of man. *Yo conozco el monstruo, he vivido en sus entrañas.*"

José Martí's famous words about the American way of life: I know the monster for I have lived in the belly of the beast.

"Then you are ready to kill your own daughter on the altar of your religion?"

He turns, disdainful, his mouth contorted.

"You wouldn't dare."

"That's the message I have from Gutiérrez. You may be saved but your daughter was found with blood up to her elbows. Co-operate with us. Or is she like the others, an expedient sacrifice? Is her name Gertrudis or Iphigenia?"

He turns abruptly, swings at me with his good arm, but all I need do is move and watch the blow go by. His face contorts in pain, he releases the hand brake and the chair rolls slowly down the slope to the shore, water rising up to the wheel hubs.

"Ekué!" he hollers, a cry muffled by his illness and his prison.

A small wave rises and breaks on him.

I watch the water splash over him and recede as he hangs his head, then I wade into the water and I begin to haul him out.

19

I HATE T.J.

Matter of fact, I don't much like Mexico at all, at least what it has become in the last fifty years—a corrupt machine for sucking money out of its people while spewing their spent carcasses up north. I'm so grateful that my grandfather left Sonora when he did, otherwise I too would have been another wretch jumping the border at San Diego with two kids and a husband in tow.

This is not to say that I'm a self-hating Mexican. I may not speak the language but I am proud of my culture, of the things we stand for, of our hard work, our patience, our endurance, the way we carry our heart on our sleeve. I even like *rancheras,* for Christ's sake, and after a couple of tequilas I get just as weepy as the rest, whistling and razzing the men who make women suffer so much.

But what the Mexican government has done to my grandfather's country is abominable. I invariably get a queasy feeling when I'm south of the border and it's not the water; it's like I can't wait to get back to L.A., get in the shower and wash off the grime of graft, hypocrisy, and injustice that surrounds me south of San Ysidro.

My irritation at Mexico only grew once I reached the airport at Tijuana. Local transportation officials, with the unctuousness the Mexicans reserve for those who hold power, directed me to a runway at the far end, by the green, smelly sewer they call the Tijuana River.

Up ahead I could see the gray DC-3 of Cubana de Aviación parked far from all the other aircraft, surrounded by a limousine and three black and white *policía* cruisers. A *policía judicial* waved me to a halt. I rolled down the window, expecting trouble. Surprisingly, the officer clicked his heels and snapped a starched salute.

The *policía* turned and yelled at a group of men huddled around one of the cruisers, then he opened my door. From among the huddle a short man in a fancy suit broke away and hurried across the fifty yards separating me from the plane. The man's hard Indian features creased into a smile while he vigorously pumped my hand as I stood there in my white cotton shift in the burning sun, the heat coming off in waves from the asphalt.

"I am Jaime Benítez, Miss Carr. Charlie has told me all about you."

"Is he here yet?" I ask.

"Oh yes, they have just landed. The Cuban government has done everything to make this possible. He should be coming down any minute now. Will you accompany me?"

We walked quickly down the burning tarmac, the small man

snapping orders at the other men, who scurried back and forth, wheeling the ladder next to the plane.

"Are you the same Benítez who is a captain with the *policía judicial?*"

"I used to be," he replied. "President Zedillo just appointed me vice governor of Baja Norte."

"Times have changed."

"It's a river, Miss Carr. You never step into the same thing twice. There is Charlie."

The airplane door opened and Charlie stepped through, looking tentatively around as though not completely sure this was his stop. He raised a hand and waved at me, then he scrambled down the stairs, embracing Benítez in a bear hug. He was followed down by the tall blond man of the videotape, who now turned and also hugged Benítez. I hadn't seen so many male *abrazos* since my cousin's wedding in Alhambra.

Charlie came up, kissed me on the cheek, and whispered, "I am exhausted beyond belief. You're going to have to carry the ball."

"That's what you pay me for."

He turned to the imitation Norseman.

"Lee Gutiérrez, my attorney, Rita Carr."

We shook hands quickly, efficiently, Gutiérrez scanning me up and down with deep blue eyes that seemed to swallow me whole.

"Thank you for your cooperation, Mr. Gutiérrez. I'm certain we would not have been able to carry this out without your good offices."

"You're welcome. It's our revolutionary duty."

Yes, I thought, to get rid of conspirators and hang them out to dry like dirty laundry on an American line. But it was time to make nice: after all, he had most likely saved Charlie's hide.

"Do you think Mr. Prado will be in any condition to testify soon?" I asked him.

Gutiérrez shrugged, touched the .38 tucked under his snowy white *guayabera.*

"Why don't you ask him? He is better," replied Gutiérrez, the

Spanish accent incongruous on such an Anglo face. "But in these kind of cases, who knows? Plus, the weight of coming here, it is very great, you know?"

"Just what is his condition?"

The squeal of a siren broke through the roar of planes flying overhead. A white van hurtled toward us, followed by yet another police car.

"Mr. Prado has had a series of strokes, ever since the incident with Charlie," he continued, watching the ambulance come to a stop at the foot of the ladder to the plane. "In Cuba we managed to give him some medication, but it is experimental. It is based on some native herbs, they dissolve blood clots and stimulate the blood flow, but we do not know for how long. Plus, his heart, it is damaged and we do not have the best equipment to test. The embargo, you know? In any case, I am here. I can testify. It is what you wanted, no?"

The van's door slammed open. A paramedic spoke into a walkie-talkie. Out of the plane's front door exited a male nurse holding a plasma bag aloft, a gun strapped to his waist. Following him two other male nurses—black, muscular, with the build of linebackers—brought out the stretcher carrying Max Prado. The nurses negotiated the ladder without difficulty and entrusted the music promoter to the care of their wiry, brown Mexican counterparts. Gutiérrez walked me over.

"This is Miss Carr, Charlie's attorney. She will be asking you a few questions later on."

It was apparent Prado had not long to live. His face was pale, and he sweated profusely in the heat, his breathing halting and noisy. But the spark of intelligence was still in his eyes.

"We'll give them a show, won't we?" he said.

"You bet."

The nurses wheeled Prado to the ambulance, two armed Mexican police boarding the van with him. Whoever tried to interfere with his testimony would get a nasty surprise. The van's doors slammed shut.

"So, I have made arrangements for our stay with a friend," said Gutiérrez, as we walked back to my Durango.

"She lives in a place I never heard of," Gutiérrez went on. "The Homebee Hills. Is that nice?"

"Holmby Hills. Yes, it's nice enough, if you can stand the rarefied air."

"It is very high?"

"No, but it is very rich. You have heard of Beverly Hills?"

"Sure! Beverly Hills nine-zero-two-one-zero. Everybody around the world knows. Even in Cuba."

"Holmby Hills is twice as rich and twice as nice."

"Oh!" he said, stunned, then added, almost to himself. "I thought radical chic was dead."

"Not in Los Angeles. People here still have fond memories of Che Guevara. Especially out on the West Side."

"Is that true? Charlie never has talked about that. We must discuss it."

Charlie came around then, having said goodbye to his policeman-turned-politico friend, who departed in the great big black limousine, trailed by a couple of squad cars. Charlie was pale and stooped, his face even more haggard than when he had left for Cuba the week before.

"BENÍTEZ TOLD me he secured all the clearances," said Charlie. "Two patrol cars are coming with us, the helicopter will keep an eye overhead."

"They're not taking any chances, are they?"

"Nor should they."

I DON'T know who took Benítez's call in Washington, but our journey through the border crossing at San Ysidro was the briefest I had ever experienced. The ambulance van was stopped for all of thirty seconds, enough time for the driver to show his papers to the Border Patrol, who scanned them and then waved the entire caravan through. The Mexican *federales* helicopter, which had been hovering above us, was replaced by a Department of Justice chopper, and the Mexican patrol cars peeled off; a few hundred yards in, two California Highway Patrol cars joined the troop, escorting us all the way into Orange County, turning back only at Mission Viejo.

Lee Gutiérrez, who had been quietly watching the rolling scene of wealthy suburbs, fancy landscaping, and undeveloped wilderness alternate during our route up the coast, watched wide-eyed what seemed like an eternal traffic jam leading into the city of dreams.

"Your traffic, it is always like this?"

"Oh, no. Sometimes it's worse. This is light, comparatively speaking," I said, clocking our speed at twenty miles an hour in the express car pool lane. "Look at it this way, we're still moving."

"Remarkable," he said, then added: "Well, then, what is the order in which you will take our statements? Will we go to the prosecutor's office first to declare and sign the affidavit?"

"No, no. Things are different here in our legal system," I said, looking at Gutiérrez through my rearview mirror.

"We don't have interrogatories before the case is heard. Everything is handled by a judge in open court."

"I hope it is not too open," muttered Charlie, who had been sitting quietly watching the building traffic. "You told Mike to get a high-security courtroom?"

"I told Winger. He said they'd find a place for us. Will you look at that!"

Ahead of us, the reason for the delay: two cars and a van had kissed, sprawled, and turned over in the middle of the freeway by Oso Parkway, pieces of metal and glass everywhere. Two Highway Patrolmen were directing traffic onto the one open lane. As we drove by the site, we could see people inside one of the cars, eyes closed, bathed in blood, sitting in their crushed vehicle, waiting for the Fire Department and its Jaws of Life.

Gutiérrez took a quick look, then returned nonchalantly to our conversation, I'm sure he'd seen far gorier scenes in Cuba. Maybe even helped create a few.

"I have a question about Prado," said Gutiérrez. "He is testifying because he thinks it is his duty to do so. But as I understand the American Constitution, there is a disposition against self-incrimination. Will that prove a problem?"

"Well, *Señor* Gutiérrez—"

"Lee, please."

"Lee, the answer is yes. That could be a problem. The DA may file charges against Prado, although it would not be too effective to file charges against a dying man. No jury would convict. In any case, he still cannot stop him from testifying, even if it is against Prado's self-interest."

"And this is not?"

Before I could answer, Charlie's cell phone came alive at the same time that the ambulance turned on its siren and pushed on through the snarled traffic. I stepped on the gas, trying to follow the white van as now it swerved out of the lane and climbed on the shoulder, plowing its way ahead. Charlie spoke furiously into the phone, snapped it shut.

"Don't let the van get away! Stay on them!" he barked.

"What's going on?"

"Prado just had another stroke!"

WE WOUND up at Queen of Angels in Hollywood, another twenty miles up the road. I suppose we could have gone to Newport or to UC Irvine but Charlie pressed them to keep driving, the cars opening before us on the freeway like floes before an icebreaker.

Dr. Yagamuchi, the head neurosurgeon, came down to see us in the waiting area, after Prado had been whisked away from the ER and settled into a private room.

"His prognosis is actually good," said the doctor with guarded warmth. We had moved over to the snack bar, and he raised the slot to get his Coke from the vending machine. He took a sip, let out an *ahh* of satisfaction. "He will most likely survive, although we don't know how many of his faculties he will retain."

"What do you mean, Doctor?" I asked.

"He has congestive heart failure. His liver and kidney functions are only about twenty percent of normal, plus he seems to have lost control over the right side of his body. But the medication your people gave him in Cuba is pretty amazing. We checked out his arteries and they are totally cleaned out. Even though his heart is a wreck, the vessels are wide open, so there is enough blood flow to sustain life. What is that stuff, anyhow?"

"We'll send you samples, Doctor," said Lee. "Perhaps we can arrange for clinical trials here?"

"Please! We'd be delighted. Let me get you my card," said the doctor, walking away with Gutiérrez to the nurses' station. Charlie and I stared at each other, then the same thought occurred to us at the same time and we hustled over to Yagamuchi.

"Will Mr. Prado be able to talk?" I asked. Yagamuchi, scrawling his name on a hospital business card, shook his head.

"We'll have to wait until he wakes up."

"When's that going to be?"

"The next forty-eight hours will tell us. If he pulls through, then, who knows?"

LATER THAT night, after the Mexican police officers and the ambulance drivers headed back to Tijuana, we dropped Gutiérrez off at the estate of the 1970s radical activist actress who married and divorced the head of the largest telecommunications company in the country. Then I drove Charlie to Los Feliz.

"Will you be all right?"

"Will you?" he asked back.

"I have Raúl, we love each other. You?"

Charlie gave me a wan smile, again, like Belmondo.

"Well, I love the truth and she loves me. The problem is . . ."

"What?"

"She's a little on the cold side."

"Anything I can do?"

He shook his head no.

"You go take care of your man. He doesn't deserve you."

"He knows that."

We waved goodbye and I drove downhill to my own life. I saw him in my rearview mirror, standing with his arms crossed, head raised, staring at the moon. I took my eyes away to slow down for a stop sign. When I looked back in my mirror, he was lost from sight.

"WHERE IS your client, Miss Carr?"

Judge Winger didn't exactly roar, but he wasn't a happy camper either. He craned over the bench, his black robe opened like a pair of bat wings, and shook his bifocals at me.

"I already imposed a five hundred dollar sanction on your client. Does he have money to burn? Because next time I will make it hurt!"

I stood, smiled, adjusted my yellow Miou Miou dress—a wasted gesture, since I knew Winger was too far gone to appreciate any token of femininity. I flushed, I fidgeted, I hemmed, I hawed, and then I lied. What else could I do?

"Mr. Morell will be here presently, Your Honor. I'm sure he's been delayed by the change of courtroom location."

That took the edge off Winger's ire. He let out a raspy breath, then scowled at the small, wood-paneled courtroom as though seeking the author of his discomfort. We had been turned out of Winger's usual spacious halls on the fifteenth floor of the Criminal Courts Building by Sheriff's deputies, who claimed our heightened security concerns necessitated the move. All the courtrooms on the much vaunted, heavily guarded ninth floor were booked up, so we were sequestered in a tiny, mildewy courtroom on the first floor of the Civil Court House, three blocks away.

In my opinion the real reason for the change had been the small but supremely loud contingent of Cuban exiles who had mounted a demonstration outside the Criminal Courts Building, complete with bomb threats, banners, bullhorns, and repeated playings of the Cuban National Anthem from an ice cream truck bearing the sign PACO'S HELADOS—*Paletas y Nieves*—parked across the street. All of this because somehow the Cuban community in Los Angeles had gotten wind that Lee Gutiérrez was testifying. Fortunately for us, only a handful of reporters from Spanish language radio and TV bothered to cover the demonstration. In spite of Elián, Cuba has been old news in California for decades. Nowadays even Iranians get better media play.

None of that was any consolation to Winger, who harrumphed, put his glasses back on.

"If Mr. Morell is not here by ten o'clock, I will issue a body attachment to be executed immediately. He better bring his toothbrush. Call your first witness."

"Thank you, Your Honor. I call Mr. Lee Gutiérrez, of the Cuban Ministry of the Interior."

As Gutiérrez took the oath, standing behind the court reporter, the two extra deputies assigned for extra security walked out of the courtroom, presumably to post themselves by the door but in reality to sneak a quick cup of coffee from their office down the hall.

Gutiérrez sat on the small wooden witness chair in the cubicle next to the judge. I was already at the lectern to start my direct when Winger swiveled to look directly at Gutiérrez.

"Please state your name and occupation for the—I just had a thought. Do you need an interpreter? *Necesita uno ese interpreta?*"

Gutiérrez gave him his most forbearing expression.

"Not if you don't speak Spanish."

The judge literally blushed, to the laughter of the handful of us in the courtroom—the clerk, the reporter, the bailiff, Mike, his law clerk, the *Daily Journal* reporter, and myself.

"Well, that's good. *Gracias.* Please continue," said Winger, retreating into judicial detachment.

"My name is Lee Gutiérrez. I am a captain in the Cuban Ministry of the Interior."

"Would you describe your job as equivalent to what in our government?" I asked. Not very grammatical but I was trying to get the point across as quickly as I could.

"In the United States the closest equivalent would be your Federal Bureau of Intelligence."

"You mean of Investigation."

"That is correct, sorry. I was thinking of your CIA but I remember it is not allowed to operate in the country, just in foreign countries."

"Like Cuba?" interjected Winger all of a sudden. "Is that right?"

"Yes."

"And you are from Cuba? Originally, I mean?"

"Yes."

"In spite of . . . never mind. Go on."

I couldn't believe the judge's obvious bias, but at least he was paying attention.

"Mr. Gutiérrez, as part of your functions as captain in the Ministry of the Interior, did you have the occasion to interview a certain Max Prado?"

"Yes. I had been investigating him for a while after his arrival in Havana because we believed he was involved in a secret religion. As part—"

"Objection, Your Honor," said Mike. "No question pending."

"Counsel, this is just a 402 hearing," warned Winger. "We have no jury present so there's no need for grandstanding. Let the man talk. Overruled. Proceed, Mr. Gutiérrez."

"What is this religion that you were talking about, Mr. Gutiérrez?" I asked.

"It is called the Abakuá, or *ñáñigos,* or the secret societies. They were imported from Africa during the time of the Spanish. They believe in blood sacrifice, in the ritual killing of people as sacrifice to their god, the she-god called Ekué Yamba O—"

"Sorry to interrupt again, counsel," begged the judge, who again turned to Gutiérrez. "Why do you call this a religion? Is it not a cult, like David Koresh or the Charlie Manson gang?"

"You can say that, Judge," replied Gutiérrez. "At the end of the accounts, I do not care what you call them or what they call themselves. I only know that they are killing innocent people and that is against our laws."

"Against the laws of any civilized country in the world, I believe, sir. My point is, in a cult, you have a central figure, the cult master, who inspires, aids, and abets in the crimes, sometimes but not always committing the crimes. Do you know of any such figure in this ABQ cult?"

"Abakuá, Sir Judge," answered Gutiérrez, breaking into a sly smile. "Yes, we did. We disposed of the leader in Cuba."

"And how did you do that?"

Gutiérrez threw his chest out, proud of the job he had undertaken.

"When Mr. Morell came to Cuba, he took us, without knowing, to the leader of that branch of the cult. She is now in the hands of the revolutionary justice."

"Excuse me," broke in the judge again, "but you just said that branch of the cult. Does that mean you believe there are others?"

"Oh, yes. The Abakuá has spread to several countries. Italy, France, Spain too."

"The United States?"

Gutiérrez turned to face Winger, *hombre a hombre,* government hack to government hack.

"According to our experts, the Abakuá has been in operation in these United States for more than fifty years now. Not just with Latinos but many other peoples too."

Winger shook his head. "Proceed, counsel."

"We were talking about a certain Max Prado, Mr. Gutiérrez. Did you detain this man while he was in Cuba?"

"Yes. Like I said, when Mr. Morell took us to this meeting of the cult, Mr. Prado was found there."

"Did he then make a confession?"

"Yes, at the hospital while we were talking to him. He believed he was dying and he wanted us to know the truth."

"And in that confession, did he mention the death of a certain woman named Olive Lane here in California?"

"I asked him. I knew Morell had been accused of that murder."

I grabbed the edge of the lectern, to drive my point home.

"So when you met Mr. Morell you knew he was being investigated for that murder?"

"Oh, much more. I knew they thought, the police and authorities here, that he had done so. I thought that was very unprobable."

"Why did you think that?"

"Well, first off, we at the Minint, we keep a record of all the high-profile writers, intellectuals of Cuban origin here in the United States. Sort of like a dossier, you understand?"

"Yes."

"This is in case the person ever tries to enter the country, we know with what we are dealing. And Mr. Morell was in no way fitting that profile. You see, this Abakuá cult has been a problem for us ever since President Castro encouraged the growth of African religions in the country. So we know there was a branch of the cult here in the United States and we had a pretty good idea who was in it."

"Who?"

The courtroom doors opened then and we all turned to see, thinking perhaps that by one of those phenomena of synchronicity loved by Carl Jung and bad writers, Charlie himself might walk in. Instead it was Sally Turner, the fiftyish actress in whose mansion Gutiérrez was staying. She sashayed into the room, not disturbed at all by our riveted looks. She worked the room until at last she sat in the front row, waving her fingers at Gutiérrez in kittenish hello. Gutiérrez nodded back, embarrassed. I pressed on.

"Who was in that cult, Mr. Gutiérrez?"

"Our information was that here in this country the other society had taken hold. You see, in Cuba the Abakuá is a secret society mostly for black people. But there is another kind, the white Abakuá, for whites only, and that is the kind that spread in this country."

"Excuse me, Mr. Gutiérrez," again interrupted the judge. "What is the difference between these two societies?"

"Not much, as we have found out. They are parallel, one for blacks, the other for whites. Same religion, same god, different races. I do not know why that is. It is a mystery to me."

"Oh, I have a pretty good idea, sir. Racism has a long history here too. Counsel?"

I walked around, picked up the tape with the fateful confession.

"And you made this video here of that confession and you sent it to Mr. Morell?"

"Yes. I thought that it might be helpful in his case. He was helpful to us so we wanted to return the favor."

"How was he helpful?"

"With his cooperation we smashed the cult in Cuba, which was spreading to all levels of government."

"Why?" asked Winger.

"Why? Because power is like a drug, Mr. Judge. This cult gives you the power you need to believe. Like the mountain men of Muhammad, who killed because they thought they would go to heaven! Only here these people got the heaven they wanted on this earth, they thought. I showed them different, though."

"Yes, sir, it sounds like you did."

Winger winked at me. I smiled, relieved. I had practically paved the way to have the confession admissible. There were just two more things to clean up.

"Did you pressure Mr. Prado to make this confession?"

"Not, in no way. He said he did it because he found Jesus and he wanted to testify."

"And where is Mr. Prado right now?"

"We brought him back because you wanted him here. Right now I believe he is in a bed at Queen of the Angels hospital. He's in bad shape."

"Thank you, Mr. Gutiérrez."

"Anything else, counsel?"

I shook my head no. Winger turned to Mike with a complaisant nod. Mike stood up, shuddering before the unpleasant task.

"Your Honor, in case I did not do so before, I would like to have my objection to this proceeding noted for the record. This witness has come here without any corroborating evidence, dumping this whole barrage of nonsense, which cannot be proven without the purported declarant, who the witness himself admits cannot be brought into court."

"No so fast, Mikey!" shouted Charlie at the door, pushing in, on a wheelchair, Max Prado, looking at least ten years younger since I'd last seen him. I opened the swing door.

"How did you do it?" I whispered.

"Lots of prayer . . . and cocaine," Charlie whispered back.

"Can he talk?"

"Try him."

"Your Honor," I said to Winger, "here is the declarant himself. Let us cut to the chase. Why don't we hear from Mr. Prado himself about this whole affair?"

Mike was apoplectic. "Your Honor, this is a travesty! Does counsel think this is *Perry Mason*?"

"Well, Mr. Cleary, this is Hollywood and we all have a weakness for happy endings. Mr. Prado certainly seems to be breathing. Can you speak, Mr. Prado?"

"I have been waiting eagerly for this moment, Judge," said Prado, his voice ringing with strength. "The good Lord Jesus has brought me back for this purpose and I intend to keep my side of the bargain."

Not to mention his bargain with the Cuban government to keep his daughter out of jail. But I certainly wasn't about to tell. I needed him as a witness, no matter what.

"Your Honor," insisted Mike, "just let it be clear to Mr. Prado that he is exposing himself to criminal prosecution if his statements under oath in this courtroom are anything like what is contained in the tape we have reviewed. I urge the court to name an attorney for Mr. Prado, if he can't afford one, to assist him in this proceeding."

"I don't know, Mr. Cleary. That's up to Mr. Prado. What do you say, sir, do you want an attorney here with you?"

"No, Judge," boomed Prado, sitting straight in his chair. "I know my rights and I give them up. Voluntarily. I am here to speak the truth about Satan's brood and to clear the names of the innocent. I am here to do the Lord's work, hallelujah, thank you Jesus!"

"Oh brother," muttered Mike, casting himself into his seat with a sigh of disgust. "Your Honor, my objection should be noted."

Winger rocked back and forth, truly enjoying the show.

"Well, counsel, I believe I can keep myself neutral in these matters. Mr. Prado has waived his right to an attorney and I don't see why we cannot go ahead. Where this will lead us is up to the Creator. And Mr. Prado, of course. Objection noted and over-ruled. Are you ready, Mr. Prado?"

"So help me Jesus!" bellowed Prado. As the clerk swore him in, he looked at me with eyes ablaze in self-righteousness. I wondered just how much cocaine Charlie had fed the man. I wanted his statement in and out, and pronto.

"Mr. Prado, are you a member of the Abakuá cult?"

"Not anymore, praise the Lord. But I was a member for many years, that I was."

"Were the tenets of your religion as you described in that tape that Lee Gutiérrez sent us from Cuba, the one shot at your hospital bed?"

"I know that a tape was made while I was in the hospital but I did not see it. But yes, the things I stated in the hospital were all true. It's Satan's workshop, the devils come and possess people to make them commit their hideous crimes. Now, thanks to Jesus, I am living the day of His Salvation and have walked away from the endless night of sin, praise the Lord!"

"I'm happy to hear that, sir. Now, could you please tell us, were you present during the murder or the ritual killing of a girl here in Los Angeles by members of that cult?"

The courtroom doors swung open again. This time it was Julian Morell, who quietly sat in the back row. Charlie waved at him to go but Julian sat stubbornly, arms crossed, paying no mind. Winger was too engrossed in what Prado had to say to give Julian much attention.

"Yes, I was, and I hope the good Lord will forgive me for my sins. She was not the first nor was she the last, but I hope that with God's almighty power, I can stop this once and for all, praise Jesus."

"Amen," I echoed, wondering how this sudden conversion would save his behind. "But how did you know the girl's name?"

"Because I saw it on TV, when Mr. Morell was accused of the murder. I laughed at the time. Charlie Morell was precisely the last person who would be involved in that. He was always fighting the gods and I thought it was funny that the gods had finally found a way to entrap him."

I should have ended the testimony right there, but I made the most egregious mistake an attorney can ever make: I asked a question without knowing the answer beforehand.

"So you know for a fact that Charles Morell did not commit that murder because you saw who committed it and Charles Morell was not that person?"

"That is correct. Mr. Charles Morell is innocent of the charges, praise the Lord. That's what I'm here to testify."

A rumble in the jury room, like a package falling to the ground. The bailiff got up from his desk, crossing the courtroom to the jury room door. I pressed on, wanting to make absolutely sure he could absolve Charlie. Who knows what would have happened had I not pressed the issue.

"And everything you're telling us today is the absolute truth?"

"So help me Jesus, amen."

I looked around, feeling inordinately proud of myself. I'd done my job, I'd gotten the tape in, I'd practically given Charlie the keys to the courthouse. I sat down.

"That is all for now, Your Honor."

"Mr. Cleary?"

Another loud thump from the jury room. For a moment I panicked, then I remembered the jury room had only one way in, through the jury door, and that the room had been cleared and inspected by Sheriff's deputies before we started. Just to be safe, I raised my shoulders at Charlie, but he was already getting up to ask the deputy to come in when Mike stood up, addressed the witness.

"So then, Mr. Prado, please tell us, who killed this girl, according to you? Who took her life?"

"He did! Satan's child!" he said, pointing at the back of the room.

"Who are you talking about?" asked Mike, who turned at that moment and saw the same nightmarish creature I had witnessed in my house and on the stairs, a creature that was half man and half cat, with almond green eyes and long whiskers, dressed all in black, who leaped out of the jury box with dreadful speed, sunk an already bloody knife in Prado's chest, then, in a second, swift motion, pulled out the blade and slit the man's throat, which sprayed crimson across the room.

"Nobody betrays Ekué, no one!" he bellowed, then lunged at counsel table.

I screamed at the top of my lungs and the judge ducked beneath his bench and pressed the emergency buzzer, summoning help from the other courtrooms and the Sheriff's office down the hall. Mike also dashed under the table as the catman slashed at Charlie, who staggered back, throwing books and files at the monster to stop him.

"No, no! Leave him alone!" screamed someone from the back of the courtroom. The creature was about to leap for Charlie all the same when two deputies rushed inside, their weapons drawn. The monster looked at the officers, then at Charlie and at Julian, as though pleased at the sight, and scurried back into the jury room before the court clerk could even bring herself to move from her desk.

Charlie vaulted over the table and raced into the jury room just ahead of the deputies, who stopped momentarily to help Prado. I kicked off my shoes, grabbed my purse, and ran after Charlie. No way I was going to let that nightmare get away.

In the jury room I saw one of the side panels upended and the body of the court bailiff on the ground, bleeding. One of the deputies rushed in.

"Help him! He's still alive!" I shouted, then I ventured into the dark hallway through the open false door. I ran as fast as I could down a set of slippery steps that had probably been installed in the 1950s as the hallway to a bomb shelter in the basement.

I jumped down into a shadowy tunnel, pipes venting clouds of vapor, puddles of brownish water on cracked concrete tiles. I heard steps behind me, the deputies, I was sure. I turned this way and that, and caught a glimpse of Charlie racing around a turn. I took off after him.

"Charlie!" I shouted. "Wait up! I can help! I've got a gun!"

But Charlie never stopped running. At the corner the tunnel plunged down at a sixty-degree-angle ramp, probably built to accommodate the big rolling bins of paper files that used to be transported underground to the different government offices. I recalled that all the buildings in the Civic Center were connected by a series of interlocking tunnels, so that someone could walk all the way from the old Hall of Justice to the Water and Power skyscraper five blocks away and even beyond without having to come up for air.

"Of course, you idiot!" I shouted at myself. That meant the same tunnels that ran under the Civic Center probably also connected to other ancient galleries, the Red Line, the Chinatown tunnels.

Now the ramp ended and three different tunnels offered themselves, doom, death, and oblivion before me. I stood there, panting, glad that all my years of dancing nonstop had prepped me for this.

I heard steps behind me, then, in the distance, inside the tunnel at the far right, I caught a glimpse of Charlie's white suit. I took off after him, splashing through the puddles, too frantic to be scared of rats and vermin in the dark. Up ahead I finally saw the end of the tunnel: a padlocked gate, and the shape of something odd and long behind it. In front of the gate, Charlie struggled with the cat-man, holding aloft the killer's arm with the knife, intent on slicing Charlie as he had two others already that morning.

"Stop or I'll shoot!"

I threw down my purse as I grabbed my .38 Colt Special and took aim.

The catman looked my way, then spit in Charlie's face, kicked him in the groin, and put him in between us, so that any bullet aimed at him would go through Charlie first. The monster brought the knife down but Charlie ducked to the right and the blade cut only air, then the catman snarled and climbed, almost walking, up the gate, and somersaulted into the darkened vault. I rushed to Charlie.

"What are you doing here?" he said, staggering from the blow.

"Come to catch a bad kitty," I said, then blew the padlock off. Charlie and I shoved open the gate and entered slowly into the foul darkness, almost gagging from the stench of piss and puke.

The vault was at least thirty feet high; at one point probably it had been some sort of storage area for the old streetcars. I could hear surface traffic from not too far away; dim light pulsed in the misty background. I stopped, held Charlie back by the arm.

The room held an enormous vat, about twenty feet high, con-structed from who knows how many pieces of old wood and crates, held together with sheets of metal and old nails discarded over the years in the bowels of downtown. The ghastliest part of all were the heads—dozens of female heads, all shrunken and shriveled, nailed to the vat like so many screaming faces of pain.

The catman suddenly fell on both of us. His cold, furry hand dropped on me and my gun went clattering on the floor. I ran for it but I felt a rubber boot stomp my face and then heard the scraping of metal as the gun was picked off the ground.

"No, not my dad!" shouted Julian, who apparently had fol-lowed us all the way down and now was running between the catman and Charlie. But it was just a fraction of a second too late, for the bullet had already left and the trajectory was unstoppable and the projectile found its way into Julian's abdomen, which exploded as the bullet coursed its way through.

Julian spun around and collapsed on the ground and then I saw something I never had imagined nor ever want to see again. A great white light filled the room, a sparkling, piercing white beam that now came out of Charlie, like he was some otherworldly klieg light and like a hand, like a laser, thrust itself against the catman and impaled him on one of the iron railings of the vat, where the catman screamed and kicked and foamed and snarled and then fell to the floor, dead.

I got up and ran to the creature, not knowing whether I could believe all that I had seen or whether I had just slipped and cracked my head and now before my death I was dreaming of the nightmare that might have happened. But as I wobbled to my feet I slipped again, and I fell down hard on the ground.

I came to a few minutes later with a ringing headache, the back of my head bleeding and my dress torn and muddy, feeling like I'd been put through the spinning cycle of a giant washer.

Charlie was keening, crooning, holding dead Julian in his arms, singing Spanish lullabies to his beautiful only son.

The deputies finally arrived. One of them walked over to a switch box, pulled down a lever. Overhead lights suddenly turned on and the whole scene was illuminated like some tragic theater of unbelievable cruelty.

I walked up to the catman, slumped on the floor. I took a better look at him, then I pulled off his rubber boots, his rubber gloves with the fake nails, the half mask he wore over his gray, stubbly scalp. I looked at him closely again.

His eyes had been surgically elongated to give him a more feline appearance, his nostrils gouged out to make them resemble a cat's. His whiskers were his own, four long waxed strands that hung limply across his cut-up face. Thin, wrinkled, and middle-aged, he was no one I had ever met or seen. He was as repulsive in death as he had been frightening in life, an instrument of evil serving ends too obscure to tell or discern.

"Who is this guy?" one of the deputies asked me.

I shrugged, the emptiness of death as harrowing as any pain I could have imagined.

The paramedics and other deputies, late like always, descended on this antechamber to hell, the noises of reality—the talking on the walkie-talkie, the curses and commands, the screeching of stretchers, and the slamming of first aid kits—stinging like antiseptic on an open wound.

I walked over to Charlie, crouched down next to him, and laid my arm on his shoulder, as he cried silently for the life he could no longer save.

21

I WAS okay after a while. A mild concussion, a laceration on my right forearm, a wound in my thigh that kept me off the dance floor for a few months. I eventually recovered but I don't know that Charlie ever will.

The last time I saw him I drove up to the monastery where he now lives. It's a Zen place up in the San Bernardino Mountains. Charlie told me the residents take turns doing the chores: cooking, laundry, cleaning windows and bathrooms, polishing floors, gardening.

We walked on the dirt road around the premises, a large Tudor house a benefactor deeded to the monks. I picked a sweet green apple from a tree; in the distance the San Gorgonio peaks were already dusted with new snow.

"It's going to be an early winter," he said, kicking a pebble down the path. He was still as thin as when I had last seen him, but now he wore his gray hair in a long ponytail, giving him a sort of patrician, Alexander Hamilton look. Not bad, considering he was only a husk of the man he used to be.

"What do you want me to do with your manuscript?" I asked him.

"You finish it. Put it together with your own story," he said, his voice as cracked and dry as the leaves the wind was scattering our way. "I don't know that I'll ever write again. That time is past."

We walked some more, the green grass in the afternoon moving like a river, raked by an invisible hand.

"How long are you intending to stay here?"

He took a deep breath, hung his head down and squinted, as though the sight of a squirrel darting across the path held the answer.

"As long as they'll have me. You can go whenever you want. Some people stay a week, others ten years. A few people go away on weekends and come back during the week, some never return. It's all up to you. It's your own path."

He glanced at me, a flicker of the old Charlie showing through: "Very Zen, you know."

"I would hope so."

We laughed. I took a bite of the apple and we walked to a wooden bench under an arbor and we sat.

"They still haven't figured out who the catman was," I told him. "Last week Fuentes called me to ask if I'd ever heard his name. Wilfred Orr. From Nebraska, originally. Ever meet anybody by that name?"

Charlie shook his head no, shivered slightly in the blustery air, hugged his thin black sweatshirt.

"Off his prints they got that he was a Marine back in Vietnam couple of years before Saigon fell," I continued. "He was reported MIA. Maybe he was captured and tortured, and he had surgery to cover the marks. Maybe he just went AWOL and this was his way to come back. Problem is, they've got a set of teeth and bones that the Vietnamese government turned over which they claim is the real Orr. Those match the records of the Orr who enlisted. This guy wore dentures, all his teeth had been pulled out, so we don't know how those teeth got with those bones. So everybody's wondering who the hell this guy was."

"The real Orr," said Charlie, amused. "Did they ever say who else was in on it?"

"They claim they don't know. They haven't found any usable prints and the DNA sample we took from the hideout was useless. They haven't even been able to identify the heads on the vat. Fuentes is inclined to believe Orr did it all by himself. Like Gacy in Chicago."

"Tell me the truth, Rita, did you ever really think they would find out? Or even want to?"

"It's all over the place, isn't it?"

"It's always been. Whether it's this thing or another, they're all in on it. I told you from the beginning. Never say I didn't warn you."

He smiled, got up. "I have to get back, I'm baking bread for tonight's supper."

We walked up the dirt path back to the house. He shook my hand, then he kissed me goodbye lightly on the cheek.

A s I drove away in my Alfa, I looked in my rearview mirror at Charlie, head down, shoulders angled forward, shivering, a rail-thin man contemplating how life goes, how death comes, how in our belief all our presents are awful and all our past times were best.

I didn't have the heart to tell him I had found out he had brain cancer when copies of his medical records were forwarded to my office after he vacated the house in Los Feliz. Thus the thinness, thus the fainting spells, thus the sadness. If he didn't want to share this final affront, that was fine by me.

I also couldn't bring myself to remind him of how the coroner had found the telltale jaguar's head tattoo on Julian's thigh. We both knew what that meant. He had joined the cult too. A young man who falls in love with a power he's never had and kills for eternal glory.

Charlie must have known all along, from the time that Kelsey showed him the pictures of his banged-up Mercedes in Palmdale. On that trip to Los Angeles, he had brought Julian along and gave him the car while he was wined and dined by a movie studio executive wanting to make a movie of his books. That's why Charlie insisted on hurrying up with the trial. He wanted to save Julian from himself, before anybody else realized who the real culprit was.

I could see why Charlie had wanted to bear the awful burden. He must have felt responsible, exposing Julian to a world he otherwise would never have known. In Miami Charlie had offered his life for Julian's, but in the end it was the son who had died for the father.

I took the long way home that day. I was enjoying being alive, driving through golden hills on a nippy autumn afternoon in the mountains above Los Angeles. I knew Raúl was waiting for me at home, that he had probably fixed me pasta and a salad to go with the crunchy La Brea bread and the Sonoma Merlot and that afterward he would probably make love, deep, slow, satisfying love to help bring a girl back from death and despair.

Maybe someday I'll tie the knot again, if Raúl will wait. I think he will.

I thought about Charlie again and that scene at the vault and even though I knew I saw what I saw, I also knew I could not accept it. I could not have seen it but if I did, what then? I didn't want to think about that so I put on a tape of Mozart's Clarinet

Concerto which I'd long ago stashed in the glove compartment and forgotten about altogether.

On my way down I took Highway 14. Passing Agua Dulce, in a spur-of-the-moment decision, I drove back to Senator Decker's house. I stopped the car, got out. The house was still vacant, the FOR SALE sign still standing. Yet somehow everything seemed lighter, more real, as though the screen of gloom that had covered the place the last time had vanished these last few months.

I walked around the courtyard until I heard a baby's cry. I hurried to the utility apartment over the old garage. A young Chinese woman sat in an old rocker, nursing her child. Startled to see me, she called out in Chinese. A young man came out of the apartment—the same young punk I'd seen months before.

"I thought you were going to go pan for gold," I said. The young man nodded, showed off the child.

"I want to but girlfriend come pregnant from China. She have baby here. I talk to Realtor, I'm care taker now until house sell."

The baby squealed, gave me a baby smile.

"What's his name?"

"Joseph. Joseph Eric Hong."

"He's beautiful." I opened my purse, took out an attorney's card, wrote down my name.

"That boy of yours is your gold mine. Call my friend. He can help you all stay here. Legal. Tell him I sent you."

"We have no money."

"It's on me. Just call me Auntie America."

It took him a few seconds to get my meaning but then he turned to his wife and explained. She cried, got up, hugged me, made me tea, gave me almond cookies, would have cooked me a seven-course Chinese dinner if I'd let her. It was all I could do to shake their hand, wish them well, and leave before it was dark.

I was at the intersection of the 5 and the 14, tooling down to Silverlake, when I wondered if Kathleen, my father's wife, really knew how to cook.

Maybe Raúl and I would take them up on that long-standing invitation and have dinner with them.

Maybe even Thanksgiving dinner.

Why not. After all, Virginia ham is bound to go with California corn.